# IT AIN'T OVER 'TIL IT'S OVER

**BASEBALL PROSPECTUS**

*The Baseball Prospectus Annual (1996–present)*

*Mind Game (2005)*

*Baseball Between the Numbers:*
*Why Everything You Know About the Game Is Wrong (2006)*

# IT AIN'T OVER 'TIL IT'S OVER

## The Baseball Prospectus Pennant Race Book

THE *BASEBALL PROSPECTUS*
TEAM OF EXPERTS

EDITED BY
STEVEN GOLDMAN

BASIC
BOOKS

A Member of the Perseus Books Group
New York

Copyright © 2007 by Prospectus Entertainment Ventures LLC
Published by Basic Books
A Member of the Perseus Books Group

Basic books are available at special discounts for bulk purchases in the United States
by corporations, institutions, and other organizations. For more information, please
contact the Special Markets Department at the Perseus Books Group, 2300 Chestnut
Street, Suite 200, Philadelphia, PA 19103, or call (800) 255-1514.

Design by Jane Raese
Text set in 10-point New Aster

A CIP catalog record for this book is available from the Library of Congress.
ISBN-10: 0-465-00284-6
ISBN-13: 978-0-465-00284-9

10 9 8 7 6 5 4 3 2 1

# Contents

# Schrödinger's Pennant Race

BY STEVEN GOLDMAN

In 1984, the Detroit Tigers got off to one of the fastest starts in baseball history, winning 35 of their first 40 games. Like the rest of their American League East rivals, the New York Yankees had been left in the dust. By the second week of May, the Tigers were 24-4 and the Yankees, 10-17, were in last place, 13.5 games out.

At that time, Yankees management had gotten in the habit of posting clever or inspirational sayings on the Yankee Stadium marquee. Some of these purportedly came directly from the owner, George Steinbrenner, who, nearly 30 years after his stint as a college football coach, had not lost his faith in the efficacy of "win one for the Gipper"–style messages, regardless of the medium. Yogi Berra managed the Yankees that year, and as the Yankees came to work that week, the marquee displayed one of his most famous aphorisms: "It ain't over 'til it's over."

In fact, for the 1984 Yankees, it was over. Though Berra's team, after some reorganization, recovered and went on to have the best second-half record in baseball that season, the Tigers had built up such a commanding lead that the Detroit team could not be caught.

Still, Yogi was right in his basic formulation. It *isn't* over until it's over. His only error, or the error of whoever ordered the message on the marquee, was not realizing that it *was* over. Like Schrödinger's cat, every race exists in an indeterminate state, undecided until the last team is eliminated. The purpose of this book is twofold: to find the moments when the status of the cat changed from indeterminate to definitive—when one team's chances of winning dwindled to nothing and another's became assured—and then to identify why things played out as they did. From these moments and their causes, we'll find lessons that have implications for the baseball teams of today. Hindsight will yield to foresight—and we'll tell some great stories along the way.

Note the use of the word *moments*. Typically, we remember a race as having hinged on one fateful error or heroic feat—Fred Merkle's Boner, Gaby Hartnett's Homer in the gloamin', and "Bucky [expletive] Dent"—

but these are the climaxes of a more involved drama. To appreciate them fully, we must first understand how the teams planned and played so that they could arrive at the point that made heroism possible.

A wonderful thing about being a baseball fan today is all the wonderful tools that we have at our disposal. It used to be that our statistical understanding of the past was limited to what we could read on the back of a player's bubblegum card. Now, thanks to work done by Bill James, countless members of the Society for American Baseball Research (SABR), Baseball Prospectus, Retrosheet, and Baseball-Reference.com (among many others), we have a constantly expanding set of information about the games and players of the past and newer, better tools with which to analyze it. It's as if all those grainy black-and-white photos have been recast in high-resolution color and placed under the world's most powerful magnifying glass. By definition, Baseball Prospectus has been a forward-looking entity, devoting its analysis to understanding the present so that we could better predict the future. With this book, we finally turn our attention—and those aforementioned tools—to the game's past.

Our first step was to identify which races we wanted to talk about. Competition for the best record among ball clubs in a league setting— the rudimentary elements of a pennant race—go back at least as far as the formation of the National Association (a predecessor of the modern major leagues) in 1871. The first pennant race that was decided on the last day of the season occurred in the National League on October 5, 1889. The New York Giants defeated the Cleveland Spiders, thereby securing the flag over the Boston Beaneaters, who were upended by the Pittsburgh Alleghenys that same day. The list of all races that were inconclusive until the last day and those, like the 1984 American League East, that were essentially concluded by the end of April runs into the hundreds. If we had covered all of them with the depth we envisioned, this book would have become the Oxford English Dictionary of Pennant Races.

How then to cut the list down to not only a manageable handful but also the *best* handful? Far be it from us, purveyors of rationalism and confirmed debunkers of the conventional wisdom, to offer readers a subjective ranking. Being Baseball Prospectus, we had to invent a formula. To that end, Clay Davenport devised what he modestly suggested we call the Davenport Method. The method has two premises:

◆ The longer a race remains undecided, the better a race it is.
◆ A three-team race is better than a two-team race.

From there we experimented, adding and subtracting various nuances. We asked if a team should get extra credit for coming from behind to win, as some of the most-talked-about races did involve big comebacks, like the 1951 Giants-Dodgers conflict or the 1978 Yankees–Red Sox battle. Ultimately, though, those would still have been great races even if both Bucky Dent's and Bobby Thomson's fly balls had been caught on the warning track. We also explicitly rejected giving any extra credit for the teams involved; there is no reason that a Kansas City–Minnesota race should be scored lower than a Yankees–Red Sox battle, however more deserving the latter pairing might seem to the fans of those teams. Popularity is an issue of perception, not science.

In the end, the Davenport Method used the Playoff Odds Report, a projection that we feature on the Baseball Prospectus Web site each year (you can find the report at www.baseballprospectus.com/statistics/ps_odds.php). Each day of the season, we take the existing standings, along with team statistics like runs scored and allowed, to rate the strength of each team—the Yankees are a .600 team, Tampa Bay is a .400 team, and so on. We then look at the remaining schedule and "play" each game inside the computer. For a game between the Yankees and Devil Rays in Tampa, for example, we'd calculate the likelihood that a .600 team would beat a .400 team on the road (about 65.6 percent). Then we would roll some electronic dice to get a random number between 0 and 1 that is either less than .656 (thuh-huh-huh Yankees win!) or not (the Rays win). We track the wins and losses and move on to the next game, right through to the end of the season.

Within the current season, we play out the season from the current date to the final game (literally) a million times. Within a million versions of the season, some strange things are bound to happen, like the Devil Rays winning the pennant once every 50 or 100 seasons. The simulation gives us a snapshot of the likelihoods that, say, on June 1 the Yankees will have established a 60 percent chance of winning the division, the Red Sox 25 percent, the Jays 10 percent, the Orioles 3 percent, the Rays 1 percent. If the race weren't competitive—what we call a dead race—we would have one team at 100 percent, and everyone else at zero. We simply measure how far a race is from being dead to get a score for that day; the highest possible score is one in which every team has an equal chance.

Ranking the pennant races using the same process as the Playoff Odds Report could be as simple as adding up the odds for all the days of a given season. Doing so produced the list in Table I-1. We also compiled a list of the *worst* pennant races by this method (Table I-2).

Table I-1 Top 10 Pennant Races as Determined by the Initial Playoff Odds Report Method

| Rank | Race | Comments |
|---|---|---|
| 1 | 1967 AL | The year of the "impossible dream" Red Sox. |
| 2 | 1904 AL | An errant spitball from New York's Jack Chesbro hands a last-minute pennant to Boston. |
| 3 | 1915 Federal League | The Whales edge the Terriers, Rebels, and Packers in a marginal major league that blinked in and out of existence. |
| 4 | 1981 AL East | A race that didn't happen, thanks to the strike. |
| 5 | 1984 AL West | The Royals, Angels, and Twins stage a season-long battle in slow motion. |
| 6 | 1983 NL East | An aging Phillies squad wheezes past the Pirates and Expos. |
| 7 | 1974 AL East | An unexpectedly weak Orioles team struggles to pass an unexpectedly strong Yankees team. |
| 8 | 1965 NL | Not as well remembered as their 1962 fight, but the Giants and Dodgers were at it again. |
| 9 | 1926 NL | The first Branch Rickey–designed pennant winner edges a Reds team with one of the great forgotten starting rotations. |
| 10 | 1966 NL | The Dodgers, the Giants, and a Pirates team still a few years from breaking through do battle. |

Table I-2 The 10 Worst Races as Determined by the Initial Playoff Odds Report Method

| Rank | Race | Comments |
|---|---|---|
| 1 | 2001 AL West | Seattle won 116 games and had a 20-game lead in July. |
| 2 | 1902 NL | The Pirates had fewer significant player defections during the contract wars with the NL, and dominated as a result. |
| 3 | 1884 Union League | This was the year Eleanor Roosevelt was born; the world had painless dentistry by then. |
| 4 | 1955 NL | The Dodgers ran away with the league on the way to their only Brooklyn championship. |
| 5 | 1939 AL | Joe McCarthy's fourth straight Yankees pennant winner; the team's only weakness was first base after Lou Gehrig stepped out. |
| 6 | 1969 AL East | One of Earl Weaver's better squads. |
| 7 | 1999 AL Central | The Indians won 97 games; no one else in the division was over .500. |
| 8 | 1995 AL Central | The same story as 1999, only the Indians were even better. |
| 9 | 1977 NL West | The Big Red Machine's pitching gave out and Tommy Lasorda's Dodgers roared past it. |
| 10 | 1885 American Association | Eleanor Roosevelt was still young, and as her dad was more into hunting and drinking than spectator sports, she probably didn't get to many games. |

These lists were not completely satisfactory. After all, we tend to think of the best pennant races as those that not only were close, but also have the most activity late in the season. Accordingly, we added a multiplier to give extra weight to the end of the season. We multiplied the daily rankings by the day of the season, so the 170th day of the season (September 18, if the season starts on April 1) counted 170 times more than the first day of the season.

This helped somewhat, but we still missed races in which one team had a big lead for most of the year but blew it in a short time; the higher scores at the end couldn't make up for all the time when the race looked like a blowout. Playing with various permutations of this system produced the list with which we began work on the book:

1. 1964 NL
2. 1967 AL
3. 1908 NL
4. 1951 NL
5. 1984 AL West
6. 1934 NL
7. 1981 AL East
8. 1974 AL East
9. 1973 NL East
10. 1995 AL West

There is often a long time between the start of a book and its completion, and as we worked, Clay kept revising his system. "I realized later that I was handling tied seasons, which required playoffs, as if they were just a regular day of the season, when they really do deserve a special emphasis," he said. "I played around with enhancing the time of the season, going to squares and cubes of the days as multipliers instead of just the day itself, making the 170th day almost 5 million times as important as the first day for scoring purposes." Ultimately, Clay's alterations produced a third, definitive list:

1. 1967 AL
2. 1959 NL
3. 1972 AL East
4. 1981 AL East
5. 2001 NL Central
6. 1948 AL
7. 1949 AL

8. 1908 NL
9. 1964 NL
10. 2003 NL Central
11. 1973 NL East
12. 1944 AL

The races discussed in this book represent an amalgamation of Clay's second and third lists. We dropped the 1981 AL East race because it didn't really happen—its ranking stems from disregarding the bifurcated schedule adopted in the wake of the players' strike. The 2001 NL Central race, a tie between the Astros and Cardinals, was booted because the wild card meant there was nothing at stake; both clubs went to the playoffs. We also elected to retain the 1934 and 1951 National League races, which dropped out of the top 10 between lists two and three, because these were landmark races about which we had useful things to say.

Despite the care put into designing the Davenport Method, the rankings are not to be taken too seriously. Which pennant races are the "best" is ultimately a subjective call. If asked to choose from memory, the typical baseball fan would probably remember first those races that give the most visceral experience—that is, the one a favorite team was in—followed by a couple of landmark races he or she might remember hearing about. The Davenport Method is merely our way of framing the question.

Framing questions in a way that makes them easier to understand is what Baseball Prospectus is all about. Consider one of our key statistics, VORP, or value over replacement player. To have any meaning at all, baseball statistics require context. If, in a given year, the average player in a league hits .300, then the player who hits .275 isn't having a good year. Conversely, if the league-average player hits only .240, the player who hits .275 is doing something moderately special. VORP goes a step beyond that, comparing a player's performance not to the average but to that of a hypothetical replacement player, by which we mean freely available talent—a Triple-A veteran or major league 25th man who is barely qualified for his job. VORP asks the question How many runs has a batter generated (or in the case of a pitcher, prevented) beyond that of his replacement?

Now, you could eyeball all this for yourself if you had all the information at hand, facts like what the league hit, what the typical player at the position in question hit, where the player played (e.g., Coors

Field or RFK?), and so on. VORP adjusts for park and league settings, providing that context for you.

Earlier we spoke of tools and magnifying glasses. In this book, we apply them to baseball's past. Some would argue that we shouldn't, that trying to gain a clearer picture of what happened (or what is happening) somehow diminishes the people or events being studied. A pleasing legend is always preferable to an unforgiving fact. Yet as we demonstrate throughout this book, if these tools had been available to the teams of the past, several great pennant races might have ended differently. As Christina Kahrl shows in her chapter on the 1934 National League pennant race, the Cubs eliminated themselves through a series of self-defeating trades that demonstrated their ignorance of park effects. In his chapter on the 1974 American League East race, Alex Belth discusses how a player "rebellion" against Earl Weaver led to the team's bunting its way to a pennant—or so the players thought.

Why are new histories written of old events? Why not just let the first draft stand forever? The answer is that as time passes, greater perspective is possible. New information is uncovered, and new ways of analyzing old information are discovered. New minds, better informed, with better analytical tools, bring (one hopes) greater understanding. Thus the stories in this book are not twice told, but reimagined and newly understood. Even better, in dragging them back out of history's attic, we had the privilege of communing with those personalities that animated the modern game—Branch Rickey, Satchel Paige, Casey Stengel, Bill Veeck, Dick Allen, Billy Martin, Earl Weaver, Tug McGraw, John McGraw, Dizzy Dean, Sig Jakucki (yes, we were shocked to see him here as well), and so many others. Baseball is the most accessible of sports: The players are not hidden behind masks or beneath helmets, not blurred by constant motion, but are knowable. In no other sport are the outcomes of games and races so susceptible to individual quirks, strengths, weaknesses, and prejudices. If "it ain't over 'til it's over," it's because the players' very humanity skews the odds, upsets predictions, causes them to delight and disappoint. This book is a celebration of those men and their Schrödinger moments, standing on the cusp of success or failure, deciding to take or swing away.

An additional word about the statistics you will find in this book. Despite the foregoing, they are actually not terribly esoteric. Most frequently you will see the "slash stats," typically rendered as (for example) .275/.367/.652. They represent the Cerberus of baseball statistics:

batting average, on-base percentage, and slugging percentage. The numbers in the example were David Ortiz's averages on the morning of April 24, 2007. They're pretty good, but not as good as Alex Rodriguez's .400/.453/1.053 on the same day. On the other hand, they're far better than Brandon Inge's .117/.194/.283. As indicated earlier, to put these statistics to good use, you need to know how the league is doing. On April 24, the average AL player was hitting .256/.327/.408, so you can see that Ortiz and Rodriguez were quite a bit above average, Inge miles below.

Some statistics have league and park context built in. We've already mentioned VORP. Another that you will come across in these pages is equivalent average, or EqA. This statistic takes a player's total offensive output, adjusts for league and park features, and divides it by outs for an end product that looks very much like batting average. In fact, EqA is scaled so that it works the same way batting average does: .260 is about average; .300 is quite good; .190 is horribly bad. In 2006, the major league leader in EqA (with 300 or more plate appearances) was Travis Hafner of the Indians with .356. Hafner's rates were .308/.439/ .659. The player with the worst EqA (in at least 300 plate appearances) was Clint Barmes of the Rockies with .206. He had batted .220/.264/ .335 while playing in Colorado. On the morning of April 24, 2007, the major league leader (minimum 75 plate appearances) was Jim Thome of the White Sox at .432 (batting .340/.553/.680). His antithesis, at .167, was Yankees outfielder Melky Cabrera (batting .200/.230/.200).

Finally, you'll see WARP, or wins above replacement, not to be confused with VORP. WARP is the number of wins the player contributed above what a replacement-level position player or pitcher would have done. WARP adjusts for park and league context, and counts all of a player's contributions—hitting, fielding, and pitching. When Ted Williams hit .406/.551/.735 in 1941, his WARP was 14.0. When third baseman Butch Hobson batted .250/.312/.408 and made 43 errors for the 1978 Red Sox, his WARP was 1.6. Visitors to our Web site, www. baseballprospectus.com, will note that WARP comes in different iterations. In this book, all uses of WARP refer to WARP3, a version adjusted to make comparisons across time possible.

At the beginning of each chapter, we've placed a Prospectus Box giving some pertinent facts about the season. Table I-3 is the Prospectus Box for the American League race of 1924, when the Washington Senators edged the Yankees by two games.

At upper left, you see the actual standings for the pennant race. The *DIF* column refers to how many days each team spent in first place.

Table I-3 Example of a League Prospectus

| 1924 American League Prospectus | | | | | | | |
|---|---|---|---|---|---|---|---|
| **Actual Standings** | | | | | Date Elim | **Pythag** | |
| Team | W | L | Pct | GB | DIF | | W | L |
| Senators | 92 | 62 | .597 | – | 52 | – | 92 | 62 |
| Yankees | 89 | 63 | .586 | 2.0 | 97 | Sept 29 | 89 | 63 |
| Tigers | 86 | 68 | .558 | 6.0 | 27 | Sept 22 | 82 | 72 |
| Browns | 74 | 78 | .487 | 17.0 | 1 | Sept 17 | 72 | 80 |
| A's | 71 | 81 | .467 | 20.0 | 0 | Sept 10 | 67 | 85 |
| Indians | 76 | 86 | .438 | 24.5 | 0 | Sept 10 | 71 | 82 |
| Red Sox | 67 | 87 | .435 | 25.0 | 16 | Sept 9 | 70 | 84 |
| White Sox | 66 | 87 | .431 | 25.5 | 6 | Sept 8 | 71 | 82 |

| **League Averages** | | | | **BP Stats Leaders** | | | |
|---|---|---|---|---|---|---|---|
| AVG | OBP | SLG | BABIP | Offense, BRAA | | Indiv WARP | |
| .290 | .358 | .397 | .307 | Tigers | 72 | Babe Ruth | 15.4 |
| ERA | K9 | BB9 | H9 | Pitching, PRAA | | Howard Ehmke | 11.0 |
| 4.23 | 2.7 | 3.4 | 10.1 | Yankees | 64 | Eddie Collins | 10.4 |

*Date Elim* is the date that each team was eliminated from the pennant race. *Pythag* is the so-called Pythagorean record for each team (technically, the Pythagenport third-order record), an "expected" win-loss record based on runs scored and allowed (this is explained in more detail in the 1908 "Paper Giants" chapter). In addition to the triple-slash league averages, the box also contains batting average on balls in play (BABIP), a measure of how the average pitcher did when he allowed hitters to make contact. There is also the more traditional ERA, strikeouts per nine innings pitched (K9), walks per nine innings pitched (BB9), and hits allowed per nine innings pitched (H9). In the lower center, we have the season's leaders in batting runs above average (BRAA), which is the number of runs the team generated beyond what an average team would have done, given the same number of outs. Pitcher runs above average (PRAA) means how many more runs the team saved than the average staff would have saved, given the same number of outs. Finally, we have the individual WARP leaders for the season in question.

Erwin Schrödinger's cat never existed; the feline was an actor in a paradox designed to illustrate the complexities of quantum physics: that a thing (a particle or a pussycat) could exist in two states at once—in the case of the cat, both alive and dead. Eventually, the concept of decoherence was proposed as a solution: While the cat is hanging around waiting for Yogi Berra to come check on it and note whether it's breathing or not, the universe is acting on the possibilities, rapidly eliminating the most improbable outcomes until all that is left is the cat's inescapable fate. In the blink of an eye, the cat traverses the distance from "It ain't over" to "It's over."

As decoherence occurred in the pennant races recounted in this book, some teams observed the collapse of their possibilities and acted. Others passively watched as the universe closed off the exits, not quite understanding what was happening or, cognizant of impending doom, still finding themselves incapable of altering the outcome. As Branch Rickey said, "Ol' man opportunity has long hair in front and he is bald behind. When he comes to you, you can snatch him and hold him tight, but when he is past, he could be gone forever." He could have put that same idea in other words, saying it ain't over 'til it's over, but it could be over at any time. The trick is to be alert to your opportunities, so you can make sure it ends in your favor.

# IT AIN'T OVER 'TIL IT'S OVER

*Baseball is a game of race, creed, and color. The race is to first base. The creed is the rules of the game. The color? Well, the home team wears white uniforms, and the visiting team wears gray.*

—Joe Garagiola

*Things don't happen without a cause. They just don't. There's a reason for pretty nearly everything that happens that I know about.*

—Branch Rickey

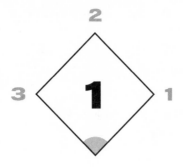

# 1967 American League

## *To Fight the Unbeatable Foe*

### JAY JAFFE

Carl Yastrzemski stepped into the Tiger Stadium batter's box in the top of the ninth inning on Monday night, September 18, 1967, with one out and nobody on base. His Boston Red Sox trailed the Detroit Tigers 5-4 in a seesaw affair that had seen the Sox jump out to a 3-0 lead in the first inning, thanks in part to a Yaz double—the first of his two hits thus far—off long-gone starter Denny McLain.

Yastrzemski's upstart club, which hadn't been in a pennant race since 1949, trailed the first-place Tigers by a game in the American League standings despite having just dropped three straight to the defending world champion Baltimore Orioles. The Sox weren't alone in nipping at Detroit's heels. At the beginning of the day, the Chicago White Sox stood just a half-game behind the Tigers, with the Minnesota Twins tied with Boston at a game back. Improbably, with just two weeks to go, the quartet was thundering down the season's backstretch, crowding each other as they vied for the pennant in the tightest four-team race ever.

A crowd of 42,674 fans watched Yaz at the plate. On the hill was Fred Lasher, the least famous among a gaggle of rookie relievers in a young Tiger bullpen that included Mike Marshall, John Hiller, and Pat Dobson, each of whom would go on to bigger things. Before his recall, the 26-year-old Lasher had yielded just five earned runs in 70 minor

## 1967 American League Prospectus

| | Actual Standings | | | | | Date Elim | Pythag | |
|---|---|---|---|---|---|---|---|---|
| Team | W | L | Pct | GB | DIF | | W | L |
| Red Sox | 92 | 70 | .568 | – | 5 | – | 93 | 69 |
| Tigers | 91 | 71 | .562 | 1.0 | 34 | Oct 1 | 92 | 70 |
| Twins | 91 | 71 | .562 | 1.0 | 43 | Oct 1 | 90 | 72 |
| White Sox | 89 | 73 | .549 | 3.0 | 92 | Sept 30 | 86 | 76 |
| Angels | 84 | 77 | .522 | 7.5 | 3 | Sept 22 | 78 | 83 |
| Orioles | 76 | 85 | .472 | 15.5 | 11 | Sept 12 | 88 | 73 |
| Senators | 76 | 85 | .472 | 15.5 | 0 | Sept 16 | 70 | 91 |
| Indians | 75 | 87 | .463 | 17.0 | 1 | Sept 13 | 74 | 88 |
| Yankees | 72 | 90 | .444 | 20.0 | 6 | Sept 10 | 69 | 93 |
| A's | 62 | 99 | .385 | 29.5 | 3 | Sept 8 | 65 | 96 |

| League Averages | | | | BP Stats Leaders | | | |
|---|---|---|---|---|---|---|---|
| AVG | OBP | SLG | BABIP | Offense, BRAA | | Indiv WARP | |
| .236 | .303 | .351 | .269 | Tigers | 107 | Carl Yastrzemski | 13.7 |
| ERA | K9 | BB9 | H9 | Pitching, PRAA | | Harmon Killebrew | 11.8 |
| 3.23 | 6.1 | 3.1 | 7.9 | White Sox | 74 | Brooks Robinson | 11.5 |

league innings at Double-A Montgomery and Triple-A Toledo. In 21.2 big-league frames, he'd surrendered just five runs while racking up nine saves. Up in the press box, in a voice loud enough for his colleagues to hear, *Boston Globe* columnist Ray Fitzgerald proclaimed, "Right now is when an MVP should hit a home run." Lasher had yet to allow one that year.

The rookie fell behind Yastrzemski 2-0 and then offered up a belt-high fastball over the center of the plate—a lollipop, as he later described it. Yaz connected, propelling the ball into the right upper deck to tie the game. His jubilant teammates poured out of the dugout to greet him at home plate as the ballpark went silent.

The Sox won the contest in the following inning when third baseman Dalton Jones, a scrub inserted into the lineup because rookie manager Dick Williams wanted another left-handed bat, led off with a solo homer off Marshall. It was Jones's fourth hit of the day. The victory, accompanied by Minnesota's 2-0 win in Kansas City, created a three-way tie atop the AL standings, with the idle White Sox still a half-game back. By the standards of this race, the tie was old hat; less than two weeks earlier, on September 6, all four teams had shared the top spot.

Despite Jones's game-winner, it was Yastrzemski's blow, his 40th of the year, that carried the day. In fact, Yaz carried just about every day from that point until the end of the season. From September 18 through October 1, the 28-year-old lefty slugger hit an astounding .523/.604/.955, one of the greatest season-ending blazes of glory in the history of baseball. With a .326 batting average, 121 RBIs, and 44 homers, Yastrzemski won the Triple Crown and the MVP award. His heroics, which included a 7-for-8, 6-RBI showing in the season's final two games against the Twins, helped the Red Sox complete the "Impossible Dream," defying the 100-to-1 odds set for them at the beginning of the year, to win their first pennant since 1946.

The 1967 pennant was the culmination of a desperately needed cultural change within the Red Sox organization. Since Ted Williams's retirement after the 1960 season, the Sox had become "as exciting as watching an accountant at work." Owner Tom Yawkey's franchise had withered under years of neglect, institutional racism, and a country-club atmosphere; in 1965 and 1966, the team had finished ninth in a 10-team league, and Yawkey even intimated that its residence in Fenway—and Boston—was not forever. That the organization could change course to avoid its self-imposed destruction was as much the "Impossible Dream" as was winning on the field.

At last, the losing shamed Yawkey into bringing in a new regime that reached beyond his inner circle of tippling toadies. He promoted executive vice president Dick O'Connell, an organization man with a distinguished military background, to the role of general manager. In 20 years of working in the dysfunctional Boston front office, O'Connell had seen enough of the bad old days to conclude, "Just get the best players, that's all." Well under Yawkey's radar before his promotion, he had hired a new generation of scouts and worked closely with Neil Mahoney, the director of minor league operations, to foster a nucleus of homegrown talent. O'Connell tabbed a no-nonsense manager, Dick Williams, for whom many of those homegrown youngsters had played in the minors, to whip his club into shape. This new regime helped shake off the cobwebs of complacency, recapturing the imagination of a New England fan base that had all but left them for dead.

Once, the Red Sox had been one of the game's elite franchises, winning five World Series between 1903 and 1918. The team soon fell on hard times, however, as owner Harry Frazee, who lacked financial liquidity, sold or traded his stars to the New York Yankees. Stars like Carl Mays, Waite Hoyt, Wally Schang, Joe Bush, Herb Pennock, and, most devastatingly, Babe Ruth were relinquished in a series of deals that laid the groundwork for the sport's longest dynasty while turning the Sox into the league's doormat. Frazee, who had bought the club in

1916, sold out to the woefully underfinanced Bob Quinn in August 1923. The Sox finished dead last in the AL nine times in 11 seasons from 1922 through 1932, winning just 36 percent of their games and exceeding 100 losses five times.

Finally, in late 1932, Quinn sold to trust-funded Tom Yawkey, whose uncle (later adoptive father) had briefly owned the Tigers. Through his Detroit connections, Yawkey had been introduced by Ty Cobb to future Hall of Fame second baseman Eddie Collins, whom he persuaded to join him in Boston as general manager. Collins spent Yawkey's money lavishly, acquiring stars like the brothers Rick and Wes Ferrell, Joe Cronin, Lefty Grove, and Jimmie Foxx. Though the Sox climbed out of the cellar, they made little headway beyond the middle of the AL pack until 1938, when they finished a distant second to the Yankees. Fueled by the arrival of left fielder Ted Williams in 1939, Boston made runner-up four times in five seasons, but it wasn't until 1946, after Williams returned from three years in the marine corps, that the Sox finally snared their first pennant since the sale of Ruth.

In those years, Yawkey was a hands-on owner, chummy with his stars to the point of maintaining a locker in the Fenway clubhouse and working out with the team, shagging flies, taking batting practice, and even carousing with the legendarily besotted Foxx. Yawkey's chumminess extended into the front office, where his crony Cronin succeeded Collins as general manager in 1948. The team endured valiant near misses under former Yankee manager Joe McCarthy in 1948 and 1949, but under Cronin, the club gradually slid toward mediocrity during the 1950s.

A key cause of that backsliding was the club's failure to integrate. The Red Sox were the last all-white team, refusing to field a black player until they brought up infielder Pumpsie Green in 1959, 12 years after the Dodgers had broken the color barrier with Jackie Robinson. Ironically, Boston had the first crack at Robinson, trying him out at Fenway Park along with two other Negro League ballplayers, Sam Jethroe and Marvin Williams, on April 16, 1945. The tryout, which occurred during the Collins regime, was the result of some political hardball by Boston city councilman Isadore Muchnick, who threatened to block the team's blue law waiver—necessary to play games on Sunday—unless they auditioned black ballplayers.

The tryout was nonetheless a sham; the Sox worked the trio for 90 minutes, but manager Cronin by some accounts couldn't even be bothered to pay attention. At one point, according to *Boston Globe* reporter Cliff Keane, a voice from the stands called out, "Get those niggers off the field!" Though unattributed, the words were assumed to come from either Collins, Cronin, or Yawkey. The Sox, hiding behind the so-called gentlemen's agreement that segregated the game, offered none of the players a contract. Six months later, the Dodgers signed Robinson to play for their Triple-A club in Montreal in 1946, and just two years and one day after the tryout, Robinson became the first black major leaguer since Moses Fleetwood Walker in 1884.

Under Collins and then Cronin, the Red Sox steadfastly held the line against integration even after Robinson reached the majors. They fumbled another golden opportunity in 1949, when, as part of a lease agreement between their affiliates, the Birmingham Barons, and the Black Barons of the Negro Leagues, the Sox were tipped off about a remarkable 18-year-old outfielder. The team sent a reluctant scout, Larry Woodall, down to Birmingham, but he departed after three days of rain, declaring, "I'm not going to waste my time waiting for a bunch of niggers." To cover his tracks, Woodall wrote an unenthusiastic scouting report on the youngster he had never even seen play, a kid named Willie Mays.

The team further reinforced its stance in 1955 by hiring as its manager Mike "Pinky" Higgins, an openly racist Yawkey drinking buddy who declared, "There will never be any niggers on this team as long as I have anything to say about it." In 1959, three weeks after Higgins was fired, the Sox finally promoted Green, who was followed a week later by pitcher Earl Wilson. Yet, like a rash, Higgins returned, overseeing the Sox's descent into the second division, first as manager (from late 1960 through 1962) and then as general manager (1963–1965). As an increasingly uninterested Yawkey distanced himself from the team, the bottom dropped out under manager Billy Herman in 1965 and 1966.

Change was in the works. Roused to action by the humiliation of the team's first 100-loss season since 1932, Yawkey fired general manager Higgins in September 1965 and replaced him with O'Connell, who had joined the organization in 1946 after striking up a friendship with Sox announcer Jim Britt while both were in the navy during World War II. O'Connell cleaned house, unloading past-prime players like Bill Monboquette, Dick Radatz, and Frank Malzone and clearing a path for the promising talent assembled by a fresh set of scouts and developed under Mahoney. Though the 1966 Sox did little to distinguish themselves in the standings, they sported two black rookies, first baseman George Scott and third baseman Joe Foy, in their starting lineup, accompanying fellow homegrown youngsters like shortstop Rico Petrocelli and right fielder Tony Conigliaro—an enviable young talent base.

Conigliaro, from nearby Revere, Massachusetts, was perhaps the team's most popular player. Tall, dark, and matinee-idol handsome, "Tony C." had homered in his first at bat in Fenway. He'd gone on to set records for the most home runs by a teenager (24 in 1964) and the youngest player to lead a league in homers (with 32 in 1965, when he was 20). On July 23, 1967, he became the youngest American Leaguer ever to reach 100 homers (22 years, 197 days).

O'Connell's masterstroke was the hiring of Dick Williams, a flat-topped hard-ass who had managed the club's Triple-A Toronto affiliate to International League championships in 1965 and 1966. A veteran of the 1963 and 1964 Red Sox, Williams was all too familiar with the Red Sox players' tendency to do little more than play out the string from Memorial Day onward. Given just a one-year contract, Williams adopted an authoritarian, my-way-or-the-highway stance guaranteed to antagonize the veterans. His philosophy was founded on hatred: "Players give you 100 percent not because they want something but because they hate something. Me, I gave 100 percent because I hated losing. Others hated failure. For the ones who treated losing and failure lightly, I figured I'd give them something even better to hate. Me. I tried to make some players win just to show me up."

There was method to Williams's madness. "He did things to make you angry," recalled center fielder Reggie Smith, a 1967 rookie who had hit .320 for Williams in Toronto the year before. "He helped us develop a kind of mental toughness that you need to play the game. ... He stressed the idea mistakes cost ballgames and winning teams just don't make mistakes."

Williams was a galvanic force that spring. "He watched you slide, or make the cutoff throw, or bat," Yastrzemski remembered. "In one intrasquad game, Williams even put on an umpire's home plate gear to work a game behind the plate. And then he called a balk on one of the rookie pitchers." For all of his irascibility, Williams saw enough potential in his new charges to declare at the outset of the season, "We'll win more than we'll lose," but even that seemed a stretch.

As if to emphasize just who was in charge, the manager eliminated the team captaincy, stripping Yastrzemski of his title. "The cruise is over and you don't need a captain anymore," he told the team. Tired of being the brightest star on a losing team, Yaz went along. The irony was that shorn of the captaincy, Yastrzemski matured into a true leader. He outgrew his own introverted ways in the locker room, befriending and offering hitting advice to youngsters Foy and Smith.

On the field as well as off, Yastrzemski took a major step forward in his age 27 season, which is generally the peak of a hitter's career. Having arrived on the big-league scene in 1961, he'd instantly been saddled with the burden of replacing the incomparable Ted Williams as the team's left fielder and lineup centerpiece. While he'd sparkled at times, earning three All-Star berths and the 1963 batting title, Yastrzemski had never hit more than 20 homers in a season, and his overall line stood at .293/.373/.458, solid but hardly impressive, given Fenway's favorable hitting conditions (Table 1-1).

Table 1-1 Yaz Favors Bean Soup: Carl Yastrzemski's Home-Road Splits, 1961–1966

| Year | Home | | | Away | | |
|---|---|---|---|---|---|---|
| | Avg | OBP | Slg | Avg | OBP | Slg |
| 1961 | .317 | .371 | .477 | .216 | .279 | .318 |
| 1962 | .342 | .402 | .563 | .252 | .325 | .379 |
| 1963 | .316 | .392 | .479 | .326 | .443 | .472 |
| 1964 | .290 | .372 | .472 | .288 | .376 | .431 |
| 1965 | .331 | .416 | .639 | .289 | .372 | .417 |
| 1966 | .325 | .400 | .521 | .228 | .334 | .336 |
| TOTAL | .320 | .392 | .525 | .265 | .354 | .390 |

Yastrzemski had met Gene Berde, the former coach of the Hungarian national boxing team, over the previous winter. Long before the era of personal trainers and year-round conditioning, Berde challenged Yastrzemski to improve his fitness under his tutelage, and Yaz showed up to spring training in the best shape of his life. In conjunction with some swing-doctoring from coach Bobby Doerr, who encouraged Yastrzemski to hold his hands higher, the left fielder transformed himself into a power hitter who could bash on the road (.321/.409/.567) as well as at home (.332/.428/.678). He could also master left-handed pitchers for one of the few times in his career (Yaz was only a career .244/.321/.371 hitter against southpaws), improving from .187/.275/.309 against them in 1966 to .338/.397/.500 a year later.

As impressive as Yastrzemski's hitting numbers are in today's context, they were even more so in 1967, when AL teams scored an average of 3.70 runs per game, the lowest level since 1918. One metric that Baseball Prospectus uses to make these numbers comparable even in different contexts is equivalent average (EqA). In one easy-to-understand statistic expressed on the scale of batting average, EqA expresses a player's ability to hit for average, hit for power, draw walks, get hit by pitches, and steal bases; .260 is defined as league average— whether the context is three runs per game or six—.300 is excellent, and .230 is replacement level. The figure includes adjustments for park and league offensive levels, enabling cross-era comparisons. Note that even hitters with superficially low triple-slash stats (batting average, on-base percentage, and slugging percentage) such as those of

Table 1-2 Within You and Without You: Yaz Among the Top Sluggers in the American League (by EqA), 1967

| Player | Team | PA | Avg | OBP | Slg | EqA |
|---|---|---|---|---|---|---|
| Frank Robinson | BAL | 563 | .311 | .403 | .576 | .350 |
| Carl Yastrzemski | BOS | 680 | .326 | .418 | .622 | .348 |
| Al Kaline | DET | 550 | .308 | .411 | .541 | .343 |
| Harmon Killebrew | MIN | 689 | .269 | .408 | .558 | .340 |
| Mickey Mantle | NYA | 553 | .245 | .391 | .434 | .321 |
| Don Mincher | CAL | 563 | .273 | .367 | .487 | .317 |
| Bill Freehan | DET | 618 | .282 | .389 | .447 | .313 |
| Frank Howard | WAS | 585 | .256 | .338 | .511 | .310 |
| Paul Blair | BAL | 619 | .293 | .353 | .446 | .302 |
| George Scott | BOS | 641 | .303 | .373 | .465 | .300 |
| Bob Allison | MIN | 576 | .258 | .356 | .470 | .298 |
| Tony Oliva | MIN | 615 | .289 | .347 | .463 | .296 |
| Dick McAuliffe | DET | 675 | .239 | .364 | .411 | .295 |
| Norm Cash | DET | 577 | .242 | .352 | .430 | .294 |
| Jim Fregosi | CAL | 651 | .290 | .349 | .395 | .288 |
| Brooks Robinson | BAL | 681 | .269 | .328 | .434 | .288 |
| Curt Blefary | BAL | 645 | .242 | .337 | .413 | .287 |
| Pete Ward | CHI | 542 | .233 | .334 | .392 | .283 |
| Rick Reichardt | CAL | 545 | .265 | .320 | .404 | .279 |
| Jim Northrup | DET | 542 | .271 | .332 | .392 | .277 |
| Rod Carew | MIN | 561 | .292 | .341 | .409 | .275 |
| Davey Johnson | BAL | 586 | .247 | .325 | .376 | .274 |
| Fred Valentine | WAS | 527 | .234 | .330 | .346 | .274 |
| Rico Petrocelli | BOS | 556 | .259 | .330 | .420 | .272 |
| Tommie Agee | CHI | 584 | .234 | .302 | .371 | .267 |

Pete Ward (White Sox) and Dick McAuliffe (Tigers) were actually among the league's more productive players in 1967 (Table 1-2).

The 1967 Red Sox produced the league's highest-scoring offense, scoring 4.46 runs per game in a league whose average was 3.70. At Fenway they bashed out 5.04 runs per game; on the road, 3.88, the third-best in the league. Besides Yastrzemski, who paced the circuit with 12.9 WARP, the offense was led by Scott, Petrocelli, and Conigliaro, all of whom were 24 or under, as were the pair of rookies who had played under Williams in Toronto the previous year, Reggie Smith and second baseman Mike Andrews. Six players reached double digits in homers as the Sox led the American League with 158.

While Fenway helped the hitters, it made for a pitcher's nightmare. With the 37-foot-high Green Monster looming just 310 feet away in left field and Pesky's Pole just 302 feet down the line in right field, the

Sox allowed a league-worst 4.38 runs per game at home, though their 3.20 runs per game on the road constituted the league's best. The staff was led by ace "Gentleman Jim" Lonborg, a 25-year-old who took a major leap forward by learning to pitch inside. Despite the nickname, his 19 hit batsmen—tallied on his glove, gunfighter style—led the league. At 22-9, with a 3.16 ERA, Lonborg tied for the league lead in wins and took home the AL Cy Young Award. The team's second-best starter, Lee Stange, pitched much better than his 8-10 record indicated, with a 2.77 ERA. The rotation was augmented by Gary Bell, who came over from Cleveland in a June 4 trade for first baseman Tony Horton and outfielder Don Demeter and went 12-8 with a 3.16 ERA. That deal, coupled with a trade two days earlier that sent reliever Don McMahon to the White Sox for utility man Jerry Adair, strongly signaled that the Sox, in fourth place at 24-22 and four games behind the Tigers, intended to do more than play out the string.

By Memorial Day, the White Sox (24-13) and the Tigers (24-14, 4.5 games ahead of the Orioles) had sprinted ahead of the pack. The Tigers had finished above .500 in five of the previous six years, averaging 88 wins during that span despite a managerial carousel that had seen new manager Mayo Smith's two predecessors, Charlie Dressen and Bob Swift, die of illnesses the previous year. (Smith had a recipe for long life: "When you smoke and drink, that tobacco doesn't mix with alcohol and you feel lousy the next morning, so I gave up cigarettes." He lived to be 62.) Led by 32-year-old All-Star right fielder Al Kaline, the Tigers boasted a powerful offense, scoring 4.19 runs per game and hitting 152 home runs, both good for second in the league. Four Tigers hit at least 20 homers: Kaline (25), first baseman Norm Cash (22), second baseman Dick McAuliffe (22), and catcher Bill Freehan (20), with left fielder Willie Horton just missing with 19. Kaline, Freehan, and McAuliffe made the All-Star team. The staff's big winner was Earl Wilson, who had been traded from Boston the previous June after speaking out about a racially discriminatory incident that had occurred at a bar during spring training in Florida. Supporting Wilson were lefty Mickey Lolich, Denny McLain, and Joe Sparma, but despite high win totals, Tiger pitchers were, at 3.60 runs allowed per game, just a hair away from league average.

The White Sox moved to the front in mid-June, after weeks of alternating with the Tigers, and stayed there for nearly two months. Piloted by Eddie Stanky, in his day a scrappy, tough infielder who was the inspirational counterexample for Leo Durocher's famous line, "Nice guys finish last," the team was founded on pitching and defense, just as it had been for the better part of the decade under Al Lopez. The White Sox had finished in the first division for nine straight years, winning at a .569 clip, but besides the 1959 pennant, all they had to show for their efforts were five second-place finishes, only one of which (1964) was close.

Quick with a quip, Stanky, nicknamed "the Brat" during his playing days, gave the race much of its flavor. In June he had called Yastrzemski "an All-Star from the neck down." Ever the bench jockey, he spent the summer chiding his opponents, wondering aloud why the Tigers weren't ahead of the league by 10 games and calling his White Sox "the dullest club in baseball" even as he complained about the lack of attention paid them.

Chicago's 2.45 ERA was not only the lowest in the league by 0.69 runs, but also the lowest since the dead-ball era. Joel Horlen (19-7, 2.06 ERA) and Gary Peters (16-10, 2.28 ERA) finished first and second in the league in ERA, with groundball specialist Tommy John (10-13, 2.47 ERA) fourth. The bullpen was even better, with knuckle-ballers Hoyt Wilhelm (1.31 ERA, 12 saves) and Wilbur Wood (2.45 ERA) as well as Bob Locker (2.09 ERA, 20 saves) and McMahon (1.67 ERA).

The offense was another story, eking out just 3.28 runs per game while hitting .225/.288/.320, unimpressive even in a league that averaged .236/.303/.351. It was as if the team were still following the "Hitless Wonder" recipe that brought them their 1906 championship. They were second in the league in steals (124) but did so at a self-defeating rate of 61 percent. As a unit, the offense was 99 runs below average according to WARP, with left fielder Pete Ward (+16 runs on a .233/.334/ .392 performance, good for a .284 EqA) and Tommy Agee (+6 on .234/ .302/.371) the only regulars above average. Shortstop Ron Hansen (6.4 WARP) and third baseman Don Buford (4.3) were the team's other top assets, more useful for their gloves than their bats.

While the White Sox took control of the race by mid-June, the defending champion Orioles were sinking below .500 for good. After averaging 96 wins a year for the previous three years under manager Hank Bauer and dethroning the Dodgers in a four-game sweep of the World Series, the O's struggled when young pitchers Dave McNally and Jim Palmer, who had combined to go 28-16 with a 3.31 ERA in 1966, succumbed to arm injuries and went just 10-8 with a 4.33 ERA in less than half as many innings. Meanwhile, defending Triple Crown winner Frank Robinson suffered a concussion in a baserunning collision on June 27 and missed a month of the season. At the same time, slugging first baseman Boog Powell slumped from 34 homers to 13. The O's would limp home with just 76 wins.

The Twins wrested the top spot from the White Sox in mid-August. Winners of 102 games and the AL pennant in 1965, Minnesota had stumbled to 89 victories in 1966, firing pitching coach Johnny Sain in the aftermath. The dismissal sent shock waves through the team; ace lefty Jim Kaat, who had won 25 games in 1966, voiced his support of the departed coach in an open letter to the public, claiming that if he were a club owner, he'd hire Sain and find a manager to complement him. It was yet another sign that skipper Sam Mele was on the hot seat, and when the club slopped to a 25-25 start in 1967, Mele was replaced by Triple-A Denver manager Cal Ermer. The Twins, who scored 4.09 runs per game, the third-best in the league, were the AL's most star-laden team, with first baseman Harmon Killebrew, rookie second baseman Rod Carew, and right fielder Tony Oliva all making the All-Star squad. But the team also had its liabilities, including .167-hitting catcher Jerry Zimmerman and shortstop Zoilo Versalles (.200/.249/.282), the 1965 MVP whose game had fallen into an abyss.

The rotation, led by another All-Star, Dean Chance, was one of the league's best. Acquired in a five-player deal from the Angels, the 1964 AL Cy Young winner bounced back from a pair of subpar years to go 20-14 with a 2.73 ERA. Jim Merritt, Dave Boswell, and Kaat rounded out a unit that didn't even have room for former All-Stars Jim Perry or Mudcat Grant, both of whom were relatively ineffective out of the bullpen; aside from top reliever Al Worthington, the rest of the pen was 0.5 wins below replacement level.

By the end of July, the Red Sox had cemented their overachiever status. A 10-game winning streak from July 14 to July 23, the latter half on the road, brought thousands of fans out to Boston's Logan Airport to welcome the players home. O'Connell continued his efforts to upgrade the team—which was now running second to the White Sox by two games. He obtained catcher Elston Howard, another African American, from the Yankees in early August, augmenting an underproducing catching corps of Mike Ryan, Russ Gibson, and Bob Tillman (though Howard didn't hit, batting just .147/.211/.198 for the Sox).

As the Twins pulled ahead of Chicago, the Red Sox fell to fourth place, trailing by 3.5 games on August 18. The game between Boston and California that night produced the season's darkest moment. In the fourth inning, California hurler Jack Hamilton drilled Conigliaro in the face with an inside fastball. From the on-deck circle, Petrocelli heard an awful sound: "It was a 'squish,' like a tomato or melon hitting the ground." Conigliaro's cheekbone was shattered, his left retina severely damaged. According to Conigliaro's doctor, had the blow been two inches higher, he would have died. The popular right fielder missed the rest of the season and all of 1968, and although he recovered to hit 20 homers in 1969 and 36 in 1970, blurred vision eventually forced him from the game.

The Red Sox tried to offset the tragic loss of their second-best slugger by picking up Ken (Hawk) Harrelson, who had been released by the Kansas City A's in the aftermath of manager Alvin Dark's firing. The A's players issued a statement voicing support of Dark. When Harrelson, the team's outspoken first baseman, reportedly called Finley "a menace to baseball," Finley responded by releasing him.

Nearly a decade before arbitrator Peter Seitz's ruling created free agency, teams engaged in a frantic bidding war for Harrelson's services. The White Sox, who had attempted to upgrade incrementally via the additions of over-the-hill veterans Ken Boyer and Rocky Colavito, offered Harrelson—who had been making $12,000 with the A's—$100,000 for the rest of the year and for 1968. The Red Sox offered $118,000, the Atlanta Braves $125,000. Finally, O'Connell won out with a breathtaking $150,000 bid—remarkable money for a first baseman hitting just .273/.330/.423. Forced to play the unfamiliar position of right field in Conigliaro's stead—reserves Jose Tartabull and George Thomas were hopelessly unproductive—Harrelson hit just .200/.247/.388 for the Red Sox; a 4-for-30 slump forced Williams to bench him in late September. Nonetheless, Harrelson's arrival was a welcome distraction for Boston as the garrulous Hawk took the spotlight away from Yastrzemski, who was only too willing to surrender it.

Despite the bidding war and Conigliaro's injury, the Sox rode a seven-game winning streak into a share of first place. On August 25 they headed to Comiskey Park tied with the White Sox at the start of a crucial five-game series that found Stanky in fine form: "We don't belong in the same league with Boston, all those hairy-chested players and their new-breed manager," he said before the teams split a Friday evening doubleheader. Afterward, when the two teams got into a war of words over brushback pitches, Stanky opined that the Conigliaro beaning was retaliation for Lonborg's hit batsmen.

Boston took the third game, roughing up Horlen for 10 hits, then split Sunday's doubleheader, with a dramatic victory. With his team down 4-3 in the bottom of the ninth, White Sox center fielder Ken

Berry led off with a double, advancing to third on a sacrifice bunt. John Wyatt, Boston's top reliever, took over for Bell. Pinch-hitter Duane Josephson lined Wyatt's first pitch to right field, where Jose Tartabull made a one-handed grab and threw home as Berry tagged up. Howard blocked the plate with his foot, and in the extra split second created by forcing Berry to reach with his hand as he hook-slid around the catcher, the veteran backstop swooped down to apply the tag for a spectacular game-ending double play.

The four teams continued to jockey for position daily, each holding a share of the top spot at least once between September 1 and September 15. Looking ahead, the league office released a schedule accounting for the possibility of postseason tiebreakers to determine a winner; the dizzying menu listed 11 permutations involving two-way, three-way, and four-way ties. In response to a playoff-related question after Boston's dramatic victory on September 18, the irascible Williams spat, "We're in a playoff every night."

◆

After another Red Sox victory the following day, none of the contenders played each other until Boston met Minnesota for the season's final two games. The result was a whirlwind of scoreboard watching as the quartet battled the league's lower echelons, providing the likes of the Indians, Senators, A's, and Yankees the opportunity to play spoiler. As the penultimate weekend approached with the Twins and Red Sox tied at 88-66, the White Sox a game back at 87-67, and the Tigers another half-game back at 86-67, the four managers went to the whip, juggling their rotations to get their top starters three starts down the stretch. The move benefited the Tigers the most, as Lolich shut out the Senators on two days' rest on September 22, blanked the Yankees on September 26, and then tossed a third straight shutout against the Angels on September 30.

In the end, none of the teams seized control so much as they simply survived the final week; from Tuesday, September 26, through Sunday, October 1, the four teams went a combined 6-12. Chicago, which with five games remaining—two more than Minnesota and Boston, one more than Detroit—had control of its own destiny, began by dropping a doubleheader to last-place Kansas City, which beat both Horlen and Peters. "GOOD GRIEF! SOX DROP TWO," blared the eight-column headline on the *Chicago Tribune* front page. The A's, losers of 99 games in 1967, had been laying in wait for Stanky. "I was up for this game," said A's pitcher Chuck Dobson after winning game 1. "That man over there called me a donkey earlier in the year and I never forgot it."

On the same night, the Twins dropped the rubber match of their three-game series with the fifth-place California Angels. Chance got spanked on two days'

Table 1-3 A Day in the Life: September 27, 1967

| Team | W | L | GB | WP |
|------|---|---|-----|------|
| Minnesota | 91 | 69 | – | .569 |
| Boston | 90 | 70 | 1.0 | .563 |
| Detroit | 89 | 69 | 1.0 | .563 |
| Chicago | 89 | 70 | 1.5 | .560 |

rest, and the Red Sox were thrashed by the eighth-place Indians, with Lonborg, also on short rest, lasting just three innings and allowing four runs. Thursday's only scheduled game, the opener of a four-game set between the Angels and the Tigers, was a washout, creating a Friday night doubleheader. As play began that day, the four teams were still snarled (Table 1-3).

Friday night's doubleheader was washed away as well, setting up back-to-back twofers on Saturday and Sunday for Detroit. By then the herd had thinned. The meager White Sox offense, shut out in the nightcap of their fateful doubleheader against the A's, ran their scoreless string to three full games when they couldn't scrape together a single run against the seventh-place Senators on either Friday night or Saturday. South Side fans must have sensed trouble was brewing, as just 4,020 witnessed their team's expiration.

The Twins could have clinched at least a playoff berth with a victory over the Red Sox on Saturday, and when they scored a run and loaded the bases with just one out in the first inning against Boston starter Jose Santiago, it looked as if they might. They couldn't pad their lead, however, and their chances took a hit in the third inning, when Kaat, leading 1-0, left the game after hearing a pop in his elbow. The Sox rallied for a pair of runs in the fifth against Jim Perry, thanks to some bounces in their favor. After Reggie Smith led off with a double, Williams put in a pinch-hitter for punchless catcher Russ Gibson: Dalton Jones reached when his grounder struck Carew in the shoulder. Two strikeouts and a game-tying single from Jerry Adair brought up Yastrzemski, who hit a grounder that deflected off Killebrew's glove to Carew. The second baseman turned to throw, but Perry didn't cover, and the go-ahead run crossed the plate. Asked afterward if he planned to fine Perry, the Twins' manager Ermer replied, "There's no punishment to fit the crime."

The Twins tied the game in the top of the sixth, but the bottom half began with Scott driving Minnesota reliever Ron Kline's first pitch into the center field bleachers. It was a shot of redemption for the weight-challenged "Boomer," who had been benched several times by Williams for his inability to stay in shape. (Williams was willing to bench anyone, even Yastrzemski—briefly, early in the season.) Once Scott conned his way back into the lineup with the connivance of the coach's weighing him, he had a torrid finish, batting .332 in August and September. Yastrzemski extended the lead with a three-run blast, his 44th of the year, in the following frame, and despite a two-run blast from Killebrew in the top of the ninth—his 44th as well (the two shared the league lead)—the Twins' sloppy fielding had let the Sox live to fight another day.

The Tigers, meanwhile, split their Saturday doubleheader. Lolich twirled a three-hit, 11-strikeout shutout in the opener, and the Tiger offense chased Angels starter Hamilton with three runs in the first inning of the nightcap. The Tigers were still leading 6-2 when Fred Lasher, who had already pitched two hitless innings in relief of Wilson, allowed the first four Angels to reach base in the eighth. Six runs and three pitching changes later, the Tigers finally escaped the inning, but the damage had been done. They would need a Sunday sweep just to force a playoff. In the first three innings, they got much of the job done when they pounded out five runs: a two-run homer by Horton and three unearned runs from a two-out error by Angels center fielder Roger Repoz. With Sparma on the hill, the Tigers held on for a 6-4 win.

At Fenway, despite the excellent seasons turned in by both starters, the pitching contest looked like a mismatch in Minnesota's favor; Chance had gone 4-1 with a 1.58 ERA against Boston, while Lonborg had gone 0-3 with a 6.75 ERA against the Twins. Minnesota scored a run in the first when Killebrew scored on an Oliva double and a wild throw by Scott on what might have been an inning-ending out at the plate. The Twins added another in the third when Yastrzemski let a Killebrew single skip past him for an error, allowing Cesar Tovar to come around from first base. The Sox squandered leadoff hits by Lonborg in the third and Yastrzemski in the fourth; the latter, who had doubled, was doubled off second base on a Scott liner.

Still trailing 2-0 in the sixth, Williams allowed Lonborg to bat for himself leading off the inning. Noticing Tovar playing deep at third base, the pitcher dropped down a bunt on Chance's first pitch, beating it out when Tovar bobbled it. Three straight singles followed, the last a sharp liner up the middle by Yastrzemski to plate the game-tying runs. Harrelson grounded to Versalles; unable to start a double play because

Yaz had been running on a full count, the shortstop threw home, wide and late—3-2 Boston. With runners on first and second, Chance departed in favor of Worthington. Trying to induce a double play, Worthington bounced his first pitch to Scott, allowing Yastrzemski and pinch-runner Jose Tartabull to advance. Three pitches later, Worthington bounced another, allowing Yastrzemski to come home. Scott struck out, but Petrocelli walked, and then a Smith ground ball bounced off Killebrew's knee, plating Tartabull with the fifth and final run of the inning.

With Lonborg still on the hill, the Sox carried their 5-2 lead into the top of the eighth, when Yastrzemski came up big yet again, this time in the field. With two outs, Killebrew and Oliva both singled. The tying run came to the plate in the form of Bob Allison. The slugging fielder roped a sure double into the left field corner, but Yaz cut the ball off before it could reach the wall. Knowing that Allison represented the tying run, he threw a perfect peg to second, where Andrews—who had just entered the game after Adair was spiked while turning a brilliant double play—applied the tag. The out—Yastrzemski's 13th assist of the year—preserved a 5-3 lead. Lonborg and the Sox held on to win, with Petrocelli squeezing Rich Rollins's popup for the final out. "And there's pandemonium on the field! Listen!" exclaimed radio announcer Ned Martin as the Fenway faithful spilled out of the stands and mobbed Lonborg.

Even amid the celebration in the Red Sox clubhouse, as beer and shaving cream sprayed everywhere, the pennant still hinged on the outcome of the Tigers' second game against California. Denny McLain, making his first start since September 18 after spraining an ankle, was staked to a 3-1 lead. But in the third inning, after giving up an RBI double to Jim Fregosi, he limped off the mound, unable to land comfortably. Don Mincher greeted reliever John Hiller with a two-run homer, and the Angels added three more runs in the fourth and another in the fifth for an 8-3 lead. The Tigers cut the margin to 8-5 in the seventh before Minnie Rojas, at 27 the league leader in saves, came on to extricate the Halos from a two-on, two-out jam. Rojas held the lead into the ninth, but after allowing a leadoff double and a walk, he gave way to lefty George Brunet, who had been knocked out of Saturday's start after just two innings. As the Red Sox huddled nervously around the radio back in Fenway, Brunet retired pinch-hitter Jim Price on a fly ball, then induced the dangerous McAuliffe, who had driven in three of Detroit's five runs, to ground into just his second double play of the year. Against all odds, the pennant finally belonged to Boston.

TABLE 1-4 Top Major League Hitters After September 1 (with a Minimum of 70 Plate Appearances)

| Year | Player | Avg | OBP | Slg | OPS | PA | HR | RBI |
|------|--------|-----|-----|-----|-----|----|----|----|
| 2001 | Barry Bonds | .403 | .607 | 1.078 | 1.685 | 117 | 16 | 25 |
| 2000 | Richard Hidalgo | .477 | .532 | .953 | 1.486 | 124 | 11 | 32 |
| 2004 | Barry Bonds | .333 | .619 | .773 | 1.391 | 118 | 7 | 13 |
| 2000 | Jason Giambi | .396 | .536 | .844 | 1.380 | 125 | 13 | 32 |
| 1992 | Barry Bonds | .392 | .537 | .833 | 1.370 | 136 | 11 | 27 |
| 1998 | Mark McGwire | .329 | .461 | .902 | 1.363 | 102 | 15 | 28 |
| 1995 | Albert Belle | .313 | .420 | .929 | 1.349 | 120 | 17 | 32 |
| 1997 | Roberto Alomar | .500 | .532 | .800 | 1.332 | 78 | 4 | 17 |
| 2005 | Randy Winn | .439 | .469 | .862 | 1.331 | 133 | 11 | 18 |
| 1999 | Manny Ramirez | .360 | .524 | .800 | 1.324 | 103 | 8 | 30 |
| 2006 | Ryan Howard | .385 | .562 | .750 | 1.312 | 137 | 9 | 21 |
| 2002 | Barry Bonds | .362 | .614 | .681 | 1.295 | 114 | 6 | 22 |
| 1995 | Mark McGwire | .288 | .470 | .822 | 1.292 | 100 | 12 | 25 |
| 1995 | Gary Sheffield | .343 | .484 | .800 | 1.284 | 93 | 10 | 27 |
| 1962 | Mickey Mantle | .409 | .557 | .712 | 1.269 | 88 | 5 | 20 |
| 1998 | Barry Bonds | .389 | .491 | .778 | 1.269 | 111 | 7 | 22 |
| **1967** | **Carl Yastrzemski** | **.417** | **.504** | **.760** | **1.265** | **113** | **9** | **26** |
| 2006 | Geoff Jenkins | .409 | .506 | .758 | 1.264 | 79 | 7 | 12 |
| 2002 | Manny Ramirez | .396 | .482 | .781 | 1.263 | 112 | 9 | 30 |
| 1998 | Edgar Martinez | .447 | .520 | .741 | 1.261 | 102 | 4 | 16 |

The Red Sox would face the St. Louis Cardinals in the World Series, nearly overcoming a 3-1 deficit before ultimately bowing in seven games to the Bob Gibson/Lou Brock/Curt Flood mini-dynasty that had captured the 1964 title and won another pennant in 1968 before losing to the Tigers in the World Series. While Boston's loss extended the team's championship drought to 49 years, the 1967 season has always been viewed as a success, exempt from the agonies conjured by the team's attempts to shake the so-called Curse of the Bambino, the near misses of 1946, 1948, 1949, 1978, 1986, and 2003.

The Sox didn't exactly enjoy unbridled success immediately after 1967. Not until 1972, when they missed the playoffs by a half-game due to scheduling havoc wrought by the spring Players Association strike, did they again come close to reaching the postseason, and not until 1975 did they win another pennant. Yastrzemski, who finished his Hall of Fame career with 3,419 hits and 452 homers, would never dominate as he had in 1967 (Tables 1-4 and 1-5). Lonborg injured his knee just months after the World Series and was little more than a league-average hurler for the rest of his career. Williams wore out his welcome by the middle of 1969, as he would do time and again at five

Table 1-5 Top Major League Hitters, Last 12 Games of the Season (with a Minimum of 35 Plate Appearances)

| Year | Player | Avg | OBP | Slg | OPS | Games | PA | HR | RBI |
|------|--------|-----|-----|-----|-----|-------|----|----|-----|
| 2001 | Barry Bonds | .448 | .698 | 1.207 | 1.905 | 12 | 53 | 7 | 10 |
| 1997 | Barry Bonds | .343 | .558 | 1.086 | 1.643 | 12 | 52 | 7 | 13 |
| 1961 | Orlando Cepeda | .487 | .583 | 1.051 | 1.635 | 11 | 48 | 6 | 15 |
| 1995 | Albert Belle | .357 | .429 | 1.190 | 1.619 | 11 | 50 | 11 | 17 |
| 2001 | Jim Edmonds | .514 | .646 | .971 | 1.617 | 12 | 48 | 4 | 11 |
| 1979 | Oscar Gamble | .472 | .525 | 1.083 | 1.608 | 11 | 40 | 6 | 15 |
| 2004 | Vladimir Guerrero | .452 | .521 | 1.071 | 1.592 | 11 | 48 | 7 | 12 |
| 1961 | Leon Wagner | .471 | .500 | 1.088 | 1.588 | 11 | 38 | 6 | 19 |
| 1962 | Harmon Killebrew | .364 | .472 | 1.114 | 1.585 | 12 | 53 | 11 | 22 |
| 2001 | Richie Sexson | .432 | .510 | 1.068 | 1.578 | 12 | 51 | 9 | 23 |
| 1995 | Mickey Tettleton | .389 | .542 | 1.028 | 1.569 | 12 | 48 | 6 | 12 |
| **1967** | **Carl Yastrzemski** | **.523** | **.604** | **.955** | **1.558** | **12** | **53** | **5** | **16** |
| 1969 | Sal Bando | .459 | .596 | .946 | 1.542 | 12 | 53 | 5 | 13 |
| 2000 | Richard Hidalgo | .475 | .563 | .975 | 1.538 | 11 | 48 | 5 | 9 |

other big-league stops while racking up four pennants, two championships, and 1,571 wins. O'Connell lasted through the 1977 season, overseeing the development of a formidable outfield of Jim Rice, Fred Lynn, and Dwight Evans and a return to the World Series. But he also made some dubious trades, sending reliever Sparky Lyle, a rookie in 1967, to the Yankees for light-hitting first baseman Danny Cater in 1972 and trading away promising first baseman Cecil Cooper to reacquire the aging and overweight George Scott in 1976.

Short-lived as it was, the O'Connell-Williams tandem made the 1967 Sox winners by running the team on meritocratic principles that had been anathema before the managers' arrival. With little to lose but another 100 or so games, O'Connell boldly built with homegrown talent and selected an ideal manager to mold a team laden with impressionable youngsters while weeding out the bad actors. The general manager never stopped trying to improve his team even after the June 15 trade deadline passed, working the waiver wire and utilizing the unprecedented avenue of Harrelson's free agency. Though that move didn't bear the intended dividends on the field, it kept Harrelson away from other contenders and showed an acute understanding of the marginal economic value of each additional win: When you're right on the edge of the pennant, each victory is worth exponentially more money than the ones that precede it.

For better or worse, the 1967 season restored the legitimacy of the Yawkey regime by producing the team's first integrated winner, although the complicated legacy of the Sox's failure to racially integrate in a timely fashion would linger like a ghost, even as black players like Rice and Luis Tiant attained stardom. Not until the days of Pedro Martinez and David Ortiz did the team's black stars receive the same unconditional love from fans that its white players did.

Ultimately, the legacy of the "Impossible Dream" season was the fan base's restored faith in the franchise. After languishing in the bottom half of the league, in terms of attendance, with just 812,160 fans per year from 1961 to 1966, the Sox drew 1.77 million fans per year over the next 12 seasons, finishing either first or second in attendance every year, despite Fenway Park's limited capacity. While the rest of the league finally caught up, the 1967 season renewed the fans' love affair with the team, marking the beginning of the modern Red Sox franchise.

## The Summer of Loving Carl Yastrzemski

JAY JAFFE

In the simplified narratives that our sports media produce, the notion of one player's carrying a team is a popular and appealing one. It puts a human—even superhuman—face on a disparate collection of players, emphasizing the strengths of one hitter's or one pitcher's accomplishments while glossing over his own weaknesses and those of his teammates. Who cares about Babe Ruth's lousy baserunning, or who was riding shotgun to Joe DiMaggio in 1941, or even Barry Bonds's peevishness unless it actually cost his team a game?

Can one player carry a team? Performances like Carl Yastrzemski's final two weeks of September 1967, when he hit a jaw-dropping .523/.604/.955, certainly suggest it's possible for a short time. In the longer term, the nature of baseball would suggest not. Aside from the obvious—the simple unlikelihood of one player's maintaining such a high level of performance over a larger time frame—there's the inherent structure of the game. The best hitter can only bat once every nine times, the most durable pitcher needs a few days' rest between starts, and even the best fielder (beyond catchers) handles the ball only a handful of times each game, making it extremely unlikely that a team could keep relying on the same player over and over again for that extra boost.

As superficial as the notion of one player's carrying a team may be, our ability to quantify the contributions of each player via an all-encompassing value metric like wins above replacement player (WARP) lends itself well to exploring the limitations of this concept as it applies to a full season. WARP measures each player's hitting, pitching, and fielding contributions against those of a freely available reserve or waiver-wire pickup. The metric calculates these contributions in terms of runs and then converts those runs into the currency of wins. Park and league contexts are built right into WARP, so that, for example, a player in a barren offensive environment such as mid-1960s Dodger Stadium and another player in a bountiful one such as turn-of-the-century Coors Field can be measured on the same scale.

With WARP in hand, we can answer questions such as the following:

1. How much impact does the presence of one great player have on a team's chances?
2. How much impact does the presence of one great player have on a team's chances if he's head-and-shoulders above all his other teammates?

To address these questions, we created a pool consisting of every AL and NL team since 1901, excluding the 1981 and 1994 strike years, for 2,082 teams in all. We logged the WARP scores of each team's top two players, the team's win-loss record, its spot in the standings (ignoring the wild card), and games behind first place. The average team in the sample had a .500 record, of course. It won its pennant or division title 14.6 percent of the time and finished an average of 16.9 games out of first place. With that baseline in mind, Table 1-6 shows a composite look at how the teams did, solely according to the WARP levels of their top-ranked players.

The sample sizes of the upper rows in the table are small enough to be dragged down by a few great seasons put up by players on horrendous

Table 1-6 The Impact of a Team's Top Player on a Team's Performance

| WARP Score of Team's Top Player | No. of Teams | W-L Record | Pennant Success (%) | GB |
|---|---|---|---|---|
| ≥15.0 | 23 | .550 | 17.4 | 10.2 |
| 14.0–14.9 | 42 | .563 | 31.0 | 6.1 |
| 13.0–13.9 | 64 | .553 | 28.1 | 6.9 |
| 12.0–12.9 | 128 | .557 | 32.8 | 7.8 |
| 11.0–11.9 | 206 | .536 | 23.8 | 10.6 |
| 10.0–10.9 | 329 | .532 | 21.9 | 10.8 |
| 9.0–9.9 | 390 | .512 | 14.9 | 14.5 |
| 8.0–8.9 | 384 | .492 | 9.9 | 18.1 |
| 7.0–7.9 | 265 | .457 | 3.8 | 24.8 |
| 6.0–6.9 | 169 | .429 | 0.0 | 29.6 |
| <6.0 | 82 | .370 | 0.0 | 39.9 |

teams—Cal Ripken Jr.'s 17.4 WARP for the 67-95 Orioles in 1991 or Steve Carlton's 15.4 WARP for the 59-97 Phillies in 1972, for example—but it's clear that having one great player greatly increases the chances of a team's winning its league or division. Having a player of at least 13.0 WARP (combining the top three rows)—say, George Brett in 1985 (.335/.436/.585) or Albert Pujols in 2006 (.331/.431/.671)—gives us 129 teams with a combined winning percentage of .556, a 27.1 percent chance of winning a pennant or division, and an average finish of 7.3 games out of first. In all, these are outcomes comparable to those of the 12.0-12.9 bracket, with slightly fewer successes but a greater number of close finishes. Once the team's best player falls below 12.0 WARP, the odds of winning take a significant hit. Once the WARP falls below 10.0, the advantage is pretty much lost, and it takes an extreme fluke to make a winner out of a team such as the 1980 Astros, led by Jose Cruz (.289/.367/.421), whose best player is worth less than 8.0 WARP.

The number of teams winning without a star of at least 8.0 WARP is just 10 out of 516, or 1.9 percent. The average WARP of the top five players on those 10 winners are 7.5, 6.8, 6.4, 6.1, and 5.6 (32.5 total for the top five). Even with a balance of players having good years, it's very tough to win without at least one player having a star-caliber year. One player can't carry a team, but *somebody* has to do the heavy lifting.

Turning to the second question, we looked at teams with the biggest WARP gaps between their best and second-best players (Table 1-7). Note how much lower the composite winning percentages are at each level than they were when we only considered the team's best player.

Table 1-7 Binary Star Power: The Impact of a Team's Top Two Players on a Team's Performance

| WARP Gap* | No. of Teams | Avg. WARP of Top Player | W-L Record | Pennant Success % | GP |
|---|---|---|---|---|---|
| ≥7.0 | 24 | 15.0 | .512 | 4.20 | 15.5 |
| 6.0–6.9 | 31 | 13.6 | .490 | 9.70 | 20.3 |
| 5.0–5.9 | 41 | 12.5 | .512 | 19.50 | 15.1 |
| 4.0–4.9 | 94 | 11.8 | .513 | 18.10 | 14.7 |
| 3.0–3.9 | 200 | 11.0 | .509 | 16.00 | 15.6 |
| 2.0–2.9 | 333 | 10.0 | .501 | 15.60 | 16.4 |
| 1.0–1.9 | 551 | 9.1 | .499 | 14.50 | 16.9 |
| 0.0–0.9 | 808 | 8.3 | .496 | 13.70 | 17.6 |

*Difference between the WARP of the best and second-best players on a team.

The lack of a supporting star clearly hampers the winning effort. If we combine all the teams with a WARP gap greater than 4.9, we have 96 teams with an average best player of 13.5 WARP. According to Table 1-6, we'd expect this group to have a winning percentage of around .553 and a pennant success of around 28 percent and be about seven games out of first. Yet the composite for the group is just .505, 12.5 percent, and 16.9 games behind. The lack of a second effective player appears to significantly lower a team's pennant chances, given a star player of a certain quality.

A simple correlation confirms these observations. Across the sample of 2,082 team-seasons, the correlation between the team-high WARP score and that team's winning percentage is 0.49. But the correlation between the team's *second-highest* WARP score and winning percentage is actually higher, at 0.60. In other words, having a second star-level player is a better predictor of winning. Furthermore, balance and depth appear to be quite important; the correlations between winning percentage and WARP score increase the deeper one drills into the roster, at least from third-highest (correlation 0.64) to fourth-highest (0.68) to fifth-highest (0.69).

That finding shouldn't be very surprising, given the reasons we have just discussed. Baseball is primarily a team sport; a team can't simply expect its best player to do the bulk of the heavy lifting and still succeed. Nonetheless, the rare situations in which a player rose far above his teammates for a winning season are instructive. Table 1-8 shows the top 10 WARP differentials for pennant or division winners.

Babe Ruth tops the list with what was, according to WARP, the greatest season of all time. Though he hit "only" 41 home runs in 1923, Ruth's .393/.545/.764 season established career highs in batting average, on-base percentage, hits (205), walks (170), and doubles (45). Ruth definitely carried the Yankees' offense that year; second baseman Aaron Ward (7.4 WARP) was the only other hitter above 4.8 WARP, and his value was largely defensive. Pitchers Joe Bush (7.8 WARP) and Herb Pennock (7.1) keyed a staff that was slightly better at preventing runs (relative to the league) than the offense was at scoring. Debuting on June 15 of that year but drawing just 26 at bats was Lou Gehrig, who would give the Bambino an effective compatriot and would keep Ruth off the upper reaches of this list, except for 1926. That year, the Babe was 21st on the list when the Iron Horse reached double digits in WARP for the first of 11 times.

Ruth also ranked fourth in his 1921 season, when he bashed 59 home runs to fuel .378/.512/.846 hitting, but he had moderate offen-

Table 1-8 Batman and Robin: Top 10 WARP Differentials Between a Team's Best and Second-Best Players

| Team Rank | Year | Team | Player 1 | WARP | Player 2 | WARP | Dif | W-L | GB |
|---|---|---|---|---|---|---|---|---|---|
| 1 | 1923 | NY-A | Babe Ruth | 18.2 | Joe Bush | 7.8 | 10.4 | 98-54 | 16.0 |
| 2 | 1945 | DET-A | Hal Newhouser | 14.4 | Roy Cullenbine | 8.0 | 6.4 | 88-65 | 1.5 |
| 3 | 1968 | STL-N | Bob Gibson | 13.9 | Lou Brock | 7.6 | 6.3 | 97-65 | 9.0 |
| 4 | 1921 | NY-A | Babe Ruth | 15.5 | Carl Mays | 9.5 | 6.0 | 98-55 | 4.5 |
| 5 | 1962 | SF-N | Willie Mays | 13.1 | Orlando Cepeda | 7.5 | 5.6 | 103-62 | 1.0 |
| 6 | 1990 | PIT-N | Barry Bonds | 13.0 | Doug Drabek | 7.5 | 5.5 | 95-67 | 4.0 |
| 7T | 1984 | CHI-N | Ryne Sandberg | 11.9 | Leon Durham | 6.5 | 5.4 | 96-65 | 6.5 |
| 7T | 1997 | SF-N | Barry Bonds | 12.2 | Shawn Estes | 6.8 | 5.4 | 90-72 | 2.0 |
| 9 | 2003 | SF-N | Barry Bonds | 13.4 | Jason Schmidt | 8.2 | 5.2 | 100-61 | 15.5 |
| 10T | 2004 | LA-N | Adrian Beltre | 12.8 | Eric Gagne | 7.7 | 5.1 | 93-69 | 2.0 |
| 10T | 1995 | CLE-A | Albert Belle | 14.0 | Jim Thome | 8.9 | 5.1 | 100-44 | 30.0 |
| 10T | 1995 | ATL-N | Greg Maddux | 13.6 | Tom Glavine | 8.5 | 5.1 | 90-54 | 21.0 |

sive help from Bob Meusel (6.8 WARP) and Ward (6.3), as well as a pitching staff with an effective one-two punch in Carl Mays (9.5) and Waite Hoyt (6.9). The Ruth-Mays tandem also ranks 16th on the list for the 1916 season, when the Bambino was exclusively a pitcher for the Red Sox. The game's future savior was 23-12 with a 1.75 ERA in 323.2 innings, helping the Sox to the third of four World Championships between 1912 and 1918.

Pitcher Hal Newhouser, second on the list, rose to prominence during World War II, when many of the major's top players were serving in the military. Newhouser had been a sub-.500 pitcher on mediocre teams, but, freed from service because of a congenital heart ailment, he rocketed to 29-9 with a 2.22 ERA in the softened balata-ball season of 1944. He went 25-9 with a 1.81 ERA in 1945, earned MVP honors in both years, and led the Tigers to the 1945 World Championship.

Bob Gibson places third with his legendary 22-9, 1.12 ERA season in 1968, the Year of the Pitcher. Though Lou Brock ran a distant second at 7.7 WARP, just a hair's breadth separates Brock from Curt Flood (7.6) and Dal Maxvill (7.5) as the Cards' second-best player that year—a good illustration of the value of balance beyond one superstar. Willie Mays, the fifth-ranked player, hit .304/.384/.615 with 49 home runs in 1962. WARP runner-up Orlando Cepeda ranked second to Mays on a talented team with five future Hall of Famers on the roster—Mays, Cepeda, Juan Marichal, Gaylord Perry, and Willie McCovey. Blocked by Cepeda at first base, McCovey was a platoon outfielder that year, hitting .293/.370/.590 overall and worth 3.8 WARP—or better than half the WARP of Cepeda in roughly 40 percent of the playing time.

Barry Bonds cracks the top 10 in three very different eras of his career. In his Pirate guise in 1990, he had no particularly outstanding teammate, but, like Gibson, had several who were close in value. Doug Drabek (7.6), Bobby Bonilla (7.4), Jay Bell (7.3), and Andy Van Slyke (7.2) proved a more-than-ample supporting cast. In 1997, before the alleged steroid use that pumped up his muscles and statistics, he had less support; besides Shawn Estes (6.8), only Jeff Kent (6.6) topped 6.0 WARP, though J. T. Snow (5.9) came close. By 2003, he'd lost Kent as a teammate, but had help from Jason Schmidt (8.2) and José Cruz Jr. (7.3). Ray Durham (6.3) might have challenged for the number two spot had he not missed nearly all of August with injury.

The all-time top differential didn't come from a pennant winner, but from the greatest season in baseball history, according to WARP. On the strength of a 36-7, 1.14 ERA season, Walter Johnson's 18.3 WARP in 1913 produced the largest gap of all, 12.4 WARP ahead of Chick Gandil's 5.9. With no supporting cast (the future Black Sox instigator Gandil should hardly count), Johnson dragged the Senators to a second-place, 90-win finish. Laboring for some wretched teams, Johnson produced five of the top 20 differentials in our study.

Yastrzemski's 1967 WARP total (12.6) was 3.6 wins better than that of teammate Rico Petrocelli, a differential that's in a five-way tie—with Sandy Koufax's WARP of 1966, Lou Gehrig's of 1936, Ron Guidry's of 1978, and Vlad Guerrero's of 2004—for 42nd place on this list. His season was unimpressive by that measure, perhaps, but the WARP gap statistics hardly lessen the magic of his accomplishment. Yaz showed that a player might spark a team for a spell of 10 or 14 games, but maintaining that kind of hot streak over a full season is the real Impossible Dream.

## Managers 2.0:
### Dick Williams and the Men Who Ate Gene Mauch's Lunch

CHRISTINA KAHRL

In becoming the manager of the 1967 Red Sox, Dick Williams enjoyed a decent amount of luck. Ditched by the Sox as a big-league ballplayer

Table 1-9  Major League Managers with the Most Games Managed, 1947 through 2006

| Manager | Career | Debut* | G | W | L | Notes |
|---|---|---|---|---|---|---|
| Tony La Russa | 1979–2006 | 34 | 4,286 | 2,297 | 1,986 | |
| Sparky Anderson | 1970–1995 | 36 | 4,030 | 2,194 | 1,834 | Hall of Fame |
| Gene Mauch | 1960–1987 | 34 | 3,942 | 1,902 | 2,037 | |
| Bobby Cox | 1978–2006 | 36 | 3,860 | 2,171 | 1,686 | |
| Joe Torre | 1977–2006 | 36 | 3,681 | 1,973 | 1,702 | |
| Walter Alston | 1954–1976 | 42 | 3,658 | 2,040 | 1,613 | Hall of Fame |
| Ralph Houk | 1961–1984 | 41 | 3,157 | 1,619 | 1,531 | |
| Tommy Lasorda | 1976–1996 | 48 | 3,041 | 1,599 | 1,439 | Hall of Fame |
| Dick Williams | 1967–1988 | 37 | 3,023 | 1,571 | 1,451 | |
| Lou Piniella | 1986–2005 | 42 | 2,939 | 1,519 | 1,420 | |
| Chuck Tanner | 1970–1988 | 41 | 2,738 | 1,352 | 1,381 | |
| Bill Rigney | 1956–1976 | 38 | 2,561 | 1,239 | 1,321 | |
| Earl Weaver | 1968–1986 | 37 | 2,541 | 1,480 | 1,060 | Hall of Fame |
| Leo Durocher | 1948–1973 | 33 | 2,494 | 1,305 | 1,181 | Hall of Fame; doesn't count 1938–1946 |
| Casey Stengel | 1949–1965 | 43 | 2,433 | 1,324 | 1,100 | Hall of Fame; doesn't count 1934–1936, 1938–1943 |
| Al Lopez | 1951–1969 | 42 | 2,425 | 1,410 | 1,004 | Hall of Fame |
| Whitey Herzog | 1973–1990 | 41 | 2,409 | 1,281 | 1,125 | |
| John McNamara | 1969–1996 | 37 | 2,395 | 1,160 | 1,233 | |
| Tom Kelly | 1986–2001 | 36 | 2,386 | 1,140 | 1,244 | |
| Jim Leyland | 1986–2006 | 41 | 2,364 | 1,164 | 1,198 | |

*Manager's age when he managed his first major league game.

at the end of the 1964 season, Williams was offered a job as a player-coach with Boston's Triple-A affiliate in Seattle for the 1965 season. He accepted, but when an unexpected affiliation switch moved the Sox's top farm team to Toronto, the Seattle manager (Edo Vani) chose not to cross the border. Williams was offered the manager's chair in Vani's place. As Williams steered the club to a pair of International League titles, he gained an intimate familiarity with many of the players he would subsequently lead as manager of the "Impossible Dream." The campaign won him *Sporting News*'s Manager of the Year award and, at the relatively young age of 38, earned him newfound job security in a three-year contract. But before the end of the contract— after his second season—he was fired, and he set out on the road to a long, successful career as a major league manager.

Consider Williams among his peers, the 20 managers with the most games managed, 1947 through 2006 (Table 1-9). The seven Hall of

Famers on the list will probably be joined by La Russa, Cox, and Torre after they retire. In this company, some of the more notable aspects of Williams's success with the Red Sox no longer seem remarkable. That he was 37 at the start of the season sounds young for a manager in abstract, especially considering the number of 37-year-old players at any nearby stadium these days, but given the average starting age of the post-1947 managers, 37 isn't young.

One common observation about managers is that age has no impact on their performance. In fact, younger managers are far more likely to be successful than older managers. Shockingly few managers have managed for any length of time past their 60th birthday. This drop-off with age is partly due to the increasing generation gap between players and managers as time passes. A young manager is a near contemporary of his players. Time passes, and he's more like a father, then a grandfather. Age was an asset for Williams in 1967—his oldest regular was 27-year-old Carl Yastrzemski. Williams's hard-core discipline and focus on fundamentals was not only something many players had already endured playing for him in Toronto, but also something that could go over more easily on a young team with no track record for success. It was part of a pattern that Williams repeated over many seasons: Find young players who would get with his program, and discard any players who could not.

Even so, Williams developed as a manager, changing over time. Moving on to Oakland, he took over another young team and helped drive an exceptional collection of talent to three division titles and a pair of pennants. Tired of dealing with interference by team owner Charlie Finley, he moved on to the Angels. Adapting to their light-hitting lineup in 1975, he called for a league-leading 220 steals. He was mentally flexible in all but one regard, his willingness to tear into players a bit more publicly than all of them cared for. This created problems for him in Anaheim, where he feuded with washed-up veterans and cranky kids alike; in Montreal, where he labeled staff ace Steve Rogers "a fraud"; and in San Diego, where he referred to pitcher Andy Hawkins as "the Timid Texan." His career ended in a futile stint in Seattle, with Williams complaining about ownership's failure to get him Dave Kingman in 1987 (Kingman had struggled to a miserable year with the A's in 1986, at .210/.255/.431) and blaming born-again Christians in the clubhouse, as he had previously blamed drugs, indolence, and laziness. Ironically, he was fired for the last time after being slammed in print by one of his players, staff ace Mark Langston.

Beyond the 20 managers listed in Table 1-9, a few notable skippers

Table 1-10 Other Notable Managers from Dick Williams's Era

| Manager | Career | Debut | G | W | L | Notes |
|---|---|---|---|---|---|---|
| Billy Martin | 1969–1988 | 40 | 2,267 | 1,253 | 1,013 | |
| Red Schoendienst | 1965–1990 | 42 | 1,999 | 1,041 | 955 | Hall of Fame |
| Jack McKeon | 1973–2005 | 42 | 1,952 | 1,011 | 940 | |
| Bill Virdon | 1972–1984 | 40 | 1,918 | 995 | 921 | |
| Don Zimmer | 1972–1991 | 41 | 1,744 | 885 | 858 | |

who came up around the same time as Williams should be listed among his peer group (Table 1-10). As a new manager, Williams was in the vanguard of a generation of young managers who went on to make names for themselves among the game's greatest. You can consider them the generation that ate Gene Mauch's lunch—the cadre that came up during the period when the game broke lose from the run-starved high-mound era and initiated baseball's most ambitious explorations of the speed game. These managers were also celebrities, the men who won the pennants and commanded top dollar in a market as novel as free agency would be in the 1970s, and some of whom made as many headlines as the players did themselves.

Following in Williams's wake were a pair of Hall of Famers and a number of other tremendously successful skippers. First up, in 1968, was Earl Weaver. The Orioles manager took over a veteran club that won the pennant and the World Series under Hank Bauer in 1966, but had dropped off since. Weaver won three straight pennants from 1969 to 1971, and while history tends to simplify his style as unimaginatively waiting around for a three-run homer, he was far more creative than that caricature allows. Not simply a big-inning manager, he had a surprising fondness for outstanding defensive players (like shortstop Mark Belanger and center fielder Paul Blair), using them as starters and not as defensive substitutes, and then pulling them when the opportunity to create a big inning presented itself. He also had an exceptional knack in setting up his rotations, showing particular creativity in breaking in young starters in middle relief. Moreover, Weaver was one of the first managers to collect data on how well his players were doing against others and to use the information in setting up his lineups and managing his pitching staff.

After Weaver, Billy Martin got his first gig in a well-traveled career with the 1969 Twins, winning the first-ever AL West title. In what became a recurrent theme, he got himself fired for his troubles. Beyond his capacity to wear out his welcome (usually by hitting someone),

Martin deserves to be considered Casey Stengel's greatest pupil. Like Stengel, Martin was a true practitioner of the tactical suppleness and in-game flexibility that had helped the old man get the Yankees past the initially favored Indians and Red Sox in the late 1940s and early 1950s. Martin's fame was for his off-field behavior, but he also built platoons and was relentlessly aggressive in his in-game tactics. Highlights of these tactics include his letting Rickey Henderson loose on the league with the Oakland A's and Martin's relishing of trick plays like delayed and straight steals of home.

In 1970, Sparky Anderson and Chuck Tanner joined the fold. Despite a nondescript résumé of managing briefly in the minors and coaching for the first Padres squad, Anderson was wooed away from the Angels before the 1970 season and helped guide the Reds to fame as the Big Red Machine. He initially had a reputation as a player's manager, deferring to a number of his veterans, but eventually became better known for a quick hook managing a pitching staff and for the incredible amount of overwhelmingly positive blarney with which he'd shower the press. At the end of that same season, new White Sox general manager Roland Hemond elevated a 41-year-old Chuck Tanner out of the Angels' organization—fresh off of skippering the Hawaii Islanders to the Pacific Coast League title—and into the manager's seat. He became infamous for his Pollyanna attitude, upbeat in the face of everything, but he was particularly aggressive with the running game; his 1976 Oakland A's still hold the all-time single-season record for stolen bases (341). He later won a pennant and the World Series with the "We Are Family" Pirates, beating Weaver's Orioles in 1979.

Whitey Herzog, a 42-year-old rookie manager with the hapless 1973 Rangers, showed up late, stepping into Ted Williams's shoes. He might have skippered the dugout sooner, but he had spent most of his time between his retirement as a player in 1963 and 1973 in player development, first scouting for Charlie Finley's A's and later serving as the Mets' director of player personnel. If both Martin and Tanner made names for themselves as erstwhile practitioners of the running game, Herzog elevated speed itself to a guiding principle in team construction. "Whiteyball" preached the value of speed afield and on the bases, and combined with the singular greatness of players like closer Bruce Sutter and shortstop Ozzie Smith, Herzog's approach wound up generating three pennants in a six-year stretch.

Some of the lesser lights who came up at this time deserve mention as well. Jack McKeon's career as a manager went in all sorts of directions, but the one unifying characteristic was his adaptability, working for one crazed owner or another, cleaning up after one equally crazed disciplinarian or another, but perhaps saving the best for last in scraping together a bullpen to help the Marlins win their 2003 championship. Don Zimmer was many things during his managerial career—reviled in Fenway, beloved in Wrigley, and just short of success everywhere, but in his last years, he was almost insane in his bold, in-game tactical creativity.

Collectively, all these managers were innovative in their own ways. Each had come up as ballplayers during the staid 1950s—a period when in-game tactics were almost obliterated by the wisdom of pursuing the big inning. And each was old enough to remember the electrifying arrival of Jackie Robinson and to have seen or played against Maury Wills. They also cut their teeth as managers, either in the minors or during the very start of their careers, during a mini–ice age for offense, the high-mound stretch from 1964 to 1968. Offensive levels dropped from 4.5 runs per team per game in 1961 to 3.4 in 1968, returning to usefulness all the one-run strategies from the dead-ball era—the running game, bunting, the hit-and-run. Exposed to that blend of experiences and playing and managing in very different offensive environments, managers ended up going in their own directions once the mounds were lowered. These manager-individualists created a diversity in managerial styles that the game had not seen before, and hasn't seen since.

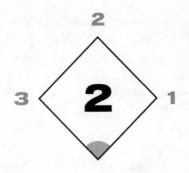

# 1959 National League

## Alston's L.A. Confidential

JAY JAFFE

Walter Alston surveyed the situation on the wet, gray afternoon of September 28, 1959, and didn't like what he saw. As a sparse County Stadium crowd of 18,297 looked on in a drizzle, the 47-year-old Los Angeles Dodgers manager had just watched the Milwaukee Braves, two-time defending champions of the National League, tie the score against starter Danny McDevitt in the first game of their best-of-three playoff.

The Dodgers had scratched out a run in the top of the first, and McDevitt had cruised through the bottom half of the frame, striking out sluggers Eddie Mathews and Joe Adcock while working around the even more dangerous Hank Aaron. But here in the second inning, the compact lefty had lost the plate and the Braves were connecting. Andy Pafko had lined out sharply to center field on the inning's first pitch, Johnny Logan had walked on four straight, and after McDevitt had fallen behind in the count to both Del Crandall and Bill Bruton, each had laced hard-hit singles, Bruton bringing Logan around to score. The pennant was on the line, and the Braves were rallying. Even with pitcher Carlton Willey due up next, it was time for the hook.

McDevitt had been an idiosyncratic choice of a starter, but then those choices in a season-ending playoff often are, given the mad scramble that precedes them. None of the Dodgers' three top winners,

## 1959 National League Prospectus

| Team | W | L | Pct | GB | DIF | Date Elim | W | L |
|---|---|---|---|---|---|---|---|---|
| | | Actual Standings | | | | | Pythag | |
| Dodgers | 88 | 68 | .564 | – | 15 | – | 82 | 74 |
| Braves | 86 | 70 | .551 | 2.0 | 89 | Sept 29 | 89 | 67 |
| Giants | 83 | 71 | .539 | 4.0 | 79 | Sept 27 | 87 | 67 |
| Pirates | 78 | 76 | .506 | 9.0 | 0 | Sept 20 | 74 | 80 |
| Cubs | 74 | 80 | .481 | 13.0 | 1 | Sept 15 | 75 | 79 |
| Reds | 74 | 80 | .481 | 13.0 | 2 | Sept 15 | 80 | 74 |
| Cardinals | 71 | 83 | .461 | 16.0 | 0 | Sept 10 | 68 | 86 |
| Phillies | 64 | 90 | .416 | 23.0 | 4 | Sept 5 | 64 | 90 |

| League Averages | | | | BP Stats Leaders | | | |
|---|---|---|---|---|---|---|---|
| AVG | OBP | SLG | BABIP | Offense, BRAA | | Indiv WARP | |
| .260 | .325 | .400 | .284 | Braves | 109 | Ernie Banks | 13.7 |
| ERA | K9 | BB9 | H9 | Pitching, PRAA | | Hank Aaron | 12.6 |
| 3.95 | 5.3 | 3.2 | 9.0 | Dodgers | 52 | Eddie Mathews | 11.9 |

Don Drysdale, Johnny Podres, and Roger Craig, was adequately rested. The most obvious alternative was Sandy Koufax, but the 23-year-old southpaw had not yet developed into the dominant ace who would lead the NL in ERAs for five straight years. Although he'd reeled off 41 strikeouts over three starts from August 24 through September 6—including an NL-record 18-strikeout game against the Giants—Koufax's ERA since then had been an unsightly 7.47, and he hadn't even gotten through an inning in his previous start on September 22. McDevitt owned a 2.41 ERA in September, but working mainly in relief, he'd made just one start since September 2.

Alston summoned 24-year-old rookie right-hander Larry Sherry from his bullpen. Later he'd tell reporters, "I had planned not to go too long with my lefthander. McDevitt was tired and a bit wild." Whether it was strategy or postgame rationalization, Alston was familiar with the drill. Forty-seven times in the Dodgers' first 154 games, he'd pulled his starter before five innings, tied for the most in the league. The average NL team won just 26.5 percent of the time in those situations in 1959, meaning that the Dodgers could have expected 12.4 victories in those 47 games. Incredibly, they had rallied to win 20 of those games, more than any other team.

They would rally again that day. Though Sherry would surrender the go-ahead run thanks to an error by shortstop Maury Wills, the

Dodgers again tied the score in the third on a trio of singles, the last by 35-year-old first baseman Gil Hodges, one of the few stars remaining from the team's days in Brooklyn. Leading off the sixth, catcher Johnny Roseboro drove a Willey pitch into the right field bleachers for a 3-2 lead. Sherry never looked back, scattering four hits over 7.2 innings while holding the Braves scoreless as the Dodgers captured the first game of the playoff.

The next day, over 1,700 miles away in sun-baked, jerry-rigged Los Angeles Memorial Coliseum, a former Olympic venue better suited for football or track and field events, 36,528 frenzied fans saw the Dodgers pull out another game after an abbreviated start. Drysdale, a six-foot-six man-child of a staff ace at just 22, had alternated stretches of brilliance and mediocrity for months; here he produced the latter. Trailing 3-2 in the fifth, he surrendered a solo home run to Mathews—the slugger's league-leading 46th of the year—walked Aaron, and left for an early shower as Podres took over.

The Braves stretched their lead to 5-2 in the eighth at the expense of reliever Chuck Churn, but the Dodgers rallied in the ninth, tying the game on four straight singles and a sacrifice fly by 37-year-old pinch-hitter Carl Furillo, the team's elder statesman. Hard-throwing Stan Williams, who had already earned a reputation as one of the league's meanest hurlers, held the Braves hitless and scoreless through three extra frames. With two outs and nobody on in the bottom of the 12th, Hodges drew a walk off Bob Rush and took second on a single by Joe Pignatano. Furillo then hit a sharp grounder over second base. Shortstop Felix Mantilla, who had replaced Johnny Logan after the latter had been shaken up in Norm Larker's futile attempt to break up a seventh-inning double play, fielded the ball awkwardly after a bad hop, and his throw was low and late. Hodges came around to score, and the Dodgers were National League Champions for the first time since moving to Los Angeles. "We go to Chicago!" exclaimed announcer Vin Scully to the transistor-toting Coliseum denizens who had stuck out the four-hour epic. There the Dodgers would face the Go-Go White Sox, whom they upset in the World Series, 4-2, as Sherry garnered MVP honors on the strength of two wins and two saves.

The Dodgers' remarkable success in overcoming those short starts was just one way that the team surpassed expectations in 1959. They had risen from a disappointing seventh-place finish in 1958 to become pennant winners in 1959, a feat never before accomplished in the NL's 84-year history. With the departure of stars such as Jackie Robinson (retired after 1956), Roy Campanella (paralyzed in a January 1958 crash), and Pee Wee Reese (retired to coaching after 1958), and with Hodges, Furillo, and Duke Snider diminished, few had even ticketed the Dodgers to finish in the first division. In March, the *New York Herald Tribune*'s Tommy Holmes declared, "It is difficult to see how even a 'gruntled' writer can detect much difference in the Dodgers this spring. ... Alston, a good Joe who deserves a front office intelligent in matters other than those involving money, might raise this club a couple of notches if he got lucky." *Sports Illustrated* was considerably more sanguine, noting the lineup's balance of speed and power, calling its hurlers "the hardest-throwing pitching staff in the majors" and declaring, "This is too good a team to be fooling around down in the second division."

All of which put Alston on the hot seat. Though he'd piloted the Dodgers to their elusive first World Championship in 1955, his second year at the helm, he had no job security due to owner Walter O'Malley's policy of keeping managers on one-year contracts. Alston's predecessor, Charlie Dressen, who had won two pennants and 298 games in his three years, had been fired for the egregious sin of demanding a three-year deal. Yet O'Malley had brought Dressen back as a coach in 1958, to keep the sword of Damocles dangling over Alston's head. Any losing streak, such as the Dodgers' five-game skid in May 1959, brought scrutiny and speculation of an imminent change.

Such speculation, and the dearth of credit Alston received, was fueled by his lacking the gift of gab. In New York, his taciturn demeanor couldn't compete with the loquaciousness of the Yankees' Casey Stengel, the Giants' Leo Durocher, or Dressen. When O'Malley brought back Dressen and Durocher (1961–1964) to coach, Alston's underlings second-guessed him in the press, most notably (in Durocher's case) for the manager's handling of pitchers in the deciding game of the 1962 Dodgers-Giants playoff.

Nonetheless, Alston's Dodgers had outlasted the Braves and San Francisco Giants in a tense three-team race that had rarely seen the L.A. club in the driver's seat. After holding a share of first place for 10 days in the first month of the season, the Dodgers had done so for just two more days before a September 19 doubleheader sweep of the Giants pulled them even with their closest rivals. The Giants, who had controlled the top spot for all but two days since August 1, dropped that pair and then five of their next six to plunge out of the pennant picture. The Braves, who had dominated the top spot from mid-May to early July, needed six wins in their final eight games to tie the Dodgers at 86-68, forcing just the fourth playoff in major-league history. The Dodgers, who had lost playoffs in 1946 and 1951, finally delivered one.

The weakest team had won. The Dodgers' .564 winning percentage was the lowest of any post-1900 pennant winner before the start of division play in 1969, as was their run differential—scoring just 35 more than they allowed, 705 to 670. By Pythagorean estimates, they won 6.6 more games than they should have, with the disparity mostly at the expense of their closest foes. The Dodgers went 14-10 against the Braves while outscoring them by just one run, and 14-8 against the Giants despite just a five-run gap, thanks to the L.A. team's winning all eight one-run games with the other two teams.

The Braves outscored their opponents by 101 runs yet underachieved by 3.6 wins, while the Giants outscored their opponents by 92 yet fell short by 2.5 wins. Both were below .500 in one-run games, compared with the Dodgers' 33-22, a big part of the Pythagorean disparities. In the preceding eight years, as the three teams had taken turns winning pennants—the Giants in 1951 and 1954; the Dodgers in 1952, 1953, 1955, and 1956; and the Braves in 1957 and 1958—the winner had averaged a run differential of +172. Only in 1951, when the Giants beat the Dodgers in the three-game playoff culminating in "The Shot Heard 'Round the World," had the team with the best differential not come out on top.

The three teams' position atop the National League in the 1950s owed much to their early investment in integration. The Dodgers, of course, were at the forefront, with general manager Branch Rickey's decision to break the color barrier in 1947 with Jackie Robinson (whom they'd actually signed in late 1945). In the wake of this decision, the Dodgers signed a remarkable collection of black talent—Roy Campanella, Don Newcombe, Dan Bankhead, Joe Black, Jim Gilliam, Sandy Amoros, Charlie Neal, Maury Wills, and Johnny Roseboro. Such was their surplus of African Americans that the Dodgers had signed Sam Jethroe and Jim Pendleton and traded both to the Braves, and signed Roberto Clemente only to lose him to the Pirates in the Rule 5 draft. While most of the remaining stars fueled Brooklyn's remarkable run of six pennants in 10 years from 1947 to 1956, Roseboro, Neal, and Wills wouldn't even crack the starting lineup until the team had moved to L.A.

The Giants, though not nearly as aggressive as the Dodgers, integrated in 1949 with Hank Thompson, who had broken the St. Louis Browns' color barrier in July 1947, and signed Monte Irvin, Willie Mays, Bill White, and Ruben Gomez as well. Even then, the Giants may have been subjecting themselves to a quota; given the opportunity to promote aged Negro league star Ray Dandridge from their Triple-A Minneapolis team in 1951 after Thompson was injured, they instead opted to move Bobby Thomson to third base. Dandridge, who had won league MVP honors the year before, never made it to the majors.

While still in Boston, the Braves traded for Jethroe late in 1949 and debuted him in 1950; they also signed George Crowe, Bill Bruton, Hank Aaron, and Wes Covington within the next three years, more fully integrating their lineup once they moved to Milwaukee. Not all these players became stars, but many played crucial roles in the three teams' collective dominance. No other NL team integrated its roster before 1953, and of the AL teams, only the Cleveland Indians and the Browns did so.

The same three teams had shaken up baseball during the 1950s by relocating. It was the Braves' move from Boston prior to the 1953 season, and subsequent success, that touched off the new-market gold rush that found six of the original 16 teams pulling up stakes within the decade—among them the Dodgers and Giants, both of which moved to the West Coast after the 1957 season. The transfers, the game's first since 1903, expanded the majors' reach considerably; before the wave, St. Louis was both the southernmost and the westernmost team. The relocations brought baseball in line with the country's shifting economic and population centers and created new demand for teams. With this demand came multiple waves of expansion, increasing the size of the majors by 50 percent by 1969 and providing representation to most of the country's major cities.

Since moving to Milwaukee, the Braves had won more games than had any other team in the league (545, two ahead of the Dodgers) while drawing record crowds from all around the Midwest. They entered the 1959 season heavily favored to repeat this feat, with a club many believed stronger than the Braves' previous two pennant winners. Certainly they had the star power. In right fielder Hank Aaron, third baseman Eddie Mathews, and lefty starter Warren Spahn, the club boasted three of the league's six most valuable players according to wins above replacement player (WARP; see Table 2-1), not to mention three future Hall of Famers. That trio and righty Lew Burdette, catcher Del Crandall, and shortstop Johnny Logan gave the team a league-best six All-Stars.

Just 25, Aaron was at his best in 1959, even better than his MVP- and World Series–winning 1957 campaign. He hit .355/.401/.636, setting career highs in all three categories and leading the league in bat-

Table 2-1 1959 NL WARP Leaders

| Player | Team | WARP |
|---|---|---|
| Ernie Banks | Cubs | 15.1 |
| Hank Aaron | Braves | 13.0 |
| Eddie Mathews | Braves | 12.9 |
| Willie Mays | Giants | 10.7 |
| Ken Boyer | Cardinals | 9.9 |
| Don Hoak | Pirates | 9.4 |
| Warren Spahn | Braves | 9.4 |
| Charlie Neal | Dodgers | 9.4 |
| Sam Jones | Giants | 9.2 |
| Don Drysdale | Dodgers | 9.1 |

ting average (his second batting title), slugging percentage, hits (223) and total bases (400, the only time this plateau would be reached between Stan Musial in 1948 and Jim Rice in 1978). "Trying to throw a fastball by Hank Aaron is like trying to sneak sunrise past a rooster," Phillies pitcher Curt Simmons once complained. Indeed, Aaron's strong wrists and quick reflexes allowed him to catch up to anyone's heat. "I looked for the same pitch my whole career," he later recounted. "A breaking ball. All of the time. I never worried about the fastball." To opponents, he was simply a headache. "More than anyone else, Hank Aaron made me wish I wasn't a manager," admitted Alston.

With a league-leading 46 homers and a robust .306/.390/.593 line, Mathews, 27, was nearly as dangerous. MVP voters actually preferred him to Aaron in 1959, placing him second behind only the Cubs' Ernie Banks. It wasn't the last time Mathews outdid Aaron; during the Braves' Milwaukee tenure, he'd actually out-homer the all-time home run leader, 452 to 398. "I've only known three or four perfect swings in my time," observed Ty Cobb on seeing the slugging third baseman. "This lad has one of them."

The Braves seized control of the race early, going 28-16 through the end of May, 2.5 games better than the Giants and 5.0 better than the fourth-place Dodgers. But the team was unable to break from the pack, its flaws already showing. From May 19 to May 29, the Braves' assortment of second basemen went hitless in 35 straight trips to the plate. The inability of the second baggers to bag hits was a problem that lingered all year. First, Hall of Famer Red Schoendienst was limited to just five games after he came down with tuberculosis. A key to the team's 1957 championship, Schoendienst had shown his age (35) in 1958, hitting just .262/.313/.328. Then there was the club's failure to make such an obvious upgrade over the winter, before Schoendienst got sick. This negligence was probably a by-product of longtime general manager John Quinn's mid-January departure for the Phillies; privately, Quinn had eyed his exit for months after being passed over for a promotion. Manager Fred Haney then frenetically shuffled seven players at the keystone, with young Mantilla and over-the-hill former

Indian star Bobby Avila (acquired via waivers in late July) both under-performing amid a dismal cast that included Casey Wise and Johnny O'Brien. This ragged bunch hit a combined .213/.289/.279 while playing second base and was 20 runs—two full wins—below average in the field.

Haney turned first base into another problem by platooning Joe Adcock and Frank Torre. Adcock was a lumbering right-handed slugger who had once hit four homers in a game and had averaged one for every 15.1 at-bats over the previous four years, but he was viewed as defensively challenged. The fielding numbers from Baseball Prospectus suggest this view was exaggerated; in 1959, Adcock had his best season as a first baseman, 12 runs above average, and he was +21 for his career there. The *Sporting News* concurred: "His work around first this season has been nothing short of first rate." The lefty Torre had enjoyed a good year with the bat and the glove in 1958, hitting .309/.386/.444 in 430 plate appearances and being 11 runs above average defensively. But nothing in his record suggested he was that good a hitter; he was completely lacking in power, having never reached double digits in home runs in either the majors or the minors. Yet Haney persisted in batting Torre in the middle of the lineup when he played, and Torre responded by hitting a miserable .228/.321/.304 with one home run in over 300 plate appearances. That was hardly better than Spahn's .231/.243/.298 with two homers, and at least Spahn had the virtue of being the team's ace. A 20-game Adcock hitting streak that began in late July marginalized Torre, but he crept back into the lineup when the slugger was sent to left field after Wes Covington's season ended with a broken leg in late August. Adcock made five errors in 21 games out there, while Torre hit .178 at first.

Even worse was the bench, which, thanks to the winter of neglect, looked like a collection of refugees from *The Great American Baseball Card Flipping, Trading and Bubble Gum Book*, with over-the-hill vets like Pafko, Mickey Vernon, Stan Lopata, Del Rice, Ray Boone, and Enos Slaughter passing through on their way to oblivion. The 38-year-old Pafko, platooned in left field with Covington, hit just .178 against southpaws, while the 41-year-old Vernon was an unproductive addition to the first base mix. Rookie outfielder Lee Maye (not to be confused with the younger Lee *May,* who came up with the Reds in 1965), who didn't arrive until mid-July, was the only reserve to bat higher than .238 or hit more than three homers.

Haney mishandled the pitching staff as well; while not exactly as focused as "Spahn and Sain, and pray for rain," the Braves depended too heavily on Spahn, now 38, and Burdette, the man they received in trade from the Yankees for Sain back in 1950. Both went 21-15, but Spahn posted a 2.96 ERA while Burdette came in at 4.07, 13 percent worse than the park-adjusted league average. Bob Buhl (15-9, 2.86 ERA) was a capable third man, but Carlton Willey couldn't live up to his solid rookie season. He took innings from promising but erratic youngsters Joey Jay and Juan Pizarro. Jay, a bonus baby languishing with the club since 1953, was just 23. Looking a little more hopeful was Pizarro, who possessed one of the best fastballs in the league and who placed second on the team in strikeouts despite throwing half as many innings as "the Big Two."

The overworking of Spahn and Burdette showed down the stretch. Having completed 55 percent of their starts for the year, they would average just six innings per start and 5.35 earned runs over the season's final two weeks. Bill James labeled Haney's 1959 effort "the worst season of any major league manager in baseball history." It was Haney's last managerial job.

The Giants, having nipped at the Braves' heels since the beginning of June, reached the top of the standings on July 4 as the Braves began to sputter. The challenger was just reemerging as a threat after hard times following its 1954 World Series win. Once manager Leo Durocher had worn out his welcome, former Giants infielder Bill Rigney ("the Cricket") had taken over for two forgettable sixth-place finishes as the Giants won just 67 and 69 games in 1956 and 1957. Despite the presence of superstar center fielder Willie Mays—"Joe Louis, Jascha Heifetz, Sammy Davis and Nashua rolled into one," marveled Durocher—attendance at the dilapidated Polo Grounds had dropped to last in the league, prompting owner Horace Stoneham to consider moving the team to Minneapolis. Eventually, Walter O'Malley had persuaded him to bring his Giants further west after the 1957 season, transferring the teams' subway-based rivalry to California freeways.

The move to San Francisco coincided with the arrival of a huge crop of homegrown talent. Rookie of the Year first baseman Orlando Cepeda, known as "the Baby Bull"—Cepeda's father, Pedro, was "the Bull" and "the Babe Ruth of Puerto Rico" during his playing career— was joined by outfielders Leon Wagner, Willie Kirkland, and Felipe Alou; catcher Bob Schmidt; and third baseman Jim Davenport. With these and others helping to create the league's highest-scoring offense, the Giants enjoyed a respectable third-place finish at 80-74.

The 1958 squad's weakness had been pitching; their 4.53 ERA was worse than the league average. Over the winter, general manager

Chub Feeney traded erratic hurler Ruben Gomez and backup catcher Valmy Thomas to Philadelphia for starter Jack Sanford, the 1957 Rookie of the Year who had endured a sophomore slump. In March, they traded first baseman Bill White and outfielder Ray Jablonski to St. Louis for pitcher "Toothpick" Sam Jones, so named because he chewed one on the mound. White had hit 22 homers as a rookie in 1956 but had missed most of the next two years in the army. Cepeda's arrival and the presence of another heavy-hitting first baseman in the minors, Willie McCovey, made White redundant.

Though White made the All-Star team five of his first six years in St. Louis, Cardinals general manager Bing Devine later admitted that the Jones trade hadn't gone over well at his home. Coming home from work one day, he found his family at the dinner table with toothpicks in their mouths. Jones, a former Negro leaguer who had been signed by the pitching-rich Indians in 1950, was a promising but erratic hurler who had led the league in strikeouts and walks as a Cub in 1955 and 1956, and again as a Cardinal in 1958. In San Francisco he emerged as a force, leading the league in both ERA (2.83) and wins (21) and combining with ace Johnny Antonelli (19-10, 3.10 ERA) to form a potent 1-2 punch at the front of the rotation. With Sanford and 20-year-old bonus baby Mike McCormick, the team may have had the strongest foursome in the NL; the staff as a whole posted a league-leading 3.47 ERA.

The potent Giant offense centered around Mays, who hit .313/.381/ .583 with 34 homers and 27 steals, great for just about anybody else but not quite up to his previous year's .347/.419/.583. Cepeda avoided the sophomore jinx, hitting .317/.355/.522, and the team got 32 homers from the right field platoon of Kirkland and Alou. But Mc-Covey's development created a logjam at first base. In 1958, his fourth year in the minors, the hulking young slugger who became known as "Stretch" hit .319 and slugged .507 at Triple-A Phoenix. He followed that up by hitting .372 with 29 homers in 95 games; clearly he was ready.

The Giants finally promoted McCovey at the end of July, and in his debut, he went 4-for-4 with a pair of triples off Phillies ace Robin Roberts. To accommodate McCovey, Cepeda, who had played third base in his first two years of pro ball, was sent on a baseball odyssey. He took over the hot corner as Davenport, the lineup's weakest hitter, went to the bench. Two days later, Cepeda made a pair of errors, and when he followed that up with an error in his next game, the experiment was abruptly halted. Not that the Baby Bull was a fan of the move; looking back, he felt it exemplified his manager's weakness: "He doesn't know baseball or ballplayers. ... At third base I am a butcher."

Sent to left field, Cepeda took time from Jackie Brandt, a better hitter than Davenport, and Wagner, who had hit .317/.371/.534 as a rookie but had become imprisoned in a pinch-hitting role. When Davenport tore cartilage in his knee, the Giants tried Brandt at third base, but after eight errors in 18 games—one more than Davenport made all year—that experiment was abandoned as well. The Giants held first place throughout this time, with McCovey bashing 10 homers and hitting .377 through his first 30 games, but with a suboptimal lineup, they were unable to run away from the pack. The positional battle between McCovey and Cepeda would linger until the latter was traded to St. Louis in 1965.

Ultimately, the Giants' collapse was best symbolized by the fate of Antonelli. The 29-year-old had endured a stormy season ever since he had complained bitterly about the team's ballpark, the quaint, 22,900-seat Seals Stadium, where Joe DiMaggio and other San Francisco Seals had roamed in the old Pacific Coast League. In late June, after losing a game to the Dodgers on wind-blown home runs by Hodges and Neal, Antonelli erupted, calling Seals the "worst ballpark in America. Every time you stand up there you've got to beat the hitter *and* a 30-mile-an-hour wind." Frisco fans took the remarks personally, booing Antonelli relentlessly; newspaper editorials excoriated him. The controversy raged as Antonelli struggled down the stretch, falling four times in pursuit of win number 20 even as the *Sporting News* had already conceded, "Pair of Giant Aces Repeats in '20-Win' Club" on the front page of its September 16 edition.

Such anticipation of the Giants' fate wasn't confined to Antonelli. As the critical week of September 14 began with the Giants holding a two-game lead on both rivals, manager Rigney spoke of the upcoming series in increasingly anxious terms. "Operation Cushion" was designed to pad the team's lead against the 70-74 Reds (they split a pair). In "Operation Clincher," against the Braves and Dodgers, the Giants split two with the former and were swept three straight at home against the latter, permanently surrendering first place. Finally, there was "Operation Frantic," the team's final five games in Chicago and St. Louis (they lost four). Worse, much had been made of ensuring the readiness of the team's new home, Candlestick Park, in the event the Giants made the World Series.

Finally, it was the plucky Dodgers, a team in transition, who won out. After the 1956 pennant—the last hurrah for Jackie Robinson, who had sparked the club to six flags—Alston's team had slumped to third place in their wrenching final season in Brooklyn. On relocating to Los Angeles, they slipped to seventh at 71-83, their lowest finish and first sub-.500 season since 1944. Concerned more about ticket sales than performance, O'Malley had brought over-the-hill boys of summer like Gil Hodges, Carl Furillo, Pee Wee Reese, and Duke Snider west. The team won at the gate, drawing 1.8 million fans to its makeshift dwelling and earning a reported $3.5 million profit despite a very un-Dodgers-like performance.

Yet even with the boys of summer in ruin, the Dodgers could draw on a wellspring of talent, including a trio of black youngsters who were signed in the early 1950s and who had patiently waited their turns. Though not the hitter Roy Campanella was, Johnny Roseboro possessed a bit of pop and was a durable receiver who cut down the running game while working well with pitchers. Charlie Neal had played 100 games at shortstop for the injured Reese in 1957 before sliding across the keystone in 1958. He was the league's top offensive second baseman, hitting .287/.337/.464 with 19 homers. The year before, he'd become just the third NL second sacker to hit at least 20 homers, and Dodger scout Al Campanis had called him "the best ballplayer in either league, pound for pound." Speedy Maury Wills, who had toiled nine years in the minors, took over at shortstop from a slumping Don Zimmer (who hit a miserable .165/.274/.249 that year). Though the rookie had no power to speak of and posted unimpressive final numbers (.260/.298/.298), he hit a sizzling .345/.382/.405 in September, keying many rallies by legging out infield hits.

The Coliseum was enormously different from the intimate bandbox of Ebbets Field. With ground for Dodger Stadium not broken until mid-September—the 1959 season would see a stormy battle over the team's deal with the city to acquire Chavez Ravine—the team was consigned to a massive 93,000-seat facility built in 1923 for University of Southern California football games. The field was asymmetrical; while dead center field was a relatively normal 420 feet away, the right field line was just 300 feet, and right-center stretched to 375 feet (reduced from an astounding 440 feet after 1958, much to Snider's relief). Left field was another thing entirely, just 251 feet from home plate, with a 40-foot screen only partly helping to compensate. *New York Times* scribe Arthur Daley, drawing on the rather racist term "Chinese homer," called the screen the Great Wall of China. It made an inviting target. In 1958, of the 193 homers hit in the Coliseum, 166 went to left field, 18 to center, and just nine to right. With the new dimensions in 1959, 115 out of 172 shots went to left field.

After battling their park's idiosyncrasies in 1958, the Dodgers embraced them in 1959. Lefty-hitting left fielder Wally Moon, acquired from the Cardinals in a trade for Gino Cimoli, rebounded from a down year by focusing on hitting to the opposite field. Fourteen of his 19 homers were hit at home, nine of them, dubbed "Moon shots," arcing over the screen. Neal hit nine of his over the screen as well; in 1958 and 1959, he hit 27 homers at home and 14 on the road.

On September 15, the Braves—who were one game behind the Giants and one up on the Dodgers—trailed the latter 5-2 in the top of the fifth, when Joe Adcock hit a ball that struck one of the steel supports of the screen and then lodged in the mesh. Second-base umpire Vinnie Smith appeared to signal for a home run, but claimed he was asking third-base ump Frank Dascoli for help with the call. Dascoli ruled the ball a ground-rule double, but when fans shook the screen and the ball fell into the seats, manager Haney asked, "How could the ball fall there if it wasn't out of the park?" Adcock was stranded at second base, and though the Braves would eventually send the game into extra innings, they lost when Wills sparked a two-run rally in the bottom of the 10th to give the Dodgers an 8-7 win. Haney protested the game, but after NL president Warren Giles flew in from Cincinnati to inspect the screen personally, he ruled against the Braves.

A change in scheduling turned the Coliseum to the Dodger pitchers' advantage as well. The Dodgers had played 46 night games in 1958, but in 1959, they upped it to a major-league record 63. The poor lighting—and the team's decision to sell tickets for the center field bleachers' "batter's eye"—served the pitching staff well. Dodger starters posted a 3.56 ERA and struck out 7.8 per nine innings under the lights; in daytime at the Coliseum, those same starters put up a 3.98 ERA with just 6.4 strikeouts per nine.

The difference between night and day wasn't lost on the Dodgers. Probably aided by the data of team statistician Allen Roth, Alston made a crucial decision involving the September 19 doubleheader that broke the Giants' back. Slated to start Drysdale in the daytime game, a makeup for the previous night's rainout, with Roger Craig going at night, Alston discovered that Drysdale's ERA was roughly twice as high in daylight (5.38 for the year) as at night (2.70), while Craig was effective under both circumstances. Craig went the distance in the opener as the Dodgers won 4-1, and Drysdale, though he lasted only six innings in the nightcap, allowed but one earned run on three hits, whiffing eight as the Dodgers won 5-3 to tie the Giants for first place.

Park effects aside, the Dodgers had embraced the religion of power pitching since the Rickey era. They'd led the league in strikeouts for

11 straight years, but in 1959, they became the first team to top 1,000 in a season, blowing away 1,077 hitters, 204 more than the second-ranked Giants. Drysdale paced the circuit with 242 strikeouts while going 17-13 with a 3.46 ERA. Koufax (8-6, 4.05 ERA) placed third with 173 despite tossing just 153.1 innings, limited by a sore shoulder and an occasional exile to the bullpen. Podres was seventh in the league with 145 strikeouts and third (among qualifiers) in strikeout rate, with 6.7 per nine innings, behind Drysdale (8.0) and Sam Jones (6.9). The pitching staff also intimidated, leading the NL with 51 hit batsmen, 17 more than second-ranked Cincinnati. Drysdale (18), McDevitt (14), and Williams (9) ranked 1-2-3 in the league.

The staff was bolstered by two call-ups from the minors. Sherry, an L.A. native who had overcome the disadvantage of congenital clubfeet, had failed in a brief test with the Dodgers in 1958. Under the tutelage of older brother Norm, a catcher in the Dodger system, he learned a slider playing winter ball in the Cuban League, and upped his minor-league strikeout rate from 4.9 in 1958 to 8.1 in 1959 before being recalled from Triple-A St. Paul in early July. With the Dodgers he went 7-2 with three saves and a 2.19 ERA in 94.1 innings split between starting and relief. Norm Sherry, incidentally, went on to help another teammate, with even more significant results; in the spring of 1961, he encouraged Koufax to take a bit off his fastball and concentrate on throwing strikes, and the left-hander took a quantum leap towards greatness.

Preceding Larry Sherry's arrival was Craig, who had come up with the Dodgers in 1955 but had since fallen on hard times. He'd spent most of 1958 and the first half of 1959 in the minors. Returning to the club on June 19, "Roger the Dodger" pitched magnificently, going 11-5 with a 2.06 ERA in 152.2 innings, just short of qualifying for the league ERA title. He tied Drysdale and six others for the league lead with four shutouts, a total that didn't include a brilliant 11-inning scoreless relief effort on July 9 against the Braves. He was particularly stellar down the stretch, posting a 1.01 ERA in September, which included three complete-game victories in the season's final nine days.

The additions of Craig and Sherry gave Alston a plethora of options, all of which he used in a very fluid staff. Six pitchers started at least 15 games, with Sherry adding nine. All saw considerable time in relief as well, whether simply throwing an inning or two between starts, working in long relief a couple of days after their patented early exits, or—in the case of McDevitt, Sherry, Craig, and Williams—shifting between roles on a longer-term basis. To some extent, every team did this, particularly with its top starters. The 29 NL pitchers who started at least 20 games in 1959 averaged 5.9 relief appearances among them; only two (Philadelphia's Robin Roberts and Pittsburgh's Bob Friend) made none, whereas the Giants' McCormick made 16 and teammate Jones 15. The Braves generally confined that strategy to their younger pitchers; Spahn and Burdette combined for just six relief appearances, but Jay and Pizarro made 30, along with 33 starts.

One way that Baseball Prospectus tracks pitcher performance is through the concept of win expectancy. This method notes the inning, score, and game state (runners on base and number of outs) when a pitcher enters and exits the game, adjusting for park and strength of opposing lineup and measuring the outcome in comparison to replacement level.

This method may seem abstract at first, but it's actually less so than the traditional measure of pitcher success, wins and losses. Win-loss records are assigned after the fact according to a set of criteria that fail to capture the pitcher's impact on the game or the support he receives from his offense and bullpen. By accounting for game situations, win expectancy gives a more appropriate weight to the context of a starter's performance.

In 1959, Antonelli tied for the NL lead in SNLVAR (support-neutral lineup-adjusted value above replacement), the starter's measure of win expectancy (Table 2-2). With 8.0 wins added, he helped the Giants lead with a combined 27.4. The Braves ranked second at 24.6, and the Dodgers third at 21.9. Turning to the bullpen version of the stat WXRL (reliever expected wins added; see Table 2-3), the Cubs led with 7.5, the Dodgers were second at 6.1, and the Braves third at 5.0. The Giants, with just 0.4, were last; aside from top reliever Stu Miller (1.4) they were actually below replacement level. Small wonder their pitching fizzled down the stretch.

The individual Dodgers' totals and positions on the leader boards aren't overly impressive, but by combining the two measures, one can see the power of their staff (Table 2-4). The Braves led the league with 29.6 wins added, with the Dodgers second at 28.0 and the Giants third at 27.8, more than four wins ahead of the fourth-ranked Cubs. Fur-

Table 2-2 1959 NL Leaders in Starter Expected Wins (Support Neutral Lineup-Adjusted Value Above Replacement, SNLVAR)

| Player | Team | SNLVAR |
| --- | --- | --- |
| Johnny Antonelli | Giants | 8.0 |
| Vernon Law | Pirates | 8.0 |
| Warren Spahn | Braves | 7.9 |
| Sam Jones | Giants | 7.8 |
| Larry Jackson | Cardinals | 7.2 |
| Don Drysdale | Dodgers | 7.0 |

Table 2-3 1959 NL Leaders in Reliever Expected Wins Added (WXRL)

| Player | Team | WXRL |
|---|---|---|
| Bill Henry | Cubs | 4.1 |
| Lindy McDaniel | Cardinals | 3.3 |
| Don McMahon | Pirates | 3.2 |
| Don Elston | Cubs | 2.4 |
| Elroy Face | Pirates | 2.2 |
| Larry Sherry | Dodgers | 2.0 |
| Danny McDevitt | Dodgers | 1.9 |

TABLE 2-4 Starter's Win Expectancy (SNLVAR) and Reliever's Win Expectancy (WXRL) for the Highest-Ranked Pitchers of the Top Three NL Finishers, 1959

| | SNLVAR | WXRL | Total |
|---|---|---|---|
| **Dodgers** | | | |
| Drysdale | 7.0 | 0.0 | 7.0 |
| Podres | 3.9 | 0.5 | 4.4 |
| Craig | 4.2 | 0.1 | 4.3 |
| McDevitt | 1.9 | 1.9 | 3.8 |
| Koufax | 2.9 | 0.7 | 3.6 |
| Sherry | 1.3 | 2.0 | 3.3 |
| **Braves** | | | |
| Spahn | 7.9 | 0.1 | 8.0 |
| Burdette | 5.6 | 0.3 | 5.9 |
| Buhl | 4.5 | −0.2 | 4.3 |
| McMahon | 0.0 | 3.2 | 3.2 |
| **Giants** | | | |
| Antonelli | 8.0 | 0.4 | 8.4 |
| Jones | 7.8 | 0.5 | 8.3 |
| Sanford | 5.6 | 0.0 | 5.6 |
| McCormick | 4.5 | 0.1 | 4.6 |

thermore, while most other teams had only three or four pitchers who combined to be at least three wins above replacement, the Dodgers had six.

Ultimately, the Dodgers could put more innings, both starting and relief, in the hands of their better pitchers, and the club enjoyed a stronger return for it. With fresh arms like Sherry and Craig shining down the stretch, the Dodgers could overcome their lack of an outstanding number two starter behind Drysdale through Alston's ability to improvise in the heat of a pennant race. "Almost everyone has the smell of fear, the hint of panic, the look of swallowed hysteria at some point or another," observed *Los Angeles Times* columnist Jim Murray. "Alston's throat was always flat. He was a man you'd most like to be next to in a lifeboat. Or a foxhole."

Indeed, for all the credit that eluded Alston, he managed four World Champions and six pennant winners from 1955 through 1966; he was clearly doing something right. He won with very different teams in very different environments. In Brooklyn, he had a star-laden club with a potent offense playing in a bandbox. In the Coliseum, he had a transitional team playing in a makeshift stadium. And in Dodger Stadium he had a pitching-dominated squad that won in an environment where runs were as plentiful as water in sub-Saharan Africa and where his penchant for one-run strategies could be put to best use.

Alston did all of this—and lasted for 10 more years, winning another pennant—while dealing with the insecurity of 23 consecutive one-year contracts and often in the presence of a ready-made successor. He had his faults, but as his 1959 job showed, his cool-headedness prevailed, and so did his ragtag but resourceful Coliseum bunch. They may have been "the weakest World Championship team of all time," according to Bill James, but they were champions just the same.

## The Braves Dynasty That Wasn't

JAY JAFFE

Whether they were known as the Beaneaters, Doves, Rustlers, Bees, or Braves, the National League franchise based in Boston knew little good fortune in the 20th century. After winning eight pennants—the most in the nascent NL—from 1876 to 1899, the Braves managed just two flags and 14 first-division finishes from 1900 to 1952, wheezing along at an overall .438 winning percentage. From 1917 through 1945—nearly a three-decade nadir—they reached the first division just three times, never climbing above fourth. Their fate at the box office mirrored their fortunes on the field; they led the NL in total attendance just once, but finished dead last 20 times.

The team's first pennant came in 1914, when manager George Stallings' "Miracle Braves" stunned the rest of the NL by climbing from a fifth-place, 69-82 finish to 94 wins and their sole world championship. Their second arrived in 1948, the team's fifth season under the ownership of a trio of contractors—the "Three Steam Shovels"—fronted by Lou Perini, and their third under manager Billy Southworth. After leading the Cardinals to three pennants and two world championships from 1942 to 1944, Southworth had improved the Braves' fortunes for two years before they won 91 games and the NL flag while drawing a pace-setting 1,455,439 fans.

The good times didn't last. Because of a heavy drinking problem, the detached Southworth clashed with his intense double-play combination of Alvin Dark and Eddie Stanky and in mid-August 1949 was sent home for the rest of the season as the Braves slumped to 75-79. That winter, general manager John Quinn traded Dark and Stanky to the Giants for four players, including star third baseman Sid Gordon. The team rebounded to 83 wins in 1950, and although Gordon enjoyed the first of four fine years, the Braves declined in 1951 and again in 1952, when they won 64 games and drew just 281,278 fans. Perini began eyeing a new home for the Braves for the 1954 season.

In March 1953, St. Louis Browns owner Bill Veeck attempted to move his similarly strapped team to Milwaukee, where he'd once owned the city's American Association franchise, the Brewers. The Braves controlled both the Brewers and the territorial rights to the city, so Perini blocked the move. Enraged local officials threatened to terminate the Brewers' lease. Fifteen days after blocking the Browns and less than a month before the 1953 season opened, Perini had not only been shamed into moving the Braves immediately but received the unanimous approval of the other NL owners.

Despite the eleventh-hour decision, the transfer paid off. The Braves drew from all over the Midwest, setting an NL attendance record with 1,826,397 in their first year and leading the league for the next five, even topping 2.0 million from 1954 to 1957. The revenue helped vault the team into contention; they finished second in three of their first four years in Milwaukee before winning back-to-back pennants in 1957 and 1958, capturing a world championship in 1957.

In fact, from 1953 through 1960, the Braves won 719 games, more than any National League team, six more than the Dodgers and 94 more than the third-place Giants. The Braves did so without ever finishing lower than third place. Yet the question remains, why didn't they win more, particularly with a talent base that included future Hall of Famers Hank Aaron, Eddie Mathews, and Warren Spahn?

To answer this question, let's first look at the team's run differentials and Pythagorean records to see if the Braves *should* have won more. Table 2-5 compares the Braves with the Dodgers, who won pennants in 1953, 1955, 1956, and 1959.

The Braves were extremely consistent from 1953 to 1960, winning between 85 and 95 games and politely finishing, on average, within about two games of their predicted records. The Dodgers were all over the map, with anywhere from 82 to 105 victories, except for their 71-win debacle in 1958. Four times they exceeded expectations by at least five wins; their 1954 differential of 12.1 wins is tied for the third-highest total of all time. Furthermore, in both 1956 and 1959, the Dodgers beat out the Braves despite having worse predicted records.

The previous chapter explored the factors that doomed the 1959 Braves. The 1956 club was a very good team, led by many of the same players—Aaron, Mathews, Spahn, Joe Adcock, Lew Burdette, Del Crandall, Johnny Logan—all of whom played up to their capabilities. The offense was the league's third-best (4.57 runs per game); Adcock

Table 2-5  Run Differentials and Pythagorean Records of Braves and Dodgers, 1953–1960

| | | Braves | | | | | | | | Dodgers | | | | | |
|---|---|---|---|---|---|---|---|---|---|---|---|---|---|---|---|
| Year | Rk | W-L | RS | RA | pW | pL | Dif | Year | Rk | W-L | RS | RA | pW | pL | Dif |
| 1953 | 2 | 92-62 | 738 | 589 | 90.2 | 63.7 | 1.8 | 1953 | 1 | 105-49 | 955 | 689 | 96.8 | 57.1 | 8.2 |
| 1954 | 3 | 89-65 | 670 | 556 | 87.9 | 66.1 | 1.1 | 1954 | 2 | 92-62 | 778 | 740 | 79.9 | 74.0 | 12.1 |
| 1955 | 2 | 85-69 | 743 | 668 | 83.5 | 70.5 | 1.5 | 1955 | 1 | 98-55 | 857 | 650 | 93.5 | 59.5 | 4.5 |
| 1956 | 2 | 92-62 | 709 | 569 | 90.0 | 64.0 | 2.0 | 1956 | 1 | 93-61 | 720 | 601 | 87.8 | 66.2 | 5.2 |
| 1957 | 1 | 95-59 | 772 | 613 | 90.6 | 63.4 | 4.4 | 1957 | 3 | 84-70 | 690 | 591 | 86.3 | 67.7 | -2.3 |
| 1958 | 1 | 92-62 | 675 | 541 | 90.1 | 63.8 | 1.9 | 1958 | 7 | 71-83 | 668 | 761 | 69.1 | 84.9 | 1.9 |
| 1959 | 2 | 86-70 | 724 | 623 | 87.3 | 68.7 | -1.3 | 1959 | 1 | 88-68 | 705 | 670 | 81.4 | 74.6 | 6.6 |
| 1960 | 2 | 88-66 | 724 | 658 | 82.7 | 71.3 | 5.3 | 1960 | 4 | 82-72 | 662 | 593 | 83.7 | 70.3 | -1.7 |
| AVG | | 90-64 | 719 | 602 | 87.8 | 66.4 | 2.1 | AVG | | 89-64 | 754 | 662 | 84.8 | 69.3 | 4.3 |

*Abbreviations:* Rk, rank; W-L, win-loss record; RS, runs scored; RA, runs allowed; pW, predicted wins; pL, predicted losses; Dif, difference.

slugged .597 and tied for second in home runs with 38, Mathews hit 37 homers, and 22-year-old Aaron hit .328/.365/.558 and rapped out 200 hits for the first time. The pitching was the league's best (3.67 runs per game). Spahn was 20-11 with a 2.78 ERA, and Burdette went 19-9 with a 2.78 ERA; at 7.2 WARP (wins above replacement player), 1956 was the second-best season of Burdette's career.

Beyond Spahn and Burdette, the 1956 club's starters weren't particularly impressive. Bob Buhl's gaudy 18-8 record belied a 3.32 ERA just 4 percent better than the park-adjusted league average. At 3.87, Ray Crone, with 21 starts, was 10 percent worse than the adjusted average. And Gene Conley, who started 19 times, was 11 percent above the adjusted average, at 3.13. Beyond the number two spot in the rotation, the Braves were at best treading water.

Meanwhile, the offense's .323 on-base percentage (OBP) was just two points above the league average. Center fielder Bill Bruton hit .272/.304/.419 in 578 plate appearances, mostly while batting second, while left fielder Bobby Thomson hit .235/.302/.408 in 505 plate appearances in the middle of the order. Crandall chipped in only a .312 OBP, but he slugged .450; from a catcher, that was a positive contribution.

These two shortcomings in the outfield could actually be traced to the same source, the February 1, 1954, trade of pitcher Johnny Antonelli to the Giants. The Braves had signed Antonelli on June 29, 1948, outbidding eight other clubs by offering a then-record $65,000.

Under the rules of the day, the 18-year-old hurler was a bonus baby who had to remain on the club's 40-man roster for two years or be exposed to waivers. Forced onto a team in the throes of a pennant race, Antonelli tossed just four innings that year. Southworth resented the youngster and used him sparingly in the following two seasons. After he was drafted into military service, Antonelli spent 1951 and 1952 pitching for a military base team in Virginia. He returned to the Braves in 1953 and joined the rotation, going 12-12 with a 3.18 ERA, fifth in the league, despite missing time with viral pneumonia.

On December 26, 1953, Quinn traded seven players, including Sid Gordon and $100,000 cash, to Pittsburgh for Danny O'Connell. It was a lopsided deal for a run-of-the-mill infielder whom Fred Haney had previously managed in Pittsburgh. Needing a left fielder, Quinn tapped the Giants for Bobby Thomson (and backup catcher Sam Calderone) and sent four players—Antonelli, pitcher Don Liddle, infielder Billy Klaus, and catcher Ebba St. Claire—plus $50,000 in return. Headlines such as "Braves See Trade As Flag Clincher" and "Thomson Brings 100 RBI to the Braves" trumpeted the deal in the *Sporting News*.

Thomson was only 30 and coming off a characteristic .288/.338/.472, 4.7 WARP season, but his best days—such as October 3, 1951, when he hit the pennant-winning "Shot Heard 'Round the World"—were behind him. He broke his ankle severely in the spring of 1954 and never got untracked in Milwaukee, hitting a combined .242/.307/.400 for 6.6 WARP—about what he'd done in 1952 alone—over parts of four seasons. His absences were more productive than his presence; his ankle injury allowed Aaron to make the team, and when the Braves sent Thomson back to the Polo Grounds in a deal for Red Schoendienst on June 15, 1957, Milwaukee left the rest of the league in the dust on its way to a world championship.

The Braves expected promising 23-year-old lefty Chet Nichols, who'd gone 11-8 with a 2.88 ERA in 1951 before losing the next two years to military service, to fill Antonelli's spot in the rotation. Nichols was a bust, putting up a 4.41 ERA in 1954, but things were different with 6 foot 8 rookie Gene Conley. The lofty hurler had gone 23-9 at Toledo in 1953 while leading the circuit in wins, ERA (2.90), and strikeouts (211); now he went 14-9 for the Braves, with a 2.96 ERA. His performance couldn't top that of Antonelli, who mastered his changeup and broke out by going 21-7 with a league-leading 2.30 ERA for the Giants, helping them to a world championship.

Table 2-6 Records of Johnny Antonelli (Giants) and Lew Burdette (Braves), 1954–1960

|  | W-L | IP | ERA | PRAA | PRAR | WARP |
|---|---|---|---|---|---|---|
| Burdette | 124-79 | 1,821.2 | 3.37 | 22 | 418 | 39.2 |
| Antonelli | 108-84 | 1,600.2 | 3.13 | 144 | 557 | 54.1 |

*Abbreviations:* W-L, win-loss record; IP, innings pitched; PRAA, pitcher-only runs above average; PRAR, pitcher-only runs above replacement; WARP, wins above replacement.

Though Antonelli's win-loss record vacillated with the varying fortunes of the Giants over the ensuing years, his ERA surpassed the league average every year through 1959. In fact, from 1954 through 1960, Antonelli compares favorably with Burdette, who was ensconced as the Braves' number two starter behind Spahn (Table 2-6).

Even though Burdette had a big edge in innings pitched and a better record owing to better teammates, Antonelli was the more valuable pitcher by roughly two WARP a year. It's as if the Braves, in considering their number two pitcher, saw only his handsome win totals (for five years running, he was in the top four) instead of his ERAs, which ballooned above the park-adjusted league average three times in that span. Had Antonelli stayed to develop into Spahn's wingman—whether or not they kept Burdette or exploited the gap between his actual and perceived values in trade—the Braves might well have collected another pennant or two.

The Braves made similar mistakes with young pitching throughout this era. After his outstanding rookie season, Conley had a few good years but was limited by shoulder soreness. After an 0-6, 4.88 ERA season in 1958, he was traded to Philadelphia and rebounded with a 12-7, 3.00 ERA effort for a team that went 64-90. Joey Jay was a $20,000 bonus baby whom the Braves signed in June 1953. Though he tossed a three-hit shutout of the Reds in his first major league start—a month past his 18th birthday—Jay pitched just 47 innings spread over three seasons before being sent to the minors, and then he didn't return (except for a cameo of less than an inning) until 1958. Shuttling between the rotation and the bullpen in 1959 and 1960, he accumulated a 22-24 record but a 3.27 ERA—7 percent better than average—in 366.1 innings over the next two years. Meanwhile, the Braves took a similarly languid approach with fireballer Juan Pizarro, limiting him to an average of 111 innings and 13 starts a year from 1956 to 1960, despite a strikeout rate of 7.4 per 9 innings, stellar for the era.

On December 15, 1960, the Braves traded Jay and Pizarro to the Reds for Roy McMillan. The 31-year-old shortstop, who replaced Johnny Logan, hit just .220/.305/.293 but generated 4.4 WARP by virtue of his excellent defense. Jay went 21-10 with a 3.53 ERA for the Reds (6.8 WARP). Pizarro, who was flipped to the White Sox in a deal for outfielder Gene Freese, went 14-7 with a 3.05 ERA (6.4 WARP). Although Jay enjoyed just one more 20-win season before descending into sore-armed mediocrity, Pizarro lasted three more years as an above-average starter. With the trades of Jay and Pizarro, the Braves had condemned themselves to a weak starting rotation. Except for Spahn and Burdette, the 1961 Braves had no pitcher who won in the double digits, and though the club finished above .500 in every year of its Milwaukee tenure, which ended in 1965, the Braves never again came so close to a pennant.

During the 1950s, the Braves spent a great deal of money and other resources on young pitchers, many of whom had solid careers. But the team struggled to harness its staff's potential and frequently cut bait at precisely the wrong time. Had they shown a bit more patience, the Braves might have added another pennant or two to their accomplishments. History shows that they were a good team, but they could have been a great one. In his autobiography, *I Had a Hammer*, Hank Aaron grapples with the club's failure to win more:

> It still bothers me that we were only able to win two pennants and one World Series with the team we had. We should have won at least four pennants in a row. ... If we had done what was there for us to do, we would be remembered as one of the best teams since World War II—right there with the Big Red Machine and the A's of the seventies and the Dodgers and Yankees of the fifties. But we didn't do it, and in the record book we're just a team that won a World Series. Damn it, we were better than that.
>
> I wish I knew what kept us from winning more, because there is no question we had the talent—three Hall of Famers, and that was just the start.

A few pages later, Aaron answers his own question:

> I've always felt that we would have won more championships if we held on to Pizarro and Jay. We needed young pitchers. ... Jay and Pizarro should have been the guys.

## The Replacement-Level Killers

JAY JAFFE

Don Zimmer began 1959 as the Dodgers' starting shortstop. After a solid April, he went into a dreadful tailspin, hitting just .133/.243/.211 in May and June. Finally, manager Walter Alston turned the job over to recently recalled rookie Maury Wills. While the speedster hit just .260/.298/.298 for the year, he did bat a blazing .345/.382/.405 in September, helping the Dodgers overtake the Giants and force the playoff with the Braves that brought Los Angeles the pennant. Had the Dodgers not stopped the bleeding, they might never have reached that playoff.

In a pennant race, every edge matters. As much as the late-season heroics of one individual can turn a close race into a tale of success writ large, it's often the failures writ small, the weak links on a team, that create the close race in the first place. All too often, and for reasons often rooted in issues beyond a player's performance, managers fail to make the moves that could help their teams, allowing subpar production to fester until it kills a club's pennant hopes. Sometimes a veteran who's passed his sell-by date persists in the lineup because he has helped the manager win in the past, and besides, the club lacks better alternatives (or thinks it does). Sometimes a regular simply isn't performing up to his established level because of injury, but tries "toughing it out" out of a misguided sense of valiance. At other times, a team will erroneously conclude that a player's defensive contributions outweigh his offensive shortcomings. Thus, a poor hitter at a key defensive position will often persist in the lineup longer than will a poor hitter at an easier defensive position. And sometimes a rookie hasn't yet adjusted to big-league pitching, yet the club doesn't want to destroy the youngster's confidence with a benching.

But there is a baseline, or replacement level, of nonproductivity. Below the replacement level—or even slightly above it—a player is actively hurting his team's chances. The definition of replacement level is controversial and varies from season to season; a simple, nonmathematical definition of replacement level is the level of a Triple-A journeyman or the least-qualified major leaguer. Baseball Prospectus's VORP (value over replacement player) defines replacement level as approximately 80 percent of the ability of an average major league hitter at his position (the percentage varies by position). In other words,

Table 2-7 Other Sins Only Speak; Murder Shrieks Out: The Replacement-Level Killers All-Star Team

| Year | Team | Player | Pos | WARP | VORP | PA | W-L | Finish | GB |
|------|------|--------|-----|------|------|-----|-----|--------|-----|
| 1984 | Angels | Bob Boone | C | 1.6 | -24.1 | 475 | 81-81 | 2nd | 3.0 |
| 1972 | Red Sox | Danny Cater | 1B | 0.3 | -6.4 | 334 | 85-70 | 2nd | 0.5 |
| 1959 | Braves | Felix Mantilla | 2B | 0.6 | -7.3 | 269 | 86-70 | 2nd | 2.0 |
| 1940 | Yankees | Frankie Crosetti | SS | 1.4 | N/A | 628 | 88-67 | 3rd | 2.5 |
| 1978 | Red Sox | Butch Hobson | 3B | 1.7 | 9.2 | 562 | 99-64 | 2nd | 1.0 |
| 1964 | White Sox | Dave Nicholson | LF | 1.7 | -2.8 | 349 | 98-64 | 2nd | 1.0 |
| 1980 | Dodgers | Rudy Law | CF | 2.0 | -0.6 | 414 | 92-71 | 2nd | 1.0 |
| 1982 | Orioles | Dan Ford | RF | 1.9 | -5.4 | 448 | 94-68 | 2nd | 1.0 |
| 1979 | Expos | Ross Grimsley | P | -1.2 | -17.1 | 678 | 95-65 | 2nd | 2.0 |

when you can say, "Just about *anybody* would be better than Smith," and the statement does not qualify as hyperbole, Smith has hit the re-placement level.

When Smith is replaced by a better player, miracles have been known to occur. Take Bobby Thomson, whose "Shot Heard 'Round the World" won the 1951 pennant for the Giants. A center fielder dis-placed by the arrival of Willie Mays, Thomson found his way back into the lineup in late July because of a spike injury to slumping third baseman Hank Thompson, who produced just 1.2 wins above replace-ment player (WARP, which is like VORP but figured in wins rather than runs) for the year. Thomson himself was hitting just .240 at the time, but he went on a tear, hitting .357 with 16 homers the rest of the way. Thompson's injury forced Giants manager Leo Durocher to make a change that dramatically upgraded the team's production at one po-sition, providing just enough extra gas for the Giants to tie the front-running Dodgers and force the three-game playoff capped by Thomson's home run.

Table 2-7 presents an all-star team of ignominy, players who for one reason or another underperformed for long enough that their teams narrowly missed the postseason. While we're singling out these re-placement-level killers, the blame must be shared by the managers who continued writing the killers' names in the lineup card, and the general managers who failed to supply an adequate array of alternatives.

Not all these players actually produced *below* the replacement level, the baseline by which we measure player value while acknowledging that alternatives from the waiver-wire or the minors could match that production. Since even the worst hitters in the big leagues can usually field their positions adequately, they generate positive WARP for field-ing value alone. Zimmer, for example, was nine runs below replace-ment level with the bat on his ghastly .165/.274/.249 performance, but 14 runs above replacement in the field—in all, worth 0.5 WARP. Gen-erally, it's asking relatively little for a full-timer to produce at least 3.0 WARP; when even one player can't meet that, teams fail to win close races.

The rest of this chapter discusses the circumstances surrounding each player's abysmal performance. To specifically highlight each player's offensive shortcomings, we've included VORP, which is solely concerned with offense and is expressed in runs (10 runs of VORP is roughly equivalent to one win above replacement).

**Catcher: Bob Boone, 1984 Angels.** A seven-time Gold Glove award winner during his 19 seasons, Boone set a career record (since eclipsed) with 2,225 games caught. That durability worked against him and the 1984 Angels, however, as manager John McNamara kept him in the lineup while Boone bled outs (.202/.242/.262 for an EqA of .189) and the club faded from a three-way race with the Royals and Twins. In 1983 and 1985, Boone was worth 4.4 and 4.5 WARP, respec-tively; had he approached that level in 1984, the Angels would have come much closer than three games out.

**First base: Danny Cater, 1972 Red Sox.** Just after the 1971 season ended, the Red Sox traded powerful, slick-fielding first baseman George Scott to the Brewers in a 10-player deal. To fill Scott's spot, they swapped ace reliever Sparky Lyle to the Yankees for Cater, who had hit .347/.371/.498 at Fenway during his otherwise undistinguished career. Already two strikes in the hole with the loss of those two popu-lar players, Cater hit a frigid .164/.205/.194 through the end of May, drawing boos from the Fenway faithful. While he heated up in June and July, his .237/.270/.372 didn't cut it in a league whose average first baseman hit .267/.346/.441. On August 22, with the Sox just two games over .500, Cater was benched by manager Eddie Kasko in favor of rookie left fielder Ben Oglivie, with Carl Yastrzemski moving from left field to first base. Neither Yaz nor Oglivie hit particularly well thereafter, but the Sox went 27-14, falling a half-game short on a schedule that left them with one less game than the AL East–winning Tigers. (Schedules were off because of the 13-day Players Association strike in the spring.) Worse, Lyle starred for the Yankees, helping to keep the Red Sox down in the later part of the decade.

**Second base: Felix Mantilla, 1959 Braves.** On the flip side of the Zimmer story, the Braves might have avoided their playoff with the Dodgers and won the pennant outright had they solved the second base vacancy caused by Red Schoendienst's tuberculosis. By April 25, manager Fred Haney had already tried four players at the keystone, but he proved constitutionally incapable of committing to anyone for more than a couple weeks. Mantilla, a poor fielder and worse hitter (though there were some oddly robust Fenway-flavored seasons late in his career), got the bulk of the work until the team acquired grizzled 35-year-old Bobby Avila in late July. Although the former batting champion had been released twice that year, he could still get on base (.238/.330/.331). Avila's fielding wasn't up to snuff, however, so Mantilla kept working his way back into the lineup. As a group, Milwaukee's keystone bunch hit a combined .213/.289/.279 and was 20 runs below average in the field, worth all of 0.9 WARP.

**Shortstop: Frankie Crosetti, 1940 Yankees.** As future teammate Yogi Berra might have put it, Crosetti got old when he was still young. Just 29 and with two All-Star appearances and five World Championships under his belt, Crosetti's production was already waning coming into 1940, as he'd dropped from .263/.382/.371 in 1938 to .233/.315/.332 in 1939, a decline of 31 runs relative to replacement level. He fell even further in 1940, hitting an anemic .194/.299/.273, nine runs below replacement, and dropped from 20 runs above average in the field to 13 runs below. As a result, his WARP fell from 6.2 to 1.4. Those missing wins helped end the four-year dominance of the American League by Joe McCarthy's Yanks, who finished in third place, two games behind the Tigers and one game behind the Indians. McCarthy had benched Crosetti in late May with the intention of calling up prospect Phil Rizzuto to replace him, but a scouting trip convinced the manager that Rizzuto wasn't yet ready and Crosetti was quickly restored to shortstop—and the leadoff spot in the batting order. "The Scooter" finally pushed "the Crow" into a reserve role in 1941.

**Third base: Butch Hobson, 1978 Red Sox.** The 1978 Red Sox, managed by the same Don Zimmer who nearly sank the 1959 Dodgers, coughed up the 14-game lead they held over the Yankees on July 18, and Hobson was a big part of the reason. Revered by Zimmer as a gamer, Hobson played the field despite bone chips that locked up his elbow when he threw and—cringe!—had to be rearranged after each play. He made 43 errors, was 21 runs below average, and fielded .899, becoming the first regular to break the .900 barrier since 1916, when gloves were little more than padded mittens. His hitting was acceptable until he missed three weeks from a hamstring strain at the beginning of July; upon returning he hit just .245/.298/.342 with two homers (he'd hit 15 prior) and made 26 errors in 65 games. Hobson wasn't the only Red Sox player who begged replacement; first baseman George Scott, whose production fell off the table because of back and finger injuries—not to mention conditioning problems and declining bat speed—hit just .233/.305/.379. Had Zimmer cut bait on Scott and left Carl Yastrzemski at first base (where Yaz had subbed for Scott), put Jim Rice in left field, and switched Hobson to designated hitter while letting utility man Jack Brohamer patrol the hot corner, Bucky Dent might now be living in obscurity.

**Left field: Dave Nicholson, 1964 White Sox.**   It may not be fair to single out Nicholson, nicknamed "Swoosh" for his penchant for striking out (he'd set a major league record with 175 whiffs in just 449 at bats in 1963), but the 1964 White Sox, who finished second to the Yankees by one game, had an appallingly unproductive outfield. While Floyd Robinson played well as he alternated in the corners (.301/.388/.408, 5.9 WARP), the remaining outfielders Nicholson, center fielder Jim Landis, and right fielder Mike Hershberger were an offensive disaster, combining for just 5.0 WARP while hitting .216/.313/.306 in 1,044 at bats. Nicholson batted .204/.329/.364, decidedly below the average American League left fielder's .262/.338/.443. The Yankees, struggling through the last year of their postwar dynasty, were beatable; Nicholson was one reason they got to play one last World Series before bowing out for 12 years.

**Center field: Rudy Law, 1980 Dodgers.**   A speedster who stole 79 bases at Triple-A in 1978, Law had little else going for him offensively. Not only did he lack power, but he rarely drew a walk, and as the old adage goes, you can't steal first base. He also had an arm weaker than a Middle East peace accord. Hitting just .269/.322/.311 through the end of July, he was finally benched in favor of fellow rookie Pedro Guerrero. Already a fantastic hitter but a man without a position, Guerrero had hit .337/.394/.579 in the 95 at bats he had received to that point. When Guerrero missed three weeks because of a knee injury, veteran Rick Monday took over. Though they mounted an impressive stretch drive, the Dodgers had to beat the Astros three straight times at the end of the year just to force a Game 163 playoff for the division title, which Los Angeles lost.

**Right Field: Dan Ford, 1982 Orioles.**   A solid if unspectacular veteran acquired from the Angels the previous winter, Ford struggled to make the transition to Baltimore. After hitting .277/.327/.440 with 15 homers—good for 4.2 WARP during the 1981 strike year—his production fell to .235/.279/.371 and 1.9 WARP. Uncharacteristically, manager Earl Weaver was unable to cobble together a solution. In the end, the Orioles, who had gone on a 17-1 tear starting in late August, still needed to overcome a four-game deficit in the final week to force a Game 162 showdown with the Brewers. Baltimore lost, 10-2.

**Pitcher: Ross Grimsley, 1979 Expos.**   In the annals of replacement-level killers, pitchers probably merit a chapter of their own, if not a book. Many a quality hurler fell apart long before his manager got the message. A free-spirited lefty signed as a free agent in the winter of 1977–1978, Grimsley went 20-11 with a 3.05 ERA for the 1978 Expos, who nonetheless went just 76-86. The arrival of Bill Lee from Boston helped make the Expos a contender in 1979, but Grimsley was unable to repeat his magic—too many innings the year before might have been the culprit. After being bombed for six runs in one-third of an inning by the Mets on August 10, he and his 5.33 ERA were dropped from the rotation, and he pitched sparingly the rest of the year; in all, he dropped from 4.0 WARP to –1.2. Despite a 17-1 run that began in late August, the Expos sputtered over the season's final two weeks and wound up two games short of the Pirates. Grimsley never recovered his old stuff.

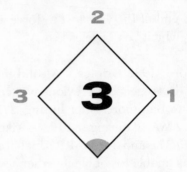

# 1948 and 1949 American League

*Tyranicide*

STEVEN GOLDMAN

Since the arrival of Babe Ruth in 1920, the Yankees had been so successful on the field that it was easier to list the years that they didn't win the pennant than the years that they did. With the promotion of Joe DiMaggio in 1936, they somehow got better. The Yankees won four consecutive World Series from 1936 to 1939. Beginning with the final contest of the 1937 series, the Yankees went over two years without losing a World Series *game*.

The Great Depression was on and teams suffered, but not equally. Yankees attendance, which had averaged over a million fans per season from 1921 to 1930, dropped under the seven-figure mark during the intensifying economic crisis and stubbornly remained there until 1946. So great was their drawing power, however, that the Yankees continued to lead the league in attendance throughout the period (Table 3-1).

The Yankees had the most lucrative ball club and the best scouting resources, and in 1932 they began building an extensive farm system. Most major league teams knew of Joe DiMaggio's prodigious talents before the Yankees obtained his rights from the San Francisco Seals for $25,000 and five minor leaguers in 1935. The acquisition has often been cast as an insightful and canny move by the Yankees, "the greatest buy in the history of modern baseball," as sportswriter Frank Gra-

## 1948 American League Prospectus

| Team | Actual Standings | | | | | Date Elim | Pythag | |
|------|----|----|------|------|-----|-----------|-----|-----|
| | W | L | Pct | GB | DIF | | W | L |
| Indians | 97 | 58 | .626 | – | 115 | – | 105 | 50 |
| Red Sox | 96 | 59 | .619 | 1.0 | 40 | Oct 4 | 95 | 60 |
| Yankees | 94 | 60 | .610 | 2.5 | 2 | Oct 2 | 99 | 55 |
| A's | 84 | 70 | .545 | 12.5 | 23 | Sept 21 | 76 | 78 |
| Tigers | 78 | 76 | .506 | 18.5 | 3 | Sept 14 | 74 | 80 |
| Browns | 59 | 94 | .386 | 37.0 | 0 | Sept 4 | 59 | 94 |
| Senators | 56 | 97 | .366 | 40.0 | 0 | Sept 3 | 54 | 99 |
| White Sox | 51 | 101 | .336 | 44.5 | 0 | Aug 29 | 50 | 102 |

| League Averages | | | | BP Stats Leaders | | | |
|-----|-----|-----|-------|------|-----|-----|-----|
| AVG | OBP | SLG | BABIP | Offense, BRAA | | Indiv WARP | |
| .266 | .349 | .382 | .283 | Indians | 130 | Lou Boudreau | 12.9 |
| ERA | K9 | BB9 | H9 | Pitching, PRAA | | Bob Lemon | 11.6 |
| 4.28 | 3.5 | 4.3 | 9.2 | Tigers | 39 | Hal Newhouser | 11.5 |

## 1949 American League Prospectus

| Team | Actual Standings | | | | | Date Elim | Pythag | |
|------|----|-----|------|------|-----|-----------|-----|-----|
| | W | L | Pct | GB | DIF | | W | L |
| Yankees | 97 | 57 | .630 | – | 164 | – | 96 | 58 |
| Red Sox | 96 | 58 | .623 | 1.0 | 7 | Oct 2 | 98 | 56 |
| Indians | 89 | 65 | .578 | 8.0 | 0 | Sept 21 | 88 | 66 |
| Tigers | 87 | 67 | .565 | 10.0 | 2 | Sept 20 | 87 | 67 |
| A's | 81 | 73 | .526 | 16.0 | 0 | Sept 16 | 77 | 77 |
| White Sox | 63 | 91 | .409 | 34.0 | 0 | Sept 3 | 68 | 86 |
| Browns | 53 | 101 | .344 | 44.0 | 1 | Aug 27 | 54 | 100 |
| Senators | 50 | 104 | .325 | 47.0 | 0 | Aug 27 | 49 | 105 |

| League Averages | | | | BP Stats Leaders | | | |
|-----|-----|-----|-------|------|-----|-----|-----|
| AVG | OBP | SLG | BABIP | Offense, BRAA | | Indiv WARP | |
| .263 | .353 | .379 | .273 | Red Sox | 92 | Ted Williams | 12.7 |
| ERA | K9 | BB9 | H9 | Pitching, PRAA | | Bob Lemon | 12.1 |
| 4.20 | 3.6 | 4.6 | 9.0 | Indians | 71 | Mel Parnell | 11.7 |

ham put it. But it was nothing of the kind. DiMaggio had injured his knee in 1934, and the Yankees were the only team that could risk the money on an injured player.

The American League was left with a competitive balance problem. The cry "break up the Yankees!" is something of a joke today, but in

Table 3-1 What Hath Coolidge Wrought? AL Attendance Before and During the Great Depression

| Team | 1921-1930 | 1931-1940 | % Change |
|---|---|---|---|
| Yankees | 10,407,836 | 8,909,698 | -14.4 |
| Tigers | 7,748,733 | 7,803,028 | +0.01 |
| Indians | 5,177,954 | 5,312,617 | +0.03 |
| Red Sox | 3,310,498 | 5,093,365 | +53.9 |
| White Sox | 5,811,009 | 4,364,150 | -24.9 |
| Senators | 5,102,573 | 3,907,187 | -23.4 |
| Athletics | 6,276,235 | 3,797,557 | -39.5 |
| Browns | 3,799,586 | 1,271,579 | -66.5 |

the late 1930s their fellow owners really meant it. In an era in which revenue sharing and salary caps hadn't yet been conceived and didn't really apply, the league couldn't figure out how to compete. In 1939, Washington Senators owner Clark Griffith proposed a rule, adopted by the American League (but not the National), to prohibit teams from trading or selling players to the previous season's pennant winner. In 1940, the Yankees yielded the pennant (barely) to the Detroit Tigers and the rule was rescinded. The Yankees then won in 1941, and 1942, and 1943, and ... back to the drawing board.

The manpower drain of World War II finally accomplished what the competition could not. The team's best players were in the service. Ownership was in transition from the Jacob Ruppert estate to the triumvirate of Del Webb, Dan Topping Jr., and Larry MacPhail. Team president Ed Barrow was aging. Manager Joe McCarthy had been a steadying influence since 1931, but couldn't coexist with the triumvirate's front man, MacPhail. The manager took to the bottle and eventually resigned. In 1946, the Yankees went through three managers—both of McCarthy's replacements had decided that if living with the mercurial, violent, alcoholic MacPhail was the price of managing the Yankees, they'd rather be unemployed.

The Yankees failed to win the pennant in 1944, 1945, and 1946. In 1947, Bucky Harris, a 50-year-old laissez-faire manager whose last success had come in 1925, was hired when MacPhail failed to lure Leo Durocher away from the Dodgers. Through May, it looked as if the Yankees would have another indifferent season. On May 21, they were in sixth place with a 13-14 record. The next day, MacPhail fined several players, including DiMaggio, for various minor disciplinary infractions. Perhaps coincidentally, the team began winning the next day, sweeping a four-game series from the second-place Red Sox. On

June 15, the Yankees moved into first place. Two weeks later and already leading by 4.5 games, they began a 19-game winning streak. At its end, they were leading by 11.5 games, and the race was over. That fall, they won an electrifying seven-game World Series from the Brooklyn Dodgers.

The Yankees were back, but the situation was different from that of 1939. The core of the team was aging and increasingly prone to injury, and the pitching staff had been patched together. MacPhail, a brilliant baseball man when sober, had pulled one too many drunken rages and had been forced out in the aftermath of the World Series. Bucky Harris had a complacent streak. Though the Yankees still had the ticket sales to accomplish anything they liked, it was clear there was an opening. If they could be knocked down now, they might panic, make a bad move, and fade. The only question was how to take advantage. How do you kill a dynasty?

Cleveland Indians owner Bill Veeck thought that Branch Rickey had shown the way.

◆

On July 5, 1948, the Indians hosted the Detroit Tigers for a doubleheader. The first game went well enough for Cleveland, with pitcher Bob Lemon scattering nine Detroit hits for a 6-3 lead. In the nightcap, the Tribe carried a 4-2 lead into the top of the eighth inning. Starter Sam Zoldak, recently acquired from the St. Louis Browns to boost the Indians' pennant chances, allowed a solo home run to Tigers second baseman Eddie Lake. Zoldak quickly vanished in favor of ace starter Bob Feller, who walked the first two batters he faced and then served up a gopher ball to right fielder Pat Mullin. Their lead gone, the Indians went on to lose the game 7-5. It was a frustrating ending to a long day.

By the time Indians' shortstop-manager Lou Boudreau got home, it was two o'clock in the morning. He collapsed into an uneasy sleep, only to be awakened by a ringing telephone just a few hours later. It was Veeck. There was a pitching prospect coming to the ballpark tomorrow. Veeck wanted his manager to personally oversee the tryout.

Boudreau groaned. Veeck, known for his flights of fancy, could have found the pitcher on the street or wandering the grounds of the local asylum. Besides, any of the coaches could run the audition and furnish Veeck with a recommendation, and Boudreau was exhausted. He asked Veeck to get someone else. Veeck insisted, so Boudreau pulled on his pants and headed to the ballpark.

He got to the park, dressed in his uniform, and found Veeck waiting for him in the home dugout. "Where's the kid?" Boudreau asked. Veeck pointed across the field to the visitor's dugout, where Satchel Paige was waiting. *The* Satchel Paige, reputed to be the hardest thrower of all time as well as the most creative; owner of a vast arsenal of unheard-of pitches with names like the bee ball, the jump ball, and the trouble ball; whose control was so impeccable that he could throw a strike over a bottle cap; who had dueled the greatest pitchers of the age from Dizzy Dean to Bob Feller and won; who was so carefree and confident that he was known to wave his defense off the field and re-tire the batters without the aid of fielders.

The manager was incredulous. It wasn't that Paige was black—Veeck, a longtime advocate of integration, had brought Larry Doby to the majors to break the American League color line less than three months after Jackie Robinson's debut with Rickey's Dodgers—but the pitcher was rumored to be somewhere between 49 and 100 years old.

In truth, Paige turned 41 just two days after the tryout, and he cer-tainly didn't *look* old. But he liked to fib about his age. Reliable records were hard to come by (to the extent that anyone bothered to look), and because he had pitched in thousands of games—Negro Leagues contests going back to 1927, barnstorming tours against white major leaguers, winter ball, politics-by-other-means contests for the benefit of dictators in the Caribbean, two-a-day exhibitions against small town semi-pro and amateur teams ("Satchel Paige, World's Greatest Pitcher, Guaranteed to Strike Out the First Nine Men")—almost certainly more than any other pitcher in the history of the game before or after, it was easy to confuse the extraordinary breadth of his career with extraordinary length.

Boudreau knew better than to refuse his boss, who, he knew, didn't think he was the most brilliant manager to begin with. He told Paige to loosen up, perhaps take a lap around the park. Paige agreed, jogged a few halfhearted steps, and returned to Boudreau. "You know," he said. "This is an awful big ballpark." Paige had never been much for running, believing, as he now told Boudreau, "I pitch with my arm, not my legs." "I don't generally run at all," he said on another occa-sion, "because of the harmful effects. I believe in training by rising gently up and down from the bench." He believed so strongly in this prohibition that he included it among his rules for "How to Stay Young," a list that became instantly famous because, if there was a formula for youth, Paige seemed likely to know it:

1. Avoid fried meats which angry up the blood.
2. If your stomach disputes you, lie down and pacify it with cool thoughts.
3. Keep the juices flowing by jangling around gently as you move.
4. Go very light on the vices, such as carrying on in society. The social ramble ain't restful.
5. Avoid running at all times.
6. Don't look back. Something might be gaining on you.

Paige was a true eccentric and individualist. "I'm Satchel," he liked to explain. "I do as I do." What that meant to Boudreau at that moment was that the manager was trying out a senior citizen who wouldn't warm up. Veeck encouraged Boudreau and Paige to have a catch, so for 10 or 15 minutes, the two threw the ball back and forth. Veeck was pleased to see that Paige was throwing easily. Finally, Boudreau squatted behind home plate to receive some actual pitches from the old man. The unshakable Paige, on the doorstep of the majors, was suddenly shaken. He had often thought that if anyone would break the color line, it would be him. Now he had been bypassed in favor of Robinson and Doby because he was too old, too strange. "When 1948 come around," he said, "and I still got my nose to the window, I realized what the club owners were thinking. They was thinking that when I was with Chattanooga, Larry Doby wasn't born." His career had been enormously successful by the standards of what was possible for an African American ballplayer in the years before integration, but it wasn't enough. "It was all so nice," Paige said, "that I almost forgot that time was passing and I hadn't begun to do what I'd always wanted." The next pitches he threw would determine the course of the rest of his life. Veeck knew it too. "As ridiculous as it was for Satchel Paige to be on trial," he remembered, "that was precisely the situation as he went out to the mound."

Paige turned to Veeck. "Man, I ain't ready for this," he said. He climbed the mound. "I just tossed a couple real easy and then I started firing," Paige remembered. "I wasn't thinking. I wasn't trying to get in the majors. I wasn't doing anything except just pitching, like I'd always done."

In that moment, something magical happened. Leroy Robert Paige, overage big league aspirant, became Satchel Paige, the legend. "Satch stopped and walked to me," Boudreau remembered. "He handed me a folded-up handkerchief, told me to put it on the plate wherever I liked.

Inside, outside, middle, wherever." Boudreau put the piece of cloth over the inside corner. Paige threw ten pitches, fastballs and sliders, and nine of them were fired over the handkerchief. He instructed Boudreau to move it to the outside corner and then repeated the trick, "all with something on them ... his fastball had a hop to it, and his slider was tremendous ... and those that missed didn't miss by much."

Finally, the 30-year-old Boudreau grabbed a bat. Hitting .368 at the time, he finished the season at .355 and was voted the league's MVP. "Against Paige he batted .000," Veeck said. "Satch threw twenty pitches. Nineteen of them were strikes. Lou swung nineteen times and had nothing that looked like a base hit." Boudreau dropped his bat. "Don't let him get away, Will," he said. "We can use him."

Paige was signed. He continued to be blessed. On July 14, J. G. Taylor Spink, publisher of the *Sporting News*, assailed the signing. "To sign a hurler at Paige's age is to demean the standards of baseball in the big circuits. Further complicating the situation is the suspicion that if Satchel were white, he would not have drawn a second thought from Veeck."

As Veeck pointed out, if Paige had been white, he would have been in the majors 25 years earlier and the point would have been moot. But Paige himself made the defense unnecessary. Pitching as a swing man, he held AL batters to a .228 average and pitched two shutouts in seven starts. Said Paige, "I demeaned the big circuits considerable that year. I win six and lose one." There was a movement to vote Paige the Rookie of the Year. "I declined the position," Paige said. "I wasn't sure which year the gentlemen had in mind."

Paige gave the Indians the deepest bullpen in the majors at a time when the very concept of a bullpen as a tactical advantage was just coming into focus. So was the idea of racial integration. For example, the Yankees' ace reliever, Joe Page, who had been decisive in 1947, was struggling with two kinds of hangovers—one from his heavy workload the year before and the other from his own self-destructive tendencies. The Yankees could have bolstered their own pennant hopes by signing Paige or any of the many other promising players of color who remained in the Negro Leagues, but the Yankees didn't believe in integration. "I will never allow a black man to wear a Yankee uniform," Yankee general manager George Weiss said once. "The truth is that our box seat customers from Westchester County don't want to sit with a lot of colored fans from Harlem."

MacPhail, Weiss's predecessor, had taken the same position in an internal report intended to provide a rationale for thwarting Rickey's plan to break the color line. "The percentage of Negro attendance at some games at Newark and Baltimore was in excess of 50%," MacPhail wrote, drawing from this statistic the conclusion that "a situation might be presented, if Negroes participate in Major League games, in which the preponderance of Negro attendance in parks such as the Yankee Stadium, the Polo Grounds, and Comiskey Park could conceivably threaten the value of Major League franchises owned by these clubs."

The establishment's conclusion was fine with Veeck, not as a manner of morals—he abhorred prejudice—but as a matter of strategy. Veeck would beat the Yankees by doing what they would not, and utilizing the best available players, not merely the best available *white* players. The Yankees had the first shot at Doby and passed. Now Veeck had Doby *and* Paige. The talent gap was narrowing.

Boston Red Sox owner Tom Yawkey was born not with a silver spoon in his mouth, but with a golden ladle, inheriting a fortune in timber and mining wealth. He wasn't inventive like Veeck, but he didn't have to be, because he could always afford to buy the best items on the market. When he first purchased the Red Sox in 1932, he bribed Connie Mack to sell him all-time A's greats like Jimmie Foxx and Lefty Grove, as well as handed to Clark Griffith a check with so many zeros on it that Griffith couldn't afford not to sell Yawkey his own son-in-law, the future Hall of Fame shortstop Joe Cronin. Yawkey's largesse had won him just one pennant (1946) and no World Series titles, but it had revived interest in his long-moribund team, which is why the Red Sox were the only team to experience a significant rise in attendance during the Depression years. (See Table 3-1.)

Yawkey had even less interest in integration than did the Yankees—the Red Sox were the last club to place an African American on its roster—but he thought he might steal a march by buying a different kind of talent the Yankees had denied themselves: a strong manager. In a major league career going back to 1926, Joe McCarthy had won nine pennants and seven World Series titles, the latter all with the Yankees. But the pressures had been mounting for him. First was the stress of managing over 3,000 major league games and dealing with egomaniacal ballplayers from Rogers Hornsby to Babe Ruth gunning for his job (Hornsby succeeded, which was how McCarthy came to the Yankees). Then there was World War II and Larry MacPhail ("There is that fine line between genius and insanity," Leo Durocher wrote, "and in Larry's case it was sometimes so thin that you could see him drifting back and forth"). Add to these a fondness for White Horse scotch, and you can see why McCarthy was driven to quit the team. "Marse Joe" had retired to his farm outside Buffalo—the Yankee Farm, he called it—to dream about the good old days of Lou Gehrig and Earle Combs. He spent the entire 1947 season this way, but the day after the season ended and the Red Sox, defending pennant winners, were in third place, 14 games behind the Yankees, it was announced that McCarthy was coming out of retirement to take over in Boston.

"I came back because baseball is in my blood," McCarthy said. "All last year I did nothing but read the *Sporting News*. ... I was like a fountain gone dry. ... I came back because I was drawn irresistibly. The Red Sox mean new problems. I want to solve those problems." You need, he said, worries to keep you young. "Connie Mack has the right system. Never retire."

Now Yawkey had baseball's best hitter in Ted Williams, a lineup of sluggers to back Williams, and one of the greatest managers in the history of the game. Everyone was ready for 1948, it seemed, except the Yankees.

At first it looked as if the 1948 pennant race would belong not to the Red Sox, Indians, or Yankees but to ancient Connie Mack's Philadelphia Athletics. Mack was 85 years old and more than a little out of it. He had last won a pennant in 1931, and his team hadn't had a first-division finish in 15 years, but the A's were still clinging to first place as late as August 12, staying ahead of the Indians by half a game, Boston by two, and the Yankees by 3.5.

The A's perseverance in the race was shocking; they had none of the star power of their three competitors for the title and not half the home run power. Nor was their pitching staff impressive, though it was a colorful lot—lefty starter Lou Brissie was the sole survivor of a German shell attack that killed 11 in Italy; reliever Alex Kellner was sunk on the USS *Callahan*, the last American ship lost in the war; reliever Bob Savage was wounded twice in Sicily; Canadian Phil Marchildon, a gunner in the RAF, was shot down and spent almost two years in German custody. Three other pitchers, Bill Dietrich, Dick Fowler, and Bill McCahan, had pitched no-hitters in the majors. What the A's did have was a patient offense led by shortstop Eddie Joost (119 walks) and first baseman Ferris Fain (113 walks). With no expectation of an extra-base hit (Joost led the club in home runs with 16), Mack—or Al Simmons, the coach assigned to protect Mack from senescence—often played for one run. Athletics left fielder Barney McCosky led the league in sacrifice bunts with 22; the team finished second in the league with 120.

This worked, for a while. What finally did the A's in was the schedule. With a single-division, 154-game balanced schedule, each team in the league played the others 22 times each season. On their last day in first place, the A's still had more than half their games with the Yankees left to play, as well as 13 games with the Red Sox and Indians and five against the Tigers, the other team in the league to finish with a winning record. This opposition would prove too strong. Starting August 13, the A's had 30 games left to play with teams in the running:

12 games against the Yankees (went 4-8)
8 games against the Red Sox (2-6)
5 games against the Indians (0-5)
5 games against the Tigers (1-4)

Against the Browns, Senators, and White Sox, the A's went 12-4.

The A's finished the season in a 19-27 slide, settling in fourth place. This was actually fine with Connie Mack, who worried that a winning club would cut into his profits. "What I like to do," he once told an umpire, "is keep my ball club in contention from first to fourth place until the first of July. By that time we have made enough money that we can tail off, and with a last-place ball club you don't have to raise anybody's salary. ... I can make more money finishing last than I can first." This transparent cynicism meant that the A's would finish higher than sixth in attendance just twice between 1933 and their eventual sale and relocation to Kansas City after the 1954 season.

The Red Sox did not expect to be looking up at the A's. Not only had they hired McCarthy during the off-season, but they had also successfully dueled Veeck for the right to rob the Browns of a player widely felt to be a difference-maker, shortstop Vern "Junior" Stephens. One of the few shortstops of this period to be a true power hitter, the 27-year-old Stephens was the animating force behind the Browns' surprising 1944 pennant, batting .293/.365/.462 with 20 home runs that year. From 1942 to 1947, Stephens had batted .292/.355/.452 with 109 home runs, more than twice as many home runs as the next-best shortstop, Eddie Miller.

The only shortstop who could claim to have as much on the bat as Stephens, though he wasn't a power hitter, was Lou Boudreau of the Indians. By 1947, Boudreau was a career .292/.374/.410 hitter and was widely recognized as the league's leading fielder, "playing shortstop as though he invented it" despite being one of the slower runners in the game. Boudreau, wrote Red Smith, "can't run and his arm's no good.

But he plays that spot the way nobody else can play it, and he gets rid of the ball so swiftly the runner never beats his weak throw. Besides which, pitchers say he is the smartest hitter in the league, the hardest to fool, the guy who hits the ball where it's pitched, pushing the outside curve to right, pulling the inside service into the left field seats."

Boudreau had also been the Indians' manager since 1942. Veeck deplored his tendency to play wild hunches and wanted to replace him with someone more reasoned like Casey Stengel, Al Lopez, or former Veeck associate Charlie Grimm. There was no way, though, to separate Boudreau the player from Boudreau the manager. If the latter went, the former had to follow. "You couldn't expose him to that embarrassment," Veeck said of asking a defrocked Boudreau to continue playing in Cleveland. "It would destroy his dignity." Veeck reconciled himself to trading his star shortstop. It just happened that the Browns needed a manager, and Stephens was the only player capable of replacing Boudreau on something close to a one-for-one basis.

Boudreau was popular, but Veeck figured he had the latitude to make a change because the ball club had been a poor performer for so long. The Indians had last won a pennant in 1920 and, except for three seasons, had finished somewhere between 12 and 43.5 games behind in the years since. But when news of the deal leaked, Veeck was confronted by a storm of hostility. "I learned how badly I had transgressed when the first of the telegrams was delivered," Veeck wrote. "It read: IF BOUDREAU DOESN'T RETURN TO CLEVELAND, DON'T YOU BOTHER TO RETURN EITHER. It was signed by a minister." Veeck backed down. He signed Boudreau to a two-year contract, unusual at the time, and hired experienced coaches—Bill McKechnie, Tris Speaker, Muddy Ruel, Mel Harder—hoping their restraint would rub off on his impulsive manager.

The moment Veeck surrendered to Boudreau, the Red Sox swept in, sending six players of very limited horizons and $310,000 of Tom Yawkey's money to St. Louis, receiving in return not only Stephens but righty Jack Kramer, the Browns' best pitcher. In a separate but nearly simultaneous deal with the Browns, also involving cash, the Sox also liberated Ellis "Old Folks" Kinder, a bibulous but effective sidearmer. Veeck fumed and Yankees co-owner Topping raged that the deals would turn the circuit into a seven-team league, a bit of hypocrisy given that it had recently been a one-team league.

Despite the move, the Red Sox began the season doing a solid impression of the eighth entry in Topping's seven-team league. Even in his highly successful Yankees years, McCarthy had avoided a consistent starting rotation, keeping only indisputable aces like Red Ruffing and Lefty Gomez on a regular schedule. The amount of work the other pitchers received depended on matchups and McCarthy's perception of who was hot. A pitcher might work every four days, every 10, or once a month. The Red Sox lacked a Ruffing or Gomez for McCarthy to build around, and he initially had trouble discerning the keepers from the chaff. At the end of May, the Sox were in seventh place with a 14-23 record, 11.5 games behind the first-place A's.

McCarthy also struggled to identify a first baseman. This was nothing new for him; from 1931 through 1938 he had the luxury of not having to think about who was playing first base—Lou Gehrig literally never missed a game (although injuries did reduce him to a cameo role on occasion). With the Iron Horse's illness and rapid decline in 1939, his position was thrown open and remained unsettled for the rest of McCarthy's term.

Like the Yankees, the Red Sox had been graced with a future member of the Hall of Fame at first base, the muscular "Double X," Jimmie Foxx. Foxx had excelled for the Red Sox from 1936 through 1941, but in June 1942, he was traded to the Cubs and ultimately became the real-life basis for the character played by Tom Hanks in *A League of Their Own*. Since then, the Sox had tried Tony Lupien (seven home runs in 1,090 at bats), Lou Finney, Catfish Metkovich, a near-retirement Joe Cronin, Rudy York (the only serviceable hitter in the group), and Jake Jones.

In a December 1947 trade that attracted far less notice than the pillaging of the Browns, Cronin had relieved his father-in-law of one of the Senators' best players, four-time All-Star center fielder Stan Spence, in exchange for a second base prospect and a fringe outfielder. Spence, who had averaged .286/.371/.470 in 1946 and 1947 (socking 50 doubles, 10 triples, and 16 home runs in 1946), would be moved to first base. Though batting as Boston's cleanup hitter (Ted Williams was batting third) at the outset, Spence then slumped and got hurt. McCarthy initially reverted to 1947's first baseman, Jake Jones, but in June, inspiration finally struck. "We've been going no place," McCarthy said. "But a little child shall lead them."

The child was 22-year-old rookie Billy Goodman. The left-handed hitter from North Carolina had given no indication that he was a nascent slugger, yielding just six home runs in 1,215 minor league at bats. But he had hit .389 for the Southern League's Atlanta Crackers in 1946 and .340 for the Louisville Colonels in 1947, and McCarthy must have reasoned that getting a bunch of singles out of his first baseman was

TABLE 3-2  Mize, Fain, and Pray for Rain: The Weak First Baseman Class of 1948

| NL | | | AL | | |
|---|---|---|---|---|---|
| Team | Player | EqA | Team | Player | EqA |
| Giants | Johnny Mize | .325 | A's | Ferris Fain | .293 |
| Braves | Earl Trogeson | .286 | Red Sox | Billy Goodman | .283 |
| Cubs | Eddie Waitkus | .278 | Yankees | George McQuinn | .264 |
| Phillies | Dick Sisler | .275 | Indians | Eddie Robinson | .251 |
| Reds | Ted Kluszewski | .266 | Tigers | George Vico | .251 |
| Dodgers | Gil Hodges | .246 | Browns | Chuck Stevens | .249 |
| Pirates | Ed Stevens | .251 | White Sox | Tony Lupien | .239 |
| Cardinals | Nippy Jones | .247 | Senators | Mickey Vernon | .232 |

better than nothing. He got what he asked for. Goodman hit just one home run in 1948, but he hit .310/.414/.387 (.283 EqA), drew 74 walks, and played good defense.

Going with Goodman at first base proved to be a decisive move; 1948 was an odd year in which nearly every team *but* the Red Sox received little production from first base, traditionally a bastion of sluggers (Table 3-2). An average major league first baseman in 1948 hit for an EqA of just .263, the lowest value since 1910. It was the first time since 1920 that major league first basemen hit less than .270 (EqA); they improved to .267 in 1949 and have been over .270 ever since. The American League was particularly starved for first base production (when reading Table 3-2, remember that a league-average EqA is .260).

With this unplanned paucity of productive first sackers, for one of the few times in baseball history, teams got more production from their shortstops (Table 3-3). This unusual flip-flop in production was particularly noticeable in the American League.

At roughly the same moment that McCarthy hit on Goodman as a solution to his first base problem, he also sorted out his rotation, dropping 1947 holdovers Mickey Harris and Boo Ferris. This left him with a rotation of Kramer and Kinder, plus sophomore lefty Mel Parnell and the veteran curveball specialist Joe Dobson, with occasional starts by veteran soft-tosser Denny Galehouse. With these changes, along with a Ted Williams hot streak that saw him hit .460 for the month, the Red Sox took off in June. They won 12 of their first 15 games that month, finally crossing the .500 mark on June 20. They played even better in July, kicking off a 13-game win streak on July 18 and going 25-9 over-

Table 3-3 Boudreau That Voodough That You Dough So Well: Shortstops of 1948

| | NL | | | AL | |
| --- | --- | --- | --- | --- | --- |
| Team | Player | EqA | Team | Player | EqA |
| Braves | Alvin Dark | .282 | Indians | Lou Boudreau | .341 |
| Dodgers | Pee Wee Reese | .273 | Red Sox | Vern Stephens | .274 |
| Pirates | Stan Rojek | .263 | A's | Eddie Joost | .283 |
| Phillies | Eddie Miller | .239 | Tigers | Johnny Lipon | .277 |
| Giants | Buddy Kerr | .228 | White Sox | Cass Michaels | .252 |
| Cardinals | Marty Marion | .226 | Yankees | Phil Rizzuto | .244 |
| Reds | Virgil Stallcup | .204 | Browns | Eddie Pellagrini | .222 |
| Cubs | Roy Smalley | .206 | Senators | Mark Christman | .221 |

all. On July 31 they stood in first place, a half-game ahead of the A's and two games ahead of the Indians and Yankees.

The Indians had stayed close throughout the season. Everything was going right for Boudreau and Veeck. Boudreau was on his way to an MVP with the best offensive season of his career. Rookie Larry Doby was establishing himself as a star (he batted .301/.384/.490 on the season) after a trying cup of coffee in 1947. The veteran second baseman Joe "Flash" Gordon was having the best season of his career at 33, joining with Boudreau to give the Indians the league's best hitting, best fielding double-play combination. Veteran third baseman Ken Keltner, 31, was setting a career high in home runs with 31.

The Indians' pitching was a surprise even to the Indians. The rotation was nominally headed up by Bob Feller, "Rapid Robert," the game's premier strikeout pitcher since he reached the big leagues as a 17-year-old phenom in 1936. When Feller enlisted in the navy on December 9, 1942, he was the most dominant pitcher in the game. When he returned on August 24, 1945, he picked up exactly where he had left off (Table 3-4).

Today we would recognize Feller as a pitcher at risk; he had thrown a terrific number of innings at a very young age. His total of 1,449 in-

Table 3-4 "Rapid Robert's" Status Quo Antebellum: Bob Feller Before and After the War

| | W | L | G | GS | CG | IP | H | BB | BB/9 | SO | SO/9 | ERA |
| --- | --- | --- | --- | --- | --- | --- | --- | --- | --- | --- | --- | --- |
| 1939–1941 | 76 | 33 | 126 | 112 | 83 | 960 | 756 | 454 | 4.3 | 767 | 7.2 | 2.88 |
| 1945–1947 | 51 | 29 | 99 | 88 | 63 | 742 | 557 | 315 | 3.8 | 603 | 7.3 | 2.41 |

Table 3-5 Fatigued Feller: All-Time Most Innings Pitched by Age 28

| Rank | Player | Years | Seasons | IP | G | GS | CG |
|---|---|---|---|---|---|---|---|
| 1 | Walter Johnson | 1907–1916 | 10 | 3,148.1 | 419 | 347 | 302 |
| 2 | Christy Mathewson | 1900–1909 | 10 | 2,966.2 | 388 | 344 | 281 |
| 3 | Bert Blyleven | 1970–1979 | 10 | 2,624.2 | 353 | 350 | 145 |
| 4 | George Mullin | 1902–1909 | 8 | 2,592.1 | 330 | 298 | 258 |
| 5 | Don Drysdale | 1956–1965 | 10 | 2,574.0 | 397 | 344 | 134 |
| 6 | Hal Newhouser | 1939–1949 | 11 | 2,458.0 | 378 | 306 | 182 |
| 7 | Catfish Hunter | 1965–1974 | 10 | 2,456.0 | 363 | 340 | 116 |
| 8 | Robin Roberts | 1948–1955 | 8 | 2,312.0 | 316 | 283 | 181 |
| 9 | Waite Hoyt | 1918–1928 | 11 | 2,250.0 | 363 | 265 | 154 |
| 10 | Vida Blue | 1969–1978 | 10 | 2,203.2 | 308 | 297 | 114 |
| 11 | Joe Coleman | 1965–1975 | 11 | 2,192.0 | 334 | 312 | 91 |
| 12 | Bob Feller | 1936–1947 | 9 | 2,191.0 | 304 | 263 | 180 |
| 13 | Chief Bender | 1903–1912 | 10 | 2,186.0 | 309 | 244 | 200 |
| 14 | Mel Harder | 1928–1938 | 11 | 2,184.2 | 390 | 260 | 122 |
| 15 | Fernando Valenzuela | 1980–1989 | 10 | 2,144.2 | 298 | 287 | 102 |

nings pitched by age 22 still stands as the most ever. Despite the interruption of the war years, he had pitched enough innings by his 28th birthday in 1947 to rank 12th on the all-time list (Table 3-5).

There was no such understanding of pitcher fatigue in 1948, so Feller's inconsistency in the first half of the 1948 season meant that he was frequently booed by the same fans who had been cheering him since he was a teenager. He shut out the Browns on two hits on opening day and pitched well throughout the first month. But in May he slumped. His velocity seemed to be down, and he continued to pitch poorly for the next two months. In late July, with his record at 10-12, he had his arm checked out by a doctor, who found nothing amiss.

Feller began to pitch better down the stretch, but by then he had ceded his position as staff ace. The Tribe was rolling, thanks to unexpected contributions by two lefty starters. Bob Lemon had come to the majors as a third baseman, but in 1946 the Indians shifted him to the mound, where he threw a variety of off-speed pitches to make up for less-than-intimidating velocity ("I was awfully brave to go out there with the stuff I had," Lemon told Russell Schneider in 1998, "and lucky"). After decent but unspectacular results as a swingman in 1946 and 1947, Lemon blossomed as a full-time starter in 1948. He won 20 games, including a no-hitter against the Tigers on June 30, and pitched 31 consecutive scoreless innings beginning in late August.

He led the league in innings pitched and shutouts (10) and finished second in strikeouts (to Feller) and third in ERA.

The pitcher who led the league in ERA was even more unexpected. Gene Bearden was a lefty with weak stuff, which had been further compromised by severe injuries suffered when his ship, the USS *Helena*, was torpedoed by a Japanese destroyer in 1943. After the war, Bearden was property of the Yankees. During the 1946 off-season, Bearden pitched in a charity game in Hollywood and acquitted himself well. Afterward, a gnomish figure hobbled over.

"So the Yankees own you, huh?" the man said. "I like your hustle. I like the way you backed up those plays. My name is Casey Stengel. I manage Oakland. How would you like to play for me?"

Bearden liked the idea, and Stengel, who was close with George Weiss, arranged Bearden's transfer to the Pacific Coast League for the 1946 season. Stengel urged Bearden, who had thrown a knuckleball only during practice, to use the pitch in games. Bearden suddenly became a prospect. That winter, Larry MacPhail offered him to Veeck as partial payment for the catching prospect Sherm Lollar. Veeck consulted Stengel. "He isn't ready yet but he will be in a year or so," Stengel said. "Get him before MacPhail regains his sanity."

Stengel's prediction was on the money. Veeck returned Bearden to Stengel and Oakland for one more year, where he again pitched well, and in 1948 he joined the Indians. Though he didn't get his first start until May 12 ("It seems every time Boudreau would schedule me to start, we'd get rained out," he remembered), Bearden had one of the great rookie seasons of all time, winning 20 games, throwing six shutouts, and posting a league-leading 2.43 ERA.

◆

The Yankees played quite well throughout the season without ever taking control of the race. They remained close to the A's and Indians, and later the Red Sox, but never found first place. They had several nagging problems—Joe DiMaggio was playing on one foot, Charlie Keller broke his hand, Bucky Harris couldn't decide if Yogi Berra was a catcher or an outfielder, first baseman George McQuinn had reached the end of the line at 38—but the slight edge they were missing came down to "Fireman" Joe Page. A struggling southpaw starter (and key source of frustration) under Joe McCarthy from 1944 through 1946, Page had been reinvented as a reliever under Harris in

1947. In return, Page gave the best performance by a relief pitcher to that point in baseball history. The bullpen had traditionally been the domain of second-class arms. Page was one of the first relievers who threw hard. In 1947, Feller led the American League with 5.9 strikeouts per nine innings. The average pitcher struck out 3.8. Page struck out 7.4. He was considered a key part of the team's successful run that year and received seven first-place votes in the MVP balloting, second to winner Joe DiMaggio (Table 3-6).

In 1948, Page was not the same. He might have been tired from his heavy usage the year before—he pitched 56 games and 141 innings— or it may have been his lifestyle. "He was probably the biggest dissipater in the history of baseball," said a contemporary pitcher. "Drinker, women ... They'd send detectives out to follow him and he'd end up getting the detectives drunk." Harris, crediting Page with the 1947 championship, refused to discipline him, out of a misguided sense of loyalty. "I don't kid myself," he said. "Page's great relief work put me back in business after I had been forgotten. I'd be an ungrateful so and so to turn on him now. This job isn't that important to me." No longer did the Yankees have the ability to hold a tie game in stasis, or save a fatigued starter from having to go an extra inning in pursuit of a win (Table 3-7).

Table 3-7 Page's Rise and Fall

| Year | W | L | G | GS | SV | GF | IP | H | BB | BB/9 | SO | SO/9 | HR | ERA |
|------|----|---|----|----|----|----|-----|-----|----|------|-----|------|----|------|
| 1947 | 14 | 8 | 56 | 2  | 17 | 44 | 141 | 105 | 72 | 4.6  | 116 | 7.4  | 5  | 2.49 |
| 1948 | 7  | 8 | 55 | 1  | 16 | 38 | 108 | 116 | 66 | 5.5  | 77  | 6.4  | 8  | 4.25 |

Given Harris's tolerance of several other carousers, George Weiss concluded the ball club had gotten away from the manager. Yet the Yankees remained solidly in contention, and their fate was in their own hands. On the morning of September 1, the Red Sox were in first place, one game in front of the Yankees and 1.5 in front of the Indians. The Yankees had but one game left with the Indians, but eight remaining with the Red Sox. The first Sox game took place on September 8 at Boston. The only difficulty was that Boston was playing tremendously well. Beginning August 29, the Yankees won nine straight games, finally losing on September 6 in the last game before an off day and the trip to Boston. During that same stretch, the Sox had gone 8-1, including seven straight wins from August 31 to September 6. The Yankees

TABLE 3-6 The First Fireman: Best Single-Season Performances by Relievers Through 1947 (by WARP)

| Player | Team | Year | W | L | G | GS | SV | GF | IP | H | BB | SO | HR | ERA | WARP |
|---|---|---|---|---|---|---|---|---|---|---|---|---|---|---|---|
| Joe Page | Yankees | 1947 | 14 | 8 | 56 | 2 | 17 | 44 | 141 | 105 | 72 | 116 | 5 | 2.49 | 7.7 |
| Joe Berry | A's | 1944 | 10 | 8 | 53 | 0 | 12 | 47 | 111 | 78 | 38 | 44 | 4 | 1.95 | 5.8 |
| Garland Braxton | Senators | 1927 | 10 | 9 | 58 | 2 | 13 | 32 | 156 | 144 | 33 | 94 | 5 | 2.94 | 5.6 |
| Clint Brown | White Sox | 1939 | 11 | 10 | 61 | 0 | 18 | 56 | 118 | 127 | 27 | 41 | 8 | 3.89 | 5.5 |
| Andy Karl | Phillies | 1945 | 8 | 8 | 67 | 2 | 15 | 41 | 181 | 175 | 50 | 51 | 7 | 2.98 | 5.5 |
| Ace Adams | Giants | 1943 | 11 | 7 | 70 | 3 | 9 | 52 | 140 | 121 | 55 | 46 | 5 | 2.83 | 5.3 |
| Joe Berry | A's | 1945 | 8 | 7 | 52 | 0 | 5 | 40 | 130 | 114 | 38 | 51 | 5 | 2.77 | 5.3 |
| Earl Caldwell | White Sox | 1946 | 13 | 4 | 39 | 0 | 8 | 37 | 91 | 60 | 29 | 42 | 2 | 2.08 | 5.1 |
| Wilcy Moore | Yankees | 1927 | 19 | 7 | 50 | 12 | 13 | 30 | 213 | 185 | 59 | 75 | 3 | 2.28 | 5.1 |
| Harry Gumbert | Reds | 1947 | 10 | 10 | 46 | 0 | 10 | 34 | 90 | 88 | 47 | 43 | 3 | 3.90 | 5.0 |

failed to gain any ground. When they finally did meet, the Red Sox took two of three, once coming from behind to defeat Page and thrashing Harris's pet pitcher Bob Porterfield in the second. Joe DiMaggio salvaged the third game by hitting a two-out, 10th-inning grand slam, but the Yankees still left town trailing by 2.5 games. The Indians were in third place, 3.5 games out. There were three weeks to play.

It was at this moment that McCarthy's team slipped just a bit. Over the next two weeks, the Sox broke even, at 7-7. Simultaneously, the Yankees won nine games and lost four, while the Indians went 10-3. Thus, on the morning of September 24, all three teams had records of 91-56 with seven games left.

The Indians had the easiest schedule of the three, playing five games with the Tigers, two on the road, three at home, these games bracketing a two-game home series against the White Sox. The Yankees and Red Sox would play each other four more times, first at Yankee Stadium and then at Fenway. In between, the Yankees would visit Philadelphia for three games. The Red Sox would host the Senators.

Boudreau tried to press his advantage. With Feller pitching better, the starting rotation was reduced to the Feller and Bearden show, with just a drop of Lemon. On September 25, Bearden beat the Tigers 9-3. The next day Feller beat them 4-1. After a day off, Boudreau came right back with Bearden, who shut out the White Sox 11-0. Feller, like Bearden working on two days' rest, beat them 5-2. At the same time, the Red Sox split with the Yankees on the 25th and 26th and then hosted Washington, a team on its way to 101 losses. The Sox dropped the first game, but took the next two. The Yankees' series with the A's went the same way. The standings on September 30 found the Indians ahead of the Yankees and Red Sox by 1.5 games.

The Red Sox and Yankees, with one less game to play than the Indians, had October 1 off before meeting at Fenway Park. If the Indians beat the Tigers that day, they would be two games up with two to play—they would have clinched a tie. Boudreau broke away from Bearden and Feller one last time, and called Lemon. The southpaw carried a 3-2 lead into the top of the ninth inning, but an error and two walks loaded the bases and Boudreau went to reliever Russ Christopher to save the game. Christopher walked in the tying run, then allowed a two-run single. The Indians lost 5-3. The Yankees and Red Sox floated a half-game closer. With two games remaining, there were three possible scenarios, with variations:

- If the Indians split with the Tigers, the Yankees or the Red Sox could tie for the pennant by winning both games.
- If the Indians lost both games, the Yankees or Red Sox could win the pennant outright by winning both games.
- If the Indians lost both games and the Yankees and Red Sox split, the season would end in a three-way tie.

"Stay with me, boys," McCarthy told his charges before sending Jack Kramer to face the Yankees' wild Tommy Byrne. "Cleveland gets knocked off by Detroit. We take the Yankees. That's the ending. That's my dream. You can't take that away from me." On cue, Ted Williams hit a two-run homer in the first, and the Red Sox cruised to a 5-1 win. Cleveland, though, didn't cooperate. Bearden, showing what he could do on three days' rest, shut out the Tigers.

The Yankees were eliminated, with nothing left to do but play spoiler. If the Indians won their final game, they took the pennant. If they lost and Boston won, there would be a tie and a playoff game. Boudreau wasn't about to use Bearden on no rest, so it was back to Feller. The Tigers responded with lefty ace Hal Newhouser, who had already won 20 games. Joe McCarthy picked Joe Dobson. Bucky Harris, managing what might be his last game for the Yankees, again went to his pet, rookie Bob Porterfield.

Porterfield sealed Harris's fate when the Red Sox erased a 2-0 Yankees lead with a five-run third. New York kept the game competitive, but Boston never again gave up the lead, winning 10-5. Meanwhile, the Tigers thrashed Bob Feller. There would be a one-game playoff for the pennant in Boston the next day. As the Boston Braves had won the National League pennant, the World Series would begin in Boston. Boudreau told his team, "We're just going to Boston a day early."

Both managers agonized over which pitcher to start in the playoff game. Boudreau chose Bearden on one day's rest. McCarthy chose a seldom-used 36-year-old veteran named Denny Galehouse. Both decisions were gambles. One worked, so its merits are never discussed. The other failed and has been second-guessed for close to 60 years.

Depending on your point of view, Galehouse was either well rested or rusty, having pitched just twice since September 12. In actuality, his inactivity was an illusion: Because the Yankees continually threatened to rally in the October 3 game, Galehouse had stayed loose in the bullpen for six innings. Rather than the least-fatigued member of the Boston staff, he was probably the most fatigued.

This seemed to escape McCarthy, as did Galehouse's status as the last man on the staff and his complete mediocrity, even in his prime. Yet McCarthy had reasons to rule out everyone else on the staff. Parnell was rested but too young and too left-handed. Kinder was rested but McCarthy didn't like the way he had pitched against the Indians earlier in the year. In later years, there was the suggestion, floated by Sox catcher Birdie Tebbetts, that some of the starters had been asked to pitch and demurred. Tebbetts died in 1999 without elaborating on his charges.

Lou Boudreau's best asset as a manager had always been his ability to write his own name into the lineup. He had also been a terror on the road, finishing the season with a .403 average away from Cleveland. With two outs and no one on in the top of the first, he homered to left field for a 1-0 Cleveland lead. In the fourth, Boudreau and Gordon singled and Keltner followed with a three-run homer, chasing Galehouse. Though the game went into the books with a final score of 8-3, it was over after the fourth. Cleveland had won the pennant.

The Indians and Red Sox had passed the Yankees. The Indians had even outdrawn the New York club, setting a new attendance record of 2.6 million. The Tribe and the Sox had succeeded partly because they had done things the Yankees wouldn't do. Now all that was left was for the Yankees to do something the Yankees wouldn't do.

In 1947, when Larry MacPhail was unable to hire Leo Durocher, George Weiss suggested his old friend Casey Stengel. MacPhail offered a two-word response: "That clown?" Now MacPhail was gone, Weiss was in charge, and the owners were willing to indulge him. In October 1948, Bucky Harris was fired and Stengel was named as his replacement.

Stengel had been in the game for almost four decades. His major league managerial experience consisted of nine uninspired seasons with the Dodgers and Braves, the public perception of which was that, as a manager, Stengel made a fine comedian. Weiss knew that Brooklyn and Boston were two of baseball's most financially precarious teams at the time that Stengel had them—the Braves had even needed to borrow money from Stengel to stay afloat. Weiss could also point to Stengel's record in the minors. In winning league championships in the high minors with Toledo, Milwaukee, and Oakland, Stengel had become noted for his ability to rehabilitate veterans, promote youngsters, and combine both into successful teams.

Pundits predicted that the Yankees were finished. "They have money, front office direction and a manager ... who should do well," wrote one. "But they will never again dominate baseball." Stengel knew better. "There is less wrong with the Yankees," he said, "than with any club I've ever had." He had seen bad teams and managed them. The Yankees, though old, didn't qualify. "There'll likely be some changes, but it's a good club and I think we'll do alright. We'll go slow because you can tear a club down a lot quicker than you can build it up."

There was not only skepticism of the ball club but doubt about Stengel himself. One writer called him "a second division manager who was entirely satisfied to have a losing ball club so long as Stengel and his wit were appreciated." Stengel had long had a reputation for comedy that exceeded that of his baseball acumen. "Because I can make people laugh," he said, "some of them think I'm a damn fool." Fifty-nine years old, five years removed from his last major league job, he knew this would be his last chance to prove that he was the equal of his late mentor, John McGraw. "Let them think it's a joke," Stengel said, "and maybe I'll laugh when I fool them."

The preseason consensus was that the Yankees would finish third in 1949. "Third ain't so bad," Stengel joked. "I never finished third before. That's pretty high up." Contrary to expectations, the club opened the season strongly. They were hotly pursued by the Red Sox. The Indians failed to make a race of it, Bearden's magic mysteriously vanishing—Veeck claimed it was because Stengel had counseled his hitters to lay off Bearden's diving knuckler. "Casey giveth," wrote Veeck, "and Casey taketh away."

The Yankees stayed a few steps ahead through late June. Injuries were a constant problem, though. Most devastating was the loss of Joe DiMaggio, who had undergone surgery to alleviate pain from a bone spur in his heel. The operation only made the pain worse. Restricted to crutches, DiMaggio sat out the first sixty-five games of the season, sullenly contemplating retirement.

The rest of the club was no better off. Stengel couldn't keep a first baseman healthy. Second basemen developed strains and sinus problems. Only shortstop Phil Rizzuto appeared in more than 130 games, though he too was hurt, his arm so weak that after he fielded the ball he would often toss it to the third baseman, who would throw across the diamond for him. Yogi Berra, whom Stengel had returned to catcher, was hit by a pitch and broke his thumb. Tommy Henrich, the team's sole remaining power hitter, persevered in the lineup despite various injuries. Stengel told him to drive carefully, avoid drafts, and "under no circumstances are you to eat fish, because them bones could be murder. Sit quietly in the clubhouse until the game begins. I can't let anything happen to you." Eventually a collision with an out-field wall took Henrich away as well.

Stengel benefited from a solid rotation led by Vic Raschi, Allie Reynolds, and Ed Lopat. At the same time, he began to apply the lessons learned from years of patching together lineups for underfinanced depression-era teams with reduced rosters. He pinch-hit early, relieved late (benefiting from Joe Page's return to form), revived the practice of platooning to maximize the contributions of his substitutes, and ran rookies into and out of games. The team continued to win.

This was the key moment in what would become known as the Yankees dynasty. Had the Yankees faded, Stengel would have vanished into obscurity, Weiss unable to protect him. Weiss too might have been replaced. The Yankees might have panicked and allowed the Red Sox or, more likely, the Indians (who would revive quickly) to sail by. They tottered but did not fall, as Stengel demonstrated that his aggressive tactics could pay off repeatedly. "People said in 1949 what terrible luck we were having with all those injuries," he said, "but that was one of the luckiest breaks I got, because I had to use the men." Rather than rely too heavily on any one player, he would cultivate versatility. "I made up my mind to have three Yankees for every position," he said, "and on this club I can do it."

In late June the Yankees went to Boston for a three-game series. With the Red Sox winning 10 of 11 games, there was a sense that a strong showing in these contests would shift the season's momentum to Boston. What happened instead was the climactic act of Joe DiMaggio's career. At precisely the moment that he had been convinced that his heel would cause him to retire, his pain vanished. DiMaggio personally buried the Sox with four homers and nine RBIs in only 11 at-bats. The Yankees swept the series, dropping Boston into third place. Before the third game, a small airplane flew over Fenway, carrying a banner that read, "The Great DiMaggio."

Still, McCarthy's team was too good to quit. The Sox turned it up a notch, going 24-8 in August. In late September, Boston finally passed New York. It wasn't that the Yankees were not playing well; the Red Sox were simply playing better. As in 1948, it was the Senators (who lost 104 games in 1949) who threw the pennant into doubt. When the Red Sox dropped a 2-1 game in Washington on September 28, they allowed the Yankees to tie the race with just three games to play. Two of those games were head to head.

On September 30, the Yankees lost 4-1 to the A's while the Red Sox beat the Senators 11-9. The Sox were up by one game with two to play.

All they had to do was win one of the last two games at Yankee Stadium, and they would go to the World Series.

Before the first game, Stengel looked across the field at his opponents and said, "I think we've got 'em. I can feel it in my bones." He had DiMaggio back (returned from more time off with the flu) and Berra as well. The Yankees' Allie Reynolds would face 25-game winner Mel Parnell.

Reynolds always issued a lot of walks, but on this day he was out of control. Already down 1-0 with one out in the third, he walked the first three men he faced and then allowed a single for another run. Stengel called for Joe Page. The move seemed to blow up in Stengel's face when Page walked the first two batters he faced to put the Yankees in a 4-0 hole, but he came back to fan the next two hitters. After that, he was untouchable, allowing only one hit in 6.2 innings of relief.

The offense took care of the rest. DiMaggio was the key figure in two rallies that tied the score. In the eighth, McCarthy relieved with one of his starters, righty Joe Dobson. (Boston had no pitcher comparable to Page. Essentially, they were missing a bullpen.) Stengel gambled again. All season long he had platooned righty outfielder Johnny Lindell. Now he let him hit. Lindell slugged the game-winning home run.

The race was tied. The winner of the final game would take the pennant. Vic Raschi, winner of 21 games, and Ellis Kinder, winner of 23, would duel. Rizzuto led off the game with a triple. With McCarthy playing his infield back, Henrich purposefully tapped a grounder to the right side to drive in the run. The score remained 1-0 through the eighth. In the top of that frame, McCarthy pinch-hit for Kinder, again exposing his team's weak bullpen. The Yankees pounced on the opportunity, scoring four runs in the bottom of the inning. Boston staged a late rally, but it was too little, too late. The Yankees were the winners of the American League pennant.

The manager, the erstwhile clown, was exultant. "I want to thank all these players for giving me the greatest thrill of my life," Stengel said. "And to think they pay me for managing so great a bunch of boys."

From that moment until 1965, the Yankees lost just two pennant races, one in 1954, the other in 1959. The Indians won the 1954 flag, the White Sox the 1959 one. The Red Sox rapidly faded from contention, Tom Yawkey having become disenchanted with baseball's many reversals. McCarthy, diminished by his poor choices in 1948 and 1949, quit the Red Sox 59 games into the 1950 season. Retired for good this time, he was inducted into the Hall of Fame in 1957.

There was still one thing that the Yankees would not do, one thing that could do them in. They would not renounce their stubborn racism—but it took years before the effects were fully felt. A window had been closed.

## The Postwar Period and Competitive Balance

### NATE SILVER

In the days before World War II, before television and expansion and the racial integration of the game, several franchises spent decade after decade in the league's basement. The Phillies had just one winning season between 1918 and 1948. The Browns went the entire decade of the 1930s without winning more than 67 games in a season. The Philadelphia Athletics were even worse, spending all but three seasons between 1935 and 1946 in last place. The Boston Braves went 30 straight years, from 1917 to 1946, without finishing higher than fourth. And the Washington Senators—though they performed a bit better than is generally remembered—did little to honor the nation's capital. Those five franchises—the Browns, Braves, Athletics, Phillies, and Senators—represented a permanent underclass during the 1930s and early 1940s. Unable or unwilling to compete, these underdogs made it far easier for teams like the Yankees and Cardinals to compile gaudy win-loss records.

Within a decade of the end of World War II, four of those five teams experienced a turnaround. The Braves won the 1948 National League pennant, and the Whiz Kid Phillies followed them in 1950. Three straight winning seasons made a refreshing change for the A's between 1947 and 1949. And the Browns were liberated, albeit slowly, by moving to Baltimore. Only the Senators' struggles continued unabated.

This thrust toward greater parity is also evident in the statistical record. Chart 3-1 displays the standard deviation of winning percentage among all major league teams from 1925 to 1965; we exclude the war years of 1942–1945, as they were played under unusual circumstances. Standard deviation is a measure of the "spread" within a given variable. Larger standard deviations indicate outcomes that are spread further apart—in this case, a lot of very good teams and a lot of very bad teams, with few teams left in the middle. Smaller standard

Chart 3-1 Standard Deviation in Average Winning Percentage of All Major League Teams, 1925 to 1965

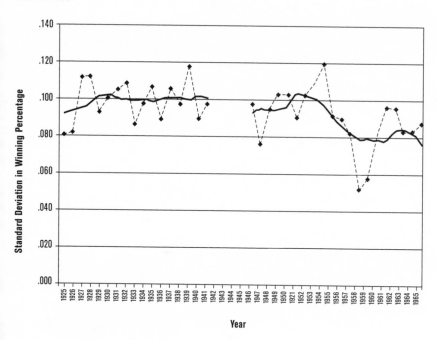

deviations indicate the opposite—that the teams are closely bunched together in talent.

As the chart indicates, the standard deviation of winning percentage fell markedly within the first ten years of the postwar era. It has essentially remained at its new, lower level ever since.

Jackie Robinson and Larry Doby debuted in 1947. Did the racial integration of the game propel the change in competitive ecology? Probably not. There is little relationship between the order in which the sixteen teams integrated and their degree of success in the prewar years (Table 3-8). Of the first three teams to integrate, the Indians had generally posted a good record in the seven seasons before World War II, the Dodgers had been about average, and the Browns had been terrible. On the other end of the spectrum, the Yankees were one of the last teams to integrate—but so too were the woeful Phillies. Integration certainly improved the quality of talent on the field, but it did not necessarily alter the competitive landscape of the game.

What, then, was driving the shift toward greater competitive balance? This question has an answer, but to get there, we have to think

Table 3-8 Racial Integration of Major League Teams

| Chronological Order of Integration | Team | W-L | Year of Integration |
|---|---|---|---|
| 1 | Dodgers | 77-76 | 1947 |
| 2 | Indians | 83-70 | 1947 |
| 3 | Browns | 58-96 | 1947 |
| 4 | Giants | 83-69 | 1949 |
| 5 | Braves | 65-88 | 1950 |
| 6 | White Sox | 79-74 | 1951 |
| 7 | Athletics | 56-96 | 1953 |
| 8 | Cubs | 85-68 | 1953 |
| 9 | Pirates | 81-72 | 1954 |
| 10 | Cardinals | 87-66 | 1954 |
| 11 | Reds | 81-72 | 1954 |
| 12 | Senators | 71-82 | 1954 |
| 13 | Yankees | 98-54 | 1955 |
| 14 | Phillies | 52-101 | 1957 |
| 15 | Tigers | 85-69 | 1958 |
| 16 | Red Sox | 82-70 | 1959 |

| League Standing | Team | W-L | Year of Integration | Chronological Order of Integration |
|---|---|---|---|---|
| 1 | Yankees | 98-54 | 1955 | 13 |
| 2 | Cardinals | 87-66 | 1954 | 10 |
| 3 | Cubs | 85-68 | 1953 | 8 |
| 4 | Tigers | 85-69 | 1958 | 15 |
| 5 | Giants | 83-69 | 1949 | 4 |
| 6 | Indians | 83-70 | 1947 | 2 |
| 7 | Red Sox | 82-70 | 1959 | 16 |
| 8 | Pirates | 81-72 | 1954 | 9 |
| 9 | Reds | 81-72 | 1954 | 11 |
| 10 | White Sox | 79-74 | 1951 | 6 |
| 11 | Dodgers | 77-76 | 1947 | 1 |
| 12 | Senators | 71-82 | 1954 | 12 |
| 13 | Braves | 65-88 | 1950 | 5 |
| 14 | Browns | 58-96 | 1947 | 3 |
| 15 | Athletics | 56-96 | 1953 | 7 |
| 16 | Phillies | 52-101 | 1957 | 14 |

about another quality that is closely related to competitive balance: efficiency.

One consistent feature of the Yankees and Cardinals dynasties of the 1930s and 1940s was their ability to place on their benches players who were better than the *starting* talent of many other teams in the league. For example, the Yankees employed an outfielder named George Selkirk, who had been Babe Ruth's replacement in 1935. Selkirk was extremely successful when he played. He batted over .300 five times, was named to two All-Star teams, and had a career on-base plus slugging percentage (OPS) that was 27 percent better than the league average.

Yet Selkirk could barely find a spot in the Yankee lineup. Blocked by Ruth, Earle Combs, and Ben Chapman early in his career, he had to wait until he was 26 to make his major league debut. But just as soon as Selkirk had gotten "rid" of Ruth and Combs, along came Joe DiMaggio, Charlie Keller, and Tommy Henrich, leaving Selkirk to fight for platoon and pinch-hit at-bats. Why didn't the Yankees deal Selkirk, when the *Sporting News* speculated they could have received more than $40,000 for him within a couple of months of his 1934 debut? The short answer is that they had the luxury to hold on to him; they already had an All-Star at virtually every position, and the cash they could give or take. Why trade a useful player to a potential rival when you could keep him forever under the reserve clause?

Teams like the Yankees and Cardinals sometimes did sell their excess talent, but when they did, it was usually to middle-tier teams like the Dodgers, Red Sox, and Cubs, rather than teams like the Phillies or Senators that might more desperately have needed it. Retrosheet, a nonprofit organization founded to computerize the play-by-play of pre-1984 major league games, maintains a historical database of transactions. Though not comprehensive, the database contains information on many prewar transactions in which money was exchanged, either as part of a trade or in an outright sale. These data suggest that the Futile Five—the Athletics, Senators, Phillies, Braves, and Browns— were far more likely to sell player talent than acquire it. Retrosheet records more than $1.3 million in player sales for these teams between 1930 and 1941, compared with $326,000 in player purchases (Table 3-9).

In other words, the rich in talent were getting richer, while the poor were quite literally serving as their farm systems. The Futile Five might not have come across premium talent very often—in fact, they

Table 3-9 Cash Transactions Between 1930 and 1941

| Team | Sales | Purchases | Net |
|------|-------|-----------|-----|
| Cardinals | $470,000 | $100,000 | $370,000 |
| Athletics* | $470,000 | $130,000 | $340,000 |
| Senators* | $350,000 | $76,000 | $274,000 |
| Phillies* | $260,000 | $15,000 | $245,000 |
| Braves* | $113,000 | $0 | $113,000 |
| White Sox | $115,000 | $102,500 | $12,500 |
| Indians | $25,000 | $27,500 | -$2,500 |
| Pirates | $8,000 | $40,000 | -$32,000 |
| Tigers | $100,000 | $135,000 | -$35,000 |
| Browns* | $50,000 | $105,000 | -$55,000 |
| Cubs | $157,500 | $250,000 | -$92,500 |
| Giants | $60,000 | $160,000 | -$100,000 |
| Reds | $55,000 | $160,000 | -$105,000 |
| Yankees | $182,500 | $337,500 | -$155,000 |
| Dodgers | $180,000 | $485,000 | -$305,000 |
| Red Sox | $207,500 | $680,000 | -$472,500 |

*Member of the "Futile Five."

generally had weak player-development capabilities. But when these teams found a diamond in the rough, the player was packaged and sold to one of the richer clubs.

So vicious was this cycle that the elite clubs often ended up with bench players who were better than the regulars on the second-division clubs. Using Clay Davenport's equivalent average (EqA), I compared the talent level of the regulars and bench players in the league at any given time. A *regular* was defined as a player who played a majority of games for his club at each of the eight primary fielding positions. A bench player was defined as the player who played in the *second*-most games for his club at that position, subject to certain requirements (for example, the player was not considered a bench player if he was in fact a regular at another position and happened to do double duty from time to time).

The goal of this exercise is to compare the true level of talent of the bench players and the regulars. Because the bench players' performances are necessarily subject to small sample sizes, we adjusted all EqAs according to the players' performances in adjacent seasons. The result of this adjustment is our best estimate of the player's true level of talent, or his TrueEqA. If a bench player posted a .300 EqA but did so in only 50 at-bats, and he did not perform as well in the years be-

Table 3-10 True Equivalent Averages (TrueEqAs) for Regular and Bench Center Fielders in 1953

| Team | Regular | TrueEqA | Bench | TrueEqA |
|------|---------|---------|-------|---------|
| Yankees | Mantle | .327 | Noren | .276 |
| Dodgers | Snider | .325 | – | – |
| Indians | Doby | .315 | Westlake | .278 |
| Phillies | Ashburn | .294 | – | – |
| Reds | Bell | .281 | Marquis | .246 |
| Giants | Thomson | .280 | – | – |
| Tigers | Delsing | .269 | – | – |
| White Sox | Rivera | .267 | – | – |
| Cardinals | Repulski | .261 | – | – |
| Senators | Busby | .255 | – | – |
| Pirates | Thomas | .254 | Bernier | .232 |
| Browns | Groth | .252 | Dyck | .239 |
| Braves | Bruton | .250 | Pendleton | .211 |
| Athletics | McGhee | .235 | Mauro | .207 |
| Red Sox | Umphlett | .221 | Evers | .234 |
| Cubs | – | – | – | – |

fore and after that season, then his TrueEqA would be much lower than .300. This process is explained at greater length in the endnotes.

Table 3-10 lists the TrueEqAs for the qualified regulars and bench players at center field in 1953. Note that the Yankees and Indians, who had two of the best regulars in the league at their position (Mickey Mantle and Larry Doby), also had backups (Irv Noren and Wally Westlake) who were better than many regulars in the league.

In general, we would probably assume that the stronger bench players should be about equal in talent to the weaker regulars. If this is *not* the case, then the competitive environment of the league is arguably inefficient, because there are opportunities for mutually beneficial trades that have not been exercised. That is, a team with a weak regular would presumably stand to gain more from "buying" a strong bench player than the selling team would lose in giving him up. Wally Westlake, for example, should presumably be more valuable to the Browns as a starter than he is to the Indians as a backup.

How we define a "strong" bench player and a "weak" regular is subject to interpretation. We certainly need to leave the teams some room for error. It is not fair to assume perfect hindsight. Moreover, the assumptions of our model are imperfect; EqA does not account for defensive acumen or a player's long-term value, for example. But we will

Table 3-11 TrueEqAs for "Weak" Regular and "Strong" Bench Players in 1953

| Position | Weak Regular 30th Percentile | Strong Bench Player 70th Percentile |
|---|---|---|
| C | .245 | .254 |
| 1B | .258 | .262 |
| 2B | .243 | .247 |
| 3B | .256 | .263 |
| SS | .234 | .228 |
| LF | .284 | .278 |
| CF | .254 | .246 |
| RF | .264 | .251 |
| AVERAGE | .255 | .254 |

start by defining a weak regular as having a TrueEqA in the 30th percentile of all qualified regulars at his position, and a strong bench player as having a TrueEqA in the 70th percentile of all qualified backups at his position. We can apply this 30/70 assumption to our set of 1953 data, for example (Table 3-11).

In this instance, the average performance of the weak regulars across all positions was almost equal to that of the strong bench players. This suggests that the competitive ecology of 1953 was fairly efficient; there were few mutually beneficial trades to be made.

In other years, however, the results did not turn out quite as nicely. In 1936, for example, the TrueEqA of the weak regulars was about 6 points below that of the strong backups under the 30/70 assumption. We will call this calculation—the difference between the TrueEqA of the weak regulars and that of the strong backups—the *efficiency index* (Chart 3-2).

What immediately stands out is the sharp increase in the efficiency of talent distribution in the decade following World War II. We have already noted a significant improvement in competitive balance in the years after the war; now we partly understand why. The weaker teams and the stronger ones were doing a better job of sharing the talent pool.

But what triggered that increase in efficiency? Before we answer this question, let's take one more cut of the data, this time using a 20/80 assumption instead of the more liberal 30/70 (Chart 3-3). That is, we'll now compare the performance of the 20th percentile regulars to that of the 80th percentile bench players.

This version of the analysis displays the same general patterns, but somewhat sharper variations in the efficiency index from year to year. It also suggests that perfect efficiency is hard to achieve; the efficiency index is usually below zero. That is, even if a league does a good job of distributing its players, its strong bench players are still likely to be better than its weaker regulars. This is probably a more realistic assumption; teams have neither perfect information nor perfect judgment, and factors like no-trade clauses and payroll restrictions might

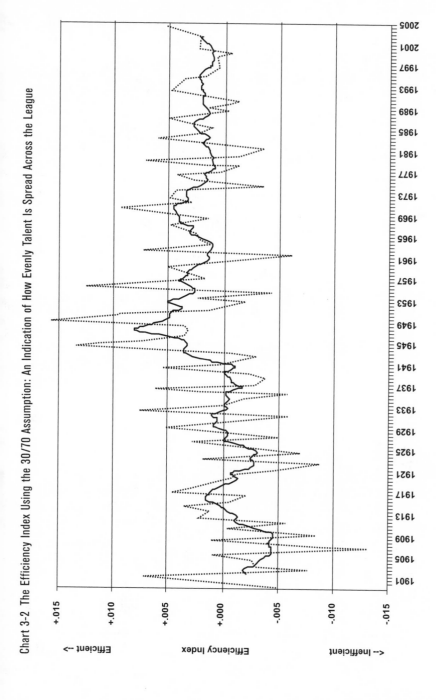

Chart 3-2 The Efficiency Index Using the 30/70 Assumption: An Indication of How Evenly Talent Is Spread Across the League

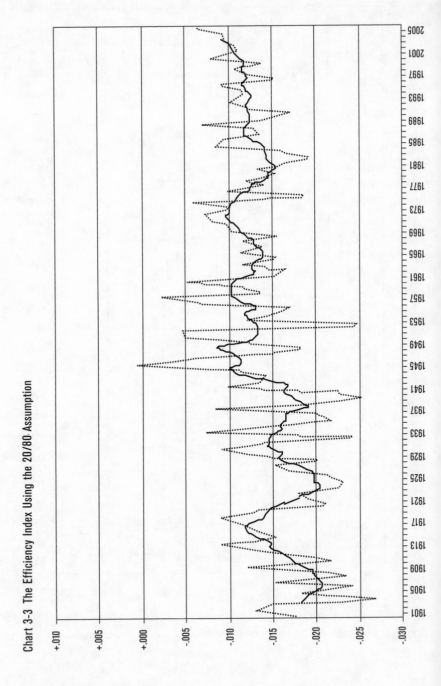

Chart 3-3 The Efficiency Index Using the 20/80 Assumption

prevent teams from completing trades that would otherwise be mutually beneficial.

Whichever version of the analysis we prefer, however, one key system regulates the ebbs and flows of the efficiency index. This regulator is the farm system. In fact, changes in the rules and practices governing the minor leagues can account for essentially every shift in the competitive ecology of the league.

## 1901–1920

At the birth of baseball's modern era in 1901, the league was chaotic. The American, National, and minor leagues took turns raiding one another's players and dishonoring one another's contracts.

In 1903, the leagues brokered peace in the form of the National Agreement. The agreement included not just the AL and NL, but also the National Association of Professional Baseball Leagues (NAPBL), which had governing authority over the minor leagues. The NAPBL agreed, in essence, to a subordinate relationship with the major leagues, including a waiver system and a draft system that allowed players to be plucked from the minors at a specified price. It took a while to iron out all the kinks, as teams gamed the system by developing "working agreements" with minor league clubs, but the competitive environment of the league became steadily more orderly, and the efficiency index rose.

## 1921–1929

All the good work done in the first twenty years of the modern era went for naught. With the creation of the Federal League in 1914, the door to widespread player movement was opened. World War I and continued efforts to cheat the system contributed to the sense of chaos. "By 1919, the major-minor agreement was dead," wrote Leonard Koppett. "In this realm, as in others ... anarchy reigned."

In 1921, a new agreement with the minor leagues was signed. It contained one crucial provision: Minor leagues were granted the right to "opt out" of letting the majors draft their players at a specified price, if the minors agreed to give up the parallel right to draft players out of lower minor league classifications. Several of the more important minor leagues took this path, and soon they had tremendous bargaining power with the majors. These minor league players had essentially become free agents who could command free-agent prices.

The effect on competition within the league was profound and immediate. Many of the poorer clubs were entirely priced out of the market for young talent, and the efficiency index reverted to its turn-of-the-century values.

### 1930–1945

The dissatisfactory conditions of the new agreement with the minor leagues and the genius of Branch Rickey, then the general manager of the St. Louis Cardinals, combined to produce the birth of the modern farm system. The 1921 agreement had failed to prohibit working agreements (affiliations) with minor league clubs or direct ownership of them, and Rickey took notice by creating dozens of affiliates for his Cardinals. A couple of other teams, notably the Yankees, followed suit.

By 1930, thanks in part to lobbying by the Cardinals, the rest of the teams had more or less resigned themselves to the legality of Rickey's maneuverings. But not all the clubs were sold on the efficacy of minor league affiliations. Thus, by 1936, the Cardinals were affiliated with 28 minor league teams, the Reds 16, and the Tigers and Yankees 11 apiece, while the Phillies and Senators had limited themselves to one.

There was some initial improvement in the competitive ecology of the league. Teams now had two choices for developing talent: They could build it, like the Cardinals, or they could buy it, like the Red Sox. Or they could do both, like the Yankees. Many teams chose to do neither, and it wasn't long before the Yankees and Cardinals had become dynastic.

### 1946–1964

Although World War II had decimated the minors—shrinking them from 304 minor league clubs in 1941 to just 66 in 1943—it had also finally proved something. Teams that invested in their farm systems stood to do tremendously well. That's what the Cardinals had done, and between 1942 and 1944, the Cardinals won 106, 105, and 105 games. During these war years, the St. Louis team had been stocked almost entirely with players from Rickey's farm system while the rest of the league was employing one-armed outfielders and 15-year-old pitchers.

Suddenly, the rest of the league began to catch on. From 1936 to 1948, the number of affiliated minor league clubs jumped by almost 250 percent (Table 3-12). The increase was buoyed by the postwar prosperity boom, which was producing record attendance at baseball games at all levels. Another leveler of the playing field was the adoption of the "bonus baby" rule in 1947, which sought to penalize teams for signing amateurs to expensive contracts. Under this rule, amateurs had to remain on the major league roster for at least two seasons.

The effects of the widespread adoption of the farm system were dramatic, as the efficiency index shot up to unprecedented levels almost immediately. Within a few years, competitive balance had followed suit. The new order was symbolized by the 1950 Phillies, who won their first pennant in 35 seasons with a roster of "Whiz Kids," like Richie Ashburn and Robin Roberts, developed almost entirely within their farm system.

### 1965–1975

After a minor loss in efficiency following the expansions of 1961 and 1962, farm systems got another boost when the amateur draft was adopted in 1965. The efficiency index followed suit in a couple years, as the players worked their way through their systems.

Table 3-12 Number of Minor League Teams Affiliated with Major League Teams, from 1936 to 1948

| | Number of Minor League Teams | | |
| --- | --- | --- | --- |
| Major League Team | 1936 | 1948 | Change |
| Browns | 3 | 20 | +17 |
| Indians | 5 | 20 | +15 |
| Yankees | 11 | 24 | +13 |
| Senators | 1 | 12 | +11 |
| White Sox | 5 | 15 | +10 |
| Red Sox | 9 | 15 | +6 |
| Tigers | 11 | 16 | +5 |
| Athletics | 5 | 10 | +5 |
| Dodgers | 5 | 26 | +21 |
| Giants | 2 | 22 | +20 |
| Pirates | 4 | 19 | +15 |
| Cubs | 5 | 19 | +14 |
| Phillies | 1 | 15 | +14 |
| Braves | 4 | 15 | +11 |
| Reds | 16 | 11 | −5 |
| Cardinals | 28 | 22 | −6 |
| TOTAL | 115 | 281 | +166 |

### 1976–2006

Thanks to the Messersmith decision and the implementation of free agency, the 1976 season was the first one played without the reserve clause. Talent development still carried significant rewards under the new economic system, but teams could no longer expect to retain players from their farm system indefinitely. As a result, there was a decline in efficiency that appears to have roughly offset the gains from the amateur draft. The efficiency index has remained in a steady state for the past thirty years.

◆

The upshot of the long and tumultuous history of baseball's relationship with the minor leagues couldn't be clearer. If you want to give teams a chance to be competitive, provide them with a cheap and equitable way to procure and develop talent from the amateur ranks.

It is no accident that baseball is extremely sensitive to any escalation in the signing bonuses of the amateur draft. These bonuses are almost certainly less than the true economic value of the players being selected, but a combination of peer pressure and compensatory draft picks for teams that fail to sign a player hold the bonuses down. If amateurs could negotiate contracts at near-market rates, we would probably see a return to the Futile Five years, with richer teams monopolizing both younger and veteran talent.

In considering the Futile Five, perhaps we can move beyond a reductionist understanding of teams like the prewar Phillies and Boston Braves as simply incompetent or cheap. These teams did sell young talent when they came across it, a practice that undoubtedly entrenched their positions at the bottom of the standings. At the same time, they probably had no choice. Under baseball's present economic structure, small-market teams like the Oakland A's and Minnesota Twins have the chance to compete by investing in their scouting and development systems, which are a heavily subsidized source of labor. The Braves and Phillies did not have that alternative, because under the majors-minors agreement of 1921, young talent could be sold to the highest bidder. Given this bottleneck, Philadelphia and Boston were too far from the goal line to have realistic hopes of contention even if they had held on to their young talent, and they were probably wise to take the money and run.

Contemporary evidence suggests that there is a substantial economic premium associated with competing for a pennant. When that is not plausible, it is overwhelmingly more profitable to behave as a seller rather than a buyer. If the same held true in the 1920s and 1930s, then the Phillies and Braves were simply behaving rationally. When the incentives changed in the 1940s and 1950s because of the development of the modern farm system, so too did the teams' behavior.

## What If Branch Rickey Had Run the Yankees?

STEVEN GOLDMAN

*None of us is color-blind, boys. Some of us just squint a little better than others.*
—Branch Rickey

As president of the Brooklyn Dodgers, Branch Rickey signed Jackie Robinson and began the desegregation of baseball. In 1947, when

Robinson reached the majors, the color line was history and the so-called gentleman's agreement that had kept African Americans out of baseball since 1887 went with it. Rickey was ahead of the nation; it would be seven years before the Supreme Court, with its decision in *Brown v. Board of Education of Topeka*, would legislate for the country what Rickey had already done for baseball. It was the sport's proudest moment. Baseball's decision to outlaw Negro players at the end of the nineteenth century was part of a nationwide trend of Jim Crowism, a trend that the Supreme Court validated by advancing the doctrine of "separate but equal" in its 1896 decision in *Plessy v. Ferguson*. Rickey unilaterally discarded that doctrine and made baseball the front-runner in a national move toward desegregation—a movement that had yet to find its voice.

Robinson's arrival resonated in every pennant race that followed in the long, glacial aftermath of integration. The competitive landscape changed overnight, with so many races now hinging on which teams allowed themselves full access to the new stream of talent entering the game. While this alteration of the terms of competition was secondary to the moral importance of integration, its impact was deeply felt.

The integration of baseball was merely the pinnacle accomplishment of Rickey's half-century in the game, which was also notable for the invention of the farm system. That he did those things is of less interest than why he did them, or why, under different circumstances, he might not have done them.

Rickey (1881–1965) spent his entire executive career in the National League, creating championship teams in St. Louis, Brooklyn, and Pittsburgh. As a player he had a passing acquaintance with the Yankees. In 1907, his last season as an active player, Rickey played 52 games as an outfielder, catcher, and first baseman for the then-Highlanders. He was coming off of an arm injury, which helps explain how on June 28 the Senators set a record by stealing 13 bases against him. After hitting only .182, Rickey retired to take his law degree and coach baseball at the University of Michigan. In 1913 he was hired as an executive assistant by the St. Louis Browns. He quickly moved up to general manager and then managed the team on the field. In 1917 he moved to the Cardinals, for whom he also served as both manager and general manager. In 1921, he began setting up the first farm system. After a few indifferent finishes, he gave up the field manager's job in 1925 and became a full-time executive. Even before that, his "chain-store baseball" system was beginning to work its magic for the Cardinals, who won a pennant and a World Series victory over the Yankees in 1926.

The preceding paragraphs describe what actually happened. Now for what could have happened, but didn't. At the end of 1914, Jacob Ruppert and Tilinghast L'Hommideau Huston purchased the Yankees. Baseball neophytes, they were unsure about whom to hire as manager and general manager. According to Frank Graham, they "turned to their friends among the baseball writers for advice." The names the sportswriters came up with were Wild Bill Donovan and Harry Sparrow. Imagine instead that the name they got back was Branch Rickey.

This scenario may conjure notions of Rickey, freed of the more provincial setting of St. Louis, tipping over the color barrier years earlier, of the first African American player being someone like Buck Leonard of the Homestead Grays, who was called "the Black Gehrig," or the great Cuban slugger Martin Dihigo. Far more likely, however, nothing at all would have happened, and integration would have come about in another place at an even later time. Had Rickey worked for the Yankees, it is unlikely that he would have accomplished anything to parallel his real achievements. He probably would have built some good teams, and perhaps gone to Cooperstown in Ed Barrow's stead (Barrow ran the Yankees from 1921 to 1945), but he would not have become the iconic figure he was. Even geniuses need motivation and inspiration, and Rickey would have lacked both in New York.

All great ideas require a seed crystal. In Rickey's case, the seed crystal was money. When he started out, young players were not developed by the major league teams but were purchased on the open market from minor league clubs owned by independent operators. Rickey found himself constantly being outbid for the best talent. That's what started his mind working. "The farm system, which I have been given credit for developing," Rickey said later, "originated from a perfectly selfish motive: saving money."

Rickey figured that if his team could buy up minor league clubs, it could control prospects from the moment the players entered organized baseball, unproven and thus inexpensive. The Cardinals could also make sure that a player received the best instruction, which increased his chances of developing, and the big-league club would have accurate scouting information all the way through the process. In this way, the Cardinals would have the pick of the litter, with excess players being used as trade bait or sold for cash. Best of all, Rickey figured the farm system would probably make enough money to pay its expenses, which meant that the whole thing wouldn't cost the Cardinals a dime.

Had Rickey been in New York, the financial incentive for the farm system would not have existed. The Yankees benefited from the open-market system, as they had the money to rule over it. Only in 1929 did Colonel Ruppert began thinking that the cost of buying minor leaguers was getting out of control; in November 1931, he finally purchased the Newark Bears (over Barrow's objections) and started the Yankees farm system in earnest.

Rickey's decision to bring Jackie Robinson to the majors was more complicated, but it also had an economic aspect. A devoutly religious man, Rickey had strong feelings about the equality of men and the injustice of the color line. In 1904, while coaching the Ohio Wesleyan baseball team, he had seen the effects of Jim Crow firsthand. The team traveled to South Bend, Indiana, to play Notre Dame. Ohio Wesleyan's one black player, Charles Thomas, was told he could not stay at the team hotel. Rickey's impassioned argument on his player's behalf earned a compromise: Thomas could share Rickey's room. Rickey remembered Thomas crying in the incident's aftermath, obsessively wringing his hands. "Damned skin ... Damned skin!" Thomas moaned. "If only I could rub it off." "That scene haunted me for many years," Rickey said later, "and I vowed that I would always do whatever I could to see that other Americans did not have to face the bitter humiliation that was heaped upon Charles Thomas."

So Rickey's eyes were wide open, but he had to find the right time to act on his feelings. He had to amass the personal prestige and power to pull off such a move. He had to survive the first commissioner, Judge Landis, who was not a proponent of integration. And Rickey had to be in the right place; St. Louis would make a poor proving ground for integration. Only when Rickey landed in Brooklyn did everything came together.

What was so special about Brooklyn? Again, it was partly economic. As much as Brooklyn loved its Dodgers, the team didn't make very much money. Farm system or not, they still weren't on a level with the Yankees and the Giants. Rickey needed an edge. "The greatest untapped reservoir of raw material in the history of the game is the black race," he said. "The Negroes will make us winners for years to come. And for that I will happily bear being called a bleeding heart and a do-gooder and all that humanitarian rot."

Branch Rickey said a lot of things—he was a baseball executive, an evangelist, and a Shakespearean actor all rolled into one—and so his statements, whether humanitarian or coldly practical, should not be taken at face value. Despite a generous spirit, he was notoriously flinty with his players. He was both lofty and mean. He was famous for being able to pull the wool over the eyes of his fellow general managers when conducting trade talks. Sportswriters called his office "the Cave of Winds" because of his grandiose pronouncements. The subject of Jackie Robinson and the integration of baseball evoked all these qualities. Rickey was a humanitarian whose high ideals and actions had a pleasingly mercenary by-product. It was Brooklyn's need for the by-product that made integration possible.

With plenty of money to sign their players, the Yankees didn't need the help that the Dodgers did. The Bronx team could afford to indulge its prejudices against African Americans and its fear of being overwhelmed by a flood of black ticket buyers. The Yankees' determination to stay lily-white would cost them in the long term, as their resistance to paying high bonuses to *white* players meant that they were also forfeiting the best talent of their preferred race. Not until 1955 did the team's management make the right decision—under pressure—and promote Elston Howard from its farm system to the major league team. Even then, it was years before a second African American player played a significant role in pinstripes.

Without a Rickey to step forward and sign Robinson in 1946, perhaps no one in baseball would have made the move that year, in which case the government would probably have stepped in. In 1945, New York State passed the Quinn-Ives Act, banning discrimination in hiring. This was followed closely by a Fair Employment Practices Act. Quinn-Ives created an investigatory committee to look into discriminatory hiring practices, and one of the committee's first moves was to call on baseball to hire black players. Simultaneously, New York's mayor, Fiorello La Guardia, made the integration of baseball part of his reelection campaign and began calling for an end to the color line.

Perhaps Bill Veeck, another owner who had long objected to the color line (and who claimed that he had attempted to buy the Phillies in 1943 with the intention of using African American players, only to be thwarted by Judge Landis), would have stepped forward. But he only became an owner in 1946, and he lacked Rickey's gravitas. Without the leadership of Branch Rickey, integration would have happened slowly and grudgingly—even *with* his leadership, it happened slowly and grudgingly. In 1947, Rickey supplied the idea and the desire to do the right thing; Brooklyn supplied the need. Perhaps in the absence of need, moral vigor would have been a sufficient motivation to act. But it's doubtful—it had never worked that way before.

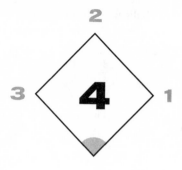

# 1908 National League

*A Foolish Inconsistency*

STEVEN GOLDMAN

Despite a half-century of practice, in 1908 baseball was still in the process of earning the designation "professional." All of the standards, laws, and folkways that now seem innate were being tested, defined, and discarded on a daily basis. In this, baseball, as it so often is, was a microcosm of the nation at that time. As historian Richard Hofstadter wrote of the period, "the processes of modern technology and machine industry—not to speak of the complex tasks of civic life—made organization, specialization, hierarchy and discipline utterly necessary." Necessary, yes, but that doesn't mean these qualities were actually present or that the urgent need for them was universally acknowledged. America was struggling with the idea that strictly enforced rules were necessary at all—that business should be restrained from anticompetitive practices; that there shouldn't be formaldehyde in the milk or rat feces in the hot dogs; that children should be in the schools and not in the coal mines—so it should come as no surprise that baseball had yet to cover its bases.

One of those naked bases was umpiring. Big league officiating was still in a primitive state at the turn of the 20th century. The big issue of the preceding 10 years was umpire abuse and intimidation—baseball couldn't be a clean, honest, family-suitable game if umpires were subject to physical threats (or worse) from the players and fans. With this

## 1908 National League Prospectus

| Team | \multicolumn{5}{Actual Standings} | Date Elim | \multicolumn{2}{Pythag} |
|------|----|----|------|------|-----|-----------|-----|-----|
| | W | L | Pct | GB | DIF | | W | L |
| Cubs | 99 | 55 | .643 | – | 90 | – | 97 | 57 |
| Pirates | 98 | 56 | .636 | 1.0 | 53 | Oct 8 | 92 | 62 |
| Giants | 98 | 56 | .636 | 1.0 | 44 | Oct 8 | 100 | 54 |
| Phillies | 83 | 71 | .539 | 16.0 | 0 | Sept 25 | 85 | 69 |
| Reds | 73 | 81 | .474 | 26.0 | 0 | Sept 16 | 70 | 84 |
| Doves* | 63 | 91 | .409 | 36.0 | 2 | Sept 11 | 67 | 87 |
| Superbas* | 53 | 101 | .344 | 46.0 | 0 | Sept 7 | 57 | 97 |
| Cardinals | 49 | 105 | .318 | 50.0 | 0 | Sept 6 | 45 | 109 |

| \multicolumn{4}{League Averages} | \multicolumn{3}{BP Stats Leaders} |
|------|------|------|-------|----------------|-----|------|
| AVG | OBP | SLG | BABIP | Offense, BRAA | | Indiv WARP |
| .239 | .299 | .306 | .236 | Giants | 159 | Honus Wagner | 18.1 |
| ERA | K9 | BB9 | H9 | Pitching, PRAA | | Christy Mathewson | 15.5 |
| 2.35 | 3.4 | 2.6 | 7.7 | Phillies | 70 | Joe Tinker | 13.5 |

*The Doves and the Superbas later became the Braves and the Dodgers.

war largely won, or at least tamped down to a series of occasional skirmishes, the game's overseers could have turned their attention to devising standards for their arbiters. They didn't. Even the four-man umpiring crew, whose need now seems so obvious, wasn't mandated until 1952. Two-man crews were not required until 1912, and three-man crews not until 1933. Until 1912, in any given game a good deal of the action on the field, some of it critical to the outcome, went unseen by the overtaxed single umpire on the field. Two-man crews were put into occasional use even before they were required by rule (though the majority of 1908's games were viewed by just one umpire), but the game had become too fast and too complex to be competently judged by even an umpiring duo.

This literal lack of oversight inevitably led to laxity about certain rules and practices. It did not occur to those running the National League at the time—the magnates and league president Harvey Pulliam—that selective enforcement of the rules could lead to inequity on the field until it was too late. As baseball historian Bill James wrote:

It is in principle most dangerous to have rules on the books which are not enforced, or to have one set of rules written down and another acted out. ... In any fascist or totalitarian state, they have laws against most everything, laws that are never enforced so long as you behave yourself. ... Having laws on the books that are not enforced puts every policeman in the robes of a judge, empowered to decide who the guilty are today.

In the National League of 1908, the entire season came down to exactly that—the arbitrary enforcement of a law by a policeman, in this case an umpire. The decision not only altered the outcome of the pennant race, but also destroyed lives.

The National League of the early 20th century was dominated by three teams, the Chicago Cubs, New York Giants, and Pittsburgh Pirates (Table 4-1).

Table 4-1    In the Money: National League First-Division Finishers, 1901–1907

| Year | 1st Place | 2nd Place | 3rd Place | 4th Place |
|------|-----------|-----------|-----------|-----------|
| 1901 | Pittsburgh | Philadelphia | Brooklyn | St. Louis |
| 1902 | Pittsburgh | Brooklyn | Boston | Cincinnati |
| 1903 | Pittsburgh | New York | Chicago | Cincinnati |
| 1904 | New York | Chicago | Cincinnati | Pittsburgh |
| 1905 | New York | Pittsburgh | Chicago | Philadelphia |
| 1906 | Chicago | New York | Pittsburgh | Philadelphia |
| 1907 | Chicago | Pittsburgh | Philadelphia | New York |

Of the three teams, only the Chicago Cubs are singled out as one of the greatest teams of all time, and some would still argue *the* greatest. In 1906, the Cubs, led by the same principles as in 1908, had won 116 games, setting a season record that still stands (the 2001 Seattle Mariners tied the mark with the help of a longer schedule). The Cubs benefited from a brilliant pitching staff, the power of Frank "Wildfire" Schulte, and the throwing of catcher Johnny Kling, but, thanks to a throwaway bit in a newspaper column, memory of the team would coalesce around three players: The pepper-pot duo of shortstop Joe Tinker and second baseman Johnny Evers, and first baseman and manager Frank Chance, "the Peerless Leader."

Newspaper columnist Franklin Pierce Adams was a Cubs fan working in New York. On July 10, 1910, Adams found himself eight lines short of finishing his *New York Evening Mail* column and filled the space with some light verse. "Baseball's Sad Lexicon" was meant to be a gentle poke in the ribs to the Giants fans among his colleagues:

These are the saddest of possible words,
Tinker-to-Evers-to-Chance

Trio of Bear Cubs fleeter than birds
Tinker-to-Evers-to-Chance
Ruthlessly pricking our gonfalon bubble
Making a Giant hit into a double
Words that are weighty with nothing but trouble
Tinker-to-Evers-to-Chance

Ironically, the trio was hardly a Three Musketeers–style unit. Tinker and Evers hadn't spoken since 1905, when they got into an on-field scuffle, the result of a quarrel over a cab, whereas Chance openly wished that Evers would play the outfield so he wouldn't have to listen to him. "They make a great deal of such differences among ball players," Tinker said. "This is pure exaggeration. You can not expect to be on intimate terms with everybody on your club and there is no reason why you should be, so long as you are playing the game."

Ever since Adams's verse, baseball writers have engaged in pedantic, angles-on-the-head-of-a-pin debates about just how many double plays went Tinker-to-Evers-to-Chance in the trio's years together, as if Adams had written a *Baseball Digest* article entitled, "Why These Three Cubs Should Be in the Hall of Fame!" that included the line, "Trio of Bear Cubs fleeter than birds, who turned exactly 28 more double plays than Jack Barry to Eddie Collins to Stuffy McInnis."

In fact, Tinkers to Evers to Chance was strong on the double play, if not always at the top of the league, but this misses the point: All three were terrific all-around players, excellent on fielding but also adept with the stick. This latter point is difficult to observe from the statistics they compiled, because of the period in which they played. The dead-ball era, which lasted from the late 1890s through the introduction of the lively ball in 1920, was named for the soft, unresponsive ball with which the game was played, a ball that was further deadened by the way teams were allowed to deface it. Umpires did not remove damaged balls from the game as they do today, so players felt free to spit, scuff, scrape, cut, and stomp on the ball until it became a misshapen, brown-gray lump.

Since this softened mass would not travel when struck, it became extremely difficult to hit a home run. From 1887 to 1897, National League batters slugged .372 and hit a home run once every 121 at bats. From 1898 through 1919, they slugged .337 and hit a home run once every 196 at bats. The offensive environment encouraged the style of play known as "inside" baseball. It was the game of the steal, the bunt, the squeeze, and the hit and run. Strategy and gamesmanship were emphasized over bashing. Inside baseball, said one observer, was "merely the outguessing of one team by another."

Evers realized this. "All there is to Evers is a bundle of nerves, a lot of woven wire muscles, and the quickest brain in baseball," said Chicago sportswriter Hugh Fullerton. "He has invented and thought out more plays than any man in recent years." Each night, Evers's bedtime ritual included a couple of candy bars (in an attempt to put weight on his 125-pound frame), the *Sporting News*, and the rule book. He was looking for an edge, a loophole.

This was the game the teams of 1908 played. In fact, 1908 was an offensively austere year even by the standards of the period. The National League ERA of 2.35 remains the lowest of all time, as do the league batting average (.239), on-base percentage (.299), and slugging percentage (.306). By modern standards, the average player of 1908 hit like your third-string shortstop's consumptive sister.

The players were also smaller then. Though the players of the early 20th century prided themselves on their hard-bitten, take-no-prisoners ethos and in their later years would go out of their way to call those who came after them effete, it's quite possible that if a 1908 Cub ran into one of today's bulky, possibly steroidal specimens, he would flee in terror (Table 4-2).

So how good were they? How would Tinker, Evers, and the rest of their primitive, diminutive lot stack up against the modern ballplayer? It's impossible to know for sure, but one can make an educated guess. Baseball Prospectus's Clay Davenport has developed a process by which statistics for all eras can be translated into a common idiom. Statistics are adjusted to

Table 4-2 Who Says Eddie Gaedel Was the Only Midget? Average Vital Statistics, 1908 Versus 2006

| Position | Year | Height | Weight |
|----------|------|--------|--------|
| 1B | 1908 | 6'1" | 188 |
|    | 2006 | 6'2" | 205 |
| 2B | 1908 | 5'9" | 165 |
|    | 2006 | 5'11" | 178 |
| 3B | 1908 | 5'10" | 166 |
|    | 2006 | 6'1" | 191 |
| SS | 1908 | 5'9" | 167 |
|    | 2006 | 6' | 175 |
| C | 1908 | 5'11" | 179 |
|   | 2006 | 6'1" | 199 |
| OF | 1908 | 5'10" | 173 |
|    | 2006 | 6'1" | 193 |
| P | 1908 | 5'11" | 180 |
|   | 2006 | 6'2" | 198 |
| DH | 2006 | 6'2" | 212 |

reflect a league context in which the average hitter bats .260/.330/.420, rates roughly reflective of the major leagues of the 2000–2006 period (in which the average hitter had rates of .266/.335/.426). While we cannot know exactly what the participants in baseball's dead-ball era would have hit with the lively ball, we can, by taking into account the results of those players whose careers straddled the two offensive eras

Table 4-3   Who Would Win, Part I: The Translated 1908 Cubs and the 2006 Cardinals

| 1908 Cubs | | Avg | OBP | Slg | HR | R | RBI | SB |
|---|---|---|---|---|---|---|---|---|
| Solly Hofman | CF | .257 | .329 | .419 | 14 | 74 | 66 | 12 |
| Jimmy Sheckard | LF | .244 | .356 | .414 | 15 | 71 | 37 | 14 |
| Frank Chance | 1B | .285 | .357 | .486 | 17 | 90 | 88 | 27 |
| Johnny Evers | 2B | .332 | .437 | .497 | 8 | 109 | 60 | 37 |
| Harry Steinfeldt | 3B | .249 | .311 | .402 | 18 | 86 | 96 | 4 |
| Frank Schulte | RF | .245 | .311 | .410 | 13 | 58 | 68 | 12 |
| Joe Tinker | SS | .270 | .320 | .520 | 32 | 95 | 107 | 28 |
| Johnny Kling | C | .279 | .324 | .503 | 22 | 71 | 91 | 12 |
| | | W | L | IP | H | BB | K | ERA |
| Three Finger Brown | RHP | 22 | 7 | 246 | 200 | 41 | 157 | 2.56 |

| 2006 Cardinals | | Avg | OBP | Slg | HR | R | RBI | SB |
|---|---|---|---|---|---|---|---|---|
| David Eckstein | SS | .296 | .354 | .349 | 2 | 64 | 22 | 7 |
| Chris Duncan | LF | .295 | .368 | .601 | 22 | 57 | 41 | 0 |
| Albert Pujols | 1B | .334 | .435 | .688 | 51 | 115 | 132 | 7 |
| Scott Rolen | 3B | .299 | .376 | .531 | 26 | 91 | 92 | 7 |
| Jim Edmonds | CF | .260 | .358 | .478 | 19 | 50 | 66 | 4 |
| Juan Encarnacion | RF | .281 | .322 | .451 | 18 | 70 | 75 | 5 |
| Ron Belliard | 2B | .237 | .294 | .376 | 5 | 19 | 22 | 0 |
| Yadier Molina | C | .215 | .273 | .325 | 9 | 29 | 47 | 1 |
| | | W | L | IP | H | BB | K | ERA |
| Chris Carpenter | RHP | 20 | 8 | 261.2 | 219 | 33 | 208 | 2.68 |

and by making adjustments to reflect the way power expressed itself before 1920, come up with a reasonable estimate. To further place these players in a modern context, a point of comparison is provided—the translated statistics of the last three (as of 2006) National League World Series winners (Tables 4-3, 4-5, and 4-6). Each lineup is arrayed in a typical batting order of the season in question.

The Cubs possessed several good pitchers, but their ace was Mordecai Peter Centennial Brown, also called "Brownie," "Miner" (for his prebaseball employment), and "Three Finger." This last was the most important. When Brown was a boy, a corn separator had gotten the best of his right hand, amputating his index finger at the first knuckle and mangling his middle finger, bending it into an S shape and leaving it paralyzed. While still healing from this injury, he had fallen on the hand, breaking the third and fourth fingers.

Brown's misshapen hand was a gift, for it allowed him to put unusual pressure on his curveball, causing it to drop sharply as it reached the plate. Ty Cobb called Brown's curve "the most devastating pitch I ever faced." Brown was once asked if his hand gave him an advantage. "I don't know," he said. "I've never done it the other way."

The Giants entered 1908 having undergone their second major restructuring in six years. When manager John McGraw took over in 1902, he had overhauled a dispirited ball club that had finished higher than seventh only once since 1894. On arriving in New York, he asked the owner for a copy of the team's 23-man roster. McGraw produced a pencil and quickly crossed nine names off the list. "You can begin by releasing these," he said. When the owner protested that the players had been expensive, McGraw replied, "They'll cost you more if you keep them. You're in last place, aren't you?"

The results were immediate; the Giants jumped from eighth place to second in 1903, then won the pennant in 1904 and 1905. In 1907, the team fell to fourth place with a mediocre 82-71 record, and McGraw, never one for complacency, again restructured his team, replacing his aging first baseman, shortstop, and left and right fielders.

This was part of a lifetime pattern for McGraw. He was loyal to his players right up to the point he thought they couldn't help him anymore. "The only popularity I know," he said, "is to win." He was prepared to fire his best friends if it would improve the team, and did. "In playing or managing," he said, "the game of ball is only fun for me when I'm out in front and winning. I don't give a hill of beans for the rest of the game."

This was not a matter of sport but of survival. Joe Tinker said that Frank Chance and John McGraw "were born to battle on baseball fields." That was because baseball was their only means of social advancement and stability. Each was born in the 1870s and came of age in an America without a social safety net during an era of constant economic upheaval. What social mobility existed was largely downward. A native of Fresno, California, Chance came from a middle-class family but never finished high school, gravitating to baseball at an early age. McGraw, son and namesake of an Irish immigrant who was a Civil War veteran and railroad maintenance worker, had seen his family destroyed when he was 11 years old. A diphtheria epidemic swept through his native Truxton, New York, carrying off his mother and four of eight siblings. After that, the family broke up amid economic hardship and harsh beatings from the embittered father. After one such beating, McGraw ran away from home, never to return.

For McGraw, Chance, and most of their contemporaries, many doors were closed. Professional baseball provided an escape for these men, who would otherwise have existed on the lowest rung of a rapidly industrializing society. Future Hall of Fame pitcher Stan Coveleski, whose older brother Harry would play a small but important role in the 1908 race, told historian Lawrence Ritter,

> It's a tough racket. There's always someone sitting on the bench just itching to get in there in your place. Thinks he can do better. Wants your job in the worst way: back to the coal mines for you pal! The pressure never lets up. Doesn't matter what you did yesterday. That's history. It's tomorrow that counts. So you worry all the time. It never ends. Lord, baseball is a worrying thing.

Chance was so eager to win, and thereby survive and prosper, that he destroyed his health, allowing himself to be hit by so many pitches that he eventually lost his hearing. His career total of 137 hit-by-pitches, though surpassed by many armor-wearing modern ballplayers, still ranks 25th on the all-time list. On May 30, 1904, Chance was hit five times in the course of a doubleheader, coming away with a black eye and a cut forehead. It was not an atypical day. He took a ball off of his body once every 37.2 times up to the plate, the 12th-highest rate of all time. John McGraw ranks 13th. He was hit by 132 pitches during his playing career.

McGraw's key triumph in overhauling his 1907 team was the reacquisition of "Turkey" Mike Donlin, an outfielder who had played for the club from 1904 to 1906. Heywood Broun wrote in the *New York World-Telegram* that "it was an important part of McGraw's great capacity for leadership that he would take kids out of the coal mines and out of the wheat fields and make them walk and talk and chatter and play ball with the look of eagles." Just as often, though, it wasn't coal-miner kids who McGraw was trying to turn into eagles but hard-core alcoholics, gamblers, and thieves. There was a saying in baseball: "If you have a bad actor, trade him to McGraw." Donlin was a bad actor in every sense, including the literal. He couldn't keep his hands off the bottle or women—after imbibing from the former, he tended to end up in jail for groping the latter without invitation. He also had an interest in acting and would periodically retire for tours on the vaudeville stage or bit movie parts. Today, Donlin would be treated as a serial sex offender with an alcohol abuse problem. In 1908 he was an eccentric and a coveted ballplayer.

Table 4-4 Turkey Mike Donlin and His Peers, 1899–1912 (with Minimum 3,000 Plate Appearances)

| | | Avg | | OBP | | Slg |
|---|---|---|---|---|---|---|
| 1 | Ty Cobb | .366 | Ty Cobb | .414 | Ty Cobb | .514 |
| 2 | Nap Lajoie | .354 | Roy Thomas | .413 | Honus Wagner | .500 |
| 3 | Honus Wagner | .345 | Honus Wagner | .412 | Nap Lajoie | .490 |
| 4 | **Mike Donlin** | .334 | Nap Lajoie | .399 | **Mike Donlin** | .469 |
| 5 | Jesse Burkett | .324 | Jesse Burkett | .398 | Buck Freeman | .461 |
| 6 | Willie Keeler | .318 | Frank Chance | .396 | Sam Crawford | .453 |
| 7 | Elmer Flick | .314 | Roger Bresnahan | .393 | Elmer Flick | .445 |
| 8 | Jake Beckley | .312 | **Mike Donlin** | .387 | Charlie Hickman | .442 |
| 9 | Sam Crawford | .312 | Elmer Flick | .385 | Sherry Magee | .437 |
| 10 | Ginger Beaumont | .311 | Topsy Hartsel | .383 | Larry Doyle | .433 |

Donlin held out for all of 1907 after McGraw refused to give in to his demand for a large bonus if he stayed sober for the entire season. It was a significant loss; somehow, amid his many distracting hobbies, Donlin was one of the best hitters of his time (Table 4-4).

McGraw's starting first baseman would be the veteran Fred Tenney, acquired from the Boston Doves (Braves) that winter (Table 4-5). But the manager saved a roster spot for a 19-year-old rookie named Fred Merkle, just in case. "Suppose Fred Tenney should be crippled. That would be a calamity, wouldn't it?" asked the *Chicago Tribune*. "Yes, it would in one way, but it wouldn't keep the Giants from winning the pennant. There is a young fellow on the bench named Fred Merkle who can fill that job better than nine-tenths of the first basemen in the league. He is crying for a chance to work." McGraw, said the *New York Evening Telegram*, "says he is the fastest man to touch runners and to touch the base he ever saw."

McGraw's pitching staff was thinner than Frank Chance's—especially after Red Ames, a right-hander who had led the league in strikeout rates from 1905 to 1907, developed kidney problems and was lost for four months. The team's ace almost made up the difference by himself. Sportswriter Grantland Rice called Christy Mathewson "the knightliest of all the game's paladins." A college man at a time when such players were rare, Mathewson stood out from the great players of the day. Ty Cobb could never be a role model the way Mathewson was.

"To me," McGraw said, "he was pretty much the perfect type of pitching machine. He had the stature and strength and he had tremendous speed." He also had the "fadeaway," a pitch we now recognize as a screwball, which Mathewson used as a changeup just a few times each game, always with devastating results. "The secret of

Table 4-5 Who Would Win, Part II: The Translated 1908 Giants and 2003 Marlins

| 1908 Giants | | Avg | OBP | Slg | HR | R | RBI | SB |
|---|---|---|---|---|---|---|---|---|
| Fred Tenney | 1B | .278 | .372 | .381 | 10 | 127 | 73 | 7 |
| Larry Doyle | 2B | .321 | .373 | .512 | 10 | 86 | 53 | 13 |
| Roger Bresnahan | C | .291 | .418 | .471 | 19 | 91 | 83 | 4 |
| Mike Donlin | RF | .337 | .374 | .589 | 37 | 101 | 161 | 25 |
| Cy Seymour | CF | .277 | .323 | .436 | 21 | 82 | 138 | 11 |
| Art Devlin | 3B | .267 | .366 | .411 | 16 | 77 | 69 | 12 |
| Moose McCormick | LF | .299 | .319 | .500 | 11 | 42 | 49 | 2 |
| Al Bridwell | SS | .312 | .397 | .395 | 5 | 65 | 66 | 15 |
| | | W | L | IP | H | BB | K | ERA |
| Christy Mathewson | RHP | 28 | 8 | 307.2 | 238 | 29 | 312 | 2.37 |

| 2003 Marlins | | Avg | OBP | Slg | HR | R | RBI | SB |
|---|---|---|---|---|---|---|---|---|
| Juan Pierre | CF | .312 | .366 | .385 | 1 | 106 | 43 | 90 |
| Luis Castillo | 2B | .326 | .392 | .414 | 5 | 98 | 38 | 24 |
| Ivan Rodriguez | C | .305 | .377 | .492 | 17 | 88 | 83 | 11 |
| Mike Lowell | 3B | .283 | .358 | .551 | 34 | 75 | 102 | 3 |
| Juan Encarnación | RF | .276 | .320 | .459 | 20 | 79 | 92 | 24 |
| Derek Lee | 1B | .281 | .389 | .535 | 33 | 91 | 92 | 26 |
| Miguel Cabrera | LF | .274 | .329 | .482 | 12 | 38 | 60 | 0 |
| Alex Gonzalez | SS | .261 | .316 | .460 | 19 | 51 | 75 | 0 |
| | | W | L | IP | H | BB | K | ERA |
| Josh Beckett | RHP | 13 | 7 | 173.1 | 157 | 63 | 159 | 2.96 |

the fade-away," remembered Giants catcher Roger Bresnahan, "was due to the change in its speed. Matty threw it overhand ... just like his fastball. He let it go shoulder high, with plenty on it, but just before it reached the plate the ball lost all its zip and just floated down over the plate."

"He was a wonderful, wonderful man," Fred Snodgrass, a reserve on the 1908 club, remembered. "Matty could do *everything* well." Mathewson was a tall right-hander ("Big Six," he was called, in apparent reference to his looking even taller than his listed height of six foot two), handsome and poised. He was intelligent and gifted with impeccable control. "That's what made him a great pitcher," catcher Chief Meyers said. "His wonderful retentive memory. Any time you hit a ball hard off of him, you never got another pitch in that spot again." His

Hall of Fame plaque says, "Matty was master of them all." To those who knew him, it was not hyperbole.

The Pirates were a good, not great team that had benefited from the confluence of three historically unique circumstances. First, when the National League contracted from 12 to eight teams during the 1899–1900 off-season, Barney Dreyfuss, owner of the defunct Louisville Colonels, bought a half-interest in the Pirates and transferred his best players to Pittsburgh. Dreyfuss was also more successful than most owners in defending his team from the American League contract raids that were prevalent until the two leagues made "peace" in 1903. Finally, it just happened that one of the players who came over from Louisville, the unassuming John Peter "Honus" Wagner, would turn out to be one of the greatest players in the history of the game.

McGraw called Wagner the greatest ballplayer who ever lived, regardless of position: "I have never heard of anybody pointing to a man as the possible peer of Wagner. He stands out above all." Wagner was at his peak in 1908. Despite playing in perhaps the most difficult hitting environment of all time, Wagner had a season that would have made Albert Pujols turn in his bat, hitting .354/.415/.542. It was, for a shortstop, or for *any* player, a towering season. "So uniformly good was Wagner," said McGraw, "that it is almost impossible to determine whether his highest point of superiority was his fielding, in his batting, or in his baserunning. He was a topnotcher in all."

"The enormous, heavy-bodied German" was bowlegged but agile and shockingly fast, with long arms and giants hands that compensated for the tiny gloves of the time. "He didn't seem to field balls the way we did," remembered his teammate, third baseman Tommy Leach. "He just ate the ball up with his big hands, like a scoop shovel, and when he threw it to first base you'd see pebbles and dirt and everything else flying over there along with the ball."

Pittsburgh had a strong pitching staff (though the team was coming to the end of its age, with one great year left in it after 1908) and decent offensive support for Wagner, including Leach, player-manager Fred Clarke, and leadoff great Roy Thomas, who was purchased from the Phillies in June (Table 4-6). But the Pirates also suffered from uncertainty in the outfield and at first base, where Clarke tried four players without success. In a tight race, giving up the one position on the field designed for pure offense was damaging, even with Wagner taking up some of the slack.

The season started uneventfully. The Cubs, defending their two straight pennants, jumped out to an early lead while the Giants strug-

Table 4-6 Who Would Win, Part III: The Translated 1908 Pirates and 2001 Diamondbacks

| 1908 Pirates | | Avg | OBP | Slg | HR | R | RBI | SB |
|---|---|---|---|---|---|---|---|---|
| Roy Thomas | CF | .264 | .364 | .459 | 18 | 68 | 39 | 4 |
| Tommy Leach | 3B | .266 | .340 | .511 | 29 | 125 | 70 | 18 |
| Fred Clarke | LF | .277 | .368 | .491 | 25 | 113 | 87 | 19 |
| Honus Wagner | SS | .366 | .434 | .745 | 51 | 146 | 176 | 56 |
| Ed Abbaticchio | 2B | .265 | .358 | .423 | 18 | 59 | 93 | 19 |
| Alan Storke | 1B | .261 | .303 | .399 | 6 | 26 | 18 | 1 |
| Chief Wilson | RF | .240 | .280 | .371 | 15 | 63 | 66 | 5 |
| George Gibson | C | .228 | .267 | .388 | 20 | 52 | 69 | 0 |
| | | W | L | IP | H | BB | K | ERA |
| Vic Willis | RHP | 15 | 12 | 240 | 238 | 66 | 126 | 4.31 |

| Diamondbacks | | Avg | OBP | Slg | HR | R | RBI | SB |
|---|---|---|---|---|---|---|---|---|
| Tony Womack | SS | .255 | .295 | .327 | 3 | 64 | 29 | 35 |
| Jay Bell | 2B | .239 | .344 | .384 | 12 | 55 | 43 | 0 |
| Luis Gonzalez | LF | .317 | .423 | .666 | 54 | 119 | 132 | 1 |
| Matt Williams | 3B | .268 | .310 | .449 | 17 | 54 | 60 | 1 |
| Mark Grace | 1B | .290 | .381 | .448 | 14 | 61 | 72 | 1 |
| Reggie Sanders | RF | .257 | .331 | .530 | 31 | 79 | 84 | 17 |
| Steve Finley | CF | .266 | .330 | .414 | 13 | 61 | 68 | 11 |
| Damian Miller | C | .263 | .332 | .409 | 11 | 42 | 43 | 0 |
| | | W | L | IP | H | BB | K | ERA |
| Randy Johnson | LHP | 27 | 4 | 284.2 | 190 | 65 | 383 | 1.93 |

gled out of the gate, getting used to what was essentially a new team. Early June found the Giants in fifth place, trailing the Cubs, Reds, Pirates, and Phillies, and struggling to stay above .500. As late as June 12, McGraw's team was idling at 23-23. The Pirates had also started slowly. Wagner had spent the winter talking seriously about retiring to become a chicken farmer. It wasn't money—money was never a priority for Wagner—but emotional fatigue and perhaps a desire to avoid spring training. The season was a week old before he was enticed to return. The Pirates went 3-3 in his absence and weren't much better on his return, finishing the month of May with a record of 18-16. In fifth place, they trailed the Cubs by four games.

On June 2, the Cubs' veteran left fielder, Jimmy Sheckard, got into a postgame scuffle with rookie Heinie Zimmerman, a reserve infielder on the club. One of the game's great human beings, Zimmerman was eventually banned for trying to fix ballgames (as a member of the Giants). In his postbaseball career, Zimmerman became involved with the mobster Dutch Schultz, who once blinded a rival by smearing a piece of gauze infected with gonorrhea into his eyes. Zimmerman anticipated Schultz by hurling a bottle of ammonia at Sheckard. The bottle shattered around the bridge of Sheckard's nose, sending ammonia streaming into his eyes. Seeing this, manager Chance and his players ganged up on Zimmerman and "gave him such a beating it was necessary to cart him to the hospital for repairs." Likewise rushed to the hospital, Sheckard had his vision saved, but he was lost for several weeks and slumped when he returned. Though inconsistent, Sheckard was expert at getting on base and had been a key member of the Cubs' pennant winners. A career .289/.373/.401 hitter through 1907, with his vision damaged he slumped to .231/.336/.305 in 1908.

With Sheckard gone, the veteran Jimmy Slagle took over in left and played just poorly enough to make 1908 his last season in the majors. The changeover didn't seem to affect the Cubs right away, but for about two weeks, from late June through early July, the team played .500 ball. They played the Pirates six times during this period and split the games with them. On June 27, as the Pirates were in the midst of sweeping a five-game series against the woeful Cardinals, the Cubs and curveball specialist Carl Lundgren were dropping a 4-1 decision to the Reds. One of many characters who might have changed the outcome of the 1908 season had he played just a little better, Lundgren had entered the season with a career ERA of 2.20, strong even in that day. In 1907 his ERA was just 1.17. A year later, no doubt suffering from an undiagnosed arm injury, he shot up to 4.22. It was a lively-ball ERA in a dead-ball year, and his career was soon over.

The June 27 loss put the Pirates and the Cubs into a tie for the league lead, with the Giants, finally hot (going 13-3 since falling to .500 on June 12), just two games behind. As the Cubs and Pirates battered each other at the beginning of July, the Giants completed a four-game sweep of the Phillies to climb within a game and a half of first.

This situation persisted into August. Chicago and Pittsburgh jockeyed for the top spot while New York stayed close. It was the Cubs who blinked first. They opened August with a 14-0 loss to the Doves, and something seemed to break; over the next two weeks, they lost 10 of 14 games, including two of three to the Giants. On August 18 they found themselves in third place, 5.5 games out of first. The Giants were second, two games behind the Pirates. The Phillies, who would play the role of spoiler to the hilt, had taken three of four contests from the Cubs in their moment of weakness and now stood just a half-game behind Chicago.

The Cubs rebounded through the rest of August, winning 12 of 13, including nine straight—all of them tight pitching duels. They swept a crucial three-game series from the Giants, 5-1, 3-2, and 2-1. Days before, the Giants had gone to Pittsburgh and swept a four-game series from the Pirates. As September 1 dawned, the Giants and Cubs were tied for first place, with the Pirates a half-game behind.

With the pennant on the line, McGraw asked Mathewson to carry the load. "Big Six" and Hooks Wiltse were the only solid starters on the staff. Now Matty would be asked to pitch every two or three days as McGraw tried to work around the weak spots in the rotation. Mathewson had done similar things before; in the 1905 World Series he had thrown three shutouts in just six days.

Mathewson was capable of such feats of endurance because he was one of the most efficient pitchers of all time. With pinpoint control, he issued few walks and rarely hit a batter. Quite similar in results to Bret Saberhagen, Mathewson walked just 42 batters in 390.2 innings in 1908. "He could throw a ball into a tin cup at pitching range," a contemporary observed. "You could catch him sittin' in a chair," Roger Bresnahan said. "If you held up your glove he'd hit it and likely wouldn't be an inch off plumb center." In the 1905 series, he walked just one batter in 27 innings. For his career, he walked just 1.59 batters per nine innings pitched and led the National League in that category seven times. He also understood that the dead ball encouraged a pitch-to-contact approach; with little reason to fear the home run and confident enough in his control to know that additional baserunners were unlikely, he could let the batters put the ball in play. It would take a great many hits in a row to create a run. "Big Six" was such a bewildering pitcher that he led the NL in strikeouts five times anyway.

A largely home-run-free game meant that Mathewson could hoard his stuff until he really needed it. McGraw once was angry with Mathewson for jeopardizing a lead in a close game by easing up. "Don't worry," Mathewson told him, and struck out the side.

Relying on Mathewson worked. Beginning on September 1, the Giants won 18 of 19 games, including 11 in a row from the 8th through the 18th. The cost was high. From September 1 until the end of the season, Mathewson threw 110.1 innings, and while he was often as dominant as he had been all year, as September turned to October, the wear started to show (Table 4-7).

On September 18, the Giants were in first place and the Cubs in second, 4.5 games out with 16 games left to play. It was around this time, with the gap looking insurmountable, that Tinker told Chance it was time to throw in the towel. "Well, Cap, I guess it's all off," he said. "Let's break training and make a good night of it."

Chance thought it over for a moment. "No," he said at last. "We were good winners last year. Let's show them we are good losers and play the string out. We may win yet."

The Giants could have put the pennant away at that moment, but they faltered. Injuries began to set in and became so numerous that Mathewson remembered McGraw's daily greeting to his players when he came to the park: "How are the cripples? Any more to add to the list of identified dead to-

Table 4-7 Christy Mathewson's Fall

|  | G | GS | IP | H | R | BB | K |
|---|---|---|---|---|---|---|---|
| Sept 1 | 1 | 1 | 8 | 4 | 0 | 1 | 7 |
| Sept 3 | 1 | 0 | 1 | 0 | 0 | 0 | 2 |
| Sept 5 | 1 | 1 | 9 | 6 | 1 | 0 | 5 |
| Sept 8 | 1 | 1 | 11 | 4 | 0 | 1 | 7 |
| Sept 12 | 1 | 1 | 9 | 10 | 3 | 1 | 5 |
| Sept 15 | 1 | 0 | 1.2 | 0 | 0 | 1 | 3 |
| Sept 18 | 1 | 1 | 9 | 5 | 0 | 0 | 3 |
| Sept 21 | 1 | 1 | 9 | 3 | 2 | 0 | 3 |
| Sept 23 | 1 | 1 | 9 | 5 | 1 | 0 | 9 |
| Sept 24 | 1 | 0 | 2.2 | 1 | 0 | 0 | 3 |
| Sept 26 | 1 | 1 | 9 | 6 | 2 | 0 | 4 |
| Sept 29 | 1 | 1 | 9 | 8 | 2 | 1 | 8 |
| Oct 1 | 1 | 1 | 9 | 10 | 3 | 0 | 5 |
| Oct 3 | 1 | 1 | 7 | 8 | 3 | 0 | 1 |
| Oct 8 | 1 | 1 | 7 | 7 | 4 | 1 | 7 |
| TOTAL | 15 | 12 | 110.1 | 77 | 21 | 6 | 72 |

Run average: 1.71
Bases on balls per nine innings pitched: 0.49
Strikeouts per nine innings pitched: 5.9

day?" No player went on the disabled list—there was none in 1908. Instead they went on playing, compromised. One key exception was Larry Doyle, the 21-year-old, second-year second baseman. The team's number two hitter was batting .309 on September 8, when he was badly spiked in a game against the Dodgers. He was on crutches for the rest of the season.

All three contenders were now playing their best baseball of the season. The tightness of the race magnified the importance of any mistake that might be made, be it a player error, an errant call by an umpire, or the inconsistent interpretation or application of the rules.

For many years it was common for fans to exit the ballpark via the field. Because of the general lack of bleachers in the early parks, overflow crowds were sometimes seated *on* the field. Further, the people of 1908 were as eager and harried as those today: When the game ended, the vast majority of attendees leaped out of their seats and headed for the nearest exit. Because of this, players made sure to get off the field the moment the winning run scored, lest they be mugged, trampled, or forced to interact with some random inebriated spectator. "The fans were part of the game in those days," Pirates third baseman

Tommy Leach remembered. "They'd pour right out onto the field and argue with the players and the umpires. It was sort of hard to keep the game going sometimes."

Fred Snodgrass recalled, "In those days, as soon as a game ended at the Polo Ground the ushers would open the gates from the stands to the field, and the people would all pour out and rush at you. Of course, all they wanted to do was touch you, or congratulate you, or maybe cuss you out a bit. But, because of that, as soon as a game was over we bench warmers all made it a practice to sprint from the bench to the clubhouse as fast as we could."

On September 4, the Cubs played the Pirates at Pittsburgh. Pirates ace Vic Willis opposed Three Finger Brown. Unsurprisingly, the game was a scoreless tie through eight and a half innings. In the bottom of the ninth, the Pirates loaded the bases with two outs, bringing rookie outfielder Owen "Chief" Wilson to the plate. He lined a single to center field, knocking home the winning run. The fans poured onto the field. The runner on first, a 29-year-old rookie first baseman named Warren Darst Gill, who had been in the majors all of nine days, knew exactly what to do: Instead of running to second, he turned and got the heck off the field.

That should have been that, but Johnny Evers had been thinking. All those nights alone in his room with his candy and his rule book had crystallized something in his mind, the difference between a custom and a law. Specifically, he was thinking about Rule 59:

One run shall be scored every time a baserunner, after having legally touched the first three bases, shall legally touch the home base before three men are put out; provided, however, if he reaches home on or during a play in which the third man be forced out or be put out before reaching first base, a run shall not count. A force-out can be made only when [a] baserunner legally loses the right to the base he occupies, and is thereby obliged to advance as the result of a fair hit ball not caught on the fly.

Evers figured that even if it was traditional for ballplayers to flee at the earliest opportunity, a run could not score on the third out of an inning. He called to center fielder Circus Solly Hofman, who relayed the ball back to the infield. Evers received it and stepped on the bag, forcing Gill out. He got the attention of umpire Hank O'Day, who was also leaving the field, and told him what had happened.

O'Day, a serious, solitary man who had been umpiring in the Na-

tional League since 1888, refused to call Gill out for the simple reason
that he had not seen the play. The Cubs protested to league president
Harvey Pulliam, but since O'Day had seen the winning run score but
could honestly assert that he had no idea what had happened with
Gill, Evers's assertion could be dismissed as hearsay. Significantly,
Pulliam did not take the opportunity to clarify Rule 59. Evers had
seemingly lost his case, but now O'Day, too, was thinking.

"That night O'Day came to look me up," Evers said later. "He told
me that my play was legal and that under the circumstances, a runner
coming down from first and not touching second on the final base hit
was out."

On Tuesday, September 22, the Giants and Cubs met at the Polo
Grounds for a doubleheader. The Giants held first place by two games
over the Cubs and three over the Pirates. That day, Three Finger
Brown and Orvie Overall pitched the Cubs to a sweep, tying up the
race, while the Pirates beat the Dodgers to climb within a game and a
half.

On Wednesday, Jack Pfiester, a side-arming lefty known as "Jack
the Giant Killer," and Mathewson were the starters. Pfiester was pitching with a strained ligament in his arm, but the results belied his
handicap. The game was scoreless into the visitors' fifth, when Joe
Tinker came to the plate. Tinker is remembered as a light hitter, but
his translated stats (career rates of .254/.304/.424, isolated power of
.170) show that he had a good deal of pop. He was also a personal
nemesis of Christy Mathewson. "For a few years we had no trouble
with Tinker," Bresnahan recalled. "We'd even pass fellows to get at
him. Finally he started hitting Matty, and we couldn't get him out. I'll
always believe Joe used to be scared of being hit. When he discovered
that Matty didn't hit one guy a season, on average, he simply took a
toehold on him." With one out in the inning and no one on, Tinker
sliced a sinking line drive to right field. Donlin tried to make a shoe-
string catch and failed, missing the ball altogether. Tinker circled the
bases for a home run.

Donlin made up for his misplay in the sixth, when he singled home
the tying run. The score remained tied into the bottom of the ninth. Cy
Seymour opened the frame by grounding out, Evers to Chance. Art
Devlin singled, then was forced by Moose McCormick for the second
out. Normally, shortstop Al Bridwell would have come to the plate, but
a last-minute scratch had forced McGraw to alter his lineup. When
first baseman Fred Tenney had come to the ballpark with a stiff back,
he was forced to miss his first and only game of the year. This meant a

start for the teenager, Fred Merkle. Merkle singled to right, chasing McCormick to third. "The single ... might have been a double or triple," Merkle remembered, "but Jack Hayden [the Cubs' right fielder] made a wonderful stab and knocked down the drive. At that, I could have gone to second easily, but with one run needed to win and a man on third, I played it safe."

Bridwell came to the plate. Swinging on the first pitch, he lined a single over second base, just past Evers and into center field. McCormick trotted home with the winning run. The crowd surged onto the field. The Giants headed for their clubhouse celebrating a big win.

Many years later, Bridwell looked back at that game-winning hit and all that came after it: "There's one thing that happened in baseball I would change if I could do it all over again. I wish I'd never gotten that hit that set off the whole Merkle incident. I wish I'd struck out instead. ... It would have been better all around." Merkle, fleeing ahead of the crowd, had never touched second base. Evers was calling for the ball.

There are many versions of what happened next. The fans never realized what was happening, but some of the Cubs and Giants did. Just as he did in Pittsburgh, Hofman threw the ball back to the infield. He missed Evers, and the ball landed near third base. Giants pitcher Iron Man Joe McGinnity, who was coaching third that day, guessed Evers's intentions and picked up the ball. Tinker and Evers grappled with him but were unable to prevent him from flinging the ball into the stands. A seldom-used Cubs pitcher named Floyd Myron Kroh spotted the fan who picked it up. After a moment of futile negotiation, Kroh struck the fan and retrieved the ball—or, possibly, *a* ball, not *the* ball.

"Why was an unannounced Chicago player on the field?" McGraw complained later, conveniently forgetting that McGinnity had handled the ball before Kroh. "His mere touching of the ball rendered it dead."

Mathewson, grasping the situation, gathered up Merkle and began walking him back toward second base, but it was too late. Kroh threw the ball to Tinker, who threw it to Evers, who stepped on second base. The base umpire, Bill Emslie, refused to make a call. Emslie had been knocked down by Bridwell's liner, and said he hadn't seen whether Merkle had touched the bag or not. He deferred to his partner, Hank O'Day. And O'Day ... O'Day might have said something. Or maybe he didn't. He waited until he was well away from the ballpark, both teams, and the crowd before he let the world know his call. At ten o'clock that night, he called Merkle out. McCormick hadn't scored. The game went into the books as a 1-1 tie.

McGraw later argued that had Merkle truly been forced out, O'Day should have had the field cleared and ordered that the game continue into extra innings. O'Day had an answer for that: It was too dark to continue play at that point. The Giants appealed to President Pulliam, a high-strung, emotional man with whom McGraw had already had many bitter conflicts. The Cubs appealed, too, saying the Giants had forfeited the game when McGinnity handled the ball. "There is no set of fair-minded men in the country who would decide the game against us," McGraw said that night. As it turned out, he was wrong. Pulliam upheld his umpire, as he had after the Gill incident. The decision was appealed upward, to the National League board of directors. After extensive deliberations lasting into October, it was ultimately decided that the game would have to be replayed.

"If this game goes to Chicago, by any trick or argument," Mathewson raged, "you can take it from me that if we lose the pennant thereby, I'll never play pro ball again!" Later, he cooled. "I don't believe Merkle touched second base," he said (knowing he had not). "It could happen to anyone. There's no sense eating our hearts out. We'll just have to beat them again."

In the 10 games they had left, the Cubs went 8-2. The Giants had 16 contests remaining, half of them against the Phillies. The Phillies had recently called up rookie Harry Coveleski from Lancaster, where he had won 22 games. On September 29 at New York, he shut the Giants out 7-0. The Phillies gave him one day of rest and on October 1 sent him out at Philadelphia, where he beat the Giants again, this time 6-2. Figuring they shouldn't mess with a good thing, the Phillies gave Coveleski another day off and then pitched him against the Giants for the third time in six days and the second time in the same series. He outdueled Mathewson 3-2. The 22-year-old had single-handedly put a huge dent in New York's pennant hopes. "Most people think it was Merkle lost the 1908 pennant for the Giants. Well they're wrong," Coveleski's younger brother Stan told Lawrence Ritter. "It was Harry Coveleski."

The Giants "were a sore lot when they left the field," wrote the *Philadelphia Inquirer* after the final Coveleski loss, "and [third baseman Art] Devlin was perhaps one of the worst ones with a grouch. As he was about to go in the clubhouse a small boy hurled a remark at him. This aroused his ire and he kicked the youngster." When Coveleski slumped in 1909, the Giants spread it around the league that they had unnerved him by discovering his secret bologna fetish.

McGraw was not happy. "No manager in a tight race has the right to play favorites. It was a lousy trick, pitching that young lefthander out of turn in his efforts to beat us out of a pennant." (Never mind that McGraw himself pitched Mathewson 15 times between September 1 and the end of the season.) In all, the Giants went 10-6 after the tie. Meanwhile, the Pirates were finishing a 28-9 September. On October 3, the penultimate day of their season, Pittsburgh, having won eight straight games, claimed first place by half a game. The Cubs were second, half a game out, and the Giants third, a game and a half back.

On October 4, in a must-win game at Chicago, the Cubs took on the Pirates. Three-Finger Brown defeated Vic Willis 5-2, putting the Cubs up by half a game with, they fervently hoped, no games left to play. Simultaneously, the idle Giants were 1.5 games out with three games to play against the Boston Doves. To stay alive, McGraw's team would have to sweep the series. This would tie up the race and trigger a replay of the Merkle game. The Giants and Red Ames held the Doves to one run in the first game; Hooks Wiltse limited them to one run in the second. On the morning of October 7, the standings remained in an indeterminate state (Table 4-8).

Table 4-8 Cubs/Giants/Pirates W/L/GB: October 6, 1908

|  | W | L | GB |
| --- | --- | --- | --- |
| Chicago Cubs | 98 | 55 | - |
| New York Giants | 97 | 55 | 0.5 |
| Pittsburgh Pirates | 98 | 56 | 0.5 |

If Ames, starting on one day's rest, lost to the Doves, but the Giants then beat the Cubs in the replay of the September 23 game, a three-way tie would result, triggering a round-robin playoff. If the Giants lost to the Doves and then lost the replay to the Cubs, the Cubs would win the pennant. If the Giants could defeat the Doves in the final game, the Pirates would be eliminated, while the winner of the replay would go to the World Series. In the event, Ames was hardly troubled by the Doves; Dan McGann, the elderly first baseman whom McGraw had dumped in favor of Tenney, tripled in two runs in the first, but Ames cruised after that, while the offense battered Boston pitching for 13 hits and seven runs.

The Pirates were eliminated. The race was down to the Cubs and Giants, with Merkle caught in between. The appellation "Bonehead" spread through the country with almost viral rapidity. *Sporting Life* lambasted him for "inexcusable stupidity." Even the National League board, in affirming Pulliam's decision, berated the young man:

The game should have been won for the New York Club had it not been for the reckless, careless inexcusable blunder of one of its players, Merkle. ... While [Rule 59] may not have been complied with in many other games; while other clubs may not have taken advantage of its provisions in the past under similar conditions, yet it did not deprive the Chicago Club of the right to do so if they so desired. ... Merkle should have had only one thing on his mind, viz.: to reach second base in safety. ... We can therefore come to no other conclusion than that the New York Club lost a well-earned victory as the result of a stupid play by one of its members.

In waiting for the resolution of the race, desperately hoping that the Giants would win enough games to take him off the hook, Merkle had lost 15 pounds.

The Giants and Cubs had been offered a choice between a five-game and a one-game playoff. With the weaker pitching staff, Mc-Graw opted for one game, betting all on Christy Mathewson's right arm, which he had allowed Matty to rest for a long four days. The October 8 replay, then, would repeat the pitching matchup of September 23, with "Giant Killer" Pfiester opposing Matty. The days of rest hadn't helped; Mathewson was all in for the season. His last two starts were shaky; he was wearing down. On October 3, the New York *American* noted, "No one can stand such constant use and Matty has worked more than his share." "I'm not fit to pitch today," Mathewson told his wife, Jane, on the morning of the October 8 replay. "I'm dog tired." He recalled years later, "When I pitched that extra play-off game against the Cubs, my arm was so sore and stiff I needed an hour's warm-up. I could barely lift it."

The scene at the Polo Grounds was one of barely restrained riot. The New York City police, having only begun exerting a presence at the ballpark on September 18, were inexperienced with crowd control. Fans without tickets had rushed past legitimate ticket-holders and filled the ballpark, including the dirt around the edge of the outfield. The police closed the gates to the park, locking out thousands more who desperately wanted in. There were severe injuries and at least one death as fans jockeyed for spots on any raised object that would grant a view of the park, and there was fighting in the park as well. One group of would-be gate crashers set fire to the left field fence.

In the top of the first, Mathewson struck out the first two Cubs he faced, then induced Evers to ground out. Pfiester struggled in the bottom of the frame. He hit Fred Tenney and walked Buck Herzog to open the inning. Although he struck out Bresnahan, Johnny Kling dropped the third strike. The runners broke, Kling throwing out Herzog. With two down, Turkey Mike Donlin doubled, scoring Tenney.

Pfiester walked Cy Seymour, putting runners on first and second, and Frank Chance called to the bullpen for Three Finger Brown. The Cubs' ace retired Art Devlin to end the inning.

Mathewson's fatigue started to show in the third, though it was Cy Seymour who put him in a bad spot. Tinker led off the frame. Legend has it that Mathewson, knowing how much trouble he had with the Cubs' shortstop, cautioned center fielder Seymour to play deep. Mathewson denied this; some accounts have McGraw instructing Seymour instead. The warning, if it was given, was ignored. Tinker hit the ball over Seymour's head and made it all the way to third. Kling drove him in with a single. Brown bunted Kling to second, and Jimmy Sheckard, playing again but not healed, flied out.

There were two outs. Mathewson needed only to retire Evers to strand Kling on second. Instead, tiring rapidly, he walked Evers. Frank "Wildfire" Schulte doubled, driving Kling home, and Chance followed with another double. When the inning was finally over, the Giants trailed 4-1, an almost impossible deficit to overcome in that season of pitcher dominance with a pitcher as good as Brown on the mound.

The Giants tried. Devlin and McCormick opened the bottom of the seventh with consecutive singles, and Bridwell walked, loading the bases and bringing Mathewson to the plate. Over his pitcher's objections, McGraw pinch-hit with Larry Doyle, who hadn't played for a month. Brown popped him up, Kling catching the ball behind the plate. Tenney hit a sacrifice fly, bringing Devlin home and narrowing the score to 4-2, but Buck Herzog grounded out to Tinker to end the rally.

The score remained 4-2 going to the bottom of the ninth. The crowd was increasingly restive. The game had to be delayed while police quelled a brawl in the stands. As Brown warmed up to pitch to Devlin, McCormick, and Bridwell, Chance came out to the mound and told him to get it over quickly, "and then run for your life." Brown wasted no time—four pitches later, the game was over.

The Polo Grounds crowd surged onto the field, the Cubs fleeing ahead of them. Tinker, Sheckard, and reserve outfielder Del Howard were hit. Pfiester was slashed on the shoulder with a knife. Someone punched Chance in the neck, crushing cartilage. He wouldn't be able to speak for awhile, but he was going to the World Series.

◆

"It is criminal to say that Merkle is stupid and to blame the loss of the pennant on him," McGraw said after. "In the first place, he is one of the smartest and best players on this ball club and, in not touching second base, he merely did as he had seen veteran players do ever since he has been in the league. In the second place, he didn't cost us the pennant. We lost a dozen games we should have won this year—yes, two dozen!—and any one of them could have saved the pennant for us. Besides, we were robbed of it and you can't say Merkle did that!" When Merkle protested that the loss was all his fault, McGraw said, "I could use a carload like you. Forget this season and come around next spring." He gave Merkle a raise. In the future, this notably autocratic manager would make it a point to consult Merkle on strategy. Perhaps regretting the way he rode Mathewson at the end of the season, he made pitcher Otis Crandall one of the game's first regular relievers starting in 1909.

National League president Pulliam suffered a nervous breakdown in February 1909, perhaps partly due to the widespread vilification he received after the Merkle decision. On July 25, 1909, he put a gun to his temple and pulled the trigger. He lingered a few hours in terrible pain before dying. John McGraw's typically sensitive reaction: "I didn't think a bullet to the head could hurt him."

His would be the only suicide as the result of the affair, though a popular rumor had Merkle taking his own life on October 8. Merkle went on to play more than 1,600 games in the majors as a regular first baseman for the Giants and Cubs. He never completely escaped the events of September 23. Years later, managing in the minors, one of his players called him "Bonehead." He walked out of the park and never returned.

"The fact of the matter is what I did was common practice in those days," Merkle said years later. "The same thing probably had been done half a dozen times during the season, but nobody was ever called on it. The umpires decided to be technical just when I did it." Roger Bresnahan had a more concise take on events. Nearly 40 years later, he insisted the Giants had been robbed: "Johnny Evers hasn't completed the force-out on Merkle yet."

## Paper Giants

CLAY DAVENPORT

In 1908 the Giants scored 652 runs to the Cubs' 624 and allowed 456 runs to the Cubs' 461. When you score more runs than another team and allow fewer, you expect to have the better record. But after a controversial playoff game, it was the Giants who went home and the Cubs who went on to win the World Series.

A favored trick of the baseball statistician is to use the relationship between runs scored and runs allowed to estimate what a team's record should be. The best-known version of this stat belongs to Bill James, who found that the results of the formula runs scored, squared, divided by the total of runs scored and runs allowed, each also squared, correlated with actual winning percentage. The squaring of all the pieces reminded James of the squares of the sides of right triangles, and so he named the relationship the "Pythagorean theorem." It looked like this:

$$\frac{RS^2}{(RS^2 + RA^2)}$$

The Pythagorean theorem is a very good estimator. James soon found, though, that you could get a slightly better fit by using an exponent of 1.81 instead of 2, which kind of ruins the tie to Pythagoras, and for a few years a hot topic in sabermetrics was discovering exactly which exponent worked best. I think I can safely claim to be the first person to figure out that the best value for the exponent depends on how many runs there are in a typical game; high-scoring environments require larger exponents. (This connection was backed up, oddly, by people trying to use a similar formula for basketball, which required an exponent of 14.) The formula I developed for the exponent was an ugly logarithmic function, but it did do a slightly better job than just saying "2" or "1.81." Humble to a fault, I called it Pythagenport.

Soon other researchers, David Smyth and someone with the online handle "Patriot," came up with a simpler formula for determining the exponent. Their way worked just as well as my log function (and sometimes even better, since it worked over a wider range of runs per game). The exponent is simply total runs per game, raised to the .287 power. Continuing the trend in naming, they called the formula Pythagenpat. To the best of my knowledge, it remains the king of the record estimators.

If we apply Pythagenpat to the 1908 Giants' 652 runs and 456 allowed in 157 games (they had some ties, a feature soon erased from major league baseball by rule changes), we find that they played in a run environment of 7.06 runs per game. Taking the 7.06 to the .287 power, we get 1.752. Using the exponent 1.752 in the runs-scored and runs-allowed formula gives them a winning percentage of .652, which rounds off to a 100-54 record.

Because the Cubs played in a lower run environment (624 and 461 in 158 games, or 6.87 runs per game), their Pythagenpat exponent is even lower, 1.738. This exponent produces a .629 winning percentage, or a 97-57 record. They should have lost the pennant by three games.

But they didn't lose; they finished at 99-55, two games better than predicted, while the Giants finished at 98-56, two games worse than expected. There is no simple explanation for why the Cubs and the Giants, or any other team, for that matter, over- or underperformed. Most attempts to find systematic discrepancies between the Pythagorean record (in whatever flavor) and actual won-lost records have failed. The Pythagorean record is fundamentally an estimate, a correlation between values and individual events. And because the estimate is not perfect, it misses, on average, by about three games in either direction. This means the Pythagorean records of the two 1908 combatants came closer to the mark than average, even though the calculations predicted the wrong order of finish.

How often the Pythagorean theorem misses is a simple thing to track, either by theory or by observation. In theory, we can easily model the distribution of errors and see how often a team that should win by three games actually does (Table 4-9).

Table 4-9 was created using a normal distribution and a standard deviation of 4.0. A team with a three-game Pythagorean advantage, like the 1908 Giants, is expected to win only about two out of three times. You have to have an eight-game advantage to get a 90 percent chance of winning, 10 games to get to 95 percent, and 14 to get to 99 percent.

By looking at every team in history from the same league-season, we can also evaluate how teams have done. All the teams with a Pythagorean difference of less than 0.5 games are assumed to have the same record, teams from 0.5 to 1.5 count as having

Table 4-9 Theoretical Chances of a Team's Winning, According to the Pythagorean Theorem

| Pythagorean Difference | Better Team Wins | Worse Team Wins | Ties |
|---|---|---|---|
| 0 | .465 | .465 | .070 |
| 1 | .534 | .397 | .069 |
| 2 | .604 | .330 | .066 |
| 3 | .671 | .268 | .061 |
| 4 | .731 | .213 | .055 |
| 5 | .787 | .166 | .047 |
| 6 | .834 | .125 | .040 |
| 7 | .875 | .092 | .032 |
| 8 | .907 | .066 | .026 |
| 9 | .934 | .046 | .020 |
| 10 | .953 | .032 | .015 |
| 11 | .968 | .022 | .011 |
| 12 | .979 | .014 | .007 |
| 13 | .986 | .009 | .005 |
| 14 | .992 | .005 | .003 |
| 15 | .995 | .003 | .002 |

Table 4-10 Theoretical Chances of a Team's Winning, Compared with Actual Performance

| Pythagorean Difference | Better Team Wins in Theory | Better Team Wins in Reality |
|---|---|---|
| 0 | .465 | .487 |
| 1 | .534 | .545 |
| 2 | .604 | .599 |
| 3 | .671 | .700 |
| 4 | .731 | .703 |
| 5 | .787 | .773 |
| 6 | .834 | .816 |
| 7 | .875 | .867 |
| 8 | .907 | .898 |
| 9 | .934 | .939 |
| 10 | .953 | .953 |
| 11 | .968 | .964 |
| 12 | .979 | .987 |
| 13 | .986 | .987 |
| 14 | .992 | .997 |
| 15 | .995 | 1.000 |

a difference of 1, and so on. The reality is very similar to our model (Table 4-10).

Historically, only three teams with at least a 14-game Pythagorean advantage have failed to beat the other team. In a reversal of the 1908 standings, the Cubs of 1936 should have beaten the Giants by three games for the pennant. Not only did the Cubs fail—the Giants won by five—but they also tied for second place with the Cardinals, whose projected record was 16 games worse than theirs. In 1967, the defending World Champion Orioles should have had an 88-73 record and been in the thick of the pennant race. Instead, they underperformed by a staggering 12 games, allowing the Washington Senators, who should have only won 70, to tie them at 76-85, making up an 18-game difference. Finally, the 2002 Red Sox should have finished 100-62 and won the American League East. They only made it to 93-69, while the Twins (projected 86-75, 14 games behind the Sox) rallied to 94-68. The Twins won the Central; the Red Sox failed even to capture the wild card and watched the playoffs from the sidelines.

Not counting the strike years of 1981 and 1994, the years 1901 through 2006 saw 306 league and divisional races. The team with the best Pythagorean record won the division 236 times, which means some other team flew the flag in 70 races. In 59 of those 70 cases, the second-best Pythagorean team claimed the title. Ten times, the third-best won. The only time that a division's fourth-best team, as measured by the Pythagorean record, ended up on top was in 1987's American League West, the most evenly matched division in the history of the majors. All seven teams had real winning percentages between .463 and .524—a spread of 10 games from top to bottom—and their Pythagorean records were even tighter, ranging from .475 to .515, a difference of just 6.5 games.

It was anybody's race, and while the Minnesota Twins ranked fourth on the merits of runs scored and runs allowed, they were only 4.5 games behind the Pythagorean-leading Royals. Overcoming that paper deficit, the Twins became only the second team ever (the Royals did it in the same division three years earlier) to make the playoffs while giving up more runs than they scored. Riding a scheduling quirk that gave the West home-field advantage in the Division Series and the AL home-field advantage in the World Series, they beat the Tigers and then the Cardinals by winning every home game and losing every road game in the postseason.

In terms of a sheer margin of difference overcome, rather than the number of teams, the Twins were far more unremarkable. Twenty of the 70 "wrong" teams that won the title overcame deficits larger than the 4.5 games of the Twins, but until almost the end of the 20th century, the limit appeared to be eight games. The record deficit overcome by any team stood at 7.5 games for more than ninety years. Nap Lajoie was a great player, but we can wonder about his management skills. Although he led his Cleveland teams to the best Pythagorean record in the AL three times—in 1904 (when Bill Armour was still the manager), in 1906, and again in 1908—he never won the pennant. The 1906 team should have beaten the "Hitless Wonder" White Sox by almost eight games, but instead lost by five. Other teams approached this record; the 1922 Yankees overcame what should have been a seven-win advantage for the Browns, and the 1959 Dodgers overtook the Braves by the same amount. But until the late 1990s, no team had overcome more than an eight-game deficit.

In 1997, the Giants became the third team to win a pennant with a sub-.500 Pythagorean record. They outplayed their 80-82 Pythagorean record by 10 games, finishing at 90-72, while the Dodgers underplayed their projected 91-71 into an 88-74 record. What should have been an 11-game walkaway for the Dodgers was instead a two-game Giant victory. Since then, the 2003 Cubs (over the Astros) and the 2004 Yankees (over the Red Sox) have also overcome margins of eight or more games in their Pythagorean records to win their divisions. The playoffs were brutal for all three teams. The Giants were swept away by the Marlins in the first round, and the Cubs endured the Bartman meltdown (leading the series 3-2 and the game 3-0, they allowed eight runs in the eighth inning to lose Game 6, then blew a 5-3 lead in Game 7). Not to be outdone, the Yankees blew a 3-0 series lead (and a 4-3 lead in the ninth inning of the fourth game) to lose the pennant to the same Red Sox they had just beaten for the division title.

The 1997 Giants may now hold the record for the biggest margin overcome to win a title, but their swing of 13 games—from their expected 11-game loss to their actual two-game win—is only the fourth-largest. Top honors go to the 1931 Athletics, who should have lost to the Babe Ruth/Lou Gehrig Yankees by three games. Instead they won going away, never leading by less than 10 games after July 22 and finally winning by 13.5—a 16.5-game difference from the expected. The 1961 Reds made up 14 games on that year's Giants, almost balancing what should have been a six-game loss with their real eight-game win. In 2006, the A's and Rangers combined to turn what looked like a half-game Ranger advantage into a 13-game triumph for Oakland.

From the opposite perspective, three teams that led their league in Pythagorean wins went on to finish in fourth place. As already mentioned, Cleveland led the league in Pythagorean percentage in 1904, but wound up losing to Boston, New York, and Chicago, at 7.5 games off the pace. The 1965 Reds finished eight games behind the Dodgers; although the Reds led the league in Pythagorean wins, the Dodgers, Giants, and Pirates were all within two games of them. And the 1969 Dodgers couldn't hold off the Braves, Giants, and Reds, underperforming by six games while the other three overachieved.

Table 4-11 lists the seventy times since 1901 that the real winner and the Pythagorean winner were different. For each team, the secret of its unexpected success or failure lies in the minutiae of its individual season. And although such disparate transcendentalists as Ralph Waldo Emerson and Casey Stengel denied the power of luck, we know that occasionally, one or two bad bounces can change the outcome of a pennant race. More often, though, these outcomes have a palpable cause, a marshaling or squandering of resources. In any of its manifestations, the Pythagorean theorem can't tell us why; it can only point out that such things are taking place.

Table 4-11 When the Predicted (Pythagorean) Winner and Actual Winner Were Different: The Complete List

|  |  | Actual Winner | | | Pythagorean Winner | | |
|---|---|---|---|---|---|---|---|
|  |  | Team | Actual | Pythagorean | Team | Actual | Pythagorean |
| 1904 | AL | Boston | 95-59 | 94-60 | Cleveland | 86-65 | 94-57 |
| 1905 | AL | Philadelphia | 92-56 | 90-58 | Chicago | 92-60 | 96-56 |
| 1906 | AL | Chicago | 93-58 | 89-62 | Cleveland | 89-64 | 98-55 |
| 1908 | NL | Chicago | 99-55 | 97-57 | New York | 98-56 | 101-54 |
| 1908 | AL | Detroit | 90-63 | 88-65 | Cleveland | 90-64 | 91-63 |
| 1909 | AL | Detroit | 98-54 | 96-56 | Philadelphia | 95-58 | 101-52 |
| 1909 | NL | Pittsburgh | 111-42 | 105-48 | Chicago | 104-49 | 107-46 |
| 1915 | AL | Boston | 101-50 | 94-56 | Chicago | 93-61 | 100-54 |
| 1915 | FL | Chicago | 86-66 | 87-65 | St. Louis | 87-67 | 89-65 |

Table 4-11 (continued)

| | | Actual Winner | | | Pythagorean Winner | | |
|---|---|---|---|---|---|---|---|
| | | Team | Actual | Pythagorean | Team | Actual | Pythagorean |
| 1916 | AL | Boston | 91-63 | 86-68 | Chicago | 89-65 | 89-65 |
| 1920 | NL | Brooklyn | 93-61 | 92-62 | New York | 86-68 | 93-61 |
| 1922 | AL | New York | 94-60 | 92-63 | St. Louis | 93-61 | 99-56 |
| 1926 | AL | New York | 91-63 | 90-65 | Cleveland | 88-66 | 90-64 |
| 1928 | AL | New York | 101-53 | 96-58 | Philadelphia | 98-55 | 97-56 |
| 1930 | AL | Philadelphia | 102-52 | 95-59 | Washington | 94-60 | 96-58 |
| 1931 | AL | Philadelphia | 107-45 | 99-54 | New York | 94-59 | 102-51 |
| 1934 | NL | St. Louis | 95-58 | 91-62 | New York | 93-60 | 95-58 |
| 1936 | NL | New York | 92-62 | 90-65 | Chicago | 87-67 | 93-61 |
| 1947 | NL | Brooklyn | 94-60 | 88-66 | St. Louis | 89-65 | 92-62 |
| 1949 | AL | New York | 97-57 | 96-58 | Boston | 96-58 | 98-56 |
| 1950 | NL | Philadelphia | 91-63 | 88-67 | Brooklyn | 89-65 | 89-65 |
| 1951 | NL | New York | 98-59 | 93-64 | Brooklyn | 97-60 | 96-61 |
| 1956 | NL | Brooklyn | 93-61 | 90-64 | Milwaukee | 92-62 | 92-62 |
| 1959 | NL | Los Angeles | 88-68 | 82-74 | Milwaukee | 86-70 | 89-67 |
| 1959 | AL | Chicago | 94-60 | 86-68 | Cleveland | 89-65 | 87-67 |
| 1960 | AL | New York | 97-57 | 89-65 | Chicago | 87-67 | 90-64 |
| 1961 | NL | Cincinnati | 93-61 | 83-71 | San Francisco | 85-69 | 89-65 |
| 1963 | NL | Los Angeles | 99-63 | 92-70 | St. Louis | 93-69 | 94-68 |
| 1964 | NL | St. Louis | 93-69 | 88-74 | Cincinnati | 92-70 | 92-70 |
| 1964 | AL | New York | 99-63 | 98-64 | Chicago | 98-64 | 98-64 |
| 1965 | NL | Los Angeles | 97-65 | 92-70 | Cincinnati | 89-73 | 93-69 |
| 1969 | NLW | Atlanta | 93-69 | 88-74 | Los Angeles | 85-77 | 91-71 |
| 1969 | NLE | New York | 100-62 | 92-70 | Chicago | 92-70 | 93-69 |
| 1970 | NLE | Pittsburgh | 89-73 | 88-74 | Chicago | 84-78 | 94-68 |
| 1971 | NLW | San Francisco | 90-72 | 88-74 | Los Angeles | 89-73 | 90-72 |
| 1972 | ALE | Detroit | 86-70 | 84-72 | Baltimore | 80-74 | 89-65 |
| 1973 | NLE | New York | 82-79 | 83-78 | St. Louis | 81-81 | 86-77 |
| 1974 | ALE | Baltimore | 91-71 | 86-76 | New York | 89-73 | 86-76 |
| 1975 | ALE | Boston | 95-65 | 89-71 | Baltimore | 90-69 | 94-65 |
| 1980 | NLW | Houston | 93-70 | 87-76 | Los Angeles | 92-71 | 90-73 |
| 1980 | ALE | New York | 103-59 | 97-65 | Baltimore | 100-62 | 98-64 |
| 1982 | NLW | Atlanta | 89-73 | 85-77 | Los Angeles | 88-74 | 90-72 |
| 1982 | NLE | St. Louis | 92-70 | 90-72 | Montreal | 86-76 | 90-72 |
| 1983 | NLW | Los Angeles | 91-71 | 86-76 | Atlanta | 88-74 | 92-70 |
| 1984 | ALW | Kansas City | 84-78 | 80-82 | California | 81-81 | 81-81 |
| 1984 | NLW | San Diego | 92-70 | 87-75 | Houston | 80-82 | 88-74 |
| 1987 | ALW | Minnesota | 85-77 | 79-83 | Kansas City | 83-79 | 84-79 |
| 1987 | ALE | Detroit | 98-64 | 96-66 | Toronto | 96-66 | 100-62 |
| 1987 | NLE | St. Louis | 95-67 | 92-70 | New York | 92-70 | 94-69 |
| 1989 | NLE | Chicago | 93-69 | 90-72 | New York | 87-75 | 91-71 |
| 1990 | ALE | Boston | 88-74 | 85-77 | Toronto | 86-76 | 92-70 |

continues

Table 4-11  (continued)

| | | Actual Winner | | | Pythagorean Winner | | |
|---|---|---|---|---|---|---|---|
| | | Team | Actual | Pythagorean | Team | Actual | Pythagorean |
| 1990 | NLE | Pittsburgh | 95-67 | 93-69 | New York | 91-71 | 98-64 |
| 1991 | NLW | Atlanta | 94-68 | 92-70 | Los Angeles | 93-69 | 93-69 |
| 1992 | ALE | Toronto | 96-66 | 91-71 | Milwaukee | 92-70 | 96-66 |
| 1992 | ALW | Oakland | 96-66 | 89-73 | Minnesota | 90-72 | 91-71 |
| 1995 | ALW | Seattle | 79-66 | 81-64 | California | 78-67 | 82-63 |
| 1997 | NLW | San Francisco | 90-72 | 80-82 | Los Angeles | 88-74 | 91-71 |
| 1997 | ALE | Baltimore | 98-64 | 94-68 | New York | 96-66 | 101-61 |
| 1999 | NLC | Houston | 97-65 | 96-66 | Cincinnati | 96-67 | 97-67 |
| 2001 | NLC | Houston | 93-69 | 89-74 | St. Louis | 93-69 | 94-68 |
| 2002 | ALW | Oakland | 103-59 | 96-66 | Anaheim | 99-63 | 102-60 |
| 2002 | NLW | Arizona | 98-64 | 96-66 | San Francisco | 95-66 | 98-63 |
| 2002 | ALE | New York | 103-58 | 100-62 | Boston | 93-69 | 100-62 |
| 2003 | NLC | Chicago | 88-74 | 85-77 | Houston | 87-75 | 94-68 |
| 2003 | ALC | Minnesota | 90-72 | 85-77 | Chicago | 86-76 | 89-73 |
| 2003 | ALW | Oakland | 96-66 | 94-68 | Seattle | 93-69 | 97-65 |
| 2004 | ALE | New York | 101-61 | 89-73 | Boston | 98-64 | 98-64 |
| 2005 | ALC | Chicago | 99-63 | 91-71 | Cleveland | 93-69 | 96-66 |
| 2006 | ALC | Minnesota | 96-66 | 93-69 | Detroit | 95-67 | 96-66 |
| 2006 | ALW | Oakland | 93-69 | 85-77 | Texas | 80-82 | 86-76 |

# 1964 National League

*There Is No Expedient to Which a Man Should Not Resort
to Avoid the Real Labor of Thinking*

CLIFFORD J. CORCORAN

On the eve of the 1964 baseball season, 232 baseball writers were asked to choose the team they thought would represent the National League in that year's World Series. Seventy percent of them named either the defending World Champion Los Angeles Dodgers or the San Francisco Giants, who had beaten the Dodgers in a three-game playoff to claim the pennant in 1962. That year, the Yankees had defeated the Giants in a dramatic, seven-game World Series in 1962 to claim the final championship of the Mickey Mantle–era dynasty, but the Dodgers had swept New York the following year, holding the Bronx Bombers to just four runs in four games.

On opening day 1964, the Dodgers appeared to pick up right where they had left off. Sandy Koufax, who had capped off the 1963 series with a complete game victory at Dodger Stadium, shut out the Cardinals in Los Angeles. It quickly became apparent, however, that the Dodgers would not repeat easily. The Dodgers' offense managed just 10 runs over the next six games as Los Angeles lost the remainder of its season-opening home stand. The team then traveled to St. Louis. In the first inning of the trip's opening game, Koufax felt something pop in his left arm on a 1-2 pitch to Cardinals first baseman Bill White. Though he hadn't told his coaches, Koufax, who had thrown more

## 1964 National League Central Prospectus

| Team | Actual Standings | | | | | Date Elim | Pythag | |
|------|---|---|---|---|---|---|---|---|
| | W | L | Pct | GB | DIF | | W | L |
| Cardinals | 93 | 69 | .574 | – | 18 | – | 88 | 74 |
| Reds | 92 | 70 | .568 | 1.0 | 17 | Oct 4 | 92 | 70 |
| Phillies | 92 | 70 | .568 | 3.0 | 140 | Oct 4 | 88 | 74 |
| Giants | 90 | 72 | .556 | 3.0 | 53 | Oct 3 | 89 | 73 |
| Braves | 88 | 74 | .543 | 5.0 | 12 | Sept 23 | 87 | 75 |
| Dodgers | 80 | 82 | .494 | 13.0 | 13 | Sept 17 | 86 | 76 |
| Pirates | 80 | 82 | .494 | 13.0 | 13 | Sept 22 | 84 | 78 |
| Cubs | 76 | 86 | .469 | 17.0 | 13 | Sept 13 | 73 | 89 |
| Colt .45s | 66 | 96 | .407 | 27.0 | 15 | Sept 7 | 64 | 98 |
| Mets | 53 | 109 | .327 | 40.0 | 12 | Aug 29 | 59 | 109 |

| League Averages | | | | BP Stats Leaders | | |
|---|---|---|---|---|---|---|
| AVG | OBP | SLG | BABIP | Offense, BRAA | | Indiv WARP |
| .254 | .311 | .374 | .286 | Braves | 156 | Willie Mays 13.9 |
| ERA | K9 | BB9 | H9 | Pitching, PRAA | | Ron Santo 13.6 |
| 3.54 | 5.7 | 2.7 | 8.7 | Reds | 94 | Dick Allen 13.0 |

than 300 innings for the first time in his career the previous season, had been experiencing pain in his pitching arm since spring training. Four batters after White reached base on what turned out to be a wild strike three, the reigning Cy Young Award winner had given up three runs and was done for the day. It was the Dodgers' seventh consecutive loss after their opening-day victory.

Nursing his aching wing, Koufax missed his next three turns and pitched with uncharacteristic inconsistency in May. Meanwhile, the already-suspect Dodgers' offense was in free fall. Only the third-year expansion Mets and Colt .45s failed to outscore the Dodgers in 1964. By the time Koufax salvaged his season with a mechanical correction in June (immediately resulting in his third no-hitter in as many years on June 4), the defending world champs had dropped to eighth place, ahead of only those two expansion teams.

With the Dodgers out of the picture, the Giants emerged as the lone favorites. Hamstrung by poor performances from their bullpen and the back of their rotation as well as clubhouse problems stemming from the organization's difficulty in accepting its growing Latin contingent, San Francisco had stumbled to a distant third-place finish in 1963, but the pitching (if not the mood) rebounded in 1964. As the Dodgers plummeted, their Golden State rivals thrived on an up-and-coming staff. Juan Marichal continued to mature, while then-reliever

Gaylord Perry, who was promoted to the rotation in August, was coming of age. The club also enjoyed a brilliant final season from former White Sox ace-turned-short-reliever Billy Pierce and solid contributions from twentysomethings Bobby Bolin and rookie Ron Herbel in the rotation and Jim Duffalo out of the pen. Between that young staff and an offense led by future Hall of Famers Willie Mays, Willie McCovey, and Orlando Cepeda and slugging rookie third baseman Jim Ray Hart, the Giants looked not only like the team to beat in 1964, but also like an emerging dynasty.

San Francisco took up residence at the top of the National League standings in early 1964, but they weren't alone. For all but one day of the first four months of the season, the top two spots in the National League standings were held by the Giants, historically one of the National League's most successful franchises, and a team that was in nearly every way their opposite, the long-suffering Philadelphia Phillies.

◆

While the Washington Senators, St. Louis Browns, and, to a lesser degree, Boston Braves and Philadelphia Athletics have gone down in history as baseball's failed franchises, salvaged only after relocation, the worst baseball club of the pre-expansion era received no such rescue and, perhaps as a result, no such notoriety. In the modern history of the National League, from 1901 to 1963, no team had won more often than the Giants had, and no team had lost more often, or had lost more games, than the Phillies had (Table 5-1). The same held true in the 62 years since the creation of the American League. Though the

Table 5-1 Phillies Phutility: The National League, 1901–1963

| Team | W | L | Pct | 100-W | 100-L | Pen | WS |
|------|------|------|------|------|------|------|------|
| Giants | 5,310 | 4,266 | .555 | 5 | 0 | 16 | 5 |
| Cubs | 5,009 | 4,594 | .522 | 5 | 1 | 10 | 2 |
| Pirates | 4,993 | 4,596 | .521 | 2 | 4 | 7 | 3 |
| Dodgers | 4,941 | 4,642 | .516 | 4 | 2 | 11 | 3 |
| Cardinals | 4,935 | 4,651 | .515 | 4 | 2 | 9 | 6 |
| Reds | 4,674 | 4,927 | .487 | 1 | 0 | 4 | 2 |
| Braves | 4,403 | 5,162 | .460 | 0 | 11 | 4 | 2 |
| Phillies | 4,167 | 5,390 | .436 | 0 | 14 | 2 | 0 |
| Astros | 130 | 192 | .404 | 0 | 0 | 0 | 0 |
| Mets | 91 | 231 | .283 | 0 | 2 | 0 | 0 |

Table 5-2 Champagne Division: Winningest Teams, 1901–1963

| Team | W | L | Pct |
|---|---|---|---|
| Yankees | 5,415 | 3,879 | .583 |
| Giants | 5,310 | 4,266 | .555 |
| Indians | 5,066 | 4,527 | .528 |
| Cubs | 5,009 | 4,594 | .522 |
| Pirates | 4,993 | 4,596 | .521 |

Table 5-3 Schlitz Division: Losingest Teams, 1901–1963

| Team | W | L | Pct |
|---|---|---|---|
| Phillies | 4,167 | 5,390 | .436 |
| Browns/Orioles | 4,212 | 5,364 | .440 |
| Braves | 4,403 | 5,162 | .460 |
| Senators/Twins | 4,476 | 5,089 | .468 |
| A's | 4,464 | 5,080 | .468 |

Yankees surpassed the Giants as the winningest team in baseball over that stretch (the Giants were second), the Phillies held on to their title as the worst, losing 26 more games than the since-relocated Browns (Tables 5-2 and 5-3).

Indeed, the Browns-cum-Orioles and Phillies were the only two pre-expansion franchises that entered the 1964 season having never won a world championship. In their first 67 years of existence, the Phillies managed just one first-place finish (the former Browns won their second AL pennant and first world championship in the franchise's 65th season). That lone Phillies flag came in 1915. Just three years after losing the 1915 World Series to the Red Sox, the Phillies were back in the second division, where they remained for the next 30 years. The stretch, from 1918 to 1948, was the worst period of losing that any major league franchise has ever endured, expansion included. Just once in this span did the Phils finish above .500, the feat coming in 1932, when they were 78-76. Their fourth-place finish that year was also their best of the era. In five seasons along the way, the club failed to win 30 percent of its games, including a combined .279 winning percentage in the almost identically dismal seasons of 1941 and 1942. The Phillies' five-year streak of 100-loss seasons from 1938 to 1942 remains a major league record.

In 1947, Branch Rickey put Jackie Robinson in a Dodgers uniform, setting in motion the long process of integrating baseball. While a few teams quickly emulated Rickey and added African American players to their rosters, for Phillies owner Bob Carpenter, general manager Herb Pennock, and manager Ben Chapman, the breaking of the color line was a nonevent. They had no intention of integrating and in fact seemed eager to see Robinson fail, Pennock telling Rickey not to "bring that nigger here." When the Phillies did play the Dodgers, the abuse Robinson received at the hands of Chapman and his players seemed excessively vituperative even by the standards of a sport that had long made room for ethnic and religious taunting on the field. "We will treat Robinson the same as we do Hank Greenberg of the Pirates, Clint Hartung of the Giants, Joe Garagiola of the Cardinals [and] Connie Ryan of the Braves," Chapman protested, at once establishing his bona fides both as a baseball traditionalist and a bigot's bigot.

Robinson immediately led Brooklyn to the pennant, the first of six in Robinson's 10 years with the team. The club's continued success arose partly from the African American talent that most other clubs had refused to avail themselves of. Yet, a strange thing happened. Though Carpenter had declined to have his team join baseball's new enlightenment, the Phillies still became competitive. After an 81-73 third-place finish in 1949 (the club's first winning season since 1932 and best record since 1917), the Phillies came out of nowhere to win the 1950 pennant with a young team led by 23-year-old future Hall of Famers Robin Roberts and Richie Ashburn and 25-year-old slugger Del Ennis. Philadelphia's "Whiz Kids" were swept by the Yankees in the World Series that year, but in a cruel irony, the fact that the Phillies went to their second-ever World Series with an all-white team (and the youngest pennant-winning team ever) further emboldened the franchise against integration.

Having dethroned the Dodgers of Robinson, Don Newcombe, and Roy Campanella (the last a Philadelphia native who had attempted to sign with the Phillies) with the all-white Whiz Kids, Carpenter foresaw the dawning of a new era for his club. Instead, his obstinacy became the team's undoing; the 1950 pennant was the last league title won by an unintegrated National League team. The Phillies didn't begin to scout black players until Carpenter hired Roy Hamey as general manager in 1954. Hamey's efforts were largely for show. In 1957, the Phillies became the last NL team to integrate, but John Kennedy, the African American who made the roster with the expectation of becoming the starting shortstop, was bounced to the bench just before opening day by the acquisition of Chico Fernandez from the Dodgers. Kennedy made just two trips to the plate in five games before being sent back to the minors. Left fielder Chuck Harmon, who made 87 plate appearances for the Phils later that season, and pitcher Hank Mason, who threw 10.2 relief innings split between the 1958 and 1960 seasons, were the only other African Americans to play for the Phillies before 1961. Meanwhile, the Phillies attempted to keep up appearances by employing a steady stream of dark-skinned Latino and Caribbean players, including Fernandez, who was Cuban. But only

Fernandez and first baseman Pancho Herrera ever played regularly, and none of the other minority players brought in between 1957 and 1959 lasted more than three seasons with the club. During this time, the team headed south in the standings.

John Quinn, the architect of three pennant-winning Braves teams in Boston and Milwaukee, replaced Hamey before the 1959 season and finally began introducing minority players who stuck. In 1960, under 34-year-old rookie manager Gene Mauch, the Phillies added Cubans Tony Taylor and Tony Gonzalez and Mexican Ruben Amaro, who would be the starting second baseman, center fielder, and platoon shortstop, respectively, for the 1964 team. In 1961, Quinn traded for his former Braves charge, outfielder Wes Covington, who quickly became the first African American regular in franchise history. The trade also made Covington and Clarence "Choo Choo" Coleman the first African American teammates in the history of major league baseball in Philadelphia.

Still, the Phillies lacked a black superstar. In the seven seasons from 1954 to 1960, four different National League teams won five world championships with African American stars such as Willie Mays, Jackie Robinson, and Hank Aaron, as well as black Puerto Rican Roberto Clemente, leading the way. The Cubs got a pair of MVP seasons out of Ernie Banks during that stretch, and in 1961, Frank Robinson led the Reds to their first NL pennant since 1940. Meanwhile, the Phillies hit rock bottom yet again, losing 107 games in 1961 low-lighted by a record 23-game losing streak on their way to their fourth consecutive last-place finish.

Unexpectedly, the Phillies began to revive. In 1962, they crossed the .500 threshold for the first time in nine years. A closer look reveals that they did so by victimizing that year's two expansion teams, compiling a 31-5 record against the Mets and Colt .45s. Still, their .400 record against the rest of the league represented a solid improvement. In 1963, the Phils made another huge leap, recovering from a 31-40 start to improve by six wins over their overall 1962 record while distributing their victories more evenly about the league. Driving the team's improvement were Gonzalez's development as an on-base threat in center, the strong platoon production of the lefty-hitting Covington in left, the emergence of slugging right fielder Johnny Callison, and the arrivals of lefty starting pitcher Chris Short and fireman Jack Baldschun.

In the winter following the 1963 season, Quinn augmented that core by trading for Detroit Tigers ace Jim Bunning, who, at 31, had posted his first below-average full-season ERA. The bait for Bunning was Don Demeter, who had a career year at third base for the 1962 Phils and then moved to the outfield in 1963 to make room for an awful year by a clearly finished Don Hoak. To replace Demeter and Hoak, Quinn handed the third-base job to a rookie outfielder who had made a handful of starts in Demeter's place in left the preceding September. The rookie's name was Richard Anthony "Dick" Allen.

In 1964, Allen emerged as the black superstar the team had sorely needed in the 13 years since the Whiz Kids won the pennant. He hit .318/.382/.557 and ran away with the Rookie of the Year award. Just 22, Allen was not a polished product—having never played third, he unsurprisingly led all major leaguers with 41 errors, led the senior circuit in strikeouts, and was unprepared to be the focal point of media and fan attention. Nevertheless, even with these small flaws, Allen instantly gave the Phillies the kind of top-tier offensive threat they hadn't had since the days of Chuck Klein and wouldn't have again until Mike Schmidt (Tables 5-4 and 5-5). Together, the homegrown rookie Allen and the veteran import Bunning (19-8, 219 Ks, 2.63 ERA, and a Father's Day perfect game) pushed the Phillies into the thick of the 1964 pennant race.

Through August 9, the Phillies and Giants were never more than 2.5 games apart atop the National League standings. Both stumbled in July. The Giants, however, failed to pull out of their slump in August. If the Giants' pitching had dashed their pennant hopes in 1963, it was their hitting that sabotaged their run in 1964. Robbing Peter to pay Paul, general manager Chub Feeney had dealt right fielder Felipe Alou to the Braves over the winter to help patch the pitching staff. Willie

Table 5-4 1964 NL VORP Leaders

| Name | Team | Pos | Avg | OBP | Slg | VORP |
|---|---|---|---|---|---|---|
| Willie Mays | Giants | CF | .296 | .383 | .607 | 74.2 |
| Dick Allen | Phillies | 3B | .318 | .382 | .557 | 69.4 |
| Ron Santo | Cubs | 3B | .312 | .399 | .564 | 66.9 |
| Frank Robinson | Reds | RF | .306 | .396 | .548 | 58.1 |
| Orlando Cepeda | Giants | 1B | .304 | .361 | .539 | 48.8 |
| Billy Williams | Cubs | LF | .310 | .368 | .527 | 46.2 |
| Roberto Clemente | Pirates | RF | .336 | .388 | .482 | 45.5 |
| Hank Aaron | Braves | RF | .316 | .382 | .499 | 44.9 |
| Denis Menke | Braves | SS | .281 | .370 | .483 | 43.0 |
| Joe Torre | Braves | C | .317 | .362 | .487 | 43.0 |

Table 5-5  The Best Rookie Seasons of All Time

| Player | Year | Team | WARP |
|---|---|---|---|
| Dick Allen | 1964 | Phillies | 13.0 |
| Christy Mathewson | 1901 | Giants | 12.0 |
| Russ Ford | 1910 | Yankees | 11.8 |
| Johnny Pesky | 1942 | Red Sox | 11.1 |
| Pete Alexander | 1911 | Phillies | 11.0 |
| Mark Eichhorn | 1986 | Blue Jays | 11.0 |
| Albert Pujols | 2001 | Cardinals | 11.0 |
| Curt Davis | 1934 | Phillies | 10.9 |
| Mark Fidrych | 1976 | Tigers | 10.6 |
| Joe Jackson | 1911 | Indians | 10.6 |
| Harvey Haddix | 1953 | Cardinals | 10.5 |
| Mike Piazza | 1993 | Dodgers | 10.5 |
| Reb Russell | 1913 | White Sox | 10.5 |
| Nomar Garciaparra | 1997 | Red Sox | 10.3 |
| Ichiro Suzuki | 2001 | Mariners | 10.3 |

McCovey, hampered by a series of injuries to his ankle, knees, groin, and ribs, struggled to deliver the production of a league-average left fielder in 1964 and slumped through the season. Lacking a meaningful contribution from their corner outfielders, the Giants' offense was reduced to the three-man attack of Mays, Cepeda, and Jim Ray Hart. After the hobbled McCovey, the next most productive player was Tom Haller, the lefty half of the team's catching platoon, at .220/.315/.393 through the end of June. Haller's power vanished in July, and the Giants fell out of first place for good on July 16.

With the Giants and Phillies slumping, the Dodgers made some noise in July, propelled by the rejuvenated Koufax. On July 18, Koufax struck out 10 Cubs on his way to a 3-1 complete game victory. The win capped a four-game Dodgers winning streak, put them two games over .500, and pulled them within seven games of first place. That would be their high-water mark. On August 8, Koufax hurled another complete game victory in Milwaukee, but jammed his pitching elbow when diving back to second base to avoid a pickoff in the fifth inning. He dominated in his next two starts, but a diagnosis of traumatic arthritis ended his season. Two years later, the injury forced him into retirement at the age of 30. In 18 starts dating back to his no-hitter against the Phillies on June 4, Koufax had gone 14-1 with a 1.31 ERA, 12 complete games, and six shutouts. Without him, the Dodgers' faint hope of salvaging their season was extinguished.

While San Francisco continued to scuffle, John Quinn made two key improvements to his club. The Phillies were already a well-rounded team. Bunning and Short were a formidable righty-lefty combination at the front of the rotation. Baldschun and veteran Ed Roebuck (purchased from the Senators in April) led the relief corps. Allen and Callison powered the offense, supported by strong platoon contributions from lefty-hitting outfielders Covington and Gonzalez and righty-hitting catcher Gus Triandos (who came over from Detroit in the Bunning deal). On July 22, what looked like a bad break turned into a good one after rookie Danny Cater, who had hit a roughly league-average .296/.325/.388 as the short side of the platoon with Covington in left, fractured his left arm in a collision with Milwaukee first baseman Joe Torre. Quinn promoted another rookie, Alex Johnson, to take Cater's place, and Johnson hit .303/.345/.495 over the remainder of the season.

Shortstops Bobby Wine and Amaro didn't hit much, but helped out with tremendous contributions on defense, while Tony Taylor managed to match the production of a league-average second baseman. That meant that the most glaring hole in the Philadelphia lineup was first base. Through August 6, rookie John Herrnstein and the rest of the Phillies' first basemen hit a combined .234/.285/.345 in a year when the average NL first baseman hit .262/.316/.422. On August 7, the Phillies traded for righty gatekeeper Frank Thomas, a home-run hitter who had fallen into a part-time role with the Mets after hitting 34 round-trippers for their inaugural edition in 1962. Installed as the full-time first sacker in Philadelphia, the veteran Thomas made an immediate impact as the Phillies won his first five games with the team and 13 of his first 16. With Johnson and Thomas in the lineup, the Phillies pulled away from the Giants, opening up a 7.5-game lead by August 20.

Surely they never saw the Cardinals coming. Rivaling the mistreatment of Jackie Robinson by Chapman, Pennock, and the rest of the Phillies, the St. Louis Cardinals threatened to boycott the games against the Dodgers in 1947 and, after league president Ford Frick forced St. Louis to play, Cardinals players Enos Slaughter and Joe Garagiola spiked the rookie first baseman. Based in the then-southernmost major league city, the only one in a former slave state, the Cardinals, along with the Phillies, are notably absent from the list of NL teams that enjoyed the production of black superstars during the 1950s. Indeed, the Cardinals made no effort to integrate until Anheuser-Busch purchased the team at the behest of August A.

"Gussie" Busch Jr. in early 1953. Busch was alarmed to discover that his new team had no black players and equally alarmed when his efforts to purchase stars such as Willie Mays and Ernie Banks from his National League rivals were met with derision.

After settling for token appearances by African Americans Tom Alston and future Phillie Chuck Harmon beginning in 1954 (from 1955 to 1957 the two combined for just 41 plate appearances), the Cardinals didn't begin to integrate in earnest until Busch hired Vaughan P. "Bing" Devine as his general manager in November 1957. One of Devine's first moves was to acquire a young center fielder named Curt Flood from the Reds. Flood became, in 1958, the Cardinals' first African American regular. He was followed the next year by Bill White, whom Devine freed from the first-base and outfield glut in the Giants' system. Still, the Cardinals' efforts to integrate were stymied by Busch's new manager, Solly Hemus, who limited the playing time of Flood and rookie pitcher Bob Gibson starting in 1959. When Johnny Keane replaced Hemus in mid-1961, Flood and Gibson were finally given full-time jobs and revealed themselves to be All-Star talents and more.

With White, Flood, Gibson, and Dominican second baseman Julian Javier, the Cardinals had finally developed a strong core of young minority players who blended well with white veterans Ken Boyer, Dick Groat, and Stan Musial. On August 12, 1963, Musial announced his impending retirement, and the young team rallied around the departing legend. Winning 19 of 20 games with Musial hitting a last-gasp .286/.327/.500, the Cardinals surged to within one game of the eventual world champion Dodgers on September 15 only to collapse in the season's final two weeks. Absent Musial, the Cardinals limped out of the gate in 1963, partly because of the gaping holes in their outfield corners. By June 15, the Cards were 28-31, had lost 17 of their last 23 games, and were languishing in fifth place, 7.5 games behind the Giants. To that point, the St. Louis corner outfielders had hit .236/.290/.373 on the season.

With the team's struggles and the behind-the-scenes maneuvering by Branch Rickey, a special consultant hired two years earlier, to have the general manager fired, Devine knew his days were numbered. He pulled the trigger on a deadline deal that sent rotation stalwart Ernie Broglio, an 18-game winner in 1963, to the Cubs for a talented young outfielder who needed a change of scenery. The youngster's name was Lou Brock. The outfielder had broken into the Cubs' lineup as a 22-year-old center fielder in 1962, but had since moved to right. Heaped with expectations and shackled by limitations—his mind confused and conflicted by the Cubs' rotating coaching staff, his great speed rendered useless by the Cubs' resistance to the stolen base, and his defense hindered by the afternoon sun at Wrigley Field—Brock had seen his production decline in two consecutive seasons. That all changed in St. Louis. Shifted to left field and set loose on the bases, Brock felt at ease in the Cardinals' fraternal clubhouse and quickly turned his worst offensive season into the most productive year in what became a Hall of Fame career. The Cardinals won Brock's first four games with the team, and their new left fielder hit .348/.387/.527 in 103 games for his new club.

Three weeks later, Devine filled right field with rookie Mike Shannon (batting .278 and slugging .434 in the International League), who joined the club during a three-game series in New York. During that same series, Bill White finally got proper medical treatment for a shoulder injury that had limited him to a .259/.307/.392 showing through July 11. The Cardinals won five of their first six games after Shannon joined the team, and after leaving New York, White broke out with five home runs in his next seven games, hitting .345/.399/.553 over the remainder of the season. Meanwhile, veteran Roger Craig, another 1962 Met, ably assumed Broglio's rotation spot. The race was on. By September 1, the Cards had pulled into a virtual third-place tie with the sinking Giants. A week later, they swept the Reds in a doubleheader at Sportsman's Park to share second place with Cincinnati. Devine was gone by then, having resigned in August.

Two days later, on September 9, the Cardinals were in Philadelphia for a Wednesday night game. St. Louis's starter, former Whiz Kid Curt Simmons, failed to make it out of the fourth inning, but the Cardinals kept it close and rallied for two runs against Baldschun in the top of the ninth to force extra innings. St. Louis then won it by dropping a five-spot on Baldschun and Roebuck in the 11th. The victory, the Cardinals' 13th in their last 16 games, put them in second place alone, five games behind the Phillies. The night before, Frank Thomas had broken his thumb diving back to second base in a futile attempt to avoid being doubled up by the Dodgers. The Phillies had scored 5.33 runs per game with Thomas in the lineup. With Thomas's right hand in a cast, they scored just 3.5 runs per game.

On September 21, the Reds came to Connie Mack Stadium in a perfect tie for second with the Cardinals, 6.5 games behind the Phillies. The Reds had spent most of the summer battling the Pirates for third place, but had also steadily improved as the season wore on, increasing their winning percentage with each successive month. Built around the core of the 1961 pennant winners, the Reds were led on offense by outfielders Frank Robinson and Vada Pinson and new first baseman Deron Johnson, and on the mound by starters Jim O'Toole, Joey Jay, Bob Purkey, and Jim Maloney. With one of the league's top defenses and a bullpen built around rookie firemen Sammy Ellis and Billy McCool, and veterans Bill Henry and Ryne Duren (who was purchased from the Phillies in May), the Reds were the stingiest team in the 1964 National League. Allowing just 3.47 runs per game against a league average of 4.01, they edged the Dodgers for the league lead, all the more impressive given the advantage conferred on the Dodgers' staff by their home park.

In the first match of the two-game series, two of the teams' less impressive starters faced off, yet the match-up of Philadelphia's Art Mahaffey and Cincinnati's John Tsitouris remained scoreless going into the sixth. In that inning, Chico Ruiz, who had spent most of the season backing up Steve Boros at third base, followed rookie second baseman Pete Rose's leadoff groundout with a single and moved to third on a single by Pinson, who was subsequently thrown out trying to stretch his hit into a double. With two outs and Frank Robinson at the plate, Ruiz stunned everyone, including his manager, Dick Sisler, by breaking for the plate. Rattled by Ruiz's charge, Mahaffey threw wild high and outside, and Ruiz slid in safely as the pitch sailed to the backstop. That would be the only run of the game as Tsitouris pitched around a leadoff Covington double in the ninth to nail down the shutout. It was a hard-luck loss that dropped the Phillies' lead to 5.5 games and was the second game in three days that they had lost on an opponent's steal of home (the Dodgers' Willie Davis had pulled the trick in the sixteenth inning the preceding Saturday). Still, at the time, the loss seemed like little more than a speed bump on the way to the Phillies' third pennant. World Series tickets went on sale in Philadelphia the following day.

The Reds beat the Phillies that night and the next by a combined score of 13-6 and left Philadelphia having pulled within 3.5 games of first place. The Braves followed the Reds into the City of Brotherly Love, outlasting Jim Bunning in the opener to drop the Phillies' lead to three games while the Cardinals swept a doubleheader from the Pirates to pull within 3.5 games. Suddenly panic set in, particularly in the manager's office of Connie Mack Stadium.

Known as the Little General, Gene Mauch had always been a micromanager. A young, intense man prone to outbursts in the clubhouse, he was operating platoons at four positions in 1964 and finished the season among the top managers in the majors in sacrifice bunt attempts, squeeze bunt attempts, pinch-hitters, pinch-runners, and overall substitutions. As Dick Allen wrote in his autobiography, "The problem with Gene Mauch as a field general in 1964—and it haunted him until his retirement—was that he held the game too tightly in his hand. ... Mauch never let us play the game instinctively." Desperate to halt the Phillies' sudden four-game losing streak, their longest since mid-July (also against Cincinnati and Milwaukee), Mauch called on Chris Short to start on two days' rest in the second game of the Braves series.

In those days of the four-man rotation, three days' rest was customary, but, like many of his early-1960s contemporaries, Mauch didn't really use a set rotation for much of the season. Bunning, the team's big off-season addition and legitimate ace, was the only starter used consistently throughout the season. Short had begun the season in the bullpen, not making his first start until May 10. By early September, however, Mauch had settled on a rotation of Bunning, Short, Dennis Bennett, and Mahaffey. The second game in the Braves series was Mahaffey's scheduled turn after his 1-0 loss to the Reds. As Mahaffey ended up starting the next day, anyway, it's unclear why Mauch felt the need to start Short on inadequate rest. Only twice before in that season had Mauch called on one of his starters on two days' rest. The first time, he had brought Short back after a disastrous outing that lasted just 1.1 innings. Having barely exerted himself in his previous start, Short had responded with a shutout. The second time, Mauch inexplicably turned to Bunning on two days' rest after a 10-inning complete game win against the Giants the week before the Cincinnati series. Exhausted, Bunning was predictably lit up by the lowly Colts.

On this night, Short pitched well through six innings, but a tenuous 1-0 Phillies lead was erased in the seventh when the Braves got two off Short and then added a third run in the eighth. With two outs in the bottom of the eighth, Dick Allen singled and Johnny Callison homered off reliever Billy Hoeft to tie the game, eventually sending it into extra innings. The Braves retook the lead in the 10th on a two-run Joe Torre home run off Phillies reliever Bobby Locke, but again Allen came through in the bottom of the 10th. With shortstop Cookie Rojas on via a single and the Phillies down to their last out, Allen delivered an inside-the-park home run to tie the game at 5-5. The Philadelphia pen couldn't hold the major league's best offense, however. Before the game, Frank Thomas, sensing his team's desperation, ripped the cast off his hand and begged Mauch to play. Mauch agreed, but Thomas clearly wasn't right at the plate. Worse, in the twelfth inning, the Braves took the lead when Eddie Mathews singled off Thomas's glove. Allen again delivered a two-out hit in the final frame, but after Callison received what was surely an intentional unintentional walk, the abysmal Herrnstein grounded out to extend the Phillies' losing streak to five games. Meanwhile, a Reds doubleheader sweep of the Mets cut the Phils' lead to 1.5 games. After the Braves game, Mauch, perhaps feeling he hadn't done enough, second-guessed his decision to pitch to Torre with first base open in the 10th.

The next afternoon, a ninth-inning Philadelphia lead evaporated on a bases-loaded triple by Rico Carty, extending the losing streak to six games and dropping the Phillies' lead to a half a game over Cincinnati. Afterward, Bunning volunteered to start the series finale on two days' rest in an attempt to keep his club's lead from evaporating completely. Though Bunning had struggled in his previous start on short rest just a week and a half earlier and was coming off a less-than-stellar six-inning loss to these same Braves in the series opener, Mauch, who was probably emboldened by Short's solid showing two nights before, accepted his ace's offer. "Hindsight dictates that we should have been rested and then pitched," Bunning later told David Halberstam. "That's obvious to everyone now, but the emotions of the moment dictated that we try for it, that we go out there and pitch on two days of rest. To say no, to refuse the ball and say that you could not pitch on short rest, was to go against every impulse superior athletes have." Bunning was creamed, of course, allowing seven runs in just three innings as the Phillies lost 14-8, unable to benefit from a three-homer performance by Callison. With the loss, the Phillies had endured their second straight series sweep and fell out of first place for the first time since mid-July. "After that, we were playing as if we were waiting to lose," remembered Callison.

A full game behind the Reds, the Phillies would have to play their final five games on the road against the very barbarians who were storming their gates, the now-first-place Reds and the Cardinals, who were now just a half-game behind the second-place Phillies. It was just as well that they play as visitors; the Philadelphia fans, 2,000 of whom had greeted the team as heroes at Philadelphia International Airport just a week earlier, had turned on the team, booing them off the field in their home finale. Meanwhile, the Phillies' rotation was in disarray as a result of Mauch's use of his two best starters on short rest. Of his four preferred starters, the only ones available to pitch the opener in

St. Louis were Bennett, who had been experiencing internal bleeding that had discolored his pitching shoulder, and Short, who would again be pitching on short rest. Sophomore Ray Culp had developed elbow soreness, which forced an early exit from his last start in mid-August and caused Mauch to write him off. Meanwhile, Mauch had lost his patience with rookie Rick Wise, pulling him after three and four batters in his last two starts. With the Cardinals throwing Bob Gibson, who was coming off eight consecutive complete games, seven of them wins in which he allowed two runs or fewer, Mauch was forced to go with Short yet again on two days' rest.

Before the game, Mauch approached *Philadelphia Inquirer* beat writer Allen Lewis and asked his opinion on the Phillies' losing streak. "Gene," said Lewis, "for 150 games I don't think anyone could have managed better than you did. But every pennant that's blown is blown because the manager screwed up the rotation by pitching guys out of turn. ... If you would have said to yourself, 'all we have to do is play .500 ball with twelve games to go to win the pennant' and planted that thought in the minds of your players, you'd have clinched it. But you insisted on winning every damn game, and that was a serious error in judgment."

"Aw, that's a bunch of bullshit!" replied Mauch, who then stormed off and refused to speak to Lewis for the rest of the year.

Considering that this was his third start in seven days, Short acquitted himself well, allowing just three runs in 5.1 innings, but Gibson allowed just one Phillies tally in eight innings to put his team into second place, a game behind the idle Reds.

The next day, faced with the alternatives of Wise or Culp, or Mahaffey on two days' rest, Mauch took a gamble on Bennett's bruised shoulder. Bennett faced nine batters, getting four outs on a pair of sac bunts and a line-drive double play. With Bennett's early exit and Callison out with a viral infection, the Phillies used 22 players to the Cardinals' 10 on their way to a 4-2 loss, their ninth straight. The game also extended the Cardinals' winning streak to seven games and pulled them into a first-place tie with the Reds, who suffered a tough loss of their own as Bill Mazeroski's two-out ninth-inning single off Billy McCool broke a scoreless tie with the Pirates in Cincinnati. It was September 29 and the first time the Cardinals had been in first place all year. After the game, Cardinals first baseman Bill White said, "Maybe it sounds ridiculous, but I think everyone in our clubhouse feels sorry for the Phillies."

The Phillies were exhausted. They hadn't had an off day since August 31 and were at the end of a stretch in which they had played 31 games in 30 days. They had made nine errors in their previous eight games, and in the series finale in St. Louis they made four more. Mauch again turned to Bunning on two days' rest. Years later the Hall of Famer and U.S. senator remarked, "I don't know if it's humanly possible to pitch effectively on two days' rest more than once." The results were again predictable. Bunning allowed six runs, only one unearned, in 3.1 innings, while Cardinal starter Curt Simmons took a no-hitter into the seventh inning. The Phillies had dropped their 10th straight. Along the way, Mauch, known for his bench jockeying and postgame outbursts, had become eerily quiet. "Mauch was wrapped so tight that we were afraid to open our mouths," Allen recalled. In 10 days the Phillies had turned a 6.5-game lead into a 2.5-game, third-place deficit largely because the Cardinals were 9-10 over that same span.

Another heartbreaking Reds loss at home to the Pirates, this one 1-0 in 16 innings, gave the Cardinals a one-game lead with just three games left at home, all against the Mets, who had already lost 108 games. Amazingly, the Cardinals lost the first two of those final three games, the first when Al Jackson out-dueled Gibson 1-0 and the second by a score of 15-5. In the second, the Cardinals used eight pitchers, none of them for as many as two full innings, and surrendered five home runs. Simultaneously, the Reds salvaged the finale of their series against Pittsburgh and then prepared for the arrival of the Phillies, who had a desperately needed off-day on October 1. That off-day did what Mauch had failed to do, allow Chris Short to start on full rest in the opener of the Cincinnati series. Despite falling behind 3-0, the Phillies, perhaps awakened by a scuffle that ensued after Short plunked Reds shortstop Leo Cardenas in the seventh inning, rallied in the eighth for four runs keyed by a two-run Dick Allen triple to finally snap their skid. Thus, the final day of the season arrived with the Reds and Cardinals tied for first place and the Phillies still alive, one game behind.

Another off-day allowed Bunning to start on regular rest in Cincinnati against Tsitouris while the Cardinals threw Simmons at the Mets and Galen Cisco. It was fitting that the season had come down to Simmons. The former Whiz Kid had been unable to pitch in the 1950 World Series, because he was called to serve his national guard duty when the Korean War began. Nine years later, Simmons suffered an arm injury and was largely ignored by rookie manager Gene Mauch when the pitcher tried to reestablish himself on the Phillies' staff in 1960. Mauch's disinterest led Quinn to release the veteran lefty. Simmons then signed with the Cardinals, posted a 2.66 ERA over the remainder of the 1960 season, and pitched like his old self thereafter. How ironic, then, that Simmons took the hill needing only one more win to make his first World Series with the Cardinals while denying the Phillies their first trip since 1950.

Things didn't quite work out that way. Simmons gave up 1-0 and 2-1 leads in consecutive innings, leaving the game in the top of the fifth, down 3-2. Meanwhile, the Phillies, whose best-case scenario involved a three-way tie should they win and the Cardinals lose, were fulfilling their part of the bargain, knocking Reds starter John Tsitouris out in the third and opening the sixth inning against Joey Jay with four singles and a Dick Allen homer to run the score to 9-0. The Phils added one more run in the seventh, and Bunning pitched his fifth shutout of the season, leaving the fate of the National League pennant in the hands of the lowly New York Mets.

Back in St. Louis, Johnny Keane, knowing a win would guarantee the pennant, brought Bob Gibson on in relief of Simmons with just one day's rest separating Gibson from his hard-luck eight-inning 1-0 loss in the series opener. Inspired by their ace's determination, the Cardinals immediately tied the game in the bottom of the fifth on a leadoff walk by Brock, a Bill White single, and a Ken Boyer RBI double that drove Cisco from the mound. Then, against reliever Bill Wakefield, the Cards took a two-run lead. Gibson allowed the Mets to get within one in the sixth, but the Cards again tallied in the bottom of the inning, building an 8-4 lead that grew to 11-4 in the eighth. A pair of walks drove Gibson from the game in the ninth, but Barney Schultz, the veteran knuckleballer turned relief ace and the one man on the Cardinals older than Simmons, finished the job. With the Cards leading 11-5 and men on first and second, Ed Kranepool popped out to catcher Tim McCarver, and the Cardinals won the 1964 National League pennant.

The Cardinals defeated the Yankees in a stirring seven-game World Series and later won two more pennants on their way to becoming one of the defining teams of the decade. The Phillies finished no higher than fourth in the ensuing nine years, while a physical confrontation between Thomas and Allen in early 1965 that resulted in Thomas's being traded soured the team's mostly white fan base on their young black superstar. It didn't matter that Thomas's racial epithet had started the fight and Thomas had hit Allen with a bat during the scuffle, injuring his shoulder. The episode and the fans' subsequent hostility to Allen also obscured one crucial fact about the team's collapse: Allen did not collapse with it, batting .341/.434/.618 from September 1 on. Nevertheless, Allen was traded in 1969.

For his part, Mauch took the blame for this infamous collapse. In the visitors' clubhouse of Crosley Field after the season's final game, Mauch told the press, "I just wore the pitching out. ... If I knew how it was going to come out, I might have done a couple of things different. When you manage the way I want to manage, you don't miss something by a game or two. All I can say is that I wish I did as well as the players did." When the team charter arrived back in Philadelphia, Mauch stood up and told his players, "I want to be the first one off. You guys didn't lose it. I did."

In Mauch's defense, Chris Short had pitched well on short rest, posting a 3.55 ERA and a 1.26 WHIP (walks plus hits per inning pitched) and striking out eight against just two walks in his two starts on two days' rest. The decision was to go with Bunning on short rest were certainly disastrous, as was the choice of the sore-armed Bennett in the penultimate game of the losing streak, but it wasn't Mauch's fault that Bennett and Culp were hurt, or that Thomas had broken his thumb and Callison came down with a virus. Just as they had in the dozen games immediately after Thomas's injury, the Phillies scored just 3.5 runs per game during their losing streak, a significant decrease from their season average of 4.28 runs per game. Perhaps Mauch's intensity resulted in his team's playing stiff. But the Phillies were a young team that had overachieved before their collapse, partly because of Mauch's ability to wring value out of his roster via platooning and taking chances on playing men such as Allen out of position.

In the end, the Phillie Phlop was less a reflection on Mauch and his team than a statistical correction translated into high drama by a fluke of streaks, slumps, illness and injury, and a distraction from the far more disappointing performances of the Dodgers, Giants, and the Pythagorean champion Reds. Curiously, those final 12 games set the Cardinals' and Phillies' franchises on radically different paths. Though both teams came late to integration, eventually succeeding with harmoniously diverse teams in 1964, the victorious Cardinals would be remembered as much for their diversity as their on-field greatness, while the Phillies, and the City of Philadelphia, continue to fight the stigma of their racial history to this day.

## Brock and Trout: The Greatest Deadline Deals of All Time

CLIFFORD J. CORCORAN

On July 23, 1922, the New York Yankees acquired third baseman "Jumping Joe" Dugan and right fielder Elmer Smith from the Boston Red Sox for $50,000 and a quartet of marginal players that included a young left-handed pitcher named Francis Joseph O'Doul. The Yankees felt the need for Dugan because their current third baseman, future Hall of Famer Frank "Home Run" Baker, was suffering a decline in what proved to be his final season. Baker had yielded more than a third of the team's starts to the execrable Mike McNally. Leading the Yankees by 2.5 games on the eve of the trade, the St. Louis Browns cried foul. The Yankees won the pennant.

A week after the Dugan deal, the New York Giants acquired right-handed starting pitcher "Handsome Hugh" McQuillan from the Boston Braves for $100,000 and two other righty hurlers. McQuillan was needed to replace veteran Fred Toney, who was suffering a decline in his penultimate season and who was one of the two pitchers sent to Boston in the deal, along with minor leaguer Larry Benton. St. Louis Cardinals manager Branch Rickey, whose team then trailed the Giants by 2.5 games, cried foul. The Giants won the pennant.

The Dugan and McQuillan deals weren't the first midseason trades by eventual pennant winners, but in mid-August, prompted by the complaints out of St. Louis, Judge Kenesaw Mountain Landis, in just his second season as baseball's commissioner, established a nonwaiver trading deadline of June 15. Thus, the deadline deal was born.

It's somehow fitting, then, that the Cardinals, with Rickey back in the fold as a special adviser to owner Gussie Busch, pulled off the greatest deadline deal of all time, and that it was pulled off by a man Rickey spent most of the season trying to get fired. Table 5-6 shows the twenty most lopsided midseason deals in major league history.

Not included in the table is the Phillies-Cubs trade of April 21, 1966. The contending Phillies sent Ferguson Jenkins (123.1 WARP), Adolfo Phillips (24.3), and John Herrnstein (–0.1) to the last-place Cubs for Larry Jackson (16.2) and Bob Buhl (0.3). The deal represented a 5.1 WARP win for the Cubs in the short term and a 130.8 win for them in the long term, as the swaps occurred just one week into the 1966 season. Also omitted is the straight-up April 30, 1989, swap of Al Leiter for Jesse Barfield. Although the deal netted the Yankees

Table 5-6  The Twenty Most Lopsided Deadline Deals in Major League History

| Date | Contender | Rebuilder | Contender Gets | Rebuilder Gets | In-Season Winner | WARP Gained | Long-Term Winner | WARP Gained |
|---|---|---|---|---|---|---|---|---|
| Aug. 28, 1983 | Braves | Indians | Len Barker (3.1) | Brett Butler (94.9), Brook Jacoby (42.5), Rick Behenna (−0.3) | Rebuilder | 0.1 | Rebuilder | 134.0 |
| July 29, 1989 | Rangers | White Sox | Harold Baines (45.2), Fred Manrique (1.5) | *Sammy Sosa (103.0)*, Wilson Alvarez (52.5), Scott Fletcher (23.8) | Rebuilder | 1.7 | Rebuilder | 132.6 |
| Aug. 31, 1990 | **Red Sox** | Astros | Larry Andersen* (8.1) | Jeff Bagwell (135.9) | Contender | 0.8 | Rebuilder | 130.8 |
| May 25, 1989 | Expos | Mariners | Mark Langston* (51.9), Mike Campbell (0.1) | *Randy Johnson (143.8)*, Brian Holman (15.4), Gene Harris (5.4) | Rebuilder | 0.6 | Rebuilder | 112.6 |
| July 29, 1996 | **Indians** | Mets | *Jeff Kent (85.5)*, Jose Vizcaino (22.4) | Carlos Baerga (5.2), Alvaro Espinoza (0.7) | Contender | 1.1 | Contender | 102.0 |
| Aug. 12, 1987 | **Tigers** | Braves | Doyle Alexander (12.5) | *John Smoltz (113.9)* | Contender | 5.2 | Rebuilder | 101.4 |
| July 31, 1997 | **Mariners** | Red Sox | Heathcliff Slocumb (7.2) | *Derek Lowe (54.7)*, *Jason Varitek (43.1)* | Contender | −1.5 | Rebuilder | 91.2 |
| June 15, 1964 | **Cardinals** | Cubs | Lou Brock (79.6), Jack Spring (0.3), Paul Toth (mL) | Doug Clemens (3.3), Bobby Shantz (1.0), Ernie Broglio (0.8) | Contender | 2.7 | Contender | 74.8 |
| July 21, 1988 | Yankees | Mariners | Ken Phelps (2.2), Rich Balabon (mL) | Jay Buhner (64.5), Troy Evers (mL) | Rebuilder | 1.9 | Rebuilder | 62.3 |
| July 31, 1993 | Royals | Pirates | Stan Belinda (14.3) | *Jon Lieber (46.2)*, Dan Miceli (22.8) | Contender | 0.8 | Rebuilder | 54.7 |
| Aug. 27, 1992 | **Blue Jays** | Mets | David Cone* (61.8) | *Jeff Kent (102.1)*, Ryan Thompson (12.7) | Contender | 0.8 | Rebuilder | 53.0 |
| Aug. 31, 1987 | Blue Jays | Orioles | Mike Flanagan (13) | *Jose Mesa (61.7)*, Oswaldo Pereza (0.2) | Contender | 1.9 | Rebuilder | 48.9 |

| Date | Team | Trade partner | Players received | Players traded | Status | WARP | Status | WARP |
|---|---|---|---|---|---|---|---|---|
| June 15, 1949 | Reds | Cubs | Peanuts Lowery (10.1), Harry "The Hat" Walker (3.1) | Hank Sauer (46.1), Frankie Baumholtz (14.1) | Contender | 1.3 | Rebuilder | 47.0 |
| Aug. 31, 1996 | **Indians** | Brewers | Kevin Seitzer (2.2) | Jeromy Burnitz (46.5) | Contender | 1.1 | Rebuilder | 44.3 |
| Sept. 8, 1969 | **Braves** | Angels | Hoyt Wilhelm (6.5), Bob Priddy (2.8) | Mickey Rivers (53.4), Clint Compton (–0.1) | Contender | 1.5 | Rebuilder | 44.0 |
| July 18, 1993 | **Braves** | Padres | Fred McGriff (52.1) | Melvin Nieves (7.8), Donnie Elliott (1.2), Vince Moore (mL) | Contender | 4.0 | Contender | 43.1 |
| June 15, 1983 | Cardinals | Mets | Neil Allen (10), Rick Ownbey (0.3) | Keith Hernandez (47.8) | Rebuilder | 3.4 | Rebuilder | 37.5 |
| July 13, 1987 | Yankees | Cubs | Steve Trout (–1.8) | Bob Tewksbury (34.2), Rich Scheid (0.7), Dean Wilkins (–1.4) | Contender | 0.1 | Rebuilder | 35.3 |
| July 28, 1995 | **Yankees** | Blue Jays | David Cone (34.1) | Marty Janzen (1), Jason Jarvis (mL), Mike Gordon (mL) | Contender | 3.7 | Contender | 33.1 |
| Aug. 31, 1981 | **Astros** | Pirates | Phil Garner (25.3) | Johnny Ray (54.2), Randy Niemann (0.9), Kevin Houston (mL) | Contender | 0.3 | Rebuilder | 29.8 |

*Note:* Teams in bold made the playoffs. Numbers in parentheses are the WARP totals for the remainder of a player's career beginning the day of the trade. Players in italics are currently active; WARP totals in italics are subject to change, because of the involvement of active players. Grey rows indicate deals in which the same team won the trade in both the short term and the long. * indicates players who signed with a third team via free agency after the given season. mL indicates a career minor leaguer.

5.7 WARP in the short term in exchange for the 48.4 WARP remaining in Leiter's career, the exchange occurred too early in the season to be properly considered a deadline deal even under the loosest definition. Trades that might soon sneak onto this table are the 1998 deal that sent Randy Johnson to Houston (Mariners 29.2 WARP gain), the 2003 deal that sent Aramis Ramirez to the Cubs (Cubs 27.6), the 2001 deal that sent Jermaine Dye to Oakland (A's 25.7), and the 2000 deal that sent David Justice to the Yankees (Indians 24.8).

Table 5-6 largely confirms that most deadline deals find contenders trading prospects for veterans they hope can guarantee them a playoff appearance in the current season. That's the case with 16 of the trades shown in the table. In the aftermath of 10 of them, the contending team did indeed benefit in the short term, making the playoffs seven times, whereas the team receiving the prospects benefited in the long term. In five other deals, the contenders were flat-out bilked in their desperate attempts to make the postseason, failing each time.

Actually, this assessment is not quite fair. The 1983 Cardinals had no illusions that they had gotten the best of the Mets when they traded Keith Hernandez to New York for Neil Allen and Rick Ownbey. Rather, Cardinals general manager and manager Whitey Herzog was determined to purge what he saw as the cancerous, cocaine-addicted presence of Keith Hernandez from his team. On June 4 of that year in Atlanta, Hernandez laid the final straw on Herzog's back. The first baseman came to the plate with one out in the ninth inning, the Cardinals down 6-4, and the tying runs on base. As Herzog recalled in *You're Missing a Great Game*, "Keith hit a grounder, a possible DP ball. It should have been close, but he jogged halfway to first, got thrown out to end the game, and laughed his ass off all the way back to the bench. And by then, his troubles were so well-known around baseball that nobody but the Mets—a last-place team going nowhere—had any interest in him. I got what I could for Keith and that's that. I never lost any sleep over that trade, and I'd make it again tomorrow." In first place by one game in the NL East on the day of the trade, Herzog's Cardinals went 49-57 without Hernandez and finished fourth, 11 games behind the Phillies. The following year, those last-place Mets who were "going nowhere" won 90 games, six more than Herzog's Cardinals. The two teams then alternated NL East titles from 1985 to 1988, but according to Herzog, "there was no question of keeping Keith Hernandez."

Only four of the 20 trades in the table were won by the contending team in both the short and the long term. The Lou Brock trade is one of those four, and two of the remaining three rank significantly lower than the Brock trade. That leaves only one true challenger to the Brock trade for the title of Greatest Deadline Deal Ever. We could define such a deal as a trade that both propelled a contending team into the playoffs and was a rewarding trade for the contender in the long term. Under this definition, the 1996 swap in which the Cleveland Indians obtained Jeff Kent and Jose Vizcaino from the Mets for Carlos Baerga and Alvaro Espinoza is the only other contender for the best deadline deal.

Several key differences between the Brock and Kent deals argue for the supremacy of the former. To begin with, the 1964 Cardinals were tied for seventh place on the eve of the Brock trade, their 28-30 (.483) record putting them 6.5 games behind the first-place Phillies. With Brock on board, St. Louis went 65-39 (.625) and won both the pennant and the World Series. Of course, the Brock trade wasn't the only reason for that improvement. The late-season surges of Bill White and Bob Gibson, the additional outfield upgrade made by the promotion of Mike Shannon, and the fine job Roger Craig did filling in for the departed Ernie Broglio also factored greatly into the Cardinals' change of direction. What's more, all this would still not have resulted in the pennant had the Phillies not collapsed down the stretch. The 1996 Indians, on the other hand, had a decisive seven-game lead in the AL Central on the eve of the Kent trade. They had played .610 ball to that point and played .625 ball the rest of the way, a slight, but not terribly significant improvement, given that they won their division by 14.5 games and had a seven-game lead over the Yankees for home-field advantage throughout the playoffs.

The respective in-season WARP gains for the Indians (1.1) and Cardinals (2.7) show that Brock had a much greater impact on the Cardinals than Kent had on the Indians. Given Kent's later career, it's shocking to learn that, over the remainder of the 1996 season, the top performer in the Kent trade was Alvaro Espinoza (0.9 WARP to Kent's 0.7 and Vizcaino's 0.6; Baerga was –0.6).

Part of the traded players' performance had to do with how they were used. Brock was installed as the Cardinals' starting left fielder and number two hitter, starting all but one of the Cardinals' remaining 103 games. Kent, likely to make the Hall of Fame as a second baseman despite his reputation for contumelious behavior, wasn't even used as the replacement second baseman for the departed Baerga. Rather, Vizcaino was installed at second base while Kent was used as a utility man, playing first, second, third, and designated hitter, in that order, and appearing in just 39 games for Cleveland. The Indians clearly didn't know what they had, and they proved it by flipping Kent (along with Vizcaino, Julian Tavarez, and Joe Roa) to the Giants for Matt Williams and Trenidad Hubbard that November (a 99.5 WARP loss, and counting, for the Indians).

We won't hold that later trade against the Indians, but there is one remaining explanation for why, above all else, the Brock trade remains the greatest deadline deal of all time: free agency. In 1964, free agency didn't exist. Note that all but three of the trades in the table occurred after the advent of free agency. Of those three, the 1949 deal between the Cubs and Reds is, as mentioned, a poor fit because it didn't involve a contending team (in fact, neither the Reds nor the Cubs won another pennant while any of the four players involved in that trade were still active). Of the remaining two deals, one was the Brock trade. The other is the curious 1969 deal between the Angels and Braves.

That trade is on the list solely because of the involvement of minor league center fielder Mickey Rivers, who had just been drafted by the Braves in the second round of the amateur draft three months before the deal. Rivers had been drafted three times by three teams before the Braves took him in the second round of the June 1969 draft, but he refused to sign each time. It's pure speculation, but it seems entirely possible that the Braves, who held a slim half-game lead over the Dodgers in the newly created NL West on the eve of the June 8 draft, selected Rivers with the explicit intention of dealing him for help down the stretch if necessary, because they knew he was a sought-after player. Indeed, the Braves had fallen to third place, two games behind the Giants (though still a half-game ahead of the Dodgers) on the eve of the trade. They then went 17-5 down the stretch to win the division by three games, with Hoyt Wilhelm posting an 0.73 ERA in eight appearances (seven in Braves wins, five of them one-run games, picking up two wins and four of those newfangled saves) over that span.

The reason the listed trades are so heavily concentrated in the free-agency era is that free agency mitigates the loss of young talent by providing wealthy teams (which contending teams often are) with the opportunity to replace the prospects they've dealt away. For example, after trading Kent to the Giants, the Indians signed Tony Fernandez to man the keystone, then two years later inked Roberto Alomar, who is just one month Kent's senior and turned in MVP-quality performances in two of his three years in Cleveland. Free agency also makes it more likely that less affluent teams will trade young talent, because they know they're likely to lose these players to free agency in time and the teams' only recourse is to attempt to get something in return via trade before that happens.

That is what makes the Brock trade so tremendous. It's not just that the Cardinals obtained the 24-year-old Brock a mere four seasons into a 19-year Hall of Fame career, but also that they did so when they (and the Cubs, for that matter) were guaranteed to control his rights indefinitely. Combine that with the dramatic upgrade Brock represented in left field, the Cardinals' radical shift in fortunes after the trade, and the team's eventual pennant and World Championship (Brock hit .300/.300/.467 in the World Series with a Game 7 homer), and one thing is certain. This trade of a 28-year-old rotation stalwart for a younger outfielder of dubious defensive abilities, who had never hit as much as league average, was the greatest deadline deal ever executed. Unfortunately, it wasn't enough to save Bing Devine's job. Thanks to Rickey's politicking, Devine was forced to tender his resignation just two months after the trade.

### Dick Allen's Aftermath

ALLEN BARRA

The amount of what-if baseball fans play is in direct proportion to how much misery their team has made them endure—obviously, because the fans don't need to ask "What If?" when their team wins. It follows, then, that Philadelphia Phillies fans have done more what-iffing than any other fans in baseball have. Sit in the bleachers today at Citizens Bank Park, and you'll hear more between-innings chat about the Phillies' fabled crashes and burns and how they might have been avoided than you will about the game being played.

The Phillies haven't just lost pennants; they've lost pennants in ugly, unforgettable ways, none of them harder to forget than the 1964 collapse. Over the decades, the bitter memory of that season has melded in the minds of many fans with the flameout of Dick Allen's career in Philadelphia to the point that the two are almost now synonymous. Among hard-core Allen haters, it is gospel that he was the primary reason the Phillies lost in 1964 and never won a pennant in the 1960s. It's possible that no player in the history of the game has been so unjustly vilified.

Richard Anthony "Dick" Allen—he never cared for "Richie," which he never hesitated to tell sportswriters, though some persist in calling him that to this day—was, in the opinion of many, one of the most talented players ever to have played the game. Bill James, one of his harshest critics, called him "probably the most gifted baseball player that I've ever seen." His talent, in fact, transcended baseball. George Will recalled, "I was at Princeton's graduate school 1964–67. During the period, probably in 1966 or 1967, I attended a party where I conversed with Princeton's basketball coach, Butch Van Breda Kolff. I asked him—he was fresh from the delights of coaching Bill Bradley—who was the finest basketball talent he had ever seen. I thought he might say Oscar Robertson. But without a moment of hesitation he said: 'A high school student from Wampum, Pennsylvania—Richie Allen.'"

Allen probably could have made it in any of the three major professional sports, but the record confirms that he chose wisely when he picked baseball. His talent was prodigious. In an era when pitchers dominated, Allen hit 351 home runs. Orlando Cepeda, a contemporary of Allen's ushered into the Hall of Fame in 1999, hit 371—but batted nearly 1,600 more times than Allen. Another contemporary who made the hall was Harmon Killebrew; Allen out-hit him .292 to .256, won three slugging titles to Killebrew's one, and hit more doubles and triples than Killebrew while batting about 1,800 fewer times. During his peak years, 1964 to 1974, Allen batted .299/.386/.554. The average major leaguer in that period batted .249/.315/.368 (Table 5-7).

Unfortunately, Allen was also what William C. Kashatus, author of *September Swoon: Richie Allen, the '64 Phillies, and Racial Integration,*

Table 5-7 Dick Allen Among the Leaders, 1964–1974 (Minimum of 4,000 Plate Appearances)

| Player | Avg | Player | OBA | Player | Slg |
|--------|-----|--------|-----|--------|-----|
| Roberto Clemente | .332 | Willie McCovey | .397 | Hank Aaron | .561 |
| Rod Carew | .323 | Carl Yastrzemski | .397 | Dick Allen | .554 |
| Pete Rose | .312 | Frank Robinson | .390 | Willie Stargell | .541 |
| Matty Alou | .310 | Joe Morgan | .389 | Willie McCovey | .541 |
| Tony Oliva | .309 | Harmon Killebrew | .386 | Frank Robinson | .524 |
| Joe Torre | .303 | Dick Allen | .386 | Willie Mays | .513 |
| Curt Flood | .300 | Roberto Clemente | .381 | Roberto Clemente | .511 |
| Lou Brock | .299 | Pete Rose | .380 | Billy Williams | .510 |
| Dick Allen | .299 | Hank Aaron | .379 | Reggie Jackson | .502 |
| Hank Aaron | .299 | Rod Carew | .377 | Harmon Killebrew | .501 |
| All Batters | .249 | All Batters | .315 | All Batters | .368 |

called "the wrong player in the wrong place at the wrong time." The long, rancorous history of Allen's relationships with an all-white Philadelphia press—most visibly represented by Bill Conlin and Larry Merchant of the *Philadelphia Daily News*, the latter sportswriter regarded by many Phillies players as a "throat-cutter"—was summed up best by Kashatus: "Dick had a very undeserved reputation as a malcontent. For his first seven seasons, he clashed with the Philadelphia press, the toughest in the country, and the fans believed what they read. The fact is that nearly all of Allen's teammates and managers liked him and regarded him as a hugely valuable player."

The incident that most colored Allen's ongoing war with the local press was his fight with teammate Frank Thomas in 1965, a clash sparked by Thomas's racial jibes, an observation that Philadelphia sportswriters, particularly Merchant, vehemently denied at the time. Thomas, an aging and unproductive player, was subsequently traded. No matter how well Allen played after that, he was subjected to lethal booing, not just in Philadelphia, and much of it tinged with racial slurs. Allen is now the first to acknowledge that he did not handle the jeers from fans and press well; he moped and sulked and got distracted, missing practices and even showing up late for games. "I'm not saying I was an angel," Allen told Edward Kiersh, "but do you know what it's like to have iron bolts thrown at you from the stands?"

As early as the spring of 1965, Allen was drinking heavily. In his 1989 autobiography, *Crash: The Life and Times of Dick Allen*, cowritten with Tim Whitaker, he talked about a spring training game in which Yankee Mickey Mantle collided with him at third base: "When the dust finally settles, the ump looks down at both of us sprawled on the ground and shakes his head. 'I've never smelled so much booze in my life' he tells me and Mantle. 'Get off your asses before you set each other on fire.'"

In his 1994 book, *The Politics of Glory*, Bill James, looking back on Allen's career, wrote that, off the field, "Allen never did anything to help his teams win, and in fact spent his entire career doing everything he could possibly do to *keep* his teams from winning. ... In 1965, when the Phillies were trying to overcome the memory of having blown the pennant in the last few days of the 1964 season, Allen got into a fight with a teammate early in the season, forcing a trade. For four yeas after that, Allen engaged in constant headline-making battles with his managers, and the Phillies, a young team at that time, never did come together and were never in position to win again."

Nearly everything James asserts in these passages is wrong, but he didn't invent any of it. Such was the prevailing attitude about Allen for a long time. Yet the assessment is unsupported by those who knew him well. Over the years, Richie Ashburn, Mike Schmidt, Pat Corrales, and other people connected with the Phillies organization past and present insisted that Allen was not the disruptive force he was portrayed as being and that they had good memories about the time they spent with him on and off the field. Later, in a remarkable piece of historical investigation published in *Baseball Research Journal*, Craig Wright traced Allen's career through the Phillies, Cardinals, Dodgers, White Sox, and then back to the Phillies in the mid-1970s, tracking down Allen's former teammates and managers. They all unequivocally rejected the image of Dick Allen as a troublemaker who hurt his teams off the field. Virtually all of them called him a great player and thought he should be in the Hall of Fame.

◆

Looking back on the 1964 Phillies, the question that probably should be asked is how they got so close to winning the pennant in the first place. The Cardinals had Bill White, Dick Groat, Ken Boyer, Curt Flood, Lou Brock, Tim McCarver, and, of course, Bob Gibson—the team even had an old Whiz Kid, Curt Simmons, who won 18 games for them. The Phillies didn't have anywhere near that depth of talent. Even the Reds, who finished the 1964 season tied for second with the Phillies—everyone seems to forget about that—had Pete Rose, Frank Robinson, Vada Pinson, Jim O'Toole, Jim Maloney, Bob Perkey, Joey Jay, and Sammy Ellis. The third-place Giants, for God's sake, had Willie Mays, Orlando Cepeda, Jim Ray Hart, Tom Haller, Juan Marichal, and Gaylord Perry—how in the world did the Phillies finish two games ahead of *them?*

The 1964 Phillies didn't lead the NL in a single major hitting or pitching category. What really galls about the memory of what happened that season is not God's unfairness but His *fairness*—we shouldn't have won after all, and we didn't. And if we had, we just would have been humiliated in the World Series by the Yankees. We all know it.

If there is one thing worse than the memory of all the Phillies' famous tank-dives, it's the aftermath of their precious few victories. You can't think of the 1950 Whiz Kids without a sigh. The season was a false dawn, and Robin Roberts, possibly the greatest pitcher of the 1950s, and Richie Ashburn, the greatest leadoff man of the decade, were subsequently condemned to years of drudgery and frustration. Even the pennant-winning years of 1980 and 1983 (1980 being the Phillies' only World Series victory) leave a bitter taste when they force us to recall the afterlives of star players on those teams: Tug McGraw's early death from brain cancer, Steve Carlton's descent into right-wing nuttiness, Mike Schmidt's postbaseball drift, Pete Rose's gambling, Joe Morgan's broadcasting career ...

If the Phillies had won in 1964, it wouldn't have changed a thing. After 1964, the pitching, except for Jim Bunning and Chris Short, fell apart. Most of the leading players on that team, particularly Tony Taylor and Clay Dalrymple, never played as well again, probably because they weren't all that good to begin with. Shortstops Bobby Wine and Ruben Amaro were good fielders, but never developed into major league hitters. Even the ones who played well in 1964 and continued to play well later, like Cookie Rojas and Tony Gonzalez, were never more than good ballplayers. Some, such as Wes Covington, Roy Sievers, Frank Thomas, Vic Power, Don Hoak, Bobby Shantz, Ryne Duren, and Cal McLish, were well past their best years in 1964 (for a team that is perceived to have been young and vigorous, the Phillies had an awful lot of washed-up geezers on the roster).

The most poignant memory for Phillies fans is of Johnny Callison— handsome, talented, second in the 1964 MVP voting behind Ken Boyer. Callison did get better, for one year in 1965, again topping 30 home runs and 100 RBIs. Then, at 27, hobbled by injuries, he began to fade. If the Phillies had won in 1964, he would probably have been the MVP instead of Boyer. But the real MVP of the 1964 season was Dick Allen. Without Allen, the Phillies would never have been in the pennant race in the first place, and without him, there would never have been even dim hopes of a Phillies dynasty in the 1960s.

On second thought, some things *might* have been different had the Phillies won in 1964. Maybe Dick Allen would have won his deserved MVP award, despite the handicap of being a rookie, and maybe that would have gotten the Philadelphia press off his back and allowed his career to develop more naturally. Perhaps then Allen's bitterness wouldn't have festered, and he never would have started drinking. It might have become obvious to fans everywhere and especially in Philadelphia that they were watching perhaps the best player in the game. Maybe all the hostility—hostility that, whether or not it was due to racial bitterness, still contributed to racial problems—would never have happened.

Maybe the Phillies then wouldn't have wanted to deal Dick Allen to the Cardinals, or maybe the Cardinals would have wanted to trade Curt Flood to the Phillies for someone other than Allen. And in that case, Flood might have found Philadelphia a more congenial place to play ball and would have never challenged the reserve clause—and maybe there wouldn't be free agency today ...

What if? No, things could not have worked out that way. Not in this universe, not in any other. Philadelphia fans booed Mike Schmidt at the peak of his career, when he was the best player in baseball, and they boo Donovan McNabb now, when he is very nearly the best quarterback in football. In itself, booing Donovan McNabb is neither worse than nor different from booing Mike Schmidt. But if the primary fan base of the Phillies and Eagles is white, then the booing of black superstar athletes tends to seem nastier than booing white stars. It's easy to forget this now, but the Phillies PR problems with their potential black fan base go back well before Dick Allen and perhaps even before the merciless racial taunting of Jackie Robinson by Phillies manager Ben Chapman in 1947. Gerald Early's mother once told him, "I'll root for the Phillies when hell freezes over," and her sentiments must have been far from atypical.

Numerous prominent athletes, black and white, have not wanted to play in Philadelphia or wanted out quickly after they got there. (We all know their names; there's no need to rehash those stories.) It's difficult to think of any other city in sports with a similar history. In some instances the blame for these sentiments, or at least part of it, can be put on the athletes, but when attitudes like these are expressed over and over, decade after decade, it's only logical to conclude that the city, press, and fans are doing something to engender them. And a rather disturbing fact: From Jackie Robinson's first major league game in 1947 until Ryan Howard's of 2006, Dick Allen was Philadelphia's only black superstar baseball player. We'll see how Howard gets on with Phillies fans when his home run total falls to, say, 32.

Meanwhile, Dick Allen and the Phillies organization have long since let bygones be bygones, and we now know that much of the disruption that Allen supposedly brought to the Phillies and his other teams in the 1970s was in reality the result of misunderstandings or misin-

Table 5-8 Allen Forever? The Top 30 Hitters of All Time by Career Equivalent Average

| Player | EQA |
| --- | --- |
| Babe Ruth | .368 |
| Ted Williams | .364 |
| Barry Bonds | .356 |
| Lou Gehrig | .346 |
| Frank Thomas | .343 |
| Albert Pujols | .342 |
| Mickey Mantle | .340 |
| Rogers Hornsby | .338 |
| Mark McGwire | .336 |
| Manny Ramirez | .334 |
| Dan Brouthers | .333 |
| Stan Musial | .333 |
| Jason Giambi | .330 |
| Mel Ott | .330 |
| Ty Cobb | .329 |
| Jimmie Foxx | .329 |
| Edgar Martinez | .329 |
| Willie Mays | .328 |
| Johnny Mize | .328 |
| Joe DiMaggio | .327 |
| Jim Thome | .327 |
| Hank Aaron | .326 |
| Hank Greenberg | .326 |
| Joe Jackson | .326 |
| **Dick Allen** | **.325** |
| Charlie Keller | .325 |
| Frank Robinson | .324 |
| Jeff Bagwell | .323 |

terpretations. Judged by his on-field performance, Dick Allen deserves to be in the Hall of Fame (Table 5-8). So if there are no strong objections, let's start the bandwagon rolling on Dick Allen in the Hall of Fame.

We can do little to ease the awful memory of 1964, but we can take it off Dick Allen's back.

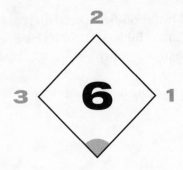

# 2003 National League Central

*Scapegoats*

JOHN ERHARDT

Many years from now, Cubs fans will recline on their psychologists' couches and be subjected to word association analysis. "Say the first thing that pops into your head," Dr. Anderson will say. "Mark Prior."

"Dusty Baker," the fans will respond, a lone tear collecting in the corner of an eye.

"Two thousand and three Cubs."

"Steve Bartman," they'll say.

Bartman, the inadvertent villain of the 2003 season, is now a permanent piece of Cubs history, a hastily drawn pencil sketch added to the Hall of Ancestors, fastened to the wall with a piece of chewing gum.

When Luis Castillo fouled a Mark Prior pitch into the left field corner of Wrigley Field during the eighth inning of Game 6 of the National League Championship Series, the Cubs were only five outs away from their first World Series appearance since 1945. Fans at the park leaned forward in their seats to see if Moises Alou could make a play on it. Many at Wrigley stood up, including a fan named Steve Bartman who was seated in the front row in the left field corner. According to photographs of the play, he was not alone in thinking the ball was hit for him; more than a few fans put on their invisible gloves and reached out toward their only chance to touch the game.

## 2003 National League Central Prospectus

| Team | Actual Standings W | L | Pct | GB | DIF | Date Elim | Pythag W | L |
|------|-----|-----|------|------|-----|-----------|------|-----|
| Cubs | 88 | 74 | .543 | – | 77 | – | 85 | 77 |
| Astros | 87 | 75 | .537 | 1.0 | 99 | Sept 27 | 94 | 68 |
| Cardinals | 85 | 77 | .525 | 3.0 | 32 | Sept 26 | 89 | 73 |
| Pirates | 75 | 87 | .463 | 12.0 | 10 | Sept 16 | 76 | 86 |
| Reds | 69 | 93 | .426 | 19.0 | 0 | Sept 12 | 62 | 100 |
| Brewers | 68 | 94 | .420 | 20.0 | 0 | Sept 12 | 66 | 96 |

| League Averages | | | | BP Stats Leaders | | | |
|------|------|------|------|------|------|------|------|
| AVG | OBP | SLG | BABIP | Offense, BRAA | | Indiv WARP | |
| .262 | .332 | .417 | .297 | Braves | 164 | Barry Bonds | 12.8 |
| ERA | K9 | BB9 | H9 | Pitching, PRAA | | Albert Pujols | 12.0 |
| 4.29 | 6.6 | 3.4 | 9.0 | Dodgers | 146 | Todd Helton | 11.5 |

What happened next has since become a symbolic distillation of the Cubs' season, indistinguishable from myth and just as realistic: Bartman reached out with his twelve-foot long retractable arm and blocked the stadium lights from illuminating the ball. Alou valiantly braved the sudden eclipse and managed to locate the tiny ball, conducted mental calculus to determine how to best time his jump, and prepared for the accolades he would receive after creating what amounted to a free out. Bartman was undeterred. He let out a maniacal laugh, selfishly lunged at the ball, and prevented Alou from catching it. Castillo was given a second life, the Marlins scored eight runs in the inning, and the series was extended another night—and that night, the Cubs lost.

For the Cubs, the entire season was reduced to a few key images, all from Game 6: Moises Alou jumping up and down in frustration after coming away from the play sans ball; Bartman sheepishly sitting in his seat and enduring the rest of the eighth-inning debacle; his eventual removal from the stadium by armed—yes, armed—men, his head tucked inside his sweatshirt like a threatened turtle. These became the symbols for the 2003 Cubs and the heartache of being just five outs from a World Series appearance.

Despite the initial outrage and hysteria (including the posting of Bartman's name on the *Chicago Sun-Times* Web site), it didn't take very long for the Bartman incident to be correctly labeled a convenient fiction. "Please leave him alone. It's not his fault," Alou later said. Dusty Baker referred to the fan's alleged interference as a "normal human reaction." Even Ryne Sandberg, no stranger to Cubs heartache himself, felt for Bartman in the aftermath: "Prior said it about as good as anybody minutes after the game. He thought that 99 percent of the fans would have had the same type of reaction down there. He didn't reach 2 or 3 feet over the wall in fair territory."

Non-Cubs fans who visit Dr. Anderson might not be able to mine their memories for word association from the 2003 regular season the way a diehard Cubs fan might. *Pitching staff, September strength of schedule,* and *strikeout* might go forever unassociated with *dominant, easy,* and *historically good* during those sessions. But while the season might forever be catalogued as the Steve Bartman Year, the real story is how the Cubs got to that point, and the performances they spent in vain.

July 2003 was still mostly an extension of that early-season ersatz parity, when most teams still look like contenders on paper, the losers haven't yet jettisoned their best players, and the winners haven't yet acquired them. By the end of the month, as the division began to take shape, it was painfully clear that the Cubs weren't a good offensive team. They could plate every runner who reached base and still lose the game 4-3; Sammy Sosa could hit four home runs in a week and have just four RBIs to show for it. Their hitters collectively managed a .259/.323/.416 line for the season, below league average in all three areas. They were 22nd in the majors in batting average, 24th in on-base percentage, and 19th in slugging. The Cubs' success did not come from their bats.

Although he provided a great deal of the offense, Sosa was no longer the superman from the summer of 1998. He still led the offense and finished near the top of the league rankings in several offensive categories, but he didn't rank quite as high as he once had: He was 10th in slugging and sixth in home runs, and his commercials didn't seem to run as frequently. His bat still moved through the zone in a blink, albeit a more languid blink. He'd swing at sliders that were just a little bit further off the plate. His hop out of the batters box was a bit less sprightly than before. Moreover, he endured the humiliation of having his bat woken up from its nap at the Hall of Fame and sawed in half on live television, all to prove it wasn't corked. This embarrassment came after he was caught using a doctored bat against the Tampa Bay Devil Rays. His excuse: "I use that bat for batting practice."

No, the offense was a problem, and if the Cubs were to reach the playoffs, they needed to find some. In July, the NL Central was winnable—even by the Reds. And the Cubs didn't wait until the trading deadline proper to improve their lineup: A week before the official deadline, they sent infielder Jose Hernandez and minor leaguer Matt Bruback to Pittsburgh for outfielder Kenny Lofton and third baseman Aramis Ramirez. (A few weeks after, "player to be named later" Bobby Hill was shipped to the Pirates, to close the books on the deal.) Ramirez was still short on performance, despite a .291 equivalent average (EqA) season under his belt (at age 23, no less). Though his acquisition meant the lineup had an injection of raw power, it didn't address two of Chicago's major needs: defense and on-base percentage. It was Lofton who delivered what was needed. His defense was often creative, but he moved Mark Grudzielanek out of the leadoff spot, hit .327/.381/.471 as a Cub, and set the table for Sosa, Alou, and Ramirez, a middle of the order that was suddenly three deep. The Cubs continued to make tactical acquisitions in preparation for their playoff roster, picking up defensive sub Doug Glanville and the vaguely credentialed Tony Womack, a desperation move after Grudzielanek broke his hand in early August and missed a month. It wasn't a great lineup either offensively or defensively, but it was better.

And "better" might be hyperbole in descriptions of the Cubs' fielding. They never did assemble much of a defense, and they finished the year with lackluster defensive numbers (Table 6-1).

Being cumulatively six runs below average isn't enough to swing your won-lost record very much; you could call this team average, and you wouldn't be wrong. But they achieved mediocrity not because they were comfortably average across the board, but because they mitigated six below-average performances (and another, exactly average performance) with one very positive contribution at short. The FRAA of 24 at shortstop (Table 6-1) was almost exclusively the product of Alex Gonzalez. Though he was not previously known as a steady defender, his contributions in the field were just about the only part of the Cubs' gloves worth the leather.

Another circumstance affecting the

Table 6-1  Cubs' Defensive Record, 2003

| Position | Fielding Runs Above Average (FRAA) | Rate* |
|---|---|---|
| P | -8 | 95 |
| C | 9 | 105 |
| 1B | -9 | 95 |
| 2B | -5 | 97 |
| 3B | -11 | 92 |
| SS | 24 | 116 |
| LF | -4 | 97 |
| CF | -2 | 99 |
| RF | 0 | 100 |

*A way to look at the fielder's rate of production, equal to 100 plus the number of runs above or below average this fielder is per 100 games. A player with a rate of 110 is 10 runs above average per 100 games, a player with an 87 is 13 runs below average per 100 games, etc.

CF row of Table 6-1 doesn't show up in the numbers of the chart. When Corey Patterson injured his knee and missed the second half of the season, the Cubs had to start cycling through center fielders. Patterson's later struggles under Dusty Baker have been well chronicled, but at the time, the outfielder was well on his way to his best season. Through 2006, the 2003 season still represents his career-high batting average, on-base percentage, and slugging percentage. Another page from the what-if files.

With few notable contributions from the offense and defense, that leaves just one possible reason for the Cubs' eventual success: pitching. The Cubs got as far as they did because of four right arms, and in spite of one left arm. Among the right-handers, Matt Clement's major virtue was that he was comfortably average. Unable to harness his stuff in Florida or San Diego, he settled into the back end of the rotation under pitching coach Larry Rothschild and did yeoman's work. Carlos Zambrano was a young, goofy, animated Venezuelan with a game plan only slightly different from that of his rotation mates: lots of walks, lots of strikeouts, and lots of ground balls. Kerry Wood was a grizzled veteran of just 25, and despite an elbow rebuilt immediately after his stellar rookie season, he could dominate a game. Mark Prior, the 2001 first-round draft choice, was in the middle of a breakout season that would have people talking Cy Young, not to mention Cy Old and Cy Forever, even though he missed some time with injury.

This left veteran southpaw Shawn Estes. Not only was Estes considerably worse than Joe Average, but he was worse than a host of pitchers who are usually cut at the end of spring training because they throw overhand with underhand results. Teams rarely have five quality starters in their rotation, so having a lousy fifth starter isn't a death sentence. For that matter, teams rarely have four quality pitchers in their rotations, either, which is why the Cubs were something special.

This rotation (or, more accurately, four-fifths of it) helped the Cubs carve out a distinguished place in history: They struck out batters at a nearly unheard-of pace. In fact, of the top five strikeout teams in baseball history, the recent Cubs occupy the top four spots (Table 6-2). In the classic baseball film *Bull Durham*, Crash Davis called the strikeout "fascist." As if to prove that, the Cubs dispatched their opposition with brutal authority. The strikeout is

Table 6-2 Top Team Strikeout Totals in Major League Baseball History

| Year | Team | SO |
|------|------|-----|
| 2003 | Chicago (N) | 1,404 |
| 2004 | Chicago (N) | 1,346 |
| 2001 | Chicago (N) | 1,344 |
| 2002 | Chicago (N) | 1,333 |
| 2002 | Arizona | 1,303 |

ferocious. It requires the batter to fail, fail, and fail. It isn't artistry; it is extermination.

First-year Brewer manager Ned Yost put it best after his team was held at bay in early September by the Cubs' staff: "It seems like every guy they bring in throws 95 to 99. With all the pitching they've got, it's a tough hole to climb out of when they get a two-run lead, let alone a five-run lead."

That they accumulated more raw strikeouts than any other team in history is impressive, but since we are currently witnessing a high-offense, high-strikeout era, the raw total loses some of its force. To place the staff in better context, we'll instead look at how the staff did in relation to its peers (Table 6-3). Two of the top 10 teams are recent Cubs squads, and the 2003 team is comparable only to two Dodgers teams of the early 1960s, featuring Koufax and Drysdale. The Dodgers' superiority can't be attributed to Dodger Stadium; in 1960 and

Table 6-3 All Time Leaders in Strikeouts Per Nine Innings Relative to League Average

| Year | Team | K/9 | K/9 League | Pct Greater |
|---|---|---|---|---|
| 1960 | Los Angeles (N) | 7.2 | 5.2 | .385 |
| 2003 | Chicago (N) | 8.7 | 6.4 | .359 |
| 1961 | Los Angeles (N) | 7.2 | 5.3 | .358 |
| 1959 | Los Angeles (N) | 6.9 | 5.1 | .353 |
| 1976 | New York (N) | 6.4 | 4.8 | .333 |
| 1990 | New York (N) | 7.6 | 5.7 | .333 |
| 1969 | Houston | 7.7 | 5.8 | .328 |
| 1971 | New York (N) | 7.1 | 5.4 | .315 |
| 1983 | Philadelphia | 6.7 | 5.2 | .288 |
| 2002 | Chicago (N) | 8.3 | 6.5 | .277 |

1961, the Dodgers were still playing their home games in the Los Angeles Memorial Coliseum, which was emphatically a hitter's park. The Dodgers top this particular list despite their home park, not because of it. So, expressed as a percentage greater than the league average, the 2003 Chicago Cubs' record sits in rare company.

But while strikeouts might be an optimal strategy, they rarely appear by themselves, and the Cubs issued many walks in the process, which was not unique to 2003. Compared with all teams from 1959 to 2006, the Cubs led the pack in how often a plate appearance resulted in the ball's not even being put in play (Table 6-4).

More than a third of the time, Cubs fielders were purely ornamental—a good thing, considering their shortcomings. Still, this strategy didn't generate wholly positive results. With more strikeouts and more walks come higher pitch counts per inning, and manager Dusty Baker never shied away from pushing his starters deep into games despite high pitch counts. So the pitching staff soldiered on, inducing batters to take mighty hacks at unhittable balls, creating wind that blew straight out into the outfield and over the lake toward northern Michigan.

Table 6-4 Pitching Staffs Allowing Fewest Balls in Play, 1959-2006

| Year | Team | PA | SO | BB | BIP % |
|------|------|-----|-----|-----|-------|
| 2003 | Chicago (N) | 6,227 | 1,404 | 617 | 64.1 |
| 2006 | Chicago (N) | 6,366 | 1,250 | 687 | 65.2 |
| 2002 | Chicago (N) | 6,236 | 1,333 | 606 | 65.3 |
| 2001 | Chicago (N) | 6,159 | 1,344 | 550 | 65.8 |
| 2004 | Chicago (N) | 6,262 | 1,346 | 545 | 65.9 |
| 2005 | Chicago (N) | 6,185 | 1,256 | 576 | 66.6 |
| 1987 | Texas | 6,390 | 1,103 | 760 | 66.9 |
| 2004 | Houston | 6,201 | 1,282 | 525 | 67.0 |
| 2001 | Arizona | 6,090 | 1,297 | 461 | 67.0 |
| 2003 | Los Angeles (N) | 6,001 | 1,289 | 526 | 67.0 |

One of the more philosophical questions surrounding team management in baseball is how to best balance the need to win now with the need to preserve players for the future. There are few better examples of this debate than the Dusty Baker–era Cubs, particularly concerning Kerry Wood and Mark Prior. Though Prior's delivery might have been consistent, all the consistency in the world won't help you if you're asked to throw 131 pitches, as Prior was on September 1. It was the opening game of a five-game set against the Cardinals, who were in first place (for the time being) when the game began. Next time out, it was 129 pitches for Prior, then 109 (in just over five innings), then 124 against the Mets, and then 131 against the Pirates, before he closed out the season with a 133-pitch outing also against the Pirates.

Prior was aware of this overwork, as are most people who either work overtime or know that they're being asked to do the job of several workers. But rather than complain about the overuse or hint that his young arm might not survive such a dramatic workload increase, Prior defended and rationalized the decision to ride starters until it was absolutely time to hand the ball off to the bullpen: "This is the time of year when you have to push yourself. Everybody's tired on every team. Dusty isn't going to send us out for 170–180 pitches, nothing crazy. If we've got to push it to 120–130 to get the job done, that's fine. If it takes 130 pitches to throw seven innings and you get it to your bullpen, then so be it."

Prior was showing his naïveté—130 pitches through seven innings is a bit on the high side, at 18.5 pitches per inning. Over nine innings, that rate becomes 166, a total that even Baker might balk at—but Prior was right about something. He specified the importance of *when* the pitches occurred, as the raw pitch total didn't tell the whole story. The fact that you were perhaps required to throw 40 pitches in one of your innings was more significant, and the consequences of pitches delivered under duress needed to be weighed differently.

Whether the nuances are important in Prior's case is immaterial: His arm has been breaking down since the 2003 season, and although we watched that year's performance, thinking it was a celebration of his arrival, we now know that he followed it up with four increasingly unhealthy seasons. (The number of Prior's major league games started since 2003 were 21, 27, 9, and 0. He underwent surgery in April 2007 and was slated to miss the entire season.) But Prior was so good that year that Cardinal reliever Steve Kline, after the season ended, hoped Prior "takes a line drive to the forehead and we never have to see him again." Kline has very nearly gotten his wish, but it didn't take a lethal line drive, just Dusty Baker.

The division race wasn't always first-rate drama. Instead of all three teams rising dramatically to the top of the NL Central with complete rosters of highly skilled warriors who put their best performances on display when it mattered most, there was an awful lot of throat clearing on stage. As we've seen, the Cubs were a flawed team, leaning disproportionately on the pitching staff. This imbalance was echoed by the other two teams in the race, as the NL Central was a flawed division.

The Astros had one of the top offenses and a good pitching staff in their own right, but the high-ranking offense hid their surfeit of empty lineup spots. The Cardinals had problems of their own, problems that were exacerbated by an injury to starting pitcher Matt Morris. So while the Cubs improved their roster and attempted to patch up their weaknesses, the Astros and Cardinals did very little to address their own needs. The Astros were criticized as being far too complacent in their preparation for the stretch drive, while the Cardinals needed to replace their existing bullpen with one that worked, required offensive upgrades at four positions, and needed a reliable arm or three in the rotation. For all of Walt Jocketty's virtues as a general manager, that's not something you can pull off at midseason. The Cardinals instead settled for Yankees castoff Sterling Hitchcock and veteran retread Mike DeJean and called it a day, hoping to ride the NL's second-best offense into the playoffs.

Despite being in first place for most of the last three months, the Astros spent that time with very little margin for error, something that became obvious in the third inning of their July 29 game against the

Braves. After two shaky innings and surrendering a home run to pitcher Russ Ortiz at the top of the third, Roy Oswalt was removed. The Astros lost the game, and Oswalt, diagnosed with a strained groin, was put on the disabled list. In typical tease fashion, Houston alternated wins and losses for almost two weeks thereafter.

Whenever a team finishes a season one game out of the playoffs, second-guessers begin to look for the one thing that would have turned the one-game deficit into a one-game lead. And while a healthy Oswalt might have closed the gap, it was the offense that was truly culpable for the shortfall. Early on, Geoff Blum and his .230 EqA saw more time at third base than did Morgan Ensberg and his .300 EqA. And the inexplicable fascination with Brad Ausmus's defensive reputation kept the equivalent of a pitcher's bat in the lineup every night. Even with the (now filed under "temporary") resurgence of Richard Hidalgo, the last really good season from Jeff Bagwell, and a solid season from Jeff Kent, you can only go so far if you write off two non-pitcher lineup spots for two months (three spots, if you count Adam Everett and his .245 EqA) while trying to score more runs. Houston's tendency to waste outs is the equivalent of an acceptably fast kid giving a faster kid a head start for a high-profile playground race. Despite its poor personnel decisions, Houston held a 1.5-game lead as late as September 19, but the guard changed soon thereafter.

Chicago's September 1 game against St. Louis represented a new beginning for the Cubs, who made it out of August with their new-look offense mustering just a .244/.307/.383 line for the entire month. That they went 15-13 was again largely thanks to their pitching, which had a 3.49 ERA during that span. But starting on September 1, they dispatched the Cardinals four times in a five-game series and then enjoyed almost a solid month of sub-.500 competition: Milwaukee (three games), Montreal (three), Cincinnati (six), the Mets (three), and Pittsburgh (seven). Meanwhile, the Cardinals had to play the Astros six times in the final three weeks of the season.

The Cubs raised their offensive game in September and continued their stellar pitching en route to a 19-8 month that vaulted them to the top of the division. Meanwhile, the Cardinals were swept by the Oswalt-led Astros and dropped to 5.5 games out of first place; they'd fall all the way to six games back before taking two of three from Houston, but that six-game deficit proved insurmountable. Just days before, against Colorado, Tony La Russa became the eighth manager in history to reach 2,000 wins. His achievement only offered personal comfort at the time, as the Cardinals were about to drop from contention; from 2000 to 2006, the year 2003 would be the only time they failed to make the playoffs.

The Astros, on the other hand, managed to stay in it until the very end. Even without Oswalt in the rotation, they drew good performances out of Ron Villone, Jeriome Robertson, and especially journeyman Tim Redding, who posted a 2.67 ERA in September. Oswalt returned in September to help take the first game against Milwaukee (the Astros would take three of four) and then beat the Cardinals twice, both times against Matt Morris. Back from the disabled list after breaking a finger, Morris was crucial to the Cards if they were to contend. Oswalt's final start of the year was a pitcher's duel against the Giants' Sidney Ponson, a battle Oswalt won 2-1. The win halted a four-game skid and put the Astros just a game behind the Cubs, with four left to play. The Cubs' opponents going into the final four days were the Reds and Pirates, and the Astros had four games against the Brewers. The top two teams in the NL Central would battle it out against the bottom three, and whoever beat up the eminently beatuppable would advance.

With both the Cubs and the Astros going 2-2 in the end, the Cubs' one-game lead was preserved. But the L-W-W-L and W-L-L-W patterns that the Cubs and Astros had, respectively, meant that for one day the NL Central was tied and that there really was a race. But after the Astros were trounced by the lowly Brewers on September 26 and the Cubs swept a doubleheader against the even lowlier Pirates the following day, it was over. The Cubs clinched their first division crown since 1989. The Astros played out the string by self-imposing Little League rules: getting 21 players into their final game against the Brewers, who used 17 themselves.

♦

After the season ended for the Cubs, Baker tried to put 2003 into perspective: "My guys performed admirably, but it took us awhile to build that Giant team to go to the World Series [in 2002]. We had more hitting. We had more power. We were number one in defense. Think about it: We did this really quickly this year. Next year is a test of how good you really are. You've got to do it in consecutive years."

They didn't. They declined every year thereafter, with win totals of 89, 79, and 66; Baker saw his team finish first, third, fourth, and sixth in his four years at the helm before being replaced in the 2006 off-season, though calls for his head began long before that. Tony La Russa, with the individual achievement of Albert Pujols's batting title fresh in his mind, was more philosophical about his team's failure to reach the postseason: "Now, the St. Louis Cardinals have been playing baseball for over 100 years and they've won nine World Series. Does that mean they've had only nine successful seasons and 90-plus failures? I think fans would have a hard time walking up to Stan Musial or Lou Brock or Bob Gibson and saying they were failures except for 1964, or whatever. The World Series is a goal and dream. A failure to get to the World Series does not mean you failed." Clearly, though, coming close to the pinnacle of the sport, as the Cubs did, and then rapidly falling away might qualify as a failure, even in La Russa's forgiving philosophy.

### Selig's Dream: The Wild Card as Enabler of Pennant Races

NATE SILVER

At precisely 4:30 P.M. on October 1, 1995, the New York Yankees made history. Steve Howe retired the Blue Jays' Randy Knorr to make the Yankees the first wild card in the history of baseball. Relieved to make the playoffs after a tumultuous season that had expected much of them, they drank Labatts and Molson in the SkyDome clubhouse. But something felt a little strange. "I'm just wondering why I'm not as excited as I wanted to be," said Don Mattingly, who had reached the playoffs for the first time in his career. Manager Buck Showalter wanted nothing to do with this attitude. "I don't want anybody to feel apologetic for getting in the playoffs this way," he insisted.

Despite the Yankees' lukewarm reactions, the wild card and the extra round of playoffs demonstrated their worth almost immediately in the form of a thrilling five-game series between the Yankees and the Seattle Mariners, the AL West champions. The winning run was scored no earlier than the seventh inning in four of the five contests, with two games coming down to the last at-bat, including Edgar Martinez's climactic double down the left-field line in the rubber match. It was just the thing baseball needed after the embarrassment of the 1994 strike. Soon enough, the wild card became so entrenched that no team needed the sort of apologetic nonapology that Showalter offered; the wild-card Marlins certainly offered no excuses after they won the 1997 World Series.

Table 6-5  2003 National League Standings Under Two-Division Format

| NL East | W | L | GB | NL West | W | L | GB |
|---|---|---|---|---|---|---|---|
| Florida | 91 | 71 | – | Atlanta | 101 | 61 | – |
| Chicago | 88 | 74 | 3.0 | San Francisco | 100 | 61 | 0.5 |
| Philadelphia | 86 | 76 | 5.0 | Houston | 87 | 75 | 14.0 |
| St. Louis | 85 | 77 | 6.0 | Los Angeles | 85 | 77 | 16.0 |
| Montreal | 83 | 79 | 8.0 | Arizona | 84 | 78 | 17.0 |
| Pittsburgh | 75 | 87 | 16.0 | Colorado | 74 | 88 | 27.0 |
| Milwaukee | 68 | 94 | 23.0 | Cincinnati | 69 | 93 | 32.0 |
| New York | 66 | 95 | 24.5 | San Diego | 64 | 98 | 37.0 |

*The Brewers and Diamondbacks were not in the National League in 1993; we have placed them in the NL East and NL West, respectively.*

A fundamental change had taken place: The goal of the baseball season was no longer to win the pennant but to reach the playoffs. It is really no accident, then, that in a book about pennant races, we've only found room for one chapter from the wild-card era. And even that season—the National League of 2003—proved undeniably how the new playoff structure could both giveth and taketh away. Although the three-division format had produced a thrilling race in the NL Central, it had perhaps deprived us of two great races: a long, tight battle between two 100-win powers in the West, and a five-way war of attrition in the East (Table 6-5).

Does the wild card, on balance, improve pennant races? It depends on what you mean by *pennant races* and what you mean by *improve*.

By most definitions, a pennant represents a league championship. Baseball has two major leagues, and so it has two pennants, which are presently won not in the regular season but in the League Championship Series. The four-division era, with its winner-take-all format, provided for some wiggle room in the characterization of a pennant. For example, in describing how the Cardinals had clinched the NL East in 1985, the *Sporting News* used the word *pennant*, but made sure to put the word in quotation marks. The introduction of the wild card blew the whole notion of a pennant to smithereens. As you will see momentarily, this is not a purely semantic distinction.

*Improve* is even trickier to define, especially when aesthetic considerations are taken into account—does a playoff race between two 100-win clubs count for more than one between three also-rans? In this

Table 6-6  Total Playoff Impact (TPLI) Example, September 22 and 23, 2003

| | Playoff Probability at End of ... | | |
| Team | September 22 | September 23 | Change |
| --- | --- | --- | --- |
| Marlins | 71.8% | 87.0% | 15.2% |
| Phillies | 25.3% | 11.1% | 14.2% |
| **Total Playoff Impact** | | | **29.4%** |

case, we will defer to the perspective offered by John Harrington, then CEO of the Boston Red Sox. "We're hoping it will enhance and maintain fan interest through the end of the season," Harrington said of the wild card after the owners voted to approve the new playoff format in September 1993.

Here is a question that we can hope to answer: Does the wild card lead to a higher percentage of important baseball games in the later part of the season? On any given day, Baseball Prospectus's Playoff Odds Report provides the probabilities of each team's making the playoffs. By comparing the results of the report from one day to the next, we can judge the importance of a particular regular-season contest.

On September 23, 2003, the Marlins defeated the Philadelphia Phillies to expand their edge in the wild-card race from one game to two. This improved the Marlins' chances of making the playoffs by about 15 percent, while reducing the Phillies' chances by 14 percent. The total playoff impact (TPLI) of this game is the sum of these two numbers, or 29 percent (Table 6-6).

Games this influential on the playoff picture are rare; there are usually only a half dozen or so every season. Still, we can certainly relax the standards a bit. Which format, for example, produces a higher percentage of games with a TPLI of 15 percent or greater: the two-division setup of 1969–1993 or the wild-card format of today?

To answer this question, I reviewed the TPLI of every game from 1969 through 2004, segregating the divisional era from wild-card play. Games were sorted into five-game bundles according to the number of days remaining until the end of the regular season, starting with 75 days to play and ending with zero. Because these results are subject to sample-size effects, smoothed curves were drawn over the individual data points to indicate the overall pattern (Chart 6-1).

As Chart 6-1 shows, a sport with a 162-game season provides few opportunities for games that jigger the playoff probabilities by 15 per-

Chart 6-1 Percentage of Games with TPLI of 15 Percent or Higher, 1969-2004

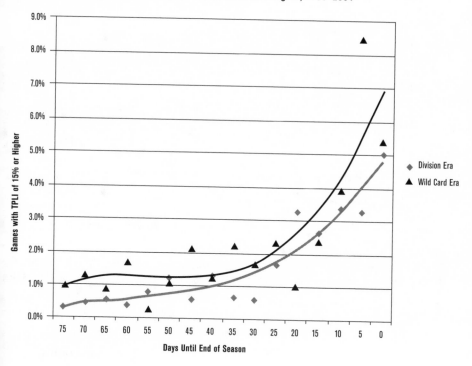

cent or more; most such games are clustered within the final 15 to 20 days of the season. Nonetheless, the wild-card format clearly produces a few more high-TPLI contests. About 6 percent of the games in the last 15 days of the season have a TPLI of 15 percent or higher under the wild-card format, versus 4 percent under divisional play.

We can run the same experiment with a somewhat more tolerant threshold, a TPLI of 10 percent or higher (Chart 6-2). These 10 percent TPLI games are quite a bit more common and more evenly distributed throughout the season's final couple of months. Still, the wild card produces a few more games of importance—about 50 percent more than the four-division format produces. This is probably to be expected. Although the wild card occasionally undermines what would have been a great divisional race (e.g., the 2003 National League), it still doubles the number of playoff spots, an advantage generally large enough to make up the difference and then some.

Here, however, the distinction between making the playoffs and winning the pennant comes into play. Suppose that instead of evaluating games for their impact on a team's chances of reaching the playoffs, we instead look at how much the games affect a team's chances

Chart 6-2 Percentage of Games with TPLI of 10 Percent or Higher, 1969–2004

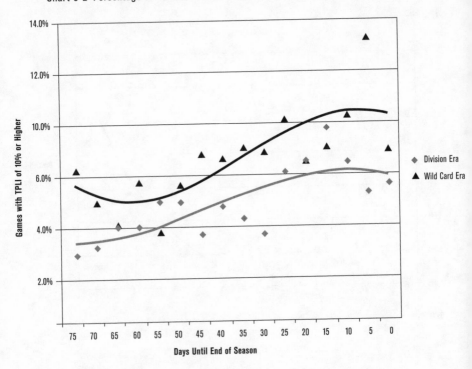

of winning its league championship. We will call this calculation TPRI, for total pennant race impact. TPRI can be defined as follows:

◆ In the divisional-play era, TPRI is equal to one-half the TPLI, since each league playoff involves two teams, each of which has roughly a 50 percent chance of winning the league's pennant and advancing to the World Series.

◆ In the wild-card era, TPRI is equal to *one-quarter* of TPLI, since there is now an extra round of playoffs to reckon with, which reduces each team's chances of winning the pennant to about one-in-four.

As you can see from Chart 6-3, which measures the percentage of games with a TPRI of 5 percent or higher, distinguishing playoff races from *pennant* races makes a huge difference. While a fair number of games from the divisional-play era meet the 5 percent TPRI threshold, they disappear almost entirely under wild-card play, appearing only during the last 15 days of the season, and then only sporadically.

We can lower the TPRI threshold to 3 percent, which gives the wild

Chart 6-3 Percentage of Games with TPRI of 5 Percent or Higher, 1969–2004

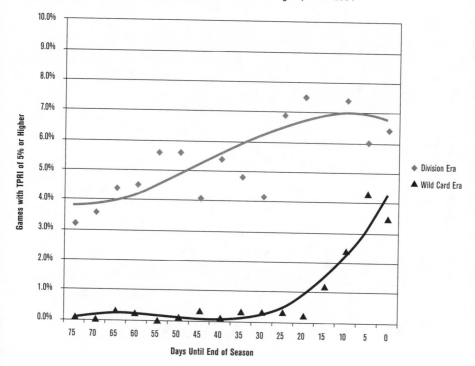

card a fighting chance (Chart 6-4). Still, regular-season games with a high degree of impact on the eventual pennant winner are far more common under the divisional-play format. The lone exception is during the final 5 to 10 days of the regular season, when divisions are liable to be clinched but the wild card tends to ensure that at least one or two playoff spots remain open for contention. From the point of view of creating dramatic pennant races, however—that is, *pennant race* as properly defined—this surge is too little, too late.

So we're stuck with two competing definitions of what makes for exciting regular-season games. If the emphasis is on creating competition for playoff spots, the wild-card format prevails. If we're focused instead on creating great pennant races, the wild card is fairly ruinous. How to break the tie?

Baseball attendance has long been subject to a September swoon, that is, the substantial decline in attendance that can be anticipated once the calendar turns past Labor Day. The decline has any number of causes, ranging from the deterioration in weather in many parts of the country, to competition from football, to the fact that the school calendar dictates that most families will become more concerned with

Chart 6-4  Percentage of Games with TPRI of 3 Percent or Higher, 1969–2004

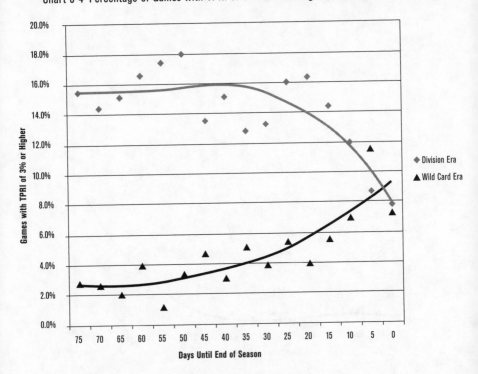

educating their children than entertaining them. What's more, with many teams out of contention by September, even the most diehard fans will have trouble suspending their disbelief for a team 32.5 games behind the Yankees.

Does the wild card reduce the effects of the September swoon? In a word, yes. And the impact is dramatic. During the final 10 years of the divisional-play era, 1984 through 1993, the average attendance in September was off by 21 percent from its levels at the zenith of the baseball calendar, June and July. In the wild-card era, by contrast, the swoon has been reduced to 8 percent (Table 6-7). This higher September attendance puts an additional $50 million in baseball's coffers each season.

It is unlikely that this shift in attendance patterns has been brought on by

Table 6-7  Decline in September Attendance Before and After Introduction of Wild Card

| Month(s) | Divisional Era (1984–1993) | Wild Card Era (1996–2006) |
|---|---|---|
| March–April | 23,777 | 27,114 |
| May | 23,939 | 27,280 |
| June | 27,269 | 30,308 |
| July | 28,127 | 31,442 |
| August | 26,970 | 30,136 |
| September–October | 21,774 | 28,295 |
| "Swoon" effect | 21.4% | 8.4% |

Chart 6-5 September Swoon Effect on Attendance, 1984–2006

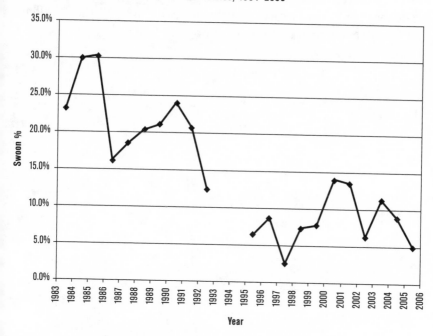

something other than the wild card, such as the stadium-building craze or baseball's improved marketing efforts. As we can see from Chart 6-5, the reduction of the September swoon occurred immediately after the introduction of the new playoff format, and the pattern has held ever since. There were a couple of minor exceptions—after 9/11, attendance dipped substantially, and a year later, several dull divisional races kept some ballpark seats empty—but even in these years, the swoon was smaller than in any divisional-play year except 1993.

Moreover, if there were some sort of rising tide lifting all boats, it would probably improve attendance early in the season as much as it improves attendance late in the season. April attendance has improved from the divisional-play era by about 14 percent, but this is nothing compared with the 30 percent boost in September.

Considering both sides of the issue, baseball strikes a remarkably good balance between the importance the league imparts to the regular season and that which it puts on the playoffs. The average wild-card entrant since 1996 has finished with a 94-68 record, which nobody would mistake for an inferior club. The wild card might not produce great pennant races, but fans are voting with their wallets, and they've concluded that it makes for great baseball.

# 1972 American League East

*The Book of Job*

CLIFFORD J. CORCORAN

Baseball is often described as a game of inches, the inches that separate a strike from a ball, a safe from an out, a hit from a catch, or, perhaps most crucially, the contact points on a bat that result in a fly out rather than a home run, or a groundout rather than a line drive.

Describing baseball as a game of inches is ultimately a flowery way of saying that the game is defined by a litany of arbitrary and often variable measurements and limits and thus often depends on luck. The variety of distances to and angles in the outfield fences of the 30 major league ballparks are only the most obvious example of variability. The individuality of umpires' strike zones, and of the rule-book strike zone itself—the vertical limits of which have been altered five times since 1950, most recently in 1996—is another.

Despite its reputation for consistency and continuity, baseball has undergone a seemingly endless series of changes over its 150-year history. Even the designation of "modern" records, which use the 1901 season as year zero and thus consign the 19th-century game to the historical dustbin, proves insufficient to compensate for the game's fluid nature. As early in the "modern" era as 1901 there was a seismic change in the game, when the American League began play, instantly diluting the major league talent pool by half. The new junior circuit failed to institute a rule that counted foul balls toward a batter's strike

## 1972 American League East Prospectus

| Team | Actual Standings | | | | | Date Elim | Pythag | |
|---|---|---|---|---|---|---|---|---|
| | W | L | Pct | GB | DIF | | W | L |
| Tigers | 86 | 70 | .551 | – | 108 | – | 84 | 72 |
| Red Sox | 85 | 70 | .548 | 0.5 | 24 | Oct 3 | 80 | 75 |
| Orioles | 80 | 74 | .519 | 5.0 | 42 | Sept 30 | 89 | 65 |
| Yankees | 79 | 76 | .510 | 6.5 | 0 | Oct 1 | 81 | 74 |
| Indians | 72 | 84 | .462 | 14.0 | 16 | Sept 20 | 72 | 84 |
| Brewers | 65 | 91 | .417 | 21.0 | 3 | Sept 11 | 65 | 91 |

| League Averages | | | | BP Stats Leaders | | | |
|---|---|---|---|---|---|---|---|
| AVG | OBP | SLG | BABIP | Offense, BRAA | | Indiv WARP | |
| .239 | .306 | .343 | .270 | Royals | 95 | Gaylord Perry | 14.7 |
| ERA | K9 | BB9 | H9 | Pitching, PRAA | | Dick Allen | 12.0 |
| 3.07 | 5.5 | 3.1 | 8.0 | Tigers | 45 | Wilbur Wood | 11.3 |

total until 1903. The height of the pitcher's mound wasn't standardized in either league until 1904. Balls didn't have cork centers until 1910. In 1920, the game adopted new rules requiring balls to be replaced if they became dirty, soggy, or scuffed, and doctored pitches such as the spitball were banned, resulting in a tremendous offensive surge that radically changed the way the game was played.

In 1925, the minimum distance of outfield fences was fixed at 250 feet. Twenty-four years later, all new parks were required to be 325 feet deep at the foul poles and 400 feet to dead center, a 30 percent increase in the minimum home run distance. Fielder's interference didn't exist until 1931. Most of the game's best players headed off to war in the early 1940s, and nonwhite players were effectively banned from the major leagues until 1947. From 1961 to 1969, each league added four expansion teams, a 50 percent increase that diluted the talent pool by another third (though one could argue that the talent pool had just been expanded by integration, the first phase of which wasn't complete until the Red Sox called up Pumpsie Green in 1959—baseball had yet to pass through tokenism and quotas). Also in 1969, in response to the dearth of offense the previous year, the pitcher's mound was lowered five inches and the upper limit of the strike zone was lowered from the top of the shoulders to the armpits.

Those changes are comparatively subtle compared with those from the Victorian age. The National League began play in 1876, but pitchers couldn't throw overhand until 1883. Hitters could request high or low pitches, but hit batsmen weren't awarded first base until both of those rules were changed in 1887. That same year, it actually took four strikes to retire a batter. Walks required more than four balls until 1889, and the pitcher's mound was just 50 feet from home plate until 1893, the same year that flat-sided bats were finally outlawed. Even the measurements that seem to have been handed down to Alexander Cartwright as if he were Moses on the mount are ultimately arbitrary. Ninety feet between bases seems like a Pythagorean ideal, but the same would be true of 85 feet had Cartwright settled on that distance; the only difference would have been more infield hits.

Perhaps the most arbitrary of all of baseball's limits is the length of its season. In the first year of the National League, the season was to be 70 games (though only one club, the Boston Red Caps, managed to play all 70). The length of the season changed 10 times in the following 24 years before finally being set at 154 games in 1904, the year *after* the first World Series was played. With the arrival of expansion in 1961, the season was stretched to 162 games, a change made infamous by Roger Maris's 61-home run season. The controversy created by commissioner Ford Frick's insistence that Maris's tater total be listed as the 162-game record in contrast to Babe Ruth's 154-game record from 1927 was a reflection of the arbitrary length of the baseball season. Did changing the length of the season make all subsequent records in cumulative categories meaningless, or at least require that they be segregated from those set over a shorter schedule? What about rate stats? Should all those .400 batting averages from the first half of the twentieth century have been set apart as 154-game averages? One wonders if anyone bothered to ask the commissioner if baseball should have applied the same reasoning to the pennant. It may not have made a difference in 1961, but the Dodgers, not the Giants, would have won the NL pennant in 1962 and the 1964 Phillies would never have phlopped had the leagues continued to recognize 154-game champions.

Another popular baseball cliché is that the six-month baseball season is a marathon not a sprint, the implication being that teams need to pace themselves and not get caught up in trying to chase down every misguided sprinter who jumps out ahead at the 12-mile mark. The best marathoners are not necessarily the fastest runners, but those who can best pace themselves and maintain their speed over the greatest distance. The question then becomes, what happens when those finely tuned marathoners get to the starting line and find out the race will only be 25 miles and won't be starting for another two weeks?

The 1960s were a particularly volatile decade in terms of how and where the game was played on the field, and who played it. Team relocation and expansion resulted in a wave of ballpark construction. There was a change in the length of the season from 154 to 162 games. The leagues were split into two divisions in 1969 and a new playoff round added, and there were rule changes affecting pitching in 1963 (when the strike zone was enlarged) and 1969. And besides the still-increasing number of minority ballplayers in the major leagues, less obvious changes off the field would have an impact every bit as significant.

In the spring of 1966, the Major League Baseball Players Association voted Marvin Miller, formerly the staff economist of the Steelworkers Union, into office as the union's first full-time executive director. Two years later, Miller negotiated the game's first collective bargaining agreement between the players and owners. The agreement included an overdue 43 percent increase in the major league minimum salary. The following winter, St. Louis Cardinals center fielder Curt Flood, in reaction to being traded to Philadelphia, decided to sue baseball over the legality of its antitrust exemption with the ultimate goal of abolishing the reserve clause that bound players to their teams in perpetuity. With Flood's case in the courts, Miller negotiated independent grievance arbitration into the second Basic Agreement in 1970, the key bargaining gain that eventually led to free agency.

Flood lost in federal court and on appeal, but the Supreme Court agreed to hear his case, which it did on March 20, 1972, just as spring training was entering its final weeks. Meanwhile, negotiations between Miller and the owners over a cost-of-living increase in the players' health care and pension benefits had reached a stalemate. The owners pulled their offer off the table, prompting the union to stage the first strike in American professional sports history on April 1, just days before the season was to begin. After 13 days, the owners relented, but 86 games had been canceled. The remainder of the season was to be played unaltered, resulting in team schedules of uneven length ranging from 153 games for the Astros and Padres to 156 for the Indians, Brewers, Mets, Cardinals, Expos, Phillies, and Tigers, with the other 15 clubs falling in between. "I don't like that uneven number of games," said Detroit outfielder Jim Northrup before the Tigers' opening tilt against the Red Sox. "I hope nobody wins or loses the pennant by a half a game." For the first time, baseball's off-the-field labor strife had a direct effect on the playing of games.

In this environment it was only fitting that one key event in the

1972 AL East race actually occurred during the previous off-season, influenced by the growing salary of one of the game's greatest stars. As 1971 drew to a close, the Baltimore Orioles were at a crossroads. As winners of the last three American League pennants and a pair of world championships, the Orioles had risen from the embarrassment of the franchise's long, lonely tenure as the St. Louis Browns to become the American League's dynastic team, filling the void left by the Yankees after the 1964 season. It's been said of the Yankees' mid-1960s collapse that everybody got old at the same time. In the winter of 1971, the Orioles were looking to avoid a similar fate.

During the 1971 season, corner outfielders Don Buford, 34, and Frank Robinson, who turned 36 on the last day of August, experienced a reduction in their playing time because of the aches and pains that come with age. Orioles manager Earl Weaver attempted to keep Robinson's bat in the lineup by giving him starts at first base, but that had the unfortunate effect of forcing Boog Powell, six years Robinson's junior and the previous year's American League MVP, to the bench. On the other hand, using Robinson at first base allowed Weaver to play 28-year-old fourth outfielder Merv Rettenmund, who soaked up the outfield starts vacated by Robinson, Buford, and center fielder Paul Blair. Already used regularly over the season's first two months, Rettenmund began playing every day on June 18 and responded by hitting .343/.441/.493 over the remainder of the 1971 season. In addition to Rettenmund, the Orioles had a 22-year-old outfielder named Don Baylor with their triple-A Rochester affiliate. The youngster was terrorizing International League pitching for the second straight season, hitting .313 with a .539 slugging percentage after posting .327 and .583 marks in 1970. Something had to give, and it was going to be either Buford or Robinson.

Frank Robinson had been the final piece of the Orioles' puzzle five years earlier, when he was acquired from the Reds for Milt Pappas, Jack Baldschun, and Dick Simpson. The Reds thought the 30-year-old Robinson, who had led Cincinnati to the NL pennant in 1961 and picked up the league MVP in the process, was on the decline. They couldn't have been more wrong. Robinson, of a piece with his NL contemporaries Willie Mays and Hank Aaron, promptly won the Triple Crown upon arriving in Baltimore, leading the Orioles to the team's first world championship and batting .286/.375/.857 in the 1966 World Series. Except for an off year in 1968, Robinson was the same perennial All-Star and MVP candidate in Baltimore that he had been in Cincinnati.

In 1970, the Orioles won their second world championship, defeating, appropriately enough, the nascent Big Red Machine. The next year, the O's claimed their third-straight AL pennant. That year, Robinson was fourth in the American League in slugging percentage, fifth in home runs, and second only to Twins slugger Harmon Killebrew in runs batted in. Robinson hit .280/.357/.520 with a pair of home runs as the Orioles battled the eventual world champion Pittsburgh Pirates over seven games in that year's World Series. A few weeks later, he finished third in the American League MVP voting.

Robinson also had the fifth-best EqA in the American League in 1971, but two of the players ahead of him were Rettenmund and Buford. Though the decision between Don Buford and Frank Robinson would seem an obvious one, even without the benefit of hindsight, Buford was both younger and cheaper than Robinson. It now seems comical that Robinson's $135,000 salary was a factor in the Orioles' decision, but this was a time when $100,000 was a superstar's salary (in the spring of 1972, Al Kaline became the first $100,000 player in Detroit Tigers history), and Robinson was the highest-paid Oriole. Emboldened by Buford's strong showing, new Orioles general manager Frank Cashen determined that Robinson, who probably had more value on the trade market as well, had to go, and proceeded to convince Weaver.

Branch Rickey once said it is better to trade a player a year too early than a year too late. Weaver took those words to heart, later writing, "Just the thought of giving up Frank Robinson scared me to death. But a manager cannot let fear deform his reason." Perhaps fear did not deform Weaver's reason, but it seems economics conspired to dent it a bit. Weaver signed off on a deal that sent Frank Robinson and reliever Pete Richert to the Dodgers for Doyle Alexander, Bob O'Brien, Sergio Robles, and Royle Stillman. Somewhere, Bill DeWitt, who had been fleeced by the Orioles in the first Robinson trade six years earlier, was smirking.

When the season finally began on April 15, Baltimore again jumped out in front of the AL East pack, thanks to a 5-1 start, but rapidly found itself mired in a dogfight. An early surprise was the performance of the Cleveland Indians, who had lost 102 games the year before. The preceding off-season had been marked by a number of lopsided trades—the Robinson deal seems perfectly reasonable compared with the swaps of Steve Carlton for Rick Wise and Nolan Ryan for Jim Fregosi. The Indians pulled off one of their own, acquiring the Giants' spitball wizard, Gaylord Perry, for southpaw Sam McDowell.

Donning new duds in 1972, Carlton and Perry won their leagues' Cy Young Awards, and Ryan recorded the fourth-highest strikeout total since the turn of the century. The Indians took over first place in the East on May 10 as Perry dominated AL batters, but after a 17-9 start, the Tribe's lack of offense began to drag them back down to their customary spot in the second division. The Orioles finally knocked the Indians out of first place for good with a four-game sweep at Memorial Stadium that concluded on May 27, but it wasn't Baltimore that took Cleveland's spot atop the division. It was the Detroit Tigers.

Cleveland may have been a short-lived menace, but Detroit posed a real threat to the defending division champions. The Tigers were the last team to win an AL pennant before the Orioles, doing so in their championship year of 1968. Some regression at the plate held the Tigers to 90 wins and a distant second-place finish behind the O's in 1969. In 1970, Detroit's pitching rotation collapsed, as did the team. Denny McClain had won 55 games for the Tigers over the previous two seasons and the league MVP in 1968, but his off-field behavior, which included investing in a Flint, Michigan–based bookmaking operation and carrying a gun on a plane, the latter a federal offense, resulted in his being suspended twice by commissioner Bowie Kuhn and missing most of the 1970 season. Of McClain's mere 14 starts in 1970, just half were quality starts (defined by Bill James as six or more innings pitched with less than four runs allowed). Meanwhile, Earl Wilson, a 22-game winner in 1967 and the team's number three starter behind McClain and Mickey Lolich in 1968 and 1969, experienced a precipitous decline and was sold to San Diego in mid-July. The Tiger players effectively gave up on the season after McClain's second suspension.

This reflected poorly on manager Mayo Smith, whom both the players and the team executives considered too passive and permissive, particularly with McClain. It thus fell to general manager Jim Campbell to right the ship. Campbell's first move was to replace the docile Smith with firebrand Billy Martin. The former Yankees World Series hero and Casey Stengel disciple had led the Minnesota Twins to the AL West title in his first year as a major league manager in 1969. But he was fired at the end of the year when his penchant for getting into fistfights with both front office personnel and his own players became too much to bear. Martin's hiring in Detroit promised a new, nononsense Tiger tenor, confirmed on the eve of the World Series, when Campbell dealt McClain, third baseman Don Wert, rookie utility man Elliott Maddox, and reliever Norm McRae to the Senators for pitcher

Joe Coleman, third baseman Aurelio Rodriguez, shortstop Eddie Brinkman, and reliever Jim Hannan. In addition to ridding the team of its principle distraction, the trade was an across-the-board win for the Tigers, as it took advantage of Washington owner Bob Short's desire to add McClain as a drawing card for his failing franchise. (Short had hired Ted Williams to manage and had later coaxed Curt Flood out of retirement, but wound up moving the team to Texas at the end of the season, anyway, after realizing that he lacked the one thing that would actually sell tickets: a winning team.)

As McClain continued to spiral out of control, both on the mound and off, Coleman gave the Tigers a sorely needed number two starter, winning 62 games in his first three years in Detroit. Rodriguez and Brinkman, meanwhile, filled the left side of the Tiger infield, upgrading the team defense by a considerable margin and even managing to out-hit the departed Wert and 1970 shortstop stop-gap Cesar Gutierrez. The Tigers allowed 86 fewer runs in 1971, while juicing their offense by 55 tallies as nearly every member of the lineup stepped up his game under the fiery Martin. In sharp contrast to the laid-back manner of his predecessor, the new manager stressed accountability and an aggressive style of play. The Orioles ran away with the division again that year, but the Tigers moved back up to second place and were emboldened when they won five of the last six head-to-head matchups between the two teams in September.

That winter, Martin lobbied Campbell to trade some of his aging veterans and extraneous arms for a top-of-the-line starting pitcher, but, besides a trio of minor moves, Campbell stood pat, forcing Martin to get creative. As 1972 got under way, Martin employed platoons at nearly every position, except for his steady left side of the infield, and clawed after every advantage he could find. Gaylord Perry's lubricated right arm may have pitched the Indians to early success in 1972, but according to rookie Bill Denehy, Martin and pitching coach Art Fowler had been teaching the Tiger pitchers how to soap up the crotches of their uniforms for similar purposes the year before (at the same time, Martin was publicly accusing the Orioles' organist of stealing signs).

Fortunately for Martin and the Tigers, the Orioles were struggling without Frank Robinson, though their problems ran deeper than being one bat short. The Orioles' offense, which had led the American League in runs scored in each of the previous two seasons, fell into a collective slump in 1972, as if Robinson were the keystone keeping the entire structure from collapsing in on itself. Buford slugged just .267 and retired after the season. Rettenmund slumped back into a part-time role from which he never reemerged. Brooks Robinson's bat suffered an untimely death at age 35. Except for a last-gasp season with Frank Robinson's Indians in 1975, Boog Powell's power was gone for good at age 30. The 23-year-old Baylor was above league average, but didn't come close to the kind of mashing he had done with Rochester, and he failed to win a full-time job in the outfield. The only encouraging sign was the arrival of 23-year-old infielder Bobby Grich, who emerged as an All-Star in his first full season.

Despite their offensive struggles, the Orioles stayed in the race on the strength of their pitching staff, in particular the four-man rotation of Jim Palmer, Dave McNally, Mike Cuellar, and Pat Dobson, each of whom had won 20 games the year before. Although the O's starters were even stingier in 1972, the collapse of the team's offense robbed all but Palmer of a repeat 20-win season. The Tigers spent the month of June fending off the Oriole attack, thrice slipping into a tie with the Birds, but, outside of a single day at the end of May, they never relinquished their grip on first place.

Then, in July, a new contender emerged. Seven-and-a-half games back with a 27-34 record at the end of June, the Boston Red Sox began July by reeling off seven straight wins. The Red Sox had preceded the Orioles and Tigers as the AL pennant winner in their "Impossible Dream" season of 1967, but, except for the Tigers' collapse in 1970, had been unable to slip by either rival during the four intervening seasons. They had even finished third behind a surprising second-place Yankees team led by Rookie of the Year catcher Thurman Munson. In 1972, though, the Red Sox had their own Rookie of the Year catcher in the person of Carlton Fisk.

"Fisk took charge of our pitching staff and really turned it around," reliever Bill Lee later recalled. "He had learned the importance of working a pitcher and nursing him along when he didn't have his best stuff. Fisk also demanded your total concentration during a game. ... Carlton always gave his best effort, and he demanded the same of everyone he played with."

Fisk could also hit, entering the month of July batting .286/.361/.571. He stepped things up from there, raking at a .337/.420/.727 pace with eight home runs as the Red Sox won 17 of their first 22 games that month. The run concluded with another seven-game winning streak. The next day, reliever Luis Tiant made a spot start in the first game of a doubleheader against the Oakland A's, pitching seven strong innings and earning a no-decision. Two weeks later, Tiant entered the rotation to stay.

If it was Fisk who got the Red Sox into the race, it was Tiant who kept them there. The pitcher had gone 21-9 with the Indians in 1968, but nearly inverted his record the following year, falling to 9-20 (though his ERA of 3.71 was only a hair off the league average of 3.63). After this, the Indians cashed him in, trading him to the Twins for a package that included young third baseman Graig Nettles. A fractured shoulder blade derailed Tiant's 1970 campaign, and when a pulled back muscle in spring training foretold more of the same in 1971, the Twins released him, as did the Braves after he spent a couple of months with their Triple-A affiliate in Richmond.

The Red Sox picked the 30-year-old Tiant off the scrap heap in May 1971 and called him up to the majors in June. Though he struggled in 10 starts that summer, he excelled after a move to the bullpen, earning a return engagement in 1972. Tiant was again effective out of the Boston pen over the first four months of 1972, but once he moved to the rotation in August, he put the team on his back and carried them the rest of the way. Over his last 11 games, all starts, Tiant went 9-2 with an 0.96 ERA, had nine complete games, six of them shutouts, and held the opposition to just 5.19 hits per nine innings.

Hot on the heels of the Red Sox were Munson and his Yankees. Answering his new rival, Munson hit .365/.430/.490 in July while catching for a pitching staff that allowed just 2.63 runs per game on the month. That staff was led by 24-year-old right-hander Steve Kline, who, from June 17 to August 25, went 10-3 with a 1.19 ERA, eight complete games, three shutouts, and an 0.85 WHIP. The Yankees also boasted a strong bullpen that was bolstered by yet another in the litany of lopsided trades from the previous winter. Amazingly, the Red Sox, craving what they saw as the Fenway-friendly bat of veteran first baseman Danny Cater, approached the Yankees about a swap of Cater for Sparky Lyle, a 27-year-old left-handed reliever. Lyle had finished 160 games for the Sox over the previous five seasons, posting a 2.85 ERA. Despite hitting just one home run there over the previous four seasons, Cater did indeed have a history of success in Fenway, but hadn't hit a lick there in 1971. The Red Sox, meanwhile, had a young first baseman named Cecil Cooper in their system and enough outfielders in the organization (Reggie Smith, newly acquired Tommy Harper, and minor leaguers Dwight Evans, Ben Oglivie, and Jim Rice) to make Carl Yastrzemski a full-time first baseman. Nonetheless, Boston general manager Dick O'Connell got his man. He probably cost his team the pennant in the process.

The Yankees swept a doubleheader in Baltimore on July 31, with

Lyle pitching the final two innings of both games for his 21st and 22nd saves of the season. With that, the Yankees leapfrogged the Red Sox into third place. Suddenly the AL East was a four-team race. In August, Yankee center fielder Bobby Murcer, already in the midst of an MVP-quality season, picked up the baton from Munson by hitting .331/.412/.692 with 10 home runs on the month. On August 13, the Yankees swept a doubleheader at home against the Brewers to pull into a second-place tie with the Tigers just 1.5 games behind the Orioles.

Over the rest of the month, the Tigers and Orioles battled over first place while the Yankees and Red Sox clashed over third, but as the Orioles and Tigers headed home from a pair of West Coast swings on the evening of September 3, Boston and New York had pulled into a three-way tie with Detroit, a half-game behind Baltimore. At least two of those teams would play each other every day for the remainder of the season.

After the four teams traded victories for most of the ensuing fortnight, the Yankees were the first team to fade, losing six of seven from September 13 to the 22nd. The lone win in that stretch was a 2-1 victory over the Orioles, who soon began to sink along with New York, losing seven of eight from the 20th to the 30th. On the penultimate day of September, the Red Sox and Orioles battled for 10 innings in Baltimore, with staff aces Luis Tiant and Jim Palmer dueling it out for the full 10 frames. Both teams had scored in the first, and the game remained knotted at 1-1 until Boog Powell broke the tie in the bottom of the sixth with a solo homer off Tiant. The Sox responded in the top of the seventh when two-out hits by Carlton Fisk, rookie Dwight Evans, and second baseman Doug Griffin knotted the game back up at 2-2. Boston manager Eddie Kasko left Tiant in to lead off the 10th inning. Though Tiant popped out, Tommy Harper followed with a double to left center and moved to third on a groundout by Luis Aparicio, who had homered for the first Boston run in the first. That brought Carl Yastrzemski to the plate with two outs and the go-ahead run on third. True to his reputation, Yaz came through with a two-run homer to left and Tiant closed out the game himself, setting down the O's in order in the bottom of the 10th. The next day Marty Pattin beat Jim Dobson 3-1 to eliminate the Orioles for the first time in four years.

The Yankees were idle for those final two days of September, but the two Red Sox victories pushed them to the brink of elimination. On October 1, Gaylord Perry and Fritz Peterson did Tiant and Palmer one better, dueling for 11 innings in the first game of a Bronx doubleheader. The Yankees scored first in the bottom of the fourth when a two-out double by third baseman Bernie Allen plated Roy White, who had been hit by what one assumes was an errant spitter earlier in the inning. That lead lasted all of two batters as Cleveland catcher Ray Fosse led off the fifth with a solo home run. With the game still tied at 1-1, Perry struck out the side in the 10th and Buddy Bell led off the 11th with a double down the left field line. Bell moved to third on a groundout by Jack Brohamer and scored on a sac fly by future Yankee hero Chris Chambliss. Like Tiant, Perry closed the game himself, setting the Yankees down in order in the bottom of the 11th and eliminating them from the race.

That night, the Red Sox flew from Baltimore, where they had taken two of three from the Orioles, to Detroit for a three-game, season-ending set against the Tigers. When the Sox arrived in Michigan, they held a slim, half-game lead on Detroit. That half-game was a result of the truncated season. Although both teams had just three games left against each other, the Tigers had played an extra game because they had lost one less to the strike than the Red Sox had. Still, all the Red Sox had to do was win the series. If they took two of three from the Tigers, they'd win the pennant.

The first game pitted 24-year-old John Curtis for Boston against ace Mickey Lolich for Detroit. Lolich had started against the Red Sox on Opening Day, which also took place in Detroit. In the top of the first inning of that springtime game, the Sox loaded the bases on singles by their first three hitters, Tommy Harper, Luis Aparicio, and Carl Yastrzemski. A subsequent single by Rico Petrocelli plated Harper, but Aparicio got hung up on his way home, eventually retreating to third as Yastrzemksi approached from second. With both runners occupying third, Yastrzemski was called out. Danny Cater struck out to end the inning, and Lolich went on to pitch a complete game, beating the Sox by a single run, 3-2. Lolich had faced the Sox twice since then, both times pitching complete games to lead the Tigers to victory. With the division hanging in the balance, the two teams acted out the same script one more time.

Al Kaline got the Tigers out to an early lead with a one-out solo homer in the bottom of the first. Then, in the top of the third, Harper and Aparicio reached on singles to put runners on the corners with one out. Yastrzemski followed with a double off the top of the center field fence to score Harper, but as Aparicio rounded the bag, he slipped and fell.

"I hit the ball off Lolich," Yastrzemski remembered years later, "and when I was rounding first, I saw it hit the center-field fence. It hit right on top and bounced back toward center field. I was thinking inside-the-park home run because it bounced so far back. It hit that top steel. Then I'm heading into third and I see Aparicio laying on the ground and I was in shock."

"When I hit the base," Aparicio explained after the game, "I landed right on top of it and that threw me off, and when I hit the wet grass beyond the base I went down. I didn't think of trying for home then. I spiked myself. I screwed up the play."

Yastrzemski continued, "He comes back to third and I'm on third and I'm still thinking I'm going to go. So I pushed him off the bag and said, 'Luis, you can still make it.' And he started running and gets halfway and falls down again. I was all set, even watching the relay, before he fell down the second time, to still go for an inside-the-park home run and follow him in. I just couldn't believe it. One of the greatest base runners who ever lived. You don't mind getting beat, but not to have the best base runner the game had ever seen fall down twice going from third to home."

After his second fall, Aparicio saw the relay throw come in to Tigers catcher Duke Sims and he scrambled back to the bag, where Yastrzemski was waiting. Yastrzemski was ruled out (8-6-2-5). Though Harper's run had tied the game, the Tigers scored in the fifth, sixth, and eighth to win 4-1 as Lolich struck out 15 Red Sox on his way to yet another complete game and his 22nd win of the year. The loss put the Tigers in first place by a half-game, and the Red Sox's backs up against the wall. They'd have to win the next night to keep their pennant hopes alive.

Tuesday night's game pitted Tiant against Woodie Fryman, a veteran lefty whom the Tigers had claimed off waivers from the Phillies on August 2. Since joining the Tiger rotation a week after joining the team, Fryman had gone 9-3 with a 2.40 ERA in 13 starts. Boston took an early 1-0 lead on Fryman when Tommy Harper led off the game with a single, stole second, and scored on an error by second baseman Dick McAuliffe. Tiant, meanwhile, cruised until the sixth, when the Tigers managed to plate a leadoff walk to Norm Cash via a sacrifice bunt by slugger Willie Horton and a Jim Northrup RBI single. The Tigers broke the 1-1 tie the next inning when McAuliffe atoned for his first-inning error with a one-out double and came around to score on a single by Al Kaline, who in turn moved to second on the throw home. With that, Kasko removed Tiant from the game and brought in southpaw reliever Bill Lee to face the lefty-hitting Duke Sims. Sims hit a ground ball to Aparicio at short. Kaline hurdled the ball on his way to third base, distracting the Boston shortstop and allowing Sims's grounder to slip through to left field for a single that put runners on the corners.

The next batter, Norm Cash, hit a grounder to Yastrzemski at first. Kaline, dancing off third base, again distracted the Boston fielder just enough to result in an error that allowed Kaline to score the third Tiger run of the game. In the next frame, Yastrzemski singled and moved to second on a Fryman wild pitch, but he was the last Boston baserunner of the game. After Fryman got Reggie Smith and Petrocelli to fly out, Chuck Seelbach came on to retire Fisk and pitch a perfect ninth to clinch the division for Detroit.

The Sox won the final game of the year behind a gem by Marty Pattin, but it was for naught. Because of the truncated schedule, both the Red Sox and the Tigers finished with 70 losses, but the Red Sox, winners of 85 games, went home and the Tigers, winners of 86, went on to face the A's in the AL Championship Series, having won the division by a half a game. Among the games canceled in April were four head-to-head matchups between the Tigers and Red Sox, one of them in Detroit, where the Tigers held a 6-2 advantage over Boston on the season, and three of them in Boston, where the two teams had split six games.

Astonishingly, history repeated itself nine years later, not once but twice, when a player strike bifurcated the 1981 season. Rather than determine the division champions by cumulative record, the league decided to award the division leaders at the time of the strike a playoff spot and have them play an additional playoff round against the teams with the best records after the strike resumed. In the NL West, the Cincinnati Reds trailed the Los Angeles Dodgers by a half-game at the time of the strike, while the St. Louis Cardinals finished the second half of the season a half-game behind the Montreal Expos in the NL East. In both cases, the two teams separated by a half-game had the same number of losses. In both cases, the team trailing by a half-game failed to make the playoffs altogether. And in both cases, that team, the Cardinals in the NL East and the Reds in the NL West, finished the season with the best cumulative record in their division. The only other time a playoff berth was decided by a half-game in the standings was in the American League in 1908, though in that case, both the pennant-winning Tigers and the second-place Indians had 90 wins, but Cleveland had one more loss.

Baseball is a game of equal chances. Though nine innings is as arbitrary a limit as any other, it is less arbitrary than the clocks used in other team sports. Unlike basketball, football, hockey, soccer, and the rest, baseball doesn't end after a given amount of time, regardless of what has transpired on the field. Rather, it ends after the trailing team has been given an equal number of opportunities to match or exceed the accomplishments of the leader. Indeed, once past nine innings, this is the only limitation placed on the game's length. In schoolyards and on sandlots, this concept of last licks is many children's first concrete lesson in fairness. This ideal of equal opportunity has been undermined in the professional game in a variety of ways over the sport's history. In that sense, the conclusion of the 1972 AL East race provided another lesson to the schoolchildren of Boston, one easier to understand than the furor over desegregation busing that would soon embroil their city. Sometimes, kids, opportunities aren't equal; the world isn't always fair.

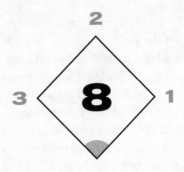

# 1973 National League East

*The Healing Power of Faith*

ALEX BELTH

The booze and smoke and good spirits were flowing at Willie Stargell's home in Pittsburgh on New Year's Eve. Some of his Pirate teammates who lived in town were there with their wives. Stargell was a warm, emotionally direct man who spoke softly and was concerned with putting his teammates at ease and having a laugh when he wasn't hitting long home runs. Soul music boomed from the stereo.

After midnight, a friend approached Stargell at the noisy party and told him something troubling he had just heard on the radio. Stargell went upstairs to listen for himself, then picked up the phone and called a friend who might have more information. By the time he hung the receiver up and walked back downstairs, people were quietly leaving.

Al Oliver had already returned home from Stargell's party and was lying in bed when the phone rang. "Scoop," said Stargell, "a plane went down in San Juan and they think Roberto was on board."

Oliver jumped out of bed and took a shower. He could not go back to sleep. Neither could any of the Pirates once they heard that their teammate, Roberto Clemente, might have been aboard a plane that had crashed outside San Juan, Puerto Rico. Pitchers Steve Blass and Dave Guisti had thrown their own raucous party across town that night. At 5:00 A.M. they drove to general manager Joe E. Brown's house, searching for more information. Later that morning they ar-

## 1973 National League East Prospectus

| | Actual Standings | | | | | Date Elim | Pythag | |
|---|---|---|---|---|---|---|---|---|
| Team | W | L | Pct | GB | DIF | | W | L |
| Mets | 82 | 79 | .509 | – | 21 | – | 83 | 78 |
| Cardinals | 81 | 81 | .500 | 1.5 | 52 | Oct 1 | 86 | 76 |
| Pirates | 80 | 82 | .494 | 2.5 | 35 | Oct 1 | 82 | 80 |
| Expos | 79 | 83 | .488 | 3.5 | 1 | Sept 30 | 77 | 85 |
| Cubs | 77 | 84 | .478 | 5.0 | 86 | Sept 30 | 76 | 85 |
| Phillies | 71 | 91 | .438 | 11.5 | 1 | Sept 21 | 73 | 89 |

| League Averages | | | | BP Stats Leaders | | | |
|---|---|---|---|---|---|---|---|
| AVG | OBP | SLG | BABIP | Offense, BRAA | | Indiv WARP | |
| .254 | .322 | .376 | .283 | Reds | 101 | Joe Morgan | 13.7 |
| ERA | K9 | BB9 | H9 | Pitching, PRAA | | Darrell Evans | 12.7 |
| 3.67 | 5.4 | 3.3 | 8.7 | Cubs | 90 | Seaver | 12.0 |

rived at Stargell's. Another teammate, Bob Moose, joined them. The four men sat there, hungover, and cried. Later, many Pirates gathered at broadcaster Bob Prince's annual New Year's Day party. "Nobody knew what to say to each other," recalled Oliver, so they acted like men and commiserated together in silence.

A major leaguer since 1955, Clemente was a perennial All-Star who felt he had been slighted by the press but had finally received his due after a brilliant performance in the 1971 World Series. Shortly after watching the Pirates win in seven games against the Orioles, Roger Angell wrote that Clemente had played "a kind of baseball that none of us had ever seen before—throwing and running and hitting at something close to the level of absolute perfection, playing to win but also playing the game almost as if it were a form of punishment for everyone else on the field."

"One couldn't face Roberto after having a bad game," Stargell later wrote. Clemente was stoic and reserved around outsiders, particularly the press, but he was engaged and at ease in a Pittsburgh clubhouse that was comfortable in its teasing, which included heavy ethnic name-calling. Guisti would scream at him in Italian, and Clemente would shout back in Spanish. Blass recalled Clemente chewing him out in jest when he found the pitcher reading a porn magazine in the whirlpool before Game 7 of the 1971 World Series. Blass was a cheerful, self-deprecating man; he and Clemente were not the best of friends, but they genuinely *liked* each other. Blass was chosen to deliver a eulogy on behalf of the Pirates at Clemente's funeral in Puerto

Rico on January 3. His words were an adaptation of a poem read at Lou Gehrig's funeral decades earlier. Like the Iron Horse, Clemente would be quickly ushered into the Hall of Fame.

◆

Joe Torre smoked a long, black cigar in the visitors' locker room in Philadelphia while he watched the live broadcast of former White House council John Dean speaking in front of a Senate Watergate Committee hearing. Torre was a grave-looking, heavyset man. It was late June 1973, and it was hot. Reserve catcher Tim McCarver remembered that of all his teammates, Torre was the most interested in the hearings. Most guys in the league paid little attention, but Torre was intrigued.

John Dean's voice was hoarse as he sat in front of the committee for the second straight day and explained in detail how his former boss, Richard M. Nixon was in on the cover-up of the Watergate break-in and how the president also kept an extensive list of his enemies. Dean was a mild-mannered man in brown tortoise shell glasses. He looked like an accountant.

The Watergate hearings were a little more than one month old, and Dean was aware that he was in a David vs. Goliath situation. A good many Americans may have suspected that the president was capable of breaking the law—he wasn't called Tricky Dick for nothing—but Nixon had not been found guilty of any misdoings yet. In charging the President of the United States with being a crook, Dean was a man alone. But he spoke "with deadly earnestness," according to the *New York Times*. "He wants to be believed."

A respected veteran hitter who had been league MVP in 1971, Torre was doggedly committed to playing by the rules, either of baseball or of government. But like Dean, he was not afraid to speak his mind, even at the risk of alienating his employers. Torre's affiliation with the Players Association had already caused him to be traded once, from Atlanta to St. Louis in 1969; he was ripped by the fans on the road and at home for his role in the strike of 1972. "I understood why they were booing, but I was hurt," he remembered years later. "I was too sensitive about it. I tried so hard there, I self-destructed so to speak."

Along with Tom Seaver and Jim Perry, Torre was the most visible player representative in the game. He had become a presence at the bargaining table alongside Marvin Miller, the executive director of the Player's Association, and Miller's head council, Dick Moss. Torre had worked on Wall Street and in the finance industry during the off-season for years. He understood power brokers and how to handle himself in their midst. John Gaherin, the owner's council, told historian Chuck Korr that Torre was "the original godfather, talking out of a cloud of cigar smoke." He recalled Torre as a level-headed optimist in a room dominated by pessimism and volatility.

The Phillies and the Cardinals were playing two that day, and Torre spoke to a *New York Times* writer about the difficulties of the St. Louis season. The Cards started the year by losing 20 of their first 25 games, and then played better-than-.600 ball for three months. Torre explained that one of the critical reasons for the team's success was improved relations with management, particularly with the Cardinals' owner, Gussie Busch.

Busch was a Nixon man. He was unable to understand the players' need for a union any more than he or the president could comprehend the protests and picketing by young Americans across the country. More than any other sport, baseball represented the Old Guard. Only a few years earlier, Dodger owner Walter O'Malley said, "These are times when people spit on the flag, when priests go over the fence. You have to understand the pattern of things today. There is rebellion against the establishment and baseball is linked to the establishment."

Busch had been good to his boys; he treated his players better than any owner in the National League. What did he get in return? Ingrates who wanted more rights and more money. In 1972, Busch finally lost his composure. "Let 'em strike," he barked to reporters in a hotel lobby shortly before the players did just that. The first major strike in American sports history lasted ten days, exposing the collective weaknesses of the owners, while fanning the resentment of fans and sportswriters alike. But it was hard for the players to feel that they had won anything when they went back out to play in front of thousands of increasingly disillusioned and spiteful fans.

Busch allowed his anger to get the better of him. He traded two pitchers holding out for more money: Jerry Reuss and Steve Carlton. Ted Simmons, a promising 22-year old catcher, could not agree to terms with the team either and played without a new contract. Under the reserve clause, his previous contract was simply renewed. But if Simmons went the entire season without coming to a new agreement, he would be able to challenge the legality of the reserve clause. That was easier said than done and his teammates admired Simmons' resolve, especially during the long, cruel baseball summer. In the end, Busch blinked first and coughed-up a new two-year deal by early August.

The owners did score a victory when former Cardinal Curt Flood lost his antitrust suit against MLB in the Supreme Court in June of 1972. Flood was old news for Busch but a constant reminder of everything that he could not comprehend about the direction America was headed. By the time his case reached the high courts, Flood had fled the country, an emotionally distraught man. In *Our Gang*, Phillip Roth's 1971 comedic novel about Nixon, Flood appears as a prominent member of the president's list of enemies.

"Flood, and his mouthpiece [former Supreme Court Justice, Arthur] Goldberg, appeared to be out to destroy the game beloved by millions," says one of the president's advisors in the novel. Marvin Miller later noted, "Roth was joking, but the point survives the exaggeration: What Flood was trying to do was perceived as a revolution."

The St. Louis clubhouse had been known for its harmony in the sixties but was now an antiseptic, cold place. However, in the off-season, Busch had a change of heart about his players. He despised Marvin Miller and the union, but Busch still had paternalistic feelings for his boys. He was a benevolent dictator and couldn't keep a grudge forever. No player saw his salary cut: general manager Bing Devine spoke to Torre and some other players during the off-season, and relations between players and management thawed considerably.

The Cards and Phils split the doubleheader that day, putting St. Louis's record at 34-36. The Redbirds were eight games out and still believed they would finish first. In this they were no different from every other team in the National League East. Earlier that spring, Yogi Berra, the Mets manager, predicted that it would take just 85 victories to win the division.

In a season in which the American League introduced the designated hitter and Hank Aaron closed in on Babe Ruth's venerated home run mark, it seemed as if nobody wanted to win the NL East. Each team except the Phillies—who had improved just slightly from their miserable 59-97 showing in 1972—had reason to believe they could win. The Pirates had the best hitting and had won the East the previous three seasons (they would win it seven times in the decade). The Cubs lineup included veteran sluggers like Billy Williams and Ron Santo as well as an ace pitcher in Fergie Jenkins; the Mets had superior starting pitching, led by Tom Seaver; even the Expos put together their best season to date, propelled by breakout seasons from outfielder Ken Singleton, fireman Mike Marshall, and rookie starter Steve Rogers.

As it turned out, the winner of the East would own the dubious distinction of having the worst record of any playoff team in baseball history (just a single game worse than the 2006 Cardinals and a half-game better than the 2005 Padres). But mediocrity in no way lessened the tension and excitement of the unpredictable, free-for-all battle that September, which saw no fewer than five of the six teams in contention for the flag in the final days of the season.

Tug McGraw, the charismatic relief pitcher for the Mets, coined the phrase, "You Gotta Believe" that summer, and, as it goes with McGraw, there was a funny story behind that one.

In a year when cynicism ran deep, in and out of the game, "You Gotta Believe" was a rallying cry that every team in the East could have applied to its season. It was a slogan made for Madison Avenue, but made innocently enough—it was intended to be taken at face value, without guile. It was a reminder that in spite of the increased labor tensions, which regularly competed with game stories for headlines, baseball still provided shelter from the troubles of every day life. Americans' belief in their government was shaken, and baseball fans' belief in the players, the owners, even their own perception of the sport as a symbol of less complicated times had been profoundly disturbed. Still, McGraw said, "You Gotta Believe." He never said in what—perhaps just the fantasy that professional sports were still a game.

The most enduring line from that summer belonged to Yogi, of course, or was at least attributed to him. (Yogi was like Carson; he had writers). Yes, if the 1973 NL East demonstrated any one thing about baseball, it would have to be that "It ain't over 'til it's over."

♦

During spring training, Clemente's absence was just beginning to hit many of his teammates; still, the Pirates were a formidable offensive team with decent pitching. Blass had an uncommonly good spring. A control pitcher just coming into his own, Blass had been the surprise hero of the 1971 World Series, but refused to let sudden success go to his head. "You can't get carried away by what happened in one week," he said in 1972. "You can't allow it to make you think you're something that you're not."

Blass won 19 games in 1972, going 8-1 with an ERA well below 2.00 over the last two months of the season. But in his first 11 starts of 1973, Blass was 3-3 with an 8.21 ERA. He was not overly concerned, as he remembered, incorrectly, having had worse stretches to start a season. But as May turned to June, something appeared to be seriously wrong. Blass's splendid control deserted him, and soon he was in something more than a slump. He had never experienced control problems in his life before; now he simply could not get his body to do what it had always done effortlessly.

For hitters, facing Blass became a frightening experience recalled Tim McCarver. The pitcher's wildness was particularly nerve-racking for right-handers, as Blass was wild up, so everything went toward their heads. In June against the Braves, he hit rock bottom. On Friday night, the 11th, he was knocked out of the box in the third inning, having allowed five runs on eight hits. Two days later, brought into the game in the fourth inning with the Pirates down 8-3, Blass pitched one and a third innings and surrendered seven runs on five hits, six walks, and three wild pitches. The Pirates ended the day 24-30, nine games out of first place.

"You have no idea how frustrating it is," Blass later told *Sports Illustrated*. "You don't know where you're going to throw the ball. You're afraid you might hurt someone. You know you're embarrassing yourself but you can't do anything about it. You're helpless. Totally afraid and helpless."

Over the course of the season, Blass received every kind of advice possible. Everybody had a theory as to what was wrong, and everyone offered a cure. He saw a shrink, tried meditation, and was grateful for the support he received, but nothing helped. He believed that he would snap out of it eventually. There was nothing physically wrong with him, and while he retained his sense of humor, he receded into the background. He became almost unnaturally calm, making a deliberate effort to take it all in stride. Perhaps he was taking it too well. Guisti remembered Blass's wife asking him to shake her husband up, but Guisti was careful not to probe too deeply and risk losing a friend in the process.

The following season, in a profile for *Sports Illustrated*, Pat Jordan said that Blass was a lot like the stock Woody Allen character. "Like Allen he is forever mocking his success and himself, as if secretly he distrusts it all," wrote Jordan. "Blass gives the impression that he feels he is losing things he has possessed fraudulently. Sooner or later he had always expected to be exposed."

◆

Blass was not the only pitcher searching for clues early in the summer. Tug McGraw, the Mets demonstrative and wildly entertaining closer, was also having the worst slump of his career. Over the previous two seasons, McGraw put up a 1.70 ERA in 217 innings. He was handsomely rewarded when the Mets made him the highest-paid relief pitcher in National League history, with a $75,000 contract. McGraw had a broad, cartoonish jaw and a mischievous smile. He was like a hyperactive child and projected a kid's love for the game. During batting practice, when pitchers shag fly balls, McGraw would hang back and then make daring dives. When he walked off the field after a big out, he would slap his glove hand on his thigh, hollering. Is it any surprise that his best pitch was the screwball? "He had four or five different words for titties," remembered Mets outfielder Ron Swoboda, "very much a California mentality."

Yet for all of his exuberance, McGraw was troubled. After the Kent State shootings in May of 1970—when National Guardsmen killed four students and wounded nine others during a demonstration—McGraw fell into a depression, and was temporarily unable to perform. That summer, he wrote in his diary:

"I want to know the difference between right and wrong: I don't. Sometimes you think you do because you have been brought up a certain way, the way of your parents or school, church or country. But every morning you wake up only to discover that your parents are divorced, your school is not with it and your church is struggling, and, worst of all, your country is falling apart."

McGraw, who served a brief stint in the Marines during the mid-1960s, was equally disillusioned with the government as he was with the student protest movement. "It must be the people that are screwed up," he wrote. "I don't know in which direction to head or what to do. Why? Because I'm a people and I'm screwed up. I think the reason I love baseball so much is because when I come into a game in the bottom of the ninth, bases loaded, no one out and a one-run lead...it takes people off my mind."

The Mets had fielded decent teams in the three years since they won the World Series in 1969, but they were not a force. Pitching was their strength. Tom Seaver was arguably the best starter in the game, Jerry Koosman was a talented number two (though he was coming off a rough season), and John Matlack was a formidable number three. But the Mets didn't have enough offense. They also had a bad habit of trading away valuable young players. Nolan Ryan was the most famous Met to be shipped off, but Amos Otis, Ken Singleton, Tim Foli and Mike Jorgenson were traded away as well.

When manager Gil Hodges died in the spring of 1972, the Mets promoted coach Yogi Berra in to replace him. Berra hadn't managed since the Yankees let him go for winning the pennant but not the

World Series in 1964. Berra was liked by his players but the running joke on the Mets was that the difference between Yogi and Hodges was three innings. In the third inning, Hodges was thinking about what he wanted to do in the sixth inning, and in the sixth inning, Yogi was thinking about what he should have done in the third. The Mets also acquired Willie Mays, another New York icon of the fifties, who was at the end of his career. In a baseball sense, Mays had returned home to die. He was well-liked by his teammates but utterly mortal on the field, a sight that pained many longtime fans.

New York was hammered by injuries during the first part of the 1973 season—catcher Jerry Grote and shortstop Bud Harrelson were two of the most crucial losses. McGraw started the season well enough, allowing two runs over eleven innings in April. Then on a Friday night in early May at Shea, the Mets were leading the Houston Astros 5-2 in the eighth inning. The bases were loaded and there was one man out when McGraw replaced Koosman and promptly walked the first batter he faced to force in a run. He struck out Lee May, then walked the following two batters to tie the game. Berra yanked him. McGraw could not get over it—both his inability to throw strikes and the fact that he was pulled from the game.

McGraw's ERA was 5.95 in May and 6.00 in June. On July 3 the southpaw came into the game in the fifth inning against the Expos. The Mets were trailing 6-5. He walked a man and then got a lucky double play. But in the sixth, McGraw gave up three walks, a single, a double, and a homer, seven runs in all.

"I didn't have any idea how to throw the baseball," McGraw wrote in his book *Screwball* (published the following spring). "It was as though I'd never played before in my entire life. I just felt like dropping to my knees and saying: Shit, I don't know what to do."

When the team returned from Montreal, McGraw went to see his friend Joe Badamo, an insurance salesman who had been close with Hodges. Badamo was something of a motivational coach, and McGraw had been meeting him regularly for years. Badamo told McGraw that he had to believe in himself and to visualize success. On his way into Shea Stadium that night, he met a group of fans waiting for the players. They asked McGraw what was wrong with the team. "There's nothing wrong with the Mets. You gotta believe!"

Shortly thereafter, M. Donald Grant, the owner's right-hand man, gave the team an old-fashioned pep talk. The team was now squarely in last place despite another brilliant season from Seaver. Grant fancied himself a baseball expert and was sincere with the players even if he came across as a stuffed shirt. During the speech, he mentioned that the team had to believe in themselves. When he left the room, Mc-Graw popped off his stool, flexed like a pro wrestler, and yelled, "You Gotta Believe! You Gotta Believe!"

He cracked his teammates up, but McGraw's performance did not improve. Finally, by the middle of July, he was "demoted" to the starting rotation. On July 17, McGraw allowed seven runs on 10 hits over six innings. The Mets scored seven in the ninth and won the game. He didn't pitch again until July 30, when he fared better this time, only giving up one run in five and two-thirds innings in a 5-2 loss.

◆

While McGraw struggled to regain his groove, the best screwball in the league was being thrown by a right-hander, fellow relief pitcher Mike Marshall. A converted infielder with a stocky body and a sharp mind, Marshal was an academic fascinated by the science of pitching and was working toward a Ph.D. He was 27 when he arrived in Montreal during the 1970 season, and he quickly hit it off with Gene Mauch, the team's tough, controlling manager.

"He was very receptive to collaboration," Marshall recalled. "I've never seen a manager more in touch with his players. He was great with the players who knew what the hell they were doing. He could also be cantankerous with the idiots on the team."

Mauch admired Bob Bailey, the team's veteran slugger, and absolutely loved Tim Foli, his volatile shortstop. Foli's nickname when he played for the Mets was "Crazy Horse." He made a name for himself fighting with coaches, teammates, opposing players, and umpires. Easygoing Eddie Kranepool once punched him in the mouth. After going 0-5 with several errors in a minor league game, Foli took his glove and record player to the field that night and slept next to second base, swearing to himself that he'd never have such a bad game again. "He had a bad night and he went home to sleep," said Mauch later. "His home is shortstop, that's all."

Mauch did not have a playoff-caliber team in 1973. Montreal's fielding was awful, and they didn't have enough starting pitching. But the emergence of Ken Singleton (.302/.425/.479), along with a thrilling second-half rookie debut by high-strung right-hander Steve Rogers (10-5, 1.54 ERA in 134 innings), gave the enthusiastic Montreal fans something to get juiced about. Marshall was a key reason for their improvement. He had been lobbying Mauch, his frequent bridge partner, to use him more often ever since he arrived in Montreal. "He was a stubborn SOB," said Marshall, who threw 111 innings in 1971 and 116 the following year; in 1973, he tossed 179 innings—all in relief—to the tune of a 2.66 ERA.

Meanwhile, in Chicago, the Cubs spent most of the summer in first place. But Chicago was an old team. Ron Santo was having a disappointing season, and though his final numbers were more than decent (.267/.348/.440), it would be his last as a Cub. Fergie Jenkins, with a losing record (14-16) after winning 20 games for six straight years, would also be traded during the winter. Still, the Cubs overachieved, thanks largely to strong first-half performances from Rick Monday (.267/.372/.469) and Jose Cardenal (.303/.375/.437). But it all came to an end in the thick of the summer; Chicago was 52-46 through July 22, 25-38 thereafter.

The Cardinals, led by Lou Brock (.297/.364/.398) and Ted Simmons (.310/.370/.438), snatched first place from the withering Cubs on July 22 and stayed there until the last day of August. But they lost their ace, 37-year-old Bob Gibson, to a knee injury on August 4. The team's record was 12-18 for the month, yet they managed to remain in first place. When the Cardinals beat the Mets 1-0 in 10 innings on August 30, Tom Seaver's record fell to 15-8 (though his ERA was 1.71). Seaver went the distance in the loss. With 23 games left in the season, the standings were fairly close (Table 8-1).

Table 8-1 National League East Standings, August 30, 1973

| Team | W | L | GB |
|------|---|---|-----|
| St. Louis | 68 | 65 | – |
| Pittsburgh | 63 | 65 | 2.5 |
| Chicago | 64 | 67 | 3.0 |
| Montreal | 62 | 70 | 5.5 |
| Phillies | 62 | 71 | 6.0 |
| New York | 61 | 71 | 6.5 |

The Pirates tied the Cardinals for first place on September 1, but then lost four of the next five games, which resulted in the firing of manager Bill Virdon. Old, reliable Danny Murtaugh, in his fourth stint as Pirates skipper, replaced Virdon. But the Pirates had struggled all season long with their roster. Catcher Manny Sanguillen replaced Clemente, his best friend, in right field. The experiment lasted through the middle of June, at which point Sanguillen returned to catching. Gene Clines was given a shot in right for a while but that didn't work out either—he had little power. They finally went with rookie Richie Zisk, their best choice. Zisk hit .344/.381/.532 as a right fielder. By then, however, the Pirates had blown some opportunities.

The Pirates couldn't decide if Sanguillen or Milt May should be the full-time catcher, whether Bob Robertson or Al Oliver should be the everyday first baseman. They also struggled to solidify their middle in-field positions. Dave Cash and Rennie Stennett platooned at second base, while Gene Alley, Jakie Hernandez, Stennett and the veteran Dal Maxvill jockeyed for time at short. Maxvill got the majority of playing time, and hit .189/.261/.235, lousy even for a shortstop. It was as if everything had gone awry in Pittsburgh.

Willie Stargell had reluctantly accepted the role of team captain earlier in the season, and was having a sensational year (.299/.392/.646), with 43 doubles, 44 homers and a 119 RBI, but the team was underachieving. "I think we needed Roberto to push us," Stargell wrote in his autobiography. "Without him, there wasn't anyone around to crack the whip. Subconsciously, we waited."

On September 11th in Chicago, Murtaugh gave Steve Blass a start, the pitcher's first in six weeks. Blass had spent most of the summer pitching batting practice. The Pirates had called up a kid named Miguel Dilone just to stand at the plate as Blass pitched. "I pounded him," says Blass today. "It got so that he'd hide in the hotel lobby when I was ready to pitch BP. He knew he was going to get it again." Blass walked around Chicago until 5:30 in the morning before the start, ob-sessing about his mechanics. He didn't perform too badly either, allow-ing just two runs on two hits and five walks in five innings. The Pirates lost, but Blass was encouraged. When he was taken out of the game he called his wife from the clubhouse and said, "I'm back!" The Pirates leap-frogged St. Louis into first place the next day and remained there when they began a five-game, home-and-away series against the Mets beginning on September 17th. They were 7-3 under Murtaugh.

For their part, the Mets had been surging, going 12-5 since that 1-0 loss to the Cards at the end of August. They were finally healthy and McGraw was on a roll. While Seaver was tiring, Koosman and Mat-lack were pitching well. But it was an unlikely lefty, George Stone (4-0, 2.15 ERA in September), who was making a major contribution, just as the normally light hitter Wayne Garrett was now the team's hottest hitter (.315/.407/.598 in September). New York began the two-game set in Pittsburgh just two and a half behind the Pirates. But Seaver was bombed, losing 10-3, and the defending champs looked primed to pull away from the rest of the division. The following night, the Mets trailed 4-1 going into the ninth inning, but then scored five runs and went on to win, 6-5.

Stone and McGraw combined to give the Mets a 7-3 victory the next night as the series shifted to New York, where Willie Mays announced that he would retire at the end of season. "It's been a wonderful 22 years," he told reporters. "I'm not just getting out of baseball because I'm hurt. I just feel that the people of America shouldn't have to see a guy play who can't produce."

On September 20, the Pirates held leads of 1-0, 2-1, and 3-2 before the Mets tied the game in the bottom of the ninth on Duffy Dyer's single to left field. The score remained even when Richie Zisk singled off of Ray Sadecki with one out in the top of the thirteenth inning. Manny Sanguillen flied out to right for the second out, and then Dave Augustine, a recent call-up from the minors, lined a shot to left over the head of Cleon Jones. The crowd at Shea gasped as the ball headed for the fence. The ball did not clear the left field wall, but hit precisely on the top of the wall. It did not skip over for a home run or ricochet wildly back onto the field of play. It bounced into Jones's glove. The left fielder spun and fired a strike to the cutoff man, Garrett, who then pegged the slow-footed Zisk out at the plate by several feet.

Catcher Ron Hodges singled home the winning run in the bottom of the inning and the Mets were suddenly just a half-game behind the Pirates. Sensing the drama of the moment, more than 51,000 New Yorkers piled into Shea the next night to watch Seaver, working on four days' rest, start the most important game of the season. Blass started for the Pirates and didn't make it out of the first inning (he later called his return start in Chicago "a head fake"). It was the second-to-last start of his big-league career. Seaver went the distance in a 10-2 laugher. Garrett and Grote each had three hits, Jones and Rusty Staub both homered. The Mets reached the .500 mark for the first time since May, and they were in first place. The Pirates were a half-game back, the Cards a game back, the Expos 1.5 games behind, and the Cubs only 2.5 games out of first.

A week later, little had changed. The Mets were still hot. Going into the final weekend of the season, they led the Pirates by 1.0, the Cards by 2.5, and the Expos by 3.5. The Cubs were technically still alive at 4.0 back. In the NL West, the Big Red Machine in Cincinnati had finally overwhelmed a talented young Dodgers club and was favored to represent the National League in the World Series, no matter what happened in the East.

The Pirates and Expos played each other, while the Cards played the Phillies and the Mets and Cubs squared off. The Expos beat Pittsburgh on Friday and Saturday, putting an ugly end to a painful season for the Pirates, although Pittsburgh came back and clobbered Montreal on Sunday. With Gibson returning and going six innings in a 5-1 win, the Cards swept the Phillies, winning their last five games in a row and finishing at 81-81. The Mets and Cubs waited in the Chicago rain. "The field is absolutely bad, almost a quagmire," said the chief umpire, "and the forecast is bad for tomorrow." When Friday's game was called, a double header was scheduled for Saturday. Saturday's rains melted any opportunity for games, and doubleheaders were set for Sunday and Monday.

"It's nice to be at home when there are delays like this," said Ron Santo. "You can just go home and relax a lot more. The Mets have to sit around the hotel and try to kill time."

With four games scheduled for two days, the Mets' lead over the Cardinals was 1.5 games on Sunday morning, just two over the Pirates. The Cubs beat the Mets 1-0 in the opener as Rick Reuschel out-dueled John Matlack, but Koosman shut the Cubs down in the second game as the Mets pounded Jenkins, 9-2, to clinch at least a tie of the division.

St. Louis was only a half-game out. Joe Torre and Tim McCarver watched the Mets game at a convention hall in Atlantic City, where they were being paid $500 to glad-hand businessmen at a paper convention. The teammates saw the game on TV and prayed for the Mets to lose. They wanted nothing more than to be in New York on the following day, facing the Mets in a one-game playoff.

Seaver took the hill late Monday morning in front of fewer than 2,000 fans at Wrigley Field. It was overcast, and the field was a soggy mess. Seaver, exhausted, allowed 11 hits and four runs over six innings while striking out only two. But in the second inning, Cleon Jones hit his seventh home run in 11 days, and Grote singled home two more runs in the fourth. Mayor John Lindsey of New York was addressing 500 recruits at the Police Academy on 20th Street that morning in Manhattan. When he gave a score update, Mets 5, Cubs 2, the auditorium erupted. Rusty Staub went 4-for-5, and Tug McGraw pitched three scoreless innings as the Mets hung on, 6-4. The Mets had won the division.

That soggy September day, a pot of chicken soup simmered in the visitors' locker room at Wrigley Field as the Mets congratulated each other. "That's the hottest champagne I've ever drunk," said one New Yorker. The Mets' celebration was muted, as there was still one game left to play. Five minutes later, the second game was called and the place went bananas. "One, two, three, you gotta bee-lieve," chanted McGraw. "Unbelievable," said Wayne Garrett. "You couldn't have convinced me two months ago we'd win."'

From August 22 on, McGraw went 5-0 with 12 saves in 40 innings, allowing 12 walks while striking out 38. He did not surrender a lead once. "It was like, we couldn't believe we had won it and that nobody wanted to win it. It got dumped in our lap," Koosman remembered.

"I hit .239 and we finished the season in Chicago," said Ed Kranepool after the game. "In 1969 I hit .239 and we finished in Chicago too. Next year I'm going to hit .239 again. In between I've hit .270 and .260 and we haven't won. I can make us all more money hitting .239."

It was still several years before Atlantic City got a gambling license. Instead of going to New York for a playoff game, Torre and McCarver were stuck by the seaside in a dead-end town. "A bad trade-off," said McCarver. Bob Gibson later said that losing the division after rebounding from such a horrid start was "agonizing." Surely the Cardinals would have won the division had Gibson not been hurt. Then again, if Clemente were alive and Blass hadn't gone from 19 wins to just three, the Pirates would still be champs. And if Chicago hadn't traded Ken Holtzman, who went 21-13 with a 2.97 ERA in 297 innings for the Oakland A's, maybe they would have won it.

McGraw and his teammates latched onto a catchy phrase with "You Gotta Believe," and it is tempting to imagine it was their collective faith that won the division, but this is too easy an answer. More likely, the Mets simply got hot at the right time, while the Pirates could not overcome a season of missed opportunities. After all, no player displayed more hope and faith than Steve Blass, but believing did him little good.

For Gibson, the sting was lessened only by the Mets' success in the playoffs—at least the Cards weren't the only ones losing to New York. The Mets beat the big, bad Red Machine in a tense five-game series and eventually came within a game of a championship against the A's. The playoffs and World Series were filled with memorable moments— the Pete Rose–Buddy Harrelson fight, Pedro Borbon literally taking a bite out of a Mets hat, Willie Mays on his knees protesting to the home plate ump—but it was New York's valiant playoff run that made the 1973 team, and the division race, famous. To this day, the most popular rallying cry at Shea Stadium remains "You Gotta Believe."

## The Great All-Time Anti-Pennant Race

CLAY DAVENPORT

*There was no "one, two, three, and away" but they began running when they liked, and left off when they liked, so that it was not easy to know when the race was over. However, when they had been running half an hour or so, and were quite dry again, the Dodo suddenly called out "The race is over!" and they all crowded round it, panting, and asking, "But who has won?"*

*This question the Dodo could not answer without a great deal of thought, and it sat for a long time with one finger pressed upon its forehead (the position in which you usually see Shakespeare, in the pictures of him), while the rest waited in silence. At last the Dodo said, "EVERYBODY has won, and all must have prizes."*

—Lewis Carroll, *Alice in Wonderland,* chapter 3

Inspired by the 1973 Mets, whose 82-79 record was the worst among pennant winners to that point in history, the Anti-Pennant Race was originally a thought experiment designed to find the worst baseball teams ever; along the way, it evolved into an actual experiment, matching up selected teams in a simulated league in a round-robin playoff race to the bottom. In a league composed of the most unlucky, underfinanced, ill-planned teams in major league history, which clubs would prove unable to withstand even this hobbled level of competition? It is very difficult to build a great baseball team. It is, perhaps, more difficult to build a perfectly bad one. Through our simulation, we would attempt to find the worst of the worst.

In choosing which teams would compete, we had to address several key issues. First is that major league baseball has, by the evidence of studies on baseball and athletics in general, been increasing in quality over time. Even a bad team from recent years would run rings around the best teams from 1900 (though perhaps not if it had to play by 19th-century rules, without gloves). Our first rule, then, is that we would only consider how bad a team is compared with its own time.

The quality of a team depends very much on the structure of its league. The National Association, which allowed any team to join as long as it paid the $10 entrance fee, found itself saddled with extremely weak teams like the 1872 Brooklyn Eckford club (3-26), the 1873 Elizabeth Resolutes (2-21), or any of the bottom six clubs of 1875, which combined to go 21-144. The National League of the 1890s allowed individuals to own more than one team, which resulted in a wave of consolidation in which virtually every team cooperated with another and then made sweetheart trades to stack the best players onto just one of the two clubs, even while both played in the same league. Most attempted to maintain a façade of legitimacy for both clubs. But ultimately, "syndicate baseball" produced the 1899 Cleveland Spiders, a team so thoroughly despoiled by the co-owned St. Louis Browns (later the Cardinals) that they stopped bothering to even schedule home games (they became known, informally, as the Cleveland Exiles), falling to a ridiculous 20-134 record. The Cleveland fiasco led to rule changes prohibiting dual ownership in following years, and four teams—including Cleveland—were contracted from the league in 1900. In view of these failings, we seriously considered excluding all teams of the 1800s from consideration.

We also decided that the Federal League would be excluded, although its only possible claimant—the 1915 Baltimore Terrapins, who were just 47-107—has great historical significance. The Terrapins were the club left out when the American and National leagues negotiated a settlement that disbanded the Federal League; the Baltimore club's subsequent lawsuit, appealed to the Supreme Court, resulted in the decision that baseball was entertainment, not commerce, and not subject to the Sherman Anti-Trust Act. An earlier lawsuit, by the Terrapins and the rest of the Federal League, had landed in the court of Judge Kenesaw Mountain Landis, whose efforts to drag out the case proved so agreeable to the existing major leagues that they eventually made him the first commissioner of baseball.

To make the league geographically diverse, we decided that no two teams from the same city would be included—saving us from a virtual flood of Philadelphia entries. For chronological spread, we tried several approaches, mandating that five, six, or seven years separate the teams to be included, but we ultimately decided that a one-per-decade approach gave us a better mix of teams for the tournament. We selected these teams on the basis of their record, as well as Baseball Prospectus's wins above replacement (WARP), which measures the sum total of a player's batting, fielding, and pitching contributions. From a team's total WARP, we can estimate what their record should have been. The teams with the lowest scores in each decade (from an average of their WARP record and their real record) would make our list, provided the team didn't come from a city already represented.

Eliminating all pre-1900 teams left us with only 11 decades to work with. This made for a thoroughly undesirable number of teams—11 is a number completely absent from major league history. We could go to 12 teams—the number of teams in the National League from 1892 to 1899, which led to the nickname "Big League"—but then we'd have to either let the Spiders back in or take in a wild-card team from somewhere. We could drop down to eight, which is the number of teams most frequently used by the major leagues, as well as a nice power of two for an elimination tournament. The temptation to see what the Spiders would do, even in a league full of losers, proved too great to resist.

Having elected to go with 12 teams, we then used the format of the 12-team major leagues from the 1970s and 1980s—two divisions, 162 games, and unbalanced schedules. The competitors, if you can call them that, are the following:

*The 1899 Cleveland Spiders.* The 1898 edition of this franchise had gone 81-68, finishing fourth in a 12-team league. Three future Hall of Famers graced the roster—Jesse Burkett, Bobby Wallace, and Cy Young. Before 1899, all three had been transported to St. Louis, as had anything else that wasn't nailed down. No other team in major league history, playing a 100-game schedule or longer, finished within 12 games of the 1899 Spiders' record; no team since 1899 has been within 16. Their batting rated 191 runs below average, their fielding was 157 runs below average, and their pitching was 244 runs below; each of those values is worse than those of any other team in the tournament. The Spiders had starting pitchers who went 4-30, 4-22, 2-17, and 1-18. The team's best hitter was below league average. From August 26, 1899, until the end of the season, the Spiders went 1-40. The last game of the season was pitched by a hotel clerk. In our league of teams that got beat, they are the team to beat.

*The 1904 Washington Senators.* The Senators have the second-worst record in the history of the American League, a dreadful 38-113. New York Highlanders (Yankees) ace Jack Chesbro by himself won three more games than did the whole Senators team. Much like a later incarnation of the Washington franchise, the Senators were wards of their league. Lacking ownership, the team had to be staffed with leftovers. "I have promised the Washington people a good club for the coming season and I will keep my word," American League president Ban Johnson said. "Every club in the American League has from four to twelve extra men they cannot use, and if Washington needs additional players they will get first call." In other words, the Senators would be populated in the same way as a latter-day expansion club. They also suffered because the team's best player, Ed Delahanty, had died jumping the club the previous summer. The pitching staff featured three 20-game losers, led by the ironically named Happy Townsend at 5-26. Rating at –130 runs defensively, the Senators are the worst fielding team in the group other than the Spiders.

*The 1916 Philadelphia A's.* You might have read about the great A's pennant winners of the 1910s, the team propelled by the "$100,000 Infield." Well, the 1916 club wasn't them. Owner-manager Connie Mack decided to hold the salary line when the formation of the rival Federal League created a short period of salary inflation. The players from his 1914 AL champion team either followed the paychecks to the new league ("Gettysburg Eddie" Plank, Charles "Chief" Bender), held out all season (Frank Baker), or demanded and received trades (Eddie Collins). Mack also hinted, somewhat mysteriously, that a clubhouse rift was a bigger motivator than the payroll in breaking up his club. Eschewing minor leaguers, Mack restocked his roster with raw players who he believed were capable of learning on the job. Unfortunately, not all of them could play. Shortstop Whitey Witt exemplified Mack's approach, both to recruitment and to salaries. The rookie infielder signed with Mack at 19 and was in the bigs at 20. In 1916 he made a remarkable 78 errors. "I signed with the A's right out of high school for $300," Witt said many years later. "I got $500 raises each year through 1921, and when I signed with the Yankees, I got $9000." At 36-117, the 1916 A's had the worst record in the history of the American League, three games behind the 1904 Senators. At one point they lost 20 straight games. "We are the little tonic team of baseball," said Mack. "We come along when any other club is sick and get it back to health." On a happier note, they were only 54 runs below their league's average offensively, making them the best-hitting team in the tournament.

*The 1925 Boston Red Sox.* A truly depressing tale of two cities: The worst-rated 19 teams of the 1920s are all Phillies, A's, Red Sox, and Braves. The 1928 Phillies were the lowest-rated team of the decade, but the 1916 A's were even worse and thereby eliminate all other Philadelphia teams. The 1925 Red Sox weren't as bad as their 1932 squad, which holds the title for worst team in the 1930s, but we didn't have to go up as far to find another city to represent the 1930s as we would have here. Fronted by the underfunded J. A. Robert Quinn, the Red Sox went 47-105. The team featured Howard Ehmke on the mound, one of the best pitchers to ever lose 20 games; his 9-20 record belies his 3.73 ERA, a half-run better than the league average, even before adjusting for the bad defense behind him. He went on to World Series glory a few years later when he was traded to the A's; his teammate Red Ruffing did the same after being traded to the Yankees. The best hitter on the team, right fielder Ike Boone, went nowhere. This minor league star was signed by Quinn after leading the Texas League in batting average (.402), hits, doubles (53), triples (26), runs, and RBIs in 1923. Although he hit .332/.404/.485 for the Red Sox from 1924 to 1925, Boone was such a poor fielder (14 runs below average in 1925) that he was allowed to return to the minors, where he continued to set hitting records through 1936.

*The 1939 St. Louis Browns.* These Brownies were the third-worst team of their decade, behind the 1932 Red Sox and 1935 Braves. But as noted, we need Boston more in the 1920s. Besides, it wouldn't be right to have a contest like this without some Brownies amid all the cup-cakes. The 43-111 Browns were a balanced bad team, not distinguishing themselves to any degree in hitting, pitching, or fielding ineptitude. They had a few competent hitters—third baseman Harlond Clift, outfielder Chet Laabs, first baseman George McQuinn—but most of the other players were weak and the pitching staff was virtually irredeemable. Rookie Jack Kramer, 21, starred for the 1944 edition of the club, but in 1939 he could only muster a 9-16 record with a 5.83 ERA. The team's best pitcher, Bobo Newsom, a 20-game winner in 1938, was dealt to the Tigers in May as part of a multiplayer deal that brought Laabs. Newsom won 20 games again in 1939, and 21 in 1940. Fred Haney, who later made a mess of managing a very talented Milwaukee Braves team in the 1950s, cut his teeth skippering this hapless crew.

*The 1948 Chicago White Sox.* The White Sox had fielded a long line of indifferent to poor ball clubs going back to 1921. With the talent loss that arose from the Black Sox affair, they treated the devastated roster like an open wound. It would be the mid-1950s before things began to look up. This edition was only the ninth-worst team of the 1940s, but seven others were from Philadelphia and the eighth was from Washington. This means that the 1948 White Sox end up being only bad, 51-101, instead of abysmal, and have the highest rating of any team in this tournament. Shortstop Luke Appling, a future Hall of Famer, was the best player on the club, hitting .314/.423/.354. He was 41 years old, which says something about the rest of the roster. The highlight of the season was the first game of the July 18 doubleheader at Philadelphia. The White Sox spotted the A's a 5-0 lead, but strikeout-prone outfielder Pat Seerey, recently acquired in a trade with the Indians, swatted a record-tying four home runs to lead the Sox to a 12-11 extra-inning victory. Of course, Seerey slumped immediately thereafter and was out of the majors the next season. "He's a strong boy and a real nice fellow," said Rogers Hornsby, whom the Indians had hired to tutor Seerey on making better contact, "but he takes his eye off the ball."

*The 1952 Pittsburgh Pirates.* This is the team whose president, Branch Rickey, famously told Ralph Kiner, "We finished in last place with you. We can finish last without you." At 42-112, the Pirates weren't close to anybody else, but that wasn't Kiner's fault. The outfielder (with a league-leading 37 home runs) and Gus Bell were the only remotely capable hitters on the team. Hoping to jump-start the team's evolution, Rickey placed 17 rookies on the roster. "Out of quantity," said the Mahatma, "we get quality." He was wrong, as Joe Garagiola, the team's starting catcher, explained: "If there was a new way to lose, we would discover it. We had a lot of triple-threat men—slip, fumble, and fall."

*The 1962 New York Mets.* The 40-120 Mets have the excuse of being an expansion team, from an era when the pickings for an expansion club were slim indeed. Having seen that the American League owners gave up some good players in the expansion draft of 1961, the National League owners rigged their draft so as to remove virtually all players of value, leaving behind, in Roger Angell's words, "culls and aging castoffs." The Mets and sister expansion club the Houston Colt .45s then drafted 22 players each, at costs varying from $50,000 to $125,000 per player. The total cost to the Mets was $1.8 million. Houston's general manager Paul Richards spoke for both expansion teams: "We have been bleeped." Hoping to endear themselves to New Yorkers, the Mets acquired familiar Dodgers and Giants faces like Gil Hodges, Don Zimmer, Roger Craig, Johnny Antonelli, Clem Labine, and Billy Loes. Loes was grateful. "The Mets is a very good thing," he said. "They give everyone a job. Just like the WPA." The Mets, said Branch Rickey, had drafted players who were "about to climb down the other side of the mountain." Said Richie Ashburn, one of the few older Mets who could still play (the 35-year-old hit .306/.424/.393 in 1962), "They [the players] are like reading an old book." As always, Mets manager Casey Stengel put it best: "I want to thank all those generous owners for giving us those great players they did not want. Those lovely, generous owners." The Mets are one of only two clubs in the tournament to be more than 100 runs below league average in both hitting and pitching. As Stengel, who had been in organized baseball since 1910, observed, "They've shown me ways to lose I never knew existed."

*The 1979 Oakland A's.* Like the 1916 A's, these A's broke up after a run of championships in a period of rapid salary escalation—this time caused by the introduction of free agency in the 1970s. Ironically, the arrival of free agency was spurred on by A's owner Charles Finley's failure to honor the details of a contract to Jim Hunter. When Hunter was made a free agent, the money he reaped on the open market showed everyone what the players were really worth. By 1979, every player of value had been traded away, the front office was basically a teenager who would later be known as MC Hammer, and the team was headed for a 54-108 finish as Finley tried to sell the club. The 1979 A's have the worst-rated hitting in the tournament, apart from the Spiders, in spite of the presence of 20-year-old rookie outfielder Rickey Henderson, who batted .274/.338/.336 (.259 EqA) and stole 33 bases in 89 games. His contribution was offset by that of starting shortstop Rob Picciolo, who walked just three times in 363 plate appearances (batting .253/.261/.328, with a .209 EqA). A defensively troubled unit, the A's were going through an error-prone phase—from 1977 through 1979, they led the majors with 543 errors. In 1979, they led the American League with 174 miscues.

*The 1988 Baltimore Orioles.* Losers of their first 21 consecutive games, the O's recovered to finish only 54-107, the best real record of all the teams in this tourney, thanks to the presence of three Hall of Famers—Cal Ripken, Jr., Eddie Murray, and Curt Schilling (even if Schilling isn't actually in yet, he will be). Since Schilling went 0-3 with a 9.82 ERA that year, you can be forgiven for forgetting that he was a part of this debacle, the result of too many years spent substituting veteran retreads for legitimate player development. Six games into the season, the Orioles changed managers, firing Cal Ripken, Sr., and replacing him with Orioles great Frank Robinson. In the midst of the long slide, President Ronald Reagan called Robinson to commiserate. When Reagan told Robinson he knew how the manager felt, Robinson replied, "No, you don't."

*The 1998 Florida Marlins.* Unfortunately for the Marlins—the only team that was defending a pennant—a fire sale intervened between the World Series defeat of the Indians and the next season. The 1916 A's were only two years removed from the World Series, the 1979 A's five years behind, and the 1988 Orioles six years. The Marlins experienced what Wall Street people call "profit taking"—the team succeeded beyond anyone's imagination in 1997, and the owners took the opportunity to rake in the cash while disposing of all the expensive players who had gotten the club there in the first place. Manager Jim Leyland, who spent the season in a state of shock, gave up. "I don't know who the hell I'm going to be pitching two weeks from now," he said in early June. "We don't know what the hell we're doing. What's the difference? We're not going anywhere." At the end of the season, he opted out of his contract.

*The 2003 Detroit Tigers.* This club, which opened its season with a nine-game losing streak, was the result of years of cost-cutting, simple bad management, a farm system that hadn't produced a starting pitcher since the late 1970s, and financial stasis induced by the wait for a new stadium to open. The Tigers went 43-119, avoiding their 120th loss on the final day of the season, triggering celebrations. First baseman Carlos Pena whined, "We're not the worst team in baseball, no matter what. ... We're going to have a better winning percentage than the Mets, and we won't beat their record. You've got to compare apples with apples, not apples with oranges, OK? They played 160 games and we'll play 162."

Table 8-2 The "Top" 12 Contenders in the All-Time Anti-Pennant Race

| Team | Actual W-L | Runs Below Average | | | |
|---|---|---|---|---|---|
| | | Bat | Pitch | Field | Total |
| 1899 Cleveland | 20-134 | 191 | 244 | 157 | 592 |
| 1904 Washington | 38-113 | 91 | 79 | 130 | 300 |
| 1916 Philadelphia | 36-117 | 54 | 110 | 117 | 281 |
| 1925 Boston | 47-105 | 120 | 24 | 76 | 220 |
| 1939 St. Louis | 43-111 | 86 | 88 | 67 | 241 |
| 1948 Chicago | 51-101 | 111 | 59 | 30 | 200 |
| 1952 Pittsburgh | 42-112 | 148 | 54 | 42 | 244 |
| 1962 New York | 40-120 | 102 | 106 | 47 | 282 |
| 1979 Oakland | 54-108 | 153 | 12 | 117 | 255 |
| 1988 Baltimore | 54-107 | 92 | 81 | 34 | 207 |
| 1998 Florida | 54-108 | 63 | 150 | 60 | 273 |
| 2003 Detroit | 43-119 | 151 | 116 | 34 | 301 |

Table 8-2 presents a statistical summary of all 12 teams. The four columns to the right of the team's actual win-loss record indicate how many runs below average they were in each category.

The teams were loaded into a league created for Diamond Mind, the computer baseball game that (in our opinion) has the best statistical engine on the planet. The program incorporates much of the information that we would use in translation. This information relates the player's statistics to the average value of his day, leveling the playing field for the contending teams, despite the disparity in eras. That's not an accident; the principal designer of the game, Tom Tippett, is one of the best baseball analysts we know. Tippett has incorporated those sabermetric concepts into the game far better than anyone else has done.

The league was split into two divisions, Eastern and Western. The Eastern teams were Boston, New York, Philadelphia, Baltimore, Washington, and Florida. As noted, we used the unbalanced schedule from the 1970s, in which each team played the other teams in its own division 18 times and played the teams from the opposite division 12 times each.

We ran an initial simulation of 12 seasons. The results were what you would have expected from Table 8-2. Chicago and Baltimore, the two strongest teams in terms of runs below average, won 14 of the 24 divisional titles. The Orioles averaged 94.7 wins and won seven titles, never failing to win fewer than 85 games. The Baltimore team was clearly the class of this league, so much so that we had a hard time remembering that it truly was a very bad team. Just to make sure we were dealing with authentically bad teams, and that they were behaving as they should, we ran one season in which the 1988 Orioles were replaced with the 1970 Orioles—108 real wins, World Series champs, three 20-game winners, league MVP Boog Powell—and left everyone else alone. The 1970s team started the year 37-3 and eventually finished 134-28. Mike Cuellar won 30 games. Yes, it was an exceptionally awful bunch of teams. Even the lowly 1988 Orioles proved too much for this competition.

At the other end of the curve were, as expected, the Spiders. Even when placed in a league composed entirely of 100-loss clubs, the Spiders managed to average—average!—107 losses a year. They finished with the worst record in their division, and in fact the entire league, for all 12 years. We ran 12 more seasons; the Spiders finished last in all those years, too. Twelve more seasons run—12 more last-place finishes. The team managed to avoid 100 or more losses in five of those 36 seasons; in their worst season, they went 41-121, which would have earned them a spot here if they had done it in regular-season play. The closest they came to finishing out of last place was a season in which they went 62-100 while the Senators were going 64-98. In another season, they actually had a lead over the A's with a week to go, but lost their final five games and finished three games back.

But we knew, going in, that the Spiders would be the champion bottom-dwellers. No one else was remotely close. The better competition was for the second-worst spot, which turned out to be a tight race indeed, for several reasons:

◆ The 1948 White Sox were the second-best team in the tournament and won 6.5 of the Western's 12 titles, averaging 92.8 wins a year.

◆ The 1952 Pirates did surprisingly well, averaging 88.2 wins a year and winning the other 5.5 titles that Chicago didn't.

◆ The 1925 Red Sox always came through with exceptional pitching; Ehmke, Ruffing, and Ted Wingfield gave them the best rotation in the tournament by far. In one season we ran, all three pitchers won 20 games. In that season, the Red Sox averaged 87 wins.

◆ The 1998 Marlins averaged 86.9 wins.

◆ The 1916 A's had, easily, the strongest offense in the league, both in real terms and because their home games were played in a model of the very hitter-friendly Baker Bowl. They also had abysmal pitching, both scoring and allowing over 1,000 runs in most years; the A's averaged 83.1 wins.

◆ The 1939 Browns turned out to be the average team of the group. Coming in at 81.2 wins, as befits their earlier description as a balanced bad team, the Browns sat right in the middle.

◆ The 1962 Mets averaged 79.7 wins, just below the Browns.

◆ The 1979 A's came close to being the only team beaten out by the Spiders on several occasions, but they managed to come in at an average of 76.3 wins.

◆ The 1899 Spiders, as already noted, averaged just 54.5 wins, 20 games behind the next worst teams.

The two teams that remain are Washington at 73.9 average wins and Detroit at 73.7. Though they appear virtually even, the numbers belie the situation. The Senators and Tigers played in different divisions, and Washington had a substantially tougher schedule, as the Eastern teams averaged about 40 wins a year more than the Western teams averaged.

So far, the race to the bottom was too close to call. To spare the Spiders further sadism, we acknowledged them as the unbeatable champion, a special case, we eliminated them from the competition. We also decided that the Orioles, White Sox, and Pirates had eliminated themselves by being too good, even though the Pirates were hardly different from the Red Sox and Marlins. By cutting those four teams, we could rerun the competition among the remaining eight in a one-league, one-division, 154-game format, to see whether the Tigers or the Senators—or some surprising team—would claim the lowliest title, along with the appropriate trophy—a dented, 17-year-old, family-sized can of chunky chicken noodle soup.

After another 20 seasons were simulated, the teams had split into two groups. Five teams averaged a record above .500; between them, they accounted for all the first-place finishes and none of the last-place finishes. The other three, well, they were the teams we were looking for. Detroit and Washington were in the bottom three, just as expected. Detroit averaged 71.8 wins through these 20 seasons and finished last six times—but it also finished above .500 five times. Washington averaged about a win less—70.9—but only had five last-place finishes. It also had only three .500 seasons.

Yet, they were not the worst. Both were beaten by the third member of their group, the surprising Oakland A's of 1979. The A's finished last in nine of the 20 seasons, averaged only 68.0 wins, and only once reached .500. A 53-win effort was the worst of the second tournament. And so we declare Oakland our worst team, with all due respect (or disrespect) to the impossibly bad Cleveland Spiders.

Table 8-3 Second-Round Standings for the All-Time Anti-Pennant Race by Average Record

| Team | W-L | Pct. |
|------|-----|------|
| 1998 Florida | 85.6-68.4 | .556 |
| 1925 Boston | 84.5-69.5 | .549 |
| 1916 Philadelphia | 79.4-75.5 | .513 |
| 1939 St. Louis | 78.5-75.5 | .510 |
| 1962 New York | 77.5-76.5 | .503 |
| 2003 Detroit | 71.8-82.2 | .466 |
| 1904 Washington | 70.9-83.1 | .460 |
| 1979 Oakland | 67.9-86.1 | .441 |

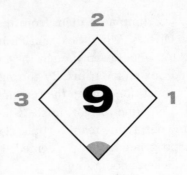

# 1974 American League East

*Mutiny on the Weaver*

ALEX BELTH

Lou Piniella rounded second base with a full head of steam. He was a big, handsome man in a square-jawed Nick Nolte kind of way, only with dark hair. It was almost the end of spring training in Florida, and Piniella was pissed off. He had been running hard for weeks and had hated every minute of it. First-year Yankee manager Bill Virdon ran the most disciplined camp that Piniella had ever been a part of. The outfielder was now completing a running drill that Virdon used to end practice sessions. Each player would run from home to first, then first to third, third to home, home to second, second to home, home to third, and to cap it off, a last turn all around the bases.

When new Yankee general manager Gabe Paul traded for the 29-year-old Piniella in the off-season, the outfielder came with a reputation as an indifferent fielder. Virdon firmly believed in conditioning and drilled his outfielders particularly hard. He knew he could make Piniella into a competent fielder and baserunner.

Piniella rumbled around third as Virdon stood with his arms folded behind home plate. Then Piniella lost his footing, wobbled, and finally wiped out. His face was red when he picked himself up off the ground and yelled at his manager. On all fours, Piniella crawled the rest of the way to the plate, cursing loudly. Virdon laughed, but later said, "As hard as I made Lou work, he never refused to do anything I asked him

### 1974 American League East Prospectus

| Team | Actual Standings | | | | | Date Elim | Pythag | |
|---|---|---|---|---|---|---|---|---|
| | W | L | Pct | GB | DIF | | W | L |
| Orioles | 91 | 71 | .562 | – | 25 | – | 86 | 76 |
| Yankees | 89 | 73 | .549 | 2.0 | 38 | Oct 1 | 86 | 76 |
| Red Sox | 84 | 78 | .519 | 7.0 | 98 | Sept 29 | 85 | 77 |
| Indians | 77 | 85 | .475 | 14.0 | 7 | Sept 23 | 77 | 85 |
| Brewers | 76 | 86 | .469 | 15.0 | 25 | Sept 22 | 80 | 82 |
| Tigers | 72 | 90 | .444 | 19.0 | 3 | Sept 20 | 65 | 97 |

| League Averages | | | | BP Stats Leaders | | | |
|---|---|---|---|---|---|---|---|
| AVG | OBP | SLG | BABIP | Offense, BRAA | | Indiv WARP | |
| .258 | .323 | .371 | .285 | Rangers | 66 | Gaylord Perry | 12.0 |
| ERA | K9 | BB9 | H9 | Pitching, PRAA | | Luis Tiant | 11.0 |
| 3.63 | 4.9 | 3.2 | 8.8 | Royals | 49 | Fergie Jenkins | 10.7 |

to do. And he became a very good left fielder." That spring, Piniella displaced Yankees veteran Roy White as the team's left fielder.

Virdon, 42, wore wire-rim glasses and had the bland but sturdy good looks of a career military man; he was unafraid to show off his physique in the clubhouse as a means of intimidation, a tactic that did not sit well with many of his players. Virdon had been a wonderful defensive center fielder in the major leagues. As a manager, he had led Pittsburgh to a division crown in his rookie campaign in 1972, but was fired the following year with two weeks left in the regular season when the team underachieved.

When the Yankees hired Virdon, he was their second choice. That off-season, owner George Steinbrenner—who less than a year earlier declared that he was not interested in the day-to-day operations of the team—very publicly courted newly available skipper Dick Williams, the Oakland A's winning manager in the 1972 and 1973 World Series. For the Yankees, it was a boffo move, the first of many for Steinbrenner. But Oakland owner Charlie Finley, arguing that Williams was still under contract, demanded lavish compensation in the form of the Yankees' best prospects. When the teams were unable to reach an agreement, the Williams deal was nullified. Explaining the Yankees' decision to hire Virdon, Paul said, "We had to do something."

In spite of his status as a consolation prize, Virdon brought a sense of organization and purpose to a Yankees team that featured some outstanding players but was chiefly comprised of likable guys who weren't particularly caught up in winning. The previous year, the team made a run for the division title only to be physically exhausted in September. "We died," said infielder Gene Michael.

The arrival of Steinbrenner, now in his second season as owner of the Yankees, had already sent manager Ralph Houk, a franchise fixture and player favorite, packing. Michael Burke, the public face of the team during the CBS years, was gone, too. Fresh flowers on the secretaries' desk were a thing of the past. Virdon was the ideal man to enforce Steinbrenner's Spartan new order on the field. Yankees players hadn't been put through this kind of rigorous spring training in years.

◆

The Yankees were going back to school, but the Orioles were already the most fundamentally sound organization in the game. The class of the American League East, the Orioles were coming off four division titles in five years. In five and one-half seasons as manager, Earl Weaver, an irascible and brilliant stump of a man, averaged 99 wins a year and three and one-half packs of cigarettes a day. Weaver never made the big leagues, but he became a part-time player-manager in the minors by the time he was 26. Harry Dalton, the assistant farm director for the Orioles, liked what he saw in the feisty young manager, who, in 11 full minor league seasons, finished either first or second eight times.

During the off-seasons, Weaver toiled in construction before landing a job as a loan officer. "Between my blue collar jobs and minor league baseball, I have been with every kind of person," Weaver told sportswriter Terry Pluto. "I know people. All types. I have heard all the sob stories about the checks being in the mail or waiting just one more week until payday. Listen, I could look into people's eyes and see if they would pay."

Weaver applied his intuitive psychological skills to managing. "Everything Earl did was calculated," remembered Pat Gillick, a star pitcher for Weaver in Fox Cities. He wouldn't ask players to do something they weren't capable of and was an avid believer in platooning. Weaver was also careful not to become emotionally attached to his players. He had no qualms about getting in their faces and berating them, ensuring that no mental mistakes went unnoticed. "I knew Earl would not be afraid to make moves," said Dalton, who became the Orioles general manager in 1966 and held the position for six years. "He is an aggressive guy who doesn't back down for anyone."

"I can't be friends with players," Weaver said later. "How can I when I may have to bench them or send them to the minors?"

And often, his players didn't like him in return. Jim Palmer, Doug DeCinces, and Rick Dempsey had celebrated rifts with Weaver over the years. "He doesn't say much to anybody," recalled Kiko Garcia, who played for Weaver from 1976 through 1980. "He talks a lot to everyone in general, but it is rare to have a conversation with him." Second baseman Bobby Grich remembered that during his rookie year in Baltimore, Weaver didn't say more than five words to him all season. "I never miss anything about the Orioles," Grich said later. "The only thing I liked about Maryland was the crabs."

Weaver was usually irritated once a game began and didn't stop grumbling, then yelling, until it was over. "You do get this negative feeling from the start," Garcia said. "But I'll say this for the man, he doesn't talk behind your backs. If he has something to say to you, he says it. And Earl let's you say whatever is on your mind. You say it and then it is forgotten."

"Earl does not have a shithouse like some managers," says Mark Belanger, who played for Weaver in the minor and major leagues. "You can argue with Earl for six hours and call him every name in the book. But if he thinks you're going to help him win, you'll play the next day." Weaver had his favorites over the years—Belanger, Don Buford, and, later, Eddie Murray and Ken Singleton—but playing for Weaver was never easy. When Oriole players were once asked what they would give Weaver for his birthday, one said, "One day in the big leagues so he'd find out that it's not so easy." Another said, "Nothing. He didn't give me nothing on my birthday," while still another teammate said, "An umpire crew which is his size so he could argue with them eye-to-eye." Weaver had a rabbinical knowledge of the rule book, and while he could abide growing pains in young players, he would not tolerate novice mistakes made by the umpires. Weaver's run-ins with the men in blue became legendary. Once, when he was manager of an Eastern League team in Elmira, New York, Weaver got so upset with a call that he carried third base off the field, then locked himself and the bag in the clubhouse. It took 10 minutes before a member of the grounds crew could get the bag back.

In the winter of 1961, the Orioles gave Weaver the task of designing the spring training regimen for the minor league program from Double-A down; his system was later adopted throughout the entire organization. The first manager in the team's brief history to rise through the ranks, he firmly believed in promoting coaches, too, rewarding performance and, more importantly, maintaining a sense of continuity throughout the system. Many of Weaver's greatest players, including Jim Palmer, Mark Belanger, Paul Blair, and Boog Powell, were from the team's farm system. They were so well versed in the fundamentals of the game—particularly the importance of mental focus—that they virtually policed themselves.

Yet for all their success, the Orioles had won the World Series only once for Weaver. They were perceived as a bland, even boring team, certainly one without a national following. Even in Baltimore, they were distinctly second-class citizens to the Colts. Attendance, which had peaked at 1.2 million in 1966, had dropped to just under 900,000 in 1972 and refused to pick back up. One night, a streaker ran across the field. He was subdued by the police and brought before the Orioles' general manager, Frank Cashen, who said, "Give him $50 and tell him to come back tomorrow night."

◆

Virtually everything about Red Sox pitcher Luis Tiant was funny: He looked funny, sounded funny, and even pitched funny. The only ones not in on the joke were the opposing hitters.

Tiant, listed at 32 but believed to be as old as 40, was a stocky, dark-skinned man with long sideburns, a Fu Manchu mustache, and a bulldog mug right out of a Looney Tunes cartoon. He had a high, piercing voice to match. When he pitched, his cheek, stuffed with chewing tobacco, puffed into a ball, emulating his ample potbelly.

Tiant's delivery was all of a piece. He twisted into a pretzel, completely turning his back to the hitter while looking out into center field. He then jerked back around and whipped the ball to the plate, throwing from three-quarters, over-the-top, and sidearm. Tiant had several fastballs, a curve ball, a palm ball, a knuckle ball, a forkball, and a hesitation pitch. His delivery would vary with the hitter and the situation. He could be deliberate, taking a long time between pitches; other times, he would sneak in a pitch before the hitter was ready. He also had a wicked pick-off move.

Oakland slugger Reggie Jackson gushed, "It's not the dancing that gets you, though. That's show business. It's the fastball on the inside corner. That's what kills you. While he's turning around doing his dance, that ball is coming in on the black."

Tiant smoked eight-inch black cigars everywhere but on the mound—sitting at his locker, in the whirlpool, even in the shower. He would stand in the clubhouse, naked except for his black socks, holding court and busting chops in a way that only a few players can. Even Carl Yastrzemski, the team's undisputed star, was not immune to Tiant's needle and was accordingly dubbed "El Polacko." Outfielder Reggie Smith once said that Tiant was "a guy who wakes up every morning of his life with something funny to say." After Red Sox outfielder Tommy Harper played a poor game, Tiant reassured him, "Tommy, don't worry because you played like shit and looked like shit. You only smell like shit."

Boston had signed the aging star pitcher Juan Marichal for $125,000 in the off-season, hoping to provide depth behind Tiant and Bill Lee, their two most reliable pitchers. Rick Wise came over for Reggie Smith, as did starter Reggie Cleveland and reliever Diego Segui. Rookie manager Darrell Johnson had a mix of veterans in Yastrzemski, Harper, Rico Petrocelli, and youngsters like Rick Burleson (shortstop), Cecil Cooper (first base), and Juan Benequiz and Dwight Evans (outfield), with the organization's two prize prospects, Jim Rice and Fred Lynn, waiting in the wings at Triple-A. But Marichal and Wise were hurt early on, and Carlton Fisk, the team's All-Star catcher, was lost for the season when he suffered a knee injury in June.

Tiant rebounded from a sluggish start, and the rest of the team followed. Yastrzemski had a strong first half (.331/.431/.502), as did Burrelson (.317/.352/.431), about whom Bill Lee later said, "I had never met a red ass like Rick in my life. Some guys didn't like to lose, but Rick got angry if the score was even tied." After starting the season 2-5, Tiant went 18-4 with a 2.22 ERA over his next 22 starts. He completed 17 of those games, tossing five shutouts in the process. The Red Sox reached first place on July 14 and remained there throughout August. Even when the team slumped, Tiant was there to save them—nine times in a row he won following a Red Sox loss.

On August 23, Tiant faced Vida Blue and the World Champion Oakland A's at Fenway Park. He was gunning for his 20th win of what the *Boston Globe* referred to as "the happy season." The paper also ran a daily "This Day in 1967" feature, a reminder that miracles really do come true. The Sox were 6.5 games in front of Cleveland and 7.0 games in front of both the Orioles and the Yankees (with Milwaukee and Detroit under .500 at the bottom of the division). For Sox fans, it was "a midsummer night's dream brought to life," wrote Leigh Montville in the *Globe*.

The largest crowd in 18 years packed Fenway Park. Tiant treated them to a vintage performance. He threw mostly breaking pitches in the early innings, saving the hard stuff for later. The A's put men on base and had their chances, but they could not score. Tiant got out of every jam, dazzling Oakland with his repertoire of pitches and deliveries. "With Luis, it's not the stats, it's the show," noted Bob Ryan after the Sox won 3-0.

With just over a month left in the season, Boston was flying high. "The Red Sox fan had forgotten his inbred pessimism," wrote Montville several weeks later, "his rooting heritage. He had stuffed it in a drawer." But there were signs of trouble. Tommy Harper's first-inning home run was the first Boston had hit since August 9.

◆

The Orioles found themselves in unfamiliar territory as well. Their ace pitcher, Jim Palmer, a 20-game winner in each of the past four seasons, was lost for a bulk of the summer with an arm injury and would post the first losing record of his career (7-12, 3.27 ERA in 178 innings). Pitchers Ross Grimsley and Dave McNally were outstanding, but Baltimore's offense was a dud. Except for second baseman Bobby Grich, everyone's season was worse than the previous one. Left fielder Al Bumbry, the league's Rookie of the Year in 1973, dropped from .337/.398/.500 (.321 EqA) to an unproductive .233/.288/.304 (.240 EqA). Another 1973 rookie, outfielder Rick Coggins, had hit .319/.363/.468 (.299 EqA). Now he slumped to .243/.299/.319 (.253 EqA).

Instead of concerning themselves with World Series shares, the Orioles were worried about surviving. In an attempt to jump-start the club, the veteran players revived the Kangaroo Court. The court had been a staple feature of the Orioles' locker room during Frank Robinson's heyday with the team. The purpose of the court, which convened only after victories, was to issue fines for infractions both real and imagined.

"The court gets everybody to relax and brings us closer together," explained outfielder Don Baylor. "It keeps guys from showering real quick and running out of the clubhouse."

Fines were one dollar. Veteran catcher Elrod Hendricks was appointed judge by his teammates. He objected but was overruled. In short order, Tommy Davis was fined for wearing a Chicago Cubs T-shirt, Paul Blair was nabbed for jogging to the outfield with a bar of chocolate in his back pocket, and Earl Williams was called out for hotdogging it around the bases after hitting a home run against the Twins. Williams said he wouldn't mind paying the dollar fine if it meant he'd keep hitting home runs. But in spite of the newfound looseness in the clubhouse, the Orioles continued to flounder.

Five days after Tiant's gem against the A's, the Orioles held a team meeting at Paul Blair's house. Baltimore had just dropped its fourth straight, its record now 63-65. Brooks Robinson and Blair led the meeting, but all the veterans spoke. They talked about doing "the little things"—stealing, sacrificing, putting on the hit-and-run—playing a brand of baseball generally disdained by their manager. Weaver had been mixing and matching combinations of lineups and platoons for weeks to no avail. The players felt they couldn't just wait around for Weaver's cherished three-run home runs. Boston's grip on first place wasn't insurmountable. If they had to defy Weaver, so be it. Most importantly, it was agreed, if they were to have any success, the players would have to be unified. After all, Weaver couldn't fight the entire team.

Don Baylor, an imposing young player who possessed both speed and power, admired the veterans on the team and didn't dare object, but later admitted, "Deep down inside, though, I was scared. There I was, my third year in the big leagues and about to enter into rebellion against Weaver and take orders from Brooks, Blair and Palmer."

The next night, with the Orioles down 2-1 in the fourth inning, right fielder Enos Cabell singled. Belanger, the number nine hitter, bunted and reached first on an error. Baltimore scored three times in the inning and won the game, 6-2. The following night, Cabell reached first on a dropped third strike leading off the top of the second inning (the O's already had a 3-0 lead). Belanger sacrificed him to second. In the fifth, with the Orioles ahead 5-1, Robinson singled and Blair bunted him to second.

The O's reeled off four straight wins after their team meeting, including one by Palmer fresh off the disabled list, and trailed Boston by just five games when the two teams met in Baltimore for a double-header on September 1. "I don't know which is harder," Weaver told reporters, "to be behind and trying to catch up, or to be ahead and always worrying about losing your lead."

"This is bad on the heart," outfielder Paul Blair said. "I'm afraid someone will hit a ball to me and I'll mess it up." "The pressure and emotional strain are exhausting," added Brooks Robinson. "I've never been through anything like this except during the playoffs and World Series."

Luis Tiant pitched the first game and had no trouble until the fourth inning, when he threw Bobby Grich a hesitation pitch with nobody on base. Grich was looking fastball but adjusted and, flat-footed, hit the ball just right, launching his 18th home run of the year. It was all the run support Ross Grimsley needed, as the Orioles beat the Sox, 1-0. Mike Cuellar and Bill Lee pitched in the second game. In the third inning, Robinson and Cabell led off with singles. Utility catcher Andy Etchebarren bunted poorly up the first-base line and the runner at third was forced out. Belanger followed with another bunt—a sound play, considering how terrible a hitter Belanger was—and reached first on a single. Blair followed with a sacrifice fly, giving the O's a 1-0 lead. Later, in the sixth inning, Belanger reached on a bunt single. Blair bunted into an out before Grich slapped into a double play. The players' small-ball strategy of playing for one run was accomplishing just that. Grimsley was sensational, and Baltimore won again, 1-0. Boston was devastated.

"That evening I lashed my hands to the bathroom sink," Lee later wrote. "My hotel room was on the eighteenth floor, and I did not want to risk the temptation of walking near an open window."

After a day off, Palmer shut Boston out again, this time 6-0. "If we have Palmer, we'll win," Grich told reporters. The Red Sox managed a total of eight hits for the entire series and had lost their last six games, while Baltimore had won its seventh in a row. Then Boston dropped the next two games to the Brewers and fell into second place behind the hard-charging Yankees.

The Orioles shut out the Indians in their next two games. The following night, George Hendrick doubled off Grimsley in the fourth inning; it was the first extra-base hit against the O's in 71 innings. Grimsley held a 3-0 lead in the ninth inning before allowing a two-run homer. The O's won again, their 10th in a row. The scoreless streak, 54 consecutive innings, was a major league record. Weaver later called it "the most amazing pitching performance by a staff" that he had ever seen.

◆

Gabe Paul, dubbed "Dial-a-Deal" by Yankee players, worked diligently to upgrade the team during the season. He used the Yankees' deep pockets to purchase outfielder Elliott Maddox and infielders Jim Mason and Sandy Alomar, all valuable contributors. Maddox, the team's best outfielder, loved the manager's fly ball drills. "He'd wear out the other guys, but I would still yell for more," Maddox recalled.

When the Yankees' best pitcher, Mel Stottlemyre, tore his rotator cuff in June—an injury that would end his career—Paul bought veteran lefty Rudy May, who went 8-4 with a 2.28 ERA in 17 games for New York. But Paul's biggest move came at the end of April, when he shipped four pitchers, starters Fritz Peterson and Steve Kline and relievers Fred Beene and Tom Buskey, to Cleveland for first baseman Chris Chambliss and pitchers Dick Tidrow and Cecil Upshaw. The quartet of Yankee pitchers had been enormously popular in the clubhouse, and the team was livid.

"How can we trade half a pitching staff?" demanded Stottlemyre.

"At this rate, the Indians are going to have a pretty good ball club soon," moaned center fielder Bobby Murcer.

During the 1974 and 1975 seasons, the Yankees played their home games at Shea Stadium while Yankee Stadium was undergoing massive renovations. "It was like we were guests there, and every game was an away game," said righty starter Doc Medich. The field, shared by two clubs, was in horrible condition, and bored Mets fans occasionally showed up simply to heckle the Yankees.

Nobody on the team suffered more than Murcer. Unable to pop home runs over a short fence in right field, as he did at Yankee Stadium, Murcer instead hit countless fly balls to the warning track at Shea. Over the previous two seasons, Murcer had hit 55 home runs. In 1974, he hit just 10, eight on the road.

At the end of May, Virdon moved Murcer to right field, replacing him in center with Maddox. It was a courageous move for Virdon, displacing the heir to Mickey Mantle. Murcer was better suited to right (his 21 assists led the league), but his ego was bruised and he was miserable: He could not sleep, and he refused to speak to Maddox.

Despite Murcer's bitterness, the move seemed to spark the Yankees, who flourished in the second half. Sparky Lyle, who, like Ted Simmons two years earlier, was playing without a signed contract, was again brilliant (9-3, 1.66 ERA in 114 innings); Graig Nettles hit 11 home runs in April and was coming into his own as a fielder, and both Piniella (.305/.341/.407) and Roy White (.275/.367/.393) were solid contributors. Maddox was a surprise offensively (.303/.395/.386), establishing career highs in doubles and on-base percentage. Before and after each game, he played Paul McCartney & Wings' "Band on the Run," a chart-topping song that June.

The biggest trouble for the team involved its not-so-absentee owner. On Friday, September 6, commissioner Bowie Kuhn ordered George Steinbrenner to sever all contact with his club. Earlier in the year, Steinbrenner had been found guilty of making illegal contributions to

Richard Nixon's reelection campaign. Now, in an uncharacteristically assertive move, Kuhn made a public example of Steinbrenner, forcing him to cut ties with the team.

The Yankees' owner liked to address his players as if they were a college football team; he had spoken with them several times after losses earlier in the season. Now, he was forced to send them prerecorded pep talks. Virdon was instructed to play the cassettes for the team in the locker room. "Goddamn it, you've got to go balls-out all the time," Steinbrenner implored on the tape. "You've got to have balls!"

◆

The Yankees and Sox were tied for first when New York arrived in Boston for a two-game series on September 11. Baltimore was just a game back. The Yankees had lost 20 of their previous 21 games at Fenway Park. "It's a little bit scary," Piniella confessed, but the Yankees won the first game, 6-3. Tiant was on the mound the following night, when Boston needed him most. "Some guys can't pick up the pot," Gabe Paul told *Sports Illustrated*, "but Luis' nostrils dilate when the money is on the table."

Tiant held the Yankees scoreless through eight innings, the Sox clinging to a slim 1-0 lead. Piniella drew a one-out walk in the ninth and was replaced by pinch-runner Larry Murray, who raced home when Chris Chambliss's line drive bounced around the right field corner. By the time right fielder Dwight Evans returned the ball to the infield, Chambliss was on third. Evans rushed in from right and screamed for fan interference. The umpires huddled and eventually sent Chambliss back to second with a ground-rule double. But they also allowed Murray to score, a dagger for the Sox.

Before Chambliss could return to second, he felt a thud in his arm. He looked down and found a steel dart embedded in it. On the ground next to him lay a half dozen more darts, thrown from the third base stands (Chambliss would need a tetanus shot, but remained in the game). Alex Johnson, a veteran slugger purchased by New York a day earlier, hit a solo home run off Diego Segui in the twelfth inning, and the Yankees were suddenly two games ahead of the Sox.

◆

The following day, the Band on the Run Yankees split a double-header in Baltimore, losing the first game in 17 innings. Grimsley surrendered just two runs in 14 innings, and Boog Powell, finally swinging a hot bat, singled home the game-winning run. A week later, the Yankees were still in first place, 2.5 games ahead of the Orioles, 3.5 in front of Boston, with Baltimore in town for a three-game series.

"If we win two out of three from Earl," Piniella told Murcer, "we win this thing." Murcer advised his teammate to stay away from the Orioles' manager. Piniella had a past with Weaver, whom he had played for in Elmira, in 1965. They had gotten into a fight the first time they met and then grew to dislike each other. Before the end of that season, Weaver suspended Piniella for insubordination. According to Weaver, Piniella had to pay for three water coolers, four doors, and at least 15 smashed batting helmets that season. The tension between the two continued throughout the years. Weaver could not resist tweaking Piniella, who always hit very well against Weaver's teams. Weaver would give Piniella a piercing whistle whenever Lou popped up or grounded out.

"Lou may be like the proverbial pile of dogshit," Weaver wrote years later. "It never bothers you until you step in it. He has to be one of the best damn 'guess' hitters I've seen. And he's a patient hitter too."

One day in 1976, Piniella almost charged Weaver, who refused to stop baiting him while he was hitting ("Don't hit a home run"). After striking out, Piniella moved toward the Orioles' dugout, only to be restrained by teammates. Weaver darted toward the clubhouse. Years later, the writer Dick Lally asked Weaver why he ran: "Did you know he was the kind of guy who would chase you?" "Worse," Weaver replied, "he's the kind of guy who'll catch you."

As the Yankees took batting practice, Weaver approached Piniella, took off his own hat, and scratched his head. Tilting his head, he looked directly at Piniella and said, "I keep reading the papers about your great catches and great throws. Why didn't you do that for me in Elmira?"

Piniella smiled and then got into the cage and took his hacks. When he was finished, Weaver was still standing there. "You know what," the manager said, "I'm going to jinx you. I know damn well there's going to be a play later on this season and you're going to screw it up and miss a ball in the outfield, and that will give us the damn pennant."

"You're crazy," said Piniella.

◆

The Orioles proceeded to sweep the Yankees, jumping into first place, with Palmer and McNally tossing shutouts. The Baltimore players congratulated themselves, feeling their rebellion had worked. Initially, Weaver was confused as to why his signals were being ignored, but he caught on soon enough. Don Baylor came to bat one night with runners on first and second against the White Sox and ignored third base coach Billy Hunter's signal for a sacrifice (issued by Weaver). Brooks Robinson, waiting on the on-deck circle, made eye contact with Baylor and indicated that he should swing away. Baylor smacked a run-scoring single to left, his third hit of the game. When he returned to the dugout, Weaver snarled at him, "You had better be glad you got that hit." Still, as the veterans had predicted, Weaver couldn't jump the whole team.

"Knowing Earl," Baylor later wrote, "he probably thought it was funny. He loved defiance. He probably said under his breath, 'Those sons of bitches ... I know what they are doing, but they're winning.' And that's the only thing that ever really mattered to Early anyway."

Had the players' rebellion really carried the Orioles? The change in play was less than revolutionary. The 1974 team was one of the weakest offensive units the Orioles had put on the field since Weaver had been manager. The team's production at bat had peaked in 1971, but since then, Boog Powell had been weakened by injuries, Brooks Robinson had declined, and slugger Frank Robinson had been traded in an ill-advised application of Branch Rickey's dictum that it's better to trade a player a year early than a year too late. Weaver said that by 1974, "it had been three years since we'd been paid an extended visit by Dr. Longball."

Weaver adjusted. Though never a fan of the bunt-and-run game ("I'd rather have more three-run homers. Then everyone can take their time and stroll home. I've never had a baserunner thrown out once a ball's been hit over the fence"), he recognized that the team could no longer slug its way to victory. The Orioles began running, leading the league with 146 stolen bases—but they did this in 1973, not 1974. When they stole 145 bases in 1974, it was a continuation, not a change of direction. The Orioles did attempt more sacrifice bunts than they had in 1973, the total rising to 119 from 104. With the acquisition of Ken Singleton and Lee May in the 1974–1975 off-season, Orioles power production rose and there was less need for the bunt. The O's made fewer attempts in 1975, but were successful far more often (73 out of 98 attempts succeeded in 1975, versus 72 out of 119 in 1974). This suggests that even if they were calling the shots on bunts in 1974, the players would have been better off leaving the decisions in Weaver's hands.

The Orioles stole more bases and had more sacrifice bunts in September than in any other month during the season. On the other hand, September brought them their second-highest home run total, their highest OBP, and their greatest number of walks of any month. The small ball certainly helped jump-start the action, but probably more responsible for the resurgence of the Baltimore offense were the strong months from Blair (.301/.377/.513), Baylor (.400/.441/.600), and Powell (.342/.528/.658).

After New York, the Orioles went to Boston and beat the Red Sox twice in three days. After the third game (a Baltimore win), at 5:05 on Sunday, September 22, a young man stood behind the Boston dugout and played taps on a bugle. The Sox were five games out of first place. New York, in the meantime, won its next four games and was a game ahead of the Orioles when Boston arrived in New York for a three-game set, beginning with a twi-night doubleheader. There was an autumn chill in the air at Shea Stadium as more than 46,000 fans watched Tiant win his first game since August 23, as the Sox blanked the Yanks, 4-0. Sportswriter Peter Gammons reported that the ensuing scene at Shea was akin to a "Chilean soccer riot":

Tennis and rubber balls showered from the upper deck, beer was poured on players, trash littered the field and all the while, fights—street brawls—broke out everywhere. They were on the field, in the stands, and one between a man and the police ended up in the Red Sox dugout. It just hadn't gone the way it was supposed to go, and the Orioles had beaten Detroit, 5-4 to take first.

Boston also won the second game, this time 4-2. The following day, the Orioles won another close one, scoring three in the ninth inning after trailing by two. Baltimore simply would not relent. Doc Medich out-dueled Bill Lee at Shea Stadium, 1-0, before a "comparatively quiet" crowd, according to Gammons. "The first fight didn't come until the fourth, the first bottle thrown from the upper deck didn't come until the sixth and Boston third base coach Don Zimmer didn't need his batting helmet until the seventh." With seven games left, the Red Sox were cooked.

◆

On Sunday, September 29, the Yankees waited out bad weather in their Cleveland hotel as they prepared to end the season in Milwaukee. With two games left, the Yankees trailed Baltimore by just one. The Orioles were in Detroit playing the Tigers. Eventually, the Yankees made it to the airport only to find that their flight had been delayed. While waiting, many of the players got loaded. By the time they finally reached Milwaukee, backup first baseman Bill Sudakis and reserve catcher Rick Dempsey, two large but thin-skinned men, were at each others throats. The two got tangled in the revolving door as the team was checking in to the hotel, and the pair emerged throwing punches. Their teammates scrambled to separate them. In the commotion, Murcer was tossed to the floor. A teammate stepped on his hand, but Murcer was too drunk to feel the pain. Sudakis and Dempsey were finally subdued, as Murcer lay pale-faced on the ground.

When Murcer woke up in the morning, his hand was in bad shape. The biggest game of his Yankee career, and he was unable to play—a fitting end to a misbegotten season. (Before the end of the month, Murcer was traded to the Angels for Bobby Bonds.) Virdon was forced to start Piniella in right.

That afternoon, the Orioles won yet another thriller, beating the Tigers by a single run. Backup catcher Andy Etchebarren doubled home the slow-footed Brooks Robinson all the way from first in the ninth inning.

It was snowing when starter Doc Medich arrived at County Stadium. Hours later, just over 4,000 people sat in the 37-degree cold to see if the Brewers could spoil the Yankees' playoff hopes. The field was a mess. In the fourth inning, with Piniella on first, Thurman Munson doubled to right. Piniella should have scored easily, but slipped in the mud rounding third. Both he and Munson were left stranded as the Brewers' Kevin Kobel and Medich threw zeros for the first six innings.

Meanwhile, at the Sheraton-Cadillac Hotel in Detroit, the Orioles coaches, a few players, and about a dozen reporters huddled in Earl Weaver's room. Weaver had been nursing a cold for days but continued to smoke cigarette after cigarette. He had asked Milwaukee owner Bud Selig to place a phone next to a radio at County Stadium so that he could follow the action. With the receiver close to his ear, Weaver listened in, hunched over and tense, providing a sketchy play-by-play for the rest of the room. When his voice became too hoarse to continue, Oriole trainer Ralph Salvon took a turn, followed by one of the day's heroes, Brooks Robinson.

The Yankees scored twice in the top of the seventh inning. In the eighth, the Brewers had a man on third with one out when Don Money sliced a fly ball to right-center field. Piniella and Maddox moved after it. "The ball seemed to switch directions in the wind," Piniella later recalled, "twist and turn and dance—damn that Earl Weaver—and nobody called for it." Maddox could have reached the ball, but pulled up at the last moment. As Piniella made a futile stab for the ball, it landed behind him. Money scored the tying run on a sacrifice fly one batter later. Piniella got even with Weaver by smashing a water cooler.

Etchebarren relieved Robinson of play-by-play duties as the Yankee game moved into extra innings. Medich was still in the game, but the Brewers loaded the bases in the bottom of the 10th with one out for first baseman George Scott. "How many out, Andy?" asked Weaver, pacing anxiously. "One, skip, and the Boomer's up." A moment later, Etchebarren jumped up and dropped the phone, a broad grin on his face. "Base hit! A hit for the Boomer. We win. We win the division!" The coaches and players hugged and shook hands, then left for the bar. Weaver fell to his knees and banged the carpet with his fists. "You mean we don't have to win tomorrow?" he said, his voice no louder than a whisper. "I don't believe it."

The Orioles had won 28 of their final 34 games. In the last 11 games of the season, they were 10-1, winning seven by a single run. Their 40 one-run wins tied a major league record they had set in 1970. "I was never happier to see a pennant race end," Weaver later wrote. But after a valiant charge, the Orioles were depleted and quickly dispatched by the A's in the playoffs.

In most of Weaver's first 14 years with the Orioles, the team's late-season record was well above .500 (Table 9-1). Baltimore averaged 91 wins a season over the next four years, but failed to make the playoffs. The Red Sox youth movement matured quickly, as Lynn and Rice led them to a World Series berth in 1975. For the rest of the decade, Boston's rivalry with the Yankees featured an intensity not seen since the

Table 9-1 Dream Weaver: Earl Weaver's Regular-Season Record in September and October, 1969-1982

| Year | W | L | Pct |
|---|---|---|---|
| 1969 | 18 | 10 | .643 |
| 1970 | 22 | 7 | .759 |
| 1971 | 20 | 9 | .690 |
| 1972 | 13 | 17 | .433 |
| 1973 | 21 | 11 | .656 |
| 1974 | 24 | 6 | .800 |
| 1975 | 17 | 9 | .654 |
| 1976 | 20 | 13 | .606 |
| 1977 | 22 | 9 | .710 |
| 1978 | 18 | 11 | .620 |
| 1979 | 15 | 12 | .556 |
| 1980 | 24 | 10 | .706 |
| 1981 | 17 | 14 | .548 |
| 1982 | 22 | 10 | .687 |
| TOTAL | 273 | 148 | .648 |

late 1940s. And once they returned to a newly restored stadium in 1976, the Yankees hit their stride, winning three consecutive pennants and two championships.

But for the moment, they were despondent. After the 3-2 loss, Yankee broadcaster Phil Rizzuto was in tears as he recapped the game. "I had a good season," Piniella told reporters after the game, "and loused it up on one play. My little boy could have caught that ball and he's five years old."

The next day, before the final game of the regular season, Piniella received a telegram in the visitor's locker room in Milwaukee. It was from Weaver. "Thanks. I knew you'd screw it up someway."

## How to Break Up the Yankees

### STEVEN GOLDMAN

From the mid-1930s through the mid-1960s, baseball struggled with how to "break up the Yankees," at one point even adopting a rule forbidding teams from trading with the previous year's pennant winner—which was always the Yankees. The rule lasted but one winter, that of 1939 to 1940. New York didn't win in 1940, Detroit did. The rule hadn't been intended to harm the Tigers, so it was quickly rescinded.

The no-trade rule had little chance of hurting the Yankees anyway, because so much of their talent was homegrown. When Branch Rickey's farm system began transforming the way major league talent was developed, Yankees general manager Ed Barrow, something of a reactionary, had been resistant to the new methods. In 1932, team owner Jacob Ruppert overruled him, buying the Newark Bears of the International League and hiring independent minor league operator George Weiss to build a complete farm system. An injection of New York revenues turned Rickey's farm into a factory. Of the key players on the champion 1939 Yankees, none of the position players were acquired via trade, and just a handful of the pitchers were acquired this way.

The factory system fed the Yankees dynasty, which was only occasionally interrupted between 1936 and 1964. Not until 1965, with the advent of the amateur draft and with ownership's cutbacks in player development on the eve of selling out to CBS (the Yankees had never been generous with bonuses anyway), did the factory shut down. The

Yankees stopped producing young players, and shortly thereafter, the team stopped winning.

Over the more than 40 years since, the Yankees have resisted getting back in the habit of producing youngsters. During its brief ownership, CBS didn't know how. George Steinbrenner, who bought the team from the Tiffany Network, didn't care to. For all Steinbrenner's financial largesse, the posture damaged the club almost from the first moment of the regime. The first test was offered by Otto Velez in 1974. The club failed it and, as a direct result, lost the division title to the Baltimore Orioles.

A key reason the team couldn't surpass the Orioles was production both at first base and at designated hitter (DH). In fact, the designated hitter was a problem from the moment of its invention. Though the Yankees are credited with having the first DH, Ron Blomberg, a *productive* designated hitter eluded them for some time (Table 9-2).

On April 26, Yankees general manager Gable Paul raided his former organization, the Indians, sending pitchers Fritz Peterson, Steve Kline, Fred Beene, and Tom Buskey to Cleveland in exchange for first baseman Chris Chambliss and pitchers Dick Tidrow and Cecil Upshaw. In the long term, it worked out to be a very good trade for the Yankees, but in 1974, Chambliss personally dragged the Yankees away from their first postseason appearance since 1964.

Chambliss was never more than a decent hitter for the Yankees, an impatient lefty who never learned to pull the ball for power. Still, from 1975 through 1979, he was mildly productive, batting .287/.328/.428. In 1974, however, the then 23-year-old seemed to panic on reaching New York, hitting a dreadful .243/.282/.343 in 110 games.

Simultaneously, the Yankees possessed a rookie first baseman named Otto Velez, one of the most promising prospects developed by the team at any time during the Steinbrenner ownership. Signed as a 19-year-old amateur free agent in 1970, the young Puerto Rican, who had been tutored by Roberto Clemente and Orlando Cepeda, batted .369/.469/.591 in rookie ball, then hit .310/.417/.510 (16 home runs in 384 at bats) in A ball (Table 9-3). Velez not only showed great hitting ability for a player just out of his teens, but also had a refined knowledge of the strike zone—unusual knowledge in one so young.

In April 1973, the Yankees gave the 22-year-old Velez the James Dawson Award, presented annually to the best rookie in camp. At the same time, they moved him from his initial position, third base, to the outfield, because the team had acquired Graig Nettles. Velez didn't mind. "I like the outfield," he said. "It gives me more time to concen-

Table 9-2  Yankee Designated Hitter and First Base Productivity, Compared with League Averages

| | 1973 | | 1974 | | 1975 | | 1976 | |
|---|---|---|---|---|---|---|---|---|
| | *Yankees* | *AL* | *Yankees* | *AL* | *Yankees* | *AL* | *Yankees* | *AL* |
| *Designated Hitter* | | | | | | | | |
| Avg | .244 | .258 | .253 | .255 | .254 | .257 | .254 | .257 |
| OBP | .306 | .328 | .319 | .327 | .317 | .327 | .322 | .325 |
| Slg | .381 | .393 | .394 | .393 | .383 | .375 | .349 | .376 |
| *First Base* | | | | | | | | |
| Avg | .306 | .271 | .244 | .262 | .300 | .267 | .295 | .262 |
| OBP | .346 | .355 | .308 | .334 | .336 | .340 | .326 | .335 |
| Slg | .429 | .416 | .351 | .409 | .428 | .422 | .444 | .391 |

trate on my hitting." Unsurprisingly, Velez proved to be an indifferent outfielder. Though he had a decent arm, his range was never very good, and he was clumsy. His abilities in left field were exemplified by a 1979 play in which Oakland catcher Jim Essian, batting with the bases loaded, ripped a grounder down the third-base line into left field. Velez charged the ball, stepped on it, and fell into the wall. Essian rounded the bases for an inside-the-park grand slam. After his tumble, Velez had to miss several games with a twisted ankle. This was in the future, but the Yankees were already thinking of moving him to a third position. They just couldn't decide where.

Velez's 1973 season was stunning. After the young slugger hit 13 home runs, including three grand slams, in Triple-A Syracuse's first 37 games, his manager, Bobby Cox, said, "He's the best hitting prospect I've ever seen. He can run, throw, and hit with power, but I don't think he's a 40- to 50-homer guy. I'd say 20 to 30 is more like it." Cox proved prescient after Velez cooled in the second half. Nonetheless, Velez was named the International League's Rookie of the Year after batting .269/.445/.562 with 29 home runs and 130 walks. That fall he made his Yankees debut. Though he didn't hit for average, batting .195/.325/.326, he did show his trademark patience and power. Manager Ralph Houk was encouraging: "The experience was good for him. I expect him to make it next year."

Unfortunately for Velez, Houk resigned under pressure from Steinbrenner. Velez then became a pawn in the team's hunt for a new skipper. When the Yankees attempted to sign the former Oakland A's manager Dick Williams, who had resigned but was still under contract, A's owner Charles Finley demanded compensation. The Yankees offered veteran second baseman Horace Clarke. But Finley demanded one of their "kids": Velez, Scott McGregor, Terry Whitfield, John Shupe, Steve Coulson, or Kerry Dineen. Gabe Paul was appalled. "Those aren't kids. Those are our crown jewels." None of them ever contributed to the Yankees.

Velez took three strikes in the managerial shuffle. Strike one was the loss of Houk, who as a long-time organization man was familiar with his strengths and weaknesses and might have made room for him. Strike two was the team's failure to sign Williams, an astute manager who would have been eager to exploit Velez's talents. The third strike came with the naming of Bill Virdon as Houk's replacement. In his 15-year managerial career, Virdon proved to be largely hostile to young players. His attitude, which jibed perfectly with Steinbrenner's own impatience with inexperienced players, set a pattern for the organization that lasted years.

Velez's minor league accomplishments should have earned him a prominent place in the Yankees' plans, especially since the team was going into the 1974 season with no established first baseman or designated hitter. Instead, when Velez struggled during the exhibition season, Virdon used the opportunity to send him back to Syracuse. "I couldn't give him a spot on the club the way he looked," said Virdon. "He simply failed to make our club." Virdon selected veterans Mike Hegan and Bill Sudakis as his first baseman and designated hitter, respectively.

Velez went back to the minors and began

Table 9-3  Otto Velez in the Minors

| Year | Age | League | G | AB | R | H | 2B | 3B | HR | RBI | BB | SO | Avg | OBP | Slg |
|------|-----|--------|---|----|---|---|----|----|----|-----|----|----|-----|-----|-----|
| 1970 | 19 | Appalachian | 53 | 176 | 49 | 65 | 10 | 4 | 7 | 44 | 33 | 36 | .369 | .469 | .591 |
| 1971 | 20 | Carolina | 113 | 384 | 82 | 119 | 21 | 4 | 16 | 73 | 72 | 75 | .310 | .417 | .510 |
| 1972 | 21 | Eastern | 122 | 409 | 64 | 102 | 17 | 1 | 13 | 68 | 80 | 98 | .249 | .369 | .391 |
| 1973 | 22 | International | 138 | 409 | 92 | 110 | 19 | 7 | 29 | 98 | 130 | 106 | .269 | .449 | .562 |
| 1974 | 23 | International | 65 | 200 | 44 | 62 | 13 | 0 | 13 | 35 | 64 | 65 | .310 | .480 | .570 |
| 1975 | 24 | International | 82 | 244 | 56 | 61 | 18 | 2 | 10 | 35 | 87 | 54 | .250 | .445 | .463 |
| TOTAL | | | 573 | 1822 | 387 | 519 | 98 | 18 | 88 | 353 | 466 | 434 | .285 | .430 | .503 |

a campaign superior to his great 1973 season, batting .310/.480/.570. At the end of June, Chambliss, batting .185 as a Yankee, was benched and Velez was recalled. Virdon wasn't keen on the move. "For now, I think he'll play first base against left-handed pitchers. It depends on how he goes and how others go whether he'll play every day. I think he can hit right-handers, too. He showed he can, but I want to give others a chance to play themselves out of the lineup before I go too far with Otto."

Velez made just one hit in his first 12 at bats, but broke out with a home run off the great Detroit closer John Hiller on July 4. By then, some of the players had objected to his presence. On July 2, pitcher Pat Dobson criticized Virdon for playing Velez. "Win or lose, you have to play your best ball club. We haven't been. That's my opinion and I'm not afraid to voice it. Sudsy should be playing first base. Stick [Michael, 36-year-old second baseman; the Yankees had been trying out a 24-year-old named Fernando Gonzalez] ought to be playing second. Last night, he pinch-hit Otto Velez when he needed a home run— and Sudsy can hit homers—when Velez hasn't even gotten the ball out of the infield." On July 1, Velez had struck out against the difficult Hiller, the same pitcher he would hit a home run against three days later.

Velez played regularly for roughly two weeks and batted .279/.389/.488 in that time (the American League hit .258/.323/.371 that year). In the 11 games after he broke his hitless streak, he batted .343/.444/.600. Despite Velez's breakthrough, it was decided to give Chambliss another try. Virdon rarely used his bench, and Velez appeared only sporadically thereafter, playing in 13 games scattered over the rest of the year.

That was the last serious audition that Velez was granted as a Yankees player. Virdon farmed him out again at the beginning of 1975. On June 8, 1975, the slugger fractured his left wrist in a home plate collision, which delayed his return to the Yankees until September, when he received a few cursory at bats. By that time, Billy Martin was the manager of the Yankees. Although he had an open mind toward Velez, Chambliss was now established, and Oscar Gamble and Carlos May had been added to the crowd of outfield and designated hitter candidates. Consequently, Martin had no plans for Velez beyond occasional use as a platoon outfielder. Velez stuck with the Yankees for all of 1976, but received just 117 plate appearances. Yankees designated hitters again performed poorly, but it didn't matter. By this time, the Yankees had just three players who had been developed by the organization: Thurman Munson, Roy White, and Velez.

Velez's Yankees experience was mercifully terminated by the 1976 expansion draft. The draft rules stipulated that the Yankees could initially protect 15 players. After each round, the team could pull back an additional three players. Velez was not among the initial 15. As the draft continued, the Yankees withdrew Fred Stanley, Fran Healy, Sandy Alomar, and Carlos May, but never withdrew Velez. The Toronto Blue Jays drafted him with their 27th pick, making him one of the last players selected.

Velez finally established himself in Toronto, though injuries and his defensive problems in the outfield would limit his playing time. "I'm not saying I will hit 30 home runs," he said in 1977, "but I would like to have 500 at bats to see what I can do." He seemed to get hurt whenever his manager was on the verge of giving him the time. Still, from 1977 through 1980, he batted .269/.375/.480 for the Jays, numbers more impressive then than now.

He had his small revenge against the Yankees as well. The newly established Jays played their first series at Yankee Stadium from April 18 to April 21, 1977. Velez pounded Yankees pitching, going 9 for 15, with two doubles, two homers, and two walks, and driving in eight runs. "I know I can swing the bat a little bit. I feel so great to show the owner," he said. "He only likes the big names."

◆

In subsequent years, Steinbrenner's hostility to young players became legendary. In 1978, he sent rookie pitcher Jim Beattie to Triple-A in the middle of a game Beattie had just started. "Did you see Beattie out there?" he told the media afterward. "He pitched like he was scared stiff." In the midst of a difficult pitching appearance by 25-year-old righty Ken Clay, reporters were called to Steinbrenner's office. "[Clay] doesn't have any heart," the owner told them. "Ken Clay has spit the bit." In March 1981, 24-year-old pitcher Mike Griffin failed to beat the Mets in an exhibition game. "Mike Griffin has fooled us long enough," Steinbrenner said. "We found out about him today. That does it for him. He won't be pitching for us this year." He was sent to Columbus the next day and soon thereafter was traded out of the organization. After making an error before Steinbrenner early in the 1984 season, rookie shortstop Bobby Meacham found himself demoted not to Triple-A, but to Double-A. "Meacham isn't ready for New York," Steinbrenner said.

In 1976, the Yankees had reached the World Series for the first time since 1964. After losing to the Cincinnati Reds that year, they returned again in 1977 and 1978 and won both times. The Yankees also reached the postseason in 1980 and 1981, but failed to capture another championship. By that time, the core of the 1976–1981 team was rapidly aging and would have to be replaced, but the delusion that somehow a player who had been developed in another organization was automatically superior to one developed within the Yankees system made rebuilding nearly impossible. Several promising young players were traded out of the organization, often for little return, among them Scott McGregor, Tippy Martinez, Jim Beattie, Tim Lollar, Willie McGee, Fred McGriff, Greg Gagne, Dennis Rasmussen, Steve Balboni, Tim Burke, Jose Rijo, Scott Bradley, Jim Deshaies, Doug Drabek, Bob Tewksbury, Jay Buhner, Al Leiter, and Hal Morris. While all organizations make a certain number of mistakes in player evaluation, the record of the Yankees organization during this period was egregious. Not only were the Yankees pathologically opposed to giving their own young players a chance, but the veterans the club was acquiring in the younger players' stead, such as outfielder Omar Moreno or pitcher Tim Leary, weren't any good.

The few prospects the Yankees were left with during this period failed to develop. The Yankees, unused to teaching youngsters, were no longer good at it. Moreover, the veterans-only strategy had neutered the farm system. In the pre-free-agency years of the Steinbrenner regime, the handling of the amateur draft was simply inept. After the advent of free agency, the league developed a compensation system in which a club losing a free agent would be awarded the first-round pick of the club that signed him. Since the Yankees signed a free agent virtually every winter, they went years without a first-round draft pick and sometimes were penalized in their second- and third-round picks as well. While baseball forbids the trading of picks, this was essentially what the Yankees were doing.

This proved to be a disastrous strategy. The first round is important because with intelligence and a little luck, a team should, at the very least, be able to come up with a serviceable major leaguer. Veteran players are more predictable than youngsters, but are also used up faster, having spent their baseball prime with their original team. In addition, certain players, such as pitchers and shortstops, proved difficult to acquire on the open market. These positions became suppurating wounds for a Yankees team that won many games in the regular season, but which, from 1982 through 1994, failed to reach the postseason (more accurately, through 1993; no one made the postseason in 1994).

In 38 annual drafts through 2003, the Yankees scored exactly four times in the first round, picking Ron Blomberg, Scott McGregor, Thurman Munson, and Derek Jeter. As Yankees picks failed, it meant that the team was forced to sign a greater number of free agents. The compensation system then kicked in, preventing the Yankees from signing better players. A vicious cycle was created, as described in the following paragraphs. Note that the "Hindsight is 20-20" section lists players available to the Yankees at various times in the draft. These picks are usually restricted to the first three rounds. In the early part of the draft, teams have more consensus about who the best talents are. In later rounds, it becomes more difficult to discern the keepers, so it's unfair to fault the Yankees for, say, not realizing that Wade Boggs was a first-round talent when he lasted until the seventh round—no team had great expectations for the third baseman. Note also that most players drafted by the Yankees were subsequently used as trade fodder, many before getting a chance to make their mark with the Yankees.

## 1973

*Douglas Heinhold, RHP, pick 13 (high school)*

*Picked before the Yankees' turn:* David Clyde (1), Robin Yount (3), Dave Winfield (4), Gary Roenicke (8).

*Picked after the Yankees' turn:* Lee Mazzilli (14).

*Later:* Heinhold tapped out in the minors. Later, the Yankees picked Mike Heath (2), Kerry Dineen (4), LaMarr Hoyt (5), Garth Iorg (8). The first three were used in deals netting Sergio Ferrer, Dave Righetti, and Bucky Dent, among others, while Iorg was lost to the Blue Jays in the 1976 expansion draft.

*Hindsight is 20-20:* Eddie Murray (Orioles 3), Fred Lynn (Red Sox 2), Floyd Bannister (A's 3).

*Overall:* In the first year of the administration, the pattern was set: Acquire talent, then deal it before giving it a chance in New York. A lasting fascination with high school players was also damaging.

## 1974

*Dennis Sherrill, SS, pick 12 (high school)*

*Picked before the Yankees' turn:* Bill Almon (1), Lonnie Smith (3), Dale Murphy (5).

*Picked after the Yankees' turn:* Garry Templeton (14), Lance Parrish (16), Willie Wilson (18), Rick Sutcliffe (21).

*Later:* Sherrill went 1-for-5 in five games with the Yankees. The Yankees took Dave Bergman (2), and Jerry Narron (6). The former was dealt for Cliff Johnson, the latter for Ruppert Jones.

*Hindsight is 20-20:* Rance Mulliniks (Angels 3), Pete Vuckovich (White Sox 3), Moose Haas (Brewers 2), Butch Wynegar (Twins 2).

*Overall:* Almost any other player the Yankees picked would have been important to the franchise, perhaps helping to save it from the malaise of the early 1980s.

## 1975

### James McDonald, 1B, 19 (high school)

*Picked before the Yankees' turn:* Rick Cerone (7).

*Picked after the Yankees' turn:* Dale Berra (20).

*Later:* The Yankees took Jim Beattie (4), Willie Upshaw (5), Mike Fischlin (7). Beattie was railroaded out of town after spotty work with the 1978 and 1979 teams. He was part of the Ruppert Jones deal. Upshaw was lost to the Jays in the Rule 5 draft. Fischlin was part of the Cliff Johnson deal.

*Hindsight is 20-20:* Carney Lansford (Angels 3), Lee Smith (Cubs 2), Don Robinson (Pirates 3).

*Overall:* The Yankees got a good return in a poor year but didn't capitalize.

## 1976

### Pat Tabler, OF, 16 (high school)

*Picked before the Yankees' turn:* Floyd Bannister (1), Ken Landeraux (6), Steve Trout (8), Leon Durham (15).

*Picked after the Yankees' turn:* Mike Scoscia (19), Bruce Hurst (22).

*Later:* Not much; Tabler was New York's only real catch. He would be dealt to the Cubs for Bill Caudill and Jay Howell.

*Hindsight is 20-20:* Alan Trammell (Detroit 2), Rickey Henderson (A's 4).

*Overall:* It's hard to imagine the devout Mormon Hurst being comfortable in New York. Some things just aren't meant to be.

## 1977

### Steve Taylor, RHP, pick 23 (college)

*Picked before the Yankees' turn:* Harold Baines (1), Bill Gullickson (2), Paul Molitor (3), Terry Kennedy (6), Richard Dotson (7),

Wally Backman (16), Bob Welch (20). Having finally won a pennant during the draft era, the Yankees were pushed down in the draft order just in time to miss out on a strong draft class.

*Picked after the Yankees' turn:* Dave Henderson (26).

*Later:* Taylor never surfaced. The Yankees took Joe Lefebvre (3), Chris Welsh (21). Both players were traded to the Padres as part of a deal for Jerry Mumphrey.

*Hindsight is 20-20:* Kevin Bass (Brewers 2), Scott Sanderson (Expos 3), Tim Raines (Expos 5), Ozzie Smith (Padres 4).

*Overall:* At least the Yankees finally took a college pitcher. It wasn't a true change of philosophy.

## 1978

*Rex Hudler, SS, pick 18 (high school)*

*Matt Winters, OF, pick 24 (high school)*

*Brian Ryder, RHP, pick 26 (high school)*

*Picked before the Yankees' turn:* Bob Horner (1), Lloyd Moseby (2), Hubie Brooks (3), Mike Morgan (4), Andy Hawkins (5), Kirk Gibson (12), Tom Brunansky (14), Nick Esasky (17).

*Picked after the Yankees' turn:* No one of significance. Despite winning the World Series, the Yankees acquired two extra picks after losing Mike Torrez and Ron Blomberg to free agency. As such, the team had all the options at the end of the first round.

*Later:* The Yankees took Steve Balboni (2), Tim Lollar (4), Andy McGaffigan (6), Brian Dayett (16), Don Cooper (17). Balboni won several minor league home run titles, then was dealt to the Royals for Mike Armstrong. Tim Lollar was included in the Mumphrey deal. McGaffigan was traded to the Giants for Doyle Alexander. Dayett got a share of the Yankees' left field job in 1984, showing power and impatience. He was dealt to the Cubs that winter as part of a deal for Ron Hassey.

*Hindsight is 20-20:* Steve Bedrosian (Braves 3), Larry Sheets (Orioles 2), Mel Hall (Cubs 2), Britt Burns (White Sox 3).

*Overall:* For many years, this seemed like the last draft. Too little came of it, and the seeds of the 1982–1992 period were sewn.

After 1978, the Yankees almost completely vanished from the first round, as shown in their first-round picks from 1979 to 1989:

1979: None, for signing Tommy John.

1980: None, for signing Rudy May.

1981: None, for signing Dave Winfield.

1982: None, for signing Dave Collins.

1983: None, for signing Steve Kemp. The Yankees also lost their second-round pick for signing Bob Shirley and their third-round pick for signing Don Baylor away from Anaheim. The Angels took Wally Joyner with the pick.

1984: Jeff Pries, pick 22 (college). When the Yankees finally had a first-round pick, they botched it, picking one of the few lemons in a deep draft class. They did find Al Leiter with their second pick.

1985: Rick Balabon, pick 28 (high school). This was a compensation pick for losing Tim Belcher because of a rather bizarre commissioner's ruling the previous winter. New York's actual first-round pick went to San Diego for signing Ed Whitson.

1986: None, for signing Al Holland.

1987: None, for signing Gary Ward.

1988: None, for signing Jack Clark.

1989: None, for signing Steve Sax.

In 1990, Steinbrenner was banned from baseball by then-commissioner Fay Vincent as a result of the owner's dealings with gambler Howie Spira. That year, the team had collapsed to last place in the American League East with a 67-95 record. Although Vincent's "lifetime" ban turned out to be temporary, general manager Gene Michael, hired in August 1990, restored some sanity to player procurement. The Yankees stopped giving away their first-round picks. In 1992, they drafted Derek Jeter. Incredibly, he was allowed to progress through the minor leagues at a normal rate, reaching the majors for a cup of coffee in 1995.

The next season, the 22-year-old rookie broke camp as the Yankees' starting shortstop, this despite trepidation by new manager Joe Torre, who like his predecessor Virdon preferred veteran players to youngsters. Steinbrenner, having resumed the active role he held with the Yankees before his suspension, publicly supported Jeter. "I would not have gone with a Jeter in the past. I think I've changed," he said. "I was too demanding. Too hasty." Privately, though, he was insisting the Yankees find an alternative. Michael faced Steinbrenner down, winning Jeter a temporary stay, and the rest is history.

Despite Jeter's success and the key role played by homegrown talents Bernie Williams, Jorge Posada, and Mariano Rivera in the four championships won by the Torre-era Yankees, player development did not become a mainstay of the Yankees' approach to team building. The battle to wean Steinbrenner from expensive free agents and to pursue products of the farm system with equal vigor is still being waged by Michael's successor, Brian Cashman. Since winning their most recent championship in 2000, the Yankees have reverted to buying off the shelf instead of building from within, spending big bucks on DOA free agents such as Carl Pavano and Jaret Wright. As in the 1980s, the Yankees have won many games but have failed to win another title. They are somehow always just a little bit short, having neglected to buy this piece or that on the open market. Developing pitching has been a particular problem; in 2007, the 2004 first-round pick Phil Hughes became just the second Yankees number one pick to pitch for the team. (The other, Bill Burbach, who pitched 37 games—badly—from 1969 to 1971, was their first pick in the 1965 draft.)

In 1974, the long-standing question of how to break up the Yankees was finally answered, and the solution played out again and again over the more than 30 years that have followed. No outside team could break up the Yankees, but it was a simple matter, through neglect of the young, for the Yankees to do it themselves.

# 1951 National League

## The Dirty, Underhanded, Compromised, Corrupt, and Perhaps Tertiary Shot Heard 'Round the World

### KEVIN BAKER

"Summarizing the 1951 race is akin to summarizing *King Lear*. Before anything else, your effort will diminish majesty," Roger Kahn wrote many years after the fact.

Nevertheless, we shall try. The race, between the New York Giants and the Brooklyn Dodgers, is remembered largely today for the second-greatest comeback (or choke) that ever was, punctuated by what remains the most famous single moment in the game's history—"The Shot Heard 'Round the World," "The Miracle of Coogan's Bluff."

No pennant race has ever ended so dramatically. It remains the only time that any team has rallied to win from three runs down in the ninth inning of a playoff or World Series game. No race was ever so extended. The Dodgers and Giants played 25 games against each other, including their three-game playoff at the end of the season, the most games any two teams played against each other in any season in any North American sport until the apocalyptic Yankees–Red Sox showdowns of 2003 and 2004. And yet, an alleged scandal still threatens to overturn how we think of the result, more than 50 years later.

The 1951 race shines bright in memory partly because of the era in which it took place. This was the golden age of New York, those halcyon days from the end of the war until both the Giants and the

**1951 National League Prospectus**

| Team | Actual Standings W | L | Pct | GB | DIF | Date Elim | Pythag W | L |
|---|---|---|---|---|---|---|---|---|
| Giants | 98 | 59 | .624 | – | 7 | – | 93 | 64 |
| Dodgers | 97 | 60 | .618 | 1.0 | 147 | Oct 3 | 96 | 61 |
| Cardinals | 81 | 73 | .526 | 15.5 | 8 | Sept 14 | 78 | 76 |
| Braves | 76 | 78 | .494 | 20.5 | 10 | Sept 11 | 83 | 71 |
| Phillies | 73 | 81 | .474 | 23.5 | 2 | Sept 7 | 77 | 77 |
| Reds | 68 | 86 | .442 | 28.5 | 0 | Aug 30 | 65 | 89 |
| Pirates | 64 | 90 | .416 | 32.5 | 5 | Aug 29 | 62 | 92 |
| Cubs | 62 | 92 | .403 | 34.5 | 3 | Aug 30 | 63 | 91 |

| League Averages | | | | BP Stats Leaders | | | |
|---|---|---|---|---|---|---|---|
| **AVG** | **OBP** | **SLG** | **BABIP** | **Offense, BRAA** | | **Indiv WARP** | |
| .260 | .331 | .390 | .272 | Dodgers | 124 | Jackie Robinson | 13.7 |
| **ERA** | **K9** | **BB9** | **H9** | **Pitching, PRAA** | | Stan Musial | 12.5 |
| 3.96 | 3.8 | 3.5 | 8.9 | Reds | 60 | Robin Roberts | 11.3 |

Dodgers left for the coast after the 1957 season. The luster of the period has been burnished by the events that preceded and followed it, but there is no denying that it was a very good moment in the history of the city. New York had become the world's capital, the biggest, richest, most glamorous city on the planet, the leader in art, fashion, literature, architecture. It was, moreover, a terrific middle-class town, a place where an astonishing array of entertainment might be enjoyed at very reasonable prices—the greatest jazz that ever was, Broadway in its heyday, any number of swank nightclubs ... and three legendary ball clubs.

Over the first 12 postwar seasons, the Yankees took a total of nine pennants and seven World Series titles and came close to winning two more flags. The Dodgers won six pennants and one World Series and were thwarted on the very last day of the season three times, losing two playoff series and dropping an agonizing extra-inning decision to the Phillies in the last game of the 1950 regular season. The Giants won two pennants and one World Series and finished second once while compiling seven winning seasons. Altogether, in the 10 years from 1947 to 1956, there were no fewer than seven "Subway Series." In 1951, the apogee of the era, all *three* teams finished first.

Yet 1951 also marked the beginning of a new era, the very first pennant race between two teams that were fielding multiple African American players in important positions—and both their presence *and* the absence of additional black players played a critical role. The race was decided as well by the rivalry between the teams' two managers, one of whom was among the very first managers to rely on statistical analysis; by the topography of the Giants' gloriously eccentric home, the Polo Grounds; and—perhaps—by sheer chicanery.

◆

The Giants and Dodgers had shared a league and a city since 1890 (technically, since 1898, when Brooklyn was merged into greater New York). Both the teams themselves and their fans seemed to genuinely hate each other. Yet Brooklyn and New York had rarely faced off in a pennant race before, finishing first and second on just two earlier occasions. The only true previous race between the two teams had been in 1924, when John McGraw's last pennant winner managed to edge out, by 1.5 games, a Dodgers club led by Zack Wheat, Dazzy Vance, and Burleigh Grimes.

This lack of head-to-head competition was due mainly to the Giants' superiority through the 1930s, but by 1951 the club had found it increasingly difficult to keep up with either of its intracity rivals. Whereas the Dodgers and the Yankees were the beneficiaries of the two founding fathers of the minor-league farm system, Branch ("the Mahatma") Rickey and George Weiss, respectively, the Giants had only Horace Stoneham, the genial imbiber who had inherited the team from his father.

"In forty-five years, the team had employed just three managers: John J. McGraw, Bill Terry, Mel Ott," Harvey Frommer wrote of the Giants. "It was a clannish, Irish-dominated organization of Sheehans, Feeneys, Brannicks."

This comfortable world was shaken to its core in 1948, when the longtime Giants star and manager, Mel Ott, was replaced as manager by Leo Durocher, himself recently fired from the helm of the hated Dodgers. Scrappy, profane, and mercurial, Durocher had a penchant for getting into trouble and making enemies—a penchant that stretched back at least to the time that, as a Yankees rookie, he stole Babe Ruth's watch. It was Durocher who first skippered the Dodgers back into the World Series, only to run afoul of Rickey, his old boss Larry MacPhail, baseball commissioner Happy Chandler, the Roman Catholic Church, and clean-living, right-thinking people everywhere with his gambling, drinking, womanizing, and general ruthlessness. "You and Durocher are on a raft. A wave comes and knocks him into the ocean," Dick Young wrote of Leo the Lip. "You dive in and save his life. A shark comes and takes your leg. Next day, you and Leo start out even."

◆

True to form, almost as soon as he arrived in Harlem, Durocher made clear his intention to rid the Giants of their many flat-footed, aging sluggers, such as Johnny Mize and Walker Cooper, and build "my kind of team." The strategy was widely applauded by sportswriters and fans alike, with their usual misguided preference for dirty uniforms over potent bats. In fact, the Giants' lineup was perfectly calibrated for the gloriously eccentric Polo Grounds, with its 279- and 257-foot foul lines and its vast, U-shaped outfield, rolling 483 feet out to the center field clubhouse. What the Giants really lacked was pitching.

Yet the New York squad Durocher inherited *was* aging, its productivity declining rapidly, and he cannily replaced it with a roster that could still hit but was vastly better in the field and on the mound. Best of all, he seems to have prodded the hidebound Stoneham into compensating for his lack of a top farm system by turning to the Negro leagues for help.

By 1951, Leo the Lip seemed to have put together a solid contender. Behind the plate for the Giants on Opening Day 1951 was Wes Westrum, one of the finest defensive catchers in the majors, a low-average hitter but one with plenty of Polo Grounds pop and an abundance of patience at the plate. At first was Monte Irvin, ranked by Bill James as the third-best left fielder in Negro league history, a power hitter who still had a great deal left at age 32. At second and short were Eddie Stanky and Alvin Dark, imported intact from the Braves. Stanky, the abrasive, hustling veteran of NL pennant-winning teams in Brooklyn and Boston, was a good fielder who compensated for his weak hitting by getting hit by pitches and drawing enormous numbers of walks; he had already led the league twice in on-base percentage. Dark was a consistent .300 hitter with some power. He compensated for his league-leading 45 errors in 1951 by topping all NL shortstops in putouts, assists, and double plays.

Filling out the infield was a Durocher project. Third baseman Hank Thompson, another Negro league star, was called "Ametralladora," or "Machine Gun," for the strong arm he showed off in Cuban winter ball. Some thought the nickname was appropriate for other reasons: Raised in a Dallas reform school, Thompson once shot and killed a man who was trying to molest his sister. Thompson carried a gun on his person even after breaking into the big leagues. His debut with the St. Louis Browns was torpedoed by his "drinking and pugnacious attitude," but he blossomed under Durocher, who in 1951 named Thompson the best third baseman he had ever managed. In 1951, though, it was Thompson's time *off* the field that proved decisive.

In the outfield, the Giants worked two similar ballplayers in the corners. Don Mueller, the right fielder, was nicknamed "Mandrake the Magician" for his supposed magic with a bat, but apart from three outstanding seasons from 1953 through 1955, his batting average and on-base percentage were ordinary to poor and his power was limited. Carroll Walter "Whitey" Lockman was a more consistent version of Mueller, with a little more power and better ability to get on base.

In center field was something of an enigma, a Scottish-born resident of Staten Island named Bobby Thomson. Blessed with speed and power, he seemed to possess all the tools necessary to be a star. He covered a great deal of the rolling prairie of the Polo Grounds center field, but after apparent breakthrough seasons in 1947 and 1949, he had slid back into mediocrity. "I was lousy at bat," Thomson recalled, "but I knew I was helping with my glove. ... I tried hard to avoid being an every-other-year ballplayer" (Table 10-1).

Table 10-1 An Every-Other-Year Ballplayer: Bobby Thomson, 1947–1951

| Year | Age | Avg | OBP | Slg | EqA | WARP |
|------|-----|------|------|------|------|------|
| 1947 | 23 | .283 | .336 | .508 | .287 | 6.2 |
| 1948 | 24 | .248 | .296 | .401 | .248 | 2.4 |
| 1949 | 25 | .309 | .355 | .518 | .299 | 9.6 |
| 1950 | 26 | .252 | .324 | .449 | .265 | 5.0 |
| 1951 | 27 | .293 | .385 | .562 | .316 | 7.3 |

What Durocher managed to improve most of all was the Giants' pitching. Sal "the Barber" Maglie had returned from Mexico and the major league blacklist at age 33 in 1950, packing his usual assortment of brushback pitches and a tight curve perfected in the 7,100-foot altitude of Puebla Angeles. Durocher used him mainly in relief his first season back, but when Maglie pitched five shutouts and 12 complete games in 16 starts, Leo got the idea and put him in the starting rotation with two more outstanding starters, Larry Jansen and Jim Hearn. Less certain was what the Giants could expect from Dave Koslo, Sheldon "Available" Jones, and spot-starter/reliever George Spencer at the back of the rotation. But in an age of Spartan pitching staffs, New York's looked as deep as any in the league. The Giants were a skillful blend of young players and veterans, a focused, opportunistic team that could pitch, run, field, and hit for both power and average. Their only real shortcoming was that they were overmatched in just about all these categories by the team that played across the East River.

Even though the Mahatma had been forced out of the front office the preceding winter by Walter O'Malley, the Brooklyn Dodgers were the epitome of a Rickey farm-fed ball club. Up the middle, the Bums boasted no fewer than four future Hall of Famers: catcher Roy Campanella, about to win the first of his three MVPs; the clutch, slick-fielding captain, shortstop Pee Wee Reese; second baseman Jackie Robinson, the fiery breaker of the color line and already a rookie of the year and MVP; and center fielder Duke Snider, the third of the three New York legends who worked the position and who would define "the Era."

At the infield corners were another near Hall of Famer, the power-hitting, smooth-handed first baseman Gil Hodges, and Billy Cox, widely considered the best NL glove at the hot corner and a respectable bat. In right field was the hard-bitten Carl Furillo, a future batting champion known as "the Reading Rifle" for his fearsome arm; in 1951 he racked up 24 assists and even threw a runner out at first base.

Only in left did the Dodgers have a weakness, plugging the gap with a revolving door of Dan Thompson, Tom Brown, Gene Hermanski, and Cal Abrams. On the mound, Brooklyn had put together a staff at least as formidable as the Giants', with a starting quartet of hard-throwing Carl Erskine; Don Newcombe, the first outstanding black hurler to pitch in the big leagues during his prime; canny veteran Elwin Charles "Preacher" Roe; and Ralph Branca, who at 25 had already won over 20 games in a season.

The Dodgers seemed, even then, to have a roster full of budding immortals, a remarkably young, talented, and charismatic team. Their biggest flaw was their manager, Charlie Dressen, a diminutive, charming egotist who had played football under George Halas and baseball under Leo Durocher—but he reserved all credit for his professional success for his favorite person. "If the letter 'I' were dropped from the alphabet, Charlie would be denuded of half his conversational talent," the *New York Post*'s Milton Gross once wrote.

Dressen was considered a solid baseball man by some of his players, and like Durocher he seemed to enjoy a special rapport with the first black players fighting their way into the majors—a sympathy that he claimed was born in seeing the Klan burn a cross on his Catholic family's lawn when he was a boy. Above all, Dressen burned to beat his old boss, but unlike Durocher, he was an intuitionist, given to eccentric, even lunatic theories. He liked to boast that he had never read a book, and he was certainly not about to read a stat sheet. Unlike

Durocher, who usually sought out advice from the Giants' team statistician before making up his lineup card during the 1951 stretch drive, Dressen had the Dodgers' pioneering stats man, Allan Roth, banished to the broadcast booth—a move that would have dire consequences.

"Hold 'em fellas, I'll think of something," Charlie characteristically told Pee Wee Reese in a game the Dodgers were losing by three runs. But in 1951, *ahead* by three runs in the most important inning of his life, he could think of nothing.

◆

Still, throughout most of the 1951 season, it didn't seem possible that Dressen, Durocher, or any other manager could stop the Dodgers. Brooklyn started unevenly, then put everything together in a 7-3 road trip in mid-May, during which the Flock hit .337 and averaged 8.2 runs a game.

Campanella, who had gotten off to a slow start, hit .417 on the trip and put himself on track for a season he would finish with 33 home runs, 108 RBIs, a .325 batting average, and a league-leading 72 assists. Robinson returned to Brooklyn hitting .415; he would finish at .338, with on-base and slugging averages of .429 and .527, respectively. He would lead all NL second basemen in putouts, assists, double plays, and fielding percentage, and—as always—run the bases like no one else in baseball. Pee Wee Reese raised his average to .384, good for third in the NL. Hodges slugged five round-trippers and batted .388 on the trip, en route to a year in which he would hit 40 home runs.

Yet no one was hotter than left fielder Cal Abrams, who returned to Brooklyn leading all major-leaguers with a .470 batting average, eliciting the deathless *Post* headline "Mantle, Shmantle—Long As We Got Abrams." And when Abrams faltered, reportedly by screwing up his swing while moonlighting as a Coney Island batting-cage instructor, general manager Buzzie Bavasi went out and snagged the Cubs' Andy Pafko at the trading deadline, giving up four reserves and has-beens for a 30-year-old outfielder who had hit 36 home runs the year before.

The Pafko deal seemed to settle things. Brooklyn was 34-18 at the time, with a six-game lead, and Pafko himself marveled, referring to his anticipated World Series share, "It's like handing me $5,000." Yet sound as the deal was, the Dodgers had unwittingly forged another link in the unlikely chain of events that led to their undoing.

◆

The Giants, by contrast, fell on their faces at the beginning of the season, getting off to a 2-12 start. When, by May 21, they were still no better than 16-17, Durocher moved Irvin, who had been highly uncomfortable at first base, back to left field and switched Whitey Lockman to first. Lockman was no more thrilled with the position than Irvin had been, but he eventually conquered it, while Irvin thrived in left.

Three days later, in a move perhaps a tad more monumental, Durocher brought Willie Mays up from Triple-A Minneapolis, where he had been thumping American Association pitchers at a .477 clip. After an 0-for-12 start that crept to just 1-for-25, Mays begged to be sent back down. But when Durocher ignored his pleas, the rookie settled in at the plate and began to amaze onlookers with his baserunning and his play in center field, as he would for the next two-plus decades.

Yet Mays's adjustment only left his manager with another conundrum. Bobby Thomson had started the season poorly, hitting just .231 by the All-Star break and repeatedly booting balls in center. Now, with Mays called up, the Flying Scot had no position. When Thomson replaced Don Mueller at the Polo Grounds for an inning on July 15, he was booed. Durocher had been eager to deal his slumping center fielder to the Cubs for Pafko and was furious at Cub manager Frankie Frisch when Frisch let the Dodgers beat him to his man.

Then, on July 17, Leo's project at third, Hank Thompson, was spiked on a pickoff play, putting him out of the lineup for 10 days. The Giants had the perfect replacement waiting in the wings at Minneapolis. Ray Dandridge was a future Hall of Famer, widely considered "the best third baseman never to make the major leagues." A lifetime .355 hitter in the Negro leagues, he was a natural shortstop but a bow-legged wizard at the hot corner; Bill James noted "the line that appears everywhere about him is that a train could go between his legs but a groundball couldn't."

Signed by the Giants halfway through the 1949 season, when he was almost 36, Dandridge batted .362 for Triple-A Minneapolis the rest of the way. In 1950 he batted .311 and was named the American Association's MVP after leading the Millers to the league title. His reward was to be relegated to Minneapolis again the following spring, a pattern that must have begun to seem almost sadistic. Perhaps the Giants were put off by his age or his relative lack of power. In *The Echoing Green*, a meticulously researched history of the 1951 season, Joshua Prager asserts that Dandridge was held back by the "unwritten quotas [that] continued to hamstring black players" in the major leagues. Indeed, when Durocher first asked Stoneham to recall Mays, Stoneham demurred. "No," he said. "We've got too many already."

We will never know for sure. Dandridge had been having yet another excellent year at Minneapolis, hitting .317 with eight home runs and 53 RBIs, but just three days before Thompson's injury, Dandridge was hospitalized with acute appendicitis and put out of action for a month. It was a sad turn for a great pro—but an opening for Bobby Thomson. Durocher paid little attention to his second-string players, but now he had a reason to think of Thomson. He remembered that Thomson had briefly played third when he was called up to the majors in 1946. Now the manager put him back at the bag and worked on his batting stance. Thomson, to his surprise, soon found that he liked the added involvement and intensity of playing the infield, and began to hit with authority again from his new stance.

Leo had finally patched up his lineup and had it humming once more—too late. In 1950, the Giants had gone 50-22 after another bad start, only to finish third behind the Phillies and Dodgers. Now it looked as if the same thing were happening. No matter what they did, the Giants seemed to be no match for the Dodgers head-to-head. On April 29, the Dodgers took their fifth straight game from the Giants at Ebbets Field, and the two teams nearly came to blows when a frustrated Larry Jansen knocked down Duke Snider and plunked Jackie Robinson with a pitch. Robinson retaliated by openly taunting Jansen on his way to first, and Don Newcombe screamed at Durocher, "Eat your heart out!" as Leo the Lip slumped, uncharacteristically lachrymose, in the Giants' dugout, burdened by a bad cold. "I've tried everything. I just can't shake it off," Durocher said in reference to his physical condition, but he might as well have been talking about the Dodgers.

After the game, Dressen was still not willing to let it go. He convinced Branca and perhaps Robinson to join him in serenading the Giants through the thin door that separated the teams' locker rooms, loudly yodeling, "Roll out the barrel! The Giants are dead!" The following day, Robinson, convinced that Sal Maglie was throwing at him, nearly set off another altercation. The second baseman laid a bunt along the first-base line and deliberately ran Maglie down when the pitcher went to field it.

An infuriated Durocher saw to it that the league ordered the door between the Ebbets Field dressing rooms bricked up. But on August 9, after the Dodgers had beaten the Giants for the 12th time in 15 meetings, Dressen insisted on needling his old boss, this time through the wall, "Leo, you in there?"

Leo smoldered—but it seemed there was nothing he could do about it. On August 11, 1951, after Robin Roberts blanked the Giants at the Polo Grounds and Branca topped Warren Spahn in the first game of a doubleheader in Boston, Brooklyn's record stood at 70-35 to the Giants' 59-51, giving the Dodgers their famous lead of 13.5 games—16 games in the loss column. Even after the Dodgers lost the second game, they remained a comfortable 13 games up at the end of the day—the largest first-place lead the franchise had enjoyed, anytime, on anyone.

No team had ever made up such a deficit, and in the years to come, only one ever would, when the 1978 Yankees came from 14 games back to beat out the Red Sox ... and that Yankees team had almost an entire extra month to work with, reaching its nadir on July 19. In 1951, the Giants had only 44 games left to play, the Dodgers, 48. Here is where the miracles, and the controversies, begin.

From August 12 through the end of the regular season on September 30, the Giants would go 37-7, to force a three-game playoff with the Dodgers, who went 26-22. This finishing kick was the second greatest in baseball history, exceeded only by the 38-6 stretch run by the 1942 St. Louis Cardinals. Only four teams have bettered the Giants' 44-game run at *any* time during a regular season, and only another five have matched it.

The comeback can be broken down into four distinct stages. First, the Giants went on a 16-game winning streak from August 12 to 27, while the Dodgers went 9-9 and watched their lead drop to five games. It was during this time that the Giants finally shook the hex the Bums had over them, sweeping the Dodgers at the Polo Grounds by scores of 4-2, 3-1, and 2-1. Durocher's newly configured lineup began to pay dividends, as Bobby Thomson saved the last game for Maglie when he made a great stop of a hard Pafko grounder up the third-base line and tagged out Robinson before he could get back to the bag. Mays scored what proved to be the winning run in the second game and preserved the lead when he made a running catch on a fly to right center, then threw Billy Cox out at the plate.

"I'd like to see him do it again," Dressen groused. "Luck, that was the luckiest throw I've ever seen," opined Carl Furillo, who even in his retirement insisted, "Willie was good, but he was not the ballplayer they built him up to be."

One is left with the distinct impression that if Carl Furillo had played piano he would have felt that Beethoven got all the breaks, but never mind. Now came the second stage, an old-fashioned horse race in which both teams played well. The Dodgers were never able to increase their lead to more than seven games again, but on September 20, with just 10 days left in the season, they still held a 4.5-game margin.

In other words, the Giants had knocked only a half-game off the Bums' lead in over three weeks of play. After Newcombe blanked the Giants, 9-0, at Ebbets Field on September 9 to give the Flock a 6.5-game lead, Dick Young wrote that "the Brooks virtually wrapped up the flag." As late as September 21, the *Sporting News* was referring to the Giants as "the '51 Runners-Up."

The real collapse came then, in stage three, as the Dodgers lost six of their last 10 games while the Giants won their last seven straight, and 12 of their last 13, to clinch at least a tie for first. Yet even then, the Dodgers did not completely fold, ensuring a playoff by winning their final two games in Philadelphia, including a scintillating 14-inning victory on the last night of the season. In those games, Jackie Robinson's hitting and fielding almost single-handedly led them back from deficits of 6-1 and 8-5. For only the second time in major league history, the regular season had ended in a dead heat.

The race was *still* not over ... but for the Dodgers, eking out a tie must have been something of a moral defeat. What had gone wrong? How could such a strong team have squandered such a big lead?

Statistically, it was clearly the team's hitting that went south. Although Brooklyn ended up leading the National League in most hitting categories by wide margins, from August 12 on the Flock batted just .249, 26 points below their season average, while their OPS plunged from .821 to .709. The worst offenders were Furillo, Reese, and Snider. Reese had batted only .217 with no home runs after previously hitting .314 with 10 homers, and Snider had hit only .228 the rest of the way with three round-trippers—and only .191 with a single home run after September 1. Pafko proved something of a disappointment throughout his stint in Dodger blue, hitting only .249 after coming over from the Cubs, although he did belt 10 home runs down the stretch.

From August 12 on, the Brooklyn pitchers, by contrast, compiled the same 3.88 ERA they had chalked up throughout the rest of the season. This number fails to show that at the first real challenge from the Giants, Charlie Dressen succumbed to the "Mauch '64 fallacy"; that is, he began pushing an overworked staff beyond its limits.

The exigencies of baseball in the age of train travel taxed the wiles of many managers. Doubleheaders, day games, and odd off-days abounded. In the last week of the season, for example, the Giants played only four games, the Dodgers seven. To compensate for such quirks of scheduling, good starting pitchers were expected to regularly throw complete games and to make relief stints when needed.

Yet even for the time, Dressen seemed oblivious to the strain he was putting on his staff. All the Dodger starters were either failing or suffering from arm strain by the end of the season. Preacher Roe had compiled a phenomenal 22-2 record by the next-to-last Sunday, but he was shelled in his last two starts, looking so shaky that Dressen did not pitch him in the three-game playoff against the Giants. Carl Erskine had also faltered badly, losing a key September game against Cincinnati and ending the year with an ERA of 4.46. Don Newcombe had left the same Cincinnati game with a "slight muscle pull" in his throwing elbow, though he would pitch valiantly down the stretch.

Most fatefully of all, Dressen pitched Ralph Branca on two days' rest in late August, while the Giants were on their 16-game winning streak. Branca responded with a pair of complete-game shutouts, the last nearly a no-hitter. But after the second start, he felt his triceps tighten, and small wonder: He had pitched a total of 54 innings in August. Branca never regained the top speed on his fastball, winning only one more game the rest of the way and running up a 6.27 ERA in September.

Behind his starters, Dressen also managed to pitch out his invaluable relief man and spot starter, Clyde King, who was 12-5 on August 11 with a 3.55 before succumbing to tendonitis and going 2-2, 6.85 the rest of the way. Dressen's replacement options were limited, and he made them more so. Erv Palica, who had filled King's role the year before, was already down with a sore arm. Clarence "Bud" Podbielan pitched well in relief all year, even winning that last, desperate regular-season game in Philadelphia, but Dressen rarely turned to him, preferring to rely on his veterans, no matter how tired they were.

Nonetheless, a rookie call-up nearly bailed the manager out. Clem Labine was an ideal replacement for King, proving to be a reliable reliever and sometime starter for the rest of the decade. Labine stepped into the rotation in late August and reeled off four straight complete-game wins. After he shut down the Phillies, 6-1, on September 16, Philadelphia skipper Eddie Sawyer called him "now the best pitcher in the league."

But in his next start, also against Philly, Labine ignored Dressen's order to pitch from a full windup with the bases loaded. When he gave up a grand slam to Willie "Puddin' Head" Jones, the angry manager benched his rookie hurler as a punishment. Labine did not pitch for over a week; Dressen used him only *in extremis* in the last game against Philadelphia and to start the second game of the playoff. (According to Roger Kahn, Dressen also never fully trusted Labine, because Labine "was an incubator baby, and no incubator baby could go nine innings.")

Yet all of Charlie Dressen's dotty notions aside, the Dodgers compiled a winning record down the stretch. Much as fans and sportswriters always like to talk about choking, it seems clear that Brooklyn did not lose the pennant but that New York came and took it. What turned the Giants around?

A currently popular explanation, one that matches the corrosive cynicism of our time, is that the Giants cheated. Even before the season ended, there were rumors that Durocher was somehow stealing pitching signs from the Polo Grounds clubhouse, which was uniquely located far out in center field. In 1990 the team's third-string catcher, Sal Yvars, finally came forward to confirm the story. He described an elaborate system whereby coach Herman Franks would decipher opposing teams' signals with the aid of a telescope mounted in the clubhouse window and convey them via an electrical system (installed, ironically, by an electrician who was a lifelong Dodger fan) to Yvars in the Giants' on-field bullpen. Yvars would then pass them on to the batter.

Joshua Prager presents persuasive evidence that Yvars was telling the truth, and the ethics of the situation seem clear. Sign stealing from the field has long been an acknowledged part of the game, but to swipe them from the clubhouse is to give the home team an unacceptable advantage. But did the practice, in fact, give the Giants such an advantage?

Durocher's sign-stealing system was put in place starting on July 20. Yet as crack sabermetrician Dave Smith points out, the Giants' hitting production actually *decreased* from July 20 through the end of the season. The team's batting average at home was .263 before that date and only .256 afterward, and its OPS similarly dipped from .810 to .761. Even during the Giants' 16-game winning streak, 13 of which were played at home, their runs scored *dropped*, from 5.1 runs per game to 4.5.

Yvars attributed the apparent sign-stealing inefficiency to the length of time it took Franks to decipher the other team's signs. The catcher also asserted that the Giants would rely on the stolen signals only in dire situations—factors that supposedly accounted for New York's ability to rally four times during the 16-game streak when trailing after seven innings.

This sounds plausible at first, but if the team was truly relying on stolen signs for all its big rallies but scoring *fewer* runs overall, then the Giants had clearly become too dependent on the whole system and were undermining themselves at the plate. A three-run rally counts as much in the first inning as it does in the ninth.

Still, could the sign stealing have helped one key player—and in one critical situation? Prager points out that Bobby Thomson batted .337 from July 17 to September 17, more than 100 points over what he had been hitting, and adds that Thomson gave different reasons at different times for his improvement: his new stance, his new bat, his mental state. Yet as Prager himself concedes, 11 of the 13 home runs Thomson stroked during that two-month span were hit on the road. For that matter, during their furious September drive to the pennant, the Giants played 18 of their final 25 games on the road—a fact that didn't put a crimp in their winning ways.

So, how did the Giants do it? The same way that winning teams have always done it, with pitching. The Giants' team ERA was 3.86 at the low-water mark of August 11; from then on it was 2.98, dropping the staff's overall season-long mark to a league-leading 3.48—or nearly half a run better than the National League as a whole. During the crucial 16-game winning streak in August the team ERA was 2.39, with Giant hurlers allowing only 35 walks in 147 innings.

And after the streak, New York's pitchers only got better. During the 12-1 run to the end of the regular season, they lowered their collective ERA to a remarkable 1.63. In the last seven consecutive wins, under the full pressure of a pennant race, they gave up a mere nine runs (six earned) and 55 hits, for an ERA of 0.86. New York's hurlers remained dominant through the end of the season, while Giant bats were not especially hot. The team won its final seven games by scores of 4-1, 4-1, 4-3, 5-1, 10-1, 3-0, and 3-2, and turned in six complete games. Durocher expertly used the team's fortuitous off-days in the last week of the season to squeeze complete game victories from Jansen, Maglie, and Jansen again.

Moreover, the Giant pitching improved across the board, with all the starters dropping their ERAs dramatically after August 11. Jim Hearn lowered his ERA by more than two runs, from 4.43 to 2.37, and ended up with 17 wins. Maglie went from 3.23 to 2.32 and finished at

23-6, 2.93, with 22 complete games—and five victories over the Dodgers. Jansen went from 3.53 to 2.02; Jones from 4.61 to 2.75; and Koslo from 3.73 to 2.20. George Spencer provided critical relief help with 10 wins and six saves, and midseason call-up Al Corwin went 5-1 as a starter and reliever.

◆

Inevitably, much of the controversy surrounding the 1951 race was telescoped, so to speak, into its fourth and final stage, the three-game playoff between the two teams. The Dodgers suffered a huge blow even before the series, when Roy Campanella pulled a hamstring running out a triple in the last game against the Phillies. After watching him hobble gamely through a hitless first game of the playoffs, even Dressen conceded that he had to sit his catcher, over Campy's vehement protests.

Moreover, Dressen perhaps blew the playoff right from the coin toss for home-field advantage. Charlie remembered that back in 1946, in the only previous playoff in major league history, Leo Durocher had opted to have the Dodgers open the three-game set in St. Louis—a move widely criticized since the Dodgers then had to take a long train ride to St. Louis and back again.

When the Dodgers won the toss in 1951, Dressen quickly announced that they would play the first game at home in Ebbets Field and thus play the next two away—apparently forgetting that the Polo Grounds, unlike Sportsman's Park, was about a twenty-minute drive away. It was a peculiar decision, given that one of Dressen's coaches, Cookie Lavagetto, *already* suspected that the Giants were stealing signs from their home clubhouse. He had tried to use binoculars to catch them at it during the Dodgers' last game at the Polo Grounds, almost a month before, only to be stopped by the umpires. "The big game is the first game," Dressen insisted. "That's the one you want at home."

Charlie's unique idea of a home-field advantage was quickly neutralized when the Giants won the opener, 3-1, with Ralph Branca pitching eight strong innings but giving up a two-run homer to Bobby Thomson. The Bums bounced back the following afternoon, trouncing the Giants by 10-0 in Harlem, as a properly chastened Labine pitched a six-hit shutout and Campanella's replacement, Rube Walker, homered twice. New York's only rally failed when Labine struck out Thomson with a wicked curveball, on a 3-2 count with the bases loaded.

In the third and final game, Thomson again played an almost uncannily central role in the action. He ran the Giants out of an early rally with a baserunning blunder, drove in the tying run with a double in the seventh, then flubbed two difficult balls at third in the top of the eighth to leave the Dodgers with a 4-1 lead. Brooklyn had the pennant within its grasp—but the last strong Dodger arm was slowly giving way.

Dressen had picked Don Newcombe to start the final playoff game, even though he had worked Big Newk to a nub in September. On the last Wednesday of the regular season, the pitcher had worked a complete-game win over the Braves, then returned to throw a shutout against the Phillies on Saturday. Nonetheless, Dressen brought him back into that desperate, 14-inning game on *Sunday*, and Newcombe responded with five and two-thirds more innings of shutout ball.

Now, after only two days of rest, Newk was on the mound again. After the Giants' seventh inning, he came back to the dugout and announced frankly, "My arm's tight," only to be upbraided by his teammate Robinson: "Bullshit, you go out there and pitch until your goddamn arm falls off." The injured Campanella tried to cajole him more gently into doing the same, and after the Dodgers scored three runs to retake the lead, Newcombe went back out and struck out the side in the eighth.

It makes a poignant picture, just four years after baseball's color line had been broken—the three black teammates huddled together in a corner of the dugout, haranguing one of their number not to look weak. But after the eighth, Newcombe still told Dressen, "It looks like I just don't have it anymore. Take me out." Charlie still left the decision up to his pitcher, and thus upbraided again, though more subtly, Newk went back out to work his 33rd inning within a week. Only then did the big right-hander finally begin to crack, giving up a pair of singles and a double that whittled the Dodger lead to 4-2 before Dressen finally pulled him for Ralph Branca.

Knowing when to replace a pitcher is the most important field decision a manager has to make, but Dressen compounded his errors in that ninth inning. Leading 4-1, he had his first baseman, Hodges, hold Al Dark on after Dark led off the frame with a seeing-eye single. The next batter, Mueller, hit a bouncer in the hole that Hodges had just vacated. The ball ticked off the first baseman's glove and rolled into right field. Mueller later told Roger Kahn, "I always checked the fielders before I swung," adding, "If Hodges had played deep, I would have swung differently and just as likely gotten a base hit." But this assertion is hard to swallow; if "Mandrake" could really hit doubles down the line at will, he should have managed more than the 10 he produced that season.

Two batters later, Dressen brought in Branca instead of Erskine to relieve Newcombe, a move he later blamed on his bullpen coach, Clyde Sukeforth, who told him that Erskine "just bounced his curveball." But there were other good reasons to choose Branca. "Oisk" Erskine had been hammered by hitters in September—and by Bobby Thomson throughout his career. The Flying Scot had hit .545 in 22 lifetime at-bats against Erskine, with five extra-base hits, as opposed to only .265 in 49 lifetime at-bats against Branca.

Yet in 1951, Thomson's luck against Branca had changed. The batter was 4-for-12 against him with a triple and two home runs, including the blast that had beaten the Dodgers just two days before—a game in which Branca had thrown 133 pitches. And Branca-Erskine was hardly the only choice Charlie had. Thomson was just 2-for-8 that year against Podbielan, 1-for-6 against Clyde King, and only a lifetime .220 hitter against Preacher Roe, who had been showing obvious fatigue but had thrown only 1.2 innings in the past five days.

For that matter, Dressen could have put in Labine—had the manager not needlessly used him for all nine innings in the Dodger rout the day before. Labine had held an 8-0 lead going into the bottom of the seventh, in a situation similar to the sixth game of the 2001 World Series. In that game, Bob Brenly showed enough foresight to pull Randy Johnson early from a rout against the Yankees, thereby enabling Johnson to pitch a crucial two innings the next night. Dressen might have similarly chosen to trade Labine's last nine outs in Game 2 of the playoff for two more in Game 3.

Of course, there remained the question of why Dressen had to pitch at all to Thomson, who was by far the Giants' hottest hitter, with first base open and a nervous rookie in the on-deck circle literally praying that he wouldn't have to hit. Willie Mays had batted just .105 against Branca in 19 at-bats and had been slumping against everyone of late, batting just .233 since September and .100 in the playoff. Statistician Roth was now sorely missed around the Dodger dugout, and Dressen preferred to live or die by the old baseball maxim "never put the winning run on base."

With a little more help from the front office, Dressen might have been able to entertain an even more intriguing option. Joe Black was a big, smart, hard-throwing right-hander who had taught school and would later become a corporate executive. He came to the Dodgers' organization after eight years with the Baltimore Elite Giants in the

Negro leagues, and in 1951 he had compiled good numbers with both Triple-A Montreal (7-9, 3.85) and Double-A St. Paul (4-3, 2.25). Black had pinpoint control and a fastball that was clocked at 96 miles per hour, and in 1952 his outstanding relief pitching would carry the Dodgers over the line after another late-season swoon.

Why wasn't Black brought up to the big club, particularly in September, after the rosters expanded? Was it another case of one black player too many? Would it have been too much for white America—or, more likely, baseball's all-white management—to have one big, smart, black fireballer relieving another and blowing away white batters to clinch the pennant?

Perhaps this is unfair. It was the Dodgers, after all, who had first broken the color barrier in baseball, and Dressen would rely heavily on Black the following season. Yet Kahn claims that even "by 1949 the Dodgers were backing away from further good black prospects," including Willie Mays, and he quotes Branch Rickey himself as cautioning, "It would not have been prudent to have had too many Negroes on any one club." Not until 1971 did a club (the Pittsburgh Pirates) field an all-minority lineup.

Instead, Dressen brought a slumping, exhausted pitcher into the ninth inning of the biggest game he would ever manage, to face a batter who had hit him well all year and beat him with a home run in his last outing. And whereas Dressen usually went over the next hitter with the new pitcher, this time he did not even remind Branca of how Labine had struck Thomson out with a curve in a key situation the day before. Dressen merely instructed his pitcher, "Get him out." It is difficult to believe that Charlie Dressen was not in some kind of fugue state throughout that ninth inning.

◆

Miracles followed. Thomson took a called strike, then turned on an inside fastball and belted a line drive into the Polo Grounds' short left-field porch, touching off pandemonium—and enduring controversy.

Dressen, perhaps alone, had no doubts. Years later, he told Red Barber that the only thing he would have done differently would have been to put Campanella in to catch despite his injury, "because he would have gotten Newcombe through"—who knows, perhaps with a tissue transplant.

Thanks to our modern preference for scandal of all kinds, attention now remains fixed on the Giants' sign-stealing system. Prager takes

Thomson's ambiguous statements over the years to imply strongly that he *was* tipped off to what pitch Branca was going to throw when he hit his famous home run.

Yet as Thomson himself points out, Branca's first pitch was a meaty fastball, straight down the pike, which he took for a strike—a pitch so fat that Erskine, back in the bullpen, shouted in horror, "Oh, no! Ralph, not down there! Good night! Not down there!"

If Thomson *did* know which pitches were coming, why would he ever take Branca's mistake pitch instead of swinging at the inside fastball the pitcher threw next? This, even Prager allows, is a "fair point." Finally, as Prager notes, Dressen himself, by the second game of the playoff, had become convinced that the Giants were stealing signs. The Dodgers changed their signals accordingly, something that helped preserve Labine's shutout. How, then, did they fail to exercise similar caution in the third game?

Many years later, Branca would accuse the Giants of "the most despicable act in the history of the game." It was an understandable outburst from a man who was forced to spend most of his life as a goat, a good pitcher who was pitched-out and put in a situation he should never have had to face. Nonetheless, it's a ludicrous claim.

For all the speculation, for all the rumors and the might-have-beens and the sheer happenstance that characterize any close pennant race, the 1951 National League flag went to the team with the best pitching—and the manager who knew best how to exploit, nurture, and husband it.

### Durocher's Obsession: Static Versus Dynamic Offenses

CLAY DAVENPORT

When Leo Durocher took the reins of the Giants in 1948, the club was coming off a historic, record-breaking season. In 1947, the Giants had hit 221 home runs, a then-modern record. (Their total was beaten by the Yankees of 1961, the Twins of 1963, the Tigers of 1987, and 35 other teams between 1996 and 2006, which showed how much the game changed in the mid-1990s.) But to the authors of the 1948 *Spink Baseball Guide*, the home run feat was more noteworthy than the debut of Jackie Robinson (Spink wasn't exactly out front on baseball's racial issues).

Durocher considered the home run record a negative, evidence of the club's devotion to power at the expense of fundamentals. Asked by owner Horace Stoneham to evaluate the team, Durocher's answer was succinct. "Back up the truck":

> "It ain't my kind of team," I told him. We had Johnny Mize, who could hit the ball a mile and couldn't run. We had Walker Cooper, who could hit the ball out of sight and couldn't run. We had Willard Marshall and Sid Gordon, who could hit the ball out of the park and could run a little, but not very much.
>
> "Horace, you're throwing your money away when you pay me. A little boy can manage this team. All you do is make out the lineup and hope you get enough home runs. You can't steal, they're too slow. You can't bunt. You can't hit and run. I can't *do* anything. I can only sit and wait for a home run."

As soon as he was on board, Durocher promptly started dismantling the team. To a certain extent, he had no choice. Despite their home run record, the 1947 Giants were not a particularly good offense for the number of home runs they hit. Their OBP, the fifth-best in the league and below average, made sure of that. In addition, the roster was old, and changes were sure to come, whether the new manager liked their offensive style or not. Top slugger Mize was 35, and in his last truly productive season. Catcher Cooper was 33 and was falling far short of his 1947 season (35 home runs, a fluke; it was the only time he ever hit more than 20). In replacing some players, the new manager envisioned a team able to do those things he had complained about to Stoneham. Durocher's team would be faster; they would steal, bunt, and take extra bases, all the little things that establishment baseball has championed and upstarts like Baseball Prospectus have disparaged. In short, Durocher wanted to swap a static offense (wait for the home run) for a dynamic one (call plays, make things happen).

Managers have often preferred the active teams, the dynamic ones, partly because these teams let the manager do something. The only real exception might be Earl Weaver, who preached the doctrine of the three-run homer. The trouble is that you can't get a really good offense without home runs. It's like trying to lose weight without exercising, or running for office without raising money. The gain from home runs is so enormous that any other way requires exceptional—and unsustainable—performances. A team would have to hit .400 to get the same offense from batting average alone.

This seems obvious; it takes a lot of singles, doubles, and walks in sequence for a team to score three runs, whereas it takes just two baserunners and a long fly to score three on a home run. But why do so many managers prefer the dynamic style of play? A purist could argue that the natural style of baseball is dynamic, that when baseball became America's pastime, it was with a fast-paced, swing-away, run-and-catch style of play, not the slow, methodical approach that the homer-and-walk-and-take-pitches crowd advocates. There has been an unfortunate trade-off between the most exciting strategies and the most effective.

The statistics of a team are a reflection of the players, and the statistics of the players are a reflection of their skills. Skills tend to come in certain packages, partly because certain skills naturally go together and partly because skills also determine how the player is taught. In the modern game, stolen bases and triples largely result from a player's speed (in the dead-ball era, triples were also an expression of power). Triples and speed have a high correlation, but the correlation is far from perfect. Stolen-base king Rickey Henderson was a poor triples hitter, largely because left-handed hitters have a huge advantage when it comes to hitting triples, and Henderson was a righty at the plate. Home run hitters, by contrast, tend to be bigger—the upper-body strength enables home runs, but it also means more weight to carry around the field and a slower overall runner. Their best drives don't go into the gaps or corners; they go over the fence—all of which means fewer triples. Home runs and triples have a negative correlation, meaning that in general the more home runs a hitter produces, the fewer triples he hits.

Fast players, lacking power, are taught to slap at pitches, to put them on the ground and use their legs to beat the throws to first. Power hitters take a ripping swing that sacrifices control for power. Sluggers have a greater need to wait on a cripple pitch (while almost any pitch can be slapped, far fewer can be effectively driven). The hitter isn't the only one whose strategies change: Pitchers, too, have choices, often throwing much more carefully to players who can reach the upper deck and trying to avoid those cripple pitches the hitters crave. It's the speed guys who get challenged, because the threat of a single is not enough of a deterrent.

You end up with dramatic differences between the quick guys and the big ones in multiple statistics. It isn't so much that the fast guys hit lots of singles, but that power hitters get very few. Triples work as a differentiator because the fast guys hit more and the sluggers hit fewer. Both walks and strikeouts line up strongly in the power hitter's favor. Doubles, however, are not useful indicators; they correlate only weakly with stolen bases and home runs, so they don't tell us what kind of skill the team relies on most.

We will explore the hidden advantages of the dynamic style of play and why Durocher and so many other managers preferred it. Looking at all the teams, we've built a scoring system that relies on the correlations just discussed. Singles, steals, and triples drive your dynamic index up; home runs, walks, and strikeouts drive it down. We're relying on translated statistics, a system of converting all the values to a common baseline, to take out the differences in the way the game has been played. We're also limiting ourselves to the years since 1920, because the translations from the true deadball era to the live one are considerably more speculative. Each of the six statistics (singles, steals, triples, homers, walks, and strikeouts) is expressed as a normalized value, meaning that we've subtracted the average score and divided by the standard deviation, eliminating the problem of determining how many singles equals a home run. The most dynamic and most static teams, by this method, are shown in Table 10-2.

It is no surprise to see Whitey Herzog's Cardinals of the 1980s on

Table 10-2  All-Time Most Dynamic and Most Static Major League Teams, Dynamic Index and Other Records

| Most Dynamic | | | | Most Static | | | |
|---|---|---|---|---|---|---|---|
| Team | Dyn. Index | W-L | Finish | Team | Dyn. Index | W-L | Finish |
| 1992 Milwaukee | 20.22 | 92-70 | 2nd, AL E | 1927 New York (AL) | -17.10 | 110-44 | 1st |
| 1985 St. Louis | 19.48 | 101-61 | 1st, NL E | 1933 Philadelphia (AL) | -16.91 | 79-72 | 3rd |
| 1975 California | 18.82 | 72-89 | 6th, AL W | 1947 New York (NL) | -16.44 | 81-73 | 4th |
| 1979 Houston | 18.78 | 89-73 | 2nd, NL W | 1932 Philadelphia (AL) | -16.24 | 94-60 | 2nd |
| 1986 St. Louis | 18.73 | 79-82 | 3rd, NL E | 1920 New York (AL) | -16.11 | 95-59 | 3rd |
| 1920 Cincinnati | 18.50 | 82-71 | 3rd | 1931 Philadelphia (AL) | -15.39 | 107-45 | 1st |
| 1944 Washington | 17.98 | 64-90 | 8th | 1992 Detroit | -14.88 | 75-87 | 6th |
| 1943 Chicago (AL) | 17.68 | 82-72 | 4th | 1922 Philadelphia (AL) | -14.85 | 65-89 | 7th |
| 1923 Chicago (AL) | 16.72 | 69-85 | 7th | 2000 Oakland | -14.83 | 91-70 | 1st, ALW |
| 1991 St. Louis | 16.49 | 84-78 | 2nd, NL E | 1999 Oakland | -14.75 | 87-75 | 2nd, AL W |

this list—the 1986 and 1989 teams rank among the top 25 teams on the extended dynamic list—as they are held up as the epitome of a team that relies on speed instead of power. The Cardinals are the most extreme such team ever assembled, and one of the few that did it successfully. The list-leading 1992 Brewers, managed by Phil Garner, hit just 82 home runs, one of the lowest non-Cardinals totals of the last 25 years, and stole 256 bases, the highest non-Cardinals total of the last 25 years. The team that beat the Brewers in the standings, the Toronto Blue Jays, stole just 129 bases that year, but hit 163 home runs.

The rest of the dynamic teams are not very good; the ten teams averaged 714 translated runs and 83.1 wins (real wins, adjusted only to a common 162-game schedule). Meanwhile, the Giants of Durocher's ire show up third on the static list, along with the most famous team of all time in first and a host of pennant winners. The static teams average 770 runs, some 56 more than their dynamic counterparts, and 91.2 wins.

A group of ten teams isn't really enough of a sample, but unfortunately for the speed lovers, in this case it's a fair sample. The top 100 static teams outscored the 100 dynamic teams by an average of 763 to 711.

So what drives managers to choose speedier teams? What makes up for the drop-off in total offense, according to these managers? If the dynamic style cannot match the totals of the static style, perhaps the speedier teams can be more efficient, squeezing more runs out of their events than the static teams can. This reasoning has some merit: Because the dynamic offenses are faster, they should be better baserunners and produce more runs.

No such trend emerges. Consider the difference between actual and expected runs for the season for the top 10, 50, and 100 static and dynamic teams as shown in Table 10-3.

Indeed, the relationship between speed and runs is quite the opposite; the static teams exceed their expected run totals by more than the dynamic teams did. The flaw in the preceding argument is that stolen bases and better baserunning don't correlate with more runs, except in faulty memory.

Another argument for dynamic offenses is timing. The most-quoted paeans to little ball speak of always being able to manufacture a run when you need it most, which suggests that

Table 10-3 Differences Between Actual and Expected Runs

|  | Top 10 | Top 50 | Top 100 |
| --- | --- | --- | --- |
| Static | +7.4 | +6.4 | +4.2 |
| Dynamic | +7.0 | +3.2 | +1.4 |

these teams can control the timing of their runs to get maximum benefit from them. If this were true, the advantage would show up as a discrepancy between estimated wins, based on runs scored and allowed, and actual wins. In this case, the evidence weakly supports the traditionalists. There is a slight advantage for the dynamic team, in terms of wins minus expected wins (Table 10-4):

Table 10-4 Wins Minus Expected Wins

|  | Top 10 | Top 50 | Top 100 |
|---|---|---|---|
| Static | -0.70 | -0.42 | -0.27 |
| Dynamic | +0.60 | +0.35 | +0.44 |

For a really good dynamic team, we are looking at about a one-win advantage over a top static team. That is, good offensive timing slightly offsets the roughly 50-run advantage of the static teams. By itself, that certainly wouldn't be enough of a reason for a team to change its style.

◆

Yet we've only been looking at half the game in this analysis. Speed is a vital part of the defensive game; fast teams could make up for their offensive shortcomings by being defensively superior, something that has worked for weak-hitting middle infielders since time immemorial (or at least since Davy Force was a star of the 1870s, entirely for his defense). Does the evidence support the idea that defense gets better with either approach?

Still recognizing that even the best defensive schemes have shortcomings, especially as we go further back in time and away from pitch-by-pitch and even play-by-play records, we see little evidence that dynamic play produces better defense. The top 10 dynamic teams allowed more runs (an average of 702 translated runs), relative to their league, than their static counterparts allowed (673). How can this be so, given what we know about defense and speed?

First of all, we are assuming that the pitchers are equivalent—after all, the selection criteria had nothing to do with pitchers or pitching stats. We may be looking at a second-order result that goes something like this: Since at least the 1920s, teams have recognized the superior value of sluggers for generating runs. Despite the occasional protests of managers, the big bats get the highest salaries and end up playing for richer teams. Speed has always been recognized as a compensation for the inability to slug. Furthermore, richer teams can also afford to get the best pitchers.

The results show this to be the case, since the defensive ratings

Table 10-5 Fielding Runs Above Average

|         | Top 10 | Top 50 | Top 100 |
|---------|--------|--------|---------|
| Static  | -3.26  | -4.8   | -3.8    |
| Dynamic | +0.29  | +4.32  | +12.3   |

Table 10-6 Pitching Runs Above Average

|         | Top 10 | Top 50 | Top 100 |
|---------|--------|--------|---------|
| Static  | +29.8  | +31.7  | +31.6   |
| Dynamic | -2.1   | -25.6  | -34.0   |

alone do provide a slight advantage to the fast teams. Let's look at Table 10-5, which shows the fielding runs above average, translated, for the top 10, 50, and 100 static and dynamic teams. Table 10-6 shows the pitching runs above average, translated.

An increasing disparity in pitchers is offset, but only partly, by improved fielding; still, the fielding appears to be worth another 10 runs or so in the balance between the two forms (Durocher, as manager of the relatively rich Giants, wouldn't have had to worry about being able to afford pitching talent). Still, the fielding and timing issues only recoup about half of the difference that was lost in having a speed-based, rather than power-based, offense. So again we have to ask why.

We'll have to speculate on that one. The question is, how much is a manager worth, with his decisions? More relevant to the argument, how much does a manager *think* the sum of his decisions over the course of a season is worth? Durocher gave the game away in his speech to Stoneham: "Horace ... I can't *do* anything." The one thing a dynamic team provides that a static team does not is opportunities for the manager to feel as if he's making a difference—he can call for stolen bases, hit and run, and sacrifice.

While it is still up to the players to produce, the manager can easily persuade himself that he made a difference. Given the selective nature of human memory (the times something worked are remembered a lot better than all the times it didn't), perhaps he feels that he "won" one game a month. That would be six games over a year, a level well above the league-average player. A static team, by contrast, offers few opportunities for in-game management, leading to the oft-maligned "push-button" manager, a job, as Durocher said, a little boy could do. Granted, it offers the comfortable out of blaming the players for any shortfalls in performance, but for someone who wants to win—and Durocher was as ferocious as managers ever came on that score—it seems that the (to them) obvious advantages of adding their own skills to those of their players must be a net winner.

## The Say-Hey Savior: Rookies and Pennant Races

JAY JAFFE

The annals of baseball history are filled with great rookies, many of whom played critical roles in the push for the pennant. In this book, we've seen the impact that players like Willie Mays, Dick Allen, and Larry Sherry had on their teams' fates—the teams may not have always won, but without these exceptional rookies, there might not have even been a race. Something about a successful prodigy stirs the blood, lending extra dimensions of excitement and novelty to a pennant race.

There's something compelling about a contending team willing to play a rookie. Pennants are routinely lost through failures of imagination and stubborn commitments to the tried and true. Relying on a relatively unproven player—one whom your scouts have judged capable—is a daring move, yet one that makes sound economic sense and offers a higher upside than does veteran mediocrity.

Mediocre play is an easy commodity to come by; the concept of the replacement level is built on this reality. Talent is not equally distributed among professional ballplayers; in fact they are the far right of a bell curve whose theoretical peak is the segment of the population that can catch up to Dad's floater in a backyard Wiffle ball game, and whose first standard deviation in ability might be a candidate for the company softball team. Further right along the curve are professional ballplayers, and those able to succeed at higher levels—Rookie League, A, AA, AAA—are smaller and smaller subsets of that population. As Bill James noted, for every player who is 10 percent above average, there may be 20 players who are 10 percent below average. A team that unsuccessfully tries to break in a rookie can easily fall back on another solution. The reward lies in taking a chance on the player who might improve on those results.

Quantifying the rookies who had the most impact on a pennant race is no easy task. Sometimes, as with Fred Lynn in 1975 (9.4 Wins Above Replacement Player, or WARP, on a Red Sox team that won the AL East by 4.5 games), a rookie made such a difference that his team won handily. Other times, as with Sherry, being recalled midseason prevents a player from amassing counting stats that chart impressively, but they make an impact nonetheless. Bob "Hurricane" Hazle combined both aspects by hitting a .403/.477/.649 in 155 plate appearances—good for 2.6 WARP—of the 1957 Braves. They were tied for first with the Cardinals when Hazle joined them on July 29, and the Braves ended up winning by eight games.

### Top Ten in Tight Spots

Moving beyond quantification, we can examine the contributions of rookies in pennant races from many other angles. In the rest of this chapter, we look at several rookies who had significant influence on their teams' performance. Table 10-7 presents the heavyweight rookie champions who made the greatest contributions—as defined by WARP, which measures each player's offense, defense, fielding, and pitching performance—to teams that finished anywhere from two games out of first place to two games ahead of the pack.

Table 10-7 Top Ten in Tight Spots: Rookies Who Made the Greatest Contributions to Their Teams in Tight Races

| Rank | Player | Pos | Year | Team | WARP | GB | Key Stats |
|------|--------|-----|------|------|------|-----|-----------|
| 1 | Dick Allen | 3B | 1964 | PHI | 13.0 | 1.0 | .318/.382/.557, 29 HR |
| 2 | Albert Pujols | 3B, 1B, OF | 2001 | STL | 11.0 | 0.0 | .329/.403/.610, 37 HR |
| 3 | Carlton Fisk | C | 1972 | BOS | 9.4 | 0.5 | .293/.370/.538, 22 HR |
| 4 | Gene Bearden | P | 1948 | CLE | 9.1 | +1.0 | 20-7, 2.43 ERA |
| 5 | Stan Musial | LF | 1942 | STL | 9.0 | +2.0 | .315/.397/.490, 10 HR |
| 6 | F. Valenzuela | P | 1981 | LA | 8.9 | +0.5 | 13-7, 2.48 ERA |
| 7 | Frank Robinson | RF | 1956 | CIN | 8.8 | 2.0 | .290/.379/.558, 38 HR |
| 8T | Don Newcombe | P | 1949 | BRO | 8.2 | +1.0 | 17-8, 3.17 ERA |
| 8T | Cal Ripken Jr. | SS | 1982 | BAL | 8.2 | 1.0 | .264/.317/.475, 28 HR |
| 10T | Paul Dean | P | 1934 | STL | 7.5 | +2.0 | 19-11, 3.43 ERA |
| 10T | Scott Williamson | P | 1999 | CIN | 7.5 | 1.5 | 12-7, 19 Saves, 2.41 ERA |

### *The Original Dick, but Not Tricky*

Dick Allen tops our list despite his Phillies' coming up agonizingly short. For all the controversy that enveloped the rest of his career, it's virtually impossible to find fault with his performance during the 1964 collapse. Allen, who played all 162 games, hit .415/.442/.634 during the 10-game losing streak, and .314/.434/.618 overall in September. Defensively, his two errors in that skid were of no consequence to the outcome either, and despite his 41 errors on the year, he was eight runs above average defensively, thanks to excellent range.

## A Prince of a Player

It's not as though Albert Pujols didn't do enough by clubbing 37 homers, winning Rookie of the Year honors and placing fourth in the MVP voting as the Cardinals won the 2001 NL wild card. Defensively, he had a value beyond his nine runs above average in the field, playing 55 games at third base, 43 at first, and 39 apiece in left- and right field. That versatility extended the roster, helped the Cards cover for injuries to Mark McGwire and J. D. Drew, and enabled the waiver-wire trade of Ray Lankford for Woody Williams, who went 7-1 with a 2.28 ERA after being acquired.

## It's All Downhill

Hurler Johnny Beazley, the teammate of rookie number five, Stan Musial, ranks 12th on this list with a 21-6, 2.13 ERA performance worth 7.4 WARP in 1942. Inducted into the air force the following year, Beazley hurt his arm in an exhibition against his old teammates—apparently, his commanding officer told him to pitch through the pain—and was never the same, generating just 0.8 more WARP in his career.

Gene Bearden was the difference-maker in the 1948 AL race. Pitching on one day's rest, the lefty knuckleballer started and won the pennant-deciding playoff in Fenway Park, tossing a complete-game five-hitter. Already 28, a refugee of both the Phillies' and Yankees' systems, and the recipient of a Purple Heart from World War II, Bearden had already peaked by that year. Bouncing to four other teams, he won only 25 more big-league games over the next five seasons, worth just 8.2 WARP.

## Three Little Indians

From a historical perspective, Bearden wasn't even the most notable rookie on the 1948 Indians. That distinction applies to Larry Doby (.301/.384/.490, 6.1 WARP, tied for 29th on our list), who broke the AL's color barrier on July 5, 1947, but got just 32 at-bats that year, leaving his rookie status intact. Fellow Negro Leagues alum Satchel Paige debuted on July 9, 1948, two days after his 42nd birthday. Paige went 6-1 with a 2.48 ERA, good for 2.6 WARP.

## We Wuz Robbed!

Carlton Fisk and his 1972 Red Sox fell victim to one of the grossest injustices in baseball history. The 13-day players' strike in April resulted in the cancellation of games that weren't rescheduled, leaving the

85-70 Sox with one less contest on their docket than the 86-70 Tigers had. Even without this disadvantage, Boston still blew the race; the Sox led by 1.5 with four games to play, but lost three of their final four, including the first two games of a season-ending three-game series in Tiger Stadium.

### Strike Two!

The seven-week 1981 strike induced a split-season format in which the prestrike division leaders were declared the "first half" winners, qualifying for an expanded playoff. The Dodgers stood half a game ahead of the Reds in the NL West at the time, and while much was made about Cincinnati's missing the postseason despite a better overall record (66-42 compared with 63-47), the run differentials—plus-94 for the Dodgers, plus-24 for the Reds, and plus-63 for the second-half-winning Astros—suggest the Reds' rough justice was somewhat earned.

Subbing for an injured Jerry Reuss on Opening Day, rotund 20-year-old Fernando Valenzuela blanked the Astros, beginning an eight-game streak in which he tossed seven complete games and five shutouts for a 0.29 ERA. Though he cooled off, that initial burst catapulted the Dodgers into the postseason and set off "Fernandomania," producing a transcendent superstar who could pack stadiums yet still couldn't speak a lick of English. Having led the circuit in innings, strikeouts, and shutouts, Valenzuela earned Cy Young honors as well as Rookie of the Year, the only pitcher to win both awards in the same season.

Another excellent 1981 rookie, Montreal left fielder Tim Raines (6.5 WARP on .304/.391/.438 hitting with 71 steals in just 88 games), ties for 20th on our list. His Expos finished half a game ahead of the Cardinals in the second half, when the stakes of the pennant race were more tangible. Raines was reduced to pinch-running by season's end, however, having broken a bone in his hand while sliding on September 13.

### It Pays to Integrate

The Brooklyn Dodgers' place at the forefront of integration enabled them to add three superstars in three years. In 1947, the team broke the color barrier with first baseman Jackie Robinson (6.4 WARP in the most courageous debut in baseball history). The next year, they added Roy Campanella (4.3 WARP in part-time duty) and, in 1949, Don Newcombe (8.2 WARP, tied for eighth on our "Tight Spots" list). From 1947 to 1956, that trio captured five MVP awards (Campanella three times), two Rookies of the Year (Robinson, the award's first recipient, and Newcombe), and the first Cy Young (Newcombe in 1956, when he also became the first pitcher to win both the Cy and the MVP) while helping the Dodgers to six NL pennants.

The Giants were the second NL team to integrate, adding both Hank Thompson (who had already broken the color barrier for the Browns in 1947) and Monte Irvin in mid-1949 and Willie Mays (.274/.356/.472, 5.9 WARP, tied for 35th on our list) in 1951. While the lily-white 1948 Braves and 1950 Phillies slipped through, the Dodgers, Giants, and Braves (the third NL team to integrate) won every other NL pennant between 1947 and 1959.

### The Nick of Time

Willie Mays's overall ranking isn't terribly impressive, but that's because he didn't debut until May 25, 1951, the Giants' 37th game of the year. Projected to a season of 157 games (including the three-game playoff that culminated with you-know-what), his 7.7 WARP would crack our top ten. Larry Sherry (7-2, 3 saves, 2.19 ERA, 4.5 WARP) didn't debut until July 4, 1959, but he was a big part of the Dodgers' catching the Giants and Braves, putting up microscopic ERAs of 1.85 in August and 1.36 in September. By year's end, Sherry was the toast of the baseball world, having won World Series MVP honors with two wins and two saves against the White Sox. Had he put in a full season consistent with his half-season of work, he'd have finished with 6.8 WARP, tied for 18th.

Nearly half a century later, another Dodger call-up made a big impact as well. Catcher Russell Martin (.282/.355/.436, 6.5 WARP) didn't debut until May 5, 2006, when the team was sputtering along at 12-17. The Dodgers won 16 of Martin's first 18 starts to catapult themselves back into the race, while Martin pipped injured Dioner Navarro out of a job.

### Too Little, Too Late

Willie McCovey (.354/.429/.656, 4.2 WARP) won Rookie of the Year honors in 1959 despite playing in just 52 games from July 30 onward. Had the Giants recalled him from Phoenix, where he had hit .372 with 29 homers in just 95 games, a few weeks earlier, they might have padded their win totals enough to withstand the late-season collapse that left them four games behind the Dodgers.

Cisco Carlos (2-0, 0.86 ERA, 1.4 WARP) didn't debut for the 1967 White Sox until August 25, but he tossed 41.2 innings in seven starts and one relief appearance, allowing just four runs. While the Sox got as close as half a game out with five left, they went winless the rest of the way and finished fourth, just three games out. Unlike McCovey and the Giants, Carlos would have been unlikely to sustain anything close to his performance even if recalled earlier; the league caught on to him the next year as he was pounded for a 3.91 ERA—very unimpressive in the Year of the Pitcher—while going 4-14.

The Expos' Steve Rogers (10-5, 1.54 ERA, 6.7 WARP) debuted on July 18, 1973, and pitched shutouts in his second and third starts. Rogers nearly carried an otherwise mediocre (79-83) Expos team through a five-way scrum for the NL East title in 1973. Would an earlier recall have helped? Rogers had gone just 2-6 with a 4.08 ERA in Triple-A the year before, and while he'd clearly made great strides earlier in the season, his 15-22, 4.47 ERA follow-up in 1974 suggests he might have struggled to carry a heavier load.

### Year of the Rookie

The 2006 season introduced a banner crop of rookies who influenced division races and cracked our expanded list. Thirteenth-ranked Francisco Liriano (12-3, 2.16 ERA, 7.2 WARP) keyed the Twins' turnaround; they were just 17-24 on May 19, when he made his first start, but they went on to pass the Tigers (featuring 20th-ranked Justin Verlander with 6.6 WARP) in the season's final week, winning the AL Central. Alas, Liriano pitched just two games after July 28, ultimately succumbing to an elbow injury that required Tommy John surgery.

Over in the NL West, the Dodgers and Padres finished the season tied for the top spot, with the Padres winning the head-to-head tiebreaker. The Dodgers featured the aforementioned Martin and closer Takashi Saito, a 36-year-old Japanese veteran in his stateside debut (7.0 WARP, 17th on the list). The Padres had second baseman Josh Barfield (6.8 WARP, 18th) as well as starter Clay Hensley (5.3 WARP, 49th).

### The Coasters

As mentioned, some rookies performed so well their teams won their league's or division's flag without nail-biting drama. No list of these would be complete without center fielder Lynn (who won MVP honors as well as Rookie of the Year), right fielder Ichiro Suzuki (10.3 WARP for the 2001 Mariners, who won a record 116 games, outdistancing the AL West pack by 14), shortstop Donie Bush (9.5 WARP for the 1909 Tigers, who won the AL pennant by 3.5 games), Jackie Robinson (whose 1947 Dodgers won by five games), and a pair of Yankees short-stops more than half a century apart: Phil Rizzuto in 1941 (8.3 WARP as the Yanks won by 17 games) and Derek Jeter in 1996 (6.0 WARP as they won the AL East by four games).

# 1984 American League West

## *Complacency*

### STEVEN GOLDMAN

When it comes to player development, teams are mostly in the business of signing and training pitching. Because modern-day roster theory, as pioneered by the bullpen-happy Tony La Russa, requires each team to carry 11 or 12 pitchers on its major league staff, plus maintain an equal number of quality replacements at Triple-A, there is a scarcity of arms. This was true even in the 1980s, when La Russa-ism had yet to run rampant and teams usually carried just 10 pitchers at a time. Twenty pitchers—10 major leaguers and 10 or more replacements—were nearly as tough to find as 24.

Like all other positions in baseball, the aggregate of pitching talent is a pyramid. Once-in-a-generation pitchers like Roger Clemens sit at the top. Cy Young–quality pitchers, perhaps even future Hall of Famers, sit a little below the apex, followed by All-Stars, ordinary above-average types, league-average pitchers, and below-average hurlers. Finally, at the pyramid's lowest and widest point (the replacement level), sit the worst possible pitchers, who might find themselves called up for an occasional week or two only to get shelled and sent back down. What makes developing pitching so difficult is that most pitchers' places within the pyramid are fluid. Depending on the pitcher's health, state of development, and myriad other factors, some not visible to the naked eye, a pitcher may be an All-Star or he may be a burden. Hitters are comparatively predictable.

## 1984 American League West Prospectus

| Team | W | L | Pct | GB | DIF | Date Elim | Pythag W | L |
|---|---|---|---|---|---|---|---|---|
| Royals | 84 | 78 | .519 | – | 26 | – | 80 | 82 |
| Angels | 81 | 81 | .500 | 3.0 | 80 | Sept 28 | 81 | 81 |
| Twins | 81 | 81 | .500 | 3.0 | 58 | Sept 27 | 81 | 81 |
| A's | 77 | 85 | .475 | 7.0 | 21 | Sept 22 | 75 | 87 |
| Mariners | 74 | 88 | .457 | 10.0 | 12 | Sept 21 | 71 | 91 |
| White Sox | 74 | 88 | .457 | 10.0 | 10 | Sept 22 | 75 | 87 |
| Rangers | 69 | 92 | .429 | 14.5 | 0 | Sept 18 | 74 | 87 |

| League Averages | | | | BP Stats Leaders | | | |
|---|---|---|---|---|---|---|---|
| AVG | OBP | SLG | BABIP | Offense, BRAA | | Indiv WARP | |
| .264 | .326 | .398 | .288 | Tigers | 121 | Cal Ripken Jr. | 13.2 |
| ERA | K9 | BB9 | H9 | Pitching, PRAA | | Eddie Murray | 10.2 |
| 4.00 | 5.1 | 3.2 | 9.1 | Yankees | 40 | Lloyd Moseby | 9.8 |

Disappointment is a way of life in the majors. Whenever a team promotes a new pitcher to the show, it hopes it has a Roger Clemens on its hands, but far more often, it has more fodder for the bottom of the pyramid. For some teams, promoting a potential ace or number two starter happens about as often as Halley's Comet drops by for a visit. For all teams, coming up with two such pitchers at once is almost unheard-of. Asking for three at one try would be an act of hubris worthy of cosmic retribution. In 1984, the Kansas City Royals completed the simultaneous development of four top pitchers. In many ways, it wasn't enough.

The 1984 American League West race is an unprepossessing contest, little remembered today, but its impact was not insignificant. The three primary participants, the Kansas City Royals, the California Angels, and the Minnesota Twins, were on the verge of doing great things. The Royals won the World Series in 1985, the Twins in 1987. In between, the Angels came within an out of going to the World Series. In 1984, these teams were still dramatically flawed, and the race is the story of how they recognized and reacted to those flaws.

◆

The most polite way to describe the Minnesota Twins in the years since 1970, when they had last won the AL West, was "inoffensive." Every year from 1972 through 1980, they had finished in third or fourth place, usually with a record right around .500. They had had a few good players in those years, though none who came close to their first baseman, Rod Carew. The future Hall of Famer, who would be traded to the Angels just before spring training began in 1979, was at his peak, winning six batting titles and an MVP award.

In the early 1970s, the Twins had pitching that varied between good and average, but lacked offensive support for Carew. From 1975 through 1977, the Twins—now managed by the ubiquitous Gene Mauch—boasted one of the better offenses in the league, notwithstanding Mauch's tendency to bunt the Twins out of big innings, but the pitching staff had fallen off dramatically. Though the Twins gave intimations of contending in some of these seasons, particularly in 1977, a season in which Carew flirted with hitting .400 before settling for .388, attendance was flat. In 1971, it dropped under 1 million for the first time since the franchise had relocated from Washington and, except for the 1977 and 1979 seasons, stayed flat. The Twins finished last in the league in attendance five times in the nine years spanning 1974 to 1982.

By the end of the strike season of 1981, the Twins were losing their battle with mediocrity. They were down to two solidly above-average position players, shortstop Roy Smalley and catcher Butch Wynegar, and a single reliable pitcher in reliever Doug Corbett. By May 1982, all three had been traded, as had four other players. Not coincidentally, the seven traded players were also the highest-salaried players on the team's roster. "This is sickening," said reliever Ron Davis, who had come over from the Yankees in return for Smalley, after Wynegar joined Smalley in New York. "I wouldn't pay $2 to watch this team play." The night of the Wynegar deal, Davis relieved in a 1-1 tie and ended up a 4-1 loser. "I'm not going to worry about it," he said. "If [owner Calvin Griffith] doesn't care about winning, why should I?"

The season, the team's first in its new home, the Hubert H. Humphrey Metrodome, was a disaster, at least as far as appearances go, with the team losing 102 games. The trades alienated fans, so the Twins failed to enjoy the boost in ticket sales that traditionally attends the opening of new stadiums. However, unlike most 100-game losers, the Twins weren't bottoming out but were starting over. The season saw the team establish four future All-Stars who would define the franchise for the rest of the decade: first baseman Kent Hrbek, third baseman Gary Gaetti, right fielder Tom Brunansky, and lefty starting pitcher Frank Viola.

In 1983 the Twins improved to 70-92. The pitching staff was still unformed. The offense was weak, with several positions, including shortstop, manned by placeholders. The Twins were more likely to lose another hundred games in 1984 than they were to contend.

The Angels were the Twins' philosophical opposites. The California team was adamantly opposed to young players. Since Gene Autry's expansion franchise had begun operations in 1961, any impulse toward sensible management had to contend with the Cowboy's impatience and then, as he aged, his seemingly imminent mortal-

TABLE 11-1 Top Homegrown Angels, 1961–1984

| Player | Games | Years | Age In | Age Out |
|---|---|---|---|---|
| Jim Fregosi | 1,429 | 1961–1971 | 19 | 29 |
| Buck Rodgers | 932 | 1961–1969 | 22 | 30 |
| Bobby Knoop | 803 | 1964–1969 | 25 | 30 |
| Dave Chalk | 732 | 1973–1978 | 22 | 27 |
| Tom Satriano | 568 | 1961–1969 | 20 | 28 |
| Rick Reichardt | 563 | 1964–1970 | 21 | 27 |
| Ron Jackson | 539 | 1975–1978 | 22 | 25 |
| | | 1982–1984 | 29 | 31 |
| Jim Spencer | 537 | 1968–1973 | 20 | 25 |
| Paul Schaal | 522 | 1964–1968 | 21 | 25 |

ity. Although successful at developing young players, management wouldn't give them the chance to grow in the majors and tended to ship them off for veterans at the first opportunity. Through 1984, just nine homegrown players had put in as many as 500 games with the club (Table 11-1).

Note that most of these players put in their time during the expansion and immediate postexpansion period. Within a few years, homegrown Angels would have no chance to take a place on the franchise's games-played list. As Autry neared his seventies, the club committed itself to shortcutting its way to a World Series ring. To Autry's general managers, Harry Dalton (1972–1977) and Buzzie Bavasi (1977–1984), this goal seemed to require fully formed veterans. Between 1977 and 1982 the Angels dealt away an entire farm system of quality players, including Mike Easler, Bruce Bochte, Thad Bosley, Jerry Remy, Richard Dotson, Ken Landreaux, Rance Mulliniks, Willie Aikens, Carney Lansford, Dickie Thon, Brian Harper, Tom Brunansky, and Dennis Rasmussen.

Simultaneously, the Angels became big players in the newly established free-agent market, signing Don Baylor, Joe Rudi, Lyman Bostock, Bobby Grich, Rick Miller, Jim Barr, Bruce Kison, and Reggie Jackson. Unlike the products of the farm system, most of these veterans stayed and stayed (Table 11-2).

The 1982 Angels had won the AL West under manager (here he is *again*) Gene Mauch. They were a terrifically old team then, with all but one member of the starting lineup 31 or older (Fred Lynn was the youngster at 30) and four-fifths of the starting rotation between 35

TABLE 11-2 The Angels Who Came to Dinner, from 1977 to Baseball Eternity

| Player | Age Games | Age Years | In | Out |
|---|---|---|---|---|
| Bobby Grich | 980 | 1977–1986 | 28 | 37 |
| Bob Boone | 968 | 1982–1988 | 34 | 40 |
| Brian Downing | 831 | 1978–1990 | 27 | 39 |
| Don Baylor | 824 | 1977–1982 | 28 | 33 |
| Doug DeCinces | 787 | 1982–1987 | 31 | 36 |
| Rod Carew | 707 | 1979–1985 | 33 | 39 |
| Reggie Jackson | 687 | 1982–1986 | 36 | 40 |
| Juan Beniquez | 504 | 1981–1985 | 31 | 35 |

and 41. The next season, the team, now managed by John McNamara, fell to 70-92 as the vets suffered a multitude of injuries—as older players are wont to do. Fourteen players hit the disabled list, forcing McNamara to write out 130 lineups. Reggie Jackson, the 37-year-old outfielder and designated hitter, slumped from .275/.375/.532 with 39 home runs to .194/.290/.340 with 14 home runs.

With most teams, this kind of season would have cued a housecleaning and an influx of youth. Indeed, Bavasi seemed to suggest this when in 1984 he re-signed McNamara, who had been working on a one-year contract, saying, "It's not his fault, and we want him to have a chance with a healthy team." "Healthy" in this context would seem to imply that Bavasi intended to add young players (the oldsters being unlikely to get younger and therefore healthier), but the Angels did nothing. The team that competed for the 1984 pennant was almost the same team that won the division in 1982, only now it was two years older (Table 11-3). Remarkably, two products of the farm system were allowed to break through. Shortstop Dick Schofield Jr. was forced on the Angels when Rick Burleson, who had been trying to recover from shoulder problems for three years, was again unable to play. And fleet center fielder Gary Pettis, a superior glove, pushed Fred Lynn to right field (allowing McNamara to keep Jackson out of the outfield). Schofield and Pettis gave the Angels two rookie starters for the first time since 1975. Of Schofield, Angels Triple-A manager Moose Stubing said, "I think he has a legitimate chance to be another Robin Yount."

As the Angels ossified, the Royals were in a state of complete upheaval, some of it caused by the natural life cycle of a team, some of it by off-field issues. By the beginning of the 2007 season, the Kansas City Royals had lost 100 or more games in four of five seasons. It is difficult to believe that the club was once one of the most successful franchises in the game. The 1969 expansion club emerged as a contender in 1975 and retained that status into the 1980s. The team's first division winner in 1976, led by manager Whitey Herzog, featured second baseman Frank White, third baseman George Brett, outfielder Amos Otis, designated hitter Hal McRae, and pitchers Dennis Leonard, Paul Splittorff, and Larry Gura. Along with faster-than-light outfielder Willie Wilson, these players were the team's mainstays through three more division titles and a World Series appearance in 1980 (a six-game loss to the Phillies).

From 1975 through 1982, the Royals boasted the third-best record in the American League, trailing only the Orioles and the Yankees. But time was not standing still. The team was aging, declining by degrees. In 1983, the Royals had gone 79-83, finishing under .500 for the first time since 1974. The offense had adopted a self-defeating impatience. Not only did they finish last by a wide margin in walks drawn, but they also became one of just 22 teams to draw fewer than 400 walks in a 162-game schedule and one of just five teams to do so despite having the benefit of the designated hitter (the others

Table 11-3 The Oldest Teams of All Time

| Rank | Year | Team | Team Age |
|---|---|---|---|
| 1 | 2005 | Yankees | 33.13 |
| 2 | 2005 | Red Sox | 32.48 |
| 3 | 2004 | Angels | 32.42 |
| 4 | 1982 | Angels | 32.14 |
| 5 | 1983 | Angels | 32.13 |
| 6 | 2002 | Diamondbacks | 32.06 |
| 7 | 2003 | Yankees | 31.94 |
| 8 | 2001 | Diamondbacks | 31.87 |
| 9 | 1998 | Orioles | 31.77 |
| 10 | 1945 | Senators | 31.70 |
| 11 | 1988 | Tigers | 31.68 |
| 12 | 2006 | Yankees | 31.63 |
| 13 | 1988 | Yankees | 31.49 |
| 14 | 1982 | Phillies | 31.47 |
| 15 | 2000 | Yankees | 31.47 |
| 16 | 2004 | Red Sox | 31.44 |
| 17 | 1945 | White Sox | 31.39 |
| 18 | 1984 | Angels | 31.37 |
| 19 | 1960 | White Sox | 31.36 |
| 20 | 1983 | Phillies | 31.35 |

are the 1975, 2002, and 2005 Tigers and the 1980 White Sox). The dearth of baserunners, combined with a below-average power quotient, severely hampered the team's ability to score runs. Simultaneously, the pitching staff, with aged starters like Splittorff (36 years old), Gura (35), Leonard (32), Steve Renko (38), and Gaylord Perry (44), lacked anyone with a semblance of a fastball. They finished last in the league in strikeouts.

Remarkably, it wasn't only baseball considerations pressing the Royals to rebuild, but also a federal matter. Pressed by government investigations, baseball was slowly being forced to acknowledge that a sizable number of the players had substance-abuse problems. In 1984, major league rosters included over 30 players who had disclosed or would, in future seasons, disclose abuse of drugs or alcohol. Seven players missed all or part of the season for drug rehabilitation, commissioner suspension, or incarceration because of drug use or being implicated in the attempt to buy drugs: Willie Aikens, Willie Wilson, Jerry Martin, Vida Blue, Rod Scurry, Pascual Perez, and Steve Howe. Aikens, Wilson, Martin, and Blue, the so-called Kansas City Four, had been sentenced to two years' prison time, all but one month of it suspended; commissioner Bowie Kuhn added his own punishment, telling the four to stay home for the entire year. The union appealed the suspensions, and an arbitrator agreed that Kuhn had exceeded his powers. All but Blue were reinstated on May 15. In a separate hearing, the arbitrator agreed with Kuhn that Blue had been more deeply involved with drugs and drug dealers than had his teammates and the enforced sabbatical was sustained.

Even before the arbitrator's decision, the Royals had divested themselves of Aiken, Blue, and Martin—other teams were happy to acquire them—while retaining Wilson, the best of the three, which just goes to show that when principles wrestle self-interest, hypocrisy is the only winner. With injuries, suspensions, and their aggressive rebuilding program, the 1984 Royals became an entirely new team. On Opening Day 1984, the only returnees from Opening Day 1983 were Frank White and Hal McRae.

In just one off-season, general manager John Schuerholz could do little to address his team's lack of depth or patience. He did, however, fleece the Yankees of slugging first-base prospect Steve Balboni in exchange for reliever Mike Armstrong, a moderately talented righty whose arm was about to permanently resign from his body. Balboni helped, but it wasn't enough; the team had more breakdowns than Zelda Fitzgerald. George Brett's knee blew out, which forced him to miss the first six weeks of the season. Frank White's leg sent him to the disabled list in July. There was no regular shortstop, because both Onix Concepcion and U. L. Washington were hurt, leaving the position in the hands of chronic nonhitter Buddy Biancalana. Third base rested in the hands of veteran understudy Greg Pryor. Propelled by a 4-for-37 May, Pryor posted a .301 on-base percentage and .356 slugging average, a far cry from what Brett would have provided. Willie Wilson's enforced vacation left the team with an outfield of Darryl Motley, Pat Sheridan, and Butch Davis. This trio of young Royals outfielders is little remembered today, and with good reason.

Schuerholz and manager Dick Howser were more successful at restoring the pitching staff. At season's outset, Kansas City envisioned its top four starters as Splittorff, Gura, Leonard, and lefty Bud Black (27 years old, and excellent). Management's best-laid plans were quickly cut down by the Grim Reaper of old pitchers: Splittorff was battered in three starts and summarily retired, Leonard missed the entire season with a knee injury, and Gura started well but then declined precipitously over the balance of the season. After 10 starts, Gura sported a 3.59 ERA. He allowed 70 runs over his next 101 innings and was yanked from the rotation.

These pitchers had to be replaced. The Royals deployed every pitching prospect they had, in the process creating the pitching staff that would get them to the World Series just a year later. The new rotation retained Black, who was pitching his way to a 257-inning, 3.12-ERA season (the league ERA was 4.00), and added Charlie Leibrandt, 27, a lefty who had been transformed at Triple-A Omaha after failing in earlier trials with the Reds; lefty Danny Jackson, 22, their 1982 first-round draft choice; righty Mike Gubicza, 21, their second-round pick in 1981; and righty Bret Saberhagen, 19, a 19th-round find in 1982.

Saberhagen proved to be one of the great control pitchers and won two Cy Young Awards, while Gubicza and Jackson both became 20-game winners. Leibrandt was also a reliable winner for years. Though it would take time for the quartet to find consistency, Kansas City had performed one of the greatest player-development feats of all time, introducing four of the best pitchers of the era simultaneously.

♦

Unlike the American League East, where the Detroit Tigers were ending the pennant race by May, no team in the AL West got off to more than a decent start. As teams reached the one-quarter mark in early May, the Royals were sixth in a seven-team division, with a record of 14-21 (.400). They were just five games back, because only two teams in the division were over .500, the Angels at 22-19 (.537) and the Twins, a half-game behind them, at 21-19 (.525). The division's malaise continued through the first half, the standings changing little (Table 11-4).

In large part, the teams in the West were evenly matched in mediocrity. The vast majority of AL talent resided in the East that year, as shown in the players' value over replacement (VORP), a measure of hitter productivity (Table 11-5). The same bifurcation was only slightly less apparent in the pitching (Table 11-6).

The VORP numbers reveal what a fractured league it was. The AL West's talent distribution began almost where that of the AL East left off.

Table 11-4 1984 AL West, Halfway Mark, July 3

| Team | W-L | Pct | GB |
|------|-----|-----|-----|
| California | 43-38 | .531 | – |
| Minnesota | 40-39 | .506 | 2.0 |
| Chicago | 39-40 | .494 | 3.0 |
| Oakland | 39-43 | .476 | 4.5 |
| Kansas City | 36-41 | .468 | 5.0 |
| Seattle | 38-45 | .458 | 6.0 |
| Texas | 36-46 | .439 | 7.5 |

Table 11-5 Listing to the Right: Talent Dominance in the East, 1984

**American League East**

| Name | Team | Pos | Avg | OBP | Slg | VORP |
|---|---|---|---|---|---|---|
| Cal Ripken Jr. | BAL | SS | .304 | .374 | .510 | 86.0 |
| Eddie Murray | BAL | 1B | .306 | .410 | .509 | 66.8 |
| Don Mattingly | NYA | 1B | .343 | .376 | .537 | 64.5 |
| Robin Yount | MIL | SS | .298 | .362 | .441 | 62.2 |
| Alan Trammell | DET | SS | .314 | .379 | .468 | 60.7 |
| Dave Winfield | NYA | RF | .340 | .393 | .515 | 54.0 |
| Dwight Evans | BOS | RF | .295 | .388 | .532 | 53.8 |
| Mike Easler | BOS | DH | .313 | .375 | .516 | 52.8 |
| Wade Boggs | BOS | 3B | .325 | .402 | .416 | 51.0 |
| Lloyd Moseby | TOR | CF | .280 | .366 | .470 | 45.6 |

**American League West**

| Name | Team | Pos | Avg | OBP | Slg | VORP |
|---|---|---|---|---|---|---|
| Rickey Henderson | OAK | LF | .293 | .399 | .458 | 53.2 |
| Kent Hrbek | MIN | 1B | .311 | .383 | .522 | 53.0 |
| Alvin Davis | SEA | 1B | .284 | .391 | .497 | 50.9 |
| Buddy Bell | TEX | 3B | .315 | .381 | .458 | 48.4 |
| Harold Baines | CHA | RF | .304 | .361 | .541 | 43.4 |
| Carney Lansford | OAK | 3B | .300 | .341 | .439 | 40.2 |
| Dave Kingman | OAK | DH | .268 | .321 | .505 | 36.0 |
| Greg Walker | CHA | 1B | .294 | .346 | .532 | 33.3 |
| Dwayne Murphy | OAK | CF | .256 | .340 | .472 | 32.0 |
| Jack Perconte | SEA | 2B | .294 | .351 | .346 | 31.7 |

Table 11-6 Even More Listing: Pitching Dominance in the East, 1984

**American League East**

| Name | Team | IP | ERA | VORP |
|---|---|---|---|---|
| Dave Stieb | TOR | 267.0 | 2.83 | 75.4 |
| Bert Blyleven | CLE | 245.0 | 2.87 | 63.0 |
| Mike Boddicker | BAL | 261.1 | 2.79 | 61.6 |
| Doyle Alexander | TOR | 261.2 | 3.13 | 60.6 |
| Willie Hernandez | DET | 140.1 | 1.92 | 52.3 |
| Storm Davis | BAL | 225.0 | 3.12 | 48.4 |
| Dan Petry | DET | 233.1 | 3.24 | 45.9 |
| Phil Niekro | NYA | 215.2 | 3.09 | 43.4 |
| Jack Morris | DET | 240.3 | 3.60 | 36.3 |
| Mike Flanagan | BAL | 226.7 | 3.53 | 32.4 |

**American League West**

| Name | Team | IP | ERA | VORP |
|---|---|---|---|---|
| Bud Black | KCA | 257.0 | 3.12 | 56.4 |
| Frank Viola | MIN | 257.2 | 3.21 | 56.2 |
| Mike Witt | CAL | 246.2 | 3.47 | 45.9 |
| Geoff Zahn | CAL | 199.1 | 3.12 | 42.2 |
| Jim Beattie | SEA | 211.0 | 3.41 | 41.8 |
| Mike Smithson | MIN | 252.0 | 3.68 | 41.2 |
| Richard Dotson | CHA | 245.2 | 3.59 | 41.0 |
| John Butcher | MIN | 225.0 | 3.44 | 41.0 |
| Ray Burris | OAK | 211.7 | 3.15 | 40.8 |
| Tom Seaver | CHA | 236.7 | 3.95 | 37.5 |

The Royals held one advantage over their divisional competition, and his name was Dan Quisenberry. The Angels had been stuck in a closer-by-committee situation for years. Between 1978, when Dave LaRoche saved 25 games, and 1985, when Donnie Moore saved 31, no single Angels pitcher had saved over 14 games. In 1983, the Angels had one of the worst bullpens in the league. Their lack of relief pitching was also a major reason they had lost the 1982 league championship series to the Brewers. Incredibly, the Halos had done nothing to address this problem. Confronted by injuries and ineffectiveness, MacNamara was unable to find a closer. He reeled from Don Aase (eight saves, five blown saves) to Doug Corbett (four saves, three blown) to Luis Sanchez (11 saves, 10 blown).

In Minnesota, the Twins had Ron Davis. A former setup man for Goose Gossage in New York, Davis was unhappy in Minnesota and was proving that being associated with Gossage did not necessarily mean that one could *be* Gossage. Davis won seven games, lost 11, and blew 14 saves in 43 chances, with eight wild pitches thrown in for seasoning. Even the worst closers generally manage to convert about 75–80 percent of their save chances, so this was a historic season. Davis was helped to this dubious accomplishment by manager Billy Gardner. In some games, Davis would be brought in too early, in others too late. He rarely started an inning but was always coming in with two on and one out, a difficult spot for pitchers with far better credentials than Davis's.

In contrast, the Royals had one of the greatest relievers of all time. "Goose is an intimidator," Quisenberry said. " [Bruce] Sutter is nasty. [Rollie] Fingers is finesse. I'm probably best described as frustrating." Quisenberry was not the traditional fire-breathing, flame-throwing closer. Instead, he was a poet who threw with an easy sidearm delivery, hoping to induce grounders. "I lull [batters] into a false sense of security by letting them watch me pitch," he said. "If overconfidence can cause the Roman Empire to fall, I ought to be able to get a ground ball." The secret was exquisite control harnessed to dizzying movement—Quisenberry walked just 162 batters in a career of 1,043.1 innings. Seventy of these were intentional—his unintentional walk rate was 0.79 per nine innings pitched. Roger Angell described his method:

Every pitch of his is performed with a lurching downward thrust of his arm and body. ... At perigee, ball and hand descend to within five or six inches of the mound dirt, but then they rise abruptly; the hand—its fingers now spread apart—finishes up by his left shoulder, while the ball, plateward-bound at a sensible, safe-driving award clip, reverses its earlier pattern, rising for about three-quarters of its brief trip and then drooping downward and (much of the time) sideways as it passes the batter at knee level or below.

In 1984, the Royals had the second-best save percentage in the game (the Tigers were first), converting 50 of 63 opportunities and finishing second in WXRL, a Baseball Prospectus estimate of the number of wins added by relievers (something not really indicated by saves). The Angels had the second-worst save percentage, covering just 26 of 48 chances (54 percent) and stranding far fewer inherited runners than would have been expected. The Twins converted 38 of 62 saves but pitched poorly enough that they were third from last in WXRL. In practical terms, this meant that the Royals went 76-9 (.894) in games in which they were ahead or tied after seven innings. The Angels went 77-14 (.846), and the Twins went 78-21 (.788).

Each team handicapped itself with some of the least productive batters in the league. As briefly explained earlier, the Baseball Prospectus statistic VORP attempts to describe how many runs a player produced beyond those that would have been generated by the worst acceptable player (the "replacement" in question) in the same amount of playing time. The "value" in VORP is actually runs, as the addition of 10 runs to a team's runs-scored column increases the team's expected wins by one (deducting 10 runs from its runs-allowed column has the same effect). Ten VORP is equivalent to the addition of one win to the team's bottom line. For example, in Table 11-5, Cal Ripken is credited with 86 VORP, which is the same as saying he was worth about nine more wins to his team than the typical Triple-A shortstop of the day.

A player with a negative VORP is so far below average that he's actively dragging his team away from winning. The Angels had the bitter honor of owning the player who was the best at being the worst (Table 11-7). Like all backstops who can't hit, veteran catcher Bob Boone's reputation as a canny defensive player and field general grew as his hitting declined. Entering 1984, Boone had never done much with the stick beyond bunting (Mauch got 23 successful sacrifices out of him in 1982), and even that was often counterproductive, but at least his career .259/.320/.359 rates offered his teams (the Phillies from 1972 to 1981, the Angels thereafter) *something*. In 1984, he slumped to .202/.239/.262, and with Dick Schofield (.193/.264/.263) batting in front of him, there was rarely any call for a signature Boone bunt.

Table 11-7 Boonesborough: 1984 American League West VORP Trailers

| Rank | Player | Team | Pos | PA | Avg | OBP | Slg | EqA | VORP |
|------|--------|------|-----|-----|-----|-----|-----|-----|------|
| 1 | Bob Boone | CAL | C | 486 | .202 | .239 | .262 | .180 | -24.1 |
| 2 | Ned Yost | TEX | C | 251 | .182 | .199 | .273 | .155 | -17.3 |
| 3 | Pat Putnam | SEA/MIN | DH | 212 | .176 | .236 | .244 | .175 | -14.9 |
| 4 | Butch Davis | KC | LF | 128 | .147 | .211 | .224 | .156 | -13.1 |
| 5 | Houston Jimenez | MIN | SS | 317 | .201 | .237 | .245 | .162 | -12.0 |
| 6 | Darnell Coles | SEA | 3B | 165 | .161 | .255 | .196 | .170 | -11.8 |
| 7 | Bill Sample | TEX | LF | 528 | .247 | .284 | .327 | .227 | -10.9 |
| 8 | Ron Jackson | CAL/BAL | 1B | 128 | .193 | .236 | .244 | .162 | -10.2 |
| 9 | John Wathan | KCA | C | 196 | .181 | .265 | .269 | .200 | -9.7 |
| 10 | Wayne Tolleson | TEX | 2B | 378 | .213 | .270 | .251 | .210 | -9.7 |
| 11 | Mike Davis | OAK | RF | 423 | .230 | .284 | .364 | .242 | -9.5 |
| 12 | Dick Schofield | CAL | SS | 452 | .193 | .257 | .263 | .197 | -8.8 |
| 13 | Bob Kearney | SEA | C | 464 | .225 | .252 | .334 | .212 | -8.7 |
| 14 | Gorman Thomas | SEA | LF | 143 | .157 | .322 | .213 | .216 | -8.6 |
| 15 | Mike Squires | CHA | 1B | 89 | .183 | .236 | .195 | .147 | -8.5 |

Shortstop was a big problem for all three teams, but particularly the Twins. From 1976 to 1981 the Twins had an All-Star shortstop in Roy Smalley Jr., an above-average hitter for a middle infielder of the day. In April 1982, Smalley was dealt to the Yankees in a trade that was partially a sop to the rebuilding effort, partially a deaccessioning of everything interesting in the Twins' collection for display in New York. The trade, in which the Twins received pitchers Davis and Paul Boris and shortstop Greg Gagne, was a short-term disaster. Davis became a data point in the argument that some pitchers can't close. Gagne ultimately became the long-term solution for the Twins, but he wasn't ready in time to replace Smalley—or so the Twins said.

Gagne came up briefly in 1983, when he had been hitting .255/.323/ .462 with 17 home runs for Triple-A Toledo. These were good power numbers for a shortstop at the time, but the next season, he went back to Toledo, where the Twins seemed to be turning him into a utility player, moving him around from shortstop to third to second. He again posted strong numbers by the standards of the day, batting .280/ .374/.441.

While ignoring Gagne, the Twins opened the 1984 season with Lenny Faedo at short. His primacy was short-lived, as he buried himself with his mouth. After a series of sloppy April plays, Faedo was quoted as saying, "I won't lose any sleep over it." Gardner benched him, sending him not just down, but also out, loaning him to the

Tigers organization to play at Double-A Evansville. The Tigers returned him six weeks later, and the Twins loaned him to Double-A Oklahoma City. The Twins could not have made their feelings more clear if they had forced Faedo wear a scarlet E-6 on his chest. He never returned to the majors.

Faedo's replacement was not Gagne but the five-foot-seven, 135-pound Houston Jimenez. Gardner was optimistic about the replacement: "With the defense he's been giving us, if Houston hits anything around .250 we'll be happy. The important thing is he's not an out." Jimenez was similarly hopeful: "Because of my size, people don't think I should be able to hit. But if I play every day, I'll hit .270 or .280." But he hit just .201/.238/.245. Late in the season, the Twins acquired the veteran infielder Chris Speier, but it was too little too late.

The Angels suffered with Schofield, who batted .235/.293/.365 in April and then never came close to .200 again. They also suffered without him; when Schofield spent three weeks on the disabled list in July, the Angels didn't bother replacing him on the roster and played with just 24 men. Similarly, when rosters expanded in September, the Angels failed to call up any players. "How can you embarrass your manager like that?" Rick Burleson asked. "The organization is bush." During Schofield's absence, the starting shortstop was Rob Picciolo, a uniquely stubborn hitter. A career .234/.246/.312 hitter, Picciolo was almost pathologically incapable of drawing a walk. In 1,720 career plate appearances, he walked 25 times. Playing for the A's in 1977, he walked nine times in 446 plate appearances. Given 363 plate appearances in 1979, he walked twice. Given 128 in 1984, he drew no walks. Playing for Schofield in July, he batted .148/.145/.241.

On July 28, the Twins went ahead of the Angels for the first time. The two traded places over the next few days, but by late August, the Twins surged ahead (Table 11-8), peaking on August 22. The only team in the division over .500, they had a 5.5-game lead over the Royals and Angels. Meanwhile, the Royals were finally getting their lineup in order after the early drug and injury problems and were playing a little better. Their improvement could not have come at a better time; the three clubs would determine the division title in head-to-head play. In September, the Royals

Table 11-8 1984 AL West, Three-Quarter Mark, August 17

| Team | W-L | Pct | GB |
|---|---|---|---|
| Minnesota | 63-57 | .525 | – |
| California | 61-60 | .504 | 2.5 |
| Oakland | 60-63 | .488 | 4.5 |
| Kansas City | 59-62 | .488 | 4.5 |
| Chicago | 58-62 | .483 | 5.0 |
| Seattle | 55-68 | .447 | 9.5 |
| Texas | 53-69 | .434 | 11.0 |

would meet the Twins six times and the Angels eight times. The Angels and Twins would not meet in September. Their season series had concluded in early August, with the Twins beating the Angels in nine of 13 meetings.

The Twins had a hard time hitting in September, batting .244/.292/.356 on the month. Ironically, they were being punished by two of their more emblematic players. Third baseman Gary Gaetti had hit 46 home runs over his first two major league seasons (then a larger total than now; only 33 players exceeded that total). In 1984 his power stroke vanished, and he hit only five home runs all season. Since Gaetti was neither fast nor selective nor capable of hitting for much of an average, his offensive game was nonexistent, making for a .238 EqA.

That May, with a hole in center field that resisted plugging, the Twins had decided to try their 1982 first-round draft pick, a strangely proportioned, almost spherical 23-year-old named Kirby Puckett. Puckett would soon show himself to be a nascent Hall of Famer, but that was still two years into the future, after Twins coach Tony Oliva showed him how to hit for power. Puckett made his debut on May 8 and was a fixture in the leadoff spot from then on. He hit .296 but drew only 16 walks and had almost no extra-base hits—12 doubles, five triples, and zero home runs. In September he slumped to .264/.276/.312. Perhaps that was the price the Twins had to pay for the two championships that Puckett would help them win in the future.

Puckett was just one of many counterproductive leadoff hitters in 1984. The construction of the batting order is one of baseball's most cherished bits of received wisdom. Managers are told, among other things, that a leadoff hitter must be fast. Yet the batting order's primary function is not to set up an arcane interaction between hitters that produces runs, but to disseminate playing time in the form of plate appearances. In each season, the leadoff position will bat more times than any other, the second spot about 25 times fewer, the third spot 25 times fewer than the second spot, and so on down the order. When a he selects a leadoff hitter, whatever statement the manager thinks he is making, what he's really saying is, "I think that this player should have more playing time than any other on my team."

Three of the greatest leadoff hitters of all time were playing at peak levels in 1984. Rickey Henderson, 25, batted .293/.399/.458 for the A's, walking 86 times and stealing 66 bases. In Montreal, Tim Raines, 24, hit .309/.393/.437 with 87 walks and 75 stolen bases (in 85 tries). Boston's Wade Boggs stole just three bases, but he hit .325/.407/.416, reaching base 292 times via hit or walk. Brett Butler of the Indians, though not quite in the Raines or Henderson class, hit .269/.361/.355, walking 86 times and stealing 52 bases. These were the exemplars of what a leadoff hitter should be, or any hitter, for that matter—superior at getting on base. Yet many managers just didn't get it.

◆

When the Twins and Royals met in Kansas City on September 3, the Twins held first place by a game over the Royals (68-68) and 1.5 games over the Angels (67-68). The Twins took the first game when an error by Royals shortstop Buddy Biancalana allowed a couple of unearned runs to get past Bud Black. Kansas City won the next two by identical 4-1 scores, Mark Gubicza and Charlie Leibrandt shutting down Minnesota's weak offense and Quisenberry saving both games. The Royals and Twins now had identical records, and the Angels, who had taken two of three games against the weak Indians, evened their record at .500 and closed to within half a game of the two leaders.

A week later, the situation was nearly the same, with the Royals and Twins tied at 74-71. The Angels had fallen back, having dropped two of three games to the same Indians they had abused the week before. The key difference was that the Angels hadn't run into the great Bert Blyleven in that earlier series. On September 12, he held the Angels to two hits, striking out 12. By September 23, with just seven games left to play, the ebb and flow of the race hadn't done anything to end the suspense. The Royals and Twins were still tied, now with records of 80-75, while the Angels trailed by 1.5 games, at 78-76.

The Royals had just four wins in the final seven games, but three of them came against the Angels. With one threat eliminated, the outcome of the race was up to the Twins, and they acted decisively: They quit. Minnesota went on a six-game losing streak, dropping an entire four-game series to the Cleveland Indians. Ron Davis took two of those losses. On September 24, the Angels went to Kansas City to face the Royals in a doubleheader. The Twins were in Chicago taking on the White Sox, the defending division winners under Tony La Russa. The Twins had won four straight games. They made it five straight, as Frank Viola out-dueled Floyd Bannister.

It was still a bad day for the Twins. Game 1 of the Angels-Royals doubleheader featured youth versus experience, with the Royals' Bret Saberhagen against Geoff Zahn. The Royals again went with a young pitcher in the second game, lefty Danny Jackson. The Angels would start Rick Steirer, a minor league veteran making his only start of the season. In the first game, which lasted just one hour, 57 minutes, Saberhagen served notice on baseball, shutting out the Angels on three hits, walking one, and striking out six. It was his first career shutout. The Angels never got a runner as far as second base. The nightcap was scarcely more troublesome. The Royals had no trouble with Steirer, who was making the last start of his major league career.

With nearly a week to go on the season, the Twins had won their last game. Their five-game winning streak was built on a three-game sweep over the Indians at the Metrodome from September 21 to the 23rd. Cleveland had a wonderfully bizarre pitching staff in 1984. On the whole it was miserable. But the club had also begun the year with a Cy Young–deserving pitcher (Blyleven) and a pitcher who did win it. Somehow, though, he won it with another team in the other league. Rick Sutcliffe started out the season with a 4-5 record and a 5.15 ERA. On June 13, the Indians dealt Sutcliffe, reliever George Frazier, and catcher Ron Hassey to the Cubs for outfielders Joe Carter and Mel Hall and pitchers Don Schulze and Darryl Banks. Sutcliffe went 16-1 with a 2.69 ERA for the Cubs, pitching them into the postseason and winning the NL Cy Young Award.

For some reason, the Indians, who were in a long period of not even pretending to be competitive, couldn't find a taker for Blyleven. Ironically, the Twins finally picked him up, though not until after the season. The Sutcliffe deal left the Indians with an odd rotation of one near–Hall of Famer and a series of youngsters and veterans of the fringiest type. In the final four games of the season, all at Cleveland, the Twins faced Blyleven and three of these fringe pitchers—Schulze, Jerry Ujdur, and Neal Heaton—and lost to them all.

On Friday, September 28, with three games left to play, the Twins became the only team in 1984 to blow a 10-run lead. Viola had started against Ujdur. The Twins knocked him out quickly and then went on to abuse relievers Jeff Barkley and Jamie Easterly. As they entered the bottom of the third inning, they led 10-0. But Viola couldn't keep the ball in the park, allowing home runs to Andre Thornton and Joe Carter. By the time the Indians came to bat in the bottom of the eighth, Viola was long gone and the score had narrowed to 10-9. With one out and none on, Billy Gardner brought in Ron Davis. The reliever retired Julio Franco (the only player mentioned in this chapter still playing in the major leagues in 2007), which brought up Carter, who hit his second home run of the ball game, tying it at 10-10. Davis then walked Thornton, but got out of the inning when George Vuckovich grounded out.

Table 11-9 The Shifting Balance of Pitching

| Year | IP | IP Start | IP Relief | IP Start (%) | IP Relief (%) |
|------|-----|----------|-----------|--------------|---------------|
| 1974 | 17,448.2 | 12,936.0 | 4,512.2 | 74* | 26 |
| * | * | * | * | * | * |
| * | * | * | * | * | * |
| * | * | * | * | * | * |
| 1986 | 20,203.1 | 14,050.2 | 6,152.2 | 70 | 30 |
| 1988 | 20,187.0 | 14,339.0 | 5,848.0 | 71 | 29 |
| 1990 | 20,057.2 | 13,653.0 | 6,404.2 | 68 | 32 |
| 1992 | 20,329.0 | 14,062.1 | 6,266.2 | 69 | 31 |
| 1994 | 14,229.2 | 9,733.2 | 4,496.0 | 68 | 32 |
| 1996 | 20,271.2 | 13,419.2 | 6,852.0 | 66 | 34 |
| 1998 | 20,194.2 | 13,650.0 | 6,544.2 | 68 | 32 |
| 2000 | 20,141.0 | 13,131.1 | 7,009.2 | 65† | 35 |
| 2002 | 20,164.0 | 13,584.0 | 6,580.0 | 67 | 33 |
| 2004 | 20,248.0 | 13,352.1 | 6,895.2 | 66 | 34 |
| 2006 | 20,121.0 | 13,224.1 | 6,896.2 | 66 | 34 |

* In this year (1974), starters pitched the highest percentage of a game's innings, from 1960 to 2006.
† In this year (2000), starters pitched the lowest percentage of a game's innings, from 1960 to 2006.

Gardner kept Davis in the game after the Twins failed to score in the top of the 10th—the manager had little choice, because of how the roster had been constructed. After Davis walked two batters to open the bottom of the frame, he was finally removed for lefty Ed Hodge, who loaded the bases and then allowed a game-winning single to Brett Butler.

Gary Gaetti's 21st error had prolonged one of the big Indians rallies. "It's tough to throw to first base with both hands around your neck," he said.

It is a measure of how much baseball has changed that Gardner did not have a Swiss army knife's worth of bullpen options available to him in extra innings and that he had to stay with Davis and then follow him with Hodge, a pitcher so good he was never seen again. In the American League of 1984, only 24 pitchers appeared in 50 or more games and just 55 pitchers worked two-thirds of all American League relief innings. These numbers changed as managers began to dramatically reduce the number of innings thrown by starting pitchers (Table 11-9).

Oddly enough, as they were asking their relievers to do more, managers were also asking these pitchers to do less. As the number of appearances by relievers rose over time, the number of batters they faced was declining (Table 11-10).

In 1984, the top 75 pitchers in relief innings pitched threw 80 percent of all relief innings. By 2006, the top 75 pitchers in relief innings threw only 68 percent of all relief innings. Because of the expansion of relief innings, the game now required 105 pitchers to cover 80 percent of the bullpen needs. The length of starter outings diminished at the same time that the workload of the best relievers was being reduced. This left a huge new pool of innings to be soaked up.

The Royals had won the race, earning the right to be dispatched by the powerhouse Detroit Tigers in the first round of the playoffs. That was no prize, but then, in this race, the ends were always less important than the means, which in future years would lead to greater glories for all three teams.

Table 11-10 AL Relief Pitchers: Batters Faced per Game

| Year | G | BFP | BFP/G |
|------|------|--------|-------|
| 1984 | 3,480 | 25,238 | 7.3 |
| 1986 | 3,769 | 26,633 | 7.1 |
| 1988 | 3,743 | 25,131 | 6.7 |
| 1990 | 4,455 | 27,557 | 6.2 |
| 1992 | 4,665 | 26,829 | 5.8 |
| 1994 | 3,600 | 20,003 | 5.6 |
| 1996 | 5,344 | 30,453 | 5.7 |
| 1998 | 5,650 | 28,564 | 5.1 |
| 2000 | 5,710 | 30,997 | 5.4 |
| 2002 | 5,557 | 28,680 | 5.2 |
| 2004 | 5,950 | 30,121 | 5.1 |
| 2006 | 6,142 | 29,975 | 4.9 |

*Abbreviations:* G, number of games; BFP, batters faced by pitchers; BFP/G, batters faced by pitchers per game.

## The Great Improvisation

KEVIN GOLDSTEIN

From 1976 to 1982, the Kansas City Royals won five American League West crowns and finished three games behind the leader in each of the other two years. But in 1983, for the first time in nine years, the Royals were totally out of it, finishing four games under .500 and 20 games behind the first-place Chicago White Sox.

Even earlier in the decade there were reasons for concern. Lacking the resources to compete with the big boys in the free-agent market, the Royals were an aging team. By the time of the 1983 downturn, five of the team's nine primary position players were in their thirties, and that was the young part of the team. The two main starting pitchers, Larry Gura and Paul Splittorff, were both in their mid-thirties, 38-year-old

Steve Renko and 44-year-old Gaylord Perry were both given rotation jobs at various points in the season, and 32-year-old Dennis Leonard and 33-year-old Vida Blue had both aged far beyond their years.

Going into 1984, it was apparent to Royals management that changes were needed, but events that winter forced them into a radical overhaul. Four Royals, Willie Aikens, Blue, Jerry Martin, and Willie Wilson, were arrested and pleaded guilty to attempting to purchase drugs. Wilson became the first active-roster big leaguer to go to jail, serving nearly three months, and the commissioner suspended the quartet for the entire 1984 season.

While the suspension was reduced to just six weeks on appeal, three of the four saw their careers destroyed. Aikens, unable to overcome his drug problems, played in just 105 more games (he is currently serving a 20-year federal prison sentence on a 1995 conviction for crack cocaine distribution). Blue sat out the entire 1984 season before making a short-lived comeback attempt with the Giants. Martin, already hampered by injuries, briefly held a bench job with the Mets on his way out of the majors. Only Wilson, just 27 at the time of his sentencing, bounced back, lasting 11 more years—though his production never recovered its pre-drug potency.

With the arrests, the off-season was tumultuous. No general manager wants to make too many changes at once, especially to a club that had recently been successful, but Royals general manager John Schuerholz felt resigned. "When it comes right down it," he said, "we had no choice."

Schuerholz had been the general manager since 1982 and had been with the team since its inception. Before taking over for Joe Burke after the 1981 season, he had spent most of his career heading up scouting or player development for the Royals, playing an integral role in turning an expansion team into a winning team within three seasons. The past gave Schuerholz some comfort going into 1984. "We had some success in the past in rebuilding, or I guess building from scratch," he said later. "That success was created with homegrown players—we did it once before, so we knew we could do it again."

Even before drafting their initial roster in 1969, the Royals developed a strategy. "We knew going in that we had a big stadium, and that we had turf," recalled Schuerholz, "so our tenets from day one were that we wanted quickness, we wanted athleticism, and we wanted guys who could pitch well—it's basically the Branch Rickey plan. That was our continual operational philosophy, and it served us well."

The reconstruction of the Royals began during the 1983–1984 winter meetings, as Schuerholz manufactured a pair of trades that would play an enormous role in the team's success the following year. Knowing Aikens would not be back with the team, Schuerholz sent Mike Armstrong, closer Dan Quisenberry's primary setup man, and a minor leaguer to the Yankees for first baseman Steve Balboni and a fringe minor league arm. Blocked by expensive veterans in the Bronx, passed by Don Mattingly, and tagged as a one-dimensional slugger, Balboni had led the International League in home runs in 1981 and 1982 but had been left to stagnate at Triple-A. In 1984, Balboni led the Royals in home runs, RBIs, and slugging, while Armstrong pitched in just 36 games for the Yankees that year because of elbow problems (George Steinbrenner appealed to the commissioner's office, claiming the Royals had known they were sending the Yankees damaged goods, but nothing came of it).

To replace Armstrong, Schuerholz acquired Joe Beckwith from the Dodgers for three minor leaguers. Over the next two years, Beckwith pitched nearly 200 innings as one of the most dependable late-inning relievers in the game, whereas none of the players sent to Los Angeles ever reached the show.

But the changes that brought the Royals their first World Series title in 1985 occurred in the rotation. In 1983, eight players made 10 or more starts for the Royals. In 1984 only two pitched more than 28 innings. Here is the disposition of the 1983 staff:

*Bud Black*
*1983:* 3.79 ERA in 161.1 innings
*1984 and beyond:* Another brilliant acquisition by Schuerholz, Black was the proverbial player to be named later in a minor league trade that sent infielder Manny Castillo to the Seattle organization before the 1981 season. Just entering his prime, Black won a career-high 17 games in 1984, and finished a 15-year career with 121 career wins.

*Vida Blue*
*1983:* 6.01 ERA in 85.1 innings
*1984 and beyond:* Between the high ERA and drug problems, the 1971 Cy Young and MVP winner spent the following year looking for a job in baseball. Nobody came calling until 1985. There were just 18 starts left in his major league career.

*Keith Creel*
*1983:* 6.35 ERA in 89.1 innings
*1984 and beyond:* The fourth overall pick of the 1980 draft, Creel never developed as expected; 1983 was his last season with the organization.

*Larry Gura*
*1983:* 4.90 ERA in 200.1 innings
*1984 and beyond:* The worst member of the 1984 rotation, Gura had been an effective junkballer in the late 1970s and early 1980s but had reached the end of the line. Gura had a 5.18 ERA in 31 games, including 25 starts, in 1984. He pitched less than 25 innings in 1985 and retired.

*Dennis Leonard*
*1983:* 3.71 ERA in 63 innings
*1984 and beyond:* A three-time 20-game winner, Leonard was a shell of his former self because of severe knee problems. He missed all of 1984 and most of 1985 recovering from surgery.

*Gaylord Perry*
*1983:* 4.27 ERA in 84 innings
*1984 and beyond:* Signed in a late-season attempt to shore up the team for a playoff run, Perry was 44, and his retirement was expected.

*Steve Renko*
*1983:* 4.30 ERA in 121.1 innings
*1984 and beyond:* At 38 and at the end of the road, Renko hung them up after the 1983 season.

*Paul Splittorff*
*1983:* 3.63 ERA in 156 innings
*1984 and beyond:* Thirty-seven and hobbled by chronic back pain, Splittorff pitched 28 innings in 1984 before retiring.

◆

Despite gaping holes in the rotation, a conversation early in spring training eased Schuerholz's mind. "I was on the field talking to Gary Blalock, a scout for us who would later become a big league pitching coach," said Schuerholz. "I was talking about how we had to rebuild the pitching staff and he said, 'I wouldn't really worry about it, we have three kids who can pitch in the big leagues right now.'"

Those three pitchers became the key to the Royals' resurgence despite being rushed through the minor league system. "When we're scouting guys, beyond baseball talent, we're looking for winning character," Schuerholz said. "We look for those kinds of guys, and those three had it."

The 34th overall selection in the 1981 draft out of a Philadelphia area high school, Mark Gubicza was a scout's dream—a 6-foot-5 power right-hander with a low- to mid-90s fastball and devastating slider. Gubicza skipped Low-A after putting up a 2.25 ERA in his pro debut, and he had a 3.08 ERA at Double-A Jacksonville as a 20-year-old. Despite control issues, he skipped Triple-A and was inserted into the 1984 Opening Day rotation. After some tough luck losses in April, he got his first big-league win on May 12 with a four-hit shutout of Boston. He finished the year with 10 wins and a league-average 4.05 ERA and then reached his prime in the late 1980s, finishing third in the 1988 Cy Young Award voting. From 1987 through 1989, Gubicza was one of the best workhorses in the game, compiling 766.2 innings.

Danny Jackson's repertoire was much like Gubicza's. He was also a power pitcher who depended on a fastball-slider combination. Unlike Gubicza, Jackson was short, left-handed, and a college product. The first overall pick in the now-defunct January draft, Jackson reached Double-A in his first professional season and made his big-league debut after just 50 minor league starts. Called up in early April, Jackson went winless in eight starts before moving into the bullpen and then down to Triple-A Omaha, where he remained until September.

Brett Saberhagen was the most surprising name on the Opening Day roster, and not only because he was still seven days short of his 20th birthday on April 4, when he fired 4.2 shutout innings of relief against the Yankees. As a high school junior in 1981, Saberhagen had been the talk of the California prep ranks, pitching the only no-hitter in the history of the L.A. City Championship game. A multi-sport star at Cleveland High in Reseda, Saberhagen had begun to suffer some shoulder problems during the basketball season and spent his senior season playing shortstop. "He basically didn't pitch as a senior, and everybody forgot about him," recalled Schuerholz—everyone, that is, except Royals scout Guy Hanson, who saw Saberhagen return to the mound just days before the draft and persuaded the club to select him in the 19th round. After luring him away from a college scholarship at the University of Southern California (Schuerholz: "The pro environment is better for pitchers than college; development takes precedence over winning"), the Royals rested Saberhagen until 1983 spring training, where he showed plus stuff to go with veteran-caliber command and control.

Knowing they had something special, the Royals began Saberhagen's career in the Class A Florida State League, where he had a 2.30 ERA in 16 starts, with just 19 walks in 109.2 innings. He spent the second half of the season at Double-A, an almost unheard-of assignment for a teenager. That would be the extent of his minor league development. Moving back and forth from rotation to bullpen to save his arm, Saberhagen had a 3.48 ERA in 38 games.

The wild card of the staff wasn't really a prospect anymore. Lefthander Charlie Leibrandt was a former Reds farmhand whom Cincinnati had given up on; they dealt him to the Royals at the 1983 trade deadline for a minor league reliever. Even Schuerholz admits he had no expectations for Leibrandt. "We needed a veteran on the staff and Leibrandt was this stable, mature guy," said Schuerholz. "He was the real stabilizer for us." Armed with an outstanding changeup and little else, Leibrandt spent all of 1983 at Triple-A and began the 1984 season there as well. But something clicked in the spring at Omaha. He had a 1.24 ERA in his first nine starts, all but forcing his way into the big leagues. Making his first start for the Royals at age 27, he limited the Twins to one run over eight innings and finished the year with 11 wins, good for third on the team despite not hitting the majors until June.

So despite a complete overhaul, the Royals returned to the top of the division, thanks primarily to young pitching. More than 20 years later, Schuerholz isn't sure he was surprised. "To be completely honest, I don't remember specifically how we felt going into the season. Our expectations were basically that we had to make some major changes and there would be some adjustments and we were going to take whatever time it took to rebuild this team properly. Luckily for us, in 1984 it only took 84 wins."

### The Break

RANY JAZAYERLI

Three-quarters into the 1984 season, the race in the American League West was dragging on, though the one in the East had long since been declared over. The Tigers finished the first 40 games of the season with a 35-5 record, ending competition for the division flag before it had really begun. From then on, the Tigers were not a great team; they were not even a particularly good one. From May 25 on, they went 69-53, not the best record in their division over that span: The Yankees were a half-game better, at 69-52. When Detroit manager Sparky Anderson was asked to comment on this piece of information, his reply was simple: "I'm old-fashioned, I like to start counting at the start of the season."

As well he should, because over the first quarter of the season, the Tigers annihilated all challengers on their way to the fastest start in modern major league history. The club started the season with nine straight victories and then, after a single loss, tacked on seven more wins to start 16-1. After splitting their next six games, they went on *another* stretch, winning 16 out of 17 games. At this point, they were 35-5 and had an 8.5-game lead on the division. Along the way, they tied or set modern major league records for numbers of victories after 20, 30, 35, and 40 games.

At some point in their six-week reign of terror, it became clear that the Tigers were not just on a hot streak; they were a dominant team having a great season, and no one in the AL East was going to catch them. And indeed, no one did; not only did the Tigers lead the division wire-to-wire, but after their 12th game of the season, they never led the division by fewer than 3.5 games. The question is, where was that point? Even the most hardened cynic would grudgingly admit that a team with a 35-5 record was probably a bit better than average. Still, the Tigers' 9-0 start was hardly proof of their greatness—just three years later, the 1987 Brewers started 13-0 and were, three weeks later, 20-15. But sometime between mid-April and late May, the Tigers were transformed from mere division leaders (a role they had not had since 1972) to the prohibitive favorite in both the division and the World Series.

In a series of columns published at BaseballProspectus.com in 2003, we attempted to answer this question: How important is a hot start? The answer was, more than you might think. Even as early as five games into the season, there's a significant difference in the fortunes of teams with good starts. From 1930 through 2002, 269 teams started 4-1 or 5-0. Of those teams, 187 (70 percent) finished with a winning record, and 71 (26 percent) made the playoffs. On the other hand, out of 236 teams that started 1-4 or 0-5, only 83 (35 percent) finished above .500, and only 15 (6 percent) advanced to the postseason.

If your favorite team gets off to a tough start, and the manager starts up with the predictable talk about how "it's still early" and "there's no reason to be concerned," don't listen to him. It's still early, but there *is* reason to be concerned. Still, five games is a guide, not destiny. The 1998 Yankees started 1-4 and arguably rank as the greatest team of all time. Of course, they followed their 1-4 start by winning 14 of their next 15 games and, after 30 games, were 23-7. As it turns out, the record of the first 30 games is a very meaningful sample. Eleven teams in our sample won at least 23 of their first 30 games. All but one of these teams then won the pennant; five of them won the World Series. (The exception was the 1945 New York Giants, who finished 78-74, in fifth place, as World War II ended and star players began filtering back into baseball from wartime duties.)

It's helpful to see that a team's record after five games carries some significance and that its record after 30 games is even more important. But can we quantify this early-lead connection a little more precisely? Maybe come up with a formula that projects a team's final record based on its performance after 10, or 30, or 50 games?

We can, and we have. After much mathematical legerdemain involving linear regression, Newtonian mechanics, and a Ouija board, here is a formula you can use to project a team's record based on their performance to date:

$$\text{Projected winning percentage} = .443 + .114x + .0057(W - L)$$

where $x$ is its current winning percentage, and $(W - L)$ is wins minus losses, or simply games above .500. (Keep in mind that this formula only works well when a team has played at least 10 games, and no more than 50.)

Don't be intimidated by the formula; it actually makes intuitive sense when you break it down into its three components:

*.443:* This term is the expected winning percentage for a team that has gone winless so far, that is, a team with a winning percentage of zero.

*.114x:* This term, when added to the preceding term, .443, raises a team's expected winning percentage based on their winning percentage so far. A team that has gone undefeated (1.000 winning percentage) would now have an expected winning percentage of .557 (or .443 + .114); a team that's .500 would be expected to finish .500 (or .443 + [.114 ∗ .500]).

*.0057(W – L):* This term adds an additional component based on how many games a team is above (or below) .500. It gives extra weight to a team that has played further into the season. For example, a team that's 30-10 would get a larger boost than a team that's 15-5 would get, even though both teams have played .750 ball to date.

Let's test the 1984 Tigers in this formula, with their 35-5 start:

Projected winning percentage =
.443 + (.114 ∗ .875) + [(35 – 5) ∗ .0057] = .443 + .100 + .171 = .714

At the high point of their season, the Tigers could have been expected to finish with a .714 winning percentage, which translates to 115.6 wins. They "only" won 104 games, but it's reasonable to suggest that they should have won more. No other team in history has ever won 35 of its first 40 games, whereas just since 1984 at least seven other teams have won 104 or more games in a season (and that doesn't include the 1995 Indians, who won 100 games in a strike-shortened campaign).

The process suffers from one fatal flaw, which is best revealed by another example. In 2003, the Kansas City Royals, who had finished with a losing record for eight consecutive seasons and had lost 197 games over the previous two years, were the talk of the majors after getting off to a 16-3 start. If we were to use the preceding formula to project their final record, we would come up with an expected winning percentage of .613, corresponding to 99.3 wins. Naturally, teams coming off a season in which they lost 100 games don't come out and win 100 games the next year. (It has never happened.) The Royals' fast start certainly meant *something,* but so did their 197 losses the two previous years. How do we reconcile the two?

The first step is to calculate a team's expected winning percentage *before* the season even begins. Using every mathematician's best friend, multivariate regression analysis, we can come up with a formula for projecting a team's winning percentage based on its record over the previous three years. (A team's record from more than three years ago has no significant impact on their projection.) That formula is as follows:

Projected record = $.1557 + .4517x_1 + .1401x_2 + .0968x_3$

where $x_1$ refers to the team's winning percentage one year ago, $x_2$ is its winning percentage two years ago, and $x_3$ is its winning percentage three years ago.

We can restate the formula in a more intuitive way. A team's projected winning percentage for the upcoming season is the sum of four parts:

.500 winning percentage: 31 percent
Record for one year ago: 45 percent
Record for two years ago: 14 percent
Record for three years ago: 10 percent

Last season's performance has the most impact on projecting this year's performance, but all teams get pulled toward .500, and a team's record from two or three years ago also has an impact. Let's use this formula on the Tigers to see what their record should have been in 1984 prior to the season:

$$\text{Tigers' projected record} =$$
$$.1557 + (.4517 * .568) + (.1401 * .531) + (.0968 * .523) = .1557 + .3815 = .537$$

The Tigers' expected winning percentage was .537, which comes out to an 87-75 record. Now that we know how the Tigers were expected to finish before the season, we can evaluate the impact of their hot start on their projected final record.

To do that, we need to use one more formula:

$$\text{Weighting factor} = .0415 + .0096G$$

where $G$ is the number of games the team has played.

In the Tigers' case, at their high point (35-5) they had played 40 games, so

$$\text{Tigers' weighting factor} = .0415 + (.0096 * 40) = .0415 + .384 = .4255$$

The weighting factor of .4255 represents how much we should weight the team's *current* winning percentage against its *expected* winning percentage at the start of the year. The Tigers were expected to win at a .537 clip, but after a 35-5 start, their actual winning percentage was .875. Using simple algebra, if you multiply their .875 record by the weighting factor of 42.55 percent, and their .537 expected record by the remainder (57.45 percent), then you arrive at a new projected winning percentage of .681, which corresponds to 110.3 wins.

While this projection still overshoots the Tigers' actual record, it is a more conservative—and more accurate—projection than the 115.6 wins calculated without taking into account their performance in previous years. The weighted formula takes into account not only the Tigers' impressive 35-5 start, but also their failure to win more than 92 games in any of the last three years.

They're not dinged as much as the 2003 Royals were, and with good reason. Our original formula projected the Royals to finish 99-63 after their 16-3 start. The new formula acknowledges that the team lost an average of 94 games the three previous years and that, before the season began, the Royals had an expected winning percentage of .431, or a record of approximately 70-92.

Kansas City's 16-3 start changes that projection, but by less than a quarter of the gap between a 70-92 record and a 16-3 record. Using the formula above, the weighting factor after 19 games is 22.4 percent. At this juncture, the Royals' expected winning percentage was .523, corresponding to 84.7 wins. They actually finished 83-79; our formula missed by less than two wins.

So to answer the question "How meaningful is a team's record in the early going?" we must respond, "It depends on how early it is."

The more games a team has played, the more difficult it is to write off their performance. The magic number is 48: After 48 games, a team's *current* record is exactly as meaningful as its *projected* record at the start of the season. Table 11-11 shows how much weight we should apply to a team's record after every 10 games, and how it would be applied to the 1984 Tigers.

So at what point should we have figured out that there wasn't going to be

Table 11-11 Weighting a Team's Early Performance by Number of Games Played: 1984 Tigers

| No. of Games Played | Weighting (%) | W-L Record | W-L Projection |
|---|---|---|---|
| 10 | 13.75 | 9-1 | 95-67 |
| 20 | 23.35 | 18-2 | 101-61 |
| 30 | 32.95 | 26-4 | 105-57 |
| 40 | 42.55 | 35-5 | 110-52 |
| 50 | 52.15 | 39-11 | 108-54 |

much of a pennant race in the AL East? At some point between 20 and 30 games into the season, it looked pretty clear that the Tigers were going to win 100 games with ease. And given that only twice in the divisional era have two teams in the same division each won over 100 games (the 1993 NL West and the 2001 AL West), the race was essentially over by the second week of May.

Considering Detroit's rather uninspired performance after its torrid start, many people before the playoffs believed that the Tigers had peaked too soon and that the team that took the field in October wasn't the same one that had run roughshod over the American League in April and May. This time, however, the common wisdom was wrong. The Tigers swept the American League Championship Series (ALCS) and won the World Series in five games; they trailed in a game for only eight innings over the entire postseason.

Were the Tigers coasting as the regular season wound down, and can a team that gets off to a great start and struggles late in the year suddenly turn it on again in the playoffs? We have no way of answering the first question, but the second question has a definitive answer: yes. Teams that back into the playoffs after getting off to a big lead have no problems shaking off the cobwebs once every team is 0-0 again.

The 1984 Tigers are one example, but newer examples are piling up. In 2000, the New York Yankees were 85-61 and had a 7.5-game lead on the Red Sox with two weeks remaining. Over the next two weeks, New York ended the regular season in perhaps the worst tailspin of any playoff-bound team ever. It's not just that they lost 13 of their last 15 games and saw almost their entire lead disappear before finally clinching the division with only two games remaining. It's how they lost: 15-4 on September 17; 16-3 two days later; and then 15-4, 2-1, 11-1, 11-3, and 13-2 in five consecutive losses from September 25 to September 29. Over the final week of the season, they were outscored 68 to 15. Naturally, they went 11-5 in the playoffs and clinched their third straight world championship.

In 2005, the Chicago White Sox zoomed out to a 16-4 start and held on to the AL Central's top spot the entire way; when they woke up on September 8, they were 87-51 and held a comfortable 9.5-game lead on the division. Twenty days later, after a 7-12 stretch, the Pale Hose had fallen to 94-63, and their lead on the Indians had crumbled to just two games with five to play, including three head-to-head.

Just as the majority of observers wrote off the team's chances to make the playoffs, let alone win anything, the Sox suddenly reversed course again. They won their last five games to knock Cleveland out and then stormed through October, winning their first World Series in 88 years with just one loss the entire postseason.

The Yankees and White Sox, at least, only faded for a few weeks in September before righting the ship. Two-thirds of the way into the 2006 season, the Detroit Tigers were shaking up the baseball world with their 76-36 record, eight games better than any other team in the majors. But over the season's final eight weeks, the Tigers collapsed, winning just 19 of their final 50 games, the fewest of any postseason team in major league history. A season-ending sweep at the hands of the lowly Royals cost the Tigers the division, forcing them to enter October as a wild-card entry against the heavily favored Yankees in the first round.

Detroit dispatched the Yankees in four games and then swept the Athletics in the ALCS, clinching their first pennant since 1984. And then ... they fell to the buzz saw that was the 2006 St. Louis Cardinals, whose 22-28 record in their last 50 games was the *second*-worst in baseball history.

The Cardinals, who led the NL Central by seven games with just 13 to play, were on the precipice of joining the 1964 Phillies as the greatest September chokers ever when they lost seven games in a row at the same time the Astros won nine in a row. With three games left to play, the Cardinals' division lead had been whittled to half a game. They recovered to win two of their last three games and squeaked into the playoffs. A month later, they earned the distinction of becoming the team with the worst record (83-78) ever to win the World Series—a distinction 29 other teams would happily have taken.

In 2006, both the Tigers and the Cardinals proved that a hot start doesn't just *disclose* the value of a team, but also *constitutes* value, because a good record early on may help a team hold on down the stretch. What's more, there's no such thing as a bad ending to a regular season so long as there's a postseason attached to it. That old adage "A win in April is as valuable as a win in September" is certainly true, but it's incomplete. A win in April is just as valuable—and it's even more revealing.

# 1934 National League

## Learning to Trust the Man in Glasses

CHRISTINA KAHRL

*I completed college in three years. I was in the top ten percent of my class in law school. I'm a Doctor of Jurisprudence. I am an honorary Doctor of Law. Tell me why I spent four mortal hours today conversing with a person named Dizzy Dean.*

—Branch Rickey

*By Judas Priest! By Judas Priest! If there were more like him in baseball, just one, as God is my judge, I'd get out of the game.*

—Branch Rickey

*But who packs 'em into the park? Mr. Rickey? No, me and Paul.*

—Dizzy Dean

Coming into the 1934 season, what might have been seen as the historical balance of power in the National League had been reasserted. Pennant-less since their four consecutive first-place finishes (from 1922 to 1924), the New York Giants had bounced back from the decline and fall of the man who had essentially *been* the Giants, John McGraw, winning the 1933 pennant under the guidance of the team's star first baseman and manager, Bill Terry. They then went on to hu-

## 1934 National League Prospectus

| Team | — Actual Standings | | | | | Date Elim | Pythag | |
|------|----|----|------|------|-----|-----------|-----|-----|
|      | W  | L  | Pct  | GB   | DIF |           | W   | L   |
| Cardinals | 95 | 58 | .621 | –    | 13  | –         | 91  | 62  |
| Giants    | 93 | 60 | .608 | 2.0  | 127 | Sept 30   | 95  | 58  |
| Cubs      | 86 | 65 | .570 | 8.0  | 25  | Sept 22   | 82  | 69  |
| Braves    | 78 | 73 | .517 | 16.0 | 0   | Sept 16   | 72  | 79  |
| Pirates   | 74 | 76 | .493 | 19.5 | 10  | Sept 14   | 77  | 73  |
| Dodgers   | 71 | 81 | .467 | 23.5 | 1   | Sept 4    | 72  | 80  |
| Phillies  | 56 | 93 | .376 | 37.0 | 0   | Aug 28    | 63  | 86  |
| Reds      | 52 | 99 | .344 | 42.0 | 0   | Aug 24    | 54  | 97  |

| League Averages | | | | BP Stats Leaders | | | |
|-----|-----|-----|-------|------------------|----|------------|------|
| AVG | OBP | SLG | BABIP | Offense, BRAA    |    | Indiv WARP | |
| .279| .333| .394| .297  | Dodgers          | 97 | Arky Vaughan | 14.2 |
| ERA | K9  | BB9 | H9    | Pitching, PRAA   |    | Mel Ott    | 12.6 |
| 4.06| 3.5 | 2.7 | 10.0  | Cardinals        | 74 | Dizzy Dean | 12.4 |

miliate the favored Senators in the World Series, winning in five games.

There seemed to be little reason not to expect the Giants to run off another series of pennants. They boasted the closest thing to a true four-man rotation in the league, with four quality pitchers making a league-high 133 of 156 starts. Despite sunny recollections of how things used to be, the four-man rotation wasn't something teams routinely had back then. With the time consumed by rail travel and scheduled doubleheaders, as well as the tactic of using some starters in relief between starts, a four-man rotation bordered on logistical impossibility. From 1920 to 1941, only four teams got as many as 30 starts from four hurlers in a single season—the 1933 Giants (who won a pennant) and the 1922 Reds, the 1925 Yankees, and the 1930 Red Sox (who didn't).

◆

The most famed of the Giants quartet was screwballing southpaw Carl Hubbell, but each starter provided different virtues: The neckless, tubby Freddie Fitzsimmons threw a hard knuckler, "Tarzan" Roy Parmelee threw a hard sinker with wicked movement, and Hal Schumacher came at hitters with overhand curves and sinkers. None of the pitchers were alike, and none of them represented a day off for opposing lineups. The league runs-per-game average was 3.97; Hubbell and Schumacher were more than 1.5 runs better than that, and Fitzsimmons and Parmelee were better than average as well.

There was also a grudging acceptance among observers from among the fourth estate that Terry, despite a certain blend of pride and condescension, was a necessary antidote to the increasingly erratic McGraw. Beyond starring on the field and managing the club, Terry also fulfilled many of the responsibilities of general manager. In his first winter in charge (after taking over for McGraw a little more than a month into the 1932 season), Terry shook up the roster with a series of minor deals, but also made one particularly decisive change: He traded his chief rival for McGraw's job, center fielder Freddie Lindstrom, acquiring veteran outfielder Kiddo Davis from the Phillies in a three-way deal that sent Lindstrom to Pittsburgh. It was a fateful move—Lindstrom, just 26, was a productive hitter and could play third base or any outfield position. In contrast, Kiddo Davis was already past 30 and not much of an offensive threat outside the Phillies' Baker Bowl, one of the most generous "band boxes" in baseball history. The trade was a mistake Terry tried to repair before the 1934 season, dealing Davis to the Cardinals for George Watkins, an even older outfielder who, unlike Davis, couldn't really play center.

Offensively, the Giants were a bit of a short-stack lineup, winning despite fielding only the fifth-best attack in the league, a problem exacerbated by the decision to deal Lindstrom lest he undermine Terry. They relied on right fielder Mel Ott to provide the power and Terry to get on base. The lone surprise performance from 1933 had been the breakout of third baseman Johnny Vergez, the Giants' only above-average hitter after Ott and Terry. By hitting .271/.332/.448 (good for a .290 EqA), Vergez had apparently blossomed as a 26-year-old regular in his third season. There was hope that things would improve, particularly that 24-year-old outfielder Jo-Jo Moore would develop as well, and that shortstop Travis Jackson's constant knee problems might finally abate enough for him to provide some offensive value. Even so, this team's defensive specialists, like second baseman Hughie Critz, were in the lineup for the support they could provide on the diamond, not at the plate.

What the Giants had was pitching and defense, with enough offense to get by. The club's defense-adjusted ERA (DERA) and normalized runs allowed (NRA) highlight the importance of its defense. (DERA means runs allowed per nine innings, adjusted for park and league effects and a team's fielding level; NRA is the runs allowed per nine in-

Table 12-1 Establishing the Favorites for 1934

| Team | Record | 3rd O. W-L | EqA | DERA | NRA |
|---|---|---|---|---|---|
| New York | 91-61 | 88.2-63.8 | .259 | 4.18 | 3.99 |
| Pittsburgh | 87-67 | 81.4-72.6 | .272 | 4.75 | 4.63 |
| Chicago | 86-68 | 87.9-66.1 | .270 | 4.40 | 4.19 |
| Boston | 83-71 | 79.2-74.8 | .253 | 4.22 | 4.17 |
| St. Louis | 82-71 | 83.8-69.2 | .266 | 4.35 | 4.38 |
| Brooklyn | 65-88 | 69.4-83.6 | .264 | 4.75 | 5.16 |
| Philadelphia | 60-92 | 62.4-89.6 | .253 | 4.86 | 4.91 |
| Cincinnati | 58-94 | 61.0-91.0 | .242 | 4.47 | 4.79 |

ABBREVIATIONS: *3rd O. W-L:* third-order win-loss record, adjusted for schedule and expected runs scored and allowed; *EqA:* equivalent average (offense); *DERA:* Defense-Adjusted Earned Run Average (4.50 is average); *NRA:* normalized runs allowed per nine innings (4.50 is average).

nings, adjusted for park and league effects. If a pitcher or team's DERA is higher than the NRA, it can safely be assumed that the pitcher or pitchers benefited from an above-average defense.) The difference between the Giants' DERA and NRA indicates that they had one of the best defenses in the league behind the best pitching; only the Cubs' defense was comparable (Table 12-1).

Not reflected in a single season's standings is that competitive balance in the National League was a joke. After the Giants' four-year run had ended in 1924, the NL pennants had been swapped between the Cardinals (four times), the Cubs (twice), and the Pirates (twice). However ill-starred they may have been from 1925 to 1932, the Giants had mostly bobbed around in the top four, usually in the company of those three rivals. There was a clear delineation between the top four teams and the second tier. Since their title in 1920, the Dodgers had finished in the top half of the league's standings only four times in 13 seasons, the Braves only twice, the Phillies once. The Reds had been a strong team at the start of the 1920s, but they made their last appearance in the first division in 1926, falling into a deepening slump afterward. The league was essentially divided up between four iterations of the Harlem Globetrotters and four patsies in the role of the Washington Generals.

Today, Bud Selig decries the fans' lack of "hope and faith" for some of Major League Baseball's poorer cousins on Opening Day, but by being born too late, he missed the era when his plaints would have had a point. For the Giants or the Cubs, playing a 154-game schedule against only seven opponents meant that more than half the season,

88 games, was against teams whose only real purpose was to fill out the calendar. Clobber those guys and you were a contender.

The expectation in 1934 was that the Giants had enough pitching, defense, and potential for offensive improvement to defend their title successfully. In a preseason poll of 97 sportswriters, the Giants drew the highest tally of first-place votes (40), followed by the Cubs, the pennant winner of 1932 (34). Before spring training, Terry said he considered the Cubs and the Cardinals his biggest rivals for the pennant. Asked about the hapless Dodgers, he answered with a question of his own: "Are they still in the league?" The remark rapidly gained a certain infamy in Brooklyn.

The rivals to the Giants each harbored their own ambitions. In 1933, the Cubs weren't that far behind the Giants in qualitative terms (as reflected in Table 12-1). And if not for the loss of their star outfielder, Kiki Cuyler, for more than half the season to a broken ankle, they may well have successfully defended their 1932 pennant. Rather than just settle for getting Cuyler back, the Cubs raided the sad-sack Phillies, throwing them $65,000 and three futureless players to acquire Triple Crown winner Chuck Klein. With Klein, Cuyler, and Babe Herman, the Cubs figured to have the league's best outfield and, with star catcher Gabby Hartnett, the league's best offense. The Cubs learned the same lesson the Giants had learned with Kiddo Davis, only writ much, much larger: Put anyone in the Baker Bowl, and he'll bop. Klein had averaged 36 homers per season over the previous five years with the Phillies; he never topped 21 with the Cubs. Moreover, Klein was already 29 when the Cubs got him—a hitter's career arc usually peaks between the ages of 25 and 29. Klein had already contributed most of his best years to the futile Phillies. Still, the idea of replacing the decrepit Riggs Stephenson with Klein was a sound one, especially with modern concerns like park factors (a stadium's propensity to affect hitting, pitching, or fielding performance) and peak age patterns removed from consideration. (These escaped the notice of all teams during this period and for a long time after.) But in 1934, it wasn't the last mistake the Cubs made from their ignorance of park effects.

The Cubs could also boast a sound pitching rotation of their own, though it wasn't as talented as the Giants' quartet. Lon Warneke's development as a young sidearming ace in his first full season had been a key factor for the team's success in 1932, giving the club a talented pitcher to match up against other teams' top starters in front of Cubs workhorses Guy Bush, Pat Malone, and Charlie Root. Unfortunately, the Cubs were about to learn that Root's days as a rotation regular were numbered, which would force them to scramble to replace him.

◆

The other team that Terry had sensibly noted as a potential challenger wasn't the third-place Pirates or the fourth-place Braves, but the fifth-place Cardinals, and for good reason. Like the Giants, the Cardinals had fallen hard in 1932, but their "business manager" Branch Rickey had taken that as an opportunity to rebuild the former pennant winners much more aggressively than Terry had in taking over for John McGraw. Despite the two teams' tying for sixth in 1932 and the Giants' rebound in 1933 to win the title, Rickey had achieved a much more thoroughgoing rebuild of the Cardinals. Consider how much Rickey had turned over his roster between his 1931 World Series winner and the team he fielded in 1934 (Table 12-2).

Keeping track of Rickey's roster shake-ups during this period is like trying to remember which players are Oakland A's in any particular year under Billy Beane; a core of Cardinals talent was carefully assembled, but everyone outside the core group was a bargaining chip in cleats, ready to be converted into something better. A year after winning the World Series, Rickey had replaced his star first baseman, Sunny Jim Bottomley, as well as his slugging left fielder, Chick Hafey.

Table 12-2 Changing of the Redbirds: Branch Rickey's Evolving Roster

| Pos | 1931 | 1932 | 1933 | 1934 |
|-----|------|------|------|------|
| P1 | Hallahan (28) | D. Dean* (22) | D. Dean (23) | D. Dean (24) |
| P2 | Derringer* (24) | Derringer (25) | Carleton (26) | Carleton (27) |
| P3 | Grimes (37) | Carleton* (25) | Hallahan (30) | P. Dean* (20) |
| P4 | Rhem (30) | Hallahan (29) | Walker (29) | Hallahan (31) |
| P5 | Johnson (30) | Johnson (31) | Haines (30) | Walker (30) |
| C | Wilson (30) | Mancuso (26) | Wilson (32) | Davis (29) |
| 1B | Bottomley (31) | Bottomley (32) | Collins (29) | Collins (30) |
| | | Collins (28) | | |
| 2B | Frisch (32) | Frisch (33) | Frisch (34) | Frisch (35) |
| 3B | Adams (36) | Open Casting | Martin (29) | Martin (30) |
| SS | Gelbert (25) | Gelbert (26) | Durocher (27) | Durocher (28) |
| CF | Martin (27) | Martin (28) | Orsatti (30) | Orsatti (31) |
| RF | Watkins (31) | Orsatti (29) | Watkins (33) | Rothrock (29) |
| LF | Hafey (28) | Watkins (32) | Medwick* (21) | Medwick (22) |

NOTE: Player age in parentheses; asterisk denotes a rookie.

In their place, he brought up first baseman Ripper Collins. The switch-hitting rookie had warmed the bench in 1931, and Rickey sensibly identified him as someone better suited to a power slot like left or first than were either of the two future Hall of Famers. When the absence of a third baseman became a problem with no obvious solution in 1933, the Cardinals moved outfielder Pepper Martin to the hot corner after an injury-marred 1932 campaign. While Martin's struggles at the position were historic (and perhaps a source of unintentional hilarity as long as you weren't in his line of fire), Rickey correctly concluded he could find an outfielder who could hit better than aging third baseman Sparky Adams. Once Joe Medwick came up from the farm, Rickey had found a slugger to slot in with Collins and fully replace both veteran power hitters from the 1931 world champs.

Not everything was by design—when Charley Gelbert went down with a leg injury early in the 1933 season, Rickey promptly snagged Leo Durocher from the Reds. It was an expensive deal—the Cardinals traded away pitcher Paul Derringer, who went on to be a major part of the Reds' pennant winners of 1939 and 1940. But however productive his assembly of a farm system had already been, Rickey had no shortstops to spare. Gelbert's career was ruined, and Durocher's glove was one of the best in the league (before 1934, "the All-American Out" had put up back-to-back seasons of 50 fielding runs above replacement, according to Clay Davenport's historical fielding metrics).

The trade with the Reds again highlighted the have/have-not divide of the period—like the decision makers of the other top teams, Rickey wasn't afraid to treat the bottom half of the league as a combination dumping ground and larder. Between the end of the 1931 season and Opening Day 1934, he made 10 deals with the Reds, and starting with his December 1933 trade that brought in catcher Spud Davis for a fading Jimmie Wilson, he made five deals with the Phillies for the 1934 season. When Rickey picked up journeyman outfielder Jack Rothrock after a big year in the 1933 American Association, it wasn't because the Mahatma expected great things—Rothrock had already washed out with the Red Sox—but he had good speed and a strong arm. It was simply a matter of good scouting and perhaps an appreciation that you can never have too many outfielders. Where the Giants were heavily dependent on their core players to score runs, the Cardinals had a lineup with only one weak spot (Durocher), two star sluggers of their own in Collins and Medwick, an underrated contributor in Davis, and four hitters who were right around average. The lineup had power and balance and was the fastest in the league.

The real achievement was the careful assembly of so much young pitching talent—between the Dean brothers and Tex Carleton, the Cardinals had carefully assembled a tremendous young group of starters. Dizzy was already a figure of public fun at the time, and as the season went on, he would develop something of a credibility problem, but on the mound, his public image took a backseat to his tremendous ability. Attacking hitters from a variety of angles, all of which were overpowering, Dean led the league in strikeouts, innings pitched, and complete games in 1932, and in strikeouts again in 1933. Before the season, Dean made a few bold observations of his own to put up alongside Terry's. Anticipating the arrival of his younger brother on the staff after a 22-7 season with 197 strikeouts with the Cardinals' affiliate at Columbus (American Association), he predicted a championship ("How are they going to stop us?") and 45 wins between the two of them. The younger Dean was another hard thrower, and filling out the front of the rotation, the Cards had Carleton (a sinkerballer happy to have Durocher in his infield) and Wild Bill Hallahan's power assortment. The result for the Cardinals was a slightly less famous quartet to match that of the Giants.

The season got under way with the league's top four teams running hot and cold. The Cubs and the Pirates got off to hot starts, but the Pirates' brief moment at the head of the pack in early May was the product of the schedule, as they rattled off a quick succession of wins against the Dodgers and Phillies. A 1-5 swing through New York and Chicago at the end of May reflected that Pittsburgh would be an also-ran this season. By the start of June, the Cubs, Giants, and Cardinals were knotted up at the front of the pack. After a weekend's play concluded on June 3, the three teams were tied, the Giants and Cubs at 27-17, the Cardinals at 26-16. The St. Louis team had been white-hot in May, winning 21 of 27 games.

After a slow start in April, Dizzy Dean won six straight starts through June 2. It wasn't all good news, though, as Dizzy's bombast and success and the success of his brother Paul ended up feeding into a near mutiny. The Deans had kvetched over Paul's compensation (set at $3,000) all through March, with Paul holding out and the 24-year-old Dizzy serving as his adviser. As the season rolled along, the Deans recognized that they were key components of whatever chance the Cardinals had and decided to take the team's fortunes hostage. Dizzy feigned a sore arm, threatening to sit out if his brother didn't get a better rate of pay. Things boiled over on June 1. Dizzy had tried to get manager Frankie Frisch in his corner the night before, and Frisch, a no-nonsense player-manager, responded, "If you don't want to pitch, go home." Dean met with Rickey that morning and heard nothing he wanted to hear. Dizzy refused to pitch, Paul announced that he too had a sore arm, and the brothers announced they wouldn't pitch again until Paul was paid an extra thousand or two. Backed by team owner Sam Breadon, Frisch and Rickey held firm. After meetings with veteran players and coaches the next day, the Deans ended their brief holdout.

It wasn't the last of this problem, however. Whether or not it's a coincidence that Dizzy pitched three of his worst games of the year in June, resentment of the Deans' popularity with the paying public and the brothers' "antics" started to boil over among their teammates. While closing out a 7-9 stretch at the end of June, the team endured a lot of distraction in-house when Dizzy was granted two wins by scorer's decision, one correctly, one not. The Gas House Gang got plenty of press for being delightful characters and one of the most colorful teams of all time, but on closer inspection, much of the "color" wouldn't wash today. Whether chasing skirts or relishing the end of Prohibition, the Cardinals were a combative, rowdy lot, which can be entertaining when a team is winning. But anyone who saw the Mets in the early 1990s might remember how ugly an undisciplined club can get when winning isn't on the menu. What the Dean brothers did—trying to blackmail their employer and derail their club's season—was monumentally stupid, a breach of faith with the fans as well as the club.

The Giants, meanwhile, avoided any drama, rattling off a 17-9 record in June. After splitting a four-game set in St. Louis—beating the Deans in the last two to break even on the series—they rolled through a pair of home-and-home sets with the Dodgers and Braves at a 7-4 clip to put themselves atop the standings at the All-Star break on July 8 (Table 12-3).

Table 12-3 NL Standings at the All-Star Break, July 8, 1934

| Team | Record | GB |
|------|--------|------|
| Giants | 48-28 | – |
| Cubs | 46-30 | 2.0 |
| Cardinals | 43-31 | 4.0 |
| Pirates | 38-33 | 7.5 |
| Braves | 39-37 | 9.0 |
| Dodgers | 31-45 | 17.0 |
| Phillies | 30-47 | 18.5 |
| Reds | 24-48 | 22.0 |

After bouncing back from a 15-14 May, the Cubs didn't really fade as the season progressed as much as they simply couldn't keep pace. Only two games behind the Giants at the break, they lost ground from there—playing .600 baseball through the end of August (28-21) wasn't enough to keep up with the Giants' 32-18 run during that same stretch. Charley Root's performance came into question

Table 12-4 Ursine Decline: Cubs Primary Pitching Starters, 1933 and 1934

| Pitcher | 1933 | | | | 1934 | | | |
|---|---|---|---|---|---|---|---|---|
| | GS | DERA | IP | PRAA | GS | DERA | IP | PRAA |
| Lon Warneke | 34 | 3.45 | 287.1 | 33 | 35 | 3.73 | 291.1 | 25 |
| Guy Bush | 32 | 4.18 | 259.0 | 10 | 27 | 4.22 | 209.1 | 7 |
| Charlie Root | 30 | 4.02 | 242.1 | 12 | 9 | 4.79 | 117.2 | -3 |
| Pat Malone | 26 | 5.32 | 186.1 | -18 | 21 | 4.10 | 191.0 | 8 |
| Bud Tinning | 21 | 4.63 | 175.1 | -3 | 7 | 4.20 | 129.1 | 4 |
| Bill Lee | – | – | – | – | 29 | 3.94 | 214.1 | 14 |
| Jim Weaver | – | – | – | – | 20 | 4.43 | 159.0 | 1 |

ABBREVIATIONS: *GS*, games started; *DERA*, defense-adjusted runs allowed; *IP*, innings pitched; *PRAA*, pitching runs above average (a defense-independent pitching value)

after the club won only two of his nine starts, and manager Charlie Grimm responded by pulling him from the rotation in mid-June. After an eight-year run as the Cubs' ace, during which he'd won 140 games, Root never again started 20 games in a season. But in his place, the team did have the benefit of a young rookie, big curveball artist Bill Lee (later "Big Bill"), whom they had purchased from the Cardinals and who had fallen from favor with Branch Rickey merely by virtue of not being Paul Dean (Table 12-4).

The Cubs' real problem was how much ground they lost in the lineup from 1933 to 1934, when they thought they were covered by adding Klein and getting Cuyler back. From their .270 equivalent average of 1933, the Cubs dropped to .263 in 1934. Getting Cuyler back had helped—playing a full season, his WARP bumped up from 3.6 to 7.8. But Chuck Klein was not the slugger they expected, and his production dropped steeply (his EqA went from .342 to .306, his WARP from 12.5 to 6.4). The drop-offs of Babe Herman and shortstop Billy Jurges were frustrating, but not debilitating, except where Jurges' struggles encouraged Grimm to play veteran infielder Woody English (displaced by Stan Hack at third) at short. Clay Davenport's fielding data suggest that English's range was nothing short of ghastly.

The real problem position in the Cubs lineup was first base, where player-manager Charlie Grimm had lost a lot to age; the club's solution was to deal for another slugging Phillie, Don Hurst, on June 11. Hurst had led the league in RBIs in 1932, but his power was almost entirely a Baker Bowl illusion. The exchange was nothing short of disastrous. The Cubs sent young Dolph Camilli—the player they should have plugged into the lineup in Grimm's stead—to the Phillies. Camilli hit another 233 homers in the major leagues; Hurst would be out of baseball after the season. With another deflated Phillies slugger plugged into the lineup, the Cubs' offense went into a tailspin down the stretch, scoring only 3.6 runs per game after August 1, up to which point they had been averaging 5.3. The pitching staff didn't kill the Cubs—it was the lineup that they'd assembled with such care.

Terry's Giants were hot and getting hotter. Deep into August, Terry and Ott were neck-and-neck for the league lead in runs scored and competing for the batting title. On August 23, Terry was leading the league at .370, trailed by the Pirates' Paul Waner at .365, Ott at .357, and Jo-Jo Moore, not far behind at .343. Moore's development as a power source justified Terry's confidence in him. Ott had a league-leading 130 RBIs, and Travis Jackson's return had been all that it was anticipated to be at the plate. Not everything was perfect—Johnny Vergez was struggling terribly, to the point that his job security was under threat from light-hitting infield reserve Blondy Ryan. Nevertheless, Terry elected to stick with one of his better bats from his 1933 pennant winner. With Moore and Jackson contributing, the lineup was better than the previous season's championship edition. On the mound, Terry had to deal with losing Roy Parmelee to illness through the first couple of months, but he got "Tarzan" back in July.

In contrast, the Cardinals seemed to be flirting with a teamwide meltdown. A sweep of a five-game series against the Braves at the end of July only closed the gap with the Giants from 5.5 games to four, and a subsequent 10-game road trip against the Giants, Cubs, and Pirates (the other good teams) produced a 4-6 record and a return to a 5.5-game deficit.

Shortly thereafter, the "Dean problem" blew up. The Deans lost both ends of a doubleheader in St. Louis on Sunday, August 12, pushing the team back to 7.5 games behind the Giants. The next day, the Cardinals were headed to Detroit to play a lone exhibition game against the Tigers and then had to double back to St. Louis to open a series against the Phillies on Tuesday. The schedule was more than a little hectic for a team in a pennant race, but this bit of interleague action was a way to make extra money for the clubs in the days before media revenue. Perhaps understandably, the Deans skipped the trip, providing all sorts of excuses—they'd forgotten to pack, they made the mistake of going to the hotel instead of realizing the club was leaving for Detroit directly after the games, and, perhaps predictably, Dizzy again decided that his arm hurt and that he might be out for weeks, which excused anything. The crux of the matter was that the Deans hadn't asked permission to skip the exhibition, and Frisch, Rickey, and Breadon agreed to lay down the law, fining the brothers. Frisch noted, "When the Yankees schedule an exhibition game, Babe Ruth is present. ... There's no hardship in a train ride ... and the mere fact that we worked Sunday is no excuse for running out on a Monday game just because it's an exhibition."

When the team returned from Detroit, the Deans showed up for work. Dizzy asked Frisch if they were really being fined and was assured they were. At this point, the Deans said they weren't going to play. Frisch suspended them. Dizzy threatened to leave for Florida, and his repeated demands that the fines be dropped were nonnegotiable for the Cardinals' brass. The response of the other players was a grim determination—they didn't rally to the Deans. Handily, the schedule offered the Cards a couple of four-game home sets against first the Phillies and then the Braves. Frisch also had the advantage of lefty Bill Walker's return from a broken wrist in July. Between having patsies on the schedule, and Walker, Wild Bill Hallahan, and Tex Carleton, the Cardinals could afford to stand on principle. Sans Deans, the club won seven of eight.

Meanwhile, on August 17, shortly after Dizzy had visited him in his Chicago offices to plead his case, commissioner Kenesaw Mountain Landis announced he would come to St. Louis to hold a hearing on the matter on Monday, August 20. Dizzy also wrote a semicoherent letter to the *St. Louis Post-Dispatch*, wheedling for understanding, but Paul had meanwhile chosen discretion that same day, accepting his fine and his forfeited salary and writing a public apology. The showdown on Monday was a rout for Dizzy and an assertion of authority—Landis upheld the Cardinals' handling of the situation, while Dizzy whined about his victimhood and the loss of almost $500.

The point made, both Dizzy and Paul were back in the rotation in time for the next series, which just happened to be against the Giants. The Deans' reinstatement availed the team little. Although they started two of the three games, the Cardinals nevertheless lost two. As August faded into September, the *Sporting News* intoned that "as far as the Cardinals are concerned, their pennant chances have been reduced to a rather hopeless degree." The paper noted that the Giants were playing almost their entire September schedule at home after posting a 41-15 record in the Polo Grounds. With a month to play, the Cardinals were tied with the Cubs, 5.5 games behind the Giants. Rumors that Frisch would be fired after the season were circulating.

What followed was a stunning reversal of fortunes. Having endured more drama than seemed possible, the Cardinals won 21 of 28, the Giants toppled with a 13-14 record, and the Cubs similarly took themselves out of the picture with a 12-14 finish. What's more, the three teams largely did not do these things playing against one another—the Giants played just a four-game set against the Cardinals that month, while the Cubs played only two games against the Cardinals; against one another, the Cubs and Giants had a single three-game series. Although the Cardinals took three of four from the Giants (September 13–16) and won both contests against the Cubs (September 1 and 24), the Giants had plenty of other games on the schedule. Nonetheless, Terry's team saw its lead dwindle: During the last week of September, the Giants watched the Cardinals overtake them when St. Louis swept the league-worst Reds in a season-ending four-game set, while the Giants themselves were suffering the humiliation of the still-in-the-league Dodgers' applying the coup de grâce to their hopes.

What happened? First, it helped that the Cardinals got to play 12 of their last 28 against the worst two teams in the league, the Reds and the Phillies. Frisch went to the whip with the Dean brothers (which must have been satisfying), starting Dizzy in eight of the last 29 games, and Paul in seven. The Cardinals had to play six games (including two doubleheaders) in four days against the Phillies before the last four-game series against the Giants. Frisch lined up his rotation with some care, spotting an ancient Dazzy Vance in the last game of the Phillies series so that Paul Dean would start the first game against the Giants; the Cards won what was the last start of Vance's career.

Frisch wasn't ignorant of the fact that the Deans had already beaten the Giants nine times that season, and Paul had just pitched a 12-inning shutout in the first game to make it 10. A rainout of the third game was a lucky break, setting up another doubleheader. Dizzy had been scheduled to start the first game; Frisch took a chance and started Paul on two days' rest in the nightcap. The Deans made it an even dozen victories over the Giants in front of the largest crowd in Polo Grounds history up to that point (62,573). Facing the last two series of the season, a pair of games against the Pirates and a four-game set against the Reds, with no off days in between the six and needing every win, Frisch started Dizzy three times and Paul twice. Dizzy won all three of his starts to reach 30 wins, shutting out the pathetic Reds twice in three days. Paul took the Cardinals' last loss of the season when Waite Hoyt threw the next-to-last shutout of his long career for the Pirates. The Cards won five of those last six, while the Giants lost six of their last seven—two each to the Braves, the Phillies, and the Dodgers—to blow it. When news of the Dodgers' victory in the elimination game reached the Cardinals' clubhouse, the players joyously chanted, "Brooklyn is still in the league! Brooklyn is still in the league!"

Some observers have suggested that the Giants lost because the club was exhausted down the stretch, and there is some truth to that. Those gaudy averages cited earlier tumbled from August 23 onward. Mel Ott fizzled, hitting .216 and driving in only five runs the rest of the way, despite playing in all 153 games. To a lesser extent, Terry and Moore also faltered, though they remained productive, hitting "only" in the .290s down the stretch. Perhaps Ott could have afforded some rest during the season, but the Giants were probably not suffering any special handicap. They played one less game than the Cardinals did in September, and because of rainouts, the Cards had to play seven doubleheaders in the last month to the Giants' four. The Giants did have to play many extra-inning games that last month (a total of seven). They also enjoyed the benefit of spending almost the entire last month in New York—after September 4, they made a three-day, four-game road trip to Boston, and that was it as far as travel for almost four weeks of season left to play.

Could Terry have fixed his club and preserved his lead? Perhaps, but the same things that had made him a successful player-manager the year before became problematic when confronted by an assiduously organizational approach like Rickey's. Terry was leading his teammates, and part of that involved his holding "skull sessions before each game, listening to every suggestion and implementing some of them." That's an admirable way to lead your fellow men, as a first among equals, but it can also create problems when you have to start sorting out how much less equal the others are and make some tough choices. In that environment, was anyone going to point out that their third-best hitter from the previous season, Johnny Vergez, had been worse than useless and needed to be benched? Or was there a basic abdication of responsibility, where nobody would make a decision and everyone just hoped Vergez would get better? Add to this dilemma Terry's decision to trade away Fred Lindstrom for the wrong reasons, and we see the penalties of personal leadership starting to add up. The previous season's antidote to John McGraw was not necessarily this season's formula for success.

The club realized it had a real problem on the left side of the infield. The aftereffects of Travis Jackson's knee injuries left him woefully ill-equipped to play shortstop; in his first full season back since 1931, his ratio of double plays to errors dropped from 79-25 to 59-43, and his fielding Rate had dropped into the 80s (100 is average). His downslide wasn't a secret. Nor was the proposed solution—by early September, the *Sporting News* was reporting rumors that the Giants would acquire shortstop Dick Bartell from the Phillies after the season, noting that Jackson would be the man who moved to third. This was exactly what happened in the winter. It was to the Giants' detriment that it hadn't happened sooner.

Still, in the middle of the summer of 1934, the Giants were holding a lead. Terry could not have known with absolute certainty that Vergez would never match his 1933 season, or that his team would blow the lead and finish behind the Cardinals. There's also a simple logistical question—did Terry have enough time to make a deal? Western Union was pretty swell, but it wasn't a cell phone. And in light of his traveling, managing, playing, and leading, we can't simply assume Terry had the same freedom of action that even Branch Rickey had with his greater investment but fewer duties.

Terry was a reflection of an older management model. Baseball had long operated with a relatively simple management system: Managers were often also active players and sometimes controlled their club's roster moves, calling the shots on the diamond, in the clubhouse, and for the entire roster. The game's decision making had been defined by the qualities of personal leadership and was a reflection of a simpler time in the game's operations, going back to its earliest beginnings. As the game rolled into the 1930s, its dugouts were populated by grand old men like Connie Mack of the Philadelphia A's, John McGraw of the New York Giants, and Wilbert Robinson of the Dodgers. All got their starts as players, slowly evolving to player-managers and assuming all responsibilities for field operations—including salary negotiations—while team presidents, investors, and sundry sons-in-law and nephews handled business operations, including ticket sales.

This division of labor was the way it was supposed to work—if you were a player, somewhat smart or famous, and gifted with some ambition, that's where you wanted to wind up if staying in the game was your goal. Whether you were Rogers Hornsby or Babe Ruth, you wanted to become a manager, perhaps a business partner, and make that big move from chattel to lordling. As the dotage of grand old men like McGraw and Robinson would eventually lead to their falls, the assumption was that the men who replaced them would achieve similarly lofty heights, becoming organizational institutions of themselves. When McGraw, sickly and dyspeptic, turned to Terry and asked if he wished to take his place at the helm, Terry accepted with alacrity. Terry was more than somewhat smart, more than somewhat famous, and ambitious.

In many respects, Bill Terry was the last great player-manager, the last manager whose brand of personal leadership depended equally on his feats on the field and his acumen in calling the shots. He won pennants in 1936 and 1937, but the 1934 pennant race exemplified why this older model of leadership was doomed. It wasn't because intelligent men could not play and manage back then, or manage and handle the responsibilities that general managers handle today, but because other intelligent men were learning the power of specializing within management. The future would belong to the teams that learned to segregate responsibilities, from dugout management to handling the front office. The game wasn't going to go back to the days of John McGraw's youth; Rickey himself had tried managing from the dugout in the 1920s and failed. He learned from that experience and got out of uniform. The future belonged to men like Rickey, Larry MacPhail, and, later, George Weiss. The future of organizational management belonged to the suits, to the men in glasses, not the heroes.

# 1944 American League

## *The Home Front*

### NATE SILVER

*Most of the men left behind to play baseball were physical culls and athletes of extraordinary youth or old age. Gradually, this state of affairs made a contender of the St. Louis Browns. Nothing short of a world war could have done so.*

—William B. Mead, *Even the Browns*

*I know you agree with me that individual players who are of active military or naval age should go, without question, into the services. Even if the actual quality of the teams is lowered ... this will not dampen the popularity of the sport.*

—President Franklin D. Roosevelt to Commissioner Kenesaw Landis,
"Green Light Letter," January 15, 1942

It has now been over six decades since the end of World War II. Though today's Americans experienced something like their own Pearl Harbor on September 11, 2001, we still have difficulty in fully understanding the pervasive effects of the war, death, and destruction unleashed on the country on December 7, 1941. Imagine that when the World Trade Center and Pentagon were attacked, Al Qaeda and its allies had taken over all the territory of continental Europe between

## 1944 American League Prospectus

| Team | Actual Standings | | | | | Date Elim | Pythag | |
|------|-----|-----|------|------|-----|-----------|-----|-----|
|  | W | L | Pct | GB | DIF |  | W | L |
| Browns | 89 | 65 | .578 | – | 128 | – | 88 | 66 |
| Tigers | 88 | 66 | .571 | 1.0 | 14 | Oct 1 | 86 | 68 |
| Yankees | 83 | 71 | .539 | 6.0 | 32 | Sept 29 | 83 | 71 |
| Red Sox | 77 | 77 | .500 | 12.0 | 0 | Sept 23 | 83 | 71 |
| A's | 72 | 82 | .468 | 17.0 | 2 | Sept 19 | 69 | 85 |
| Indians | 72 | 82 | .468 | 17.0 | 0 | Sept 20 | 73 | 81 |
| White Sox | 71 | 83 | .461 | 18.0 | 2 | Sept 17 | 63 | 91 |
| Senators | 64 | 90 | .416 | 25.0 | 0 | Sept 9 | 69 | 85 |

| League Averages | | | | BP Stats Leaders | | | |
|------|------|------|-------|------|-----|------|-----|
| AVG | OBP | SLG | BABIP | Offense, BRAA | | Indiv WARP | |
| .260 | .325 | .353 | .280 | Indians | 91 | Dizzy Trout | 15.9 |
| ERA | K9 | BB9 | H9 | Pitching, PRAA | | Snuffy Stirnweiss | 14.8 |
| 3.43 | 3.4 | 3.2 | 9.0 | Tigers | 81 | Lou Boudreau | 14.3 |

Stalingrad and the Iberian Peninsula; much of Southeast Asia, including Japan, Korea, Thailand, and urban China; and parts of North Africa and the Mediterranean. The resultant conflict would not be one of choice but of national survival.

That is what the world was like in 1944, and yet in our imaginings, we're still only halfway there. In mid-2007, Americans were living through a war in Iraq that, despite far-reaching consequences, could all too easily be dismissed to the recesses of the mind with the flick of a remote control. World War II was different; there were too many absent friends. Over 16 million Americans served at some point during the conflict, and more than 400,000 died. Daily life was transformed. In 1944, pleasure driving was forbidden because of gasoline rations. Cities like New York were blacked out at night because of fear that lights would aid Axis destroyers and submarines in an amphibious attack on our shorelines. Every resource—literally every available resource—was somehow marshaled for the war effort.

Baseball was no exception. It couldn't have been. Though President Roosevelt's Green Light Letter of January 15, 1942, ensured that major league baseball would continue to be played, the letter made no such promises about which men would be playing it. The government was willing to grant Hollywood figures exemption from military service (actors could be granted a 2-A deferment for serving in an essential national industry), but from Pearl Harbor onward, there were no serious calls to exclude baseball from the war effort. Unlike actors, producers, and directors, baseball players were men in the prime of their lives who made a living with their physical and mental gifts. They were exactly the sort of men the army and navy needed. And the military needed all the men it could get.

Occasionally, a ballplayer's enrollment in the service was deferred for a few weeks so that he could complete his season, but no major league baseball player could entirely avoid service as a result of his fame, influence, or chosen profession. In fact, because of their highly public profiles, baseball players were probably less likely than others of comparable fitness to be exempted from the war effort. The public pressure was too great, and these men were too patriotic. Players who were initially rejected for military service because of physical deficiencies would frequently attempt to volunteer. "There was no joy if you were declared 4-F (unfit for duty)," recalled Dom DiMaggio. "Every man in his twenties or thirties wanted to do his part."

Moreover, for some months during the latter years of the war effort (1944–1945), the government adopted a policy of compelling into service the professional athletes who were called to the draft, even if they might have otherwise been rejected. By then, when the size of the active armed forces had mushroomed, the presumption was that a baseball player would have been drafted for the military or he would have volunteered for it. A major league baseball player in those years might have been deferred from military service for only a handful of reasons:

- He was too young or too old.
- He was classified as 1-C, meaning that he had dependents who might have been put at hardship if he served.
- He was classified as 1-B, meaning that he had an essential, non-baseball civilian occupation.
- He was a resident alien who hadn't registered for the draft.
- He had completed his tour of duty and been honorably discharged.
- He was a 4-F, unfit for military service.

*Too young or too old.*   In October 1940, with war under way in Europe and Asia but with the United States remaining on the sidelines, all men between ages 21 and 36 were required to register for the draft. A new law enacted after Pearl Harbor and the declaration of war on the Axis powers expanded registration from ages 18 to 64, though men younger than 20 or older than 45 could not be drafted. These policies were soon revised further, lowering the age of conscription to 18, while establishing an effective upper bound at 38.

Thus, a handful of players aged 39 or older, some former stars and others who had never established themselves in the big leagues, played important roles with their clubs during the war years. This effect is not to be overstated; in 1945, the year in which the talent pool was most profoundly affected by the war effort, just 31 men aged 39 or older appeared in a major league uniform. Most of them—like Lloyd Waner of the Pirates and Leo Durocher of the Dodgers—played token roles. And although the era is remembered for the 1944 debut of the 15-year-old Joe Nuxhall, teenage prodigies were even rarer. Just four players listed at age 17 or younger appeared on major league rosters in 1945, though none of these youngsters played in more than 57 games.

*Class 1-C, deferred because of dependents.*   A complicated series of protocols made single men with no dependents more likely to be drafted than married men with children or other dependents; the latter group of men could hope for a Class 1-C deferment. As the size of the military grew, however, 1-C exemptions became rarer, and many players, like Joe DiMaggio, who had initially been granted 1-C status, volunteered to serve. Others had their 1-C status revoked and were drafted.

These policies were enforced by hundreds of local draft boards and were often applied inconsistently. Thus, the Yankees' Red Ruffing, who was 38, lacked four toes, and had a wife, children, and a dependent mother-in-law, was drafted, while the Cardinals' Stan Musial, far younger and healthier, was deferred until after the 1944 season. (Musial, who had an ailing father and mother to attend to, did serve in 1945.) By the end of the 1944 season, there were few 1-Cs left to play major league baseball.

*Class 1-B, deferred for essential civilian position.*   Many baseball players moonlighted in other occupations during World War II, either to help pay the bills or because they wanted to contribute to the war effort. In some cases—the player worked in a shipyard or a munitions factory, for example—this earned him a Class 1-B deferral.

The trouble was that the more essential the player's non-baseball job, the less likely he would be able to play baseball full-time. Thus, while the Indians' Ken Keltner managed to play through the 1944 season because of a 1-B classification (he joined the service in 1945), the

Brownies' Chet Laabs and Denny Galehouse were limited to playing baseball on weekends on account of their civilian jobs. Additionally, a few others forsook baseball entirely for civilian duties.

*Resident aliens.* Some owners, most notably the Senators' Clark Griffith, sought to recruit Latin American talent to overcome the player shortage; eight Cubans and one Venezuelan appeared in a game for the 1944 Senators. In practice, however, there was little to exempt these players from the draft—resident aliens could not volunteer for the draft, but they were theoretically expected to register and could be called on to serve. In July 1944, three of Griffith's Cubans—Roberto Ortiz, Fermin Guerra, and Gilberto Torres—were told they must register for the draft or leave the country. All three initially returned to Cuba before reporting to the Senators (and Selective Service) a couple of weeks later. Other foreigners, such as Dick Fowler and Phil Marchildon, a pair of Canadian pitchers on the Philadelphia Athletics, went on to serve the Allies under their own nation's flag.

*Tour of duty completed.* The expanding size of the army made it difficult for enlisted men to return home unless they had been injured severely, had proven themselves unfit for duty, or were temporarily discharged after basic training and awaiting further instructions. A few players had also served during the peacetime years of the 1920s and 1930s and had been honorably discharged. This group of players made for notable exceptions here and there—including Dick Wakefield and Sig Jakucki, two key figures in the 1944 pennant race—but most players in the service did not return until the waning days of the 1945 season or the start of 1946.

*Class 4-F, physically, mentally, or morally unfit for military service.* With the other reasons for avoiding military service rendered impractical or impossible by 1944, the most common reason that a player could continue playing major league baseball was his 4-F classification—physically, mentally, or morally unfit for military service. Reasons for 4-F status included a heart defect (Hal Newhouser, Tigers), poor teeth (Morrie Arnovich, Giants), an arthritic ankle (Lou Boudreau, Indians), or inadequate eyesight (Dizzy Trout, Tigers), but more common were chronic problems with a player's back, joints, or feet. The 4-F classification could and would be revoked; Arnovich was reclassified as 1-A and enlisted, while Boudreau was reclassified as 1-A but managed to stay with the Indians.

This was the great irony of the 1944 pennant race—most men who were able to play major league baseball were doing so because of one or more severe physical limitations. It was natural selection in reverse, survival of the weakest. And this turn of events greatly favored the St. Louis Browns, a team that had been playing in the mud when the rest of baseball emerged from its primordial gene pool. With more than 60 percent of the league's 1941 starters away in the service, the Browns led baseball in misfits; 18 of the team's players either held a 4-F classification or had been honorably discharged from the service. There was shortstop Vern Stephens, the closest thing the Browns had to a star, out of the service because of a broken kneecap; first baseman George McQuinn, who had back problems; and pitcher Jack Kramer, who had joined the navy in 1943 but received a discharge for asthma.

And there was Sig Jakucki. Jakucki had served in the army. In fact, in the apparent desire to see the world, he'd joined the service in 1927 at age 16, having lied about his age at a Philadelphia recruitment station a few miles from his Camden, New Jersey, home. (Some sources dispute Jakucki's age, placing his birth date in 1909 rather than, as Jakucki claimed, in 1912. It's still likely that Jakucki lied about his age, but with the intention of seeming younger for baseball, not older for the service.) Jakucki spent most of his five years of service at Schofield Barracks in Hawaii, and played baseball much of that time. While stationed there, he established a reputation as one of the most feared sluggers on the army teams of that era. "He became so good that during his second enlistment," the *Sporting News* said in a gushing profile of June 22, 1944, "a Honolulu sports promoter bought his release from the Army so that Jakucki could play with his Honolulu Braves."

Jakucki excelled in Hawaii and proved to be so popular that a group of Honolulu enthusiasts bought him a tryout with the San Francisco Seals of the Pacific Coast League. But Jakucki was as big a misfit as they came. Rejected by the Seals, he bounced around the minor leagues for several seasons, including a stop in Galveston, where manager Billy Webb moved him from the batter's box to the pitcher's mound. Although Jakucki did well enough as a pitcher to earn a cup of coffee with the Browns in 1936, an 0-3 record and the beginnings of a drinking problem did not endear him to manager Rogers Hornsby. Jakucki failed to break camp with the Browns in 1937, and by the next season, he was out of organized baseball entirely. He found himself back in Galveston, where he worked as a contractor, played semipro ball, fished, and drank. Mostly he drank: The travel restrictions of the wartime era were not a good fit for his wanderlust.

Jakucki made his way back to the Browns. Acting on a tip from a Texas friend, general manager Bill DeWitt had invited Jakucki to training camp in 1944. The hurler made the team and proved capable of retiring big-league hitters, compiling a 13-9 record and a 3.55 ERA. On the last day of the season, Jakucki found himself on the spot at Sportsman's Park. He was set to start in a sold-out game that the team had to win to clinch the first pennant in its history. His opponents were the Yankees—and his sobriety.

◆

The war gave and took from the Browns. The second team in a one-team market, the Browns had sought throughout 1941 to relocate to Los Angeles, by then already a city of a million and a half people. It was a complicated arrangement. First there was a payout from Sam Breadon, the owner of the Cardinals, who wanted the St. Louis market to himself. Then there would be a payout to Phil Wrigley, the owner of the Pacific Coast League's Los Angeles Angels, who were then a Cubs affiliate. And finally, there was a nightmarish schedule involving trips on the *Super Chief*, the flagship passenger train of the Santa Fe Railway, which embarked from Chicago and arrived in Los Angeles some 40 hours later. But the Browns had fully expected approval from American League owners at the winter meetings, which were scheduled to begin in Chicago on December 10, 1941.

That weekend, Pearl Harbor was attacked. Like so many other things, the idea of transporting baseball teams across the country to California, on trains that would soon be overcrowded with soldiers reporting to duty, would have to be placed in abeyance "for the duration."

But in other ways, the war benefited the Browns. The club had come to depend on an allotment of nighttime games to pay the rent in working-class St. Louis, a practice that had become widespread in the minors but was opposed by an influential cadre of major league traditionalists, including Commissioner Landis. Under pressure from President Roosevelt, who recognized that men would be working long hours in the shipyards and factories of major league cities, the owners agreed to reverse an earlier halving of the nighttime schedule.

The Browns also benefited from the unusual circumstances of spring training. With trips to Florida ruled out because of travel restrictions, teams trained instead at sites concentrated in New England and Indiana. The Browns and Cardinals, then the geographic outliers of their leagues, were allowed to stay closer to home, provided that they remained north of the Ohio River. And so the Cardinals landed at Cairo, Illinois, at the intersection of the Ohio and Mississippi, and the Browns at Cape Girardeau, Missouri, about sixty miles upstream.

Cape Girardeau offered several distinct advantages. It was more southerly than other spring training sites—and therefore milder. It was only 120 miles from St. Louis. And it featured indoor training facilities—one of the few spring training sites that did—including a gymnasium at a local college and an arena built for horse shows. The zealous city fathers of Cape Girardeau were only too happy to lend these civic landmarks to the Browns.

The Browns made a habit of taking advantage of their comparatively comfortable training conditions. They had won their first four regular-season games in 1942 and their opening series in 1943. In 1944, they again won their first four in a row, sweeping the Tigers in Detroit, with Jakucki bettering MVP Hal Newhouser in the finale. They then took their home opener against the White Sox before a crowd of just 2,300 at Sportsman's Park. Although the Browns had faded after their successful 1942 and 1943 starts, this time they kept on going, completing a sweep of the White Sox and rolling through the Indians. By April 28, they had won nine straight, breaking the American League record for victories to start the season, and had opened up a 3.5-game lead over the Philadelphia Athletics (Table 13-1).

It wouldn't take long, however, for the Browns to start playing like the Browns. With the rest of the league

Table 13-1 American League Standings at the End of Friday, April 28, 1944

| Team | W | L | GB |
|------|---|---|-----|
| St. Louis | 9 | 0 | – |
| Philadelphia | 4 | 2 | 3.5 |
| New York | 3 | 3 | 4.5 |
| Boston | 3 | 4 | 5.0 |
| Washington | 2 | 3 | 5.0 |
| Detroit | 3 | 5 | 5.5 |
| Cleveland | 2 | 5 | 6.0 |
| Chicago | 1 | 5 | 6.5 |

warming up, literally and figuratively, they lost first place to the Yankees after dropping both games of a doubleheader to the Athletics on May 14. What was more troubling, on May 9 the army laid claim to the Browns' pitcher Steve Sundra, who had led the team in victories in 1943 and was slotted in as second starter. Without the services of Sundra, the Browns surrendered 48 runs over their next eight contests, bottoming out at 17-15 on May 21 (Table 13-2).

But the Browns reclaimed first place soon afterward, benefiting from one time-tested baseball ingredient: home cooking. After their doubleheader loss to the Yankees, the Browns were set to play their

Table 13-2 American League Standings at the
End of Sunday, May 21, 1944

| Team | W | L | GB |
|------|-----|-----|-----|
| New York | 17 | 10 | – |
| St. Louis | 17 | 15 | 2.5 |
| Washington | 15 | 14 | 3.0 |
| Detroit | 15 | 16 | 4.0 |
| Boston | 14 | 15 | 4.0 |
| Cleveland | 14 | 17 | 5.0 |
| Chicago | 13 | 17 | 5.5 |

next 19 contests at Sportsman's Park. The Browns played especially well at home throughout 1944, compiling a 54-23 record in St. Louis while managing only a 35-42 mark on the road.

Although the home field advantage was generally larger in the 1940s than it is today, the Browns' home performance arose from two very real advantages. The first is geography. St. Louis represented the western frontier of the American League in those days; it was about 290 miles by train from Chicago, its closest AL counterpart, and some 1,200 miles from Boston. This might not have been a big deal during the ordinary course of business, when baseball players traveled in luxury coaches on superliners, but railway travel was different during wartime. Because of restrictions on automobile travel and the rapid movement of military supplies throughout the country, trains were overcrowded, slow, and unreliable. Teams frequently arrived in faraway cities exhausted.

Table 13-3 looks at the impact of travel on teams during the war years. Three AL teams had an especially large home advantage at this time: the New York Yankees, who drew the most fans of any AL club during the period, and the St. Louis Browns and Boston Red Sox, who were at the southwestern and northeastern corners of the league map, respectively. The team with the smallest difference in home-versus-road winning percentage was the Cleveland Indians, who were closest

Table 13-3 Home and Road Records, 1942–1945, American League

| Team | Home Record | Road Record | Home-Road Difference | Average Distance to Other AL Cities (miles) |
|------|------|------|------|------|
| St. Louis | 185-120 (.607) | 139-164 (.459) | .148 | 764 |
| Boston | 181-125 (.592) | 128-178 (.418) | .173 | 664 |
| Chicago | 160-136 (.541) | 130-179 (.421) | .120 | 604 |
| Detroit | 181-126 (.590) | 146-162 (.474) | .116 | 509 |
| New York | 207-101 (.672) | 158-148 (.516) | .156 | 496 |
| Philadelphia | 130-174 (.428) | 98-210 (.318) | .109 | 470 |
| Washington | 165-142 (.433) | 132-173 (.433) | .105 | 467 |
| Cleveland | 166-143 (.537) | 136-161 (.458) | .079 | 431 |

to the map's center and could reach any AL destination overnight. The correlation between travel distance and home field advantage is very strong, and stronger still if New York—Yankee Stadium was an intimidating place even then—is removed.

The Browns' general manager Bill DeWitt also had a second, more peculiar reason to prefer that his team play at home. Besides Jakucki, several other Browns had a fondness for drink and enjoyed the favorable gender ratios of wartime America. Center fielder Mike Kreevich and shortstop Vern Stephens were noted for their appreciation of the bottle and Victory Girls, respectively. At home, many of the Browns had wives or girlfriends, families, and perhaps even part-time jobs. On the road, they behaved like a bunch of teenagers on spring break. DeWitt and manager Luke Sewell tried their best to keep the Browns under control, with little success.

The Browns also benefited from a couple of reinforcements. Outfielder Chet Laabs, an All-Star in 1943, was working in an Akron war plant, and pitcher Denny Galehouse was doing the same in Detroit. Neither man was playing baseball in 1944. But the Browns' fast start, coupled with the slow road trip, had whet the team's appetite for the pennant. So DeWitt did what he could to draft Galehouse and Laabs for baseball duty. Galehouse agreed to be a Sunday pitcher, making the commute from Akron each weekend. Meanwhile, DeWitt arranged for Laabs to take a plant job in St. Louis, where the outfielder would assemble pipes for the atomic bombs that would eventually be dropped on Hiroshima and Nagasaki. Other teams would not have considered such maneuvers. Yankees president Ed Barrow, known equally for his bombast and patriotism, refused to let top relief pitcher Johnny Murphy perform in such a capacity (and therefore lost Murphy's services for the entirety of 1944 and 1945).

The Browns were not assisted by their new players immediately; Laabs did not reach St. Louis until June 1, and Galehouse did not record his first win until July 20. Still, the club was playing better baseball, finishing the home stand at 11-8, while the rest of the American League was exhibiting the parity that had come to be expected of wartime baseball. The entire league was separated by fewer than five games on June 11, with the Browns barely out on top (Table 13-4).

Little would change over the next month. American League teams took their turns sharing train cabins, four-game winning streaks, and news from the war front, including Allied progress in the Battle of Normandy. On July 13, the Browns held a 2.5-game lead over the Boston Red Sox, a lead barely changed from a month earlier.

Table 13-4 American League Standings at the
End of Sunday, June 11, 1944

| Team | W | L | GB |
|------|-----|-----|-----|
| St. Louis | 28 | 23 | – |
| Boston | 25 | 23 | 1.5 |
| Detroit | 25 | 24 | 2.0 |
| Chicago | 22 | 22 | 2.5 |
| New York | 22 | 22 | 2.5 |
| Cleveland | 24 | 26 | 3.5 |
| Philadelphia | 22 | 24 | 3.5 |
| Washington | 22 | 26 | 4.5 |

The exception to this rule was the Detroit Tigers. Perhaps the closest thing to a favorite in 1944 because of the presence of star pitchers Dizzy Trout and Hal Newhouser, the Tigers had dropped to eight games behind the Browns, just barely ahead of the cellar-dwelling Athletics. On the 13th, the Tigers were jolted by the return of slugging outfielder Dick Wakefield to their lineup. Having been honorably discharged from the navy after completing his squadron training, he was eligible to play until called back into the service (which he was, but not until 1945). Wakefield made his impact felt immediately, keying an eight-run rally off White Sox starter Orval Grove to propel the Tigers to a 9-1 victory in his first game back. The Tigers then won nine of Wakefield's first 11 games with the club, cutting their deficit with the Browns in half (Table 13-5). The 23-year-old Wakefield went on to hit .355/.464/.576 in 78 games.

But the Browns were soon to enjoy a streak of their own. Starting with the second game of a doubleheader on July 23, they won 14 contests in 15 tries. True, they were facing weak opposition—most of the damage was done in home games against the Senators, Athletics, and Indians—but taking advantage of manager Luke Sewell's hunches, the Browns strung together rallies at just the right time. On July 26 against Philadelphia, the Browns tallied just six hits, but were propelled to a 4-2 victory on the strength of a three-run homer by catcher Red Hayworth—his only long ball of the season. Four days later, in the first game of a doubleheader against the Senators, the Browns headed into extra innings deadlocked at zero, but gave up a run in the top of the 10th. But in the bottom half, Frank Mancuso singled, pinch hitter Tom Hafey drew a walk, and Don Gutteridge doubled to bring Mancuso and pinch runner Tex Shirley home. On August 6 against the Indians, before a large crowd at Sportsman's Park, the

Table 13-5 American League Standings at the
End of Saturday, July 22, 1944

| Team | W | L | GB |
|------|-----|-----|-----|
| St. Louis | 50 | 40 | – |
| New York | 45 | 40 | 2.5 |
| Boston | 46 | 42 | 3.0 |
| Detroit | 45 | 44 | 4.5 |
| Cleveland | 45 | 45 | 5.0 |
| Washington | 42 | 45 | 6.5 |
| Chicago | 40 | 43 | 6.5 |
| Philadelphia | 37 | 50 | 11.5 |

Table 13-6 Runs Created Versus Actual Runs Scored for 1944 American League

| Team | BA/OBP/SLG | RC | R | Difference |
|------|-----------|-----|-----|-----------|
| Yankees | .264/.330/.387 | 686 | 674 | -12 |
| Red Sox | .270/.334/.380 | 682 | 739 | +57 |
| Indians | .266/.329/.372 | 664 | 643 | -21 |
| Tigers | .263/.330/.354 | 617 | 658 | +41 |
| Browns | .252/.321/.352 | 592 | 684 | +92 |
| Senators | .261/.321/.330 | 562 | 599 | +37 |
| Athletics | .257/.311/.327 | 537 | 525 | -12 |
| White Sox | .261/.320/.330 | 514 | 543 | +29 |

Browns managed the devilish feat of scoring six runs in the sixth inning twice, winning both legs of a doubleheader 9-6 and 6-4.

It was these sorts of games that the Browns won all season. Statisticians have a couple of ways of telling whether a team gets lucky (or performs well in the clutch, depending on your perspective). One of these is the Pythagorean record—comparing a team's runs scored and runs allowed to its wins and losses. The 1944 Browns' run totals (684 scored and 587 allowed) implied a Pythagorean record of 88-66, a good match for their actual record of 89-65.

By another measure, however, the Browns were very fortunate. St. Louis ranked seventh out of eight American League teams in batting average (.252), sixth in on-base percentage (.321), fifth in slugging average (.352), and seventh in stolen bases (44). By any metric, they were a below-average offensive club, but somehow, the Browns finished with 684 runs scored on the season, the second-highest total in the league.

We can combine the individual elements of offensive performance into an estimate of how many runs a team "should" have scored by using Bill James's runs-created formula (Table 13-6). The formula estimates, for example, that the Yankees' offensive inputs in 1944 would usually add up to an output of 686 runs; they actually scored 674. The White Sox had 514 runs created, versus 543 runs scored. The runs-created formula estimates that the Browns should have scored 592 times. They actually scored 684 runs, some 92 more than anticipated. That's the rough equivalent of replacing the performances of first baseman George McQuinn and center fielder Mike Kreevich with those of Hank Greenberg and Joe DiMaggio.

It isn't uncommon for pennant-winning teams to exceed the sum of their statistical parts, in part through luck. In fact, it's more the rule than the exception, and the Browns weren't alone in having things come together for them. The Tigers (41 runs above their runs-created formula for the season) were doing it, too.

Led by Wakefield, who would finish fifth in the MVP balloting in spite of playing in fewer than half his team's games, Detroit was streaking, going 13-6 on a five-city road trip that concluded on August 22. The Yankees were playing good baseball as well, having their best month of the season in August, while the Red Sox remained in the hunt, taking advantage of an extended home stand.

The Browns couldn't have picked a worse time for their longest road trip of the season. It had started well enough, with the Browns winning three games from the Yankees and earning a series split in Boston. Then St. Louis dropped three out of four in both Washington and Philadelphia. The schedule at this point offered a blessing and a curse: The entire league had three days off between the 22nd and 25th. But the Browns spent the break in Detroit, with plenty of time for rabble-rousing in between, while the Tigers were headed home, with Newhouser and Trout fresh for the four-game series.

The Tigers took the first game of the series 1-0, the lone run coming on a double-steal in the third inning, with Trout earning the shutout and his 21st victory of the season. The Browns were shut out again in the second game as Jakucki got shelled, yielding two home runs to Rudy York. After Newhouser took the first game of the Sunday double-header, the Browns earned some redemption, their bats coming alive for 17 runs in the nightcap. But they woke up the next morning to find the Tigers, Yankees, and Red Sox all within four games of them (Table 13-7).

Table 13-7 American League Standings at the End of Sunday, August 27, 1944

| Team | W | L | GB |
|------|-----|-----|------|
| St. Louis | 70 | 54 | – |
| New York | 65 | 56 | 3.5 |
| Boston | 66 | 58 | 4.0 |
| Detroit | 65 | 57 | 4.5 |
| Cleveland | 60 | 66 | 11.0 |
| Philadelphia | 60 | 67 | 11.5 |
| Chicago | 57 | 66 | 12.5 |
| Washington | 52 | 71 | 17.5 |

Thanks to the War Department, one of those teams had reached its high-water mark. Tex Hughson, the Red Sox's ace, had made his last start of the season on August 9 before being inducted into the navy. That was hard enough to stomach, but barely two weeks later, on the 27th, catcher Hal Wagner left for the service. A week after that, second baseman Bobby Doerr, named 1944's MVP by the *Sporting News*, played his last game of the year before heading off to Gold Beach, Oregon, for his army physical. The team hoped that Doerr, who had been rejected for service twice that summer because of a perforated eardrum, would again be failed, but by that point it would have been too little and too late. Dazed and demoralized by their losses, the Red Sox won just seven of their final 25 games after Doerr's departure.

The Browns weren't losing players—when platoon outfielder Al Zarilla was drafted, DeWitt successfully persuaded Zarilla's commanding officer to let him take a leave until the season was complete—but they were losing ballgames. After splitting a two-game set with the Indians, the Browns returned home ready to play a four-game weekend series against the Tigers. Dizzy Trout performed double duty in the first game of the series, relieving Stubby Overmire in the seventh and sparking a rally with a leadoff single in the ninth, giving the Tigers the 4-3 victory. Newhouser won the next game to give the Tigers sole possession of second place, and they climbed to within one of the Browns by winning again on Saturday. Only Jack Kramer's outstanding performance in the Sunday finale prevented the Tigers from tying the standings.

It was but a temporary reprieve. The next day was Labor Day, when the league played a set of doubleheaders. The Browns split theirs against the Indians while the Yankees romped over Philadelphia 10-0 and 14-0, which gave the New York club eight wins in the last nine tries. The Browns had been in first place since May 31; now they had been leap-frogged by the Yankees (Table 13-8).

Still, the Tigers looked like the team of destiny. They took advantage of home-and-home series against the Indians, winning six of eight games, to pull into first place on September 17. Then they took two out of three in a critical series against the Yankees—the wins going, of course, to Trout and Newhouser—and swept four games from the slumping Red Sox.

Table 13-8 American League Standings at the End of Monday, September 4, 1944

| Team | W | L | GB |
|------|-----|-----|------|
| New York | 74 | 59 | – |
| St. Louis | 73 | 59 | 0.5 |
| Detroit | 70 | 60 | 2.5 |
| Boston | 71 | 62 | 3.0 |
| Cleveland | 64 | 69 | 10.0 |
| Philadelphia | 63 | 72 | 12.0 |
| Chicago | 60 | 70 | 12.5 |
| Washington | 55 | 79 | 19.5 |

The Browns resorted to the Browns' way of keeping pace: by picking a fight. Red Smith described it in the *Sporting News*:

During Washington's batting practice on the night of September 21, Turner sat on the bench and sought to calm his nerves by playing a word game. This consisted of digging interesting words with a Biblical flavor out of his vocabulary and flinging them at the Senators.

[Roberto] Ortiz, Cuban student of Pan-American diplomacy, walked to the mouth of the Browns' dugout and spoke briefly for the defense, and apparently remembering Luke Sewell's use of a bat, brandished one of George Case's Louisville Slugger models. ... Turner suggested that if Roberto would discard the shillelagh, they could do the rest of their talking with their hands.

"Turner" was Tom Turner, the Browns' third-string catcher, who played the equivalent of a hockey goon. Not often used by Luke Sewell, but notorious for his dislike of Latin players, Turner got the better of his round with Roberto Ortiz, the Senators' Cuban outfielder, taking a cheap shot in the groin but leaving Ortiz with a broken thumb. Reviewing baseball brawls in *Mind Game*, Steven Goldman wrote that "we could find no clear examples of teams that were propelled into the post-season by physically abusing an opponent." The fight in St. Louis might have been the exception. The Browns went on to win 9-4 that night, then swept three games from Philadelphia and two more from Boston before finally succumbing to the Red Sox on September 27.

And so three teams headed into the final weekend of the season with a chance to win the pennant: the Tigers, who had the most favorable matchup of the weekend at home against the Senators; the Browns, who trailed the Tigers by one game; and the Yankees, the Browns' opponent, left for dead a week earlier but keeping their hopes alive by winning six of seven games from the White Sox and Indians (Table 13-9).

TABLE 13-9 American League Standings at the End of Wednesday, September 27, 1944

| Team | W | L | GB |
|------|-----|-----|------|
| Detroit | 86 | 64 | – |
| St. Louis | 85 | 65 | 1.0 |
| New York | 83 | 67 | 3.0 |
| Boston | 75 | 75 | 11.0 |
| Cleveland | 72 | 78 | 14.0 |
| Chicago | 69 | 81 | 17.0 |
| Philadelphia | 68 | 82 | 18.0 |
| Washington | 62 | 88 | 24.0 |

The Browns' odds were longer than that one game might have suggested. Given the standings and the games remaining, the Browns had only a 17 percent chance of winning the title, with the Tigers at 82 percent and the Yankees with the mathematical leftovers. Moreover, the league had determined by coin flip that a one-game tiebreaker against the Tigers would be played in Detroit, a horrifying prospect for the road-weary St. Louis team. The Browns knew that nothing less than a four-game sweep of the Yankees would do.

After rainouts in both cities on the 28th, the weekend got under way with doubleheaders in Detroit (against Washington) and St. Louis (against New York). The Tigers split theirs; Trout, who was working on just two days' rest, got shelled in the second game by the Senators. The Browns were more fortunate. Their first win, which eliminated the Yankees from contention, came with relative ease, but the second was a nail-biter. The Browns scored once in the bottom of the first when second baseman Don Gutteridge doubled, advanced to third on a wild pitch, and came home on a groundout. Yankees starter Hank Borowy yielded just one hit the rest of the way, but that would be enough: Kreevich and Gutteridge made spectacular defensive plays to end the Yankees' rallies in the eighth and ninth innings, and the Browns took the game 1-0.

Each of the home teams won the next afternoon, the Browns getting a shutout from Galehouse, who by then had quit his war plant job. St. Louis and Detroit headed into Sunday with identical records of 88-65. It would be a long 24 hours for Sig Jakucki, who had drawn the final start against the Yankees. Jakucki found ways to work around the club's rules for his own personal comfort, as Browns' trainer Bob Bauman observed:

So Sig comes into the hotel about 11 o'clock at night carrying a big bag. A bag of whiskey; that's the way he carried it. [Zack] Taylor was a coach, and he hollered at him, "You're not going to take that to your room!" Jakucki says, "You're not going to take it away from me!" Taylor says, "You're not going to drink that tonight, I tell you that." ... Jakucki says, "I promise you I won't take a drink tonight. But don't try to take the liquor away, or there'll be trouble."

So the next thing I saw of Jakucki was at the ball park the next day. ... I can see he's been drinking. He says, "I kept my promise last night. I told him I wouldn't take a drink last night but I didn't promise him I wouldn't take one this morning."

This was wartime baseball: The Browns, who two years earlier had hoped to fold their cards and move to Los Angeles, were playing the Yankees, who two years earlier had nine All-Stars, all but one of whom were unavailable for the game because of the war. The Browns' pitcher was Sig Jakucki, a misfit among misfits—and Jakucki was drunk.

The game in Detroit had started a time zone earlier than the St. Louis game. Battling on the mound in Detroit were Trout, this time working on just one day's rest, and the Senators' Dutch Leonard, the veteran knuckleballer who in a phone call just that morning had told a mysterious man from a gambling syndicate to "go to hell." The Senators had pushed ahead of the Tigers in the fourth inning on a two-run homer by Stan Spence and had added a third run by the time the Browns, back in St. Louis, took the field in front of their first sellout of the season at Sportsman's Park.

The Yankees landed the first blows in St. Louis, scoring in the first inning on a triple and a Vern Stephens error, and again in the second on a series of defensive misplays. But in Detroit, the Senators' Leonard was cruising. Though he later claimed to have been shaken by the call he received that morning, his demeanor on the mound belied any unease. Through eight innings, he held the Tigers to two hits and no runs.

Meanwhile, at Sportsman's Park, Mike Kreevich singled in the fourth inning against Yankees starter Mel Queen, giving the Browns their first hit of the day. The next man up was Chet Laabs. When he hit a home run to left field, the game was tied.

Around this time in Detroit, the Tigers were finally cracking Leonard in the bottom of the ninth. Pinch hitters Chuck Hostetler and Don Ross strung together singles to lead off the inning, and the Tigers scored their first run of the game on a sacrifice fly. But that was all they would get. Leonard retired the last two batters, and the Senators won 4-1.

The Detroit score was posted at Sportsman's Park between the fourth and fifth innings. Shortly thereafter, Kreevich singled again, and Laabs hit another home run, putting the Browns ahead 4-2. The rest was up to Jakucki, who was strengthening (or sobering up) as the game went along. The Yankees could not put together a rally, while the Browns added a run on a Vern Stephens home run in the eighth. The final score was Browns 5, Yankees 2, and Browns 89 wins, Tigers 88.

Said the *New York Times* the next day: "It was, perhaps, the most dramatic finish any championship campaign has ever known, one which even the most gifted scenario expert could scarcely have improved upon."

◆

Any team that wins the pennant by exactly one game can point to any number of fortunate moments during its season. But the Browns' season had been a cacophony of serendipity. The most direct effect of the war—the loss of player talent—had hurt the Browns far less than it had their primary rivals. When the Browns' talent had been threatened, DeWitt did what other general managers couldn't or wouldn't do, working his connections to ensure that his players could play out the season. There had been the favorable circumstances of geography, which allowed the Browns to train close to home in the spring and which meant long journeys by their opponents into Sportsman's Park in the summer. There had been the Browns' propensity to string run elements together, which resulted in the team's scoring almost 100 more runs than the numbers would suggest. There had been the parity of the American League, which allowed the Browns to win the pennant with the worst winning percentage of any champion in league history. There had been the tip that brought Sig Jakucki to St. Louis from a contracting job in Galveston. There had been Tom Turner and his pugilism, Dizzy Trout and his tired arm, Chet Laabs and his home runs. For one season, the Browns, a cursed franchise before such curses existed, had been the luckiest team on the face of the earth.

But just what would have happened if the season had played out as normal, with each team allowed its full contingent of players? Would the Yankees, with their lineup full of All-Stars, have cruised to their fourth pennant in a row? Would the Red Sox, with Ted Williams and Johnny Pesky on hand, have mounted a challenge to their rivals? Would the Tigers, with Hank Greenberg joining Wakefield, Newhouser, and Trout, seen a happier outcome in the season's final days? The Browns wouldn't have won the pennant—that much we know. But would they have been competitive?

There is no way of knowing for certain, but we have the tools for comparing a counterfactual pennant race with the real one. The basic steps are as follows:

1. Determine, to the best of our ability, what each team's starting lineup and pitching staff would look like if no players were unavailable because of the war or war-related activities.
2. Estimate how much better than their actual 1944 counterparts these lineups would have been.

*Determination of starting lineups.* For each American League team, we attempted to determine which players would be deployed at each of the eight standard fielding positions, the top five slots in the pitching rotation, and the team's "ace" relief pitcher. In some cases, this determination is straightforward: Joe DiMaggio was absent from the Yankees in center field and was replaced by Johnny Lindell. In other cases, it requires more finesse. For example, although Charlie Gehringer, the great Tigers second baseman, was enlisted in the service while nominally remaining the property of the Tigers, he probably would have retired by 1944.

In general, we asked two groups of questions to decide whether a player deserved a place in a team's idealized lineup:

◆ For how many years was he the regular at his position before entering the military? In particular, was he the regular immediately before departing for the war? Did he again become the regular after returning from the service?

◆ If the player was one of several who might have been considered at his position, how well did he perform in the years before and after his military service? Would he have been in the prime of his career in 1944?

Our bias is conservative. Just because a player was a regular in 1941 or 1942 and left to serve in the war doesn't necessarily mean that he'd have been a regular in 1944. Player turnover in baseball is inherently high, with players losing their starting roles because of age, injury, new acquisitions, the development of minor league talent, or poor performance. For example, in 2003 there were 268 position players who played in at least 100 games. Only 138 (51 percent) of those players also played in 100 games in 2006. Similarly, 122 pitchers made at least 20 starts in 2003; fewer than half of them (60 of 122) made 20 starts three years later. We generally have not listed a player unless he was a definitive favorite to have held on to his starting job.

We also need to determine which players who played in 1944 would have been *out* of a job. For example, if a team lost three prominent members of its starting rotation to military service, we must select three pitchers to bump from the team's actual 1944 rotation. The questions we ask here are similar:

◆ Was the player a major league regular immediately before and after the war years?

◆ How well did the player perform before, after, and during the war years?

◆ Is there any anecdotal evidence that a player got his job opportunity specifically because of wartime absences?

Teams often resorted to platoons or a series of irregular performers if their starter was absent because of the war. In these cases, we might assign the playing time from several replacement players to one war-bound counterpart. An effort was made to match the playing time of the war-bound player. For example, if the absent player started almost every game in the years before and after his service, we assign him almost all the playing time at his position, even if it requires several players to do so. If the player was used as part of a platoon, received regular days off, or often missed time due to injury, we might assign him only his primary replacement at each position but not his secondary replacements.

*Estimating the impact of wartime absences.* The basic idea behind our process is simple: figuring out how many more runs a team would have scored or prevented if the regulars had been available. Contributions are broken down into batting, fielding, and pitching performance.

The application of this concept is more involved and is described at greater length in the endnotes. In short, we form a *projection* for the war-bound player using his age and his statistics in the three years before and after the war. We then compare that projection against the actual performance of his replacement. Baseball Prospectus has a particularly convenient tool for this process—the Davenport Translations. The translations build in an adjustment for league difficulty, including the diminished level of competition during the war. Thus, we can make an apples-to-apples comparison between a player who served as a replacement during the war years and the projected statistics of his absent counterpart.

Two additional problems required reconciliation.

*The addition-by-subtraction problem, that is, the Snuffy Rule.* Occasionally, the performance of the replacement player actually exceeded that of the absent regular. For example, Joe Gordon was the regular second baseman for the Yankees during the late 1930s and early 1940s, but he was drafted while in spring training and unavailable for the 1944 season. Our system projects Gordon at a .292 equivalent average (EqA) in 1944, a high figure that would qualify him as an All-Star second baseman in many seasons. Nevertheless, Gordon's replacement, Snuffy Stirnweiss, hit even better, posting a .306 EqA in 1944. After accounting for both the replacement's offensive and defensive contributions, we determined that Stirnweiss's actual performance was about 30 runs better than Gordon's projected performance during the 1944 season.

When such situations arise, we subtract *half* the difference in performance between the regular and his replacement. In the Stirnweiss/Gordon case, for example, we deduct about 15 runs from the Yankees rather than 30.

This solution, which we will call the Snuffy Rule, is the least imperfect alternative to a vexing problem. It would not be fair to deduct nothing at all when the replacement player turned out to be better than the regular. In 1944, as today, teams were often stubborn about promoting a rookie or giving a chance to a bench player. Sometimes, only something as cataclysmic as a war would have made teams see the light. On the other hand, deducting full credit is probably too much. The replacement player might have found a way to establish his value even without the war, as often happens during regular baseball business. And even if he was blocked at his position, the team might have been able to accommodate him by way of a trade, creating value at another position. Gordon, for example, was traded to the Indians for pitcher Allie Reynolds after the 1946 season in part because of Stirnweiss's emergence.

*The Cecil Travis Quandary.* One final ambiguity relates to players whose abilities might have atrophied as a direct result of their wartime service. Ballplayers, as a group, were remarkably fortunate during World War II. No established regular died or was gravely injured in the war, and most stars picked up right where they left, once they returned. The most frequently cited exception is Washington shortstop Cecil Travis, who had made the All-Star team in 1938, 1940, and 1941, but played in just 226 more major league games after returning from the service as a 31-year-old in 1945. Travis had suffered from frozen feet in the Battle of the Bulge, and this injury is generally considered the cause of a substantial decline in his reflexes at the plate and his mobility in the field. For this reason, our projections weight a player's performance in the years before the war somewhat more heavily than the years that followed it.

### The Impact of the War on the Browns
The Browns' wartime losses are summarized in Table 13-10. We estimate that they lost about 40 runs at the plate, nine in the field, and six on the mound as a result of their missing players. The total impact was 54 runs—or, since 10 runs are roughly equal to one win under the Davenport translations, between 5 and 6 wins.

Does this imply that the Browns should actually have gone 94-60 in

1944 instead of 89-65? Not really. If players like Wally Judnich and Joe Grace had been available to the Browns, but *no other teams got their wartime players back*, then 94 wins is a reasonable estimate of their performance. This projection, however, fails to consider the seven other AL teams, most of which lost much more talent than St. Louis did.

### The Impact of the War on the Tigers

Although they are generally remembered as having been fortunate because both Newhouser and Trout were classified as 4-F, the Tigers in fact lost an above-average amount of talent to the war (Table 13-11). The most prominent loss was Hank Greenberg, who in 1941 had been one of the first major league players to be called into the service. But Dick Wakefield also lost half his season, while scrappy center fielder Barney McCosky, who hit .311 or better three times between 1939 and 1941, was replaced by the 38-year-old Doc Cramer. The Tigers' pitching staff was affected as well. Although Newhouser and Trout stayed, Al Benton, Tommy Bridges, and Virgil Trucks were highly effective starters in their own right, having combined for 10 All-Star appearances over the course of their careers. All of them were overseas.

Without the war, the Tigers might have had one of the best starting rotations of all time, and one of the better outfields of the era. They would certainly have finished far ahead of the Browns. Only their middling infield would have prevented them from being a team for the ages.

### The Impact of the War on the Yankees

The conventional wisdom is that the Yankees lost more talent to the war than did any other club. Indeed, all eight of the positional regulars who made up their pennant-winning lineup in 1942 were unavailable because of military service or related duties. The pitching staff was affected, too, with starters Red Ruffing and Spud Chandler (who made just one start before being drafted) and closer Johnny Murphy all out of action.

Although the Yankees probably did lose more talent to the war than any other team lost, they also did a creditable job of replacing it (Table 13-12). In addition to having a good replacement at second base in Snuffy Stirnweiss, the Yankees were also fortunate in center field, where Johnny Lindell did a fair job replacing Joe DiMaggio, and in the rotation, where replacement pitchers Monk Dubiel and Atley Donald had ERAs of 3.38 and 3.34, respectively.

TABLE 13-10  St. Louis Browns Wartime Replacements, 1944

| Pos | Starter | Replacement | G/IP | Bat | Field | Pitch | Total | Comments |
|---|---|---|---|---|---|---|---|---|
| CF | Wally Judnich | Kreevich/Byrnes | 135 | 15.3 | 11.5 | | 26.8 | Judnich's replacements were clumsy defenders. |
| RF | Joe Grace | Gene Moore | 96 | 26.7 | -3.0 | | 23.7 | The aging Moore had played just one major league game in 1942 before being forced back into regular duty. |
| SP-4 | Denny Galehouse | Hollingsworth/ Shirley | 500 | | | | 10.5 | Galehouse was limited to 24 appearances because of weekday work at a defense plant. We have assigned him 25 innings from each of Hollingsworth and Shirley as a result. |
| LF | Chet Laabs | Al Zarilla | 46 | -2.2 | 0.3 | | -2.0* | Laabs's defense plant job limited his playing time early in the season, but Zarilla made the most of increased playing time. |
| SP-2 | Steve Sundra | Sig Jakucki | 198.0 | | | -4.9 | -4.9* | Sundra made three starts before being called to serve; Jakucki surprised everyone with his frequent effectiveness and occasional sobriety. |
| **Total** | | | | 39.8 | 8.7 | 5.6 | 54.1 | |

*NOTE: Subject to Snuffy Rule, an adjustment to the runs-lost statistic when a replacement player performs better than the starter would have done.

Table 13-11  Detroit Tigers Wartime Replacements, 1944

| Pos | Starter | Replacement | G//IP | Runs Lost | | | Total | Comments |
|---|---|---|---|---|---|---|---|---|
| | | | | Bat | Field | Pitch | | |
| LF/RF | Hank Greenberg | Hostetler/Outlaw/Ross | 154 | 77.5 | -11.5 | | 66.0 | If both Wakefield and Greenberg had been available, it is unclear which of the two would have played left field and which right field. The impact would have been substantial either way; Greenberg was projected for a .329 EqA. |
| CF | Barney McCosky | Doc Cramer | 137 | 26.6 | 9.0 | | 35.6 | Cramer, 38 in 1944, was long past his peak offensively and defensively. |
| LF/RF | Dick Wakefield | Outlaw/Metro | 78 | 33.8 | -0.2 | | 33.6 | Wakefield returned to the team in July. |
| SP-5 | Tommy Bridges | Johnny Gorsica | 162.0 | | | 32.4 | 32.4 | Bridges was nearing the end of his career, but had been highly effective in 1943 (2.39 ERA). |
| SP-4 | Virgil Trucks | Rufe Gentry | 203.2 | | | 17.2 | 17.2 | Gentry was a regular only in 1943 and 1944. |
| SP-3 | Al Benton | Stubby Overmire | 199.2 | | | 12.1 | 12.1 | Overmire was effective but would probably have remained in the minors, given the Tigers' deep staff. |
| RP | Hal White | Boom-Boom Beck | 74.0 | | | 3.9 | 3.9 | White worked as a starter in 1943 but became a reliever after wartime players had returned. |
| SS | Billy Hitchcock | Joe Hoover | 118 | -3.7 | -0.6 | | -4.2* | Hitchcock was no star, but Hoover played only during the war years (1943–1945). |
| C | Birdie Tebbetts | Paul Richards | 89 | -1.4 | -3.1 | | -4.5* | Tebbetts saved the hits left in his bat for the Red Sox a few years later. |
| 2B | Jimmy Bloodworth | Eddie Mayo | 142 | 0.8 | -7.3 | | -6.5* | Transitional period at the position. Charlie Gehringer would probably have retired even without his military service. |
| **Total** | | | | 133.6 | -13.7 | 65.6 | 185.5 | |

*Subject to Snuffy Rule.

TABLE 13-12  New York Yankees Wartime Replacements, 1944

| Pos | Starter | Replacement | G/IP | Runs Lost | | | | Comments |
|---|---|---|---|---|---|---|---|---|
| | | | | Bat | Field | Pitch | Total | |
| RF | Tommy Henrich | Metheny/ Stainback/Derry | 143 | 40.8 | 21.8 | | 62.6 | Henrich's replacements combined for a .241 EqA. |
| LF | Charlie Keller | Martin/Levy/ Derry/Metheny | 137 | 52.7 | 7.9 | | 60.6 | Keller, at his potential age-27 peak in 1944, was serving in the coast guard. |
| SS | Phil Rizzuto | Milosevich/Crosetti | 136 | 22.5 | 14.4 | | 36.9 | Losing Rizzuto's glove—fantastic early in his career—worsened the blow. |
| 3B | Billy Johnson | Grimes/Savage | 154 | 0.3 | 33.8 | | 34.1 | Johnson's replacements were adequate offensively, brutal defensively. |
| CF | Joe DiMaggio | Johnny Lindell | 145 | 32.4 | −11.5 | | 20.9 | Lindell limited damage with career year (.291 EqA), earning some postwar playing time with the Yankees. |
| C | Bill Dickey | Mike Garbark | 83 | 21.5 | −1.7 | | 19.8 | Dickey was nearing the end of his career and needed frequent rest, but still projected for a .294 EqA. |
| SP-1 | Spud Chandler | Monk Dubiel | 232.0 | | | 19.1 | 19.1 | Chandler made just one start in 1944 before leaving for the army. |
| SP-5 | Marius Russo | Joe Page | 102.2 | | | 13.9 | 13.9 | Page became an effective reliever with the Yankees, but was inconsistent in his 1944 debut. |
| RP | Johnny Murphy | Turner/Johnson | 57.1 | | | 11.7 | 11.7 | Murphy was one of the few 1940s-era pitchers whose usage resembled modern closers. |
| SP-2 | Red Ruffing | Atley Donald | 159.0 | | | 11.5 | 11.5 | Ruffing's career was winding down, but he was better suited for the ball field than the battlefield. |
| 2B | Joe Gordon | Snuffy Stirnweiss | 154.0 | −6.6 | −6.9 | | −13.6* | Taking nothing away from Gordon (.290 projected EqA), Stirnweiss had an MVP-caliber season. |
| **Total** | | | | 163.6 | 57.8 | 56.2 | 277.5 | |

*Subject to Snuffy Rule.

One ambiguity relates to the first-base position, where Buddy Hassett had played in 1942 before being drafted. After failing to complete a deal for the Indians' Hal Trosky, the Yankees instead had settled on Nick Etten of the Phillies. Etten had a very effective season in 1944, hitting .293 with 22 home runs—in fact, he outperformed Hassett's projection by about 50 runs.

We could apply the Snuffy Rule in this instance, as the draft status of Hassett was the immediate reason for Ed Barrow's desire to pick up Etten. Considerable evidence, however, suggests that Hassett would not have been the Yankees' regular first baseman by 1944:

♦ Hassett himself was a wartime replacement. Although he had been a regular first baseman with the Brooklyn Dodgers and Boston Braves before the war began, the Yankees picked him up for the 1942 season because Johnny Sturm, their primary first baseman in 1941, had been drafted.

♦ Hassett was viewed as a transitional solution at the position. According to contemporaneous newspaper accounts, he had had to fight for the first-base job in spring training after having been picked up from the Braves.

♦ Hassett simply wasn't very good. His EqA in 1942 was .256, well below average for a first baseman, and would probably have been worse still by 1944, given two additional years of aging.

♦ Hassett was promptly released after returning from the service in 1946.

The Yankees of the 1940s, just like the current iteration of the franchise, weren't a team to tolerate a subpar performance. Whether Etten in particular would have been acquired is an open question, but they would almost certainly have found someone better than Buddy Hassett.

Even with the noble performances of players like Etten, Stirnweiss, and Donald, however, the Yankees' losses were substantial. Although Lindell filled in well in center field, DiMaggio represented just one-third of the Yankees' star-studded outfield. Charlie Keller and Tommy Henrich, the hard-hitting corner outfielders, were also hard to replace. Shortstop Phil Rizzuto and third baseman Billy Johnson were also missing, while Barrow compounded his team's problems by refusing to let top reliever Johnny Murphy pitch while the hurler was engaged in his civilian job. All told, the Yankees lost some 277 runs' worth of talent to the war.

## The Impact of the War on the Red Sox

The Red Sox were the Yankees' primary rival in the peacetime 1940s. It is fitting that they were the only team that could rival the Yankees' suffering in wartime. Any discussion of Boston's losses must begin with Ted Williams. After struggling to find a solution at left field in 1943, the Red Sox acquired "Indian" Bob Johnson in 1944 to fill Williams's shoes. Johnson had an outstanding season, compiling a .324 batting average and a .431 on-base percentage and joining the ranks of All-Stars. Even so, Williams would almost certainly have been nearly 10 wins better than Johnson in 1944.

But Williams was not the only player the Red Sox missed. Dom DiMaggio, their center fielder, proved to be a more costly loss to the Red Sox than older brother Joe was to the Yankees, because of Dom's outstanding defense and the Red Sox's inferior replacements. Johnny Pesky lost some of his best seasons to the war. And although pitchers Mickey Harris and Charlie Wagner were not stars, their replacements were simply inadequate (Table 13-13).

To make matters worse, the Red Sox continued to bleed talent as the season wore on. Tex Hughson carried an extremely heavy workload in those days, having pitched 266 innings in 1943. He missed about a third of the season after being recalled to the draft in early August 1944, and his replacements from the Pacific Coast League, Rex Cecil and Clem Dreisewerd, yielded nearly 30 extra runs in the process. Bobby Doerr missed the season's final month, costing the Red Sox 10 runs; at least the loss of platoon catcher Hal Wagner could be tolerated. Though he had batted .330/.415/.436 for the Sox in 1944, this was a small-sample fluke; he normally wasn't much of a hitter. In total, the Red Sox lost more than 300 runs' worth of production, or about 40 more runs than the Yankees lost, to the war.

## The Rest of the American League

Three teams can make a credible claim to the counterfactual 1944 pennant: the Tigers, Yankees, and Red Sox. But we will briefly consider the impact the war had on the league's second division:

*The Indians.* The only team besides the Red Sox and Yankees to bring a peacetime pennant home in the 1940s, the Indians took the crown in 1948. Except for Bob Feller, their wartime losses were minimal (Table 13-14). The Indians' best position players in that era were Lou Boudreau and outfielder Jeff Heath. Boudreau maintained a 4-F classification through most of the war and was

Table 13-13  Boston Red Sox Wartime Replacements, 1944

| Pos | Starter | Replacement | G/IP | Runs Lost Bat | Field | Pitch | Total | Comments |
|---|---|---|---|---|---|---|---|---|
| LF | Ted Williams | Johnson/McBride | 154 | 95.0 | 4.1 | | 99.1 | "Indian" Bob Johnson was named an All-Star (.331 EqA). Williams's absence still cost the Red Sox 10 wins. |
| CF | Dom DiMaggio | Metkovich/Culberson/McBride | 145 | 34.8 | 22.6 | | 57.4 | The Little Professor's defense was better than that of older brother Joe. |
| SS | Johnny Pesky | Newsome/Lake | 154 | 48.9 | 0.3 | | 49.2 | Pesky's replacements could match his great glove but not his stick. |
| SP-3 | Mickey Harris | Emmett O'Neill | 151.2 | | | 36.4 | 36.4 | O'Neill went 15-26 between 1943 and 1945 as one of the worst regular starters in the league. |
| SP-1 | Tex Hughson | Cecil/Dreiswerd | 87.7 | | | 29.4 | 29.4 | Hughson was lost to the draft in early August. Two replacements recalled from the Pacific Coast League were inadequate. |
| SP-5 | Charlie Wagner | Yank Terry | 132.2 | | | 13.9 | 13.9 | Wagner's career was just getting on track when he was drafted; he made just four big league starts after returning. |
| RP | Mace Brown | Frank Barrett | 90 | | | 10.9 | 10.9 | Brown was coming off a 93 IP, 2.12 ERA season in 1943. |
| 2B | Bobby Doerr | Jim Bucher | 25 | 5.7 | -3.9 | | 9.6 | Doerr left the Red Sox on September 2 to be inducted into the army; Sporting News named him its MVP, anyway. |
| SP-2 | Joe Dobson | Pinky Woods | 170.2 | | | 8.2 | 8.2 | Woods had a decent 3.27 ERA in spot duty, but only pitched from 1943 to 1945. |
| C | Hal Wagner | Hank Partee | 18 | 1.7 | -1.4 | | 0.4 | Wagner missed the final 30 games of the season after entering the navy. |
| Total | | | | 186.1 | 29.5 | 98.8 | 314.5 | |

TABLE 13-14  Cleveland Indians Wartime Replacements, 1944

| Pos | Starter | Replacement | G/IP | Runs Lost | | | | Comments |
|---|---|---|---|---|---|---|---|---|
| | | | | Bat | Field | Pitch | Total | |
| SP-1 | Bob Feller | Gromek/Bagby | 282.2 | | | 59.4 | 59.4 | Feller pitched so many innings during his peak that we have assigned him two pitchers to match his missing playing time. |
| LF | Hank Edwards | Seerey/Hockett | 99 | 11.7 | -5.2 | | 6.5 | It's unclear how the Indians would have handled this situation had Jeff Heath been healthy, but Heath managed only 60 games between injury and holdout. |
| **Total** | | | | 11.7 | -5.2 | 59.4 | 65.9 | |

fortunate enough not to be called for the draft once that status was revoked in 1944. Heath missed much of the 1944 season, but this was the result of a spring training holdout and a midseason injury rather than military service. When Bob Lemon was drafted, he was a minor league third baseman rather than a Hall of Fame pitcher. Catcher Jim Hegan was drafted as well, but he was too young to be an everyday player. Although the Indians were an up-and-coming team by the late 1940s, they would have been in the midst of a rebuilding phase in 1944 with or without the war.

*The Athletics.* This team lost a handful of players, including Benny McCoy, Elmer Valo, and Sam Chapman, but probably suffered more from Connie Mack's deteriorating sensibilities than from anything to do with the war itself. Several of the Athletics' better players, including 21-year-old third baseman George Kell, Cuban outfielder Bobby Estalella, first baseman Dick Siebert, and pitcher Louis "Bobo" Newsom, received deferments. Table 13-15 shows how the lineup changed during the war.

*The White Sox.* This Chicago club lost a couple of stars (Table 13-16). Shortstop Luke Appling, an underrated player then and now, could not adequately be replaced. But the White Sox were more fortunate with Hall of Fame pitcher Ted Lyons, who volunteered for the U.S. Marines at age 41, as his departure helped Eddie Lopat pitch himself into the big leagues a season sooner than he might have done otherwise.

*The Senators.* Clark Griffith's club tried to stem its losses by signing players from

Table 13-15  Philadelphia Athletics Wartime Replacements, 1944

| Pos | Starter | Replacement | G/IP | Runs Lost Bat | Field | Pitch | Total | Comments |
|---|---|---|---|---|---|---|---|---|
| 2B | Benny McCoy | Hall/Rullo | 127 | 32.7 | 9.9 | | 42.7 | McCoy did not play after returning from four years of service in the navy, but his replacements were woefully inadequate. |
| RF | Elmer Valo | White/Garrison/ Epps/Rosenthal/ Burgo | 112 | 24.8 | 2.0 | | 26.8 | Connie Mack's outfield lineups were a rotating, three-ring circus during the war years. |
| LF/1B | Sam Chapman | Garrison/McGhee/ Burgo/White | 142 | 32.2 | -8.5 | | 23.7 | Since Dick Siebert split his time in 1944 between LF and 1B, we are taking 31 games of backup first baseman Bill McGhee's playing time at 1B (equivalent to Siebert's playing time in LF) and placing it here. |
| SP-3 | Dick Fowler | Luke Hamlin | 190.0 | | | 8.2 | 8.2 | An effective starter with the Dodgers in the late 1930s, Hamlin was on his last legs. |
| SS | Pete Suder | Busch/Hall | 147 | -5.2 | 8.1 | | 2.9 | Suder was regarded as a defensive specialist, but our statistics find his defense to have been below average. His replacements, however, were even worse. |
| SP-2 | Phil Marchildon | Russ Christopher | 215.1 | | | 2.4 | 2.4 | Marchildon and compatriot Fowler joined the Canadian armed forces and served with the Allies in 1943 and 1944. |
| **Total** | | | | 84.5 | 11.6 | 10.6 | 106.7 | |

TABLE 13-16  Chicago White Sox Wartime Replacements, 1944

| Pos | Starter | Replacement | G/IP | Bat | Field | Pitch | Total | Comments |
|---|---|---|---|---|---|---|---|---|
| | | | | | Runs Lost | | | |
| SS | Luke Appling | Webb/Michaels | 150 | 72.7 | 3.5 | | 76.2 | We rate Appling as the second most costly wartime loss after Ted Williams. |
| LF | Taffy Wright | Carnett/Curtright/ Hodgin | 124 | 28.0 | 0.7 | | 28.7 | A similar player to Trot Nixon, Wright was projected at a .290 EqA in 1944. |
| 2B | Don Kolloway | Roy Schalk | 140 | 18.4 | 7.2 | | 25.6 | Unrelated to White Sox catcher Ray Schalk, second baseman Schalk played just three games outside the 1944–1945 period. |
| SP-2 | Johnny Rigney | Orval Grove | 234.2 | | | 18.7 | 18.7 | Of Grove's 63 career wins, 43 came between 1943 and 1945. |
| SP-1 | Ted Lyons | Ed Lopat | 210.0 | | | 8.6 | 8.6 | Lopat won 166 games in his major league career, but did not debut until age 26 at 1944. The debut might have been delayed further without the war. |
| SP-3 | Eddie Smith | Johnny Humphries | 169.0 | | | –3.9 | –3.9* | An All-Star in 1941 and 1942, Smith had just one good season after the war. |
| 3B | Bob Kennedy | Hodgin/Clarke | 125 | –7.6 | 2.6 | | –5.0* | Kennedy was a major league regular at age 19, but struggled to hit early in his career. |
| Total | | | | 111.5 | 14.0 | 23.4 | 148.9 | |

*Subject to Snuffy Rule.

Latin America, but the Senators probably suffered the most of the second division clubs. Virtually the entire infield, including shortstop Cecil Travis and second baseman Jerry Priddy, was lost. Pitcher Sid Hudson and outfielder Buddy Lewis, an All-Star in 1938 and 1947 on either side of the war years, were gone, too (Table 13-17). Still, part of the problem was that the Senators simply didn't bother to put adequate replacements on the field, even by the standards of wartime competition.

### The Counterfactual Pennant Race

The counterfactual American League of 1944 would have been one of the tougher associations of all time. The Red Sox and Yankees had a myriad of stars near their peak, including DiMaggio and Williams. With Greenberg and their outstanding pitching staff, the Tigers would have been right there with the top two. Though not at the top of the heap, the Browns would surely have been plucky. Even the also-rans had their stars in players like Feller and Appling. As many as 20 Hall of Famers might have filled out the league's rosters.

But every pennant race, even a hypothetical one, must have its winner. Table 13-18 summarizes the number of runs and wins that the AL teams missed because of wartime activities. World War II had the largest effect on the Red Sox—not necessarily because they lost the *most* talent, but because they lost a lot of talent and had great trouble replacing it. The Yankees were next, followed by a middle tier consisting of the Tigers, Senators, and White Sox. The Browns, by comparison, got off scot-free.

What really counts, of course, is not the absolute number of wins missed because of the war but the relative number. The average AL team lost between 16 and 17 wins to the war. The Browns were hurt by World War II—but every other team in the league was hurt much worse (Table 13-19).

The Red Sox, for example, would have won about 15 more games if all the league players had been available for duty. Since their actual record in 1944 was 77-77, this implies that their counterfactual record would be 92-62. But, alas, the Red Sox would have been slight underdogs to the Yankees, who were projected to finish at 94-60 (Table 13-20).

Given the degree of uncertainty in our estimates, a case can be made for any of the top three teams: the Yankees, Red Sox, and Tigers. In all probability, the counterfactual American League of 1944 would

TABLE 13-17 Washington Senators Wartime Replacements, 1944

| Pos | Starter | Replacement | G/IP | Runs Lost | | | | Comments |
|---|---|---|---|---|---|---|---|---|
| | | | | Bat | Field | Pitch | Total | |
| RF | Buddy Lewis | Ortiz/Powell/ Case/Boland/ Monteagudo | 145 | 44.2 | 17.1 | | 61.3 | Lewis was one of the more underrated players of his era; he lost his age 25-27 peak to the war. |
| SS | Cecil Travis | John Sullivan | 137 | 15.3 | 23.9 | | 39.3 | Travis's bat was gone after he returned from the service. |
| SP-3 | Sid Hudson | Roger Wolff | 155.0 | | | 32.1 | 32.1 | Wolff went 4-15 with a 4.99 ERA in 1944, but 20-10 with a 2.12 ERA in 1945. |
| 2B | Jerry Priddy | Myatt/Vaughn | 142 | -3.0 | 27.5 | | 24.5 | Priddy was a fine fielder early in his career; the Senators greatly missed his defense. |
| 1B | Mickey Vernon | Kuhel/Butka | 147 | 16.0 | -2.2 | | 13.7 | Vernon (.288 projected EqA) would have been near his peak, but veteran Kuhel filled in adequately. |
| RP | Walt Masterson | Alex Carrasquel | 134.0 | | | 8.9 | 8.9 | One of Clark Griffith's more effective Latin American acquisitions, Carrasquel nevertheless pitched just 3.2 innings after the war concluded. |
| C | Jake Early | Rick Ferrell | 96 | -1.9 | -0.4 | | -2.3* | The Senators probably benefited from getting the last three years of Hall-of-Famer Ferrell's career. |
| Total | | | | 70.6 | 65.9 | 41.0 | 177.5 | |

*Subject to Snuffy Rule.

Table 13-18   Runs and Wins Lost Because of Wartime Absences, 1944 American League

| Team | Runs Lost Batting | Fielding | Pitching | Total | Wins Lost |
|------|---------|----------|----------|-------|-----------|
| Red Sox | 186.1 | 29.5 | 98.8 | 314.4 | 31.4 |
| Yankees | 163.5 | 57.7 | 56.2 | 277.4 | 27.7 |
| Tigers | 133.6 | -13.7 | 65.6 | 185.5 | 18.6 |
| Senators | 70.6 | 65.9 | 41.1 | 177.6 | 17.8 |
| White Sox | 111.5 | 14.1 | 23.3 | 148.9 | 14.9 |
| Athletics | 84.5 | 11.6 | 10.7 | 106.7 | 10.7 |
| Indians | 11.7 | -5.2 | 59.4 | 65.9 | 6.6 |
| Browns | 39.8 | 8.7 | 5.6 | 54.1 | 5.4 |
| AVERAGE | 100.2 | 21.1 | 45.1 | 166.3 | 16.6 |

Table 13-19  Relative Gain from Recovering World War II Talent

| Team | RS | RA | Wins |
|------|------|------|------|
| Red Sox | +120.0 | +28.1 | +14.8 |
| Yankees | +97.3 | +13.7 | +11.1 |
| Tigers | +67.5 | -48.3 | +1.9 |
| Senators | +4.4 | +6.9 | +1.1 |
| White Sox | +45.3 | -62.8 | -1.7 |
| Athletics | +18.4 | -77.9 | -6.0 |
| Indians | -54.4 | -46.0 | -10.0 |
| Browns | -26.4 | -85.9 | -11.2 |

NOTE: RS indicates Runs Scored and RA indicates Runs Allowed.

Table 13-20 Counterfactual American League Standings, 1944

| Team | W | L | GB |
|------|-----|-----|------|
| New York | 94 | 60 | – |
| Boston | 92 | 62 | 2.0 |
| Detroit | 90 | 64 | 4.0 |
| St. Louis | 78 | 76 | 16.0 |
| Chicago | 69 | 85 | 25.0 |
| Philadelphia | 66 | 88 | 28.0 |
| Washington | 65 | 89 | 29.0 |
| Cleveland | 62 | 92 | 32.0 |

have provided one of the best pennant races ever, just as the real American League did.

The Browns, however, would not have been included in that race; they would have finished closer to .500. Indeed, considering that the Browns' actual 1944 season involved a fair amount of luck, their true level of talent would probably have been below average in a fully stocked league. The year 1944 might have been one of the more competitive seasons in the franchise's sad history, but no more than that.

◆

There was no pennant race in the National League that year. The Cardinals led their league by 8.5 games at the end of June, 15 by the end of July, and 18.5 by the end of August. They coasted through the rest of their schedule, winning just 14 of their 33 games in September, but by then, the race was over and the Cardinals finished at 105-49.

It was the same record they had posted the year before. Indeed, the 1942–1944 Cardinals are the only team in modern baseball history to have won at least two-thirds of its games in three consecutive seasons. Such an accomplishment would not have been possible without both tremendous luck and tremendous design.

The Cardinals were fortunate that many of their stars avoided the draft. Stan Musial was exempted because of his 1-C status and his off-season job at a war plant. Shortstop Marty Marion, named the MVP that season as a reward for his stellar defense, was 4-F because of his bad knees. The same was true of pitching ace Mort Cooper. Indeed, we have identified only four definitive Cardinal regulars who missed the season because of the war. Only one of those losses—Hall of Famer and 10-time All-Star Enos Slaughter—was of much consequence.

The Cardinals also benefited from their tremendous farm system, which had developed under Branch Rickey. Center fielder Terry Moore was serving overseas; his absence opened up a spot in the lineup for first baseman Ray Sanders. The replacement infielder did nothing but hit for the Cardinals, posting a .279 batting average and a .372 on-base percentage over portions of four seasons and receiving some MVP consideration in 1944, but as soon as Moore and Slaughter had returned from the war, Sanders was sold to the Boston Braves for $25,000.

Pitcher Howie Pollet, who would probably have been the Cardinals' number four starter, also found his name on a draft notice. His replacement was Ted Wilks, who went 17-4 with a 2.64 ERA in 1944. But once Pollet returned in 1946, Wilks was relegated to bullpen duty and made only six starts with the Cardinals over the rest of his career.

The Cardinals enjoyed a farm system that produced replacement players who were better than many of the league's regulars under peacetime conditions—this in spite of the fact that nearly three-quarters of the minor leagues had been lost to the war as well (Table 13-21). The minor leagues experienced a boom immediately after the war years, reaching all-time peak attendance in 1949. Very likely, the success of the Cardinals during the war years was a driving force in the minor league's later success. The shortage of talent brought on by the war had removed the Band-Aid and exposed just how thin some organizations were under the surface.

◆

So the Cardinals had lost some talent to the war, but the deficiency had only a minimal impact on their position in the standings: between four and five games, by our estimates. Whether the counterfactual Cardinals would have been favored over the counterfactual Yankees or the counterfactual Red Sox is an open question. What is more clear is that the actual St. Louis Cardinals of 1944 were heavy favorites over the actual St. Louis Browns—two to one, according to bookmakers before the World Series.

The Browns had one more trick up their sleeves, surprising the Cardinals 2-1 in Game 1 of the Streetcar Series. Although the Browns managed only two hits in the game, they were timed perfectly, with Gene Moore singling in the bottom of the fourth and George McQuinn knocking him home with a round-tripper that barely cleared the short porch in right field. Denny Galehouse held on for the victory, just the sort of minor miracle that had characterized the Browns' season.

Their luck ran out soon afterward, however. Early in Game 2, the Browns gave up two runs, each of which had been allowed to score as the result of errors. Tying the score in the seventh and sending the game to extra frames, the Browns were poised to pull ahead when McQuinn led off the top of the 11th with a double. But a failed bunt attempt by Mark Christman resulted in a fielder's choice. McQuinn's position was sacrificed, and Blix Donnelly retired the last two Browns batters to end the threat.

Table 13-21  St. Louis Cardinals Wartime Replacements, 1944

| Pos | Starter | Replacement | G/IP | Runs Lost | | | | Comments |
| | | | | Bat | Field | Pitch | Total | |
| --- | --- | --- | --- | --- | --- | --- | --- | --- |
| LF | Enos Slaughter | Litwhiler/Bergamo | 153 | 33.0 | 1.6 | | 34.6 | Slaughter's replacements combined for a decent .272 EqA. |
| RP | Murry Dickson | Freddy Schmidt | 109.0 | | | 9.0 | 9.0 | Dickson was used primarily in the bullpen early in his career. |
| SP-4 | Howie Pollet | Ted Wilks | 207.2 | | | 5.6 | 5.6 | Wilks went 17-4 with a 2.64 ERA in his debut in 1944. |
| CF/1B | Terry Moore | Ray Sanders | 154 | -3.1 | 0.0 | | -3.1* | Sanders played well enough during war to warrant additional playing time, but the Cardinals' depth buried him. |
| Total | | | | 29.9 | 1.6 | 14.6 | 46.1 | |

*Subject to Snuffy Rule.

The Cardinals were more fortunate, winning the contest in the bottom of the inning when pinch hitter Ken O'Dea singled home Ray Sanders.

Bad defense and a bad bunt had cost them the game; it was just like the Brownies of old. And although they came back to win Game 3 of the series 6-2, it was as though the air had been let out of their sails. The Cardinals won the last three games to clinch the title, limiting the Browns to two runs scored in the process.

The St. Louis Browns' only appearance in the World Series had come and gone. By 1946, the players were back from the war, Sig Jakucki was back in Galveston, and the Browns were back in seventh place. The world was once again at peace.

# The Great Pennant Race Abstract

DAN FOX

WITH JASON PARE

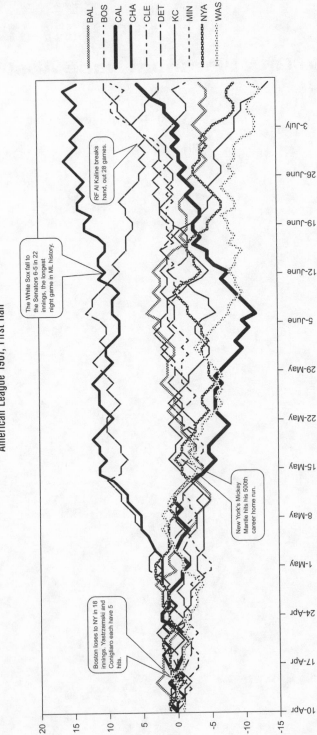

American League 1967, First Half

## American League 1967, Second Half

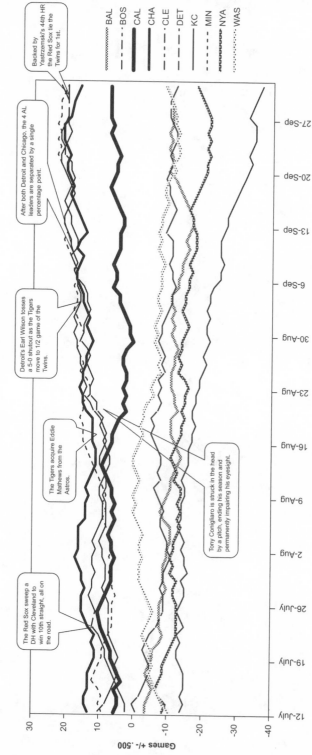

Legend:
BAL, BOS, CAL, CHA, CLE, DET, KC, MIN, NYA, WAS

Backed by Yastrzemski's 44th HR the Red Sox tie the Twins for 1st.

After both Detroit and Chicago, the 4 AL leaders are separated by a single percentage point.

Detroit's Earl Wilson tosses a 5-0 shutout as the Tigers move to 1/2 game of the Twins.

The Tigers acquire Eddie Mathews from the Astros.

Tony Conigliaro is struck in the head by a pitch, ending his season and permanently impairing his eyesight.

The Red Sox sweep a DH with Cleveland to win 10th straight, all on the road.

Y-axis: Games +/- .500 (30, 20, 10, 0, -10, -20, -30, -40)

X-axis: 12-July, 19-July, 26-July, 2-Aug, 9-Aug, 16-Aug, 23-Aug, 30-Aug, 6-Sep, 13-Sep, 20-Sep, 27-Sep

National League 1959, First Half

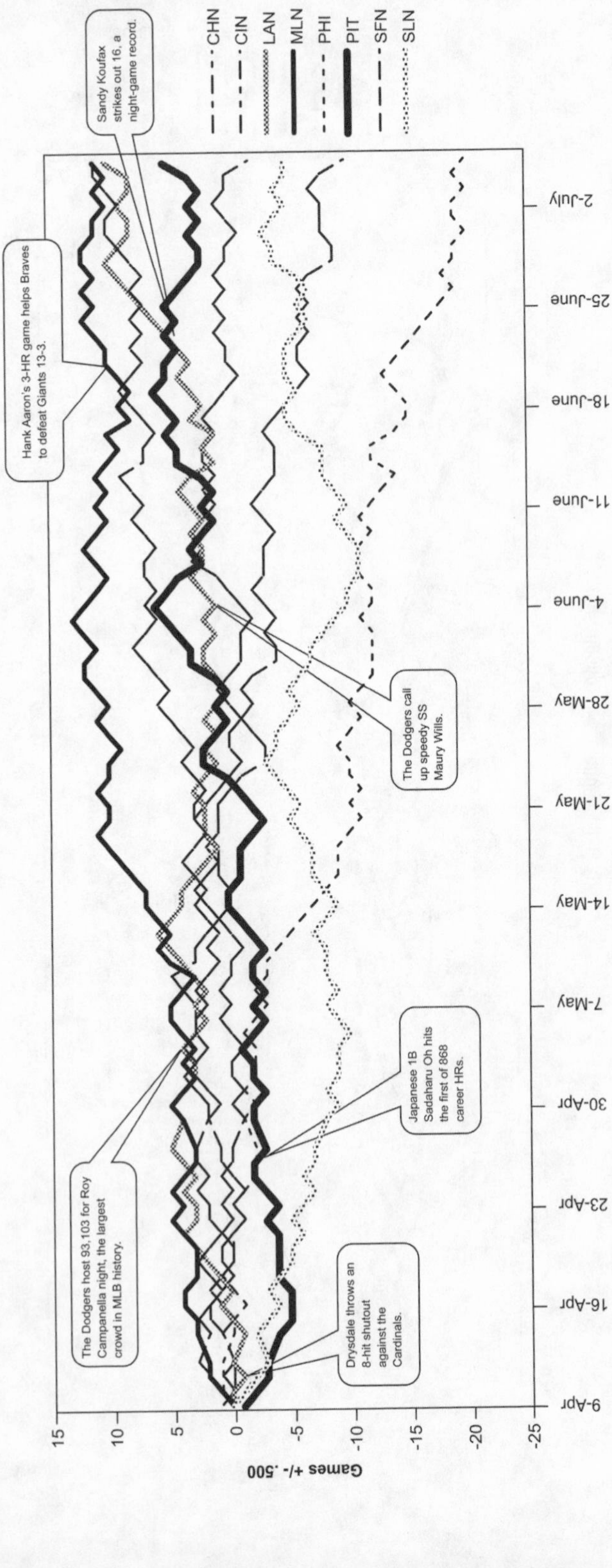

Sandy Koufax strikes out 16, a night-game record.

Hank Aaron's 3-HR game helps Braves to defeat Giants 13-3.

CHN
CIN
LAN
MLN
PHI
PIT
SFN
SLN

The Dodgers call up speedy SS Maury Wills.

The Dodgers host 93,103 for Roy Campanella night, the largest crowd in MLB history.

Japanese 1B Sadaharu Oh hits the first of 868 career HRs.

Drysdale throws an 8-hit shutout against the Cardinals.

Games +/- .500

15
10
5
0
-5
-10
-15
-20
-25

9-Apr
16-Apr
23-Apr
30-Apr
7-May
14-May
21-May
28-May
4-June
11-June
18-June
25-June
2-July

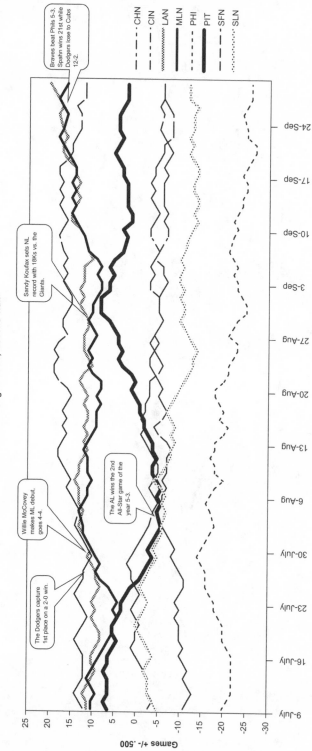

National League 1959, Second Half

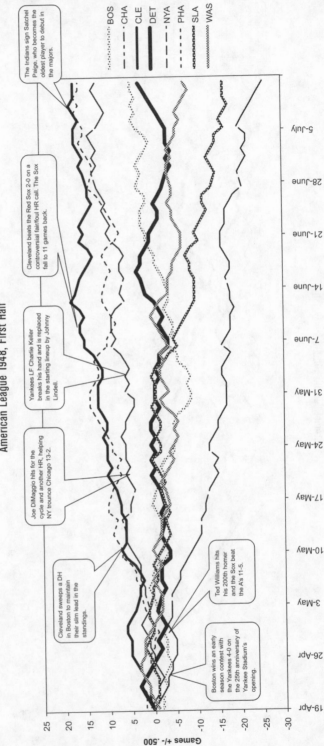

American League 1948, First Half

The Indians sign Satchel Paige, who becomes the oldest player to debut in the majors.

Cleveland beats the Red Sox 2-0 on a controversial fair/foul HR call. The Sox fall to 11 games back.

Yankees LF Charlie Keller breaks his hand and is replaced in the starting lineup by Johnny Lindell.

Joe DiMaggio hits for the cycle and another HR, helping NY trounce Chicago 13-2.

Cleveland sweeps a DH in Boston to maintain their slim lead in the standings.

Ted Williams hits his 200th homer and the Sox beat the A's 11-5.

Boston wins an early season contest with the Yankees 4-0 on the 25th anniversary of Yankee Stadium's opening.

BOS
CHA
CLE
DET
NYA
PHA
SLA
WAS

Games +/- .500

25
20
15
10
5
0
-5
-10
-15
-20
-25
-30

19-Apr
26-Apr
3-May
10-May
17-May
24-May
31-May
7-June
14-June
21-June
28-June
5-July

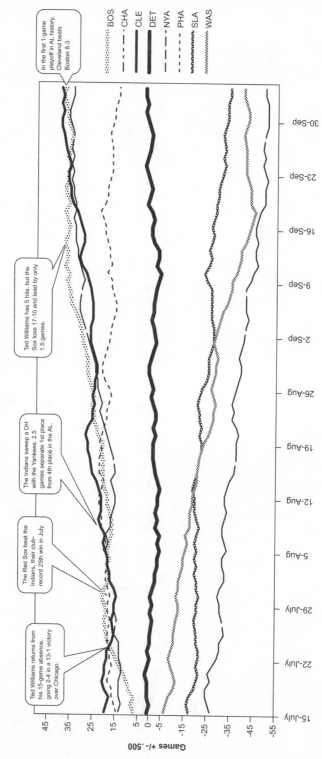

American League 1948, Second Half

In the first 1-game playoff in AL history, Cleveland beats Boston 8-3.

Ted Williams has 5 hits, but the Sox lose 17-10 and lead by only 1.5 games.

The Indians sweep a DH with the Yankees. 2.5 games separate 1st place from 4th place in the AL.

The Red Sox beat the Indians, their club-record 25th win in July.

Ted Williams returns from his 15-game absence, going 2-4 in a 13-1 victory over Chicago.

BOS
CHA
CLE
DET
NYA
PHA
SLA
WAS

Games +/- .500

15-July
22-July
29-July
5-Aug
12-Aug
19-Aug
26-Aug
2-Sep
9-Sep
16-Sep
23-Sep
30-Sep

45
35
25
15
5
-5
-15
-25
-35
-45
-55

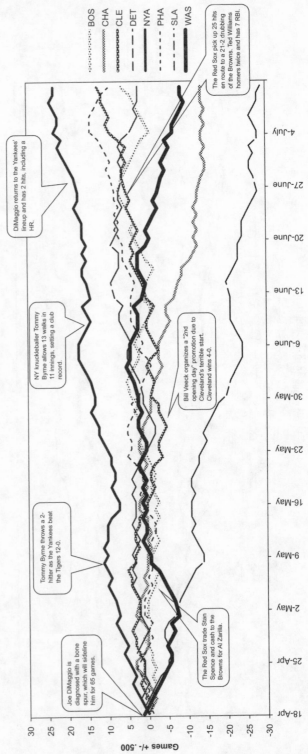

American League 1949, First Half

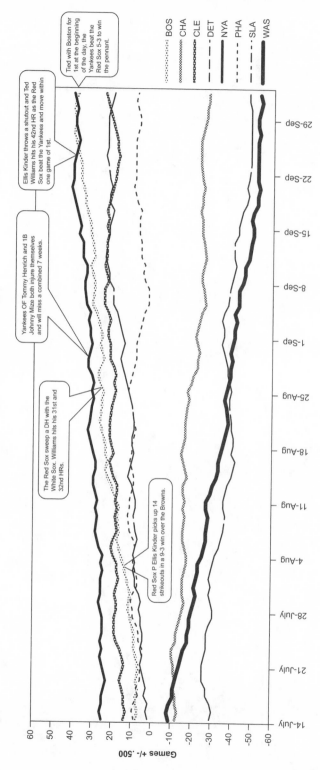

American League 1949, Second Half

National League 1908, First Half

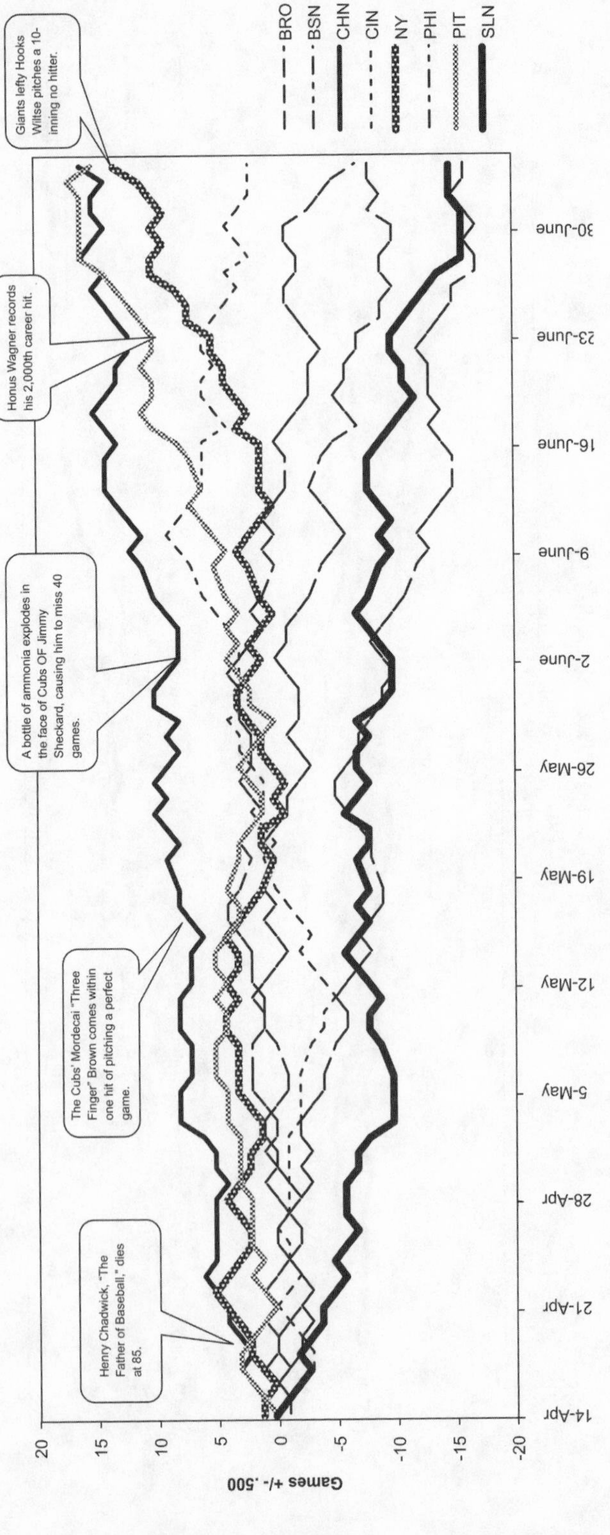

Giants lefty Hooks Wiltse pitches a 10-inning no hitter.

Honus Wagner records his 2,000th career hit.

A bottle of ammonia explodes in the face of Cubs OF Jimmy Sheckard, causing him to miss 40 games.

The Cubs' Mordecai "Three Finger" Brown comes within one hit of pitching a perfect game.

Henry Chadwick, "The Father of Baseball," dies at 85.

BRO
BSN
CHN
CIN
NY
PHI
PIT
SLN

Games +/- .500

20
15
10
5
0
-5
-10
-15
-20

14-Apr
21-Apr
28-Apr
5-May
12-May
19-May
26-May
2-June
9-June
16-June
23-June
30-June

National League 1908, Second Half

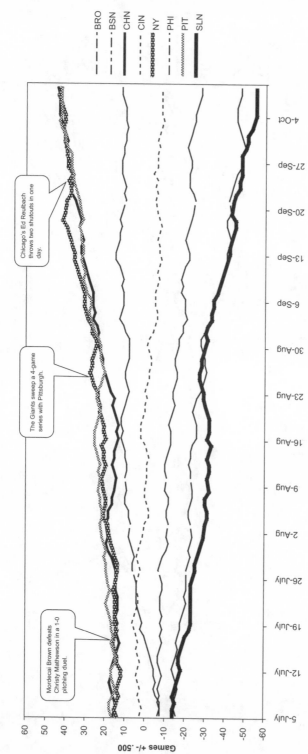

Mordecai Brown defeats Christy Mathewson in a 1-0 pitching duel.

The Giants sweep a 4-game series with Pittsburgh.

Chicago's Ed Reulbach throws two shutouts in one day.

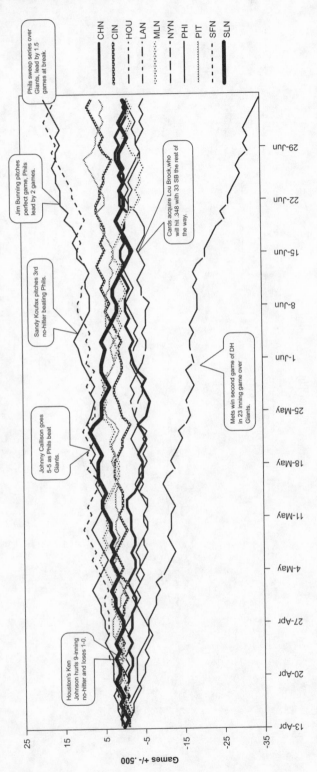

National League 1964, First Half

CHN
CIN
HOU
LAN
MLN
NYN
PHI
PIT
SFN
SLN

Phils sweep series over Giants, lead by 1.5 games at break.

Jim Bunning pitches perfect game, Phils lead by 2 games.

Cards acquire Lou Brock, who will hit .348 with 33 SB the rest of the way.

Sandy Koufax pitches 3rd no-hitter beating Phils.

Johnny Callison goes 5-5 as Phils beat Giants.

Mets win second game of DH in 23 inning game over Giants.

Houston's Ken Johnson hurls 9-inning no-hitter and loses 1-0.

Games +/- .500

25
15
5
-5
-15
-25
-35

13-Apr
20-Apr
27-Apr
4-May
11-May
18-May
25-May
1-Jun
8-Jun
15-Jun
22-Jun
29-Jun

## National League 1964, Second Half

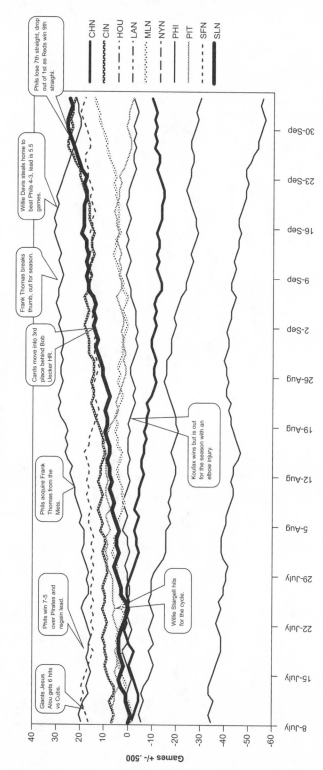

CHN
CIN
HOU
LAN
MLN
NYN
PHI
PIT
SFN
SLN

Phils lose 7th straight, drop out of 1st as Reds win 9th straight.

Willie Davis steals home to beat Phils 4-3, lead is 5.5 games.

Frank Thomas breaks thumb, out for season.

Cards move into 3rd place behind Bob Uecker HR.

Koufax wins but is out for the season with an elbow injury.

Phils acquire Frank Thomas from the Mets.

Phils win 7-5 over Pirates and regain lead.

Willie Stargell hits for the cycle.

Giants Jesus Alou gets 6 hits vs Cubs.

Games +/- .500

40
30
20
10
0
-10
-20
-30
-40
-50
-60

8-July
15-July
22-July
29-July
5-Aug
12-Aug
19-Aug
26-Aug
2-Sep
9-Sep
16-Sep
23-Sep
30-Sep

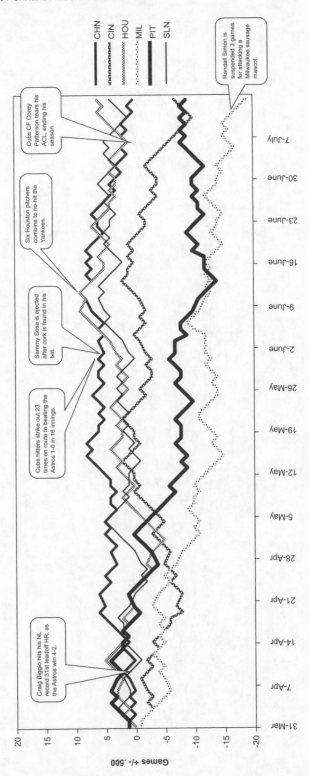

National League Central 2003, First Half

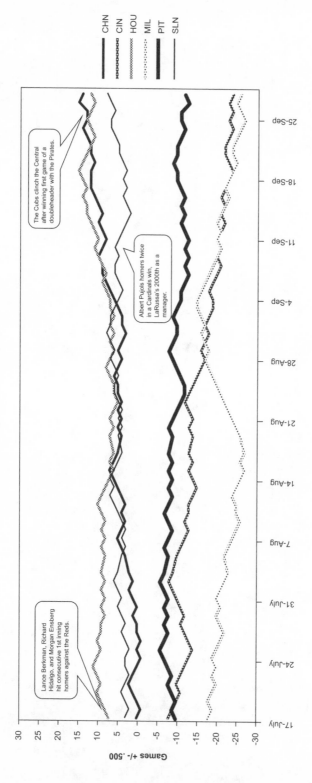

National League Central 2003, Second Half

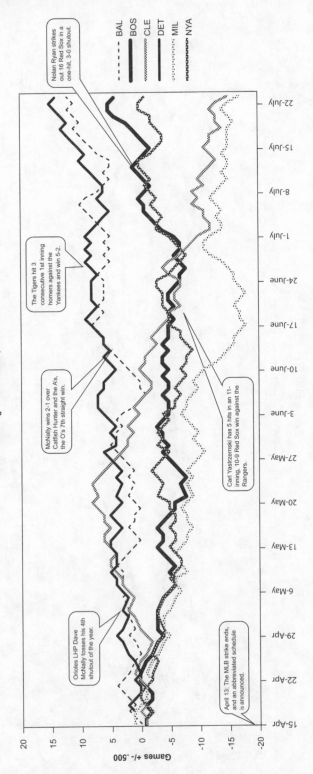

American League East 1972, First Half

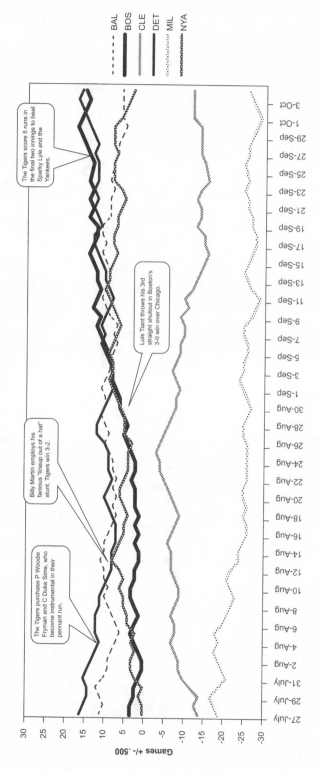

American League East 1972, Second Half

BAL
BOS
CLE
DET
MIL
NYA

The Tigers score 5 runs in the final two innings to beat Sparky Lyle and the Yankees.

Luis Tiant throws his 3rd straight shutout in Boston's 3-0 win over Chicago.

Billy Martin employs his famous "lineup out of a hat" stunt. Tigers win 3-2.

The Tigers purchase P Woodie Fryman and C Duke Sims, who become instrumental in their pennant run.

Games -/+ .500

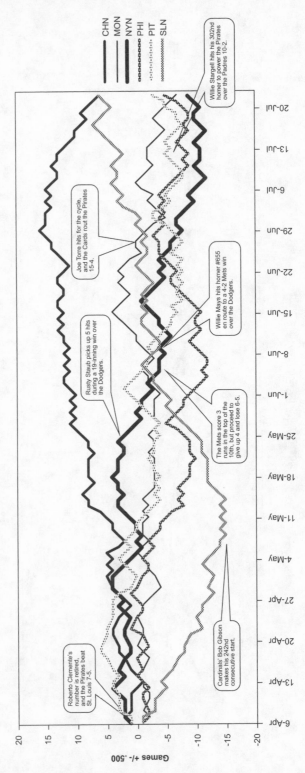

National League East 1973, First Half

CHN
MON
NYN
PHI
PIT
SLN

Games +/- .500

Willie Stargell hits his 302nd homer to power the Pirates over the Padres 10-2.

Joe Torre hits for the cycle, and the Cards rout the Pirates 15-4.

Willie Mays hits homer #655 en route to a 4-2 Mets win over the Dodgers.

Rusty Staub picks up 5 hits during a 19-inning win over the Dodgers.

The Mets score 3 runs in the top of the 10th, but proceed to give up 4 and lose 6-5.

Roberto Clemente's number is retired, and the Pirates beat St. Louis 7-5.

Cardinals' Bob Gibson makes his 242nd consecutive start.

6-Apr  13-Apr  20-Apr  27-Apr  4-May  11-May  18-May  25-May  1-Jun  8-Jun  15-Jun  22-Jun  29-Jun  6-Jul  13-Jul  20-Jul

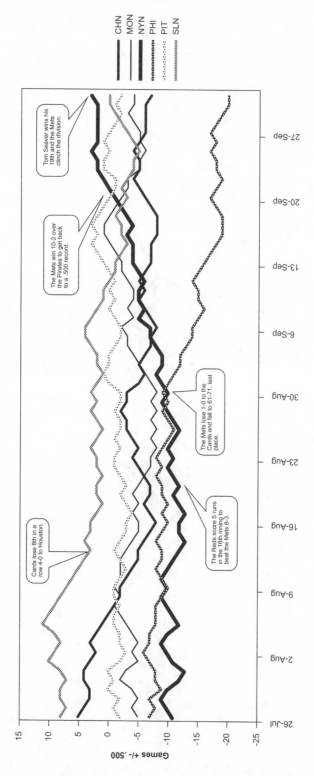

National League East 1973, Second Half

CHN
MON
NYN
PHI
PIT
SLN

Tom Seaver wins his 19th and the Mets clinch the division.

The Mets win 10-2 over the Pirates to get back to a .500 record.

Cards lose 8th in a row 4-0 to Houston.

The Mets lose 1-0 to the Cards and fall to 61-71, last place.

The Reds score 5 runs in the 16th inning to beat the Mets 8-3.

Games +/- .500

15
10
5
0
-5
-10
-15
-20
-25

26-Jul
2-Aug
9-Aug
16-Aug
23-Aug
30-Aug
6-Sep
13-Sep
20-Sep
27-Sep

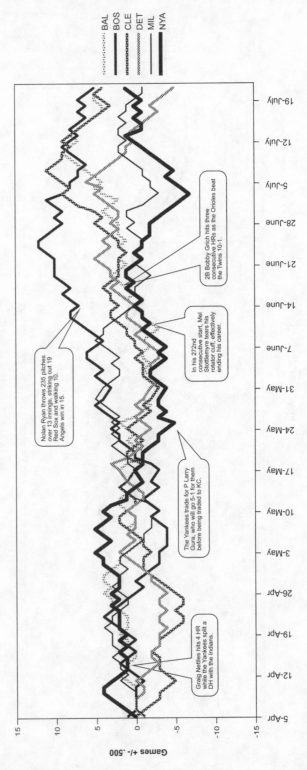

American League East 1974, First Half

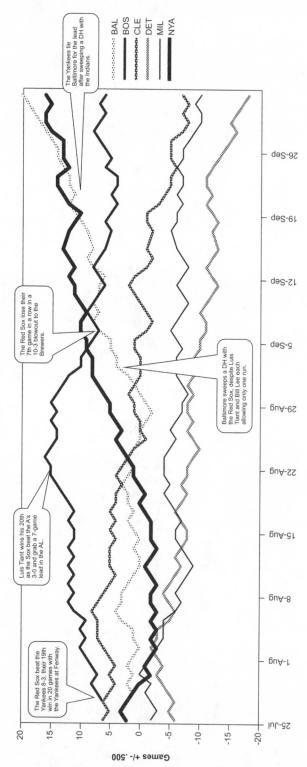

American League East 1974, Second Half

The Yankees tie Baltimore for the lead after sweeping a DH with the Indians.

The Red Sox lose their 7th game in a row in a 10-3 blowout to the Brewers.

Baltimore sweeps a DH with the Red Sox, despite Luis Tiant and Bill Lee each allowing only one run.

Luis Tiant wins his 20th as the Sox beat the A's 3-0 and grab a 7-game lead in the AL.

The Red Sox beat the Yankees 8-3, their 19th win in 20 games with the Yankees at Fenway.

BAL
BOS
CLE
DET
MIL
NYA

Games +/- .500

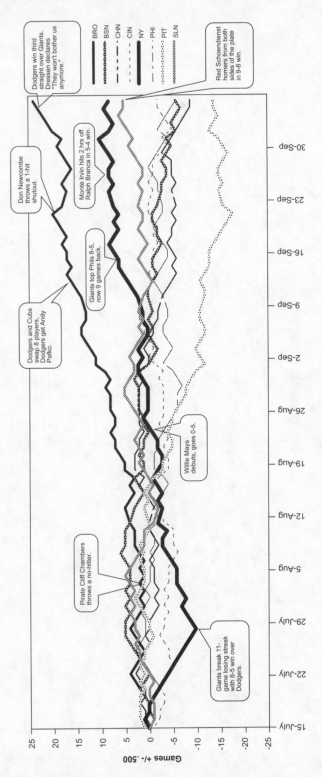

National League 1951, First Half

Games +/– .500

BRO
BSN
CHN
CIN
NY
PHI
PIT
SLN

Dodgers win third straight over Giants. Dressen declares "They won't bother us anymore."

Red Schoendienst homers from both sides of the plate in 9-8 win.

Don Newcombe throws a 1-hit shutout.

Monte Irvin hits 2 hrs off Ralph Branca in 5-4 win.

Dodgers and Cubs swap 8 players. Dodgers get Andy Pafko.

Giants top Phils 8-5, now 9 games back.

Willie Mays debuts, goes 0-5.

Pirate Cliff Chambers throws a no-hitter.

Giants break 11-game losing streak with 8-5 win over Dodgers.

15-July  22-July  29-July  5-Aug  12-Aug  19-Aug  26-Aug  2-Sep  9-Sep  16-Sep  23-Sep  30-Sep

25  20  15  10  5  0  -5  -10  -15  -20  -25

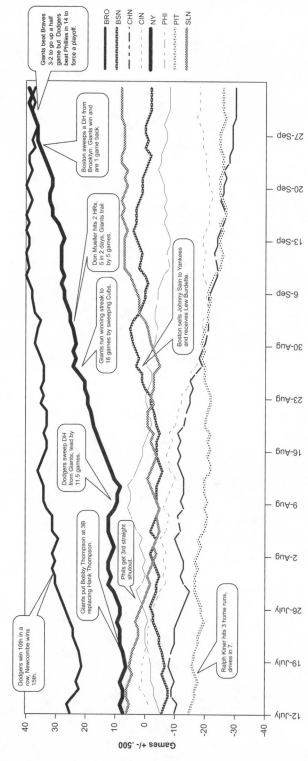

National League 1951, Second Half

Giants beat Braves 3-2 to go up a half game but Dodgers beat Phillies in 14 to force a playoff.

BRO
BSN
CHN
CIN
NY
PHI
PIT
SLN

Boston sweeps a DH from Brooklyn. Giants win and are 1 game back.

Don Mueller hits 2 HRs, 5 in 2 days, Giants trail by 5 games.

Giants run winning streak to 16 games by sweeping Cubs.

Boston sells Johnny Sain to Yankees and receives Lew Burdette.

Dodgers sweep DH from Giants, lead by 11.5 games.

Giants put Bobby Thompson at 3B replacing Hank Thompson.

Phils get 3rd straight shutout.

Dodgers win 10th in a row, Newcombe wins 15th.

Ralph Kiner hits 3 home runs, drives in 7.

Games +/- .500

40
30
20
10
0
-10
-20
-30
-40

12-July
19-July
26-July
2-Aug
9-Aug
16-Aug
23-Aug
30-Aug
6-Sep
13-Sep
20-Sep
27-Sep

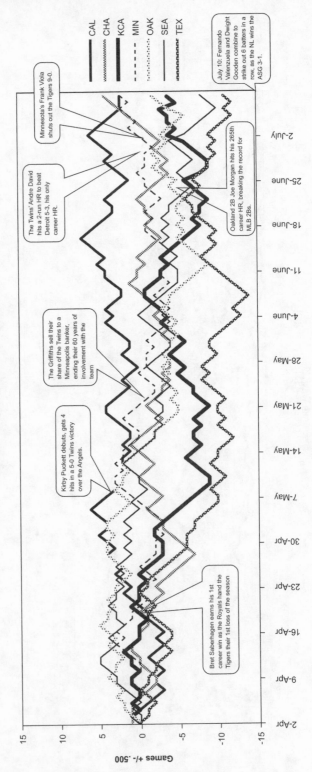

## American League West 1984, First Half

CAL
CHA
KCA
MIN
OAK
SEA
TEX

Kirby Puckett debuts, gets 4 hits in a 5-0 Twins victory over the Angels.

The Griffiths sell their share of the Twins to a Minneapolis banker, ending their 60 years of involvement with the team

Minnesota's Frank Viola shuts out the Tigers 9-0.

The Twins' Andre David hits a 2-run HR to beat Detroit 5-3, his only career HR.

Bret Saberhagen earns his 1st career win as the Royals hand the Tigers their 1st loss of the season

Oakland 2B Joe Morgan hits his 265th career HR, breaking the record for MLB 2Bs.

July 10: Fernando Valenzuela and Dwight Gooden combine to strike out 6 batters in a row, as the NL wins the ASG 3-1.

Games +/- .500

15
10
5
0
-5
-10
-15

2-Apr
9-Apr
16-Apr
23-Apr
30-Apr
7-May
14-May
21-May
28-May
4-June
11-June
18-June
25-June
2-July

American League West 1984, Second Half

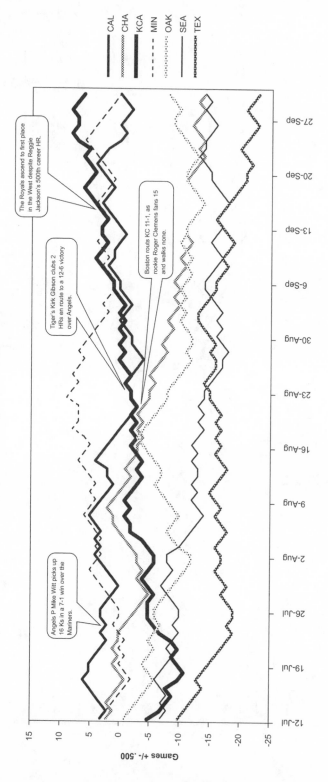

CAL
CHA
KCA
MIN
OAK
SEA
TEX

The Royals ascend to first place in the West despite Reggie Jackson's 500th career HR.

Boston routs KC 11-1, as rookie Roger Clemens fans 15 and walks none.

Tiger's Kirk Gibson clubs 2 HRs en route to a 12-6 victory over Angels.

Angels P Mike Witt picks up 16 Ks in a 7-1 win over the Mariners.

Games +/- .500

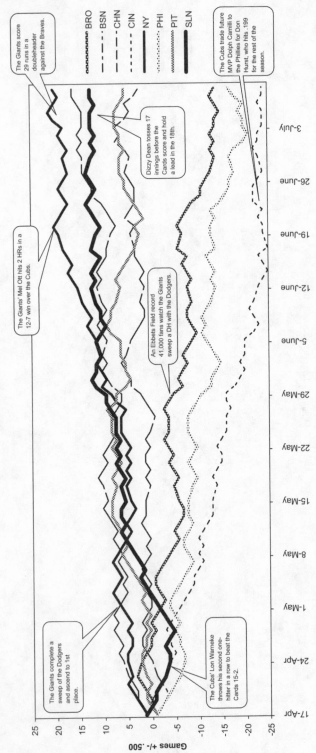

National League 1934, First Half

BRO
BSN
CHN
CIN
NY
PHI
PIT
SLN

The Giants score 29 runs in a doubleheader against the Braves.

Dizzy Dean tosses 17 innings before the Cards score and hold a lead in the 18th.

The Cubs trade future MVP Dolph Camilli to the Phillies for Don Hurst, who hits .199 for the rest of the season.

The Giants' Mel Ott hits 2 HRs in a 12-7 win over the Cubs.

An Ebbets Field record 41,000 fans watch the Giants sweep a DH with the Dodgers.

The Giants complete a sweep of the Dodgers and ascend to 1st place.

The Cubs' Lon Warneke throws his second one-hitter in a row to beat the Cards 15-2.

Games +/- .500

25
20
15
10
5
0
-5
-10
-15
-20
-25

17-Apr
24-Apr
1-May
8-May
15-May
22-May
29-May
5-June
12-June
19-June
26-June
3-July

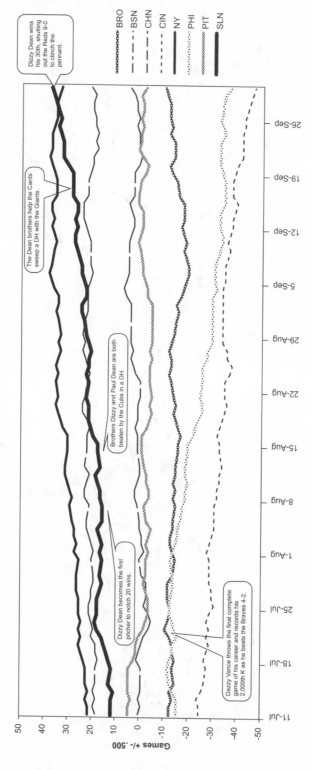

National League 1934, Second Half

Games +/- .500

BRO
BSN
CHN
CIN
NY
PHI
PIT
SLN

Dizzy Dean wins his 30th, shutting out the Reds 9-0 to clinch the pennant.

The Dean brothers help the Cards sweep a DH with the Giants.

Brothers Dizzy and Paul Dean are both beaten by the Cubs in a DH.

Dizzy Dean becomes the first pitcher to notch 20 wins.

Dazzy Vance throws the final complete game of his career and records his 2,000th K as he beats the Braves 4-2.

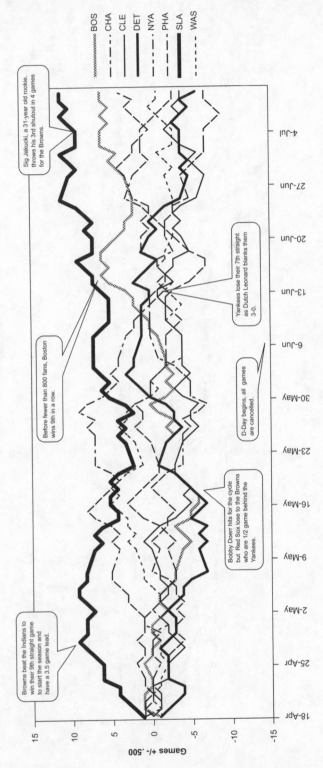

American League 1944, First Half

Browns beat the Indians to win their 9th straight game to start the season and have a 3.5 game lead.

Sig Jakucki, a 31-year old rookie, throws his 3rd shutout in 4 games for the Browns.

Before fewer than 800 fans, Boston wins 9th in a row.

Bobby Doerr hits for the cycle but Red Sox lose to the Browns who are 1/2 game behind the Yankees.

Yankees lose their 7th straight as Dutch Leonard blanks them 3-0.

D-Day begins, all games are cancelled.

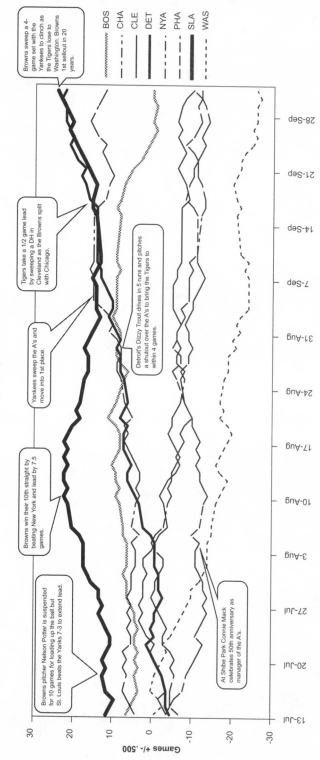

American League 1944, Second Half

# Notes

## Introduction
### Schrödinger's pennant race

xi    "The marquee displayed one of his most famous aphorisms": Moss Klein, *Sporting News*, May 21, 1984, 25.

xii    "Competition for ... 1871": Peter Morris, *A Game of Inches: The Game Behind the Scenes* (Chicago: Ivan R. Dee, 2006), 286–287.

xiii    "The first pennant race decided on the last day": Jonathan Fraser Light, *The Cultural Encyclopedia of Baseball* (Jefferson, N.C.: McFarland, 1997), 537.

## Chapter 1: American League 1967
### To Fight the Unbeatable Foe

2    "Right now is when an MVP should hit a home run": Bill Reynolds, *Lost Summer: The '67 Red Sox and the Impossible Dream* (New York: Warner Books, 1992), 206.

2    "A lollipop": Ken Coleman and Dan Valenti, *The Impossible Dream Remembered: The 1967 Red Sox* (Lexington, Mass.: Stephen Greene Press, 1987), 192.

3    "As exciting as watching an accountant at work": Glenn Stout and Richard A. Johnson, *Red Sox Century* (Boston: Houghton Mifflin Company, 2004), 297.

4–5    "Get those niggers off the field!": Howard Bryant, *Shut Out: A Story of Race and Baseball in Boston* (Boston: Beacon Press, 2002), 32.

5    "I'm not going to waste my time waiting for a bunch of niggers": Al Hirshberg, *What's the Matter with the Red Sox?* (New York: Dodd, Mead and Company, 1973), as quoted in ibid., 45.

5    "There will never be any niggers on this team as long as I have anything to say about it": ibid., 3.

6    "[P]layers give you 100 ... Plaschke": *No More Mr. Nice Guy: A Life of Hardball* (New York: Harcourt Brace Jovanovich, 1990), 78.

6    "We'll win more than we'll lose": ibid., 318.

6    "The cruise is over and you don't need a captain anymore": Stout and Johnson, *Red Sox Century*, 317.

10    "An All-Star from the neck down": Dave Anderson, *Pennant Races: Baseball at Its Best* (New York: Doubleday, 1994), 298.

10 "The dullest club in baseball": Reynolds, *Lost Summer,* 171.

12 "It was a 'squish,' like a tomato or melon hitting the ground": Bob Ryan, "Unforgettable Moment Hit Home 39 Years Ago," *Boston Globe*, August 18, 2006

12 "A menace to baseball": Stout and Johnson, *Red Sox Century,* 326.

12 "We don't belong … manager": Coleman and Valenti, *Impossible Dream Remembered,* 165.

13 "We're in a playoff every night": Anderson, *Pennant Races,* 296.

14 "There's no punishment to fit the crime": ibid., 315.

## Managers 2.0

26 "A fraud": Dick Williams with Bill Plaschke, *No More Mr. Nice Guy* (New York: Harcourt Brace Jovanovich, 1990), 215.

26 "The Timid Texan": ibid., 250.

26 "ironically he was fired … Langston": ibid., 310. Williams, not one to turn the other cheek, refers to Langston as "a gutless wonder."

27 "Showing particular creativity in breaking in young starters in middle relief": Earl Weaver with Terry Pluto, *Weaver on Strategy* (Dulles, Va.: Brassey's, 2002), 74. This was Weaver's "Eighth Law" of ten that he suggested were timeless truths in managing.

28 "For the incredible amount of overwhelmingly positive blarney he'd shower the press with": Well, almost entirely positive. Sparky also once quipped of one of his backup catchers, John Wockenfuss, "The problem with [him] getting on base is that it takes three doubles to score him."

29 "He was almost insane in his in-game creativity": Bill James and Mike Kopf, "The Gerbil Strikes Back," in *The Baseball Book 1990* (New York: Villard, 1990), 40-41.

## Chapter 2: National League 1959
### *Alston's L.A. Confidential*

31 "I had planned … wild": Louis Effrat, "Sherry's Successful Pitching Traced to Winter Experience," *New York Times*, September 29, 1959.

32 "We go to Chicago": Gordon Edes and Maryann Hudson, "That Championship Season," *Los Angeles Times Magazine*, April 9, 1989.

38 "The worst season of any major league manager in baseball history": Bill James, *The Bill James Guide to Baseball Managers from 1870 to Today* (New York: Scribner, 1997), 202.

40 "[w]orst ballpark in America. Every time you stand up there you've got to beat the hitter *and* a 30-mile-an-hour wind": Bob Stevens, "Verbal Blast by Antonelli Jars Frisco," *Sporting News*, July 29, 1959.

40 "Pair of Giant Aces Repeats in '20-Win' Club": Fred Lieb, "Pair of Giant Aces Repeats in '20-Win' Club," *Sporting News*, September 16, 1959.

40   "Operation Cushion": Jack McDonald, "Giants Eye Pennant Parlor Minus Davenport," *Sporting News*, September 16, 1959.

41   "Chinese homer": ibid.

41   "The Great Wall of China": Arthur Daley, "The Great Wall of China," *New York Times*, January 12, 1959.

41   "115 out of 172 shots went to left field": These numbers contradict numerous previously published totals but are based on the most recent play-by-play data on baseball-reference.com via Retrosheet.org.

42   "How could the ball fall there if it wasn't out of the park": "Giles Nixes Braves' Protest, Rules Adcock's Rip a Double," *Sporting News*, September 23, 1959.

45   "He was a man you'd most like to be next to in a lifeboat. Or a foxhole": Jim Murray, "Alston Quietly Goes from Darrtown to Cooperstown," *Los Angeles Times*, March 12, 1983, in *The Great Ones* (Los Angeles: Los Angeles Times, 1999), 6.

46   "The weakest World Championship team of all time": James, *Guide to Baseball Managers*, 225.

### The Braves Dynasty That Wasn't

51   "It still bothers me": Hank Aaron, *I Had a Hammer* (New York: HarperCollins, 1991), 197.

51   "I've always felt": ibid., 216.

### The Replacement-Level Killers

52   VORP (Value Over Replacement Player) defines the replacement level": Rob Neyer, "The World According to VORP," http://sports.espn.go.com/mlb/hotstove06/columns/story?columnist=neyer_rob&id=2751842.

55   "McCarthy had benched Crosetti": Allan Levy, *Joe McCarthy* (Jefferson, N.C.: McFarland, 2005), 271.

## Chapter 3: American League 1948 and 1949
### Tyranicide

59   "The greatest buy": Frank Graham, *The New York Yankees* (New York: Putnam, 1943), 217.

61   "It was two o'clock in the morning": Lou Boudreau, *Clearing All the Bases* (Champaign, Ill.: Sagamore, 1993), 112.

62   "Where's the kid": Bill Veeck, *Veeck as in Wreck* (New York: Putnam, 1962), 187.

62   "Including the bee ball": Bill James and Rob Neyer, *The Neyer/James Guide to Pitchers* (New York: Simon and Schuster, 2004), 333.

62   "Going back to 1927": Dick Clark and Larry Lester, eds., *The Negro Leagues Book* (Cleveland: SABR, 1994), 328.

62 "Satchel Paige, World's Greatest Pitcher": Richard Donovan, "The Fabulous Satchel Paige," in *The Baseball Reader*, ed. Charles Einstein (New York: McGraw-Hill, 1983), 98.

62 "You know … This is an awful big ballpark." Satchel Paige, *Maybe I'll Pitch Forever* (Lincoln, Neb.: Bison, 1993), 197.

62 "I pitch with my arm, not my legs": Boudreau, *Clearing All the Bases*, 112.

62 "I don't generally run at all": Donovan, *Fabulous Satchel Paige*, 101.

62 "How to Stay Young": ibid., 140.

63 "I'm Satchel … I do as I do": ibid., 127.

63 "Veeck was pleased to see": Veeck, *Veeck as in Wreck*, 188.

63 "When 1948 come around": Donovan, *Fabulous Satchel Paige*, 134.

63 "It was all so nice": ibid., 133.

63 "As ridiculous as it was": Veeck, *Veeck as in Wreck*, 188.

63 "Man … I ain't ready for this": Mark Ribowsky, *Don't Look Back* (New York: Da Capo, 1994), 248.

63 "I just tossed a couple real easy": Paige, *Maybe I'll Pitch Forever*, 197.

63 "Satch stopped and walked to me": Boudreau, *Clearing All the Bases*, 112–113.

64 "Against Paige he batted .000": Veeck, *Veeck as in Wreck*, 188.

64 "As Veeck pointed out": ibid., 189.

64 "I demeaned the big circuits": Donovan, *Fabulous Satchel Paige*, 134–135.

64 "I will never allow": Peter Golenbock, *Dynasty* (New York: Prentice-Hall, 1975), 206.

64 "The truth is": Roger Kahn, *The Era* (New York: Houghton Mifflin, 1993), 45n.

65 "The percentage of Negro attendance": Jules Tygiel, *Baseball's Great Experiment* (New York: Oxford, 1997), 83–84.

65 "The first shot at Doby": Glenn Stout and Richard A. Johnson, *Yankees Century* (New York: Houghton Mifflin, 2002), 210.

65 "There is that fine line": Leo Durocher, *Nice Guys Finish Last* (New York: Simon and Schuster, 1975), 105.

66 "The day after the season": Alan H. Levy, *Joe McCarthy* (Jefferson, N.C.: McFarland, 2005), 323.

66 "I came back": Stan Baumgartner, *Sporting News*, October 8, 1947, 12.

66 "Lou Brissie was the sole survivor": Shirley Povich, *Sporting News*, April 14, 1948, 9.

67 "What I like to do": David Kaiser, *Epic Season* (Amherst: University of Massachusetts, 1998), 32.

67 "As though he invented it": Stanley Frank, "They're Just Wild About Boudreau," in *The Third Fireside Book of Baseball*, ed. Charles Einstein (New York: Simon and Schuster, 1968), 142.

67 "Can't run and his arm's no good": William Marshall, *Baseball's Pivotal Era* (Lexington: University Press of Kentucky, 1999), 177.

68 "You couldn't expose him": Frank, *Wild About Boudreau*, 142.

68 "I learned how badly": Veeck, *Veeck as in Wreck*, 154.

69 "We've been going no place:" Ed Linn, *The Great Rivalry* (New York: Ticknor and Fields, 1991), 184.

70 "A Ted Williams hot streak": Stout and Johnson, *Red Sox Century*, 262.

71 "When Feller enlisted": Russell Schneider, *The Boys of the Summer of '48* (Champaign, Ill.: Sports Publishing, 1998), 61.

72 "His velocity seemed to be down": John Sickels, *Bob Feller* (Washington, D.C.: Brassey's, 2004), 190.

72 "He had his arm checked out": ibid., 195.

72 "I was awfully brave": Schneider, *Boys of the Summer*, 123.

73 "So the Yankees own you": Steven Goldman, *Forging Genius: The Making of Casey Stengel* (Washington, D.C.: Brassey's, 2005), 234.

73 "It seems every time Boudreau": Schneider, *Boys of Summer*, 126.

74 "He was probably the biggest dissipater": Goldman, *Forging Genius*, 10.

74 "I don't kid myself": ibid., 22.

77 "If the Indians split": Linn, *The Great Rivalry*, 190.

78 "Kinder was rested": Stout and Johnson, *Red Sox Century*, 265.

78 "He had also been a terror on the road": Bill James, *The Bill James Historical Baseball Abstract* (New York: Villard, 1987), 192.

## *The Postwar Period and Competitive Balance*

85 "When the *Sporting News* speculated they could have received more than $40,000 for him within a couple of months of his 1934 debut": *Sporting News*, November 22, 1934, 5.

85 "Retrosheet records more than $1.3 million in player sales for these teams between 1930 and 1941, compared with $326,000 in player purchases (Table 3-9)": These figures do not include purchases or sales involving minor league clubs, for which Retrosheet's records are rarely complete.

86 "A regular was defined as a player who played a majority of games for his club at each of the eight primary fielding positions": The "eight primary fielding positions" exclude pitcher and DH.

86 "Subject to certain requirements": Specifically, the requirements to be a qualified bench player were as follows:

1. The bench player must have played at least five adjusted defensive games (AdjG) at his position.
2. The bench player must have played at least 10 AdjG between *all* defensive positions.
3. The bench player's AdjG total between all positions must be no greater than 60 percent of the total number of games played by his team.
4. The bench player must have had a qualified regular at his position. If no player had accumulated a majority of his team's AdjG at a given position that season, then neither the regular nor the bench player was considered eligible.

AdjG builds in an estimate of instances in which the player played for only a portion of the game. For example, if the player were brought in as a defensive substitute in the ninth inning, he would be given credit for one-ninth of an AdjG.

87    "This process is explained at greater length in the endnotes": I evaluated a player's EqA over a span of five years that were centered around the current season. For example, in determining a player's TrueEqA in 1959, we would look at his performance over 1957 through 1961. This EqA performance was *age-adjusted* and *weighted* for each season. An example of these adjustments (Richie Ashburn in 1959) can be found in Table A-1.

Table A-1  Richie Ashburn

| Year | 1957 | 1958 | 1959 | 1960 | 1961 |
|---|---|---|---|---|---|
| EqA | .282 | .318 | .250 | .296 | .255 |
| Age | 30 | 31 | 32 | 33 | 34 |
| Age-Adjusted EqA | .272 | .312 | .250 | .302 | .266 |
| Absolute Weight | 2 | 3 | 5 | 3 | 2 |
| Outs Made | 455 | 421 | 436 | 400 | 237 |
| Adjusted Weight | 42.7 | 61.6 | 104.4 | 60 | 30.8 |
| TrueEqA | – | – | .278 | – | – |

The *age adjustment* operates according to aging curves that I developed for the PECOTA forecasting system. In the Richie Ashburn table above, we note he was 32 years old in 1959. Our aging curves specify that the typical player will have an EqA about 10 points lower at age 32 than he had at age 30. Therefore, in evaluating Ashburn's EqA in 1957, when he was 30, we subtract 10 points to adjust it to an age-32 baseline. This result is the player's *Age-Adjusted EqA*.

Each season is also assigned a *weight*. This weight is based on two components: the *absolute weight* and the player's playing time. The absolute weight is fixed: 5 for the current season, 3 for the seasons immediately before and after the current season, and 2 for the seasons two years before and two years after the current season.

The weight is adjusted according to a player's playing time—specifically, the *square root* of the number of outs that the player made that season. This number is multiplied by the absolute weight for that season to produce the *adjusted weight*.

If the sum of the player's adjusted weights totals less than 100—indicating a very limited sample size—we build in additional plate appearances for him until the total adjusted weight equals 100. These plate appearances are assessed as replacement-level appearances at his position. Replacement-level EqAs are assumed to be .208 for catchers, .247 for first basemen, .222 for second basemen, .232 for third basemen, .217 for shortstops, .242 for corner outfielders, and .219 for center fielders. It is appropriate to regress to replacement level rather than to the league average, because a very limited sample of playing time indicates that the player was not good enough to maintain a regular job in the major leagues.

The player's *TrueEqA* is determined by multiplying his age-adjusted EqAs by his adjusted weights to create a weighed mean, including any "bonus" playing time assigned to him at replacement level. In Ashburn's case, this projection works out to a TrueEqA of .278 in 1959, which is quite a bit better than his actual EqA of .250. This is because Ashburn's performance was much better in the seasons before and after 1959, indicating that he underachieved his true level of talent.

Additional information about EqA is available in the Baseball Prospectus Glossary at www.baseballprospectus.com/glossary.

91  "With the creation of the Federal League in 1914, the door widened": Note that players from the Federal League are not considered for purposes of calculating the efficiency index.

91  "In this realm, as in others ... anarchy reigned": Leonard Koppett, *Koppett's Concise History of Major League Baseball*, 2004 ed. (New York: Carroll and Graf, 2004), 175.

91  "These minor league players essentially had become free agents, who could command free-agent prices": The players themselves, of course, were not the primary beneficiary of this form of free agency. Instead, the teams selling the players benefited by securing large transfer frees. These transfer fees were often much larger than the salary actually paid to the player.

92  "While the Phillies and Senators had limited themselves to one": *Total Baseball*, 407.

93–94  "These bonuses are almost certainly less than the true economic value of the players being selected": Nate Silver, "Lies, Damned Lies: Valuing Draft Picks," August 25, 2005, in www.baseballprospectus.com/article. php?articleid=4368.

94  "It is overwhelmingly more profitable to behave as a seller rather than a buyer": Nate Silver, "Lies, Damned Lies: Defending Jeffrey," November 22, 2005, in www.baseballprospectus.com/article.php?articleid=4618.

### Chapter 4: National League 1908
*A Foolish Inconsistency*

99  "The processes of modern technology": Richard Hofstadter, *Age of Reform* (New York: Vintage, 1960), 215–216.

100  "The majority of 1908's games": David W. Anderson, *More than Merkle* (Lincoln: University of Nebraska, 2000), 88.

100  "It is in principle most dangerous": Bill James, *The Bill James Historical Baseball Abstract* (New York: Villard, 1987), 191.

102  "They make a great deal of such differences": F. C. Lane, *Batting* (Cleveland: SABR, 2001), 19.

102 "In fact, Tinkers to Evers to Chance was strong": James, *Historical Baseball Abstract,* 344.

102 "Merely the outguessing of one team": Charles Einstein, *Our Game* (New York: MJF, 1991), 87.

103 "All there is to Evers is a bundle of nerves": Anderson, *More than Merkle,* 65.

103 "Each night, Evers's bedtime ritual": Lee Allen and Tom Meany, *Kings of the Diamond* (New York: Putnam, 1965), 119.

105 "The most devastating pitch I ever faced": Tom Simon, ed., *Deadball Stars of the National League* (Washington, D.C.: Brassey's, 2004), 104.

105 "I don't know. I've never done it any other way:" David Pietrusza et al., eds., *Baseball: The Biographical Encyclopedia* (Ontario: Sports Media, 2003), 135.

105 "You can begin by releasing these": Noel Hynd, *Giants of the Polo Grounds* (Dallas: Taylor, 1995), 111.

105 "The only popularity I know": David Gallen, ed., *The Baseball Chronicles* (New York: Carroll and Graf, 1991), 245.

105 "Were born to battle on baseball fields": Daniel Okrent and Harris Lewine, eds., *The Ultimate Baseball Book* (New York: Houghton Mifflin, 2000), 61.

105 "Never finished high school": Gil Bogen, *Tinker, Evers, and Chance* (Jefferson, N.C.: McFarland, 2003), 7.

106 "It's a tough racket": Lawrence Ritter, *The Glory of Their Times* (New York: Vintage, 1985), 123.

106 "On May 30, 1904": Eddie Gold and Art Ahrens, *The Golden Era Cubs* (Chicago: Bonus Books, 1985), 46.

106 "It was an important part": Paul Dickson, *Baseball's Greatest Quotations* (New York: HarperCollins, 1991), 64.

106 "If you have a bad actor": Gallen, *The Baseball Chronicles,* 234.

107 "Suppose Fred Tenney should be crippled": Geoffrey C. Ward and Ken Burns, *Baseball: An Illustrated History* (New York: Knopf, 1994), 92.

107 "He is the fastest man to touch runners": G. H. Fleming, *The Unforgettable Season* (New York: Simon and Schuster, 1981), 14.

107 "To me he was pretty much the perfect type": Joseph Durso, *Casey & Mr. McGraw* (St. Louis: Sporting News, 1989), 61.

107–108 "The secret of the fade-away": John Kuenster, ed., *From Cobb to Catfish* (Chicago: Rand McNally, 1975), 66.

108 "He was a wonderful, wonderful man": ibid., 96.

108 "That's what made him a great pitcher": Ritter, *Glory of Their Times,* 176.

109 "I have never heard of anybody": John McGraw, *My Thirty Years in Baseball* (Lincoln: University of Nebraska Press, 1995), 217.

109 "So uniformly good was Wagner": ibid., 202.

109 "He just ate the ball up": Glenn Dickey, *The History of National League Baseball* (New York: Stein and Day, 1979), 74.

111 "Would become involved with the mobster Dutch Schultz": Simon, *Deadball Stars,* 128.

112 "He could throw a ball into a tin cup": Ward and Burns, *Baseball,* 71.

112 "You could catch him sittin'": Kuenster, *From Cobb to Catfish*, 66.

112 "Don't worry": John Thorn and John Holway, *The Pitcher* (New York: Prentice Hall, 1987), 82.

113 "Well, Cap, I guess it's all off": Bogen, *Tinker, Evers, and Chance*, 88.

113 "How are the cripples?": Christy Mathewson, *Pitching in a Pinch* (New York: Putnam, 1912), 190–191.

113 "The fans were part of the game": Ritter, *Glory of Their Times*, 27.

114 "In those days, as soon as the game ended": ibid., 106.

114 "One run shall be scored": Blanche McGraw, *The Real John McGraw* (New York: David McKay, 1953), 217.

115 "Dismissed as hearsay": G. H. Fleming, *The Unforgettable Season* (New York: Simon and Schuster, 1981), 224.

115 "Significantly, Pulliam did not take the opportunity": Anderson, *More than Merkle*, 162.

115 "That night O'Day came to look me up": Simon, *Deadball Stars*, 100.

117 "If this game goes to Chicago": Robinson, *Matty*, 102.

117 "Most people think it was Merkle": Ritter, *Glory of Their Times*, 117.

118 "The game should have been won for the New York Club": W. W. Aulick, *New York Times*, October 7, 1908, 7.

119 "No one can stand such constant use": Ray Robinson, *Matty* (New York: Oxford, 1993), 104.

119 "I'm not fit to pitch today": Bob Broeg, *Superstars of Baseball* (South Bend: Diamond Communications, 1991), 305.

119 "When I pitched that extra play-off": Grantland Rice, *The Tumult and the Shouting* (New York: A. S. Barnes, 1954), 47.

119 "The scene at the Polo Grounds": Peter Golenbock, *Wrigleyville* (New York: St. Martin's, 1999), 144.

120 "Get it over quickly": Gold and Ahrens, *The Golden Era Cubs*, 58–59.

120 "Brown wasted no time": Bogen, *Tinker, Evers, and Chance*, 95.

120 "It is criminal to say that Merkle is stupid": Frank Graham, *McGraw of the Giants* (New York: Putnam, 1944), 48.

121 "I could use a carload like you": Charles C. Alexander, *John McGraw* (Lincoln: University of Nebraska, 1988), 139.

121 "Though a popular rumor": Mathewson, *Pitching in a Pinch*, 185.

121 "The fact of the matter is": Kuenster, *From Cobb to Catfish*, 162.

121 "Johnny Evers hasn't completed the force-out": Golenbock, *Wrigleyville*, 150.

## Chapter 5: National League 1964
*There Is No Expedient to Which a Man Should Not Resort
to Avoid the Real Labor of Thinking*

129 "There is no expedient": Sir Joshua Reynolds said, "There is no expedient to which a man will not resort to avoid the real labor of thinking." The implication here is the Phillies would have been better off if they had

proved him right. Nugent had accrued $256,000 in debt (David Pietrusza, *Judge and Jury: The Life and Times of Judge Kenesaw Mountain Landis* [South Bend: Diamond, 1998], 420). By 1920, Philadelphia was home to the largest African American population in the United States (population by county, taken from Historical U.S. Census data from the University of Virginia Library Geospatial & Statistical Data Center).

141  "The problem with Gene Mauch as a field general": Dick Allen with Tim Whitaker, *Crash! The Life and Times of Dick Allen* (New York: Houghton Mifflin, 1988), 54.

142  "Hindsight dictates that we should have been rested": David Halberstam, *October 1964* (New York: Villard, 1994), 306.

142  "After that, we were playing as if we were waiting to lose," William C. Kashatus, *September Swoon: Richie Allen, the '64 Phillies, and Racial Integration* (University Park: Pennsylvania State University, 2004), 131.

143  "Gene, for 150 games" and "Aw, that's a bunch of bullshit": ibid., 133.

143  "Maybe it sounds ridiculous": ibid., 134.

144  "I don't know if it's humanly possible": ibid., 138.

144  "Mauch was wrapped so tight": Allen with Whitaker, *Crash!* 57.

146  "I just wore the pitching out" and "I want to be the first one off": Kashatus, *September Swoon*, 2–3.

### Brock and Trout

150  "Keith hit a grounder, a possible DP ball": Whitey Herzog, *You're Missin' a Great Game* (New York: Simon and Schuster, 1999), 188–189.

### Dick Allen's Aftermath

155  "Allen told Edward Kiersh": Edward Kiersh, *Where Have You Gone, Vince DiMaggio?* (New York: Bantam, 1983), 199.

### Chapter 6: National League Central 2003
#### Scapegoats

161  "Please leave him alone. It's not his fault": Drew Olson, "Ill-Fated Fan Tries to Grab Some Pardon; Focus of Furor Says He Never Saw Alou," *Milwaukee Journal-Sentinel*, October 16, 2003.

161–162  "Normal human reaction": ibid.

162  "Prior said it about as good as anybody minutes after the game": Henry Schulman, "Cubs' Fan Is 'Truly Sorry'; Apology Given for Messing Up Alou's Chance," *San Francisco Chronicle*, October 16, 2003.

162  "I use that bat for batting practice": "Unsplendid Splinter: Cubs Rally Past Rays after Sosa's Ignominious Ejection," June 3, 2003, in http://sportsillustrated.cnn.com/baseball/news/2003/06/03/sosa_ejected_ap, or

"Sosa banned over bat," June 6, 2003, in http://news.bbc.co.uk/sport2/hi/other_sports/us_sport/2970198.stm.

165 "It seems like every guy they bring in throws 95 to 99": Neil Milbert, "Simon Slugs 2 Homers As Win Streak Reaches 5," *Chicago Tribune,* September 7, 2003.

166 "This is the time of year when you have to push yourself": Mark Prior, quoted in *Arlington Heights Daily Herald,* reprinted in "The Week in Quotes: September 8–14," ed. Ryan Wilkins, September 15, 2003, in http://www.baseballprospectus.com/article.php?articleid=2313.

167 "Takes a line drive to the forehead and we never have to see him again": Paul Sullivan, "Cardinals' Kline Reheats the 'Feud,'" *Chicago Tribune,* September 30, 2003.

169 "My guys performed admirably, but it took us awhile to build that Giant team to go to the World Series": John Shea and Bruce Jenkins, "Not the Return Trip That Baker Wanted," *San Francisco Chronicle,* October 20, 2003.

170 "Now, the St. Louis Cardinals have been playing baseball for over 100 years": Rick Hummel, "La Russa Reaffirms Intention to Return; Rumors About White Sox Have No Basis, He Says," *St. Louis Post-Dispatch,* September 30, 2003.

## Selig's Dream

170 "Steve Howe retired the Blue Jays' Randy Knorr to make them the first wild card in the history of baseball": The Colorado Rockies clinched the first National League wild card later that day, but their game started and ended later.

170 "I'm just wondering why I'm not as excited as I wanted to be": Don Mattingly, quoted in *New York Times,* October 2, 1995.

170 "I don't want anybody to feel apologetic for getting in the playoffs this way": ibid.

171 "By most definitions, a pennant represents a league championship": The *American Heritage Dictionary,* for example, defines a *pennant* as a "flag that symbolizes the championship of a league, especially a professional baseball league."

171 "The *Sporting News* ... used the word 'pennant'": *Sporting News,* October 14, 1985, 17.

172 "We're hoping it will enhance and maintain fan interest through the end of the season": John Harrington, quoted in *New York Times,* September 10, 1993.

172 "I reviewed the TPLI of every game": Technically speaking, this statement is incorrect. Doubleheaders were excluded from the analysis because Clay Davenport's report updates the playoff odds at the end of every day of the season, rather than the end of every game played, creating ambiguities if more than one game is played in a day. In addition, the strike years of 1981 and 1994 were removed from the analysis.

174 "In the wild-card era": Although technically within the wild-card era, 1994 and 1995 were eliminated from consideration because of the impacts of the strike.

176 "This higher September attendance puts an additional $50 million in baseball's coffers each season": This is calculated by comparing the actual attendance in September games over 1996–2006 with the expected attendance assuming a 21.4 percent decline from June and July levels, as was experienced during divisional play. The difference amounts to about 4,000 fans per game. Assuming that 430 games are played in September and October (this was the number played in 2006) and that the average ticket price is $30, this works out to $51.6 million in additional attendance revenues.

178–179 "Which nobody would mistake for an inferior quality club": By contrast, the average divisional winner has finished with a 95-67 record.

## Chapter 7: American League East 1972
### The Book of Job

182 "I don't like that uneven number of games": Hal Butler, *Al Kaline and the Detroit Tigers* (Chicago: Henry Regnery, 1973), 258.

184 "Just the thought of giving up Frank Robinson scared me to death": Earl Weaver with Barry Stainback, *It's What You Learn After You Know It All That Counts* (New York: Fireside, 1983), 199.

186 "according to rookie Bill Denehy, Martin and pitching coach Art Fowler": Peter Golenbock, *Wild, High and Tight* (New York: St. Martin's, 1994), 183.

187 "Fisk took charge of our pitching staff": Bill Lee, *The Wrong Stuff* (New York: Viking, 1984), 94.

190 "I hit the ball off Lolich," "When I hit the base" and "He comes back to third": Dan Shaughnessy, *The Curse of the Bambino* (New York: Dutton, 1990), 108.

## Chapter 8: National League East 1973
### The Healing Power of Faith

194 Stargell phone call to Al Oliver: Al Oliver, interview with author, November 2006.

195 Pirates at Bob Prince's New Year's Day Party: ibid.

195 Clemente's performance in 1971 World Series: Roger Angell, *The Summer Game* (New York: Ballantine Books, 1972), 275.

196 "One couldn't face Roberto": Willie Stargell and Tom Bird, *Willie Stargell: An Autobiography* (New York: Harper and Row, 1984), 160.

196 "With deadly earnestness": Douglas Kneeland, "Dean at Witness Table: A Calm and Cool 'David,'" *New York Times*, June 27, 1973, 49.

196  "I understood why they were booing": Joe Torre, interview with author, September 2006.

197  "The original godfather": Charles P. Korr, *The End of Baseball as We Knew It: The Players Union 1960–81* (Chicago: University of Illinois Press, 2002), 128.

197  "Torre spoke to a *New York Times* writer": Joseph Durso, *New York Times*, June 27, 1973.

197  "These are times when people spit on the flag": Robert Lipsyte, *Sports-World: An American Dreamland* (New York: Quadrangle Books, 1975), 47.

198  "Flood and his mouthpiece": Phillip Roth, *Our Gang* (New York: Random House, 1971), 62.

198  "Roth was joking": Marvin J. Miller, *A Whole Different Ball Game* (New York: Simon and Schuster, 1991),183.

199  "You can't get carried away": Milton Gross, *New York Post*, March 3, 1972.

200  "For hitters, facing Blass became a frightening": Tim McCarver, interview with author, November 2006.

200  "You have no idea how frustrating it is": Pat Jordan, *Sports Illustrated*, April 15, 1975, 64.

200  "Guisti remembers Blass's wife": Roger Angell, *Five Seasons: A Baseball Companion* (New York, Popular Library, 1977), 254.

200  The following season, Pat Jordan wrote: Pat Jordan, *Sports Illustrated*, April 15, 1975, 67.

201  "He had four or five different words for titties": Peter Golenbock, *Amazin': The Miraculous History of New York's Most Beloved Baseball Team* (New York: St. Martin's Griffin, 2002), 202.

201  "I want to know the difference between right and wrong": Tug McGraw and Joseph Durso, *Screwball* (Boston: Houghton Mifflin, 1974), 155.

201  "It must be the people that are screwed up": ibid., 157.

202  "I didn't have any idea how to throw the baseball,": ibid., 22.

202  "There's nothing wrong with the Mets": ibid., 25.

202  "You gotta believe!": ibid., 26.

203  "He was very receptive to collaboration": Mike Marshall, interview with author, November 2006.

203  "He had a bad night ... Mauch" Pat Jordan, *Sports Illustrated*, June 9, 1975, 32.

204  "He was a stubborn S.O.B.": Mike Marshall, interview with author, November 2006.

205  "I think we needed Roberto to push us": Stargell and Bird, *Willie Stargell*, 160.

205  "I pounded him": Steve Blass, interview with author, November 2006.

205  "I'm back!": Jerome Holtzman, *Chicago Tribune*, June 16, 1988.

205–206 "It's been a wonderful 22 years": Willie Mays, quoted in *New York Times*, September 21, 1973, 27.

205–206 "Head fake": Jerome Holtzman, *Chicago Tribune*, June 16, 1988.

207 "The field is absolutely bad": Joseph Durso, *New York Times*, September 30, 1973, 209.

207 "It's nice to be back at home": George Langford, *Chicago Tribune*, September 30, 1973, B1.

207 "That's the hottest champagne": Robert Markus, *Chicago Tribune*, October 2, 1973, C1.

207 "Unbelievable ... Wayne Garrett": George Langford, *Chicago Tribune*, October 2, 1973, C1.

208 "It was like ... Jerry Koosman": Peter Golenbock, *Amazin': The Miraculous History of New York's Most Beloved Baseball Team* (New York: St. Martin's Griffin, 2002), 310.

208 "I hit .239": Ed Kranepool, quoted in *New York Times*, October 2, 1973, 50.

208 "A bad trade-off": Tim McCarver, interview with author, November 2006.

208 "Gibson ... agonizing": Bob Gibson and Lonnie Wheeler, *A Stranger to the Game* (New York: Viking, 1994), 242.

### The Great All Time Anti-Pennant Race

210 "They became informally known": George Robinson and Charles Salzberg, *On a Clear Day They Could See Seventh Place* (New York: Dell, 1991), 21.

211 "New York Highlanders (Yankees) ace Jack Chesbro": Robinson and Salzberg, *On a Clear Day*, 44.

211 "I have promised the Washington people": Morris Beale, *The Washington Senators* (Washington, D.C.: Columbia, 1947), 60.

212 "I signed with the A's right out of high school": ibid., 74.

212 "We are the little tonic team": ibid., 86.

214 "He's a strong boy and a real nice fellow": Jack Ryan, *Sporting News*, August 4, 1948, 10.

214 "We finished in last place with you": Andrew O'Toole, *Branch Rickey in Pittsburgh* (Jefferson, N.C.: McFarland, 2000), 97.

214 "Out of quantity," Robinson and Salzberg, *On a Clear Day*, 185.

214 "If there was a new way to lose": ibid., 182.

214 "Culls and aging castoffs": Jonathan Fraser Light, *The Cultural Encyclopedia of Baseball* (Jefferson, N.C.: McFarland, 1997), 239.

214 "We have been bleeped": Norman MacLean, *Casey Stengel* (New York: Drake, 1976), 142.

214 "The Mets is a very good thing": Jimmy Breslin, *Can't Anybody Here Play This Game?* (New York: Ballentine, 1970), 17.

214 "About to climb down the other side of the mountain": Peter Bjarkman, ed., *Encyclopedia of Major League Baseball: National League* (New York: Carroll and Graf, 1993), 346.

214 "They are like reading an old book": Maury Allen, *Now Wait a Minute, Casey* (New York: Doubleday, 1965), 20.

214 "I want to thank all those generous owners": Breslin, *Can't Anybody?* 82.

215 "No, you don't": John Eisenberg, *From 33rd Street to Camden Yards* (New York: Contemporary Books, 2001), 396.

## Chapter 9: American League East 1974
### *Mutiny on the Weaver*

220 "As hard as I made Lou work": Phillip Bashe, *Dog Days: The New York Yankees' Fall from Grace and Return to Glory 1964–1976* (New York: Random House, 1994), 286.

221 "We had to do something": ibid., 269.

222 "We died ... Gene Michael": ibid., 271.

222 "Between my blue collar jobs and minor league baseball": Terry Pluto, *The Earl of Baltimore* (New Century Publishers, 1982), 28.

222 "Everything Earl did was calculated": ibid., 36.

223 "I can't be friends with players": ibid., 168.

223 "He doesn't say much to anybody": ibid., 152.

223 "I never miss anything about the Orioles": ibid., 156.

223 "You do get this negative feeling from the start": ibid., 152.

223 "Earl does not have a shithouse like some managers": Earl Weaver with Barry Stainback, *It's What You Learn After You Know It All That Counts* (New York: Fireside, 1983), 65.

223 "When Oriole players were once asked what they would give Weaver for his birthday": Pluto, *The Earl of Baltimore*, 186–187.

224 "Give him $50 and tell him to come back tomorrow night": Mark Kram, *Sports Illustrated*, July 15, 1974, 25.

224 "Oakland slugger Reggie Jackson gushed": Leigh Monteville, *Boston Globe*, August 25, 1974.

225 "Outfielder Reggie Smith once said that Tiant": Myron Cope, *Sports Illustrated*, May 7, 1973, 44.

225 "Tommy Harper played a poor game, Tiant reassured him": Howard Bryant, *Shut Out: A Story of Race and Baseball in Boston* (Boston: Beacon Press, 2002), 128.

225 "I had never met a red ass like Rick in my life": Bill Lee and Dick Lally, *The Wrong Stuff* (Penguin: New York, 1984), 118.

225 "The happy season": Leigh Monteville, *Boston Globe*, August 25, 1974.

225 "Midsummer night's dream": ibid.

226 "With Luis, it's not the stats": Bob Ryan, *Boston Globe*, August 24, 1874.

226 "The Red Sox fan had forgotten": Leigh Monteville, *Boston Globe*, September 3, 1974.

226 "It keeps guys from showering ... Don Baylor": Doug Brown, "O's Sock It to Sinners ... Revive Kangaroo Court," *Sporting News*, September 14, 1974.

227 "Deep down inside, though": Don Baylor and Claire Smith, *Nothing But the Truth: A Baseball Life* (New York: St. Martin's Press, 1989).

227 "I don't know which is harder": Larry Whiteside, *Boston Globe*, September 3, 1974, 29.

227 "This is bad on the heart": Doug Brown, *Sporting News*, October 12, 1974, 4.

227 "The pressure and emotional strain are exhausting": ibid.

228 "That evening I lashed my hands to the bathroom sink": Lee and Lally, *The Wrong Stuff*, 121.

228 "If we have Palmer, we'll win": Ray Fitzgerald, *Boston Globe*, September 5, 1974.

228 "The most amazing pitching performance by a staff": Earl Weaver with Barry Stainback, *It's What You Learn After You Know It All That Counts* (New York: Fireside, 1983), 216.

228 "He'd wear out the other guys": Dick Lally, *Pinstriped Summers* (New York: Arbor House, 1985), 135.

229 "How can we trade half a pitching staff?": Phil Pepe, *Sporting News*, October 19, 1974, 9.

229 "At this rate, they are": Bashe, *Dog Days*, 273.

229 "It was like we were guests there": ibid., 275.

230 "Goddamn it, you've to go balls-out all the time": ibid., 287.

230 "Some guys can't pick up the pot": Myron Cope, *Sports Illustrated*, May 7, 1973, 44.

231 "If we win two out of three from Earl": Lou Piniella and Maury Allen, *Sweet Lou* (New York: G. P. Putnam's Sons, 1986), 132.

231 "Lou may be like the proverbial pile of dogshit": Earl Weaver with Barry Stainback, *It's What You Learn After You Know It All That Counts* (New York: Fireside, 1983), 23.

231 "Don't hit a home run … ": Pluto, *The Earl of Strategy*, 91.

231 "Years later, the writer Dick Lally": Dick Lally, interview with author, December 2006.

231 "I keep reading the papers about your great catches": Piniella and Allen, *Sweet Lou*, 132.

231 "I'm going to jinx you": ibid., 133.

232 "You had better be glad you got that hit": Baylor and Smith, *Nothing but the Truth*.

232 "Knowing Earl … he loved defiance": ibid.

233 "Chilean soccer riot": Peter Gammons, *Boston Globe*, September 25, 1974, 51.

233 "The first fight": ibid., 55.

235 "The ball seemed to switch directions": Piniella and Allen, *Sweet Lou*, 134.

235 "How many out, Andy?": Doug Brown, *Sporting News*, October 19, 1974.

235 "You mean we don't have to win tomorrow?": ibid.

235 "I was never happier to see a pennant race end": Earl Weaver with Barry Stainback, *It's What You Learn After You Know It All That Counts* (New York: Fireside, 1983), 217.

236 "I had a good season": Joseph Durso, *New York Times*, October 3, 1974.

236 "Thanks. I knew you'd screw it up someway": Piniella and Allen, *Sweet Lou*, 134.

### How to Break Up the Yankees

237 "The James Dawson award": Jim Ogle, "Velez Is Dawson Winner," *Sporting News*, April 21, 1973, 11.
237 "I like the outfield": Bill Reddy, "Fence Corrals Chiefs' Velez Following Hot Hitting Start," *Sporting News*, May 12, 1973, 32.
238 "His abilities in left field": Neil MacCarl, *Sporting News*, June 30, 1979, 22.
239 "He's the best hitting prospect I've ever seen": Bill Reddy, *Sporting News*, May 12, 1973, 32.
239 "The experience was good for him": Jim Ogle, *Sporting News*, April 21, 1973, 11.
239 "Those aren't kids": Phil Pepe, *Sporting News*, December 22, 1973, 38.
240 "I couldn't give him a spot on the club": Phil Pepe, *Sporting News*, July 27, 1974, 22.
240 "Win or lose, you have to play your best ball club": *Sporting News*, July 20, 1974, 22.
241 "As the draft never withdrew Velez": Jack Lang, *Sporting News*, November 20, 1976, 34.
241 "I'm not saying I will hit 30 home runs": Neil MacCarl, *Sporting News*, May 24, 1980, 12.
241 "I know I can swing the bat": Neil MacCarl, *Sporting News*, May 14, 1977, 29.
242 "Did you see Beattie out there": Bill Madden and Moss Klein, *Damned Yankees* (New York: Warner, 1991), 184.
242 "Meacham isn't ready for New York": Joel Sherman, *Birth of a Dynasty* (New York: Rodale, 2006), 53.
247 "Steinbrenner, having resumed the active role": ibid., 61.
247 "I would not have gone with a Jeter": ibid., 60.
247 "Michael faced Steinbrenner down": ibid., 52.
247 "Phil Hughes became just the second Yankees number one pick": Tyler Kepner, "When Needed Most, Pettitte Can't Steady Sliding Yankees," *New York Times*, April 28, 2007.

### Chapter 10: National League 1951
*The Dirty, Underhanded, Compromised, Corrupt, and Perhaps Tertiary Shot Heard 'Round the World*

248 "Summarizing the 1951 race": Roger Kahn, *The Era* (New York: Ticknor and Fields, 1993), 268.
250 "In forty-five years, the team had employed": Harvey Frommer, *New York City Baseball: The Last Golden Age, 1947–1957* (New York: Atheneum, 1985), 85.

250 "You and Durocher are on a raft": Bill James, *The Bill James Guide to Baseball Managers* (New York: Scribner, 1997), 123.

251 "And build 'my kind of team'": Dave Anderson, *Pennant Races, Baseball at Its Best* (New York: Doubleday, 1994), 214.

251 "At first was Monte Irvin, ranked by Bill James": Bill James, *The New Bill James Historical Baseball Abstract* (New York: Free Press, 2001), 188.

251 "Hank Thompson, was Negro League star": James A. Riley, *The Biographical Encyclopedia of the Negro Baseball Leagues* (New York: Carroll and Graf Publishers, 1994), 780.

252 "His 'drinking and pugnacious attitude'": Frommer, *New York City Baseball*, 85.

252 "Perfected in the 7,100-foot altitude of Puebla Angeles": Joshua Prager, *The Echoing Green: The Untold Story of Bobby Thomson, Ralph Branca, and the Shot Heard 'Round the World* (New York: Pantheon Books, 2006), 200.

253 "Who had played football under George Halas, and baseball under Leo Durocher": Peter Golenbock, *Bums: An Oral History of the Brooklyn Dodgers* (New York: Pocket Books, 1984), 388.

253 "If the letter 'I' were dropped from the alphabet": Prager, *The Echoing Green*, 85.

253 "Dressen was considered a solid baseball man by some of his players" Golenbock, *Bums*, 387–388.

253 "Seeing the Klan burn a cross on his Catholic family's lawn": Kahn, *The Era*, 303.

253–254 "Unlike Durocher, who usually sought out advice from the Giants' team statistician": Prager, *The Echoing Green*, 221.

254 "Dressen had the Dodgers' pioneering stats man": ibid., 185–186.

254 "Hold 'em fellas, I'll think of something": Kahn, *The Era*, 303.

254 "Mantle, Shmantle—Long as We Got Abrams": *New York Post*, May 25, 1951.

254 "Moonlighting as a Coney Island batting instructor": Frommer, *New York City Baseball*, 107.

254 "It's like handing me $5,000": Anderson, *Pennant Races*, 219.

255 "The Giants, by contrast, fell flat on their faces": ibid., 216.

255 "Durocher moved Irvin": ibid., 219.

255 "Durocher brought up Willie Mays": ibid.

255 "Bobby Thomson had started the season poorly": Prager, *The Echoing Green*, 5.

255 "Furious at Cubs manager Frankie Frisch": Anderson, *Pennant Races*, 219.

255 "Ray Dandridge ... 'the best third baseman never to make the major leagues'": Riley, *Negro Baseball Leagues*, 210.

255 "A train could go between his legs but a groundball couldn't": James, *Historical Baseball Abstract*, 184.

255 "The American Association's MVP after leading the Millers to the league title": Riley, *Negro Baseball League*, 211.

255–256 "Unwritten quotas [that] continued to hamstring black players": Prager, *The Echoing Green*, 6.

256 "Dandridge ... acute appendicitis, and put out of action for a month": ibid., 7.

256 Durocher remembered that Thomson had briefly played third: Anderson, *Pennant Races*, 219.

256 "In 1950, the Giants had gone 50-22 after another bad start": Prager, *The Echoing Green*, 16.

256 "Robinson retaliated by openly taunting Jansen": *New York Post*, April 30, 1951.

256 "I've tried everything. I just can't shake it off": ibid.

256 "Roll out the barrel! The Giants are dead!": Prager, *The Echoing Green*, 85–86.

256 "Ran Maglie down when the pitcher went to field it": *New York Post*, May 1, 1951.

257 "Leo, you in there?": Prager, *The Echoing Green*, 85–86.

257 "The largest lead the franchise had ever had, anytime, on anyone": ibid., 85.

257 "This finishing kick was the second greatest in baseball history": Dave Smith, "1951 NL Pennant Race," in www.retrosheet.org , 3.

257 "First, the Giants went on a 16-game winning streak": Anderson, *Pennant Races*, 222.

257 "Thomson managed to tag out Robinson before he could get back to the bag": ibid., 211.

257 "Mays scored what proved to be the winning run": ibid., 221.

257 "I'd like to see him do it again": ibid.

257 "Luck, that was the luckiest throw I've ever seen": ibid.

257 "Willie was good, but he was not the ballplayer": Golenbock, *Bums*, 358.

258 "In other words, the Giants had knocked only a half-game": Anderson, *Pennant Races*, 225–226.

258 "Dick Young wrote that 'the Brooks virtually wrapped up the flag'": ibid., 225.

258 "Statistically, it was clearly the team's hitting that went south": Smith, "1951 NL Pennant Race," 4–8.

259 "All of the Dodger starters were either foundering or suffering": Anderson, *Pennant Races*, 226.

259 "But after the second start, he felt his triceps tighten": Prager, *The Echoing Green*, 184.

259 "Branca never regained the top speed on his fastball": ibid., 114.

259 "Clyde King, who was 12-5 on August 11": Golenbock, *Bums*, 345–346.

259 "Labine stepped into the rotation": Prager, *The Echoing Green*, 227.

260 "Now the best pitcher in the league": ibid.

260 "Dressen also never fully trusted Labine": Golenbock, *Bums*, 389.

260 "The team's batting average at home was .263": Smith, "1951 NL Pennant Race," 7.

260 "Even during the Giants' 16-game winning streak": Prager, *The Echoing Green*, 100.

260 "Yvars attributed the apparent sign-stealing": ibid.

261 "Prager points out that Bobby Thomson batted .337": ibid., 109–110.

261 "For that matter, during their furious, September drive": Smith, "1951 NL Pennant Race," 4.

261 "The Giants' team ERA was 3.86 at the low-water mark": ibid.

261 "During the crucial, 16-game winning streak": Prager, *The Echoing Green*, 100.

261 "And after the streak, New York's pitchers": Smith, "1951 NL Pennant Race," 4.

261 "In the last seven consecutive wins": Anderson, *Pennant Races*, 230–236.

261 "Jim Hearn lowered his ERA by more than two runs": Prager, *The Echoing Green*, 199.

262 "Jansen went from 3.53 to 2.02": Smith, "1951 NL Pennant Race," 9.

262 "After watching him hobble gamely through a hitless": Anderson, *Pennant Races*, 241.

262 "Moreover, Dressen perhaps blew the playoff right from the coin toss": ibid., 232–233.

262 "It was a peculiar decision, given that one of Dressen's coaches, Cookie Lavagetto": Prager, *The Echoing Green*, 103; and Golenbock, *Bums*, 344–345.

262 "The big game is the first game": Anderson, *Pennant Races*, 233.

263 "My arm's tight": Kahn, *The Era*, 274.

263 "It looks like I just don't have it anymore. Take me out": Golenbock, *Bums*, 369.

262 "Mueller later told Roger Kahn": Kahn, *The Era*, 279.

264 Sukeforth told him that Erskine 'just bounced his curveball': Anderson, *Pennant Races*, 246.

264 "The Flying Scot had hit .545 in 22 lifetime at-bats": Prager, *The Echoing Green*, 214.

264 "A game in which Branca had thrown 133 pitches": ibid., 187.

264 "By contrast, Thomson was 2-8 that year against": ibid., 214–215.

264 "Literally praying that he wouldn't have to hit": ibid., 221.

264 "Willie Mays had batted just .105 against Branca in 19 at-bats": ibid., 216.

264 "Joe Black was a big, smart, hard-throwing right-hander, who had taught school": Golenbock, *Bums*, 402.

264 "Would later become a corporate executive": Riley, *Negro Baseball Leagues*, 86–87.

265 "He had compiled good numbers with both Triple-A Montreal": ibid.

265 "Black had pinpoint control and a fastball that was clocked": Kahn, *The Era*, 283.

265 "Yet Kahn claims that even 'by 1949 the Dodgers were backing away'": ibid., 246–247.

265 "Dressen merely instructed his pitcher, 'Get him out'": Prager, 217.

265 "Because he would have gotten Newcombe through": Golenbock, 371.
266 "Erskine, left back in the bullpen, shouted in horror": Prager, *The Echoing Green*, 220.
266 "This, even Prager allows, is a 'fair point'": ibid., 334.
266 "the most despicable act in the history of the game": ibid., 353.

### Durocher's Obsession

267 "It ain't my kind of team": Leo Durocher, *Nice Guys Finish Last* (New York: Simon and Schuster, 1975), 255.

## Chapter 11: American League West 1984
### Complacency

282 "This is sickening": *Sporting News*, May 24, 1982, 23.
283 "The Angels dealt away an entire farm system": Joseph L. Reichler, *The Baseball Trade Register* (New York: Macmillan, 1984), 277–280.
284 "Fourteen players hit the disabled list": Ross Newhan, *The Anaheim Angels* (New York: Hyperion, 2000), 237.
284 "McNamara ... 130 different lineups": "1983 California Angels," Baseball Reference Web page, at www.baseball-reference.com/teams/CAL/1983_lu.shtml.
284 "It's not his fault": Newhan, *The Anaheim Angels*, 239.
284 "I think he has a legitimate chance": Tom Singer, "Quiet Schofield Defies His Age," *Sporting News*, April 16, 1984, 15.
289 "Goose is an intimidator": Mike McKenzie, "Quip Artist, Rescue Ace," *Sporting News*, July 12, 1982, 44.
289 "I lull [batters] into a false sense of security": Tim McCarver, *The Perfect Season* (New York: Villard, 1999), 61.
289 "Every pitch of his is performed with a lurching downward thrust": Roger Angell, *Season Ticket* (New York: Ballentine, 1989), 196.
292 "With the defense he's been giving us": Patrick Reusse, *Sporting News*, March 21, 1984, 21.
292 "How can you embarrass your manager like that": Tom Singer, "Burleson Could Be in Autumn of Career," *Sporting News*, September 17, 1984, 16.
296 "It's tough to throw to first base": Patrick Reusse, "Twins' Title Hopes Go Up in Smoke," *Sporting News*, October 8, 1984, 17.

### The Great Improvisation

All quotes are from John Schuerholtz, interview with author, February 23, 2007.

## Chapter 12: National League 1934
### Learning to Trust the Man in Glasses

311 "The most famed ... sinkers": Entries for Fitzsimmons, Hubbell, Parmelee, and Schuhmacher, in *The Neyer/James Guide to Pitchers*, by Rob Neyer and Bill James (New York: Fireside, 2004).

312 "In a three-way deal that sent Lindstrom to Pittsburgh": Peter Williams, *When the Giants Were Giants* (Chapel Hill, N.C.: Algonquin, 1994), 127–128.

314 "In a preseason poll ... 1932": G. H. Fleming, *The Dizziest Season* (New York: Morrow and Co., 1984), entry for Wednesday, April 11, 58. Of course, the 1932 Cubs famously lost to the Yankees, with Charlie Root surrendering the "Called Shot" (or not) to Babe Ruth.

314 "The Cubs raided the sad-sack Phillies, throwing them $65,000 and three futureless players to acquire Triple Crown winner Chuck Klein": Reichler, *The Baseball Trade Register*, transaction from November 21, 1934, 50. In the Phillies' defense, the money was relatively important to the club. The Great Depression had forced industrywide pay cuts in 1932, and attendance had fallen to barely 2,000 per game at the Baker Bowl. If the Phillies existed to fill out other teams' schedules, they may also be forgiven for existing also to fill the gaps in other teams' rosters.

316 "Rickey sensibly identified him as someone he'd rather have playing in a power slot like left or first than either of the two future Hall of Famers": Inducted in 1971, Hafey probably owed his induction to Frankie Frisch, his former teammate. Frisch died before Bottomley was inducted in 1974, but given Frisch's permanently corrosive influence on the standards for Hall of Fame status during his reign of error with the Veteran's Committee, you can fairly ask whether Bottomley's induction was almost a posthumous bequest. Though Collins eventually became one of the innumerable hellraisers of the Gas House Gang, Rickey operated in happy ignorance of this unfortunate future, and simply picked the better ballplayer.

316 "As long as you weren't in his line of fire": Editors of Total Baseball, *Baseball: The Biographical Encyclopedia* (Kingston, N.Y.: Total Sports Publishing, 2000), entry for Pepper Martin, 716.

316 "And perhaps an appreciation that you can never have too many outfielders": Fleming, *The Dizziest Season*, 60.

317 "And 45 wins between the two of them": *Baseball: The Biographical Encyclopedia*, entry for Dizzy Dean, 275.

318 "If you don't want to pitch, go home": Fleming, *The Dizziest Season*, 102.

318 "One correctly, one not": ibid., 133.

319 "Who had only fallen from favor with Branch Rickey merely by virtue of not being Paul Dean": *Baseball: The Biographical Encyclopedia*, entry for Big Bill Lee, 652.

321 "Frisch, Rickey, and Breadon agreed to lay down the law, fining the brothers": ibid., 204–205. Dizzy was initially fined $100; Paul $50.

321 "When the Yankees ... exhibition": ibid., 204.

321 "As far as the Cardinals are concerned, their pennant chances have been reduced to a rather hopeless degree": *Sporting News*, August 30, 1934, 1.

321 "After posting a 41-15 record in the Polo Grounds": "Terrymen Favored by Long Home Stay," *Sporting News*, September 6, 1934, 1.

323 "There is some truth to that": Williams, *When the Giants Were Giants*, 176–177.

323 "Skull sessions before each game, listening to every suggestion and implementing some of them": Williams, *When the Giants Were Giants*, 135.

324 "This was exactly what happened in the winter, but why couldn't it have been done sooner": Reichler, *The Baseball Trade Register*, 129. When the Giants finally did nab Bartell from the Phillies, it was for a particularly noxious package—a lot of cash, with a quartet of players for ballast: Vergez, utility infielder Blondy Ryan, the ubiquitous George Watkins, and southpaw Pretzels Pezzullo.

324 "With his greater investment with fewer duties": That's not to say Rickey didn't have distractions of his own; flanking team owner Sam Breadon, he had to attend a hearing of St. Louis city aldermen on August 24 in an attempt to defeat a proposal to levy a 10 percent tax on tickets. Breadon and Rickey complained to the city fathers that the club had lost $100,000 in both 1932 and 1933, called the tax onerous, and (perhaps inevitably) threatened to skip town. "The club chief gave figures to show that only 250,000 attended the home games last summer (1933). Breadon asserted that the Cardinals should be seen as a civic asset from the standpoint of the advertising they give the city and hinted it might be necessary to move the club if the tax was imposed." It was ever thus. *Sporting News*, August 30, 1934, 8.

325 "The last manager whose brand of personal leadership depended equally on his feats on the field and his acumen in calling the shots, and achieve success": Williams, *When the Giants Were Giants*, 135–136.

### Chapter 13: American League 1944
*The Home Front*

327 "Over 16 million Americans served": Richard Goldstein, *Spartan Seasons: How Baseball Survived the War Effort* (New York: Macmillan, 1980), 3.

328 "There was no joy if you were declared 4-F (unfit for duty)": Dom DiMaggio, quoted in Bill Gilbert, *They Also Served: Baseball and the Home Front, 1941–1945* (New York: Crown, 1992), 22.

328 "The government adopted a policy ... laymen": Not every ballplayer was forced to enlist, of course, but those who had their draft number called and failed their physical might still be required to enlist because of the so-called professional athlete exemption.

329 "Lowering the age of conscription to 18, while establishing an effective upper bound at 38": William B. Mead, *Even the Browns* (Contemporary Books, 1978), 87–91.

329 "Most of them ... token roles": Ages provided are "baseball ages" as of July 1, 1945, as provided on baseball-reference.com.

331 "With more than 60 percent of the league's 1941 starters away in the service": Gilbert, *They Also Served*, 113.

331 "18 of the team's players either held a 4-F classification or had been honorably discharged from the service": *Sporting News*, May 4, 1944, 1.

331 "And there was Sig Jakucki": Much material in this section is from *Sporting News*, June 22, 1944, 3.

332 "Scheduled to begin in Chicago on December 10, 1941": Mead, *Even the Browns*, 33.

334 "And some 1,200 miles from Boston": Distances by train are approximated by means of contemporary driving distances.

335 "The correlation between travel distance and home field advantage is very strong ... removed": Specifically, the correlation is .70, or an astonishing .86 excluding the Yankees.

335 "Refused to let top relief pitcher Johnny Murphy perform in such a capacity": Mead, *Even the Browns*, 119.

336 "Eligible to play until called back into the service (which he was, but not until 1945)": *Sporting News*, July 20, 1944, 11.

337 "By using Bill James's runs-created formula": The version of runs created used here is the so-called stolen base version: RC = (H + BB – CS) (TB + .55SB) / (AB + BB).

338–339 "It was hoped that Doerr, who had been rejected for service twice that summer for a perforated eardrum": *Sporting News*, September 7, 1944, 4.

339 "DeWitt successfully persuaded Zarilla's commanding officer to let him take a leave until the season was complete": Mead, *Even the Browns*, 165.

339 "During Washington's batting practice ... hands": *Sporting News*, September 28, 1944, 1.

340 "Taking a cheap shot in the groin but leaving Ortiz with a broken thumb": Mead, *Even the Browns*, 167.

340 "We could find no clear examples of teams that were propelled into the postseason by physically abusing an opponent": Steven Goldman, ed., *Mind Game* (New York: Workman, 2005), 173.

341 "Kreevich and Gutteridge ... took the game 1-0": *New York Times*, September 30, 1944, 19.

341 "So Sig comes into the hotel ... morning": Mead, *Even the Browns*, 175.

341–342 "Leonard ... a phone call just that morning had told a mysterious man from a gambling syndicate to 'go to hell'": Mead, *Even the Browns*, writes that Leonard was offered $20,000 to throw the game, while Gilbert, *They Also Served*, claims $2,000. Gilbert's account is probably more likely; $20,000 would have ranked as one of the top annual salaries in baseball that season.

342 "It was, perhaps, the most dramatic finish any championship campaign has ever known, one which even the most gifted scenario expert could scarcely have improved upon": *New York Times*, October 2, 1944, 14.

343 "Determine, to the best of our ability ... activities": The lists of active-duty major leaguers provided in David S. Neft and Richard M. Cohen, *The Sports Encyclopedia: Baseball*, were of significant help in compiling these lineups.

343 "The top five slots in the pitching rotation": It is slightly improper to refer to a five-man pitching rotation in the context of 1944 baseball. Schedules were very different from what they are today, including more off-days but also more doubleheaders. Moreover, pitchers were often used on less than four days' rest. Nevertheless, most teams frequently used at least five starters. Among the American League teams, the number of starts made by the fifth-most-used starter ranged from 14 for the White Sox to 23 for the Athletics.

343 "The team's 'ace' relief pitcher": *Ace relief pitcher* generally means the pitcher who finished the most games for his club.

344 "He probably would have had retired by 1944": Gehringer would have been 41 at the time, had seen only limited action in 1942, had played poorly in 1941, and did not play for the Tigers after returning from his tour of duty.

345 "The application of this concept is more involved and is described at greater length in the endnotes": Our projections operate by evaluating the performance of the player in three key statistical categories—equivalent average (EqA), normalized run average (NRA), and defensive rate (Rate)—over any seasons that he played between 1941 and 1947. These categories relate to hitting, pitching, and defense, respectively.

Each of these categories is a member of the Davenport translations (DT) family of statistics. The DTs adjust historical statistics to put players on a level playing field. In particular, the figures account for a player's run-scoring environment (the average number of runs scored in his ballpark, his league, and his era) and—more importantly, for our purposes—the quality of competition in his league. Thus, through the DTs, a .300 batting average in 1944 is treated as less valuable than a .300 batting average in 1941, because the .300 average in 1941 came in peacetime and therefore against tougher competition.

A player's DT performance is *age-adjusted* and *weighted* for each season. An example of these adjustments (Joe DiMaggio) is found in Table A-2 on the following page.

The *age adjustment* operates based on aging curves that I developed for the PECOTA forecasting system. Separate curves are used for EqA, Rate, and NRA. In the DiMaggio example in the table, we note that he would have been age 29 in 1944. Our aging curves specify that the typical player will have an EqA about 5 percent higher at age 29 than he does at age 32. Therefore, in evaluating DiMaggio's EqA in 1947, we adjust it upward by approximately 5 percent, from .325 to .341 (the assumption is that a player who posted a .325 EqA at age 32 would most likely have posted a .341 EqA at age 29). This result is the player's age-adjusted EqA. Note that

Table A-2  Joe DiMaggio

| Year | 1941 | 1942 | 1943 | 1944 | 1945 | 1946 | 1947 |
|---|---|---|---|---|---|---|---|
| EqA | .365 | .313 | – | – | – | .312 | .325 |
| Age | 26 | 27 | 28 | 29 | 30 | 31 | 32 |
| Age-Adjusted EqA | .356 | .307 | – | – | – | .322 | .341 |
| | | | | | | | |
| Absolute Weight | 2 | 3 | 5 | 7 | 3 | 2 | 1.5 |
| Outs Made | 353 | 443 | DNP | DNP | DNP | 367 | 385 |
| Adjusted Weight | 37.6 | 63.1 | 0 | 0 | 0 | 38.3 | 29.4 |
| | | | | | | | |
| Projected EqA | – | – | – | .327 | – | – | – |

the age adjustment does not always work upward. For example, DiMaggio's performance in 1942 is adjusted downward, because he was 27 in 1942, and the typical player is better at age 27 than he is at age 29.

Each season is also assigned a *weight*. This weight is based on two components: the *absolute weight* and the player's playing time. The absolute weight is fixed at 2 for 1941, 3 for 1942, 5 for 1943, 7 for 1944, 3 for 1945, 2 for 1946, and 1.5 for 1947. These weights reflect the fact that the closer a season is to 1944, the more the season can tell us about a player's probable level of performance in 1944. Seasons before the war, however, are given somewhat more weight than seasons after the war, because of the Cecil Travis Quandary.

The weight is adjusted according to a player's playing time—specifically, the number of outs that a hitter makes, the number of innings that a pitcher tosses, or the number of games that a fielder plays at his primary defensive position. For hitting and pitching performances, the *square root* of the number of outs made or innings pitched is used. This number is multiplied by the absolute weight for that season to produce the *adjusted weight*. (For fielding performances, we do not take the square root, because fielding statistics stabilize less quickly and the square-root method places comparatively larger emphasis on smaller sample sizes; instead, we simply multiply the number of defensive games played by the absolute weight to produce the adjusted weight). Seasons consisting of fewer than 40 plate appearances or 10 innings pitched are discarded.

The player's *projected EqA* (or NRA or Rate) is determined by multiplying the age-adjusted EqA by the adjusted weight to create a weighed mean. In DiMaggio's case, this projection works out to an EqA of .327.

Note that we run a projection for a player even if he actually had some playing time in 1944. For example, Dick Wakefield played about half the season in 1944 and had an EqA of .351. This EqA was much higher than the EqAs that Wakefield recorded in the seasons before and after 1944, and it is therefore unlikely that he would have been able to sustain this performance had he played the full year in 1944. Therefore, Wakefield's projected EqA of .315 is used rather than his actual EqA of .351 in evaluating the effects of his missing playing time.

The final step is comparing a player's projection to the actual performance of his replacement. The goal is to determine how many more runs the player would have produced or prevented, given the same number of outs made, innings pitched, or defensive games played as his replacement. DiMaggio's replacement, for example, was Johnny Lindell, who had an EqA of .291 in 1944 and made 413 outs. By translating EqA into equivalent runs (EqR), we find that DiMaggio's .327 projected EqA would have resulted in 32.4 additional runs for the Yankees, given 413 outs (an analogous process is used for NRA and Rate). Where more than one replacement is matched to a player, we take the weighted average of the performance of all such replacements before making this calculation.

Additional information about the DT family of statistics is available in the Baseball Prospectus Glossary at www.baseballprospectus.com/glossary.

346 "This injury is a substantial decline in his reflexes at the plate and his mobility in the field": Goldstein, *Spartan Seasons,* 254.

351 "After failing to complete a deal for the Indians' Hal Trosky": *Sporting News,* January 28, 1943, 6.

351 "He had to fight for the first base job in spring training after having been picked up from the Braves": *Sporting News,* March 26, 1942, 10.

352 "His replacements from the Pacific Coast League, Rex Cecil and Clem Dreisewerd, yielded nearly 30 extra runs in the process": We have assigned 80 percent of the total innings pitched in 1944 to Cecil and Dreisewerd to make up for Hughson's missing playing time.

352 "At least the loss of platoon catcher Hal Wagner could be tolerated": Wagner missed the final 30 games of the season; we have assumed that he would have made 60 percent of the starts in those games, with Hank Partee getting the rest.

357 "As many as 20 Hall-of-Famers might have filled out the league's rosters": There were nine Hall of Famers who played in at least one game in the 1944 American League, while another 11 were listed on service rolls. A few of these cases are marginal. Al Simmons and Paul Waner received just a couple at-bats in 1944 with the Athletics and Yankees, respectively. Charlie Gehringer is counted here, but would probably have been retired. Bob Lemon is counted, too, but he might have been in the minors. On the other hand, a few players, like Cecil Travis, might have had a chance at the Hall of Fame if not for the war.

357 "Table 13-18 summarizes the number of runs and wins that the AL teams missed because of wartime activities": Again, we have assumed that 10 runs are equal to one win.

357 "The average AL team lost between 16 and 17 wins to the war": The majority of this loss appears to have come from positional rather than pitching talent; our replacement players represent 44 percent of the total games played in the league at the eight primary fielding positions, but

about 32 percent of innings pitched. (Each of these figures would be higher if we accounted for the loss of backup talent in the league in addition to the primary starters.) It also appears that the positional talent lost was slightly stronger than the pitching talent on a per-capita basis.

360 "His absence opened up a spot in the lineup for first baseman Ray Sanders": If Moore had been available to the 1944 Cards, the most likely scenario is that he would have played left field, Johnny Hopp would have played right field instead of center, and Stan Musial would have played first base instead of right, as he did frequently early in his career. Thus, we assume that the departure of center fielder Moore opened up a spot for first baseman Sanders. Because of the ambiguities of the potential defensive alignment, we have not attempted to evaluate the effect of Moore's absence on the Cardinal defense.

360 "Nearly three-quarters of the minor leagues had been lost to the war as well": Goldstein, *Spartan Seasons*, 156.

360 "The minor leagues experienced a boom immediately after the war years, reaching all-time peak attendance in 1949": "Minor League Baseball Timeline, 1901–2001: A Century of Memories," Minor League Baseball Web page, www.minorleaguebaseball.com/milb/history/timeline.jsp.

361 "What is more clear is that the actual St. Louis Cardinals of 1944 were heavy favorites over the actual St. Louis Browns—two to one, according to bookmakers before the World Series": Mead, *Even the Browns*, 180.

361 "With a round-tripper that barely cleared the short porch in right field": Sportsman's Park's distances in that era were 310 feet to the right field pole and 354 feet to right-center.

# Acknowledgments

Baseball Prospectus books are by their nature collaborative projects, and though one of us is credited as editor, it must be admitted that he stands on the shoulders of giants. The very existence of this book is due to the successful collaboration of Basic Books' Bill Frucht and BP's Jonah Keri on *Baseball Between the Numbers*. Jonah has since moved on to other things but continued to be supportive of *It Ain't Over*. Bill lived up to Jonah's glowing advance reviews, offering guidance, calm, and a seemingly bottomless well of patience despite an unforgiving schedule.

Within Baseball Prospectus, executive vice-president Nate Silver was terrifically supportive and was always available to proffer advice when an intractable problem arose. Clay Davenport served ably as our statistics guru on this project. Bill Burke was Johnny on the spot with the answers to complicated statistical research questions. BP intern Jason Pare did dependable utility work when called upon. Christina Kahrl, veteran of more books as author and editor than can be easily counted, offered the benefit of her experience, as did the indefatigable editor of the BP annuals Cliff Corcoran. Both Cliff and Jay Jaffe not only delivered great work but made themselves available to pinch-hit whenever needed. When managing a large cast of writers, one sleeps easier knowing that if anything goes wrong he can rely on such loyal and talented friends to bail him out. Kevin Goldstein, Marc Normandin, and Ben Murphy checked in on a nigh-daily basis to offer assistance and good cheer.

Allen Barra and Kevin Baker, friends, colleagues, and heroes, both made excellent contributions to this volume and were free with advice and bonhomie on innumerable subjects. Andrew Baharlias and Dr. Richard Mohring took time away from their own busy lives to bend an ear or an elbow.

Stefanie Goldman, Sarah Goldman, and Clemens Goldman were, each in their own way, spectacularly indulgent of the editor, who leaped from *Baseball Prospectus 2007* to this book without a break and served as a constant reminder that when one has a family, he must always strive for excellence, for his name and work no longer represent only himself.

BP's agent, Sydelle Kramer, always makes herself available to us, a rare thing. At Basic, Courtney Miller was a pleasure to work with, as were Christine Marra, Jane Raese, and Patricia Boyd of Marrathon Production Services. If this book looks sharp and reads cleanly it is overwhelmingly due to their diligence, patience, and professionalism.

The authors would also like to thank the following: Dr. James Andrews, Dr. William Carroll, Alex Ciepley, Samuel Clemens, John Coppolella, Carl Erskine,

Dr. Glenn Fleisig, Jonah Fried, Dr. Ralph Gambardella, Fred Harner, Pat Jordan, Matthew Kleine, Richard Lally, Rich Lederer, Dr. Donald Peyser, John Schuerholz, Natasha Simon, Melissa Stone, and Glenn Stout.

*Steven Goldman*
April 2007

# About the Authors

**Kevin Baker** is the author of the City of Fire trilogy of historical novels about New York: *Dreamland, Paradise Alley,* and *Strivers Row.* He has written on baseball for the *New York Times, Harper's Magazine,* and several anthologies and is currently working on a history of New York City baseball, to be published by Pantheon.

**Allen Barra** writes about sports for the *Wall Street Journal* and the *Village Voice.* His last book, *The Last Coach: A Life of Paul "Bear" Bryant,* was a national best seller, and *Clearing the Bases: The Greatest Baseball Debates of the Last Century,* was named the *Sports Illustrated* Best Book of the Year in 2002. He is currently working on a biography of Yogi Berra.

**Alex Belth,** having worked in the postproduction end of the New York film business for filmmakers like Ken Burns, Woody Allen, and the Coen brothers, started Bronx Banter, a blog about living in New York and rooting for the Yankees. He wrote *Stepping Up: The Story of Curt Flood and His Fight for Baseball Players' Rights* and is currently editing *The Very Best Sports Writing of Pat Jordan.* Alex writes about baseball for SI.com and lives in the Bronx with his wife, Emily, and their cat, Tashi.

**William Burke** (statistical research) is a software engineer and has been part of the Baseball Prospectus tech crew since 2004. Previously, he developed software for STATS Inc. He lives with his wife, Amanda, and son, Joey, in Indianapolis.

**Clifford J. Corcoran** is the coauthor of Bronx Banter, the Yankee blog at BaseballToaster.com, and writes the "Wild Card" portion of SportsIllustrated.com's Fungoes blog. He also contributed to *Mind Game* and *Baseball Prospectus 2006* and is the in-house editor of the Plume editions of the *Baseball Prospectus* and *Pro Football Prospectus* annuals. A book editor by day, he has also freelanced as a music critic. Cliff's earlier baseball writing can be found on the now-dormant Clifford's Big Red Blog. He is currently living happily ever after in northern New Jersey with his beautiful wife, her cat and turtle, and the world's sweetest dog.

**Clay Davenport** is a meteorologist living in Maryland, and one of the founders of Baseball Prospectus.

**John Erhardt** is a Web editor for BaseballProspectus.com and was a contributor to the 2006 and 2007 *Baseball Prospectus* annuals. His baseball writing has also appeared in the *New York Sun*. An instructional designer, he lives in Canandaigua, New York, with his wife, Cheryl.

**Dan Fox** writes the "Schrödinger's Bat" column for Baseball Prospectus, focusing on sabermetric analyses. He is also a part-time stats stringer for Major League Baseball Advanced Media. A graduate of Iowa State University, Dan works as a software architect for Compassion International and lives in Colorado Springs with his wife and two daughters.

**Steven Goldman** is the creator of the long-running "Pinstriped Bible" column and companion "Pinstriped Blog" at www.yesnetwork.com, and the "You Could Look It Up" column for www.baseballprospectus.com. He is a baseball columnist for the *New York Sun* and the author of the biography *Forging Genius: The Making of Casey Stengel*. Steven is the editor of Baseball Prospectus's book *Mind Game* and a contributor to BP's *Baseball Between the Numbers*. He is also a coauthor of the *New York Times* best-selling *Baseball Prospectus* annual and co-edited the 2006 and 2007 editions. Steven lives in New Jersey with his wife, Stefanie; daughter, Sarah; and son, Clemens.

**Kevin Goldstein** covers prospects, scouting, and player development for Baseball Prospectus. Kevin earned national acclaim for his independently published *Prospect Report*, before spending three years at *Baseball America*. He joined Baseball Prospectus in the spring of 2006. Kevin lives in Chicago with the love of his life, Margaret, who thinks baseball would be more interesting if all home runs were considered outs.

**Jay Jaffe** is the founder of the six-year-old Futility Infielder Web site (www.futilityinfielder.com), one of the oldest baseball blogs. In addition to covering the annual Hall of Fame ballot for Baseball Prospectus, he writes the weekly Prospectus Hit List during the season. In recent years, he's contributed to two *Baseball Prospectus* annuals; *Mind Game*; *The Juice*, by Will Carroll; *Bombers Broadside 2007*; and *Fantasy Baseball Index*. A Brown University graduate who works as a graphic designer in New York City, he's married to Andra, the most supportive gal in the world, and once came in third in the famous Milwaukee Brewers sausage race.

**Rany Jazayerli** was a first-year medical student when he joined the original team that founded Baseball Prospectus in 1995. He is now a dermatologist in private practice in the western suburbs of Chicago. He lives with his wife, Belsam, and daughters Cedra and Jenna.

**Christina Kahrl** is one of the founding five members of Baseball Prospectus, and is one of three who has been involved in the creation of all 12 editions of the annual. Beyond her regular "Transaction Analysis" column at BP.com (entering its 12th year in the spring 2007), she's written about baseball and football for *Playboy*, the *New York Sun*, Salon.com, Slate.com, SportsIllustrated.com, and ESPN.com and contributed to BP's *Mind Game* and *The ESPN Pro Football Encyclopedia*. She also published a few dozen cutting-edge books on almost every sport imaginable during her five years as Sports Acquisitions Editor at Brassey's/Potomac Books, helping launch the careers of several contemporaries. A graduate of the University of Chicago with a Master's degree from Loyola University (she went into the lucrative field of history for both), she now lives in the Washington, D.C., metro area with somebody else's dog, and roots to this day for the team of her childhood, the Oakland A's.

**Nate Silver** is the executive vice president of Baseball Prospectus and the inventor of the PECOTA forecasting system. In addition to his duties for BP, Nate has written for *Sports Illustrated*, ESPN.com, and Slate.com. Nate lives in Chicago and claims that rooting for the White Sox, Cubs, and Tigers is no greater a sin than wearing unmatching socks.

# Index